# Encyclopedia of the
# McCarthy Era

# Encyclopedia of the
# McCarthy Era

William K. Klingaman

# Facts On File, Inc.

AN INFOBASE HOLDINGS COMPANY

**Encyclopedia of the McCarthy Era**

Facts On File, Inc.
11 Penn Plaza
New York NY 10001

**Library of Congress Cataloging-in-Publication Data**
Klingaman, William K.
Encyclopedia of the McCarthy era / William K. Klingaman.
p.   cm.
Includes bibliographical references (p.   ) and index.
ISBN 0-8160-3097-9 (alk. paper)
1. Subversive activities—United States—Encyclopedias.   2. Anti-
communist movements—United States—Encyclopedias.   3. McCarthy,
Joseph, 1908–1957—Encyclopedias.   4. Internal security—United
States—Encyclopedias.   5. United States—Politics and
government—1945–1953—Encyclopedias.   I. Title.
E743.5.K57   1996
973.918′03—dc20                    95-23574

Jacket design by Vertigo Design

This book is printed on acid-free paper.

Printed in the United States of America

VB VC 10 9 8 7 6 5 4 3 2 1

# Contents

Introduction     **vii**

Entries A to Z     **1**

Chronology     **409**

Bibliography     **413**

Appendix I:  Executive Order 9835, March 21, 1947     **415**

Appendix II:  Testimony before HUAC     **418**

            J. Edgar Hoover, 1947     **418**

            Ronald Reagan, 1947     **421**

            John Howard Lawson, 1947     **423**

Appendix III:  The Waldorf Statement, December 3, 1947     **431**

Appendix IV:  Whittaker Chambers' Statement to
         the FBI, December 3, 1948     **432**

Appendix V:  Speech at Wheeling, West Virginia, Senator Joseph
         McCarthy, February 9, 1950     **434**

Appendix VI:  Declaration of Conscience Speech, Margaret Chase
         Smith, June 1, 1950     **436**

Appendix VII:  The McCarran Act (excerpts)     **439**

Appendix VIII:  Veto of the Internal Security Act of 1950, President
         Harry S. Truman, September 22, 1950     **441**

Appendix IX:  U.S. Attorney General's List of Subversive
         Organizations, 1950 (excerpt)     **443**

Appendix X:  FBI Files and Memos, Harry Gold and
         David Greenglass, 1950–51     **446**

Appendix XI:  Sentencing of Julius and Ethel Rosenberg, Judge Irving
         Kaufman, April 5, 1951     **448**

Appendix XII:  Lillian Hellman—Letter to HUAC, May 19, 1952,
         and *Red Channels* List of Alleged Political Affiliations
         (1950)     **450**

Appendix XIII:  Memo to President Truman from Dean Acheson re:
         John Carter Vincent     **453**

Appendix XIV: Executive Order 10450, April 27, 1953    **455**
Appendix XV: Albert Einstein Letter, 1953    **459**
Appendix XVI: Presidential News Conference, 1953
       (excerpt)    **460**
Appendix XVII: Communist Control Act of 1954 (excerpts)    **461**
Appendix XVIII: Resolution of Censure, Documents, 1954    **462**
Index    **473**

# Introduction

Between 1946 and 1954, the issue of Communist subversion—and, in a broader sense, Communist influence in American life—came to dominate political debate in the United States. Public concern over a potential Communist threat to the nation's security was fueled by a series of shocks at home and abroad that stunned and confused the American people and left them searching for villains to explain these unanticipated postwar misfortunes.

As early as the autumn of 1945, Americans were shaken by accusations of Soviet espionage in the U. S. atomic research program. The Soviet Union's announcement in August 1949 that it had exploded its first nuclear device shattered the U.S. monopoly on atomic weapons and further eroded the public's sense of security. The subsequent victory of Communist forces in the civil war in China and the invasion of South Korea by North Korean troops in June 1950 dealt additional blows to American strategic interests in the Far East. Meanwhile, the Soviet Union had extended its political and military control over Eastern Europe and threatened to push southward into Greece and Turkey until the Truman administration rushed emergency aid to those beleaguered nations in 1948.

Yet, this succession of diplomatic crises, as dispiriting as they certainly were, fails to explain the virulence of the anti-Communist fervor that swept over the United States in the late 1940s and early 1950s. Equally significant was the conservative reaction, particularly in Congress, against nearly two decades of liberal reform at home. The Republican Party had lost its traditional position as the nation's majority party in the wreckage of the Great Depression, and the coalition of interest groups assembled by Franklin Delano Roosevelt to support the New Deal had dominated American politics since 1933. By 1946, however, Republican partisans were eager to regain their former position of primacy, and they—along with their conservative Democratic allies in the House and Senate—welcomed the opportunity to roll back some of the more controversial reform measures of the Roosevelt and Truman administrations.

The task of discrediting liberal reforms was made far easier by the fact that a significant segment of mainstream American liberalism had cooperated with socialists and Communists during the Popular Front period of the 1930s. In the context of the antifascist crusade of that time, such cooperation did not necessarily bear any sinister implications; yet, in the heightened tensions between the United States and the Soviet Union during the postwar period, when the international Communist movement had resumed its hard-line stance against cooperation with the Western democracies, the legacy of the 1930s tainted liberals with an ineradicable Red stain.

Once the stage was set, it needed only actors to put the drama into motion, and by the end of 1947 the House Committee on Un-American Activities (HUAC) had moved to center stage in its highly publicized quest for Communist infiltration of American society. HUAC's efforts were supplemented by numerous anti-Communist organizations outside the government and by a growing number of ambitious conservative politicians in Congress. By the time Senator Joseph McCarthy made his famous Lincoln Day speech on February 9, 1950, charging the Truman administration with harboring Communists and Communist sympathizers in the federal government, the crusade was well under way. McCarthy did not create the fear and anxieties upon which his career depended; he merely played upon the public's growing hysteria more astutely than any other politician of his time.

In this volume, I have attempted to provide readers and researchers with a general overview of the most prominent personalities and issues of this controversial period in U.S. history. Some entries were obvious candidates for inclusion in any reference work on the McCarthy era. Others were included because of the light they shed on different aspects of American life during this time, including education, religion, and even sports. Most entries, however, emerge from the areas where the anti-Communist crusade had its greatest impact: domestic politics, law, foreign policy, and—largely because it was a highly visible target—the entertainment industry.

Even with a volume of this size and scope, limitations of time and space necessarily preclude a completely comprehensive view of the subject. My hope is that readers will find sufficient information herein to provide them with a solid basis for further research in primary sources and monographs, including those listed in the bibliography. The McCarthy era remains a highly fruitful area of historical research, open to widely divergent interpretive viewpoints. As more domestic and foreign documentary sources become available, our assessments of this period will continue to change and evolve, the better to enhance our understanding of American society in the late twentieth century.

# Encyclopedia of the
# McCarthy Era

# A

**Acheson, Dean** (1893–1971) As secretary of state in President Harry S. TRUMAN's second administration (1949–1953) when the United States suffered a number of shocks and setbacks in world affairs, Dean Acheson became one of the primary targets of Senator Joseph MCCARTHY and his followers.

Acheson was born in Middletown, Connecticut; his father was an Anglican priest and later bishop of Connecticut, and his mother was the heiress to a Canadian distillery fortune. Acheson attended Groton Preparatory School and took his undergraduate degree at Yale University, where his classmates included songwriter Cole Porter and poet Archibald MacLeish. In 1915, he entered Harvard Law School and studied under Felix Frankfurter. After serving as an ensign in the U.S. Navy during World War I, Acheson obtained a position as clerk to Associate Supreme Court Justice Louis Brandeis. After two years with Brandeis, Acheson joined the prestigious Washington law firm of Covington, Burling and Rublee, becoming a partner of the firm in 1926.

Shortly after President Franklin D. Roosevelt took office in March 1933, Acheson was appointed to the post of undersecretary of the treasury. Acheson's outspoken opposition to Roosevelt's decision to devalue the dollar led to his dismissal after only a few months at Treasury, though he remained loyal to the Roosevelt administration. In 1940, Acheson helped lead the fight to send military aid to Britain and France and drafted a public brief supporting Roosevelt's right to trade U.S. destroyers for British bases in the Western Hemisphere. Roosevelt subsequently rewarded him with another appointment as assistant secretary of state for economic affairs; in that post Acheson helped supervise the lend-lease program, chaired the committee that established the United Nations Relief and Rehabilitation Agency, and represented the United States at the Bretton Woods interna-

Secretary of State Dean Acheson, a frequent target of Senator Joseph McCarthy and other conservative Republican congressmen.

tional financial conference in 1944. In December 1944, Acheson was named assistant secretary of state for congressional relations, a post which provided him with valuable experience in obtaining legislative support for the administration's foreign-policy initiatives.

At the end of World War II in August 1945, Acheson left government service to return to private practice. Much to his surprise, he soon received a telephone call from President Truman's recently appointed Secretary of State James Byrnes, asking him to accept an appointment as undersecretary of state, the number two job in the department. Acheson readily accepted, and for the following two years he often served as acting secretary while Byrnes was

1

abroad on business. (Byrnes' travels took him out of Washington for nearly half of his tenure at State.) In the immediate postwar period, Acheson believed that the United States and the Soviet Union could reach some sort of diplomatic accommodation—or at least coexist peacefully. "Today you hear much talk of absolutes," Acheson told a group of officers at the National War College. "People say that two systems as different as ours and that of the Russians cannot exist in the same world . . . that one is good and one is evil, and good and evil cannot exist in the world. . . . Good and evil have existed in this world since Adam and Eve went out of the Garden of Eden."

Toward that end, Acheson advocated an atomic partnership with Britain and the U.S.S.R., as well as international control of atomic power. Acheson also pressed for the establishment of a federal civilian commission to control all domestic sources and uses of atomic energy, a policy that attracted the fire of conservative Republicans in Congress who wanted the military to retain control of nuclear power. Yet, Acheson also favored American development of a hydrogen bomb—the so-called "super-bomb"—over the opposition of liberals within the Truman administration. He possessed no illusions about the intentions of the Soviet Union, especially after several confrontations with his Russian counterparts. In dealing with the Soviets, Acheson explained, "You say to yourself, 'What are the specific things they are trying to accomplish?' And then you make it as inconvenient for them as possible. . . . When they finally see they're getting nowhere and they know you know they're getting nowhere, then they come around and say, 'Let's talk about these specific things.' And then you say, 'Fine.' "

Unlike many of his critics, Acheson understood that the postwar world was a very complex place and that there were no easy answers to difficult problems. In June 1946, he warned the American public that the nation's task in the postwar world was "a long and tough job and one for which we as a people are not particularly suited. We believe that any problem can be solved with a little ingenuity and without inconvenience to the folks at large. We have trouble-shooters to do this. And our name for problems is significant. We call them headaches. You take a powder and they are gone. These pains about which we have been talking are not like that. They are like the pain of earning a living. They will stay with us until death." In the emotional atmosphere of the McCarthy era, when many Americans were searching for simple panaceas and scapegoats, Acheson's views—however realistic—were not calculated to earn him popularity.

Acheson again left the State Department in 1947, only to be recalled by Truman in December 1948. Truman, who defeated Republican presidential candidate Thomas E. Dewey in November 1948 to win reelection (an upset victory that enraged congressional Republicans and portended acrimonious relations between the executive and the minority party in Congress for the next four years), asked Acheson to serve as secretary of state in his second administration. Acheson demurred, saying that he was not qualified to handle the job. Truman replied that Acheson might be right, but that in the present state of world affairs, he could say the same about himself or anyone else.

Acheson eventually accepted the position, and the two men developed an excellent working relationship. Acheson probably had more influence with Truman than any other cabinet officer. They met on a regular basis twice a week and spoke on the telephone nearly every day. Truman allowed Acheson—whom he considered the "top brain man" in his cabinet—to serve as the administration's spokesman on foreign affairs and relied on the secretary to keep him fully informed on world events. For his part, Acheson provided Truman with frank, forthright counsel while always deferring to Truman to make final policy decisions. "I never thought I was the President, and he never thought he was the Secretary," Acheson observed. "It is important that the relations between the President and his Secretary be quite frank, sometimes to the point of being blunt. And you just have to be deferential. He is the President of the United States, and you don't say rude things to him—you say blunt things to him. . . . You don't tell him only what he wants to hear. That would be bad for him and for everyone else."

Soon after he became secretary of state, Acheson found it necessary to tell the American people some blunt news about China. Since the 1930s, a considerable segment of public opinion in the United States had viewed Chinese Nationalist leader CHIANG Kai-shek as the best hope for democracy in the Far East. Despite massive amounts of American aid, however, the inefficient and corrupt Nationalist regime crumbled under the assault of the Communist Chinese armies under the leadership of MAO Zedong in the civil war that broke out shortly after the conclusion of World War II. By the summer of 1949, it was clear that the Nationalist cause was doomed to defeat; in fact, Chiang already had abdicated as president and had gone into seclusion. In an attempt to preempt criticism for any American responsibility for Chiang's defeat, Acheson and Truman decided to publish a thorough documentary account of U.S. policy toward China, demonstrating that the Nationalist collapse was due to the failings of Chiang's regime and not to mistakes in U.S. policy. Nevertheless, the administration's account, known as the CHINA WHITE PAPER, failed to assuage members of the CHINA LOBBY, Chiang's most fervent supporters in the United States; the inauguration of the government of the People's Republic of China in October 1949 led Republicans in the Senate to call for Acheson's resignation.

The Truman administration's "loss" of China also provoked a search for scapegoats, and conservative critics believed that the real responsibility lay with veteran Far East experts in the foreign service who had deliberately and disloyally aided the Communist cause in China. On January 21, 1950, a State Department official named Alger HISS, whose brother Donald had once served on Acheson's personal staff, was convicted of perjury after he denied during a congressional investigation that he had ever belonged to the COMMUNIST PARTY. At a press conference shortly after Hiss' conviction, Acheson declared that "whatever the outcome of any appeal which Mr. Hiss or his lawyers may take in this case, I do not intend to turn my back on Alger Hiss." Acheson added that his conduct in the Hiss affair would be governed by the words of Jesus in the Gospel according to St. Matthew 25:34: "I was a prisoner and ye came unto me."

Acheson's defense of Hiss enraged the anti-Communist crusaders in Congress (Republican Richard M. NIXON of California termed it "disgusting") and encouraged them to intensify their attacks on the State Department. Acheson's aristocratic appearance and demeanor only added fuel to the conflict: Invariably dressed in British-tailored suits and British handmade shoes, wearing a neatly clipped brush mustache, and possessed of a lofty patrician demeanor, the elegant Acheson personified to isolationist members of Congress the deleterious effects of foreign influence in U.S. affairs. "I look at that fellow," complained Republican Senator Hugh Butler of Nebraska; "I watch his smart-aleck manner and his British clothes and that New Dealism in everything he says and does, and I want to shout, 'Get out! Get out! You stand for everything that has been wrong in the United States for years!' "

On February 9, 1950, Senator Joseph McCarthy of Wisconsin joined the growing American anti-Communist movement with a speech in Wheeling, West Virginia, accusing the State Department of harboring "card-carrying Communists" in its ranks. Not surprisingly, McCarthy focused his attacks upon Acheson. "When this pompous diplomat in striped pants, with the phony British accent, proclaimed to the American people that Christ on the Mount endorsed Communism, high treason, and betrayal of a sacred trust," McCarthy said, "the blasphemy was so great that it awakened the dormant indignation of the American people." For the following four years, McCarthy continued his personal attack upon Acheson; the senator's devoted followers sent so much threatening mail to Acheson that Truman decided to post guards at the secretary's house twenty-four hours a day.

Acheson attempted to fight McCarthy and "the primitives," as he called the senator's allies, with a rational defense of U.S. policy and appeals to facts and reason. His carefully calculated approach, however, failed to deter McCarthy and won few points with the American public, nor was Acheson's cautious policy toward federal employee loyalty review boards calculated to deflect criticism in the increasingly hysterical atmosphere of the McCarthy era. When Truman appointed former Republican Senator Hiram BINGHAM to head the U.S. Civil Service Commission's LOYALTY REVIEW BOARD in November 1950, Bingham was appalled at the lax standards applied by the Department of State in uncovering potential subversives among the department's employees. "I think it is fair to say," observed Bingham in Feburary 1951, "that the State Department, as you know, has the worst record of any department in the action of its loyalty board. The loyalty board, in all the cases that have been considered in the State Department, has not found one—shall I say 'guilty' under our rules. It is the only board which has acted in that way." Yet, Acheson refused to permit emotion to overrule his considered judgment or his trust in veteran career foreign-service officials. Among the targets of the anti-Communist crusaders whom Acheson refused to dismiss were John Paton DAVIES, Jr., Oliver CLUBB, and John Carter VINCENT, although he did dismiss John Stewart SERVICE after revelations in the *AMERASIA* affair made it clear that Service was guilty at least of indiscretion and extremely poor professional judgment.

The outbreak of the KOREAN WAR in June 1950 produced further congressional demands for Acheson's resignation, but Truman refused to give in. Despite the persistent and continued attacks upon his record and his loyalty, Acheson remained in office through the end of Truman's tenure in the White House. He subsequently served as an adviser on foreign policy to the Democratic Party and was recalled to the White House to provide experienced counsel in crisis situations during the administrations of John F. KENNEDY and Lyndon B. JOHNSON. Acheson's distrust of the Soviet Union and his conviction that the United States needed to maintain an active role in world affairs led him to favor American military intervention in Vietnam during the mid-1960s, though a tour of Vietnam in 1968 convinced him that the situation was far worse than he had envisaged and that President Johnson "was being led down the garden path by the Joint Chiefs of Staff."

On October 12, 1971, Acheson died of a heart attack at his farm in Sandy Spring, Maryland.

**After the Fall** (1964)   A drama set during the McCarthy era, *After the Fall*—written by Arthur MILLER and directed by Elia KAZAN— was first performed at Lincoln Center during 1963–64, the center's opening season.

The play revolves around a character named Quentin (originally played by Jason Robards, Jr.), an ex-Communist attorney who is subpoenaed to testify before the HOUSE COMMITTEE ON UN-AMERICAN ACTIVITIES (HUAC). Among the other characters are two additional former Communists; one (Lou) refuses to cooperate with the committee, and another (Mickey) decides to inform on his former comrades—including Lou. When an incredulous Quentin and Lou ask Mickey why he will name names before the committee, he replies, "I want to. Fifteen years, wherever I go, whatever I talk about, the feeling is always there that I'm deceiving people." He argues that all three men have come to despise the Communist Party; therefore, Mickey claimed, "I ought to be true to myself now. And the truth, Lou, my truth, is that I think the party is a conspiracy. . . . I think we were swindled; they took our lust for the right and used it for Russian purposes. And I don't think we can go on turning our back on the truth simply because reactionaries are saying it."

To Lou, such reasoning was anathema. "If everyone broke faith," he argues, "there would be no civilization! That is why that committee is the face of the Philistine! And it astounds me that you can speak of truth and justice in relation to that gang of cheap publicity hounds!" Following Mickey's public identification of him as a former Communist, Lou commits suicide.

Among other things, *After the Fall* offered a retrospective view—in a more dispassionate atmosphere—of the passions generated by the anti-Communist crusade of the late 1940s and early 1950s. For Miller, "The play was about how we—nations and individuals—destroy ourselves by denying that this is precisely what we are doing." The theater critic of *The New York Times* wrote that the play recalled "those who would name names and those who wouldn't. . . . *After the Fall* seeks to understand, not to judge." The character of Mickey clearly seemed to be based on Elia Kazan himself—he had testified to HUAC in 1952 and named numerous former political associates. This testimony had temporarily destroyed the working relationship between himself and Miller, and *After the Fall* marked their first collaboration in nearly fifteen years. During rehearsals, Kazan reportedly attempted to recast the play to focus instead on the character of Maggie, whom most critics took to be a representation of Miller's second wife, film star Marilyn Monroe. (Monroe committed suicide several months before the play opened.) "The very point of it all," observed Miller, "was that Maggie might be saved if she could cease to blame either herself or others and begin to see that like everyone else she had essentially made her own life, an awesome fact toward which one had to feel humility and wonder rather than such total remorse as was implied in her denial of any decisive part in her calamity."

By the time the play was produced, the anti-Communist hysteria that had swirled through the United States during the McCarthy era had subsided. Miller had ambivalent feelings about working with Kazan again, but he felt that Kazan's decision to testify should not exclude him, in Miller's words, "from a position for which he was superbly qualified by his talent." Nevertheless, Miller's willingness to work with Kazan earned the playwright widespread criticism among liberals in the theatrical profession. "He gave the Kazan character a flag of honesty and then he attacked the people who took the Fifth Amendment," complained director Kermit Bloomgarden. Writer Norman Rosten noted that "The irony of Kazan doing *After the Fall* was that Miller thought he was getting the same man who directed *Death of a Salesman,* and Kazan was not the same man. It was not the same setup. Miller was looking for a replay of his past triumphs and the plays were different, the times were different. Kazan—because of what he had gone through—was not the same man and the chemistry was different."

**Amerasia**  A low-circulation, left-wing journal devoted to a discussion of U.S. relations with the Far East, *Amerasia* was written primarily for professional diplomats and students. In 1945, its editor was Philip Jaffe, a journalist and businessman who had liberally supported Communist causes in the past and whom the FBI suspected of having ties with COMMUNIST PARTY leaders in the United States. Under Jaffe's leadership, the magazine frequently published articles sympathetic to the Communist forces in the ongoing civil war in China.

In its February 1945 issue, *Amerasia* carried an article on British-American activities in Siam. Upon reading the article, an analyst for the Office of Strategic Services (OSS, the wartime U.S. intelligence service and precursor to the CENTRAL INTELLIGENCE AGENCY) recognized it as a summary—and in some parts an exact duplicate—of a classified report he once had written for OSS. The analyst relayed his concerns to his superiors, and the OSS launched an investigation of *Amerasia*'s operations.

When a team of agents led by Frank Bielaski, the OSS director of security in New York, obtained entrance to the *Amerasia* offices at 225 Fifth Avenue, they discovered an extensive array of sophisticated photocopying equipment, along with stacks of original classified documents and recently made photocopies. "There were so many we could not list them," Bielaski later testified. "These documents were from three or four to 150 pages. There were 300 documents. Every one of them bore the stamp that possession of these documents is a violation of the espionage act. It was stamped all over them." According to Bielaski, the cache included a top-secret report describing in detail Allied plans for bombing Japan, a document revealing that the U.S. Navy had broken the Japanese code, and another report showing the disposition of Nationalist Chinese troops on the mainland.

Because the United States was still at war, the unauthorized possession of material so critical to the war effort appeared to be an offense of the utmost gravity. Following further investigation by the FBI—including illegal wiretaps of telephones and surreptitious break-ins into the apartment of at least one suspect—six people were arrested on June 6, 1945, and charged with violations of the espionage act: Philip Jaffe; his co-editor, Kate L. Mitchell; low-ranking State Department employee Emmanuel Larsen, who had given classified materials to *Amerasia;* a naval intelligence officer; a writer for *Collier's* magazine; and John Stewart SERVICE, a State Department career officer who had been assigned to posts close to both the Chinese Nationalist commander CHIANG Kai-shek and Chinese Communist leader MAO Zedong, and who had knowingly used *Amerasia* to disseminate material detrimental to the Nationalist cause.

Government prosecutors decided that they would not be able to convict any of the six on espionage charges because they had found no evidence that the stolen documents had been passed on to a foreign government. Indeed, the combination of illegal entries and wiretaps without warrants had tainted the entire case. A grand jury did indict Jaffe and Larsen on the lesser charge of illegal possession of government property, but when Larsen's attorney discovered that the FBI had entered his client's apartment illegally, the case against Larsen was dropped. Before Jaffe could find out that this had been done, prosecutors struck a deal with him; in return for a plea of nolo contendere (not contesting the charge), he was fined $500 and released.

Such a light penalty for a seemingly serious violation of security regulations struck many Republicans in Congress as evidence of irresponsibility within the Truman administration, or worse, as evidence of treasonous pro-Soviet activity at the highest levels of the Executive Department. In fact, the administration (in the person of Tommy Corcoran, a long-time adviser to Democratic presidents) did work behind the scenes to persuade prosecutors to treat John Stewart Service lightly. Further, the episode coincided with a power struggle within the State Department between one faction—led by Undersecretary Joseph Grew—which advocated a tough policy against Soviet expansion and the Chinese Communists, and an opposing group led by Dean ACHESON. Soon after the *Amerasia* case was dismissed, Acheson replaced Grew as undersecretary.

Pressure from the FBI, the pro-Nationalist CHINA LOBBY, right-wing newspapers (including editorial cartoons which showed a trail of footprints labeled "*Amerasia* Fix" leading into the White House), and conservative Republicans in Congress kept the case alive. In June 1947, a House Appropriations Subcommittee investigating Communist influence in the State Department referred to the *Amerasia* affair when it expressed its alarm over "a deliberate, calculated program being carried out not only to protect Communist personnel in high places, but to reduce security and intelligence protection to a nullity." Questions about John Stewart Service's loyalty resurfaced periodically, and when Senator Joseph MCCARTHY delivered his famous Wheeling, West Virginia, speech on February 9, 1950, Service was one of four whom McCarthy cited by name as evidence of Communist subversion in the federal government. As McCarthy noted, Service, "who had been picked up by the FBI and who had previously urged that Communism was the best hope of China, was not only reinstated in the State Department but promoted and finally, under Acheson, placed in charge of all placements and promotions."

Led by Senator Millard TYDINGS, a subcommittee established by the Senate to investigate McCarthy's charges launched its own investigation of the *Amerasia* case in April 1950, and a grand jury subsequently undertook its own independent search for criminal wrongdoing. In response, the Justice Department reiterated its original conclusion that the evidence had been insufficient to warrant convictions. Tydings concurred and released a summary of the prosecution's testimony, but McCarthy refused to let the matter rest. He termed the alleged cover-up "Operation Whitewash" and insisted that the six people arrested in the case be questioned by the subcommittee.

Tydings did call Jaffe to testify, but the editor refused to answer any questions, invoking the protection of the Fifth Amendment more than 100 times. In the end, the Democratic majority of the subcommittee concluded that Service had been "extremely indiscreet" in his relations with Jaffe but that the State Department official was neither disloyal nor a security risk. Further, the Tydings report maintained that there was "not one shred of evidence to support the unwarranted charge that the [*Amerasia*] case was 'fixed' in any manner." In defending the government's conduct of the case, the majority report also took time to condemn McCarthy, thereby dividing the Senate further along partisan lines. McCarthy responded by charging that the case had been "one of the foulest coverups in history."

On June 15, 1950, a grand jury cleared John Stewart Service of any wrongdoing, and a security clearance was granted to Service for the sixth time.

**American Association of University Professors** As the largest organization of college teachers in the United States, the American Association of University Professors (AAUP) was intimately involved in the attempts by anti-Communist crusaders to limit academic freedom. During the political and intellectual ferment of the 1930s, a number of college and university professors had adopted radical ideals or joined left-wing organizations, with the objective of effecting thoroughgoing reforms in American society. Some teachers were possibly also disaffected with the capitalist system's inability to reward intellectual achievement with commensurate salaries. In any case, a sizable percentage of major American universities did employ at least a few Communists on their teaching staffs, although the number had dwindled by the late 1940s.

The presence of Communist professors on college campuses provided the HOUSE COMMITTEE ON UN-AMERICAN ACTIVITIES (HUAC) with an attractive target, particularly because it had long been fashionable for intellectuals to treat HUAC with contempt and scorn. Further, the committee's investigations of Soviet atomic espionage in the United States kept uncovering names of physicists who were still on the faculties of prominent American universities.

When Congressman Harold VELDE assumed the chairmanship of HUAC in 1953, he vowed to lead a search for COMMUNIST PARTY members or sympathizers at the nation's institutions of higher learning. Although there was no uniform response among university administrators to this incursion of the federal government into the hitherto sacrosanct academic world, enough professors were dismissed by their employers for present or past Communist Party membership—or for refusing to sign LOYALTY OATHS or for taking the Fifth Amendment when subpoenaed to testify about their political affiliations—to lead the American Association of University Professors to enter the dispute in the spring of 1956.

Since its inception in 1914, the AAUP had acted as the primary guardian of academic freedom in the United States. By the mid-1950s, the organization had grown to nearly 37,500 members. In response to the threat posed by HUAC and state and local anti-Communist crusaders to the integrity of the teaching profession, the AAUP established an eight-man committee to investigate the records of various campuses where professors had been dismissed for political reasons and to propose a resolution to the full membership on the question.

At the forty-second annual meeting of the AAUP on April 6, 1956, the special committee presented its recommendations. Membership in the Communist Party, it stated, should not be sufficient grounds for dismissal of a teacher, nor was the invocation of the protection afforded by the Fifth Amendment. The only way a school could justly fire a professor was to prove that he or she was unfit to teach because of "incompetence, lack of scholarly objectivity or integrity, serious misuse of the classroom or of academic prestige, gross personal misconduct, or conscious participation in conspiracy against the government." The burden of proof lay with the school, and no final decision should be imposed until the accused teacher had been judged by his or her academic peers. After sharp debate, the report was accepted by the full association. To emphasize its point, the AAUP censured eight universities (including the University of California, Ohio State, Rutgers, Temple, and the University of Oklahoma) for dismissing professors who had either refused to testify before Congressional committees or who pleaded the Fifth Amendment.

**American Civil Liberties Union**   Originally established to provide legal protection to pacifists in the United States during World War

I, the American Civil Liberties Union (ACLU) found itself in a difficult position during the McCarthy era. On the one hand, the ACLU opposed Communism and refused to allow known Communists to sit on its board of directors. In May 1940, the ACLU removed from its board one Elizabeth Gurley Flynn, a member of the COMMUNIST PARTY OF THE UNITED STATES OF AMERICA, on the grounds of this membership; by definition, argued ACLU officials, no Communist could honestly support civil liberties.

As tensions rose between the United States and the Soviet Union in the years immediately following World War II, the ACLU sought to distance itself publicly from *any* association with Communism. The organization gave its hearty endorsement to the Truman administration's efforts to prohibit and punish "the conspiratorial-action part of the Communist Party's activities." Like the AMERICANS FOR DEMOCRATIC ACTION, the ACLU formed part of the militantly anti-Communist American Left.

Yet, the ACLU also sought to uphold its traditional defense of civil liberties under the onslaught of anti-Communist zealots. It opposed the passage of the SMITH ACT of 1940, which made membership in the Communist Party a crime. In its annual report of 1948, entitled "The Shadow of Fear," the ACLU surveyed the American scene and concluded that the crusade against Communism had already begun to trample on the rights of Americans: "The imagined insecurity of the strongest democracy in the world in the face of the COLD WAR with Communism has created an atmosphere in which fear makes the maintenance of civil liberties precarious," observed the ACLU. "Not only the liberties of real or suspected Communists are at stake. Far beyond them, the measures to protect our institutions from Communist infiltration have set up an unprecedented array of barriers to free association, of forced declarations of loyalty, of blacklists and purges, and, most menacing to the spirit of liberty, of taboos on those progressive programs and principles which are the heart of any expanding democracy."

Specifically, the ACLU condemned the dismissal of Communist professors from university faculties, the excesses of the federal employee loyalty program, political deportations, the growing abuse of the attorney general's list of subversive organizations, and the expansion of the functions of the FBI, which, according to the ACLU, threatened to create "for the first time in our history . . . a secret political police system with its array of informers and undercover agents."

Over the ensuing decade, a struggle within the top leadership of the ACLU nearly paralyzed the organization and precluded it from taking a more active role in the most controversial court cases of the McCarthy era. The ACLU never became involved in the original trial or appeals of Ethel and Julius ROSENBERG because it claimed that civil liberties were not an issue in the case. (The ACLU's reticence in the Rosenberg affair sparked the formation of a bolder spin-off group, the EMERGENCY CIVIL LIBERTIES COMMITTEE.) When it appeared that State Department official Owen LATTIMORE's right to due process was being violated during his trial for perjury, the ACLU hesitated so long before offering its assistance to Lattimore that defense counsel Abe FORTAS finally told the organization not to bother.

The ACLU's ambivalent approach could be observed outside the courtroom as well. One faction of ACLU staffers regularly provided the FBI with copies of confidential ACLU memoranda and correspondence in return for information about the involvement of any of its local or national board members in Communist or Communist-front organizations. When the KOREAN WAR broke out in 1950, the ACLU dropped for the first time in its history its opposition to military conscription.

On less controversial matters, however, the ACLU maintained its traditional libertarian stance. In April 1953, the organization voiced its opposition to EXECUTIVE ORDER 10450 establishing the Eisenhower administration's rigorous federal-employee loyalty program. Three months later, the ACLU asked the Senate to investigate McCarthy's effort to ban purportedly Communist volumes in the State Department's overseas libraries, and in August 1956, ACLU Executive Director Patrick Malin declared that the hunt for Reds must not confuse subversive speech with subversive action. "It is even more than ever true," Malin wrote, "that the best defense and offensive weapon in the arsenal of democracy is its unique capacity for truth and intelligence."

**American Committee for Cultural Freedom**  Established in the late 1930s by liberal intellectuals such as John Dewey and Sidney Hook, the American Committee for Cultural Freedom (ACCF) was the American branch of the international Congress for Cultural Freedom. Disillusioned by the hard line adopted by the Soviet Union in 1945, the ACCF dedicated itself in the postwar years to the exposure of "Stalinism and Stalinist liberals wherever you find them." Along with the AMERICAN CIVIL LIBERTIES UNION and AMERICANS FOR DEMOCRATIC ACTION, the ACCF provided a home for staunchly anti-Communist liberals.

During the early 1950s, the ACCF's membership rolls included Elia KAZAN, Arthur SCHLESINGER, Jr., J. Robert OPPENHEIMER, Whittaker CHAMBERS (who joined in 1954, despite his misgivings about joining any group that included Oppenheimer), Irving Kristol, Diana Trilling, and Elliot Cohen, the editor of *Commentary*. The executive director of the ACCF was Sol Stein, a former analyst for VOICE OF AMERICA, who later helped found the publishing firm of Stein & Day. As Stein saw it, the duty of the ACCF was to attack "the residues of Communist influence frontally." Officials of the committee insisted that one was automatically tainted by any association with Communists; in their view, those who were not anti-Communist were necessarily suspect.

ACCF spokesmen defended the guilty verdict in the trials of accused Soviet spies Ethel and Julius ROSENBERG and claimed that the evidence against the Rosenbergs was "so incontrovertible that the DAILY WORKER did not even bother to inform its readers that the trial was taking place." Yet, the ACCF also denounced Senator Joseph MCCARTHY for his use of "smearing tactics" and condemned his censorship crusade against purportedly pro-Communist works in State Department libraries overseas.

One publication subsidized by the ACCF, *McCarthy and the Communists* by Moshe Decter and James Rorty (1954), further criticized McCarthy for his slipshod methods in combating the Communist menace. For Rorty and Decter, the true heroes in the battle against Soviet infiltration were those ex-Communists who informed on their former associates. These witnesses, the authors wrote, "may be patriots who place the highest value on safety of their countrymen. They may be persons who believe so deeply in the value of freedom and democracy that they will sacrifice the comfort of their own silence and the emotional ties of personal attachment to the ideals they honor."

By 1955, the ACCF had become so obsessed with its anti-Communist mission that moderate members began to resign from the organization. Weakened by defections, it disintegrated completely in the late 1950s.

**American Legion**   Founded in 1919 by a group of American veterans of World War I, the American Legion had evolved by the late 1940s into one of the largest, best-organized, and well-financed right-wing organizations in the United States. From the time the HOUSE COMMITTEE ON UN-AMERICAN ACTIVITIES (HUAC) was established in 1938, the American Legion served as one of HUAC's staunchest supporters.

As the anti-Communist drive gathered momentum in the postwar years, the legion—which by that time had 17,000 local posts and nearly 3 million members—joined the movement with enthusiasm. In August 1948, the legion's national commander, James F. O'Neil, authored an article entitled "How You Can Fight Communism," suggesting that the most valuable patriotic service a legionnaire could render this country was to protect the American public against "new commie fronts" and "the ever-changing [Communist] party line." Specifically, O'Neil recommended that local posts of the legion establish advisory services to identify newspaper articles with a Communist slant and alert the public to pro-Soviet guest speakers in their communities. O'Neil further suggested that legionnaires demand that their state legislatures set up investigating committees to ferret out Communist influence wherever it existed. "If 75,000 fanatical Communists can indoctrinate, control, and activate an estimated million dupes and camp followers," concluded O'Neil, "surely the American Legion's more than 3 million members can arouse, warn, and instruct the remaining 139 millions of our citizens."

Certainly the legion's national headquarters did its best to achieve O'Neil's goals over the following decade. It held antisubversive seminars, issued lists of suspected subversives in Hollywood, organized boycotts of motion pictures made by blacklisted film makers, and published articles in the legion's publications, *Firing Line* and *American Legion Magazine,* warning that "Your Child Is Their Target." One local legion post claimed that Girl Scouts were being taught subversive pro-Soviet material. Another staged a mock Communist coup in a small town in Wisconsin on May Day (May 1), 1950, as part of a well-publicized attempt—complete with library purges and a diet of potato soup and black bread—to demonstrate how somber life would be behind the Iron Curtain.

In the summer of 1951, President Harry TRUMAN chose the occasion of the dedication of the American Legion's new Washington headquarters to deliver a blistering speech against "scaremongers and hatemongers" who had "created such a wave of fear and uncertainty

Democratic presidential candidate Adlai Stevenson addresses the American Legion at its annual convention in 1952. (American Legion)

that their attacks upon our liberties go almost unchallenged." For the most part, the legionnaires in the audience remained silent or responded with only a scattering of polite applause. The legion's sympathies clearly lay instead with the aggressive anti-Communist campaign waged by Senator Joseph MCCARTHY. In 1953, for instance, the Wall Street post of the legion voted McCarthy its Bill of Rights gold medal, which it awarded annually to the citizen or organization "whose outstanding Americanism has provided exceptional protection to our way of life."

Following the publication in *American Legion Magazine* of an article entitled "Did the Movies Really Clean House?" in December 1951, a group of leading Hollywood studio officials led by Eric Johnston met with American Legion National Commander Donald Wilson on March 31, 1952. The goal of the producers was to avoid a public clash with the legion over alleged subversives in Hollywood. The method it chose was to establish a procedure whereby any screenwriters, directors, and actors suspected of Communist activities could be cleared in advance by the legion or its representatives; the studios could then proceed to make films without constant interference from the legion.

Toward that end, Wilson provided Johnston and his colleagues with the names of 300 individuals in the motion picture industry whose loyalty had been called into question, and the studios immediately initiated a wholesale investigation of their backgrounds. One hundred of these individuals chose to clear themselves by answering a series of questions about their past political associations ("Why did you join the listed organization? Who invited you to join? Whom did you invite to join? Did you resign? When?") The responses were then sent to a designated "clearing agent"—one of whom was former legion commander O'Neil—for review. If the answers were deemed complete and satisfactory, the person could return to work. The remaining 200 were placed on a "graylist," which made it more difficult for them to obtain work in Hollywood until they agreed to submit to the clearance process.

## American Library Association

As the leading organization of professional librarians in the United States, the American Library Association (ALA) was one of the few groups willing to challenge the power of Senator Joseph MC-CARTHY of Wisconsin in the early 1950s.

In the spring of 1953, McCarthy launched an investigation of the libraries operated overseas by the U.S. State Department. McCarthy's associates informed him that certain libraries carried books that were written by Communists or suspected Communist sympathizers or that dealt critically with problems in American society. McCarthy publicly objected to the use of American tax dollars to purchase such works, and staff members of his Senate subcommittee made a tour through Europe to inspect State Department libraries and remove any volumes they found offensive.

At its annual meeting in Los Angeles at the end of June 1953, the American Library Association took a stand against McCarthy's book purges. On June 25, 1953, the president of the ALA opened the convention with a ringing denunciation of McCarthyism, and the following day the association approved a "Declaration of Principles" supporting the free expression of ideas and condemning McCarthy's actions as a threat to liberty and democracy.

Following negotiations with the White House, the ALA also elicited a formal statement from President Dwight David EISENHOWER, reaffirming the principles he had recently put forth in his DARTMOUTH COLLEGE SPEECH. In his message to the association, the president applauded the ALA for recognizing that freedom "cannot be censored into existence" and warned against the zealots who "with more wrath than wisdom . . . would try to defend freedom by denying freedom's friends the opportunity of studying Communism in its entirety."

## Americans for Democratic Action

A liberal political-action organization, Americans for Democratic Action (ADA) was formed in January 1947 by a group of New Deal liberals including Eleanor ROOSEVELT, Senator Hubert H. HUMPHREY of Minnesota, theologian Reinhold Neibuhr, actor Melvyn DOUGLAS, and historian Arthur J. SCHLESINGER, Jr. Originally, the ADA represented an attempt to put visible distance between Communism and mainstream American liberalism. The founders of the ADA believed that a combination of political naivete and a lack of vigilance in the 1930s had allowed Communists to infiltrate traditionally liberal organizations. It had therefore become difficult for simplistic anti-Communist zealots to distinguish between liberals, fellow travelers, and actual Soviet agents.

In the increasingly emotional atmosphere of the late 1940s, ADA leaders deemed it essential for liberal groups to purge themselves of Communist elements so that conservative critics would have no grounds to attack their loyalty; the ADA, therefore, specifically banned Communists from its membership lists. Further, it insisted that the most effective means of combating the Soviet threat was a program of moderate social reform on the domestic front and "muscular anti-Communism" abroad. In its own terms, the ADA hoped to represent a "vital center" of liberalism between the excesses of the far Right and the far Left: "We reject any association with Communists or sympathizers with Communism in the United States," read the ADA's initial public proclamation, "as completely as we reject any association with fascists or their sympathizers."

Along those same lines, the ADA took pains to distance itself from the 1948 presidential candidacy of Progressive Party nominee Henry Wallace, going so far as to publish leaflets claiming that Wallace was influenced by Communist advisers. Its repudiation of Wallace left the ADA with no viable candidate to support in 1948 other than President Harry TRUMAN, although the organization's endorsement of the incumbent was lukewarm at best.

Despite its efforts to avoid association with radicals and Communists, the ADA found itself increasingly under attack, first by the HOUSE COMMITTEE ON UN-AMERICAN ACTIVITIES (HUAC)—which the ADA condemned for its "careless and callous investigating methods"—and then in the early 1950s by Senator Joseph MCCARTHY and his allies. In his Wheeling, West Virginia, speech in February 1951, McCarthy cited one of the ADA's founders, David Lloyd, as a security risk, even though Lloyd had long since severed his ties with left-wing organizations.

The ADA picked up the gauntlet and launched an intensive counterattack against McCarthy personally, working to defeat him in his bid for reelection in 1952. The annual convention of the ADA that year urged "a full disclosure of the senator's public record in the hearings now being conducted so that the people of Wisconsin may be fully informed as to his performance against the public interest and retire him from the Senate." Toward that end, the ADA reprinted 7,000 copies of an internal Senate subcommittee report accusing McCarthy of embezzling, income-tax cheating, bribery,

accepting kickbacks, and illegal use of classified documents. McCarthy, in response, cited the ADA as a "left-wing" organization, and condemned Democratic presidential candidate Adlai Stevenson for his membership in it.

Undaunted, ADA national chairman Francis Biddle, former attorney general in the Truman administration, called upon the Justice Department to launch a full-scale probe of McCarthy's personal financial affairs. McCarthy promptly replied with a charge that the ADA had "viciously attacked the FBI; has attacked the SMITH ACT, which makes it a crime to 'conspire to teach and advocate the overthrow of this government by force and violence'; has urged the recognition of Red China; and in many other respects has followed the COMMUNIST PARTY line."

Although the McCarthy era was not its finest hour, the ADA certainly outlasted the Wisconsin senator and his colleagues and has continued to promote liberal causes in the United States into the 1990s. Its influence has grown and waned according to the political climate in the nation at any given moment, but for the most part it has found itself on the defensive since the late 1960s, attempting to preserve and extend federal programs to aid the less fortunate members of American society.

**American-Soviet Science Society**   Formed in 1945 as the successor to the Science Committee of the National Council of American-Soviet Friendship, the American-Soviet Science Society (ASSS) was intended to facilitate relations between scientists in the United States and the Soviet Union by publishing scientific articles by Russian authors in American journals and by circulating Soviet scientific journals, books, and reprints in the United States. In its *Bulletin*, the ASSS also sought to acquaint American scientists with recent and contemporary Soviet scientific research; therefore the flow of information was designed to be almost exclusively one way.

In June 1946, the ASSS severed its relationship with the National Council of American-

Soviet Friendship largely because the ASSS objected to the increasingly pro-Soviet stand of the council on political and diplomatic matters. (At approximately the same time, other nonscientific members of the council withdrew from membership, including former Secretary of the Interior Harold Ickes, Judge Learned Hand, Senator Arthur Capper of Kansas, and New York Congressman Joseph C. Baldwin.) The board of trustees of the Rockefeller Foundation granted the ASSS $25,000 to continue its work after its split with the national council, though the grant was contingent upon the acquisition of a tax-exempt certificate from the U.S. Treasury. Because the national council's science committee had obtained such a certificate, the ASSS assumed that it, too, would receive one in due course.

In the winter of 1946–47, however, the ASSS became entangled in the controversy between the HOUSE COMMITTEE ON UN-AMERICAN ACTIVITIES (HUAC) and Dr. Edward CONDON, director of the Bureau of Standards and a member of the executive committee of the ASSS. On April 28, 1947, the Internal Revenue Service (IRS) rejected the American-Soviet Science Society's request for tax-exempt status. "It appears from newspaper articles recently published," wrote an IRS official, "that the Committee on Un-American Activities of the House of Representatives proposes to investigate the matter of whether your activities and those of certain of your leaders are detrimental to the interests of the United States. Under these circumstances a definite ruling on your status for Federal income tax purposes is being deferred pending further development of facts."

Although Attorney General Tom CLARK did place the National Council of American-Soviet Friendship on his list of subversive organization, he did not do so until December 1949, long after the ASSS had broken away from the council. Still, the government's refusal to grant tax-exempt status to the ASSS as a nonprofit educational organization made it impossible for the society to continue its work. In announcing the demise of the ASSS, a group of present and former society officers lamented that "The atmosphere of suspicion created by the Thomas Committee [HUAC], which, in the absence of any inquiry, has by insinuation alone sufficiently influenced a department of the Government to prevent our receiving the material support needed for our work."

**American Youth for Democracy**   One of the first organizations cited by the HOUSE COMMITTEE ON UN-AMERICAN ACTIVITIES (HUAC) in 1944 as a Communist front, American Youth for Democracy (AYD) was allegedly the successor to both the Young Communists League and the American Youth Congress. On December 4, 1947, the AYD was also listed by Attorney General Tom CLARK as a Communist-front organization.

The House Committee on Un-American Activities accused the American Youth for Democracy of subverting American college and high school students by turning them "against religion, the American home, against the college authorities, and against the American government itself." According to the committee, AYD was connected to the International Union of Students and the World Federation of Democratic Youth, two parent organizations allegedly sponsored by the Soviet Union. The AYD further incurred the ire of the committee by sponsoring a rally in June 1946 for a strike by maritime workers in New York. One of those who performed at the rally was actor Zero MOSTEL, who was later BLACKLISTED for his left-wing activities (including his alleged membership in AYD).

By the early 1950s, the AYD—which had never been more than marginally effective as a Communist propaganda or training organization—had faded into obscurity.

**Anti-Defamation League**   An organization of B'NAI B'RITH that provided assistance during the McCarthy era to any blacklisted Jewish entertainer or writer who wanted to clear his or her name, the Anti-Defamation League (ADL) refused, however, to help anyone who had taken the Fifth Amendment and declined to testify. According to the general counsel of the ADL, a BLACKLISTED individual who wanted the organization's assistance had to be willing to "follow our suggestion to communicate voluntarily with the FBI or HUAC [the HOUSE COMMITTEE ON UN-AMERICAN ACTIVITIES] and offer to answer all questions."

Typically, the ADL would first attempt to arrange a hearing before HUAC and then work behind the scenes to help its clients get their jobs back. Officials of the ADL also offered to meet privately with investigators from HUAC before Jewish witnesses testified to make sure that the committee had its facts straight about the witnesses' backgrounds.

**Appendix Nine**   A seven-volume collection of documents published in late 1944 from the files of the HOUSE COMMITTEE ON UN-AMERICAN ACTIVITIES (HUAC), Appendix Nine was officially entitled *Communist Front Organizations with Special Reference to the National Citizens Political Action Committee.* This sampling of nearly 2,000 pages of material, covering more than 100 private organizations, became known as Appendix Nine simply because it was the ninth addendum to the subcommittee's series of reports for the year. Consisting of 245 sections in 6 volumes, the appendix described alleged Communist-front organizations, with text and documents (identified as "exhibits") from HUAC files; the seventh volume was an index of approximately 22,000 names, mostly of individual U.S. citizens whose loyalty had been called into question by committee informants. At that time, mere suspicion seemed sufficient reason to include their names on the lists. Upon further investigation, committee staff members later acknowledged that many of the individuals identified in the appendix were neither Communists nor Communist sympathizers.

The publication of these documents appears to have been motivated by a fear on the part of certain subcommittee members that their records were about to be destroyed. Seven thousand sets of Appendix Nine were printed and delivered to the subcommittee, which then distributed a number of them to federal government agencies. Other sets were sold by the Government Publications Office to private citizens. When the members of the full committee discovered that the records had been published, they ordered all existing copies destroyed, but by that time too many had been distributed. During the following two decades, the material included in Appendix Nine was employed by congressional staffs and private investigators as evidence of Communist activity on the part of the individuals identified in the documents.

**Army-McCarthy Hearings**   The Army-McCarthy hearings were a series of confrontations in the spring of 1954 between U.S. Army officials and Senator Joseph MCCARTHY of Wisconsin over the issue of Communist influence in the U.S. armed forces. Partly because McCarthy displayed such arrogance and vindictiveness toward Army officials and partly because the hearings were televised to a national audience, the hearings marked the beginning of the decline in McCarthy's political fortunes and led directly to his censure by the Senate in December 1954.

In late 1953, McCarthy began to press Army officials for access to the service's confidential personnel files. Specifically, McCarthy stated that he wished to investigate allegations of espionage among civilian scientists at the Army Signal Corps Engineering Laboratories at FORT MONMOUTH, New Jersey. Dissatisfied with the Army's response to his demands for documents, McCarthy threatened in January 1954 to subpoena the members of the Loyalty and Security Appeals Board, which supervised security inquiries at Fort Monmouth. The Eisenhower administration stoutly resisted McCarthy's demands; given McCarthy's past record of engaging in far-flung fishing expeditions in security and loyalty files, few observers believed McCarthy would limit his inquiry to any one locale.

Meanwhile, one of McCarthy's top assistants, a wealthy young man named G. David SCHINE, had been drafted by the Army, and McCarthy and Roy COHN had pressured Secretary of the Army Robert T. STEVENS to obtain preferential treatment for Schine. Schine did, in fact, receive special privileges, including extra passes; he also was regularly excused from drill to receive telephone calls.

Tensions between McCarthy and Army officials rose in February 1954 when McCarthy learned that an Army dentist named Irving PERESS had been promoted to the rank of major despite Peress' refusal to answer routine questions regarding his political beliefs. Peress' insistence upon invoking his Fifth Amendment rights against self-incrimination convinced McCarthy that he was, or had been, a Communist. McCarthy thereupon embarked upon a crusade to discover "who promoted Peress." By that time, Peress had actually received an early discharge from the Army, but that circumstance did not dissuade McCarthy from discovering who had been responsible for promoting Peress in the first place.

On February 18, 1954, McCarthy questioned Brigadier General Ralph ZWICKER and asked Zwicker to provide him with the names of all officers involved in the Peress affair. When Zwicker refused, on the advice of counsel, to divulge the names, McCarthy flew into a rage and shouted that Zwicker did not have "the brains of a five-year-old." Secretary Stevens met with a group of conservative Republican senators on February 24 in an attempt to smooth over the controversy, but he succeeded only in creating the public impression that the administration was unwilling to stand up to McCarthy's bullying tactics. McCarthy continued to insist that he had evidence that "certain individuals in the Army have been promoting, covering up, and honorably discharging known Communists," while Secretary of Defense Charles Wilson—who termed McCarthy's charges "just damn tommyrot"—responded by accusing McCarthy of attempting to obtain privileged treatment for Schine.

The tangled controversy between the Army and McCarthy was finally resolved during the hearings, which opened on April 22, 1954. The hearings were conducted by the Permanent Subcommittee on Investigations, which normally would have been chaired by McCarthy; because the Wisconsin senator was both the accuser and the defendant in this case, Senator Karl MUNDT of South Dakota, one of McCarthy's staunchest allies, was appointed chairman for the duration of the hearings, much to Mundt's subsequent discomfort. Television networks carried the hearings live, providing millions of Americans with their first opportunity to observe McCarthy's tactics firsthand.

During the hearings, McCarthy sought to smear as many of his antagonists as possible by throwing out wild charges of subversion and disloyalty. His attacks were not limited to Army officials and their relatives: McCarthy also attempted to intimidate Democratic members of the committee, including Senators Henry Jackson of Washington and Stuart SYMINGTON of Missouri. For instance, McCarthy charged at one point that Symington had formerly belonged to a study group that included at least one Communist and that this was the reason why Symington was attempting "to force an end to our investigation."

Nor was McCarthy reluctant to fabricate evidence to advance his cause. Early in the hearings, he introduced a cropped photograph of Secretary Stevens and Schine that provided the false impression that Schine and Stevens were close friends. To support his charge that Stevens had impeded investigations into alleged Communist sympathizers at Forth Monmouth, McCarthy later submitted a two-and-a-half page letter that he claimed was a note from FBI Director J. Edgar HOOVER to an Army general, alerting him to security problems at a number of military laboratories as early as 1951. McCarthy then insisted that Stevens had done nothing about the situation since that time, despite Hoover's warning.

McCarthy's primary antagonist during the hearings was the Army's special counsel, a 63-year-old Boston attorney named Joseph WELCH. Throughout the hearings, Welch displayed a dry wit and avuncular disposition that contrasted sharply with McCarthy's blustering, slashing image. Part of Welch's strategy was to anger McCarthy, to make the senator lose his temper and commit a tactical blunder that Welch could use to discredit McCarthy. To that end, Welch objected to McCarthy's use of the cropped photograph, pointing out that it had been altered. Perhaps, Welch suggested, a pixie had been responsible for doctoring the original. When McCarthy asked Welch sarcastically to give the committee a definition of a pixie, Welch blandly replied, "I should say, Mr. Senator, that a pixie is a close relative of a fairy." Because rumors about the precise nature of the relationship between Cohn and the handsome Schine had been swirling around Washington for months, Welch's remark stung McCarthy and left the senator eager for an opportunity to even the score.

Welch also proved that the alleged Hoover note to Stevens was, in fact, a retyped, abridged copy of Hoover's original fifteen-page note. Again, it seemed obvious that someone on McCarthy's staff had altered evidence to suit the senator's purpose. Welch pressed McCarthy to tell him from whom he had obtained the photo, but McCarthy angrily refused to divulge his source.

The climactic confrontation between Welch and McCarthy occurred on June 9 when McCarthy exacted his revenge by revealing on national television that a young lawyer named Frederick G. Fisher—an associate in Welch's law firm of Hale & Dorr—had belonged to the NATIONAL LAWYERS' GUILD, a liberal organization that, according to McCarthy, had been identified as "the legal bulwark of the COMMUNIST PARTY."

As the nationwide audience watched, McCarthy continued to press his point while Welch sat disconsolately nearby, holding his head in his hands. When he finally composed himself sufficiently to reply, Welch spoke with a measure of sadness and weariness in his voice. "Until this moment, Senator," he said, "I think I never really gauged your cruelty or your recklessness." After conceding that Fisher had, in fact, belonged to the guild in the past, he informed McCarthy that Fisher was currently serving as secretary of his local chapter of the Young Republican League and appeared to have a brilliant future with Hale & Dorr. Yet, Welch feared that Fisher would always bear a scar needlessly inflicted by McCarthy. "If it were in my power to forgive you for your reckless cruelty," Welch added, "I would do so. I like to think I am a gentle man, but your forgiveness will have to come from someone other than me." When McCarthy attempted to interrupt, Welch cut him off. "Let us not assassinate this lad further, Senator. You have done enough. Have you no sense of decency, sir, at long last? Have you no sense of decency?"

A long moment of silence followed. Then the spectators in the hearing room rose to their feet and burst into applause, and reporters rushed out to telephone the story to their editors. Welch had put into words the outrage that the public and many of McCarthy's colleagues in the Senate had felt after observing the recklessness and irresponsibility of McCarthy's method of operations.

The incident marked a turning point in McCarthy's fortunes. Although a number of Republican senators had begun to desert McCarthy in the preceding weeks, the televised spectacle of the hearings hastened the process and emboldened President Eisenhower to invite Welch to the White House to congratulate him personally. When Senator Ralph FLANDERS of Vermont introduced a motion on July 20 calling upon the Senate to censure McCarthy for his actions, one of the specific charges against the Wisconsin senator was his possession of a classified FBI document during the Army-McCarthy hearings. Another charge centered on McCarthy's abusive treatment of General Zwicker. Following several months of testimony, a special Senate committee recommended that the Senate condemn McCarthy for his actions, and on December 2, 1954, the Senate voted to approve the committee's recommendation.

**Atomic Energy Commission**   Established in 1947, the Atomic Energy Commission (AEC) bore responsibility for research and control of atomic energy—including the development and production of nuclear weapons—in the United States. As a result of President Harry S. TRUMAN's conviction that "the release of atomic energy constitutes a new force too revolutionary to consider in the framework of old ideas," the AEC was placed under civilian control from its inception. In opposition to Truman, conservative members of Congress argued that the control of atomic energy properly belonged to the U.S. military establishment; Representative J. Parnell THOMAS, for example, considered the civilian administrators of the AEC "a group of Milquetoasts."

Revelations of Communist atomic espionage in Canada and the United States, from the allegations of Soviet diplomat Igor GOUZENKO to the discovery of the FUCHS-GOLD-GREENGLASS-ROSENBERG spy ring, added further fuel to the debate over civilian control of atomic energy. (Right-wing critics of the Truman administration frequently neglected to notice that most lapses in security occurred during World War II, when the U.S. Army enjoyed control over the American atomic-research program.) When President Dwight D. EISENHOWER assumed office in 1953, the Atomic Energy Commission—under the chairmanship of Admiral Lewis STRAUSS—tightened its standards for employee loyalty in an attempt to prevent further leaks of vital information. The most notable AEC security case during the Eisenhower administration involved J. Robert OPPENHEIMER, former head

scientist of the wartime Manhattan Project. Doubts about Oppenheimer's loyalty, exacerbated by his opposition to the development of a hydrogen bomb, led the commissioners of the Atomic Energy Commission in June 1954 to vote, by a 4–1 margin, to deny Oppenheimer further clearance to atomic-research efforts.

**AWARE, Inc.**   Established in 1953 to "combat the Communist conspiracy in entertainment communications," AWARE, Inc., was an organization that issued its own decisions on the loyalty of radio, television, and film performers. The founder of AWARE, an aspiring television producer named Vincent Hartnett, had earlier joined with three ex-FBI agents in forming American Business Consultants; together, they published the weekly newsletter COUNTERAT-TACK, as well as RED CHANNELS, the loyalty handbook of the entertainment industry.

AWARE's primary role in the BLACKLIST procedure was to act as a clearinghouse for information about performers. (For the record, Hartnett and his associates steadfastly denied that there was ever such a thing as a blacklist.) When a network or sponsor wished to hire a performer, it would submit the performer's name to AWARE (or to an advertising agency, who would then pass along the name to AWARE). For a fee, AWARE would check the name against its membership lists of subversive organizations. If the name did not appear on any of its lists, AWARE notified the network that the performer was acceptable. If the performer's name did appear on a list, AWARE would inform the network that it would run "a serious risk of adverse public opinion" by featuring the performer.

AWARE's list of subversive organizations (drawn primarily from reports of congressional investigative committees) was considerably more extensive than the official list compiled by the attorney general. The company also claimed that its investigations were more rigorous than those conducted by the FBI. As one representative of

AWARE explained, "We at AWARE had different standards of clearance than the United States Government's agencies. We are a little more stringent. We feel they are a little too lenient." Moreover, Hartnett and his staff did not check to determine whether a performer actually did belong to an organization to which his or her name had been linked. Occasionally, confusion resulted; actor Everett Sloan, for instance, found it impossible to find work for months because he had been confused with another performer named Alan Sloane.

In 1955, the American Federation of Television and Radio Artists (AFTRA) attempted to break the power of the blacklist. When a slate of candidates for the executive board of AFTRA promised to fight AWARE, the company responded by denouncing the slate as a "Communist-FRONT apparatus" and published information from the performers' dossiers as proof. After AFTRA did, in fact, pass a resolution condemning AWARE, the chairman of the HOUSE COMMITTEE ON UN-AMERICAN ACTIVITIES (HUAC)—encouraged by Hartnett—launched an investigation of AFTRA and summoned twenty-seven actors, directors, producers, and writers to testify about their political associations. Following the conclusion of the HUAC probe, actor Philip LOEB, one of those who had been blacklisted by AWARE, committed suicide.

AWARE also sought retribution against radio humorist John Henry FAULK for his role in AFTRA's campaign against AWARE. After pressuring CBS to cancel Faulk's network show in 1956, AWARE was sued by Faulk for libel. Six years later, a jury returned a verdict in favor of Faulk and awarded him damages of $3.5 million. By that time, the entertainment industry blacklist was no longer a powerful weapon, and AWARE had already lost virtually all of its influence in the industry.

# B

**Bailey, Dorothy** (1907– ) A personnel officer in the United States Employment Service, Dorothy Bailey found herself facing charges of disloyalty in the spring of 1948 as a result of reports to the FEDERAL BUREAU OF INVESTIGATION by several anonymous informants. For the previous fourteen years that she had been working for the federal government, there had been no adverse reports in Bailey's file. She was, however, president of her local chapter of the United Public Workers of America, and her activities on behalf of the union may have provoked the accusations against her.

In her hearing before the Civil Service Commission's LOYALTY REVIEW BOARD in 1949, Bailey was accused of membership in the COMMUNIST PARTY. All the accusations came from unnamed informants, none of whom were present at the hearing to confront Bailey. The evidence against her consisted entirely of statements similar to the following, taken directly from the transcript of the hearing:

> Here is a statement that it was ascertained you were a member of the Communist Party in the District of Columbia as early as 1935, and that in the early days of her Party membership she attended Communist Party meetings. . . . Here is another that says you were a member of the Communist Party, and he based his statement on his knowledge of your association with known Communists for the past seven or eight years.

Bailey was not allowed to know the names of the individuals who had made the accusations against her. Indeed, Loyalty Review Board Chairman Seth RICHARDSON admitted that he himself did not know the names of her accusers; "I haven't the slightest knowledge as to who they are or how active they have been in anything," he told Bailey's defense counsel. Their names, Richardson added, were confidential and could not be disclosed, nor were their accusations made under oath.

Bailey steadfastly denied that she had ever been a member of the Communist Party. Still, the Loyalty Review Board ruled against her, and she was subsequently dismissed from her job. She took her case to the District of Columbia Circuit Court of Appeals, but the court ruled against her, 2–1. The justices in the majority admitted that Bailey had not received a fair trial but claimed that she was not entitled to a trial over the loss of her job in the first place. As Richardson had explained earlier, employment by the federal government was "a privilege, not a right." Although convictions such as Bailey's were not typical of the operation of the board under Richardson's leadership, the episode did portend a more rigorous examination of employee backgrounds and an increasingly limited interpretation of the rights of those accused of disloyalty.

**Ball, Lucille** (1911–1989) A television comedienne whose loyalty was briefly called into question by overly zealous anti-Communist informants, Lucille Ball defended herself twice before the HOUSE COMMITTEE ON UN-AMERICAN ACTIVITIES (HUAC) during the early 1950s. Her first appearance came on April 3, 1952, as part of HUAC's second intensive investigation of Communist influence in Hollywood. When committee investigators asked Ball if she had ever been a member of the COMMUNIST PARTY, she admitted that she had registered as a Communist in the 1936 elections, but she claimed that she had done so solely to placate her eccentric grandfather, a longtime socialist. She said she had never actually belonged to the Communist Party, nor had she ever voted for a Communist candidate.

There the matter rested until Ball was subpoe-

**Actress Lucille Ball was briefly accused of Communist sympathies.**

naed again and asked to testify on September 4, 1953, just one week before the third season of her hit television show, *I Love Lucy,* was scheduled to begin filming. This time, the committee claimed to have a registration card signed by Ball, identifying her as a voting member of the Communist Party. During her two-hour meeting with a HUAC investigator in Los Angeles, Ball reiterated her contention that "I am not a Communist now. I never have been. I never wanted to be. Nothing in the world could ever change my mind. At no time in my life have I ever been in sympathy with anything that even faintly resembled it." Once again she said she had only registered as a Communist voter in 1936 to please her grandfather, who had been seriously ill at the time. "In those days," she said, registering as a Communist voter "was not a terrible thing to do. It was almost as terrible to be a Republican in those days." At the end of the session, the investigator assured Ball that she had been cleared of all suspicions.

Two days later, columnist Walter Winchell informed his nationwide Sunday-evening radio audience that Lucille Ball had been "confronted with her membership in the Communist party." He followed this bombshell with a similar item linking Ball to the Communist Party in his syndicated column on September 7. One Los Angeles newspaper carried a headline announcing "LUCILLE BALL NAMED RED," accompanied by a photocopy of a document that purported to be her 1936 Communist Party registration card.

Ball and her husband, Desi Arnaz, immediately met with anxious executives of the CBS television network to reassure them of her loyalty. While they awaited word from the show's sponsor, Philip Morris, Arnaz contacted California Representative Donald L. Jackson, chairman of HUAC; Jackson consented to hold a press conference stating that Ball "had never had a role in the Communist Party." That evening, Arnaz made an emotional speech to the audience that had come to watch the filming of the season's first show. "Lucille is no Communist," he swore. "We both despise the Communists and everything they stand for. Lucille is one hundred percent an American."

The matter was laid to rest when Winchell carried the news of Jackson's press conference, adding that J. Edgar HOOVER, head of the FBI, had also cleared Ball of all charges. But Ball never forgave the people in Hollywood who had suddenly deserted her when it appeared that she might be blacklisted because of a single incident in her past.

**Baseball**    During the McCarthy era, baseball received renewed attention as one of the strongest cultural symbols of Americanism. The sport was deemed incompatible with Communism; as Republican Senator Herman Welker of Idaho put it, "I never saw a ballplayer who was a Communist." Eddie Stanky, the manager of the St. Louis Cardinals, put forth the prevailing view when he argued that Russians could never excel at baseball because it was a game of "give and take. The Russians like to dish it out, but they can't take it." Baseball, said Stanky, was "the big game of a free people" because it combined teamwork, sportsmanship, free discussion (i.e., rhubarbs), and opportunities for players of a wide variety of talents.

The sport enjoyed a surge in popularity on all levels during the early 1950s, due partly to the tremendous financial support of youth leagues by the AMERICAN LEGION and the Veterans of Foreign Wars as part of their anti-Communist program. Spokespersons for these patriotic organizations contended that baseball built teamwork and helped a boy learn "to subordinate his own personal interests to those of the team as a whole," just as adult Americans elevated the country's interests above their own. Baseball therefore purportedly helped boys take "an important step toward adulthood and good citizenship."

One anxious moment occurred when officials of the CINCINNATI REDS major-league team succumbed to the growing anti-Communist hysteria and changed its name to the "Redlegs" to avoid identification with the Marxist enemy. Eventually common sense prevailed, and the team's original name was restored.

**Bentley, Elizabeth** (1909–1965)    One of the most famous informers to the HOUSE COMMITTEE ON UN-AMERICAN ACTIVITIES (HUAC), Elizabeth Bentley was a former Communist courier who recanted her radical past and provided more than a score of names of alleged former comrades to government investigators.

According to her own testimony, Bentley first became involved with Communist causes in the mid-1930s, following her graduation from Vassar College (1930) and a brief period of study in Italy. Her repugnance for the Italian Fascist regime of Benito Mussolini led her to join the growing antifascist movement upon her return to the United States, and it was in those circles that she met several Communists in New York, including Jacob Golos, a Soviet agent posing as president of a travel agency known as World Tourists, Incorporated.

Bentley fell in love with Golos, and after Germany invaded the Soviet Union in 1941, she agreed to serve as a courier for him, bringing Golos and his associates a variety of classified government documents from several groups of sympathetic federal employees in Washington. Bentley later claimed that one of the Washington espionage groups was headed by Nathan Gregory Silvermaster, an economist who worked for a number of government agencies (including the Board of Economic Warfare) between 1935 and 1947. Silvermaster was, in fact, identified in a Civil Service Commission Report of 1942 as a member of the COMMUNIST PARTY and a likely Soviet agent who used his house as a photographic laboratory and transfer point for confidential documents. As Bentley recalled, she visited Silverman every other week at his home and collected from him material that he had assembled from other members of his group. She claimed that among the documents he gave her were statistics on aircraft production and allocation as well as Allied plans for the invasion of Normandy. (Although Bentley claimed to have received "information as to when D-Day would be," the Allied military command did not finally settle on June 6 as the date of the invasion until June 5.)

Bentley said that her second circle of Washington contacts was led by Victor Perlo, a government economist who worked for the Office of Price Administration and the War Production Board. She further maintained that she established contact during the war years with additional individuals who were not members of either group. One such government employee was William W. REMINGTON, who also worked for the War Production Board; Bentley later claimed that Remington had sent her information on U.S. military-aircraft production, along with a classified formula for making rubber out of garbage.

Golos' death in 1944 seemed to remove the aura of romance from these clandestine operations for Bentley, and by 1945 she had ceased her espionage activities. "Having worked with Mr. Golos, whom I took to be a great idealist, a man who was working for what I considered to be the betterment of the world, I had been terrifically shielded from the realities behind this thing," she explained to HUAC several years later. "When he died I was thrown in direct contact with Russians who had just come over from Russia. . . . The international communist movement, I realized, was in the hands of the wrong people."

In August 1945, Bentley went to the office of the FEDERAL BUREAU OF INVESTIGATION in New Haven, Connecticut, and told agents her story. They took no action. In the summer of 1947, however, she began to give testimony to a New York grand jury investigating Communist spy networks in the United States. As a result of that probe, a dozen leaders of the Communist Party were indicted for violations of the SMITH ACT, which made it unlawful for any person knowingly to teach or advocate the overthrow of government by force of violence or to help organize or to become a member of any organization advocating the overthrow of government. (The same grand jury would later indict Alger HISS on perjury charges.)

In July 1948, Bentley repeated part of her account of her wartime service to a Senate subcommittee, again implicating Remington. Despite the Justice Department's doubts about the accuracy of her testimony, HUAC—seeking a weapon to use against the Truman administration—subsequently summoned Bentley to testify. It was her appearance in public before

HUAC that vaulted Bentley into national prominence. Dubbed "the blonde spy queen" by a New York journalist, Bentley's stories of Communist infiltration of government agencies made front-page news across the country. Her use of specific detail and colorful anecdotes added to both the impression of veracity and the sensationalism of her testimony.

This time, however, she added to her list of Communist sympathizers in Washington the names of Lauchlin Currie, a longtime adviser to President Franklin Delano Roosevelt, and Harry Dexter WHITE, former assistant secretary of the Treasury and one of the chief founders of the International Monetary Fund. Bentley acknowledged that she had never met either Currie or White, but she had heard their names mentioned by her Communist comrades, and she claimed that they had used their influence to place and protect Communist sympathizers in strategic positions within the federal government. In one of his press conferences, President Truman responded that all of Bentley's allegations were already known to the FBI, and that her testimony was nothing more than a frivolous diversion from the real problems Congress should have been tackling.

Members of HUAC asked for no documentation of Bentley's charges; for them, her recollections seemed sufficient, despite the fact that she occasionally changed the details of her testimony against several alleged former comrades, Remington in particular. Following Bentley's appearance before HUAC, Remington challenged her to repeat her accusations away from the protection of a congressional committee. She did so on the NBC radio show *Meet the Press*. Remington then sued Bentley for libel; the case was settled out of court by NBC's attorneys with an award of $9,000 to Remington. For the moment, the settlement damaged Bentley's credibility, upon which so much of the case against Communist espionage agents depended. To repair the damage, government prosecutors assembled another grand jury that indicted Remington for perjury, and Bentley's antagonist was subsequently convicted for denying that he had been a member of the Communist Party.

Between 1948 and 1956, Bentley testified eight times before congressional committees, identifying more than forty individuals as members of Communist espionage networks. Besides Remington, three of her targets were convicted, and numerous others were dismissed from their jobs. In 1956, HUAC hired Bentley as a consultant. She supplemented her income with the fees she earned as a speaker and writer on the Communist threat in the United States. Bentley subsequently disappeared from public view as the anti-Communist fervor subsided in the final years of the Eisenhower administration.

Bentley's memoirs, *Out of Bondage*, published in 1951, recount the story of her conversion to Communism and her subsequent abandonment of the Soviet cause.

**Benton, William Burnett** (1900–1973)
One of the first members of the U.S. Senate to confront Senator Joseph MCCARTHY openly, William Benton was a businessman, educator, and politician who had compiled an impressive list of credentials even before he entered Congress as a senator from Connecticut in 1949.

An honors student at Yale University who continued his studies as a Rhodes Scholar at Oxford University, England, Benton joined with Chester Bowles in 1929 to form the advertising agency of Benton & Bowles. By brilliantly exploiting the possibilities of advertising on radio—including the extensive use of the singing commercial—Benton and Bowles became millionaires in six years during the depths of the Great Depression. In 1937, Benton accepted an appointment as vice-president of the University of Chicago. He remained in that position for eight years; in 1943, meanwhile, Benton also became chairman of the board of *Encyclopaedia Britannica*. Two years later, Benton left the University of Chicago to serve as assistant secretary of state for public affairs in the first administration of President Harry S. TRUMAN, with

Democratic senator William Benton of Connecticut, an early foe of Joseph McCarthy.

responsibility for the supervision of the department's overseas information programs.

In 1949, Bowles—who had meanwhile been elected governor of Connecticut—appointed Benton as a temporary replacement for former Senator Raymond Baldwin, who resigned from Congress following a confrontation with Joseph McCarthy. When Connecticut voters went to the polls in November 1950 to choose a candidate to fill the remainder of Baldwin's unexpired term, Benton emerged victorious by a narrow margin of slightly more than 1,000 votes.

Perhaps because he was not a career politician, Benton—who proved himself to be one of the more independent and liberal members of the Senate—was less reluctant than most of his colleagues to challenge the growing power of McCarthy. When a Senate subcommittee issued a report in August 1951 criticizing McCarthy for his unethical, "back-street" tactics in contributing to the electoral defeat of former Maryland

Senator Millard TYDINGS in November 1950, Benton was moved to submit a resolution calling upon the Senate Rules Committee to launch an investigation into McCarthy's activities to determine whether he should be expelled from the Senate. Specifically, Benton suggested that the Rules Committee examine McCarthy's role in the campaign against Tydings, his questionable financial affairs, and his reckless practice of character assassination while protected by senatorial immunity. "In my opinion," declared Benton, "Senator McCarthy has weakened the respect of decent people for representative government by his attacks upon the character of respectable citizens from the sanctuary of the Senate floor." Although numerous other senators may have agreed with Benton, only New York Democrat Herbert Lehman rose to support his call for a full-scale inquiry.

Not surprisingly, McCarthy responded with a personal assault upon Benton, whom he referred to as a "mental midget." "Tonight, Senator Benton has established himself as the hero of every Communist and crook in and out of government," announced McCarthy. "I am sure that Owen LATTIMORE and all the Alger HISSes and William REMINGTONs still in government will agree with the resolution. I call the attention of all honest Democrats to how men of little minds are destroying a once great party." In a thinly veiled threat, McCarthy also warned Benton—who would stand for reelection in 1952—that "the people of Connecticut do not like Communists and crooks in government any more than the people of Maryland like them." Benton seemed unimpressed by McCarthy's bluster. "I can only reply," he told one journalist, "that I would rather be right than be senator."

The Senate referred Benton's resolution to a subcommittee headed by Senator Guy Gillette of Iowa. As submitted by Benton in September 1951, the list of charges totaled 59 pages and 10 specific counts, including an accusation of perjury against McCarthy for denying that he had said that he possessed a list of 205 Commu-

nists in his February 9, 1950, speech at Wheeling, West Virginia; a charge that McCarthy had diverted a campaign contribution of $10,000 to his own personal use; accusations of unethical campaign activities during the Maryland senatorial campaign; and allegations that McCarthy had acted in a contumacious manner during the hearings held by the Tydings committee, which had investigated McCarthy's charges at Wheeling. Benton recommended that the Senate turn over to the Justice Department any information obtained during the inquiry: "If that is done, I concede cheerfully that my resolution asking for Senator McCarthy's expulsion from this body becomes somewhat academic," said Benton. "After all, a senator in jail, for all practical purposes, has been expelled. Freedom to lie is not a freedom which membership in the United States Senate confers upon any man."

For his part, McCarthy professed unconcern with the Senate's inquiry. "I am not in the least concerned with what this subcommittee does insofar as my fight to expose communism and corruption in Washington is concerned," McCarthy told reporters. "This subcommittee cannot in the slightest influence my activities. . . . The Benton type of material can be found in the *DAILY WORKER* almost any day of the week and will continue to flow from the mouths and pens of the camp followers as long as I continue to fight against Communists in government." McCarthy followed up this statement with allegations that "Several U.S. representatives and senators have known Communists on his staffs," a charge that clearly appeared designed to frighten any potential opponents from launching a serious investigation.

Nevertheless, the subcommittee's investigation continued, albeit in a desultory manner, over the next four months. On January 18, 1952, the subcommittee issued its preliminary report recommending that hearings be held on five of the ten charges submitted by Benton. While the Senate tried to decide whether or not to proceed with the hearings, McCarthy repeatedly assailed the integrity and motives of the members of the subcommittee. Outraged, Benton compared McCarthy's tactics to those of the Nazi regime of Adolf Hitler and offered to waive his right to senatorial immunity by repeating his September 1951 charges against McCarthy in public, away from the Senate floor. McCarthy challenged him to do so, and when Benton accepted the dare, McCarthy promptly sued Benton for libel and slander, seeking $2 million in damages.

On April 8, 1952, the Senate voted 60–0 to allow the Gillette subcommittee investigation to proceed. For the rest of the year, McCarthy and Benton continued to spar on the Senate floor. At one point, McCarthy accused Encyclopaedia Britannica Films, Inc., of employing numerous writers with a "fantastic record of Communist activities." He also claimed that Benton, during his tenure at the State Department, had provided jobs to "fellow travelers, Communists, and complete dupes." Benton responded by describing McCarthy as "a hit-and-run propagandist of the Soviet type." Despite the best efforts of Benton and his Democratic colleagues, however, the subcommittee's hearings failed to turn up any significant, solid evidence of illegal activities by the Wisconsin senator. By the end of the year, the inquiry had struggled to an inconclusive end. The subcommittee's final report, issued on January 2, 1953—the final day of the Eighty-second Congress—contained considerable evidence suggesting that McCarthy had engaged in highly questionable financial and political practices and condemned McCarthy for deliberately attempting "to thwart any investigation of him by obscuring the real issue and responsibility of the subcommittee by charges of lack of jurisdiction, smear, and Communist-inspired persecution." Yet the subcommittee failed to recommend any specific action against McCarthy. "The record should speak for itself," the report declared lamely. "The issue raised is one for the entire Senate."

Benton, meanwhile, lost his bid for election to a full Senate term and subsequently returned to his position as chairman of the board of *Encyclopaedia Britannica*. In the spring of 1954,

McCarthy dropped his libel suit against Benton, claiming that his attorney, Edward Bennett WILLIAMS, had been unable to find anyone who believed anything Benton said; therefore, McCarthy said, he had no basis for claiming that he had been damaged by Benton's statements. Benton, however, pressed McCarthy to revive the suit. "I told the truth about him and he knows it," Benton declared. "McCarthy was guilty of fraud and deceit in 1951 and he hasn't improved with age." By that time, however, the issues involving McCarthy's performance in the Senate had moved far beyond Benton's charges. McCarthy was preparing to challenge the U.S. Army in a series of televised hearings that would eventually lead to his censure by the Senate before the end of the year. For his part, Benton never reentered national politics, preferring to serve as chairman of *Encyclopaedia Britannica* until his retirement in 1967.

**Berle, Adolf A., Jr.** (1895–1971)   In the early years of the first Roosevelt administration (1933–1937), Adolf Berle served as an unofficial adviser to President Franklin D. Roosevelt. Although Berle did help shape the New Deal program of domestic reforms, his special area of expertise was in Latin American affairs, and by the late 1930s Berle had become assistant secretary of state.

It was in that capacity that he was approached in September 1939 by Whittaker CHAMBERS, a journalist who claimed to have personal knowledge of Communist activities in the United States. Berle and Chambers later gave conflicting reports of precisely what Chambers told Berle at their meeting. In testimony before the HOUSE COMMITTEE ON UN-AMERICAN ACTIVITIES (HUAC) in August 1948, Chambers recalled that he had given Berle the names of numerous government officials—including a high-ranking State Department officer named Alger HISS—who were members of the COMMUNIST PARTY. Chambers further maintained that he had accused Hiss of being a Soviet espionage agent and that Berle had shown "considerable excitement" at this information.

Former assistant secretary of state Adolf A. Berle was reportedly told, by Whittaker Chambers, of Communist infiltration of the federal government.

Berle, on the other hand, told the committee that there had been no mention of espionage, nor had Chambers specifically identified any government employees as members of the Communist Party. According to Berle, all Chambers had told him was that certain government officials in Washington were Communist sympathizers who formed a sort of Leftist underground and were trying to recruit other people to their cause. In support of Berle's version of the meeting, Alger Hiss later testified that he had visited Berle's home two months after Berle's meeting with Chambers and that Berle had not mentioned anything about any accusations concerning his (that is, Hiss') loyalty.

The truth appeared to lie somewhere between the two men's recollections. Berle's notes of the meeting, introduced at one of Hiss' trials for perjury, revealed that Chambers had named both Alger Hiss and his brother as Communist Party members: under Alger Hiss' name there appeared the notation in Berle's handwriting: "Ass't to Sayre—CP-1937—Member of the Underground Com.-Active Baltimore Boys." Nowhere in the notes, however, was there any indication that Chambers had connected Hiss with Soviet espionage activity.

In any event, Berle did not act upon Chambers' information in 1939 or at any time thereafter, although he maintained in his testimony to HUAC that he did advise Secretary of State Dean ACHESON of Chambers' suspicions when Alger Hiss became Acheson's executive assistant. (On this point, at least, Berle was mistaken because Alger Hiss was never Acheson's assistant.)

When one member of HUAC asked Berle in August 1948 if he had suspected Hiss of being a Soviet agent, Berle replied that he had only become concerned about Hiss' loyalty in the closing months of World War II because Hiss was part of a State Department faction that favored a conciliatory policy toward the Soviet Union. "There was a difference of opinion in the State Department," recalled Berle. On one side were Berle and Undersecretary Joseph Grew, who headed a coterie who felt "the Russians were not going to be sympathetic and cooperative"; therefore, Berle and Grew were "pressing for a pretty clear-cut show-down when our [i.e., the United States'] position was strongest. The opposite group in the State Department was largely the men in Mr. Acheson's group, of course, with Mr. Hiss as his principal assistant in the matter." At that time, continued Berle, "Mr. Hiss did take what you would call today the pro-Russian point of view. That was a cause for worry." Berle and Grew lost the policy battle. Berle was subsequently appointed U.S. ambassador to Brazil, and Acheson replaced Grew as undersecretary of state.

Berle went on to become one of the founders of the Liberal Party in New York. Like other militantly anti-Communist liberals, he supported the premise that liberalism should look upon the far Left as its primary opponent. In 1973 his wife published his memoirs, *Navigating the Rapids: 1918–1971.*

**Bessie, Alvah** (1904–1985)  A left-wing screenwriter and member of the HOLLYWOOD TEN, Alvah Bessie attended Columbia University before embarking on a career as an author. He began by writing short stories and in 1935 received a Guggenheim fellowship for creative writing. For the following two years, Bessie served as drama and book editor for the *Brooklyn Daily Eagle;* he interrupted his writing career in 1938 to fight on the side of the Republican government in the Spanish Civil War as a member of the Abraham Lincoln Battalion of the International Brigade. Upon returning to the United States in 1939, Bessie spent several years as a reporter and drama critic for the Communist publication *New Masses.* His enthusiasm for left-wing causes outweighed the financial hardships imposed by his minuscule salary; he had to live on a farm in Vermont because he could not afford to live in New York City. "We need writers," Bessie once explained, "who will joyfully impose upon themselves the discipline of understanding and acting upon working-class theory."

In the winter of 1943, executives from the Warner Bros. studio offered Bessie $300 a week to come to Hollywood to write scripts for motion pictures. He completed several movie scripts (including *Objective Burma, Hotel Berlin,* and *Northern Pursuit*) between 1943 and 1945. For the most part, however, his work failed to impress producers, and Bessie's only film credit after 1945 was for a small independently produced movie titled *Smart Woman.* By that time, he was known as an active and quite vocal member of the COMMUNIST PARTY in Hollywood.

In September 1947, while Bessie was barely eking out a living in Hollywood, the HOUSE COMMITTEE ON UN-AMERICAN ACTIVITIES (HUAC) subpoenaed him, along with the other members of the Hollywood Ten, to testify in Washington about his alleged Communist activities. The fourth member of the Ten to testify before HUAC, Bessie attempted to defend his political affiliations and activities aggressively. He charged the committee with trying to "smear New Dealers" and accused it of leading a drive to prepare "a fascist America" by taking part in "precisely the identical activities engaged in by un-Spanish committees, un-German committees, and un-Italian committees which preceded it in every country which eventually succumbed to fascism." His protests failed to move either the committee or the federal district court that convicted him of contempt of Congress in early 1948 for his refusal to tell HUAC whether he was a Communist. Bessie subsequently served a one-year prison term at Texarkana, Texas. While in jail, he expressed his bitterness and disillusionment in a letter to a friend: "I curse the day that Warner Brothers called me in New York in January 1943 and asked me if I would like to write motion pictures."

Following his release from prison, Bessie had difficulty finding employment. He expressed no interest in working in Hollywood; instead, he obtained a position as a publicist at the headquarters of the Longshoremen's and Warehousemen's Union. After spending five years with the union, Bessie was dismissed when the union found it necessary to reduce its staff, and he subsequently took a job as a stage manager and lighting technician at the "Hungry I" nightclub in San Francisco. In 1965, his personal account of his confrontation with HUAC, entitled *Inquisition in Eden,* was published.

Although Bessie adamantly refused to return to southern California, he wrote an adaptation of his novel *The Symbol* for television (it was shown as an *ABC Movie of the Week)* and subsequently wrote another account of his journey through radicalism entitled *Spain Again.*

**Biberman, Herbert** (1900–1971)  One of the most talented members of the HOLLYWOOD

TEN, Herbert Biberman grew up in Philadelphia and graduated from the University of Pennsylvania before working briefly for his family's textile business. In 1924, Biberman arrived at Yale University to study theater, and four years later he joined the Theater Guild in New York as assistant stage manager. Biberman quickly rose to the position of director with several outstanding productions (including *Miracle at Verdun* and Maxwell Anderson's *Valley Forge*) among his credits.

He arrived in Hollywood in 1935 under contract to Columbia Pictures as a director, but never achieved much commercial success. By 1948, he had only eight films to his credit, including three as a director and five as a screenwriter.

Biberman was far more active, however, in the political affairs of the film community, as was his wife, actress Gale SONDERGAARD. He was a member of the COMMUNIST PARTY and a founder of the Screen Directors Guild and the Hollywood anti-Nazi League. He also joined several antifascist POPULAR FRONT organizations and worked to raise funds to improve the lot of farm laborers in California. In April 1939, Biberman helped establish the Motion Picture Guild, Inc., a group dedicated to the production of "socially relevant" movies. His own contributions to this effort included documentaries on the evils of fascism and the plight of migrant agricultural workers.

In March 1940, a Los Angeles County grand jury subpoenaed Biberman as part of an investigation of Communist influence in the motion picture industry. The inquiry was poorly organized, however, and ended almost before it began. When the HOUSE COMMITTEE ON UN-AMERICAN ACTIVITIES (HUAC) launched its own investigation into Hollywood in the autumn of 1947, Biberman was one of the unfriendly witnesses it called to Washington to testify. Like the other members of the Hollywood Ten, Biberman failed to answer the questions of the committee and was subsequently indicted for contempt of Congress. In 1948, a

federal district court convicted Biberman on this charge and sentenced him to six months in prison and a fine of $1,000.

While he waited for the U.S. Supreme Court to hear his appeal, Biberman helped establish the Freedom from Fear Committee, an organization dedicated to raising funds and arousing public support for the defense of the Ten. Biberman also organized a production company called Film Associates, Inc., created to produce films that would combine technical excellence and progressive political themes. The expenses of legal fees for the Ten and continued pressure from HUAC, however, forced the company to fold within a year.

In the spring of 1950, the Supreme Court denied Biberman's appeal, and he entered a federal prison at Texarkana, Texas. When asked by his parole adviser if he would repeat his hostile behavior if he were summoned before HUAC again, Biberman replied, "How could a man who conceived of citizenship and duty as I do *not* challenge what he was deeply convinced his duty impelled him to challenge as evil and destructive?"

Following his release from prison, Biberman joined with other BLACKLISTED members of the motion picture community to form yet another film company, Independent Productions Corporation. The company's first and only release, *Salt of the Earth,* was a stirring drama about striking miners in New Mexico. It was shown in only one theater in the United States, however, because union projectionists refused to show it when they discovered that Biberman had been blacklisted by the motion picture industry. (The sole exception was the 86th Street Grande Theater in New York.) Nevertheless, French critics voted *Salt of the Earth* the best picture of the year, and after political passions had died down, the film finally was shown in the United States in the mid-1960s.

Although Biberman remained involved in political affairs—he publicly supported Julius and Ethel ROSENBERG in the appeal of their conviction on espionage charges—he drifted out of the film industry for a time and took a job as an assistant buyer for the Pacific Coast Textile Company at a salary of $100 per week. He later returned to Hollywood and in the late 1960s made one more film entitled *The Slaves,* which garnered critical acclaim at the Cannes Film Festival in 1969.

**Bingham, Hiram** (1876–1956)   A former senator from Connecticut (1924–1933) and a longtime friend of Herbert Hoover, Hiram Bingham was selected by President Harry S. TRUMAN in November 1950 to head the United States Civil Service Commission LOYALTY REVIEW BOARD. The Truman administration had come under increasing attack from congressional Republicans for allegedly harboring disloyal employees, and Truman hoped that the selection of Bingham would help mute partisan criticism of federal personnel security standards. "They wanted an old-fashioned conservative Republican," Bingham acknowledged. "They told me so."

Both Bingham and his predecessor, Seth RICHARDSON, urged the adminstration to grant the Loyalty Review Board broader powers to investigate and dismiss suspected subversives, including those who had been cleared by the review boards of individual executive departments. Bingham was particularly appalled at the lax standards applied by the Department of State. "I think it is fair to say," observed Bingham at a meeting of the board in February 1951, "that the State Department, as you know, has the worst record of any department in the action of its loyalty board. The loyalty board, in all the cases that have been considered in the State Department, has not found one—shall I say 'guilty' under our rules. It is the only board which has acted in that way. . . . I called [Secretary of State Dean] ACHESON's attention to the fact that his board was out of step with all other agency boards."

Truman complied with Bingham's request in April 1951 with his EXECUTIVE ORDER 10241, which allowed the Loyalty Review Board to dismiss any federal government employee when there appeared a "reasonable doubt" of his or her allegiance in the present or at any time in the past. (The previous standard had required "reasonable grounds" to doubt an employee's loyalty in the present.) Bingham used this change to move aggressively to reopen cases that had already been dismissed for lack of evidence. By March 1952, 2,756 of the 9,300 federal employees who had been cleared under the prior standard were again under scrutiny. Among the reopened cases were those of Stephen BRUNAUER (who was suspended by the Navy Department and then resigned), Esther BRUNAUER (suspended and then fired by the State Department), John Paton DAVIES (suspended by State), and John Stewart SERVICE (fired by State).

Shortly after the Eisenhower administration took office in January 1953, the President—under pressure from Senator Joseph MCCARTHY to prove that he was tougher on Communists in government than his predecessor—broadened the powers of the Loyalty Review Board further through EXECUTIVE ORDER 10450, making it still easier to dismiss federal employees suspected of disloyalty. This time, even Bingham believed that the standards had been loosened too far; it was, he declared, "just not the American way of doing things," and he predicted a "Pandora's box of troubles." Bingham was replaced as head of the board later that year.

In light of the U.S. Senate's censure of McCarthy in December 1954, it was perhaps ironic that Bingham was one of only three other senators ever censured by the Senate prior to that time. Bingham had been censured in 1929 for bringing the assistant to the president of the Connecticut Manufacturers Association, disguised as his aide, into an executive session of the Senate Finance Committee.

**blacklist**   The practice of proscribing certain individuals from employment, based upon their political activities or affiliation, was used in the entertainment industry during the McCarthy era. Typically, an actor, director, or other performer was identified by an informant as having belonged to or supported the COMMUNIST PARTY or certain Communist-front organizations. Sometimes, evidence of a performer's association with left-wing causes was nothing more substantial than an organization's letterhead with the performer's name on it or an advertisement for a benefit show for which the performer had agreed to be a sponsor or participant. An accused performer was seldom afforded any opportunity to deny or explain any allegations of Communist sympathies. Once individuals had been publicly identified as Communist sympathizers, they found it impossible to obtain work in their chosen field.

Blacklisting began in earnest after the appearance of the HOLLYWOOD TEN before the HOUSE COMMITTEE ON UN-AMERICAN ACTIVITIES (HUAC) in October 1948. Following the Ten's refusal to testify, executives from the leading Hollywood movie studios gathered at the Waldorf-Astoria Hotel in New York City and issued the WALDORF STATEMENT, in which the studios—in an attempt to block further congressional interference in the film industry—pledged not to employ any members of the Ten until they had repented and cleared themselves of contempt charges; further, the studios promised not to employ knowingly any actors or directors with Communist sympathies. The practice of blacklisting subsequently became institutionalized in the early 1950s, following the second round of investigations by the HUAC into Communist influences in the motion picture industry. As Victor Navasky, the leading authority on the Hollywood blacklist during the McCarthy era, explained, "No Hollywood Communist or ex- who had ever been accused, or called to testify, or refused to sign a studio statement would get work in the business—or at least under his own name—unless he went through the ritual of naming names."

Numerous conservative organizations, including the AMERICAN LEGION, developed their own blacklists of suspected subversives whose name on any movie, television or radio show, or consumer product would produce calls for a boycott. There were also publications that existed solely for the purpose of identifying allegedly subversive individuals. In 1947, three former FBI agents created a company known as American Business Consultants. With financial assistance from industrialist Alfred KOHLBERG, a leading member of the anti-Communist CHINA LOBBY, and the CATHOLIC CHURCH, the agents launched a publication known as COUNTERATTACK. The editors of Counterattack simply compiled a list of Communist front organizations from reports issued by congressional committees, the federal government, private organizations, and state legislatures, as well as old copies of the Communist Party newspaper, the DAILY WORKER. The editors then identified in their newsletter individuals who had been listed as members of any of these organizations without making any attempt to discern whether the original listing was accurate.

In June 1950, American Business Consultants launched a second publication, a handbook entitled RED CHANNELS, which focused exclusively on the entertainment industry. The original edition of Red Channels contained the names of 151 performers and authors who allegedly belonged to one or more organizations that the editors had identified as Communist fronts; the names included Edward G. ROBINSON, Abe BURROWS, Jose FERRER, Orson Welles, Garson Kanin, and Gypsy Rose Lee.

Radio and television executives and their corporate sponsors soon discovered that the path of least resistance was to abide by the judgments delivered by professional and amateur blacklisting organizations. "The advertising agency simply does not hire a person listed in Red Channels or does not renew a contract upon its expiration," explained one contemporary industry analyst. "The individual is not even told in so many words that the Red Channels listing is responsible. . . . The individual is just out of a job." Blacklisting organizations made a further profit by offering to "vet" performers or writers for producers or network executives; that is, they would run a performer's name through its files before he or she was hired to determine whether there was any hint of subversive activity in the performer's background. Further, the blacklisters would set themselves up as judges and confessors when accused individuals desired to repent and clear themselves to reestablish their credentials as loyal Americans.

Among the performers whose careers were ruined by blacklists were Mady CHRISTIANS (who suffered a nervous breakdown as a result and died a year later), Jean Muir, Gale SONDERGAARD, and Philip LOEB, who committed suicide. Others who were blacklisted for varying amounts of time included Robinson, Lee J. COBB, director Carl FOREMAN, radio humorist John Henry FAULK, actor Jack Gilford, theatrical producer Joseph PAPP, and Zero MOSTEL. Charlie CHAPLIN was effectively barred from further film projects in Hollywood, and folksinger Pete SEEGER did not appear on network television for twelve years following his refusal to answer the questions of the House Committee on Un-American Activities.

In 1956, an organization known as the FUND FOR THE REPUBLIC, originally sponsored by the Ford Motor Company, published a two-volume study entitled *Report on Blacklisting,* written by John Cogley, a former executive editor of *Commonweal* magazine. In his report, Cogley pointed out that the entertainment industry had abdicated its responsibility for assessing the loyalty of performers and writers, giving that duty wholly to the blacklisters themselves. In one case after another, Cogley proved that the blacklisting procedures depended heavily upon suspicion, innuendo, and anonymous tips rather than facts and that cases of mistaken identity were common.

Not surprisingly, the House Committee on Un-American Activities objected to Cogley's conclusions and opened hearings on July 10, 1956, on its own "Investigation of So-Called 'Blacklisting' in the Entertainment Industry." The committee summoned Cogley as its first witness and sought (albeit unsuccessfully) to discredit his evidence and conclusions. HUAC subsequently called numerous blacklisters themselves to testify and permitted them to defend their procedures at length. In the end, HUAC chairman Francis Walter concluded that "The Fund for the Republic report is a partisan, biased attack on all persons and organizations who are sincerely and patriotically concerned in ridding the movie industry and radio and television of Communists and Communist sympathizers."

The power of the blacklist continued long after the political downfall of Senator Joseph MCCARTHY in 1954. In 1960, actor/singer Frank SINATRA attempted to hire blacklisted screenwriter Albert MALTZ to write the script for a film but was forced to cancel his arrangement with Maltz following a series of vocal protests by the American Legion and the Catholic War Veterans. In that same year, however, producer Otto Preminger announced that Dalton TRUMBO, like Maltz a member of the Hollywood Ten, had written the screenplay for his film *Exodus,* and actor Kirk Douglas insisted that Trumbo be hired to write the screenplay for the movie *Spartacus.* A further blow to the blacklist was dealt by the courts in 1962 in awarding Faulk a $3.5 million judgment in his libel suit against several fanatical anti-Communist individuals and an organization that had been responsible for blacklisting him six years earlier. By 1963, the practice of blacklisting had become the subject of television dramas and published memoirs.

In 1976, a film about the blacklisting era entitled THE FRONT, starring Woody Allen, was released, featuring numerous writers and actors who had been blacklisted during the 1950s. The use of blacklists in the entertainment industry has also been the subject of numerous historical studies, including Victor Navasky's *Naming Names* (1980).

**Blankfort, Michael** (1907–1982) A prominent left-wing novelist, playwright, and screenwriter in the 1930s and 1940s, Michael

Blankfort graduated from the University of Pennsylvania in 1928 and taught psychology for two years at Princeton University before turning to writing as a full-time career. Blankfort's first novel, *I Met a Man,* was published in 1936; subsequent works included *The Brave and the Blind* (1938) and *A Time to Live* (1942).

Although Blankfort never joined the COMMUNIST PARTY, he regularly wrote drama and film reviews for two Communist publications, the *DAILY WORKER* and *New Masses.* He was dropped by both journals in 1934–35 because, in his words, "I refused to fit my play reviews into the political theory of the moment." (Specifically, party officials objected to his negative reviews of two plays by Clifford ODETS.) As what he termed an "independent radical," Blankfort served as a member of the board of the Theatre Union, an organization founded in 1932 to bring drama with socially relevant themes to a broad working-class audience. During the mid-1930s, he also visited the Soviet Union to witness the Marxist experiment firsthand.

Blankfort moved to Hollywood in 1937 and became a successful screenwriter (*Broken Arrow; The Halls of Montezuma*) and an active supporter of left-wing causes. One of his closest friends in the motion picture industry was fellow screenwriter Albert MALTZ. According to Blankfort, a Communist Party recruiter attempted to persuade him to join the party in 1937, but he refused. Nevertheless, Blankfort did support numerous Communist front organizations during the late 1930s; "I believed, at that time, that the Communist movement represented a progressive force in the American life," he later explained. After the signing of the NAZI-SOVIET PACT in 1939, Blankfort abandoned his antifascist activities and, following the lead of the Communist Party, worked to keep the United States out of war. His most notable contribution toward this end was as coauthor of a "Living Newspaper on Peace," presented to an audience of 8,000 at a noninterventionist rally at the Olympic Auditorium in Los Angeles on April 6, 1940.

Immediately after the Japanese attack on Pearl Harbor in December 1941, Blankfort enlisted in the Marine Corps. He served for two-and-a-half years and received an honorable discharge as a captain. His past leftist associations brought his loyalty into question in the postwar period, however, as did his support of the HOLLYWOOD TEN through his membership in the COMMITTEE FOR THE FIRST AMENDMENT and his signature on an amicus curiae ("friend of the court") brief to the Supreme Court on behalf of John Howard LAWSON and Dalton TRUMBO. In January 1952, former Communist Party member Louis BUDENZ named Blankfort as a Communist in testimony before the HOUSE COMMITTEE ON UN-AMERICAN ACTIVITIES (HUAC).

When he appeared before the committee to rebut Budenz' charges on January 28, 1952, Blankfort answered all questions and firmly denied that he had ever been a member of the Communist Party. He also told the committee that he did not know any Communists, although when he was asked whether he had "any relatives who are or have been members," he reportedly answered, "You are referring to my ex-wife Laurie and my cousin Henry—I have no knowledge of either."

This slip, later expunged from the record, earned Blankfort the contempt of Maltz and other members of the Hollywood community who had refused to answer HUAC's questions or inform on their former associates. For his part, Blankfort received the thanks of the committee and resumed his film career, working with another cooperative Hollywood witness, Edward DMYTRYK, on the movie version of *The Caine Mutiny.* He later served as president of the SCREEN WRITERS' GUILD.

**Blau v. United States**   In 1949, a federal grand jury investigating Communism called Patricia Blau, a minor COMMUNIST PARTY official in Colorado, as a witness. Pleading the Fifth Amendment, Blau refused to state whether she knew anything about the Communist Party. She was subsequently tried for contempt, convicted, and sentenced to a year in jail.

Blau appealed the verdict, and in December 1950, the Supreme Court overturned the lower court and ruled 8–0 in favor of Blau. Because the SMITH ACT of 1940 had made Communist activities a basis for criminal charges, Justice Hugo Black, writing the majority opinion for the Court, reasoned that a witness asked to testify about such actions might justifiably invoke the Fifth Amendment to avoid self-incrimination.

The ruling was greeted with approbation by a host of reluctant witnesses in congressional investigations who were then facing jail terms for refusing to answer questions about their Communist activities. The Supreme Court's opinion also underlined the flaw in the strategy of the HOLLYWOOD TEN, who had chosen to stand on their First Amendment rights instead of pleading the Fifth.

Blau's victory also encouraged resistance to the INTERNAL SECURITY ACT OF 1950 (also known as the McCarran Act), which required members of the Communist Party to register with the government as Communists. If party membership were illegal under the Smith Act, the mere act of registration as a Communist would necessarily violate the protection of the First Amendment.

The principle of *Blau v. U.S.* was subsequently modified by the outcome of *Rogers v. U.S.*, which required a witness to plead the Fifth Amendment at the outset of questioning. It could not be invoked in the midst of a line of questions inching toward incrimination.

### Block, Herbert L. (1909– )

One of Senator Joseph MCCARTHY's earliest and most persistent critics in the press, Herbert Block began his career with the Chicago *Daily News* at the age of nineteen as the newspaper's editorial cartoonist. Four years later, Block accepted a position with the Newspaper Enterprise Association in Cleveland. His cartoons attracted nationwide

Cartoonist Herbert Block, who coined the term "McCarthyism."

publicity, and in 1942, Block—who had adopted the pseudonym "Herblock" on his father's advice—won the Pulitzer Prize for editorial cartooning. The following year he joined the United States Army and spent most of World War II in New York and Florida, drawing cartoons for the Army's Information and Education Division. Discharged in 1946 as a sergeant, Block obtained a position as editorial cartoonist for the *Washington Post*.

The nation's capital provided Block with a virtually unlimited supply of subjects to lampoon. Two of Block's favorite targets were Senators Patrick MCCARRAN of Nevada and Joseph McCarthy of Wisconsin. Block was appalled by McCarthy's practice of vilifying individuals through innuendo, unsubstantiated reports, and hearsay evidence—hence his artistic condemnation of the tactics which he called "fear and smear" and "the screaming whimwhams."

In March 1950, the *Post* published a Herblock cartoon that introduced a new word—"MCCAR-

THYISM"—into the nation's political language. The cartoon featured right-wing Republican leaders trying to drag a noticeably recalcitrant elephant (the cartoonist's symbol for the Republican Party) toward a teetering stack of buckets dripping with tar, with the top barrel labeled "McCarthyism." "You mean I'm supposed to stand on that?" asked the incredulous elephant in the caption. Another anti-McCarthy Herblock cartoon featured a man labeled "Hysteria" armed with a bucket of water, climbing the Statue of Liberty in an attempt to extinguish the torch of freedom.

Block invariably portrayed McCarthy as a sort of Neanderthal in modern guise: squat, beetle-browed, with a menacing leer and a perpetual stubble of beard. The parody apparently caused McCarthy considerable anguish. During the 1952 presidential campaign, Block satirized Republican candidate Dwight D. EISENHOWER's attempt to benefit from McCarthy's accusations against the TRUMAN administration while maintaining a discreet distance from the Wisconsin senator. In one cartoon, a simian McCarthy stood in a pool of filth holding a sign that read, "Anything to Win." Eisenhower stood nearby, explaining to a distraught voter that "Our differences have nothing to do with the end result we are seeking." In a later commentary on the duel between Eisenhower and McCarthy for control of the Republican Party, Herblock pictured McCarthy wielding a bloody meat cleaver while Eisenhower was armed with only a feather.

Although McCarthy and his allies accused Block of Communist sympathies, the cartoonist also frequently turned his pen against the leaders of the Soviet Union and the People's Republic of China. In fact, Block won his second Pulitzer Prize in 1954 specifically for a cartoon published upon the death of Soviet dictator Joseph STALIN. In his drawing, a skeletal figure—the grim reaper—accompanied Stalin as the dictator walked along toward the netherworld, carrying a sickle soaked in blood. "You always were a great friend of mine, Joseph," read the caption.

**B'nai B'rith**   See ANTI-DEFAMATION LEAGUE.

**Bogart, Humphrey** (1899–1957)   A popular Hollywood film star, Humphrey Bogart was a member of the COMMITTEE FOR THE FIRST AMENDMENT, a coalition of performers, directors, and writers who protested in the autumn of 1947 against congressional encroachments upon artistic freedom. A native of New York City, Bogart first acted on the stage in 1920. He worked steadily in a succession of theatrical roles for the next decade before landing his first part in a motion picture in 1930. Bogart made his biggest impression on audiences as a gangster in the film version of *The Petrified Forest* in 1936; that triumph was followed by *Dead End* (1937), *King of the Underworld* (1939), *High Sierra* (1941), *The Maltese Falcon* (1942), and *Casablanca* (1942).

Active in liberal political causes during the 1930s, Bogart testified about his activities and beliefs before the HOUSE COMMITTEE ON UN-AMERICAN ACTIVITIES (HUAC) in California in August 1939. During this session, Bogart assured the chairman of the committee, Martin DIES, that he was not a Communist and did not

Humphrey Bogart (right), a Hollywood liberal who was forced to publicly prove his anti-Communist credentials.

have any sympathy with the Communist movement. The issue remained in abeyance until 1947 when HUAC, at the behest of chairman J. Parnell THOMAS, launched another probe into Communist influence in the motion picture industry. Nineteen "unfriendly" witnesses—actors, directors, and writers whom committee investigators suspected of being Communists—were called to Washington to answer questions about their political associations. Faced with the threat of congressional interference in the film industry, a group of Hollywood liberals headed by William Wyler and John Huston formed the Committee for the First Amendment (CFA) to protest HUAC's inquiry.

To publicize their cause, the CFA sent a delegation of film stars—including Bogart, Lauren Bacall, and Danny Kaye—to Washington at the end of October 1947. Bogart participated in the nationwide radio broadcasts sponsored by the CFA to put its case before the American public. The hostile attitude of the first ten unfriendly witnesses (who later became known as the HOLLYWOOD TEN) turned public opinion against their cause, and Bogart, like many members of the CFA, decided to withdraw his support of the Ten to keep from being accused of Communist sympathies himself.

Accordingly, Bogart dispatched a letter to newspaper columnists across the country, stating unequivocally that "I am not a Communist." "I am not a Communist sympathizer," Bogart continued. "I detest Communism just as any other decent American does. My name will not be found on any Communist front organization as a sponsor for anything communistic. I went to Washington because I thought fellow Americans were being deprived of their constitutional rights and for that reason alone. That trip was ill-advised, even foolish, I am very ready to admit. At the time it seemed like the thing to do."

Yet, even this statement was not sufficient to end the threat to Bogart's career. In a further effort to clear his name, Bogart wrote an article entitled "I'm No Communist" for the March 1948 issue of *Photoplay* magazine. In the article, Bogart admitted that he had been a "dope" to go to Washington for the CFA, but he insisted that he was an "American dope." Bogart's public repentance helped establish a pattern for other performers who wished to clear themselves of suspicion. His career revived without further delay, and in the next nine years Bogart starred in such classic films as *The Treasure of the Sierra Madre* (1948), *Key Largo* (1948), and *The African Queen* (1951), for which he won an Academy Award as best actor. Bogart died of cancer in 1957.

**Bohlen, Charles E.** (1905– ) A career State Department officer who was nominated by President Dwight David EISENHOWER in February 1953 to be the United States ambassador to the Soviet Union, Charles "Chip" Bohlen became the focal point of the first confrontation between Eisenhower and Senator Joseph MC-CARTHY of Wisconsin. Although Bohlen was a personal acquaintance of Eisenhower, who respected him as one of the nation's leading experts on the Soviet Union, his selection as ambassador caused an uproar in conservative Republican circles. The problem was that Bohlen had served as translator for President Franklin D. Roosevelt at the YALTA Conference in 1945. To right-wing stalwarts such as Senators McCarthy and Styles BRIDGES, Yalta symbolized the perfidious Democratic policy of appeasement of Communism. They wanted Eisenhower to repudiate the Yalta agreements; instead, he had chosen a member of Roosevelt's conference staff as the new American ambassador.

Undersecretary of State Walter Bedell Smith urged the Senate Foreign Relations Committee to move quickly to approve Bohlen's nomination. Bohlen appeared before the committee in March and seemed to assuage its concerns. Then Scott MCLEOD, McCarthy's friend and the recently appointed assistant secretary of state for security affairs, revealed that an FBI investigation had produced adverse information on Bohlen.

Charles Bohlen's nomination as U.S. ambassador to the Soviet Union touched off the first confrontation between Joseph McCarthy and the Eisenhower administration.

(Later, it was revealed that most of this material was nothing more than hearsay reports and anonymous letters, along with one report from an informant who claimed to have a "sixth sense" that discerned immorality in Bohlen.)

In the unsettled atmosphere of early 1953, such rumors were sufficient to place the nomination in jeopardy. The Foreign Relations Committee announced that it would delay action on Bohlen and scheduled another hearing. McCar-

thy and Senator Pat MCCARRAN told reporters that they would oppose the nomination. Even Secretary of State John Foster DULLES wavered in his support, but Eisenhower insisted that the administration stand firmly behind Bohlen. After Dulles told the committee that he was personally convinced of Bohlen's loyalty, the nomination received preliminary approval by a vote of 15–0.

Furious, McCarthy and his allies launched an attack on Bohlen when the nomination reached the floor of the Senate on March 23. Bridges referred to Bohlen as an "exponent of appeasement and containment" and called him an "experienced failure." McCarthy suggested that Bohlen submit to a lie-detector test about the allegations in the FBI's files. "In our opinion," McCarthy charged, "he is a bad security risk."

Outraged by McCarthy's attack on a man who enjoyed his respect and full approval, Eisenhower nonetheless consented (over the objection of Attorney General Herbert BROWNELL, who feared it would set a damaging precedent) to open Bohlen's FBI file to any two senators chosen by the chamber. The Senate selected Robert TAFT and John J. Sparkman to review the documents; they subsequently reported that they had found nothing that cast doubt on Bohlen's loyalty.

On the eve of the final Senate vote on the nomination, Eisenhower held a press conference to reiterate his support for Bohlen and to express his concern that excessively zealous investigations of an individual's loyalty might reach a point where they would imperil the national security. The President refused to criticize McCarthy by name, however, believing that such publicity would benefit the senator.

The Senate approved Bohlen's nomination by an overwhelming majority, 74–13. Although the administration won the battle, the long-term effects of the nomination fight were less one sided. The incident demonstrated clearly that McCarthy and his allies would not desist from their anti-Communist crusade simply because there was now a Republican in the White House.

Despite Eisenhower's best efforts, the heated fight over the Bohlen nomination provided McCarthy with a generous measure of publicity in the nation's newspapers. It also made Senate Majority Leader Robert Taft wary of supporting future White House initiatives without prior consultation with Congress.

**Boorstin, Daniel J.** (1914– )   When the HOUSE COMMITTEE ON UN-AMERICAN ACTIVITIES (HUAC), under the chairmanship of Harold VELDE, launched an investigation of Communist influence in American colleges and universities in February 1953, one of the first witnesses they called was Daniel Boorstin. At that time, Boorstin was a professor of history at the University of Chicago, but the committee was interested primarily in Boorstin's membership in Communist organizations at Harvard University in the late 1930s.

Boorstin appeared before the committee in public session on February 26, 1953, one day after the testimony of Robert Gorham DAVIS. Boorstin acknowledged that he had been a member of a Marxist study group while he was attending Oxford University as a Rhodes Scholar in 1936–37. There were, according to Boorstin, about a hundred students in the group who spent their time discussing Marxist literature. "It was not," claimed Boorstin, "an important episode in my life in the sense that I had any position of leadership, or anything of that kind."

Upon his return to the United States in 1938, Boorstin accepted a position as an instructor at Harvard College. There he joined the COMMUNIST PARTY, partly because the notion of a POPULAR FRONT against fascism appealed to him and partly because the Communists were taking a strong stand against the anti-Semitic policies of Hitler and the Nazis. Boorstin added that his decision to join the party was also influenced by the prestige of Granville HICKS, an admitted Communist and eminent scholar of American literature who was then serving as a counselor in American studies at Harvard.

Boorstin confirmed Davis' testimony that the Communist Party members among the faculty never made a concerted effort to impart Marxist doctrines to their students. Boorstin also followed Davis' example in providing the committee with the names of individuals with whom he had associated during his membership in the party.

Following the announcement of the NAZI-SOVIET PACT in 1939, Boorstin left the party. He informed the committee that he had since sought to express his opposition to Communism through his participation in religious activities ("because I think religion is a bulwark against Communism") and by discovering and extolling through his teaching and writings "the unique virtues of American democracy."

In response to a question from a member of the committee, Boorstin stated that he believed active members of the Communist Party should be barred from teaching in American public schools and colleges. "My feeling," Boorstin said, "is that no one should be employed to teach in a university who was not free intellectually, and, in my opinion, membership in the Communist Party would be virtually conclusive evidence that a person was not intellectually free." At the conclusion of his testimony, Boorstin left the committee with the assurance that its questions "had not in any way impinged on my academic freedom."

Boorstin currently serves as Librarian of Congress.

**Brecht, Bertolt** (1898–1956)   One of the outstanding playwrights and poets of the early twentieth century, Bertolt Brecht was known for his cynical contempt for capitalism and the values and politics of the bourgeoisie, as well as his steadfast opposition to the Nazi regime that came to power in Germany in 1933. Born in Augsburg, Germany, Brecht first achieved prominence with his antiwar poetry in 1918–19. At the end of World War I, he participated in the short-lived Marxist regime of Eugene Levine in Munich. When the revolution collapsed, Brecht migrated to Berlin where he helped mold the distinctively dark, radical artistic culture of Weimar Germany. His most successful play was *The Threepenny Opera*, first produced in public in 1928.

When his antiwar poem "The Dead Soldier" marked him as an enemy of the Nazis, Brecht fled Germany in February 1933, one day after the Reichstag fire. He lived in Scandinavia for the next eight years, trying to stay one step ahead of the Nazis advance, until he left Europe in May 1941, making his way eastward by train across the Soviet Union and then boarding a ship for the United States. To his disappointment, Brecht very soon decided that cultural life in southern California was virtually nonexistent. "The intellectual isolation here is enormous," he wrote to a friend. "In comparison to Hollywood, Svendborg [Denmark] was a world center."

During the next six years, Brecht sold only one idea—the story that became a film called *Hangmen Also Die*—to a movie studio. He did complete several of his best-known plays in this period, however, including a biographical drama of Galileo, in the English version of which Brecht castigated those who cooperated with the forces of the inquisition.

When the HOUSE COMMITTEE ON UN-AMERI- CAN ACTIVITIES (HUAC) launched its investigation of Communist activities in Hollywood in 1947, it targeted Brecht as one of its initial list of nineteen "unfriendly" witnesses, largely because of his left-wing activities in Weimar Berlin and his continuing friendship with suspected Communist agents Hanns and Gerhart EISLER. Since he was not an American citizen, Brecht assumed that the protection afforded other witnesses by the First and Fifth Amendments did not apply to him, and he decided to cooperate with the committee, at least on the surface. Besides, Brecht had already obtained an exit visa for Switzerland, and he did not want any legal squabbles to delay his departure.

Unlike the first ten "unfriendly" witnesses (known collectively as the HOLLYWOOD TEN),

all of whom had refused to state whether they were members of the COMMUNIST PARTY, Brecht readily informed the committee that "I was not a member, or am not a member, of any Communist Party." He admitted receiving Gerhart Eisler as a guest in his home, but he said that they had merely played chess and discussed German politics.

Brecht spent most of the remainder of his time on the witness stand debating whether the committee's translations of his plays from German into English were accurate, while evading committee attempts to reduce his writings to a simplistic pro-Communist or anti-Communist formula. On occasion, the language barrier between Brecht and HUAC staff, compounded by Brecht's deliberate efforts to obfuscate the issues, enlivened the proceedings with a touch of absurd humor. Consider the following exchange between Brecht, Robert E. STRIPLING, chief investigator for HUAC, and committee chairman J. Parnell THOMAS:

> Mr. Stripling: Mr. Brecht, since you have been in the United States, have you attended any Communist Party meetings?
> Mr. Brecht: No, I don't think so.
> Mr. Stripling: You don't think so?
> Mr. Brecht: No.
> Mr. Stripling: Well, aren't you certain?
> Mr. Brecht: No—I am certain, yes.
> Mr. Stripling: You are certain you have never been to Communist Party meetings?
> Mr. Brecht: Yes, I think so. I am here six years—I am here those—I do not think so. I do not think that I attended political meetings.
> The Chairman: No, never mind the political meetings, but have you attended any Communist meetings in the United States?
> Mr. Brecht: I do not think so, no.
> The Chairman: You are certain?
> Mr. Brecht: I think I am certain.
> The Chairman: You think you are certain?
> Mr. Brecht: Yes, I have not attended such meetings, in my opinion.

At last the committee gave up, commended Brecht for his cooperation, and dismissed him from the hearing. Brecht promptly boarded a flight for Switzerland and, two years later, moved to East Berlin, where he founded the Berliner Ensemble.

**Bridges, Harry** (1901–1990)   As head of the International Longshoremen's and Warehousemen's Union (ILWU) and West Coast regional director of the CIO, Australian native Harry Bridges (born Alfred Renton Bridges) acquired a well-deserved reputation as one of the most aggressive labor leaders in the United States from the 1930s to the 1970s.

Shortly after the House of Representatives authorized the establishment of the HOUSE COMMITTEE ON UN-AMERICAN ACTIVITIES in 1938, committee chairman Martin DIES (who harbored a pronounced dislike for the American labor-union movement) singled out Bridges as one of his initial targets. Blaming Bridges for labor unrest on the West Coast, Dies sought first to prove that Bridges was a member of the COMMUNIST PARTY and then initiated deportation proceedings against him. Dies never succeeded in proving that Bridges was a Communist, although, like most CIO officials in the late 1930s, Bridges certainly considered Communists his allies in the labor movement. Even if he had established Bridges' Communist credentials, however, Dies would have run afoul of a U.S. Court of Appeals decision in a separate 1938 case that stated that "membership in the Communist Party is not grounds for deportation."

Dies' failure notwithstanding, Justice Department officials—prodded by Congress—took up the cause and twice attempted to deport Bridges as a Communist. (Bridges' comment that "There are more Hitler agents to the square inch in Congress than there are to the square mile in Detroit," did nothing to endear him to the legislature.) The government's first deportation effort, in 1939, foundered upon the unreliability of the witnesses against Bridges. Moved in part by its hostility toward Bridges—he was actually named in the original legislation—Congress passed the SMITH ACT in 1940, one provision of which made it a deportable offense to belong to any group that advocated the overthrow of the United States government.

After a second hearing and 7,724 pages of evidence, the government succeeded in acquiring a deportation order against Bridges in 1941 on the testimony of witnesses who claimed they had heard him admit to being a Communist, supported by evidence of Bridges' membership in numerous Communist-front organizations. The following four years were spent in court appeals and rehearings, until the United States Supreme Court finally quashed the deportation order in 1945. An individual, the Supreme Court ruled, could not be deported solely because he had belonged to the Communist Party in the past. "Seldom, if ever, in the history of this nation," wrote Justice Murphy in a concurring opinion, "has there been such a concentrated and relentless crusade to deport an individual because he dared to exercise the freedom that belongs to him as a human being and that is guaranteed to him by the Constitution." The government's harassment of Bridges, added Murphy, might "stand forever as a monument to man's intolerance of man."

Still the government refused to give up. Amid the labor unrest that accompanied reconversion to a peacetime economy, the TRUMAN administration found Bridges' confrontational tactics a particularly bothersome thorn in its side. In June 1949, a federal grand jury indicted Bridges for perjury, claiming that Bridges had lied when he claimed during his citizenship hearings that he was not a Communist and had never belonged to the Communist Party. Following a near three-month trial, a judge accepted the testimony of several dozen witnesses, found Bridges guilty of perjury, and sentenced him to five years in prison. Bridges appealed the verdict.

Following the outbreak of the KOREAN WAR in 1950, the government intensified its efforts to deport Bridges, fearing that his union might tie up vital war-related shipping along the West Coast. Therefore, it revoked Bridges' bail while his case was on appeal. The verdict was eventually reversed, and the government subsequently launched a fourth, fifth, and sixth effort to deport the union leader. All of them failed. At the end of the 1950s, Bridges was still alive and active as head of the ILWU.

Between court battles, Bridges took time to encourage the resistance of the HOLLYWOOD TEN in their confrontation with HUAC. When Senator Joseph MCCARTHY joined the anti-Communist crusade in the winter of 1950, one of the criteria he employed as proof of Communist sympathies was an individual's friendship with Bridges or membership in groups that supported Bridges' efforts to avoid deportation, such as the Harry Bridges Defense Fund. Yet, Bridges endured and continued to provoke anti-Communist politicians through his labor union activities and outspoken advocacy of left-wing political causes. For instance, HUAC cited Bridges as a threat to American security interests in 1959 following his pledge to disrupt shipping on the West Coast if the United States ever provided assistance to Nationalist Chinese leader CHIANG Kai-shek (whom Bridges described as "a bum") in an attempt to restore Chiang to supremacy on the mainland of China. "I would do what I could to oppose America engaging in such a suicidal enterprise," admitted Bridges. Also when Soviet premier Nikita KHRUSHCHEV visited the United States in 1959, Bridges was one of the few American labor leaders to embrace Khrushchev publicly. In 1960, Bridges managed to negotiate one of the first major U.S. labor contracts containing provisions for workers who lost their jobs due to automation.

## Bridges, Styles (1898–1963)

A leader of the conservative Republican faction in the United States Senate, Henry Styles Bridges served as senator from New Hampshire from 1937 until his death in 1963. Born in West Pembroke, Maine, Bridges grew up on a farm and earned the cost of his college tuition at the University of Maine by working for fifteen cents an hour in the university's dairy barns. Follow-

Styles Bridges (left), conservative Republican senator from New Hampshire.

ing his graduation from the university, Bridges served as an instructor in agriculture at Sanderson Academy in Ashfield, Massachusetts. In 1921, he became the U.S. agricultural agent for Hancock County, Maine, and subsequently was appointed a member of the University of New Hampshire agricultural extension staff. From 1922–24, Bridges was executive secretary of the New Hampshire State Farm Bureau Federation, and in 1924, he became editor of the New Hampshire journal *Granite Monthly,* as well as director and secretary of the New Hampshire Investment Company.

Bridges first entered public service in 1930 when he was appointed to the New Hampshire Public Service Commission. Four years later, Bridges was elected governor of New Hampshire; at the age of thirty-six, he became the youngest governor in the history of the state. In the midst of the Great Depression, Bridges acted vigorously to balance the state's budget, establish a state planning-and-development board, sponsor state unemployment insurance and benefits for the elderly (New Hampshire was the first state to qualify under the Federal Social Security Act), and develop a new agricultural standards act.

In 1936, Bridges won election to the United States Senate—despite the Democratic landslide nationwide—where he quickly earned a reputation as a "conscious, unashamed" conservative. He mounted an unsuccessful campaign for the Republican presidential nomination in 1940 (changing his name in the process from "Henry Styles Bridges" to "Styles Bridges" to avoid confusion with radical labor leader Harry BRIDGES) but won reelection to the Senate two years later. As a member of the Senate Foreign Relations Committee, Bridges steadfastly opposed concessions to the territorial ambitions of the Soviet Union. In the immediate postwar period, he bitterly criticized the YALTA accords, which gave to the Soviet Union territory that traditionally had been a part of Poland. When the Chinese Nationalist government of CHIANG Kai-shek began to lose ground to the Communist forces of MAO Zedong in 1946–47, Bridges joined the other members of the pro-Chiang CHINA LOBBY in supporting calls for investigations of Communist influences in the United States Department of State.

Although President Harry S. TRUMAN had long considered Bridges a friend, the New Hampshire senator became one of the most vocal critics of Secretary of State Dean ACHESON during Truman's second administration (1949–53). Bridges, who was one of only six senators to vote against Acheson's confirmation, was especially outraged by Acheson's defense of State Department official Alger HISS, who was convicted of perjury after denying that he had formerly belonged to the COMMUNIST PARTY. During one of Acheson's appearances before the Senate Appropriations Committee, which Bridges chaired, the New Hampshire senator asked Acheson coldly whether he would consider "a friend of a person convicted of perjury in connection with a treasonable act" a security risk. ("I think it would be a matter to be looked into," replied Acheson.) At one point, Bridges came close to accusing Acheson of disloyalty. "We must find the master spy who moves the puppets Hiss and [H. Julian] Wadleigh and the others in and out of office in this capital of the United States," said Bridges, "using them, and using our State Department as

he wills." Bridges' repeated assaults upon Acheson eventually led Truman to describe the senator as one of "the Kremlin's biggest assets" in the COLD WAR.

As a member of the Senate hierarchy, Bridges had not favored the frequently reckless and unpredictable activities of Senator Joseph MCCARTHY of Wisconsin. But when McCarthy accused the State Department in February 1950 of harboring a number of "card-carrying Communists," Bridges helped organize a coalition of conservative members of Congress to provide McCarthy with ammunition to justify his charges. Although he had a reputation as a loyal member of the Republican Party, Bridges broke with the administration of President Dwight David EISENHOWER when he joined McCarthy in opposing the nomination of Charles BOHLEN as United States ambassador to the Soviet Union in the spring of 1953, largely because Bohlen had attended the Yalta conference as an interpreter. "If we approve the nomination of Mr. Bohlen," claimed Bridges, "we put the seal of approval on the sellout of Poland, and we slap in the face every citizen of Polish descent in this nation and every free man in this country."

In November 1954, as the Senate moved toward a vote of censure against McCarthy, Bridges sought to substitute less condemnatory measures for the resolution proposed by Senator Ralph FLANDERS of Vermont. When all efforts at compromise failed and the Senate voted to condemn McCarthy's actions, Bridges rose and asked Vice President Richard M. NIXON, who was then presiding over the Senate, whether the motion specifically mentioned the word *censure*. Informed by Nixon that the word did not appear in the final version of the motion, Bridges announced that "then it is not a censure resolution." Democratic Senator William FULBRIGHT of Arkansas responded by pointing out that, in his dictionary, *condemn* was actually a harsher term than *censure*.

His steadfast defense of McCarthy notwithstanding, Bridges remained a respected member of the Senate Republican establishment, easily winning a fifth term in 1960. He died soon afterward of complications following a severe coronary attack.

**Brookings Institution**   In early 1945, the Brookings Institution—a prestigious liberal policy analysis and research organization located in Washington, D.C.—prepared for the HOUSE COMMITTEE ON UN-AMERICAN ACTIVITIES a memorandum to guide its forthcoming investigation of subversive activities in the United States. Entitled "Suggested Standards for Determining Un-American Activities," the pamphlet recommended that the committee focus its efforts on five objectives:

1. To determine whether existing law against un-American activities was adequate, or whether further legislative action was desirable;
2. To publish the results of the committee's investigations so that the American people could have "accurate and comprehensive information" about the un-American activities of individuals and associations;
3. To inform government officials of un-American activities and potentially subversive actions;
4. To disclose the un-American activities of individuals who were or might become candidates for public office; and
5. To detect and give to the American public "accurate and reasonably complete information of un-American activities of any person holding any public office."

Although there is no direct evidence that the committee based its investigative approach upon the Brookings memorandum (later published by Brookings and offered for sale to the public), HUAC did focus its probe upon individuals, a strategy that was clearly consistent with the Brookings recommendations. The assistance rendered by Brookings to HUAC provided another demonstration (see the AMERICAN CIVIL LIBERTIES UNION and AMERICANS FOR DEMO-

CRATIC ACTION) that mainstream American liberal organizations were prepared to cooperate with the committee, at least at the outset of the postwar period.

**Browder, Earl**   (1891–1973)   Known within the American Communist movement as "the quiet man from Kansas," Earl Browder served as general secretary of the COMMUNIST PARTY OF THE UNITED STATES OF AMERICA (then officially known as the Communist Party, U.S.A.) during World War II. From the time he first rose to prominence within the movement in 1935–36, Browder advocated a "soft" line that called for collaboration with other left-wing groups and a muting of differences between Communism and American liberalism. He helped lead the drive to create a POPULAR FRONT of leftist organizations against fascism in the mid-1930s, supporting the New Deal initiatives of President Franklin D. Roosevelt and downplaying the Communist Party's subservience to Moscow. "We Communists claim the revolutionary tradition of America," Browder stated. "We are the Americans, and Communism is the Americanism of the twentieth century."

Browder campaigned as the Communist Party candidate in the U.S. presidential election of 1940 (the last time the party nominated a candidate of its own), but his campaign was interrupted by his arrest and conviction on charges of traveling on false passports. He was sentenced to five years in prison; in May 1942, however, Roosevelt commuted Browder's term.

Between 1942 and 1945, Browder personified the wartime era of good feelings between the United States and the USSR. He became the symbol of the policy of peaceful coexistence and was awarded a preeminent position among American Communists in Moscow, pushing former leader William Z. FOSTER (who still opposed cooperation with capitalist nations, even in wartime) into the background. In keeping with his softer approach, Browder even changed the name of the Communist Party in America to the Communist Political Association.

When Stalin ordered an end to the Soviet wartime policy of collaboration in the spring of 1945, Browder was deposed and subsequently expelled from the Communist Party in February 1946 as a "social imperialist." His abrupt dismissal shook the faith of many American leftists who had accepted his assurances about Communist intentions and inaugurated an exodus of disillusioned radicals from Communist-front organizations.

In an effort to understand the implications of Browder's removal from a position of leadership, the HOUSE COMMITTEE ON UN-AMERICAN ACTIVITIES (HUAC) summoned the former general secretary to testify in September 1945. The committee's questions were so disorganized, however, that they elicited little useful information. Browder's name thereupon passed from the headlines, except when he was mentioned by witnesses before congressional committees as proof of a suspect's Communist associations.

Browder resurfaced in April 1950, following Senator Joseph MCCARTHY's allegations that Owen LATTIMORE was one of the top Soviet agents in the United States. In an appearance before Senator Millard TYDINGS' subcommittee investigating McCarthy's charges, Browder claimed that he did not know Lattimore, that he had never met Lattimore, that he had never (to the best of his knowledge) even seen Lattimore, that he did not know Lattimore as a member of the Communist Party, and that he had never heard Lattimore's name mentioned at Communist Party gatherings.

Six months later, McCarthy managed to strike back at Tydings by using Browder's brief appearance before the committee. During the 1950 congressional elections, a campaign tabloid known as "For the Record," written in part by members of McCarthy's staff, published a photograph that purported to show Tydings and Browder whispering together, engaged in an intimate conversation. Although later analysis proved the photograph to have been a composite of two separate cropped photos, the ploy helped defeat Tydings in his bid for reelection to the Senate.

Excluded from the leadership of the American Communist Party, Browder explored the possibilities of cooperation with the Socialist Party. In 1959, he reportedly discussed the formation of a "new Fabian Society" with Socialist leader Norman THOMAS, but no organization ever emerged from the talks. Browder spent the remainder of his life in relative obscurity until his death in 1973.

**Brownell, Herbert** (1903– )   As attorney general under President Dwight David EISENHOWER, Herbert Brownell worked to establish the anti-Communist credentials of the Eisenhower administration as a means of fending off attacks from right-wing Republican extremists in Congress.

A native of Nebraska, Brownell graduated from the University of Nebraska and Yale Law School, working as an attorney in a prestigious Wall Street law firm before winning a seat in the New York State legislature in 1931. In 1942, Brownell directed Thomas E. Dewey's successful campaign for governor; he subsequently served as Dewey's campaign manager in both the 1944 and 1948 presidential campaigns.

Four years later, General Eisenhower chose Brownell to guide his presidential election campaign as well. Following Eisenhower's victory, Brownell advised the president-elect on appointments and then accepted a cabinet post as attorney general. Eisenhower considered Brownell one of his most trusted advisers, a man of impeccable honesty and respected judgment who would make an excellent chief executive. (Brownell was, in fact, considered by the moderate wing of the Republican Party as a possible successor to Eisenhower.)

At the initial cabinet meeting of the Eisenhower administration on January 23, 1953, Brownell declared that he was not satisfied with the existing loyalty program for federal employees. Republican candidates had attacked the

Truman administration relentlessly during the 1952 election campaign for its allegedly lax security standards, and Eisenhower clearly felt compelled to tighten up the federal loyalty program. Brownell recommended that the White House put less emphasis on LOYALTY OATHS, which he felt were both ineffective and a logistical nightmare to administer, and focus its attention on the question of whether an employee was a security risk. Brownell said that he could envision employees who were perfectly loyal and yet were susceptible to blackmail because of past indiscretions. Eisenhower approved the change, and thereafter security rather than loyalty became the test for appointing and retaining federal employees.

In the autumn of 1953, Brownell attempted to take the initiative in the anti-Communist crusade away from Senator Joseph MCCARTHY by reopening the case of the late Harry Dexter WHITE, a former high-ranking government official in the Truman administration. In a speech to the Executives Club in Chicago on November 6, Brownell said that President Truman had ignored reports from the FEDERAL BUREAU OF INVESTIGATION that proved that White was a Soviet espionage agent. Not only had Truman refused to dismiss White; the President had actually promoted him to be head of the International Monetary Fund. The White case, Brownell concluded, was "typical of the blindness which infected the former Administration on this matter," and showed "why the present Administration is faced with the problem of disloyalty in government."

Brownell predicted to Eisenhower that his attack on Truman "would take away some of the glamour from the McCarthy stage play" and establish the administration's credentials for fighting the Red menace, thereby capturing control of the anti-Communist crusade from McCarthy, whom both Eisenhower and Brownell disliked and distrusted. By reopening the White case, Brownell also hoped to steal the spotlight from McCarthy's subcommittee and place it instead on Indiana Republican Senator William JENNER's internal security subcommittee of the Judiciary Committee.

Unfortunately for Brownell, his strategy misfired. Pressed by reporters to prove White's guilt, Eisenhower promised to supply the relevant evidence, but Brownell found it necessary to object on principle to the release of raw FBI files. The administration was thus placed in the uncomfortable position of reneging on its promise to be more open with the public on the issue of Communists in government. Further, McCarthy seized the headlines by calling former President Truman to testify in the White case. Truman refused on the grounds of executive privilege and bitterly criticized Brownell and Eisenhower for dredging up a case that had long been resolved. Nor did Brownell's initiative persuade McCarthy to relinquish his leadership of the anti-Communist crusade. Instead, McCarthy awarded Eisenhower faint praise for being more vigilant than his predecessor, all the while insisting that even this Republican president employed Communists in office, as witnessed by the posting of John Paton DAVIES as counselor to the American embassy in Lima, Peru.

Brownell was more successful in defending the privileges of the Executive Department during the ARMY-MCCARTHY HEARINGS in the spring of 1954. When McCarthy urged federal employees and military personnel to provide him and his subcommittee with all information they possessed regarding "graft, corruption, communism, [and] treason" in government, Brownell swiftly responded with a public statement that the President—and the President alone—was responsible for the execution of the laws of the nation and "that responsibility can't be usurped by an individual who may seek to set himself above the laws of our land."

Meanwhile, Brownell moved to commit the Eisenhower administration to a far-reaching revision of internal subversion legislation. Frustrated by the frequent invocation of the Fifth

Amendment by suspected Communists, Brownell proposed in October 1953 that Eisenhower ask Congress for legislation that would give the office of the attorney general authority to grant immunity to witnesses so that the government could compel witnesses to testify. Brownell also sought authority to employ wiretaps in national security cases without prior judicial authorization—evidence obtained by wiretaps in intelligence investigations would therefore be made admissable in criminal cases—and to expedite the deportation of naturalized and alien subversives.

The sweeping provisions of Brownell's wiretap proposal alarmed even Republican conservatives, who condemned it as "an invasion of privacy and a violation of American tradition." Although his wiretap measure did not pass Congress, Brownell did win approval of a modified expatriation bill, along with witness-immunity legislation that vested in the courts, rather than the attorney general, the authority to grant immunity. At the same time, Brownell opposed the passage of the major piece of congressional anti-Communist legislation of 1954, the COMMUNIST CONTROL ACT. Brownell correctly pointed out that this bill, which made membership in the COMMUNIST PARTY a crime and required Communists to register with the Subversive Activities Control Board, would actually permit Communists to defy the registration requirements because admission of party membership—if it were a crime—would violate their rights under the Fifth Amendment.

Ultimately, Brownell provided Eisenhower with a militant anti-Communist who helped to deflect criticism from senatorial conservatives during the height of the anti-Communist hysteria, although Brownell's excesses cost Eisenhower support among moderate Democrats. In 1958, Brownell resigned and was replaced by William Rogers, who shared his reputation as a hard-line opponent of Communism.

## Brunauer, Esther Caulkihn (1901–1959)

Dr. Esther Brunauer and her husband, Stephen BRUNAUER, were among the first individuals named by Senator Joseph MCCARTHY when he launched his crusade against Communists in America in 1950.

A native of California, Esther Caulkin received a Ph.D. from Stanford University and served for seventeen years as head of the American Association of University Women's program in international education. In 1931 she married Stephen Brunauer, a Hungarian-born chemist. During the mid-1920s, Brunauer had belonged to a Communist-front organization known as the Young Workers' League. He had never joined the COMMUNIST PARTY, however, and in 1927 he quit the league.

The Brunauers spent several months studying in Germany shortly after the Nazis came to power in 1933; their personal experiences with Naziism converted Esther to the antifascist cause upon her return to the United States. She worked to further the American rearmament effort throughout the late 1930s and enlisted public support for the victims of Nazi aggression after the outbreak of World War II. During the war, her husband served in the U.S. Navy Bureau of Ordnance and became an expert on high explosives. In 1944, Esther Brunauer accepted a position with the State Department, helping to carry out programs for postwar international organizations. It was in that capacity that she attended the San Francisco conference in 1945 at which the United Nations was founded. Following the war, Esther Brunauer became the State Department's liaison with the United Nations Educational, Scientific, and Cultural Organization (UNESCO), while Stephen remained in the Navy as a commander in the naval reserve. He also participated in the planning for the U.S. atomic-bomb tests at Bikini in the immediate postwar years.

Questions about the loyalty of the Brunauers had first surfaced in 1941 when a Senate committee briefly questioned them before security officers granted them a clearance. Six years later, isolationist Illinois Congressman Fred Busbey attacked Esther Brunauer and several other alleged "pro-Communist fellow travelers and muddle heads" in the State Department; investigators for the HOUSE COMMITTEE ON UN-AMERICAN ACTIVITIES examined her records at length, but a review board reaffirmed her loyalty in 1948 following a full field investigation by the FBI.

Then McCarthy entered the picture. Someone had passed Esther Brunauer's name along to the senator, and he first mentioned her to reporters—off the record—as a possible security risk during his famous trip to Wheeling, West Virginia, on February 9, 1950. In a subsequent speech on February 20, McCarthy identified Esther Brunauer as a Communist sympathizer; he repeated the charge in greater detail on March 13 in his testimony before the TYDINGS subcommittee that was established to investigate the spectacular charges made by McCarthy in his Wheeling speech. McCarthy informed the Tydings subcommittee that during her tenure at the American Association of University Women, Esther Brunauer had directed the association toward pro-Communist consumer activities. Further, he claimed that she had been Alger HISS' first assistant at the San Francisco Conference and charged her with membership during the 1930s in a Communist-led organization advocating rearmament. "This is, in my opinion, one of the most fantastic cases I know of," McCarthy concluded. To make matters worse, in McCarthy's opinion, Stephen Brunauer had been granted access to what McCarthy termed "some of the topmost defense secrets which the armed forces of this country possess." He therefore asked the subcommittee to obtain collaborative evidence about the Brunauers from the files of Naval Intelligence and the State Department.

Dr. Esther Brunauer asked Tydings for permission to respond to McCarthy's charges, and on March 27 she testified before the Tydings committee. She denied that she had ever been a Communist or a Communist sympathizer; she pointed out that she had actually served as Congressman Sol Bloom's assistant at the San Fran-

cisco conference and knew Hiss only slightly. She also explained that McCarthy had confused two different organizations from the 1930s—the group to which she belonged had not been associated with the Communist Party in any way. Brunauer adamantly insisted that she had never knowingly associated with Communist-front organizations, and she submitted letters from Dr. Milton Eisenhower (the brother of General Dwight David EISENHOWER) and two United States senators attesting to her loyalty. Moreover, Brunauer defended her husband, pointing out that he had severed his connections with the Young Workers' League more than twenty years earlier and had since adopted a fervently anti-Communist stance.

Despite Esther Brunauer's rebuttal of McCarthy's charges and the Tydings subcommittee's conclusion that there was "no evidence that Mrs. Brunauer is disloyal, or a Communist sympathizer, or a security risk," the couple received scores of obscene and threatening telephone calls and letters at their home. One newspaper ran a photograph of Dr. Brunauer above the caption, "TOP RED?" Perhaps frightened of more inquiries by McCarthy and his colleagues, the Navy suddenly suspended Stephen Brunauer's security clearance on April 10, 1951, pending further investigation. Almost simultaneously, the State Department suspended Esther Brunauer. By this time, the standards of federal security boards had been tightened, in part because of the publicity afforded McCarthy's charges. Convinced that the Navy intended to dismiss him, Stephen Brunauer resigned from the naval reserve in June. Esther Brunauer, however, continued the fight to clear her name. A State Department review board affirmed her loyalty once again, but in June 1952 she was fired from her job on the grounds that she was a security risk. The most damning evidence against her was her "close and habitual association" with her husband.

Stephen Brunauer left Washington, moved to Chicago, and obtained a position as a chemist with the Portland Cement Association. Esther worked for a brief time with the Library of Congress before joining her husband in Illinois, where she worked as an editor at several publishing firms.

It has been suggested that the case of Esther Brunauer reflected a definite gender bias inherent in the McCarthy crusade. Because women had long been prominent in social reform and humanitarian organizations—which McCarthy and his allies often singled out as Communist fronts—they were especially vulnerable to attack on their past associations. In any event, the fate of the Brunauers clearly demonstrated that by 1951, outside pressures had tilted the federal government's loyalty-review procedures to favor the prosecution.

**Brunauer, Stephen** (1903– )   A Hungarian-born chemist who emigrated to the United States at the age of eighteen and subsequently became one of the U.S. Navy's top experts on high explosives, Stephen Brunauer was accused by Senator Joseph MCCARTHY in 1950 of harboring Communist sympathies. Brunauer acknowledged an association with Communists in Europe in the 1920s but claimed that he had never joined the COMMUNIST PARTY and had broken all ties with his former Communist associates before 1930. In an attempt to refute McCarthy's charges, Republican Senator Joseph Ball described Brunauer as "perhaps the most violently anti-Communist person I know."

Nevertheless, McCarthy continued to assail Brunauer in his speeches, and in the spring of 1951, Brunauer was suspended by the Navy pending the outcome of a security investigation. He resigned from government service in June 1951. (See also BRUNAUER, Esther.)

**Buckley, William F. Jr.** (1925– )   An ardent defender of Senator Joseph MCCARTHY and the HOUSE COMMITTEE ON UN-AMERICAN ACTIVITIES (HUAC), William F. Buckley, Jr., has been one of America's leading conservative intellectuals since the early 1950s. The son of a

wealthy Texas oil speculator, Buckley grew up in New York City and attended Millbrook Academy before entering the United States Army in the final year of World War II. Upon his discharge from the Army with the rank of second lieutenant, Buckley resumed his studies at Yale University. Before graduating from Yale, Buckley completed a book entitled *God and Man at Yale,* which attacked the university's curriculum for its alleged bias against religion and in favor of liberalism. Buckley attempted to distribute the volume at Yale's commencement exercises in 1951.

Shortly after his graduation from college, Buckley launched a series of attacks upon liberal Democratic Senator William BENTON of Connecticut, claiming that Benton—who was emerging as one of the leading foes of McCarthy in the United States Senate—was a Communist sympathizer. "Buckley is a smart, able, aggressive young man," Benton replied. "He is a potentially dangerous young man." Besides his attacks upon Benton, Buckley lent his talents to a private group dedicated to the eradication of Communist influence in the federal government. By 1953, Buckley had become a protege of McCarthy. In that year, he drafted a Senate speech for McCarthy attacking the prospective appointment by President Dwight D. EISENHOWER of former Harvard University President Dr. James B. Conant as U.S. high commissioner for West Germany. Conant had angered Buckley and his conservative colleagues by opposing congressional inquiries into Communist activities on the nation's university campuses. Although McCarthy never delivered Buckley's speech, he did draft a strongly worded letter to Eisenhower opposing the Conant nomination.

Buckley remained close to McCarthy throughout the remainder of the senator's life, despite Buckley's misgivings about McCarthy's increasingly erratic behavior in the spring and summer of 1954. That year, Buckley and a conservative attorney named Brent Bozell published a lengthy defense of McCarthy entitled *McCarthy and His Enemies.* Although they ac-

**William Buckley (right, with President Richard Nixon), ardent defender of HUAC.**

knowledged that McCarthy did not possess sufficient evidence to support some of his charges of subversion, Buckley and Bozell argued that evidence of Communist sympathies would be difficult for anyone to obtain. "Probatory evidence of Party membership is *ipso facto* hard to come by," they wrote. "If we have learned anything about the scope and the techniques of the Communist conspiracy, it is that only a small percentage of the Communist faithful take out membership cards; and that, what is more, many Communists are not identifiable on the basis of their overt political activities." Buckley and Bozell then proceeded to extend their argument by attacking American liberals, "not because they are treacherous like the Communists, but because . . . we will conclude 'that they are are mistaken in their predictions, false in their analyses, wrong in their advice, and through the results of their actions injurious to the interests of the nation.' " Rejecting the accusations of liberal critics that McCarthy had employed a reckless, scattershot approach to fighting Communist influence in the United States, Buckley concluded that "as long as MCCARTHYISM fixes its goal with its present precision, it is a movement around which men of good will and stern morality can close ranks."

McCarthy's censure by the Senate in December 1954 and his ensuing political decline dimmed Buckley's enthusiasm for the anti-Communist crusade not a whit. In 1955, Buckley founded *National Review,* a journal of opinion and commentary which provided conservative ideologues with a forum to promote their political and cultural agendas. Seven years later, Buckley and the editors of *National Review* published a volume defending the record of the frequently maligned (in liberal circles, at least) House Committee on Un-American Activities. Entitled *The Committee and Its Critics: A Calm Review of the House Committee on Un-American Activities,* the book included articles on the case of Alger HISS, the liberal campaign against HUAC, and the nature of Communist subversion in the twentieth century.

In his introductory article to the volume, Buckley suggested that the United States in 1962 had drifted back to the complacent atmosphere of the immediate post-World War II era. Bemoaning "the general indifference to the problem of Communist subversion," Buckley proceeded to defend the work of HUAC, which he claimed had displayed "an intuitive apprehension of Communism which by empirical standards seems truer than that of some of our most conspicuous and learned academic and journalistic Kremlinologists." Moreover, Buckley claimed that HUAC was responsible "for the development of more serious information, of a didactically useful kind, than the typical department of political science in the typical university." The academic community, he argued, had failed to develop any practical means of divining political heretics from Communist conspirators, and therefore the task had fallen by default to HUAC. For Buckley, the issue of whether HUAC had violated constitutional rights of suspected Communist sympathizers seemed to be largely irrelevant. "It is nothing short of preposterous willingly to tolerate an active conspiracy in our midst," Buckley decided, "and if the Constitution is not, as presently understood, resilient enough to cope with the contemporary requirements of survival, then the Constitution should be modified, as it has been before."

In 1965, Buckley ran for mayor of New York on the Conservative party ticket and won only 13 percent of the vote in a three-way race. The following year, he launched a weekly television interview program called *The Firing Line,* which subsequently became the longest-running show on the Public Broadcasting System. President Richard M. NIXON, a former member of the House Committee on Un-American Activities, named Buckley to the U.S. delegation to the United Nations in 1973. While continuing to write his political columns for a variety of forums, Buckley also authored a series of moder-

Louis Budenz (right) and Elizabeth Bentley, two former Communists who testified frequently before congressional committees about former associates and activists.

ately successful spy novels in the late 1970s and 1980s.

**Budenz, Louis F.** (1891–1967)   A former COMMUNIST PARTY official who had served as managing editor of the official party newspaper, the *DAILY WORKER,* Louis Budenz became one of the leading witnesses against accused Communists in trials and congressional committee hearings during the McCarthy Era. A native of Indianapolis, Indiana, Budenz attended a series of Catholic and Jesuit educational institutions in his youth, including St. John's High School, St. Xavier College in Cincinnati, Ohio, and St. Mary's College in Kansas.

Although he was admitted to the bar in 1913, Budenz practiced law on a full-time basis for less than a year. Appalled by the sight of working Americans who were "too poor to live as they should," Budenz became active in the labor union movement. At the age of 21, he became an editor of the official journal of the Brotherhood of Carpenters and Joiners. Over the next twenty-two years, Budenz served as secretary of the St. Louis Civic League, publicity director of the AMERICAN CIVIL LIBERTIES UNION, editor of a pro-union publication entitled *Labor Age,* as the New Jersey state campaign manager of Progressive Party presidential candidate Robert M. LaFollette in 1924, and as a labor organizer in New Jersey and in Kenosha, Wisconsin. His union activities eventually earned him a total of twenty-one arrests, though each time Budenz was brought to trial he was acquitted of the charges against him.

Beyond his membership in various radical labor organizations, Budenz also joined the COMMUNIST PARTY in 1935. On the recommendation of Earl BROWDER, then secretary general of the Communist Party of the United States, Budenz openly acknowledged his party membership in October 1935 and was subsequently appointed labor editor of the *Daily Worker.* Two years later, Budenz was named editor of the *Midwest Daily Record,* though that publication folded when the party shifted its line on American intervention in the European war following the announcement of the NAZI-SOVIET PACT of August 1939. In 1941, Budenz became managing editor of the *Daily Worker* and a member of the Communist Party's national committee.

In the closing months of World War II, Budenz began to meet with the well-known and fervently anti-Communist Roman Catholic prelate Monsignor Fulton J. Sheen, who helped persuade Budenz to renounce his Communist beliefs and return to the CATHOLIC CHURCH. On October 10, 1945, Budenz announced that he had left the Communist Party. Within months the FBI had contacted Budenz and persuaded him to provide it with information against his former colleagues. Budenz later claimed that it took him more than 3,000 hours—"the staggering equivalent of 375 eight hour days"—to tell the authorities everything he knew about Communist Party activities in the United States. There should have been no questions, claimed the articulate Budenz, about his veracity. According to Budenz, ex-Communists made excellent witnesses; indeed, he ar-

gued that they were "the most truthful people in the world" because "they have learned how utterly incorrect is the morality of Lenin, the morality of deceiving for a cause. They have learned in pain and suffering . . . they have [had] a resurrection within themselves." After recanting his Communist allegiance, Budenz accepted a position on the faculty of Notre Dame University. He later left Notre Dame and joined Fordham University as an assistant professor of economics.

In October 1946, Budenz delivered a radio speech during which he claimed that the Communist International continued to exist "in fact, if not in form," that the International gave instructions to Communist parties throughout the world—including the United States—and that a man named Gerhart EISLER, also known as Hans Berger, was the Comintern's representative in the United States. One month later, Budenz appeared to testify before the HOUSE COMMITTEE ON UN-AMERICAN ACTIVITIES (HUAC). At that time, the committee was still beginning to obtain basic information about the nature of the Communist movement in the United States. Budenz's testimony on that occasion amounted to a virtual monologue on the relationship between the International and the Communist Party of the United States, including tantalizing tidbits about the "conspiratorial apparatus" which the party employed to advance its interests and protect its officials' identities. Clearly Budenz's former membership in the party added a cachet of veracity to the material he provided the committee.

During the course of his testimony, Budenz informed the committee that American intellectuals were particularly susceptible to Communist propaganda. He claimed that Communists referred to liberal intellectuals as " 'soft-headed and soft-hearted liberals,' and to some extent that is a correct designation. They rush out to defend the communist line, without any responsibilities on their part. It is a very comfortable position to be in, by the way. You do not have any of the responsibilities of the Communist leadership, and on the other hand you have the satisfaction of acting very progressively. . . . The liberals are the first line of defense for the Communists."

Budenz elaborated upon his HUAC testimony in his autobiographical account of his years in the Communist Party, *This Is My Story,* published in 1947. One newspaper reviewer wrote that Budenz's personal witness of Communist machinations represented "the most damaging evidence of the conspiratorial character of the American Communist Party ever published." Over the next several years, Budenz testified at numerous court trials and congressional inquiries about individuals he reportedly had known during his years in the party. In 1948, Budenz joined another ex-Communist, Whittaker CHAMBERS, in accusing former State Department official Alger HISS of membership in the Communist Party. The following year, Budenz served as a key witness in the prosecution's case against eleven leading officials of the Communist Party in the United States. He subsequently provided the House Committee on Un-American Activities with the names of nearly 400 individuals whom he claimed were Communists. Meanwhile, Budenz continued to write columns for popular magazines and newspapers and embarked upon a series of lecture tours. By the end of 1950, Budenz had earned nearly $40,000 from speaking and writing about Communism.

Not surprisingly, Budenz became closely acquainted with millionaire industrialist Alfred KOHLBERG, the leader of the CHINA LOBBY, a loose coalition of politicians and businessmen who wished to advance the cause of Chinese Nationalist leader CHIANG Kai-shek. Budenz claimed that he and Kohlberg met at least once a week following Budenz's departure from the Communist Party. It was Kohlberg who introduced Budenz to Senator Joseph MCCARTHY of Wisconsin and who brought Budenz into the controversy over the loyalty of Far East experts Owen LATTIMORE and John Carter VINCENT.

Budenz was, in fact, the sole witness who claimed that Lattimore—whom McCarthy identified as the foremost Soviet espionage agent in America—had been involved in the innermost circles of the Communist Party leadership in the United States. (Budenz had not, however, mentioned Lattimore as a former member of the Communist Party in previous debriefings with federal authorities.) Although he had never met Lattimore, Budenz told a special Senate subcommittee chaired by Senator Millard TYDINGS of Maryland that Lattimore had been identified by the code letter *L* or *XL* on secret documents sent to the national committee of the Communist Party. He also claimed that party functionaries had relied upon Lattimore to establish the party line on events in China; in fact, Budenz said that in 1945 one party official had told him that he should "treat as authoritative anything which Lattimore wrote or advised." Budenz acknowledged, however, that McCarthy's charge about Lattimore's significance as a top Soviet spy was "not technically accurate."

Lattimore replied that Budenz's story was "a plain, unvarnished lie," and he denounced Budenz as "a man who had turned a sordid past into a lucrative present of writing and lecturing . . . [and] who had built up a morbid and almost hypnotic reputation as a kind of 'finger of doom.' " Although Lattimore's case was later taken up by the Senate Internal Security Subcommittee, no concrete evidence was ever discovered to support Budenz's charges that Lattimore had been a member of the Communist Party or that he had played an integral role in the party hierarchy. In part because of the lack of evidence to support his charges against Lattimore, the FBI later acknowledged that it harbored substantial doubts about Budenz's credibility as a witness.

Undaunted, Budenz continued to testify against other enemies of the China Lobby, including Vincent, whom Budenz identified as a member of the Communist Party. In August 1951, Budenz told the Internal Security Subcommittee that he had heard "in official Communist Party circles" in 1944 that Vincent was a Communist and that he and Lattimore were trying to guide U.S. Far East policy along Communist lines. Informed of Budenz's testimony, Vincent reportedly retorted, "That . . . son of a bitch should be in jail or hell!" Although Vincent, too, was later exonerated of the charge of Communist Party membership, he was forced to resign from the foreign service.

In neither the Lattimore nor the Vincent case did the Internal Security Subcommittee openly question the credibility of Budenz as a witness, despite the fact that other witnesses—including columnist Joseph Alsop—contradicted Budenz's sworn testimony. Budenz thus continued to make unsubstantiated charges of Communist infiltration in the United States. He claimed that there were approximately 400 members of the Communist Party entrenched in the American motion picture, radio, and newspaper industries, an accusation which was repeated by Senator McCarthy. As the Internal Security Subcommittee broadened its probe of Lattimore to include the INSTITUTE FOR PACIFIC RELATIONS, Budenz identified as Communists 46 other individuals who had been associated with the institute at one time or another. When McCarthy began his search for subversives within the U.S. Army in 1954, he turned to Budenz as an expert witness, to testify that two Army publications on the USSR were "the work of a concealed Communist" within the military hierarchy.

By 1956, the diminishing hysteria over Communist influence in America and the increasingly preposterous nature of Budenz's allegations had limited his usefulness as a witness. During the congressional inquiry into the activities of the FUND FOR THE REPUBLIC in 1956, for instance, Budenz claimed that all such foundations supported "socialist trends" and were Communist infiltrated. During the late 1950s, Budenz appeared frequently on television where he warned his viewers that "the surface has only been scratched" in uncovering Communist espionage networks in the United States. Budenz also

wrote occasional columns for the New York *Herald Tribune,* in which he frequently denounced the decisions of the U.S. Supreme Court—led by Chief Justice Earl WARREN—that upheld the civil liberties of individuals accused of subversive activities. Budenz charged that such decisions demonstrated "the effectiveness of the line laid down by KHRUSHCHEV." At the time of his death, Budenz was still highly regarded as a writer and intellectual within the far right-wing community in the United States.

**Bulletin of Atomic Scientists**   Founded in 1946 by a group of prominent American scientists including Albert EINSTEIN, J. Robert OPPENHEIMER, Edward CONDON, and Linus PAULING, the *Bulletin of Atomic Scientists* provided a forum for members of the American scientific community to express their views on contemporary political issues. Under the editorial direction of Dr. Eugene Rabinowitch, the *Bulletin* generally published articles critical of the nuclear-arms race, proposing instead the path of international cooperation. Science was viewed by the authors as a sphere of intellectual activity that could be separated from political tensions. As Soviet-American relations deteriorated in the late 1940s, the *Bulletin* lamented the narrowing opportunities for contact between scientists of the two nations, and in May 1953 Oppenheimer contributed an article calling for more open discussion of atomic weapons within the United States and for the sharing of nuclear secrets between the United States and the United Kingdom.

While the *Bulletin* adopted an unequivocally hostile stand against Communism, it also condemned the excesses of the anti-Communist hysteria that swept over the United States during the McCarthy era. In May 1954, forty American scientists, including Einstein, expressed their solidarity with the embattled Oppenheimer in his struggle to retain his security clearance with the Atomic Energy Commission. The following year, the *Bulletin* devoted an entire special issue to a review of the loyalty/national security issue in which it repudiated "Communists and fellow travelers" while simultaneously castigating the anti-Communist inquisition for "flinging its net too widely." Even after McCarthy had faded from public prominence, the *Bulletin* continued to monitor the deleterious effects of his work. In 1958, for instance, it estimated that in the State Department alone there were still more than 1,000 employees who were informing on their colleagues.

**Burnham, James** (1905–1987)   A former radical political scientist who had joined the COMMUNIST PARTY in his youth, James Burnham left the party to become a leading critic of Communism in the United States in the early 1950s. In the years following World War II, Burnham urged Congress to pass legislation outlawing the Communist Party in the United States (a move which the FEDERAL BUREAU OF INVESTIGATION (FBI) opposed). In testimony to the HOUSE COMMITTEE ON UN-AMERICAN ACTIVITIES (HUAC) on February 19, 1948, Burnham claimed that "the experience of the past thirty years proves that in the end education and exposure will not be a sufficient defense against Communism. The Communist movement will have to be outlawed." Burnham rejected the notion that attempts to outlaw the Communist Party would simply drive the movement underground. "The fact is that the most serious part of the Communist movement is already underground," Burnham told the committee. "Illegalization would deprive the underground apparatus of the cover and protection and funds that they now enjoy from the legal organizations."

Even after the anti-Communist movement lost much of its momentum following the censure of Senator Joseph MCCARTHY in 1954, Burnham continued to press the cause forward. In 1956, he joined Representative Francis WALTER of Pennsylvania and several dozen other anti-Communist zealots in issuing a warning to the American public not to relax its vigilance against Communist infiltration in the wake of the anti-Stalinist movement in the Soviet Union.

A professor of philosophy at New York University, Burnham was the author of numerous works on political science and management, including *The Managerial Revolution* (1940), *The Machiavellians* (1942), and *The Struggle for the World* (1947). In 1954, Burnham published *The Web of Subversion*, which sought to explain the methods used by Communists to achieve their goals. Burnham also provided an article defending HUAC to *The Committee and Its Critics* (1962), a collection of essays edited by conservative ideologue William F. BUCKLEY, Jr. In his article, Burnham argued that liberal attacks on HUAC failed to recognize the historical precedents for an active investigatory function in Congress. Citing numerous examples to support his case, Burnham claimed that HUAC, with its investigative powers, "did not differ in any significant way from . . . other Congressional committees of the present and past" and actually served a valuable function in limiting the growth of executive power and secrecy. From 1955–1978, Burnham also served as a leading member of the editorial board of the conservative journal *National Review*.

**Burrows, Abraham** (1910–  )   A comedian and writer who achieved considerable popularity in the late 1940s and 1950s, Abe Burrows was accused of membership in the COMMUNIST PARTY and was forced to testify before the HOUSE COMMITTEE ON UN-AMERICAN ACTIVITIES (HUAC) to clear his name.

Burrows grew up in New York City and attended the New York University School of Finance, graduating with a degree in accounting. He found the life of an accountant unsatisfying and worked briefly as a clothing-industry salesman before he entered show business in 1938 as a comedy writer. Burrows spent most of 1939–45 in California writing for various radio programs, including a five-year stint for *Duffy's*

*Tavern,* earning approximately $40,000 a year. After starring in his own short-lived radio show in 1947, Burrows worked for a year and a half in night clubs. He also used this time to coauthor the musical *Guys and Dolls.*

On March 20, 1951, Burrows appeared before HUAC in closed session to answer questions about his membership in left-wing political associations. At that time, Burrows claimed to be unable to remember the names of any Communist Party members he might have met in Hollywood or New York. More than a year and a half later, another witness, an ex-Communist radio writer named Owen Vinson told the committee that he recalled seeing Burrows at Communist Party meetings in 1945–46, and that Burrows had paid party dues to Vinson. Meanwhile, Burrows had also been named as a Communist sympathizer in the entertainment industry's loyalty handbook, RED CHANNELS.

Burrows asked permission to return and testify to HUAC in public session to deny Vinson's allegations. "I have no recollection at all of ever applying for Party membership," he declared. "I have no recollection of ever having possession of a Communist Party card, although I have been told by a private source that somebody had seen a card with my name on it. I have never seen such a card and I don't believe it. I have no recollection of paying dues or anything that could be called dues. I have no recollection of any formal participation in anything that could be called this organization."

Burrows did admit that he had associated with Communists during the life of the American-Soviet alliance during World War II, "when the Communists weren't Communists as we know them or knew them before." He acknowledged attending study groups with Communists, belonging to Communist-front organizations, attending lectures by Communist speakers, and contributing to Communist-front causes. Vinson's testimony also appears to have jogged Burrows' memory about his past associates because this time he provided the committee with names of individuals whom he believed to be Communists or Communist sympathizers. Still, Burrows adamantly maintained that he had never taken "the final step" by joining the party.

Burrows' obsequious performance before the committee amounted to a virtual plea for forgiveness and absolution and earned him the scorn of other Hollywood witnesses who had refused to inform on their former radical associates. Nevertheless, Burrows was able to continue his television and playwriting career unimpeded by further doubts about his loyalty. He subsequently became a popular guest on several television shows and helped create the popular situation comedy *Get Smart* in the late 1960s.

# C

**Cain, Harry P.** (1906–1979)   A much-decorated combat veteran of World War II, Senator Harry Cain of Washington gained fame during the McCarthy era for expressing his disillusionment with Senator Joseph MCCARTHY and the anti-Communist crusade. During his single term in the Senate from 1947 to 1953, Cain was one of McCarthy's staunchest supporters. After his defeat at the polls and his subsequent appointment by President Dwight David EISENHOWER as head of the Subversive Activities Control Board, however, Cain concluded that the atmosphere of suspicion and hysteria that McCarthy had encouraged was having a markedly deleterious effect on American society.

Cain was born in Nashville, Tennessee, raised in the Pacific Northwest, and received a bachelor's degree from the University of the South. He worked briefly as a journalist for an Oregon newspaper before embarking upon a career as a banker from 1929 to 1939, during the Great Depression. In 1940, Cain was elected mayor of Tacoma, Washington; unlike most of the political leaders on the West Coast, Cain opposed the internment of Japanese American citizens in detention camps during World War II. After serving two terms as mayor, Cain enlisted in the U.S. Army and fought in Europe, working his way up to the rank of colonel. Upon his return to the United States, Cain received the Washington Republican Party's nomination for U.S. senator. Campaigning on a platform that emphasized his determination to oppose Communism at home and abroad, Cain emerged victorious—part of the "class of '46," as the ultraconservative Republican newcomers to the Senate were called—as voters across the nation expressed their dissatisfaction with the seemingly inept administration of President Harry S. TRUMAN.

Once in the Senate, Cain redeemed his campaign pledges by pursuing suspected Communists so zealously that Wisconsin Senator Joseph McCarthy once described Cain as "perhaps more hated by Communists, Communistic and fellow-traveler elements than any man alive." In 1947, for instance, Cain demanded the deportation of actor Charlie CHAPLIN when Chaplin asked Spanish artist Pablo Picasso ("the self-admitted Communist Picasso," in Cain's words) to organize European protests against the persecution of composer Hanns EISLER by the HOUSE COMMITTEE ON UN-AMERICAN ACTIVITIES (HUAC). On another occasion, Cain declared that "if the [Truman] administration is indifferent to the infiltration of Communists and misguided liberal poison within the bloodstream of America, Joe McCarthy is alert to its evils and dangers."

By the end of 1950, however, Cain had begun to entertain doubts about the integrity of some members of the anti-Communist crusade. In December of that year, Cain was appointed to head a subcommittee to investigate allegations of disloyalty that an ex-Communist informer had leveled against Assistant Secretary of State Anna ROSENBERG, a prominent liberal Democrat. After hearing all the relevant testimony, Cain concluded that Rosenberg's accusers had committed perjury. "Among the chief witnesses," Cain declared, "were some who sought to inflict deep injury on Mrs. Rosenberg and further divided the nation by giving false testimony under oath. . . . These witnesses call themselves men, but they were cowardly, dishonest and traitorous in their conduct and testimony before the committee. I have urged the committee to seek to prefer perjury charges against these individuals."

The Rosenberg incident did not prevent Cain from labeling his opponent in the 1952 senatorial election, Congressman Henry R. JACKSON, a supporter of the State Department's left-wing clique that had purportedly sold out China to the Communists and "approved each step the Administration took on the road to Korea." For his part, Jackson scorned Cain's attempts to attack his loyalty as "the last plaintive cries of a politician going down for the last time." Nevertheless, Communism remained a peripheral issue in the campaign, despite the fact that McCarthy appeared in the state several times to personally endorse Cain. Although the national Republican ticket, headed by General Dwight David Eisenhower, swept to victory in a landslide that brought the Republicans control of both houses of Congress, Jackson defeated Cain by a margin of 52–48 percent.

Eisenhower subsequently appointed Cain to head the five-member, bipartisan Subversive Activities Control Board (SACB), a federal agency that had been established by the INTERNAL SECURITY ACT of 1950. The Internal Security Act required the Communist Party and all individuals who belonged to Communist front organizations to register with the SACB, which also was responsible for barring Communists and Communist sympathizers from employment with the federal government. Each day, Cain's office received hundreds of letters of denunciation of one citizen by another for alleged subversive opinons or actions, as well as a smaller number of protests from former government employees who claimed they had been fired unfairly from their jobs. One former postal-service employee in Baltimore wrote to Cain repeatedly, in semiliterate prose, charging that he had been accused falsely as a subversive. Assuming that a real Communist would probably be able to spell better than the author of the letters, Cain invited the worker to come to his office to discuss the matter. Upon further investigation, Cain discovered that the worker had the same name as another individual who had contributed to a Communist-front organization.

Cain managed to get the postal-service worker his job back, but the incident—combined with other similar cases of mistaken identity and his own experience in the Anna Rosenberg fiasco—shook his faith in the integrity of the entire federal LOYALTY REVIEW BOARD system. In a speech to a Republican club in Spokane, Washington, Cain criticized the "ruthlessness, smugness, and brutality" of the system and claimed that "a whole clique of spies could hardly do as much damage to us as could our failure as a government to have confidence in our people." Cain followed this talk with numerous other speeches in which he attempted to alert Americans to the excesses that were occurring daily. The attorney general's list of subversive organizations, argued Cain, was "misleading and unfair." "The problem," he informed Attorney General Herbert BROWNELL, "remains that of taking action in ways to better protect individuals from unintended repression."

Eventually Cain concluded that the potential for abuse in the system was so great that the government should remove itself altogether from the business of policing the political ideologies of its employees. "I have seen how much damage a person in Congress can do by orating without knowing what he is talking about," Cain stated. After Cain confided his misgivings to President Eisenhower, the President decided not to renominate Cain to his position with the SACB. In response to critics who charged that he was merely responding to a shift in the political winds following the censure of McCarthy by the Senate in December 1954, Cain noted that he had always been a conservative who respected individual rights, including the fundamental right of free speech.

After teaching political science for several years at Yale University in the mid-1950s, Cain moved to Florida, where he entered the real estate business and served as a political commentator on a television station. He returned to New York in 1958 to testify on behalf of playwright Arthur MILLER, who had been denied a passport by the State Department on the grounds that he maintained Communist sympathies. Cain told a federal district court that he had read Miller's plays and decided that they contained such contradictory political views that the author could not possibly be under the single-minded, ideological control of the Communist Party. Despite

Cain's testimony, the judge ruled in favor of the State Department and denied Miller's passport.

In 1972, Cain was appointed to the Dade County (Florida) Commission, but lost his bid for reelection in 1976. He died three years later.

**Catholic Church**    During the twentieth century, the Catholic Church has been one of the most staunchly anti-Communist institutions in the United States. The church's opposition to Communism began during the nineteenth century as a succession of popes denounced Communist theory as atheistic and materialistic. The violently anticlerical bent of the Russian Revolution of 1917–20 and the persecution of the Catholic Church in the Soviet Union during the 1920s and 1930s confirmed church officials in their hatred of Communism.

In the United States, the Catholic hierarchy generally supported the liberal New Deal initiatives of President Franklin Delano Roosevelt, and certainly Catholic voters—particularly those in urban areas—formed one of the major segment of support for Roosevelt and the Democratic Party in the 1930s. Nevertheless, the church began to grow concerned in the late 1930s over the extent of radical influence in the federal government, labor unions, and reform organizations. Indeed, Communist infiltration of unions and social reform groups during the period of the POPULAR FRONT gave Church officials substantial cause for concern. Catholic Church leaders broke further with American liberals over the Spanish Civil War of 1937–38, as liberals supported the Republican Loyalist cause while the church backed General Francisco Franco.

Following the defeat of Nazi Germany in 1945, the church denounced the Soviet takeover of the nations of Eastern Europe, particularly because the advent of Communist governments in that area was invariably accompanied by savage persecution of the local Catholic leadership. The Soviet occupation of Poland in 1945 brought protests from thousands of American Catholics, and the torture and imprisonment of Cardinal Joseph Mindszenty by the Communist regime in Hungary in 1948 provided the church with a martyr for the anti-Communist cause.

The leaders of the anti-Communist crusade among the Catholic hierarchy in the United States were Francis Cardinal Spellman of New York City and his assistant, Bishop Fulton J. Sheen. Both Spellman and Sheen supported the efforts of Senator Joseph MCCARTHY of Wisconsin, himself a member of the Catholic Church. In fact, it was a Catholic priest, Father Edmund Walsh of Georgetown University, who helped persuade McCarthy in early February 1950 to employ anti-Communism as a viable partisan political tactic. Beginning in 1945, the church sponsored education programs—known as "labor schools"—to alert labor-union members to the dangers of Communist infiltration of the union movement. This effort was supplemented by the work of the so-called "waterfront priests," who labored among dockworkers to encourage them to resist the appeals of Communist organizers and racketeers. (For an excellent example of a waterfront priest, one need look no further than the movie *On the Waterfront*—directed by ex-Communist sympathizer Elia KAZAN—in which Karl Malden played an anti-Communist priest battling the machinations of Rod Steiger and Lee J. COBB.)

Support for anti-Communist initiatives also came from organizations such as the Catholic War Veterans and the Knights of Columbus. In 1947, for instance, the Knights of Columbus sponsored a series of national radio broadcasts entitled *Safeguards for America* that were intended to provide listeners with the truth about Communism. When the Communist newspaper the *DAILY WORKER* complained that the series was the "biggest and most vicious scare hoax in the history of radio," the Knights of Columbus replied that "Communism is a lie and a lie hates the truth." Even liberal Catholic publications such as *Commonweal* adopted a stoutly anti-Communist stand during the late 1940s and early 1950s, although *Commonweal* rejected the sort of repressive legislation and witch hunts that characterized the anti-Red crusade during the McCarthy era; instead, it suggested that an expansion of social programs represented the best means of fighting Communism.

**Central Intelligence Agency**  Established in 1947 to coordinate American intelligence activities abroad, the Central Intelligence Agency played only a minimal role in the crusade against Communist influence in the United States in the late 1940s and early 1950s. The presence and prestige of the agency did, however, produce jealousy in FBI director J. Edgar HOOVER, who accordingly redoubled his efforts to discover domestic subversives in the United States. The agency also served as a target for Senator Joseph MCCARTHY of Wisconsin in the summer of 1953.

Concerned that Soviet espionage agents had infiltrated the CIA and frustrated by his inability to compel the appearance of a CIA official named William Bundy before his GOVERNMENT OPERATIONS COMMITTEE, McCarthy vowed to launch an investigation of the agency. President Dwight David EISENHOWER moved immediately to quash any such inquiry, and in the Senate, Democrat Mike Monroney of Oklahoma warned that a probe of the CIA would give McCarthy "carte blanche authority to fully explore . . . the innermost secrets" of the nation's intelligence community, thereby releasing critical security information "that even the Kremlin's best spy apparatus could not get." CIA Director Allen DULLES, brother of Eisenhower's Secretary of State John Foster DULLES, reportedly threatened to resign if McCarthy were granted access to the agency's personnel files.

Eventually Vice President Richard M. NIXON intervened in the dispute and convinced McCarthy to abandon his investigation of the agency, but only after the administration promised to carry out an extensive purge of the agency's personnel to satisfy the Wisconsin senator.

**Chambers, Whittaker**  (1901–1964)  A troubled, enigmatic man who joined the COM-

Whittaker Chambers (right), the ex-Communist who claimed to have known Alger Hiss as a Communist during the 1930s.

MUNIST PARTY in the late 1920s and subsequently became a leading anti-Communist witness several decades later, Whittaker Chambers was born Jay Vivian Chambers in New York City, the son of an actress and an advertising artist. Chambers' childhood and youth were full of horrors: his father deserted the family when Chambers was still a boy, leaving them in poverty, and then returned to carry on an icy and occasionally violent relationship with his wife and children; Chambers' brother attempted to commit suicide several times and was thwarted only by Chambers' vigilance—finally he succeeded on an evening when Chambers was meeting with a Communist friend; for years Chambers' grandmother, who had gone insane, lived with the family and haunted them with her ravings and hallucinations.

A loner for most of his life, Chambers left home after graduating from high school and set out for Mexico. He never made it that far, stopping first in Washington to work as a laborer and then ending up in New Orleans, living with a prostitute whom Chambers later described as "as ugly a woman as I have ever seen." He returned to New York to attend Columbia University briefly, leaving after he published an atheist drama under a pseudonym. By this time, Chambers had taken his mother's maiden name, Whittaker, as his first name, replacing the name of his father and the hated middle name of Vivian. He obtained a job at the New York Public Library and attempted to resume his collegiate career at Columbia, but left again after attending classes for less than a year.

According to his later testimony, Chambers decided to become a Communist in the winter of 1925. Throughout his life, he tended to view events as episodes in a grand, apocalyptic scheme, and he had convinced himself at that point that the old world of capitalism and democracy was dying. Communism, Chambers believed, offered the best if not the only hope for the future, and so he joined the Communist Party, dropped out of Columbia once again, and began to write for the Communist publication, the *DAILY WORKER*. After several years with the *Daily Worker,* Chambers departed following a dispute over its editorial policies. He earned a living through freelance writing for magazines before landing another job with a Communist journal entitled *New Masses.* In the early 1930s, Chambers appears to have joined the Communist underground, participating in espionage activities of a not terribly significant nature.

Chambers later stated that in 1934–35, he made contact with a group of bright young New Deal officials in Washington, D.C., whom he believed were sympathetic to the Communist cause. Among those Chambers named as members of this group were Alger HISS, Donald Hiss, Victor Perlo (who was later also accused of being a Communist spy by Elizabeth BENTLEY), labor lawyer Lee PRESSMAN, Harry Dexter WHITE, and Harold Ware. In his dealings with these young men, Chambers—partly for security reasons and partly for his love of cloak-and-dagger devices—called himself "George Crosley" or simply "Carl." Initially, these men purportedly used their influence within the government to provide whatever help they could to the Soviet Union and the cause of Commu-

nism abroad; according to Chambers, they later also became members of an espionage ring.

The precise nature of the relationship between Chambers and Hiss later became a critical issue during the McCarthy era. It seems clear that Chambers and Hiss did have extensive contacts during the mid-1930s. At that time, Hiss was serving as a staff member on the Nye Committee, the U.S. Senate committee established to investigate the relationship between the munitions industry and American involvement in World War I. Chambers (posing as Crosley) told Hiss that he was a freelance writer and asked Hiss to provide him with material for articles. Because cooperation with the press was part of Hiss' job, he passed along unclassified material to Chambers. Hiss also allowed Chambers to use his apartment after Hiss and his family had moved into a house in downtown Washington and gave Chambers access to Hiss' old Ford automobile.

Chambers claimed that Hiss had actually given the automobile to the Communist Party for its use and that the small favors Hiss did for Chambers during these years were not performed out of sympathy for Chambers—who clearly was less financially fortunate than Hiss—but were the type of assistance rendered by one Communist Party member to another. Far more significant was Chambers' charge that Hiss, who became an official in the State Department in 1937, had transmitted to him copies of classified government documents. Some of the documents, stated Chambers, had been copied in Hiss' own handwriting; others were retyped by Hiss' wife on an old Woodstock typewriter in the Hiss home; the remainder were microfilmed and then returned. Chambers then passed along copies of the documents to a Soviet contact.

In 1937 or 1938—Chambers' memory was hazy as to the precise date—Chambers decided to leave the Communist Party, largely because he was horrified by the Stalinist purges and trials in Moscow. Although he still was not sanguine about the prospects for democracy, Chambers decided that "it is better to die on the losing side than to live under Communism." Chambers later claimed that he met with Hiss about this time and urged him, too, to quit the party, but Hiss refused. (Hiss adamantly denied that such a meeting ever took place.) In any event, Chambers obtained an appointment in 1939 with Assistant Secretary of State Adolf BERLE and informed him that he had personal knowledge that several officials within the State Department had Communist sympathies and that several of them might have been involved in pro-Soviet espionage activities. In the absence of any hard evidence to substantiate Chambers' allegations, Berle declined to take any action at that time. Three years later, Chambers repeated his story to FBI Director J. Edgar HOOVER, who would later pass it along to prosecutors investigating Communist subversion in the United States.

By that time, Chambers had obtained a position with *Time* magazine, published by Henry LUCE, who subsequently became a leading member of the fervently anti-Communist CHINA LOBBY. Chambers rose through the magazine's hierarchy to become a senior editor by 1948. In August of that year, Chambers was contacted by Robert STRIPLING, the chief investigator for the HOUSE COMMITTEE ON UN-AMERICAN AC-TIVITIES (HUAC). The committee had recently heard testimony from admitted ex-Communist Elizabeth Bentley, who informed HUAC that she had participated in a Soviet espionage ring in Washington during the war. Stripling's subordinates had previously questioned Chambers in connection with the case of Edward CONDON; now—searching for corroboration for Bentley's accusations—they subpoenaed Chambers to testify before the committee.

Although the overweight, rumpled Chambers did not make a particularly impressive appearance, the substance of his testimony did not disappoint the committee. On August 3, 1948, he recounted for them the story of his own conversion to Communism and his contacts with Alger Hiss and the other members of the

Washington group, most of whom also had been named by Bentley. President Harry S. TRUMAN responded to Chambers' allegations against Hiss by describing them as a "red herring" designed to deflect the public's attention from the failure of the Republican-controlled Congress to achieve anything of consequence. Yet, aside from Hiss, few of those named by Chambers sought to refute publicly the allegations in detail. Hiss, however, stoutly maintained his innocence, and his subsequent appearance before the committee was sufficiently impressive to persuade a majority of HUAC that Chambers had been mistaken.

Representative Richard M. NIXON, however, refused to allow the issue to fade away and arranged a second meeting with Chambers. On August 7, Nixon and two of his HUAC colleagues met Chambers in executive session in New York. During that meeting, Chambers revealed a detailed knowledge of Hiss's personal life—his furniture, family nicknames, hobbies, and reading matter—which convinced Nixon that the two men had in fact, been closely acquainted. To establish the nature of their relationship, Nixon arranged a confrontation between Chambers and Hiss in a New York hotel room. Chambers remained calm, though there seemed something slightly disconcerting about his performance. When Hiss asked him twice whether he had ever used the name "George Crosley," Chambers replied each time, "Not to my knowledge," and gave Hiss a slight smile.

On August 25, both Chambers and Hiss testified once more before HUAC. Chambers repeated his story in a direct and convincing fashion. When a committee member asked him why he was testifying against Hiss, Chambers replied that "We were close friends. But we got caught in the tragedy of history. Mr. Hiss represents the concealed enemy we are all fighting. I am testifying against him with remorse and pity. But in this moment of historic jeopardy at which this nation now stands, so help me God, I could not do otherwise." Some observers appeared unmoved by Chambers' allegations; the *Nation,* for instance, noted that "any neurotic exhibitionist who can claim to have been a Communist is now assured of absolution, soul-satisfying publicity, and probably more material rewards in the shape of payment for exclusive newspaper stories, lecture contracts and good jobs." Yet, as public and press reaction revealed itself to be generally favorable to Chambers, Hiss challenged Chambers to repeat his allegations outside a congressional committee hearing room, where he would not be protected against libel.

On September 4, 1948, Chambers did precisely that. During an appearance on the NBC radio program, *Meet the Press,* Chambers stated that Alger Hiss "was a Communist and may be one now." Nearly a month later, Hiss sued Chambers for defamation of character. To defend himself, Chambers had to produce evidence that Hiss had been a member of the Communist Party. Chambers thereupon produced a sheaf of classified State Department documents, which he claimed Hiss had given him during the late 1930s. Several weeks later, Chambers took members of HUAC on a tour of his Maryland farm, where he reached into a hollowed-out pumpkin and produced three strips of microfilmed documents which Hiss allegedly had passed along to him.

Hiss was subsequently indicted for perjury for denying that he had ever been a member of the Communist Party and for denying that he had transmitted classified documents to Chambers. Although Chambers' testimony during Hiss' two perjury trials (the first ended in a hung jury) revealed him to be subject to delusions of persecution, and—according to three psychiatrists retained by defense counsel—an habitual liar with a borderline psycopathic personality, Hiss was eventually convicted and sentenced to a term in federal prison. For his part, Chambers viewed the confrontation between himself and Hiss as part of a climatic struggle between universal forces of good and evil. In that struggle, Chambers saw himself as an unconventional sort of martyr. "I am a man who reluctantly, grudgingly, step by step, is destroying himself, so that this country and the faith by which it lives may continue to exist," Chambers wrote. Nor did he possess any illusions that he represented a sympathetic figure. "The world's instinctive feeling," he observed, "was against the little fat man who had stood up to testify for it, unasked. The world's instinctive sympathy was for the engaging man who meant to destroy it, was for Alger Hiss."

Following Hiss' conviction, Chambers remained in the nation's headlines by testifying on numerous other occasions about his former colleagues in the Communist movement. In late 1948, he informed the House Committee on Un-American Activities that former State Department official Lawrence DUGGAN had been one of the other individuals he had mentioned to Assistant Secretary Berle in 1939, although he admitted that he had no direct knowledge that Duggan was a Communist, nor did he recall receiving any classified documents from Duggan. Several weeks later, Duggan fell to his death from the sixteenth floor of an office building in Manhattan.

By 1950, Chambers had become a sort of elder statesman in the anti-Communist crusade. After Senator Joseph MCCARTHY of Wisconsin announced in February 1950 that the State Department harbored a number of card-carrying members of the Communist Party, McCarthy visited Chambers at his Maryland farm to receive instruction on the intricate details of Soviet espionage, along with Chambers' opinions on the identity of the top Soviet agents in the United States.

Disconcerted by the fact that a substantial number of skeptics refused to believe that Hiss had actually been guilty, Chambers published accounts of his confrontation with Hiss in several memoirs, including *Witness* (1952) and *Cold Friday* (1964). In *Witness,* Chambers revealed his tendency toward apocalyptic imagery when he asked whether there were "people who still believe that in 1948 Alger Hiss, impenitent and defiant to this hour, was still not an active Communist, working as such in close touch with some of the highest power centers in the country? Are there people who still do not see that in removing his power for evil in 1948, the secret apparatus that I failed to smash singlehanded in 1938 was at least damaged?"

In a similar vein, Chambers proclaimed in *Cold Friday* that Western society—bereft of any compelling faith or "rallying idea . . . capable of being grasped and so overmastering millions of men"—was approaching complete destruction. The agent of its demise, Chambers believed, would be the hydrogen bomb.

To the end, Chambers remained a staunch anti-Communist. Like many of the most fervent supporters of the anti-Communist crusade during the McCarthy era, Chambers refused to believe that the reaction against Stalinism in the Soviet Union during the late 1950s was anything more than a sham. In 1956, Chambers joined with thirty-eight other conservatives (including fellow ex-Communist Louis BUDENZ and publisher William Randolph Hearst), to issue a report entitled *The Great Pretense*, which put forth the proposition that "anti-Stalinism is but a political artifice, fraudulent and more dangerous than any other produced by the Kremlin thus far." Although the emotions of the McCarthy era had faded by the early 1960s, the continuing controversy over the relative veracity of Hiss and Chambers refused to disappear, and doubts over the truth of his testimony followed Chambers to his grave in 1964.

## Chaplin, Charles Spencer (1889–1977)

One of America's most beloved film stars, Charlie Chaplin was an Englishman who had grown up in the East End of London. He began to act in a traveling vaudeville troupe that, in 1913, toured the United States, where he caught the attention of film producer Mack Sennett. Five years later, Chaplin had become the most popular movie actor in the world, with a $1 million contract and complete artistic freedom.

Chaplin was never as successful in talking pictures, which became popular in 1927, as he had been in silent films. Yet two of his greatest cinematic achievements, *Modern Times* and *The Great Dictator* (the latter a satire on Adolf Hitler and the Nazi regime in Germany) were produced after the advent of sound films. Even in semiretirement, during the 1930s and 1940s, Chaplin remained an institution in Hollywood; it was considered a great honor for anyone, no matter how famous, to be invited to visit Chaplin's home.

He had always dabbled in politics—*The Great Dictator* featured a stirring oration against fascism at the close of the film—but Chaplin had never participated in organized politics in anything more than a cursory fashion. Certainly, there was no evidence that he had ever belonged to the COMMUNIST PARTY. Yet many of his closest friends in Hollywood, including Clifford ODETS, John GARFIELD, Theodore Dreiser, John Howard LAWSON, and Donald Ogden Stewart, had been Communists or Communist sympathizers at some point in their lives. During World War II, Chaplin made several public speeches praising the Soviet military effort on the Eastern Front, and at one San Francisco rally for Russian War Relief he addressed his audience as "comrades."

Chaplin's wartime eagerness to aid the Soviet Union, combined with his association with known Hollywood radicals (including film composer Hanns EISLER, brother of Communist International (Comintern) representative Gerhart EISLER), made him suspect in the minds of anti-Communist zealots in the postwar years. His flippant attitude toward the anti-Red crusade further angered his opponents. When FBI agents came to his house to ask if he had actually used the word *comrades* in his San Francisco speech, Chaplin replied that he was far too much an amateur to discuss Communism with such experts. His well-publicized attraction to younger women—which made headlines in 1946, when Chaplin was found guilty of fathering a child out of wedlock—added one more strike against him in the minds of many conservatives. Representative John RANKIN of Alabama, for instance, who was a member of the HOUSE COMMITTEE ON UN-AMERICAN ACTIVITIES (HUAC), once referred to Chaplin as that "seducer of white girls" who had "loathsome paintings" hanging in his home.

When HUAC launched an investigation into the loyalty of his friend Hanns Eisler in 1947, Chaplin bitterly criticized the committee and cabled Pablo Picasso in France to organize protests in Europe. HUAC considered calling Chaplin himself to testify about his political activities and did subpoena him as one of the nineteen "unfriendly" Hollywood witnesses in September 1947. When the committee first leaked word that he would be asked to appear, Chaplin responded with a bitterly sarcastic public message to HUAC Chairman J. Parnell THOMAS: "In order that you may be completely up to date on my thinking I suggest that you view carefully my latest production, *Monsieur Verdoux.* It is against war and the futile slaughter of our youth. I trust you will not find its humane message distasteful. While you are preparing your engraved subpoena I will give you a hint on where I stand. I am not a Communist. I am a peacemonger."

Three times the committee postponed Chaplin's appearance, perhaps partly due to the actor's announced intention to appear in his famous "little tramp" guise so that he could "burlesque the burlesque." After the third postponement, Chaplin sent HUAC a telegram in which he stated that "I am not a Communist, neither have I ever joined any political party or organization in my life." Apparently the committee accepted his statement for it wrote back to Chaplin that it considered the matter closed and that his testimony would no longer be necessary. "I almost wish I could have testified," Chaplin noted later. "If I had, the whole Un-American Activities thing would have been laughed out of existence in front of the millions of viewers who watched the interrogations on TV."

Chaplin's leftist connections and his failure to take the anti-Communist issue seriously cost him public support, however. When his film, *Monsieur Verdoux,* was released in 1947, theaters were picketed by protesters carrying signs that read, "SEND CHAPLIN TO RUSSIA," and "CHAPLIN'S A FELLOW TRAVELER." To help repair Chaplin's image, United Artists studio arranged a press conference, during which reporters naturally questioned Chaplin about his political sympathies. "I have no political persuasion whatsoever," the actor replied. "I've never belonged to any political party in my life, and I have never voted in my life!" He had sympathized with the Soviet Union during the war, Chaplin admitted, "because I believe that she was holding the front, and for that I have a memory and I feel that I owe her thanks. I think that she helped contribute a considerable amount of fighting and dying to bring victory to the Allies. In that sense I am sympathetic."

En route to London in 1952 to promote his next film, *Limelight,* Chaplin learned that Attorney General J. Howard McGrath had announced that he would be subject to an investigation upon his return to the United States, "as a salutary lesson to the youth of our land." In fact, the government decided that Chaplin would not be able to return at all until he had proved his "moral worth." During his absence, FBI agents interrogated the servants at his home in an attempt to obtain information about Chaplin's political beliefs, or at least evidence of wild orgies rampant with naked women. Outraged, Chaplin decided to remain in Europe, where he was treated like royalty; France inducted him into its Legion of Honor, and the British Parliament honored him with a banquet in London.

While Chaplin and his family settled into their new residence at a chateau at Lake Geneva, Switzerland, the AMERICAN LEGION insisted that American theaters prohibit all of Chaplin's films. The attorney general followed up his threat to refuse Chaplin reentry into the United States with darkly ominous statements about the actor's character, accusing him of "making leering, sneering statements about the country whose gracious hospitality has enriched him." In Switzerland, Chaplin received news of the spreading anti-Communist hysteria with sadness. "America is so terribly grim in spite of all that material prosperity," he said. "They no longer know how to weep. Compassion and the old neighborliness have gone, people stand by and do nothing when friends and neighbors are attacked, libeled and ruined. The worst thing is what it has done to the children. They are being taught to admire and emulate stool pigeons, to betray and to hate, and all in a sickening atmosphere of religious hypocrisy."

Chaplin did not return to the United States until 1972, when he was awarded an honorary Oscar by the Academy of Motion Picture Arts and Sciences. He was granted a knighthood by Queen Elizabeth II in 1975.

## Chiang Kai-shek (1887–1975)

Born in Chekiang Province in southern China during the last years of the Manchu Dynasty, Chiang Kai-shek (the name may be translated into English as "Firm Rock") was the son of a salt merchant and a concubine. His father died when Chiang was nine years old, leaving the family in poverty; Chiang later credited his mother, a devout Buddhist, with saving the family "from utter ruin" through her perseverance and kindness. At the age of 19, Chiang embarked upon a military career, spending a year at the Paoting Military Academy and two more years in advanced study in Japan. It was there he met Chinese revolutionary leader Sun Yat-sen, who was elected provisional president after the successful rebellion against the Manchus, which erupted in 1911.

By 1922, Chiang had become Sun Yat-sen's chief of staff. After Sun Yat-sen's regime agreed to accept material assistance from the recently established Soviet Union, Chiang traveled to Moscow to coordinate relations between the two new governments. Within China, Sun Yat-

Chiang Kai-shek, leader of the Nationalist forces in the Chinese civil war.

sen established a tenuous coalition between Communists and conservative nationalists such as Chiang. Following Sun Yat-sen's death in 1925, however, the coalition was shattered when Chiang suddenly turned on his erstwhile allies and slaughtered thousands of Communists in Canton and Shanghai. As the Communists retreated to the mountains of northern China, Chiang—working in partnership with powerful allies in the Shanghai financial and business community—established the National Revolutionary Government with its capital at Nanking.

Aided by military advisers from Nazi Germany, Chiang attempted to eradicate his Communist opponents, but his repeated expeditions into the north met with little success. Outside the immediate area around Nanking, meanwhile, Chiang struck deals with local warlords; in return for their nominal professions of loyalty to him, Chiang allowed the military chieftains to retain virtually autonomous control of their regions. When the Japanese armies invaded Manchuria in 1931, Chiang refrained from challenging them in force, nor did he launch a particularly staunch resistance when the Japanese moved south along the Chinese coast in 1937. Instead, Chiang retreated into the interior of China, establishing a new capital at Chung-king, where he spent the remainder of World War II carrying out occasional raids against Japanese positions while imploring the United States for additional military assistance.

From 1942 to 1945, President Franklin D. Roosevelt repeatedly pressed Chiang to take the offensive against Japanese forces in China. Early in 1942, Roosevelt dispatched General Joseph W. "Vinegar Joe" Stillwell to serve as Chiang's chief of staff, but Stillwell's relations with Chiang deteriorated rapidly because the Nationalist regime refused to move more forcefully against Japan. By 1944, Roosevelt had grown so frustrated that he warned Chiang that "with further delay, it may be too late to avert a military catastrophe tragic both to China and to our Allied plans for the early overthrow of Japan." A mission led by Vice President Henry WALLACE to persuade Chiang to reconcile with the Communists for the duration of the war foundered on the Nationalists' determination to exterminate their Marxist enemies. Chiang was convinced that the United States failed to understand that the Chinese Communists, whom some American experts viewed as democratic agrarian reformers, were part of an international Communist movement and were actually more communistic than their counterparts in the Soviet Union.

Unlike State Department and military officials in Washington, who had become totally disillusioned with Chiang by 1945, a significant segment of the American public viewed Chiang as the savior of modern China. On the one hand, he embodied traditional Confucian values, including a belief in the efficacy of moral rectitude ("If the ruler is virtuous," Chiang observed, "the people will also be virtuous"), a tendency toward spiritual self-examination (he set aside time every day for prayer and meditation), and an austere lifestyle (unlike many of his corrupt advisers, Chiang did not gamble or smoke, and he almost invariably appeared in public clad in a simple plain brown tunic with matching trousers). At the same time, Chiang appeared

to have absorbed Western values. He had joined the Methodist Church in 1931 and regularly attended Sunday worship services; his wife, the sister of powerful Shanghai banker T.V. Soong, had been educated at Wellesley College; and Chiang posed as the champion of democracy in Asia.

Following the surrender of Japan in August 1945, Chiang's Nationalist government resumed its civil war against the Communist armies led by MAO Zedong. Instead of concentrating upon the effective administration of the areas under their control, the Nationalist forces tried to seize as much territory as quickly as they could. As a result, they rapidly lost public support due to the extravagant corruption and inefficiency of their rule. Even $3 billion in American military assistance to Chiang could not stem the advancing Communist tide, and on January 1, 1949, Chiang resigned as president of the Chinese Republic. "I must put the blame on myself," Chiang admitted shortly after his defeat. "The disastrous military reverses on the mainland were not due to the overwhelming strength of the Communists, but due to the organizational collapse, loose discipline, and low spirits of the [Nationalist] party members." Later that year, Chiang fled to the island of Taiwan, where his supporters had prepared the way by forcibly displacing the native political and economic leaders. On March 1, 1950, Chiang declared from his capital at Taipei that he had resumed the presidency of China.

Chiang's defeat caused considerable consternation among American conservatives—particularly the loose coalition of political, military, and business leaders known as the CHINA LOBBY—who blamed the outcome of the Chinese civil war on pro-Communist officials in the State Department. Through an efficient network of contacts in the United States, Chiang helped keep alive the debate over who was responsible for the loss of China to the Communists. The outbreak of hostilities in Korea in June 1950 and the subsequent entry of Communist Chinese troops into the war on the side of North

Nationalist leader Chiang Kai-shek reviewing his troops in the Chinese civil war (1946–1949). (China)

Korea bolstered Chiang's hopes for increased American support and a triumphal return to the mainland. That opportunity never presented itself, though as late as 1966 Chiang was still threatening to "exterminate Mao Tse-tung and his cohorts, liberate our mainland compatriots and establish on the ruins a new country of unity and freedom."

In 1971, Nationalist China lost its struggle to keep the mainland Chinese Communist government out of the United Nations. The following year, President Richard M. NIXON, one of Chiang's staunchest supporters during the McCarthy era, made an official diplomatic visit to Beijing (Peking) to establish ties with the Communist regime. Chiang was sworn in for his fifth term as head of the Nationalist government in 1972 but fell ill soon afterward and turned over most of his duties to his son, Chiang Chingkuo. Chiang died three years later.

**China**    During the McCarthy era, the fate of China became one of the most controversial topics in American politics. Ever since a coup established the Nationalist government of CHIANG Kai-shek at Nanking in 1927–28, China had been divided into spheres of influence governed respectively by the Nationalists, the Communist forces of MAO Zedong in northern China, and various warlords and military chieftains who governed their own local regions in return for nominal recognitions of Chiang's sovereignty. The Japanese incursion into Manchuria in 1931 added another element to the mix; in 1937–38, Japanese troops turned southward and drove the Nationalist forces out of key coastal cities, forcing Chiang to relocate his capital at Chungking in the interior of China.

Despite massive American aid, the Nationalist government exerted relatively little effort to oust the Japanese invaders during World War II; in the latter stages of the conflict, General Joseph W. "Vinegar Joe" Stillwell, the U.S. military official who served as Chiang's chief of staff during the war, described the Nationalist military effort since 1938 as "practically zero." Instead, Chiang simply waited and relied upon the Allies to defeat Japan, a strategy that bore fruit with the surrender of the Japanese government in August 1945. Meanwhile, the Communist armies of Mao had been battling both the Japanese and occasional assaults by the Nationalist forces, while carrying out a series of land-reform measures that won the Communists the support of a substantial segment of the Chinese peasantry.

The exodus of the Japanese invaders in 1945 signaled the resumption of civil war between the Nationalists and the Communists. In December of that year, President Harry S. TRUMAN dispatched General George C. MARSHALL to China on a mission to unify and pacify the country. By alternately cajoling and threatening Chiang and Mao, Marshall succeeded in arranging a cease-fire on January 10, 1946, but violations by both sides sabotaged his efforts. The numerical superiority of the Nationalist forces—3 million soldiers to 1 million Communist troops—earned Chiang a series of victories in the early stages of the civil war, but the Communists launched their own offensive in the spring of 1947. From that point on, the Communists steadily strengthened their control over the country, despite the infusion of $3 billion in American aid to the Nationalist regime (much of which ended up in the hands of the Communists), until Chiang and his associates fled the mainland in December 1949. They settled on the island of Taiwan, where Chiang proclaimed on March 1, 1950, that he had resumed the presidency of China.

U.S. military officials and diplomats with firsthand knowledge of Chinese affairs were virtually unanimous in their conclusion that the Nationalist government lost the civil war because it was corrupt, inefficient, antidemocratic, and vastly unpopular with the Chinese people. They had therefore rejected the option of massive military intervention on the mainland to crush the Chinese Communists and suppress the widespread popular discontent that Chiang adamantly refused to ally with any significant program of reform. In the aftermath of defeat, Chiang himself acknowledged the deficiencies

of his regime when he stated that "I must put the blame on myself. The disastrous military reverses on the mainland were not due to the overwhelming strength of the Communists, but due to the organizational collapse, loose discipline and low spirits of the [Nationalist] party members."

The Truman administration agreed. In its CHINA WHITE PAPER, issued in August 1949, the administration tried to prove that the upheaval in China was the result of massive internal changes which the United States could not control. If blame for the Communist victory were to be apportioned, the paper placed the largest share squarely on the Nationalist regime. It noted that "a large proportion of the military supplies furnished the Chinese armies since V-J Day has fallen into the hands of the Chinese Communists through the military ineptitude of the Nationalist leaders, their defections and surrenders, and the absence among their forces of the will to fight. . . . A realistic appraisal of conditions in China, past and present, leads to the conclusion that the only alternative open to the United States was full-scale intervention in behalf of a Government which had lost the confidence of its own troops and its own people." Yet, such was the prevailing suspicion of Communism in the late 1940s and early 1950s that American policymakers could not attempt any rapprochement with Mao's Communist regime in Peking.

The Communist victory in China set off a domestic debate within the United States that raged for more than a decade. The question "Who lost China?" reflected a presumption that events in China were determined by external influences; indeed, Chiang's leading American supporters—known collectively as the CHINA LOBBY—refused to admit that the outcome of the civil war was the result of deficiencies within the Nationalist regime. Instead, they concluded that Chiang had been the victim of willful pro-Communist decisions within the State Department. If the United States had failed to control the Chinese revolution, so the argument ran, it meant simply that the government of the United States was infested with Communists. Specifically, the leaders of the China Lobby charged the foreign service's Far East career experts, such as John Paton DAVIES, John Carter VINCENT, and John Stewart SERVICE, with Communist sympathies. Other targets of the China Lobby included Owen LATTIMORE and Secretaries of State Dean ACHESON and George Marshall.

From the outset, Senator Joseph MCCARTHY used the Communist victory in China to bolster his charges of Communist influence in the federal government. The issue of the United States policy toward China provided McCarthy with invaluable publicity and public support, particularly following the outbreak of the KOREAN WAR in June 1950. Once the Chinese Communists entered the conflict on the side of North Korea, the implications of Chiang's defeat for U.S. interests in the Far East seemed to become more ominous and, for many Americans, more sinister.

Events in China continued to influence U.S. Far East policy throughout the 1950s and 1960s. The United States was wedded to support of the Nationalist regime on Taiwan. Any threat to the security of Chiang's government—such as the Communist bombardment of the Nationalist-controlled offshore islands of Quemoy and Matsu in 1958—automatically resulted in increased commitments to Taiwan. Moreover, the savage domestic criticism that the Democratic Party endured for allegedly failing to support Chiang sufficiently between 1945 and 1949 led the administrations of John F. KENNEDY and Lyndon Baines JOHNSON to commit massive amounts of American resources to the survival of equally corrupt and undemocratic regimes in South Vietnam.

**China Lobby** The China Lobby was an amorphous coalition composed of American businesspeople, conservative Republican politicians, church leaders, and journalists, along with representatives of the government of Nationalist China. These anti-Communist groups found a common focus in the cause of Generalissimo CHIANG Kai-shek, the Nationalist leader who lost to the Communists in the Chinese civil war of 1945–49 and subsequently established his own regime on the island of Taiwan.

Although it is impossible to assign a precise date to the formation of the China Lobby, it was certainly operating as an effective propaganda organization by 1945. Its leaders included industrialist Alfred KOHLBERG; right-wing Republican Senators Styles BRIDGES of New Hampshire and William KNOWLAND of California; journalists Freda UTLEY and John T. Flynn; editor William Loeb; Henry LUCE, publisher of *Time, Life,* and *Fortune* magazines; Congressman Walter Judd of Minnesota; General Claire Lee Chennault, who had led the famous "Flying Tiger" air squadrons during World War II; William J. Goodwin, a former registered agent for the Chinese government who had become a consultant for the China Supply Commission; and Chinese financiers T.V. Soong and H.H. Kung, both of whom were relatives of Chiang with close ties to his inner circle of advisers. These individuals' motives for supporting Chiang were diverse: Kohlberg, a lace importer, had extensive economic interests in China; both Luce—the son of missionaries to China—and Judd, who had been a missionary himself, backed Chiang's efforts to promote Christianity in the Far East; Bridges and Knowland used the China issue as a partisan political weapon against the Truman administration; Chennault operated a profitable airline in China subsidized in part by American dollars; Goodwin was on the payroll of the Chinese News Service, the propaganda arm of the Nationalist government; and Soong and Kung shared business interests that depended upon U.S. foreign aid.

Between 1945 and 1948, the China Lobby worked tirelessly to persuade Congress to dispatch massive amounts of military and economic aid to Chiang's Nationalist regime. It succeeded in obtaining nearly $3 billion in assistance for Chiang; yet, even that amount proved insufficient as the Communist armies led by MAO

Zedong repeatedly routed the Nationalist troops. By December 1949, Chiang had fled the mainland for Taiwan, and the China Lobby—unwilling to permit any blame for the debacle to fall upon Chiang—began its search for subversives in the Truman administration. If the Communists had emerged victorious in China, the China Lobby argued, it was only because U.S. policy had been influenced by pro-Communist officials in the State Department.

An indefatigable zealot, Kohlberg led the attack upon the government's Far East experts. Kohlberg later claimed that he had suspected as early as 1943 that Communists were subverting American policy in China. In 1945, Kohlberg attempted to seize control of the INSTITUTE FOR PACIFIC RELATIONS, of which he was a director, because he believed its officials were following the Moscow line. When the IPR continued to publish articles favorable to the Chinese Communists, Kohlberg helped found an alternative policy-research organization, the China Policy Association, and published a journal called *China Monthly*. Kohlberg frequently supplied *China Monthly* with articles, and as Chiang's fortunes dimmed, Kohlberg intensified his crusade against the State Department. When the Truman administration released its CHINA WHITE PAPER in August 1949, Kohlberg declared that "the real purpose of the White Paper seems . . . to be to reveal to the chancellories of the world the story of the American betrayal of the Republic of China. What could be of greater aid to the Soviet Union than this?" Later that month, Kohlberg described Ambassador at Large Philip JESSUP as "the initiator of the smear campaign against Nationalist China and Chiang Kai-shek and the originator of the myth of the democratic Chinese Communists." Other prominent targets of the China Lobby were Secretary of State Dean ACHESON, General George C. MARSHALL, Alger HISS, Harry Dexter WHITE, career foreign-service officers John Stewart SERVICE and John Carter VINCENT, and China expert Owen LATTIMORE.

The China Lobby solidified its alliance with the Republican Party in the presidential election of 1948 when it supported the candidacy of Governor Thomas E. Dewey on the assumption that Dewey would provide increased assistance to Chiang. Over the next six years, members of the China Lobby (particularly Kohlberg) contributed significant amounts to the campaign chests of right-wing Republican congressional candidates, including Bridges, Knowland, Senator Kenneth Wherry of Nebraska, and Richard M. NIXON. Less than a month after Senator Joseph MCCARTHY delivered his 1950 Lincoln Day speech in Wheeling, West Virginia, Kohlberg had met privately with the Wisconsin senator to provide him with additional ammunition to employ in his anti-Communist crusade. In fact, it was the China Lobby that fed McCarthy most of the material about alleged subversives in government that he employed so effectively during his rapid rise to prominence.

Not surprisingly, the China Lobby had its detractors. Owen Lattimore once described it as a "bitter and implacable group of people" who sought "to intimidate people like me and even officials of the United States government from expressing views that are contrary to their own. Their weapon of intimidation is McCarthy's machine gun." The power of the China Lobby seemed so ominous to Senator Mike Mansfield of Montana that he called for a thorough Senate investigation of the coalition, but his colleagues refused to support his request. As late as 1970, the China Lobby was strong enough to prevent U.S. recognition of Communist China, even though it was obvious to most objective observers that Chiang Kai-shek had no viable chance of returning to power on the mainland.

**China White Paper**    In the spring of 1949, as the Nationalist Chinese forces of CHIANG Kai-shek neared their final collapse in the civil war against the Communist armies led by MAO Zedong, the Truman administration decided to publish a thorough account of U.S. policy toward China, focusing especially on the years since 1944. Prepared by a group of State Department officials under the leadership of W. Walton Butterworth and edited by Dr. Philip C. JESSUP (then serving as Ambassador at Large), the compilation of documents and analysis was delivered to President Harry S. TRUMAN on June 26, 1949. Formally entitled *United States Relations with China with Special Reference to the Period 1944–1949,* the report came to be known simply as the China White Paper.

The report itself totaled 409 pages and was accompanied by 645 pages of documentary material. In releasing the White Paper on August 4, Truman declared that his "primary purpose in having this frank and factual record released at this time is to ensure that our policy toward China, and the Far East as a whole, shall be based on informed and intelligent public opinion." The fundamental theme underlying the White Paper was that the military defeat of the Nationalist forces was due to the incompetence and corruption of Chiang's regime and not to mistakes in American policy. In a separate preface to the report, Secretary of State Dean ACHESON essentially absolved the Truman administration of all blame for the Communist victory in China:

> The unfortunate but inescapable fact is that the ominous result of the civil war in China was beyond the control of the government of the United States. Nothing that this country did or could have done within the reasonable limits of its capabilities could have changed that result; nothing that was left undone by this country has contributed to it. It was the product of internal Chinese forces, forces which this country tried to influence but could not. A decision was arrived at within China, if only a decision by default.
>
> And now it is abundantly clear that we must face the situation as it exists in fact. We will not help the Chinese or ourselves by basing our policy on wishful thinking.

Truman's comment to Senator Arthur Vandenburg about the outcome of the Chinese civil war was more succinct. In backing Chiang, Truman said, "We picked a bad horse."

To prove the administration's contention that it had done everything within reasonable limits to support Chiang, the White Paper pointed out that between 1945 and 1949, the United States had provided the Nationalist government with more than $2 billion in grants and credits and had sold it more than $1 billion worth of nonmilitary material at a fraction of the actual cost. More than half of Chiang's military forces had been equipped with American weapons. Nevertheless, the Nationalists had lost seventeen divisions armed with American military equipment in the space of three months alone in late 1948. In all, State Department experts estimated that 60 percent of American military aid to Chiang had been captured intact by the Communists. The report closed with a letter dated May 5, 1949, from the acting president of the Nationalist regime to Truman. (Chiang had resigned the presidency and was temporarily in seclusion at the time.) "It is regrettable," the letter read, "that, owing to the failure of our then Government to make judicious use of this aid and to bring about appropriate political, economic, and military reforms, your assistance has not produced the desired effect. To this failure is attributed the present predicament in which our country finds itself."

Truman and Acheson had hoped that a presentation of the facts behind the dispiriting course of events in China would quell criticism of the administration's Far East policy as the nation awaited the inevitable collapse of the Nationalist armies. They were badly mistaken. The White Paper was denounced by the administration's critics as "a smooth alibi for the pro-Communists in the State Department who . . . aided in the Communist conquest of China." Even the moderate *New York Times* stated in an editorial that "This White Paper, an attempt at vindication, is actually a sorry record of well-meaning mistakes." Amid the growing public furor over Communist influence in the Truman administration, the release of the White Paper fueled the controversy over the fate of China and encouraged the search for Communist sympathizers in the State Department.

**Christians, Mady** (1900–1951)   A victim of the entertainment industry's BLACKLIST during the McCarthy era, Mady Christians was born in Austria in 1900. She began her acting career at the age of sixteen with a performance at her father's German theater in New York City. She returned to Germany to study with noted drama teacher Max Reinhardt and subsequently starred in numerous European films. Christians emigrated to the United States in 1931 and continued her career in New York and Hollywood, appearing in more than sixty films and stage productions. The highlights of her career were her roles on Broadway in the antifascist drama *Watch on the Rhine*, in Maurice Evans' production of *Hamlet*, as Mama in *I Remember Mama*, and—on film—in Arthur Miller's *All My Sons*.

During the Nazi occupation of Europe, Christians supported numerous organizations dedicated to assisting refugees and exiled artists. However, one of those groups, the American Committee for the Protection of the Foreign-Born, was cited by Attorney General Tom CLARK in 1949 as a Communist-front organization. Consequently, the entertainment industry handbook known as *RED CHANNELS* included Christians in its listing of suspected subversives. Following an investigation by the FBI and staff of the HOUSE COMMITTEE ON UN-AMERICAN ACTIVITIES (HUAC), Christians suddenly found herself without any offers of employment.

Her health deteriorated. At one point, she was scheduled to play the lead role in a televised version of *The Mother*, but one week before rehearsals began the producer withdrew his offer. Shortly thereafter, Christians suffered a nervous breakdown and was hospitalized. "I cannot bear yet to think of the thing which led to my breakdown," she wrote to a friend. "One day I shall put them down as a record of something unbelievable." Christians died on October 28, 1951, the victim of a cerebral hemorrhage. Associates who had seen her in the last days of her life maintained that the industry's blacklist had ruined her health.

**Cincinnati Reds**   See BASEBALL.

**Clark, Tom C.** (1899–1977)   A fervent anti-Communist who served as attorney general of the United States during the first administration of President Harry S. TRUMAN, Tom Clark subsequently was named to the U.S. Supreme Court, where he served for eighteen years. Born in Dallas, Texas, Clark served briefly as a sergeant in World War I before completing his undergraduate studies at the University of Texas. In 1922, Clark obtained his law degree from the University of Texas and joined his father's law firm in Dallas. Partly as a result of

U.S. Supreme Court justice Tom Clark.

his friendship with Senator Tom CONNALLY, Clark obtained an appointment as district attorney of Dallas County in 1927. He resumed private practice in 1932 but accepted a position with the U.S. Department of Justice in 1937 as a special assistant in antitrust cases. Following the entry of the United States into war in 1941, Clark helped organize the evacuation and internment of thousands of Japanese-American citizens on the West Coast.

During World War II, Clark worked closely with Senator Truman on the Senate War Investigating Committee, the body which vaulted Truman into public prominence. When Truman sought the vice-presidential nomination at the Democratic Party's national convention in 1944, Clark proved one of the Missouri senator's strongest supporters. Although he had been selected to head first the Justice Department's antitrust division and subsequently its criminal division during the war, Clark maintained a relatively low profile in Washington and was not well known to the public when Truman selected him in the summer of 1945 to become attorney general.

Attorney General Clark urged Truman to institute a comprehensive loyalty review program to protect the administration against charges that it was "soft" on communism. Although he conceded that there probably were very few federal employees who were actually disloyal, Clark argued that even one subversive employee could pose a threat to the nation's security. Moreover, the sweeping victory of the Republican Party in the congressional elections of 1946 convinced Clark that the Truman administration needed to bolster its public image in the area of internal security. As a result of pressure from Clark and FBI Director J. Edgar HOOVER, Truman issued EXECUTIVE ORDER 9835 on March 21, 1947, establishing the nation's first comprehensive loyalty program. The measure did not assuage Republican critics of the adminstration, however, and so Clark continued to press for further anti-Communist measures. He persuaded Truman to maintain electronic surveillance of potential subversives in cases where the national security was involved and personally supervised the government's pursuit of Judith COPLON, a political analyst in the Department of Justice who was arrested in March 1949 on suspicion of passing confidential government data to Soviet espionage agents in New York.

As the presidential election of 1948 neared, Clark repeatedly emphasized the Truman administration's commitment to clearing disloyal employees out of the federal government. He pointed particularly to the successful prosecution under the SMITH ACT of twelve leaders of the COMMUNIST PARTY OF THE UNITED STATES OF AMERICA. Clark had pressed U.S. Attorney John McGohey to launch the Smith Act cases, and he used the conviction of the Communist leaders in July 1948 to demonstrate the administration's commitment to the cause of anti-Communism.

In September 1949, Truman named Clark to the U.S. Supreme Court to replace the late Associate Justice Frank Murphy. Despite opposition from civil-rights officials, the Senate confirmed Clark by an overwhelming majority. During his first few years on the Court, Clark consistently voted in support of Chief Justice Fred Vinson, whose conservative philosophy never had appealed to civil libertarians. Because Clark had initiated the prosecution of the defendants while attorney general, he took no part in the Court's consideration of the lower courts' decisions in DENNIS V. UNITED STATES in which a majority (led by Vinson) upheld the conviction of the Communist Party officials. In 1957, however, Clark dissented in YATES V. UNITED STATES objecting to the majority decision that overturned the conviction of a different group of Communist Party leaders under the Smith Act. Clark also opposed the Supreme Court's decision in 1957 to grant defendants in subversion cases the right to obtain access to certain prosecution documents.

During the 1960s, Clark gradually modified his views on civil liberties and authored several civil-rights decisions that upheld the provisions of the Civil Rights Act of 1964. Clark resigned from the Supreme Court in 1967 to clear the way for the appointment of his son, Ramsay Clark, as attorney general in the administration of President Lyndon JOHNSON. For the following decade, Clark served on various circuits of the U.S. Court of Appeals, becoming the only retired justice in history to sit on all eleven circuits. He died in 1977 at the age of 77.

**Clubb, Oliver Edmund** (1901–1989)  A twenty-four-year veteran of the U.S. foreign service, Oliver Edmund Clubb was director of the Office of Chinese Affairs in the Department of State when he was called to testify before the HOUSE COMMITTEE ON UN-AMERICAN ACTIVITIES in June 1951. Clubb had previously been identified by Whittaker CHAMBERS as the foreign-service employee who had visited the offices of the Communist publication *New Masses* in 1932, bearing a letter of introduction from Agnes SMEDLEY, an American journalist in China who was suspected of harboring Communist sympathies. Committee investigators asked Clubb—a close friend of Owen LATTIMORE, another Far East specialist whose loyalty had been called into question—about the purpose of his visit in an attempt to discover whether he had been part of a conspiracy to aid the Chinese Communist army of MAO Zedong in its civil war with CHIANG Kai-shek. (The issue had taken on additional importance following the fall of China to Communist forces in 1949.)

After Clubb testified, he was suspended by the State Department pending an investigation to gauge his loyalty and to determine whether he was a security risk. The departmental LOYALTY REVIEW BOARD found that Clubb was indeed loyal but that he represented a security risk, and they recommended that he be dismissed. Clubb appealed the decision to Secretary of State Dean ACHESON. Acheson, who claimed that he never had time to personally review employee files in security cases, asked an old friend, former Ambassador Nathaniel P. Davis, to examine the documentation and make a rec-

ommendation. David recommended that Acheson overturn Clubb's dismissal. Acheson did so on February 11, 1952, praising Clubb as "one of our most experienced and trusted officers." But Acheson did not return Clubb to the Far East Division; instead, he reassigned him to the State Department's Division of Historical Research. Clubb promptly retired from the foreign service.

At this point, Senator Joseph MCCARTHY began his own probe of the affair, claiming that Acheson and Clubb had struck a deal that allowed Clubb to retire voluntarily and save his pension. To McCarthy, Acheson's decision to overturn the unanimous finding of the loyalty review board represented yet another piece of evidence that the top officials of the Truman administration protected Communist sympathizers in the government. The incident proved a public embarrassment to the White House, forcing Acheson to explain his actions at length at a press conference on March 5, 1952.

**Cobb, Lee J.** (1911–1976)  A well-known stage and motion picture star who participated in left-wing political activities as a young actor in New York, Lee J. Cobb was named as a Communist by fellow actor Larry PARKS in testimony before the HOUSE COMMITTEE ON UN-AMERICAN ACTIVITIES (HUAC) in March 1951.

Cobb had grown up on the Lower East Side of New York and might have become a professional musician had he not broken his wrist as a young man. At the age of 17, Cobb ran away to Hollywood, only to return several months later. He studied accounting at New York's City College but never took a degree. In 1934 he joined the Group Theatre, where he became acquainted with a number of left-wing political activists who invited him to join the COMMUNIST PARTY.

By his own admission, Cobb became a member of the Communist Party in 1940 or 1941. At that time, he did not view membership in the party as requiring a thoroughgoing commitment to Marxist ideology: "The atmosphere in the country as a whole at that time lent itself to rather a loose liberal, if not leftist, interpretation of events, local and international," Cobb later explained, "and at that time we took each other for granted as subscribing generally to a similar interpretation of history." Cobb remained a member of the Communist Party in New York for less than a year.

He moved to Hollywood in the summer of 1942, where he established contact with Communist Party members in the motion picture community. One of the projects he undertook as a party member there was an effort (in collaboration with John Howard LAWSON) to inject Communist ideology into Stanislavski's method on acting; "The excuse," noted Cobb, "was that however good Stanislavski was, he would be so much better if he were a Communist." Not surprisingly, the attempt failed miserably. For the next two years, Cobb served as a private in the U.S. Army. Upon his discharge, he resumed his attendance at party meetings, but when Moscow changed direction in 1945 and started to move away from its wartime collaborationist policy, Cobb grew disillusioned and ceased attending party meetings.

In 1949, Cobb made his professional breakthrough with his portrayal of Willy Loman in Arthur MILLER's drama, *Death of a Salesman*, directed by Elia KAZAN. Then came Parks' testimony citing him as a Communist. For the following two-and-a-half years, congressional investigators met periodically with Cobb, trying to persuade him to testify and name other individuals who had been his associates in the party. During that time, according to Cobb, his telephone lines were tapped, his grocery bills were intercepted, and he was shadowed by government agents. In the spring of 1953, Cobb's wife was hospitalized for alcoholism. "I was pretty much worn down," Cobb recalled. "I had no money. I couldn't borrow. I had the expenses of taking care of [two small] children. You are reduced to the position where you either steal or gamble, and since I'm inclined more to gamble than steal, I gambled."

Cobb agreed to meet in executive session with HUAC investigators on June 2, 1953, in a Hollywood hotel room. During his testimony, he acknowledged his past ties to the Communist Party, and he named twenty individuals, most of them fellow members of the motion picture industry, as Communists. Shortly afterward, Cobb suffered a massive heart attack.

Cobb subsequently defended his decision to testify voluntarily and provide the committee with names. His former associates, Cobb claimed, abandoned him "when the chips were down." "They ran when I was named," Cobb said. "The very people I was protecting were beneath contempt. . . . You became a thinly disguised pariah. You were really bereft of those closest to you. They threw in the towel, gave up. They would sympathize with me as I died—*that* human they would allow themselves to be. There wasn't a single exception to that statement. I'm talking about breakfast, not moral support. . . . I decided it wasn't worth dying for, and if this gesture was my way of getting out of the penitentiary I'd do it. I had to be employable again. There were no two ways about it."

Cobb did resume his career, appearing in such successful productions as *On The Waterfront* (a film about informants and Communist infiltration of the labor movement, directed by Kazan) and *The Brothers Karamazov*. Cobb subsequently starred in several television series as well.

## Coburn, Charles (1877–1961)

A veteran stage and screen actor, Charles Coburn served as an officer of the right-wing MOTION PICTURE ALLIANCE FOR THE PRESERVATION OF AMERICAN IDEALS. The model of a dapper, sophisticated leading man, Coburn accumulated scores of credits in successful theatrical productions before appearing in his first motion picture in 1937. In 1943, Coburn won an Academy Award as best supporting actor for his performance in *The More the Merrier*.

Although he was not one of the original members of the executive committee of the Motion

Picture Alliance, Coburn subsequently served as one of the alliance's officers, along with such other conservative entertainers as John WAYNE, Adolphe MENJOU, and Gary COOPER. He enthusiastically supported the organization's determination to fight "Communists, radicals, and crack-pots," and to oppose "any effort of any group or individual to divert the loyalty of the screen from the free America that gave it birth."

**Cohn, Roy** (1927–1986)   Chief counsel to Senator Joseph MCCARTHY's Permanent Investigations Subcommittee from 1953 to 1955, attorney Roy Cohn became one of the most hated and feared public figures in the United States during the McCarthy era.

The son of a New York State supreme-court justice, Cohn was a precocious student who graduated from Columbia Law School at the age of 20. Instead of joining a private law firm, Cohn accepted an offer to serve on the staff of the U.S. attorney in New York City. From the start, Cohn preferred to specialize in the investigation of subversive activities, and from 1948 to 1952 he played an integral role in the successful prosecution of William REMINGTON, Julius and Ethel ROSENBERG, and the eleven top officials of the COMMUNIST PARTY OF THE UNITED STATES.

In 1952, during the waning months of the Truman administration, Cohn was named special assistant to Attorney General James McGranary. From that post in Washington, Cohn continued his pursuit of alleged subversives. Along the way, he also criticized what he considered to be a lack of zeal by his superiors in the Justice Department in prosecuting suspected Communists among the U.S. delegation to the United Nations. Following a prolonged investigation of Far East expert Owen LATTIMORE by the Senate INTERNAL SECURITY SUBCOMMITTEE, Cohn prepared an indictment of Lattimore for perjury. Cohn was notably less successful in this case than in his previous efforts, however; two of the seven perjury charges were dismissed even before the case went to a jury, and the other five were later dropped by the government.

Nevertheless, Cohn had attracted the attention of Senator McCarthy, and after the Republicans gained control of Congress in the elections of 1952, McCarthy named Cohn chief counsel of the Permanent Investigations Subcommittee of the GOVERNMENT OPERATIONS COMMITTEE. To McCarthy, Cohn was "one of the most brilliant young men I have ever met," and Cohn returned the compliment by treating McCarthy with far more respect than he afforded anyone else in public life. In fact, Cohn's evident disdain for virtually everyone else around him led *Time* magazine to remark that he showed "contempt of all but the top boss." Cohn subsequently wangled an appointment for a personal friend, G. David SCHINE (the son of a millionaire businessman), as the subcommittee's unpaid "consultant on psychological warfare."

One of McCarthy's first targets in early 1953 was the INTERNATIONAL INFORMATION AGENCY (IIA), the branch of the State Department that operated more than a hundred libraries overseas and supervised the radio broadcast activities of the VOICE OF AMERICA. To obtain evidence against the IIA, McCarthy dispatched Cohn and Schine on a fact-finding tour of State Department libraries in Western Europe to view first-hand the content of the library shelves and determine whether they contained books written by Communists or Communist sympathizers.

Cohn and Schine disgraced themselves by their raucous performance on the tour—at one point Schine was seen chasing Cohn through a Berlin hotel lobby, whacking him over the head with a rolled-up magazine—and provoked an uproar by their reckless allegations of disloyalty among State Department officials. "Their limited vocabulary, their self-complacency, and their paucity of ideas," wrote a correspondent of the *Manchester Guardian*, "coupled with the immense power they wield, had the effect of drawing sympathy for all ranks of the United States diplomatic service who have to submit to this sort of thing."

The sight of American officials actually burning or destroying books to avoid Cohn's wrath caused such a furor that President Dwight David EISENHOWER found it necessary to issue a statement in defense of intellectual freedom at the commencement exercises at DARTMOUTH COLLEGE in June 1953. Years later, Cohn acknowledged that he and Schine had quickly realized, "although neither of us could admit to the distressing fact, that [the tour] was a colossal mistake." There were also allegations, largely by McCarthy's critics, that the relationship between Cohn and Schine—and McCarthy, as well—was more than mere friendship; author Lillian HELLMAN, for instance, referred to the three men as "Bonnie, Bonnie, and Clyde."

In November 1953, Schine was drafted into the U.S. Army. Cohn promptly began badgering Army officials to obtain special treatment for his friend. Schine did, in fact, receive special privileges, including extra evening passes; he also was regularly excused from routine drills and kitchen duty to receive telephone calls. Eventually, however, the Army balked at Cohn's demands. Cohn warned that he would "wreck the Army" if it failed to reconsider, and McCarthy threatened to launch a full-scale investigation of Communist infiltration of the Army. For his part, Secretary of the Army Robert T. STEVENS retaliated by releasing a thirty-four-page report summarizing the outrageous demands made by Cohn and McCarthy on behalf of Schine.

The question of the Army's treatment of Schine combined with McCarthy's investigations of alleged Communist espionage at the Army Signal Corps Engineering Laboratories at FORT MONMOUTH, New Jersey, to produce a nationally televised confrontation between McCarthy and the Army hierarchy. During these ARMY-MCCARTHY HEARINGS, Cohn played a vital role as both an investigator and a witness, and millions of Americans received their first opportunity to get a close look at Cohn, with his dark complexion, heavy-lidded eyes, and black hair slicked straight back. Cohn's aggressive, abrasive style provoked fireworks both on camera and behind the scenes. When Senator Henry Jackson of Washington made a critical remark denigrating McCarthy's motives, Cohn threatened to "get" Jackson; assistant subcommittee counsel Robert KENNEDY overheard Cohn's remark, and the two men nearly came to blows before bystanders broke up the argument.

Near the end of the hearings, Army special counsel Joseph WELCH subjected Cohn to a lengthy cross-examination to determine precisely how he and Schine had conducted their inquiries into reports of disloyalty at Army bases in the United States and abroad. Although Cohn held up reasonably well against Welch's questions, McCarthy was growing visibly upset at the persistent interrogation of his protege. Finally, McCarthy interrupted Welch's questions by announcing that an associate in Welch's law firm of Hale & Dorr, Frederick G. Fisher, had belonged to the NATIONAL LAWYERS GUILD, which, according to McCarthy, had been identified as "the legal bulwark of the Communist Party." This outburst violated a private agreement that Cohn and Welch had negotiated several days earlier: in return for Welch's promise not to ask Cohn about his own military record (Cohn had failed the physical exam for entrance to West Point), Cohn had promised to keep Fisher's name out of the hearings; McCarthy had accepted that agreement, but had now broken the bargain. Welch's emotional response to McCarthy's outburst—"Have you no sense of decency left, sir? Have you no sense of decency?"—left McCarthy at a loss for words for one of the few times in his public career and helped turn public opinion against the bullying tactics of the Wisconsin senator.

By the time the hearings concluded in June 1954, the revelations of Cohn's attempts to obtain special favors for Private Schine had virtually assured his departure from the Permanent Investigations Subcommittee staff. Accordingly, Cohn resigned on July 20, much to the regret of Senator McCarthy, who believed that millions of Americans who had watched the hearings shared his feelings of sadness. "I know," McCarthy said, "that they will resent as deeply as do I the treatment to which he has been subjected." At a banquet in Cohn's honor at the Hotel

Astor in New York the following week, guests included such right-wing luminaries as columnists Westbrook PEGLER, Fulton Lewis, Jr., author William F. BUCKLEY, and millionaire industrialist Alfred KOHLBERG.

Cohn, in turn, described the Senate's subsequent censure of McCarthy in December 1954 as "the blackest act in our whole history." In his autobiographical account of his relationship with McCarthy, Cohn concluded that "McCarthy used the best methods available to him to fight a battle that needed to be fought. The methods were far from perfect, but they were not nearly as imperfect as uninformed critics suggest. . . . He may have been wrong in details, but he was right in essentials. Certainly few can deny that the Government of the United States had in it enough Communist sympathizers and pro-Soviet advisers to twist and pervert American foreign policy for close to two decades."

McCarthy, Cohn claimed, "was a man of a peculiar time: the COLD WAR. . . . He came forward at the time of Communist aggression in Korea and the triumph of MAO's revolution. The job he felt he had to do could hardly have been done by a gentle, tolerant spirit who could see all around a problem. What is indisputable is that he was a courageous man who fought a monumental evil. He did so against opposition as determined as was his own attack—an opposition that spent far more time, money, and print seeking to expose *him* than Communism."

Although Cohn's detractors predicted that he would become "the biggest has-been since Jackie Coogan" following his departure from Washington, Cohn joined a prestigious New York law firm and became an extremely successful attorney, attracting such famous and wealthy clients as Francis Cardinal Spellman, organized crime boss Carmine Galante, and, later, real estate millionaire Donald Trump. Cohn also retained his flair for controversy. On three separate occasions (1964, 1969, and 1971), he was indicted on a variety of offenses including fraud, conspiracy, and bribery. Each time he was ac-

quitted, and Cohn publicly blamed the prosecutions on the malice of Justice Department officials from the days when his longtime adversary, Robert KENNEDY, had served as attorney general. Cohn also had a long-running battle with the Internal Revenue Service, which audited his tax returns for twenty years in a row.

Shortly before Cohn's death, a panel of judges from the New York State Supreme Court disbarred him from the practice of law in the state, due to conduct that the panel called "unethical," "unprofessional," and "particularly reprehensible." Cohn died on August 2, 1986, of a heart attack. Although he had claimed that he was suffering from liver cancer, doctors noted that his symptoms indicated that he also suffered from the HIV virus that causes acquired immune deficiency syndrome (AIDS).

**Cold War**  At the end of World War II, the wartime alliance between the United States and the Soviet Union quickly deteriorated into an icy hostility and long-term rivalry that came to be known as the Cold War.

The term itself was coined by columnist Walter Lippmann, whose 1950 book, *The Cold War,* criticized the foreign policies of the Truman administration, but the state of affairs that it described existed as early as the spring of 1945. In April of that year, an article by Communist writer Jacques Duclos signaled Moscow's intention to return to a hard-line policy of confrontation with the Western democracies. The ensuing Soviet occupation of Eastern Europe in the wake of the defeat of Nazi Germany angered American public opinion, though Soviet dictator Joseph STALIN viewed the move as an essential measure for the security of the USSR. Tensions were exacerbated further by angry exchanges between American and Soviet diplomats at the Potsdam Conference, by the discovery of a Soviet spy ring in Canada led by Igor GOUZENKO, and by Soviet sponsorship of guerrilla insurgencies against the postwar governments of Greece and Turkey.

The Cold War. Escalating tension between the United States and the Soviet Union, as symbolized by the division of Berlin into eastern and western sectors, helped fuel the anti-Communist crusade in postwar America.

As U.S.–Soviet hostility increased, so did suspicion of leftist radicals in the United States. Fears of Communist aggression abroad were mirrored by concern over Communist subversion from within the United States. In 1946, Republican congressional candidates garnered a significant number of votes by charging that the Democratic administration of Harry S. TRUMAN was "soft" on communism. The following year, the HOUSE COMMITTEE ON UN-AMERICAN ACTIVITIES (HUAC) began to step up the frequency and scope of its investigations.

Further diplomatic defeats in the Far East and Eastern Europe, combined with the Soviet Union's acquisition of a nuclear capability and the continuing uneasiness created by the inability of the Truman administration to end the Cold War decisively in favor of the United States, intensified the search for scapegoats within the federal government. A comprehensive system of LOYALTY OATHS and security checks was instituted by Truman and was refined by his successor in the White House, Dwight David EISENHOWER. Although few spies were discovered within the government, the celebrated cases of Judith COPLON and Julius and Ethel ROSENBERG contributed to the atmosphere of paranoia.

Given the prevailing climate of suspicion, it was not surprising that Senator Joseph MCCARTHY of Wisconsin obtained a ready audience when he launched his own anti-Communist crusade in February 1950. Only when Cold-War tensions abated temporarily in the late 1950s did the accusations of Communist influence in American life subside significantly.

**Cole, Lester** (1904–1985)   A motion picture screenwriter and member of the HOLLYWOOD TEN, Lester Cole was convicted of contempt of Congress and sentenced to jail for his refusal to answer questions before the HOUSE COMMITTEE ON UN-AMERICAN ACTIVITIES (HUAC).

Born into a trade-unionist family, Cole grew up in a very class-conscious atmosphere, listening to his father propound socialist views on contemporary political issues. After dropping out of high school, Cole turned to the theater, where he became a respected playwright for the legitimate stage in New York. In 1932, Cole moved to Hollywood, where he became involved almost immediately in left-wing political causes, particularly the organization of labor unions. Cole served as one of the founding members of the resuscitated SCREEN WRITERS' GUILD in 1933 and three years later helped found the Motion Picture Artists Committee to Aid Republican Spain. During the following decade, Cole worked as a screenwriter for virtually every major Hollywood studio except RKO, amassing an impressive list of credits. In 1946, he signed a long-term contract with MGM, then the largest studio in Hollywood, at a salary of $1,350 per week. Louis Mayer was so impressed with Cole's work that he reportedly informed Cole in early 1947 that he would soon be promoted to a position as writer-producer.

Cole was also a longtime member of the COMMUNIST PARTY OF THE UNITED STATES and was well known as one of Hollywood's leading radicals in the 1930s and 1940s. When HUAC began to look into Communist influence in the motion picture industry in the spring of 1947, it was not surprising that Cole was one of the Committee's first targets. At that time, a HUAC investigator warned MGM that the studio might be subjected to a full-scale probe if it did not dismiss Cole. Mayer subsequently suggested to Cole on several occasions, in an increasingly pointed manner, that he should consider curtailing his radical political activities.

In September 1947, HUAC subpoenaed Cole to testify as an unfriendly witness. Cole became the last member of the so-called Hollywood Ten to take the witness stand in the last week of October, and, like the other nine members of the group, Cole refused to answer the committee's questions about his membership in political organizations. He was subsequently cited for contempt of Congress and joined the rest of the Ten in appealing the verdict to the U.S. Supreme Court.

For several weeks after his appearance before HUAC, Cole continued to work at MGM. Following the release of the WALDORF STATEMENT on December 3, however, MGM suspended Cole indefinitely on the grounds that he had violated the "morals" clause in his contract. At the same time, Cole lost his position on the executive board of the Screen Writers' Guild. To help clear the air, Cole issued his own statement, declaring that he "did not believe in violence and force to overthrow our government, . . . and was not an agent of a foreign power," but he pledged to continue to resist the efforts of HUAC to subvert the First Amendment. Despite his protestations of loyalty, for the next two years Cole could only find work on the black market under an assumed name and at a salary considerably below the wages he had previously earned at MGM.

While he was waiting for the Supreme Court to hear his appeal, Cole filed a civil suit against Loew's Incorporated, the parent company of MGM, claiming that he had been fired solely because of his refusal to testify before HUAC. Although a jury found in Cole's favor in December 1948, Loew's appealed the verdict; an appeals court subsequently overturned the original ruling, stating that the HUAC hearings had made Cole "a distinct liability to his employer."

After the Supreme Court refused to hear the appeal of the Ten in their contempt case, Cole entered federal prison in Danbury, Connecticut, to serve a one-year term. There, he encountered former HUAC chairman J. Parnell THOMAS, who had been convicted of accepting kickbacks from relatives whom he had placed on his congressional staff payroll. Thomas, who had been assigned to duty cleaning out the prison chicken yard, overheard Cole propounding his political views and muttered, "I see that you are still spouting radical nonsense." "And I see," Cole retorted, "that you are still shoveling chicken shit."

Following his release from prison, Cole worked for a while in a warehouse and later obtained a job as an assistant copywriter for the Sealy Mattress Company, composing advertisements at a salary of $400 per month. Eventually, he resumed his Hollywood career, albeit in a limited fashion. His most notable work in later years was his screenplay for the movie *Born Free*. Unlike most of the other members of the Hollywood Ten, Cole maintained his faith in Communism into the 1970s.

*Cole v. United States* In *Cole v. United States*, the U.S. Supreme Court ruled in 1956 that the Department of Health, Education, and Welfare had exceeded its authority in dismissing a food and drug inspector as a loyalty risk. The Court's decision was based upon its conviction that the Summary Suspension Act of 1950, the statute upon which EXECUTIVE ORDER 10450 depended, had been intended to cover only "sensitive" positions within the federal employment service. Because HEW was not a sensitive agency, the dismissal of employee Cole was ruled invalid.

This ruling effectively vitiated the federal government's LOYALTY REVIEW PROGRAM because 80 percent of federal employees worked for "nonsensitive" agencies. For this reason, President Dwight David EISENHOWER and Senator Joseph MCCARTHY both vigorously protested the Court's decision. Nevertheless, the Cole ruling stood, and the decision had far-reaching consequences. Partly because of the Cole decision and partly because of the moderating temper of the times, no federal employees were dismissed or suspended from their jobs under the terms of Executive Order 10450 between 1957 and 1961, when the order expired.

**Committee for the First Amendment**  A brief-lived organization formed by Hollywood directors, writers, and performers to protest the activities of the HOUSE COMMITTEE ON UN-AMERICAN ACTIVITIES (HUAC), the Committee for the First Amendment (CFA) represented the first and only attempt by Hollywood liberals to fight the rising tide of anti-Communist sentiment in the United States in the late 1940s.

In September 1947, as HUAC launched its investigation of Communist influence in Hollywood, a group of four prominent members of the motion-picture industry—directors John Huston and William Wyler, screenwriter Philip Dunne, and actor Alexander Knox—decided to organize the CFA. Huston, Wyler, Dunne, and Knox were concerned that HUAC's tactics of intimidation would cast a pall over the right of free speech in Hollywood. The committee held its first formal meeting at the home of songwriter Ira Gershwin; shortly thereafter, the committee issued a statement claiming that "not only the freedom of the screen, but also freedom of the press, radio, and publishing are in jeopardy" from the HUAC investigation.

While the membership of the committee quickly grew to more than 500 individuals, its leaders were careful to exclude all Communists so that the committee would not be tainted by association with known radicals. "We were going to be called Communists or Comsymps [Communist sympathizers] anyway," noted Dunne, "and [we] weren't anxious to give the opposition real grounds for saying so." The committee sponsored full-page advertisements (written by Huston, Dunne, and Wyler) in newspapers across the nation, attacking HUAC's investigations into the motion picture industry. On the eve of HUAC's hearings in late October 1947, members of the committee—including Wyler, Huston, Frank SINATRA, Humphrey BOGART, Gene Kelly, Paul Henreid, Katharine HEPBURN, and Danny Kaye—chartered an airplane called the *Star of the Red Sea* for a highly publicized trip to Washington, D.C., to demonstrate their support for the constitutional right to free expression.

On October 26, the CFA aired a broadcast ("Hollywood Fights Back") over the ABC radio network, attacking HUAC's tactics and mission. Another CFA radio presentation was broadcast on November 2; in the meanwhile, CFA members had presented a petition to Congress accusing HUAC of infringing upon the American right of free speech. The poor impression made by the truculent HOLLYWOOD TEN at the HUAC hearings dampened the enthusiasm of the committee, however, and pressure from the major film studios convinced most CFA members to retreat from their brief foray into political activism. In early 1948, the committee merged quietly into the short-lived Committee of One Thousand.

**Communist Control Act** (1954)   The Communist Control Act originated in legislation proposed on August 11, 1954, by Senator Hubert H. HUMPHREY, Jr., a Democrat from Minnesota. A liberal anti-Communist and a founder of the AMERICANS FOR DEMOCRATIC ACTION, Humphrey was frustrated by the failure of conservative critics to distinguish between traditional American liberalism and Communism. By introducing this bill, Humphrey sought to demonstrate beyond question his own anti-Communist credentials, to wrest control of the anti-Communist crusade from Senator Joseph R. MCCARTHY and his allies, and ultimately to defuse the issue by removing it from politics and giving it to the courts, where issues of civil liberties could be decided in a calmer, more dispassionate environment. Humphrey later stated that he also wanted to "give the back-row red-hunters on the other [Republican] side some real legislation to chew on."

Prior to the passage of the Communist Control Act, the COMMUNIST PARTY OF THE UNITED STATES had been allowed to operate as a legally constituted political party. The INTERNAL SECURITY ACT of 1950, popularly known as the MCCARRAN ACT, did not define membership in the Communist Party as a crime; instead, it required Communists and members of Communist-action organizations to register with a Subversive Activities Control Board and precluded Communists from holding jobs in the federal government or any defense industry.

The Communist Control Act, however, declared that the Communist Party of the United States was not, in fact, a political party; rather, it was "an instrumentality of a conspiracy to overthrow the Government of the United States." "It constitutes an authoritarian dictatorship within a republic," continued the act, "demanding for itself the rights and privileges accorded to political parties, but denying to all others the liberties guaranteed by the Constitution. . . . Unlike political parties, the Communist Party acknowledges no constitutional or statutory limitations upon its conduct or upon that of its members."

The danger posed by the party, according to the text of the Communist Control Act, was that it was dedicated to the proposition that the constitutional government of the United States "must be brought to ruin by any available means, including resort to force and violence. Holding that doctrine, its role as the agency of a hostile foreign power renders its existence a clear present and continuing danger to the security of the United States." As a result, the act proposed that the Communist Party be outlawed, and anyone who "knowingly and willfully" joined the Communist Party would be subject to fine and imprisonment and potentially a loss of citizenship.

In introducing his legislation, Humphrey told the Senate that he was "tired of reading headlines about being 'soft' toward communism. I am tired of having people play the Communist issue. I am tired of having people play the Communist issue as though it were a great overture which has lasted for years. I want to come to grips with the Communist issue. I want senators to stand up and to answer whether they are for the Communist Party or against it." Only one senator, Republican John Sherman Cooper of Kentucky, rose to object to the bill on constitutional grounds. Terming Humphrey's legislation "shameful," Cooper argued that it would "depart from precedents and principles held since the adoption of the Constitution." Nevertheless, the measure passed the Senate by a vote of 85–0 after being combined with another anti-Communist bill sponsored by Senator John Marshall Butler of Maryland, which added the category of "Communist-infiltrated" to the list of subversive organizations proscribed under the McCarran Act.

During the debate on the bill in the House of Representatives, Department of Justice officials sought to remove the clause that made membership in the Communist Party a crime. For years, FBI director J. Edgar HOOVER had opposed the outlawing of the Communist Party, fearing that it would drive the Communist movement underground and therefore make it more difficult for the FBI to maintain surveillance on Party members. Moreover, if membership in the Communist Party were made illegal, the government would be unable to require Communists to register with the Subversive Activities Control Board because admission of party membership would constitute a violation of their Fifth Amendment rights.

Amused by the Eisenhower administration's opposition to his measure, Humphrey played the role of anti-Communist crusader to the hilt. It was puzzling, he said, to note that after "all the speeches we have heard on communism," a Republican administration was "backing away" from an opportunity to act effectively against the Communist Party. In rejecting the provision that outlawed the party, Humphrey claimed that the House had defined *communism* as "a man-eating bear" and then "went forth with a powder puff and touched the bear on the nose." By a narrow margin, the Senate reinstated the provision making the party illegal, and the House finally agreed to accept the Senate version of the measure. When the bill came up for final consideration, Senator Estes Kefauver of Tennessee voiced his fear that it might penalize individuals for holding unorthodox beliefs. "If they want to be different," Humphrey replied, "let them join the party of Mars or the party of Jupiter." The Senate then approved the Communist Control Act by a vote of 79–0, and the House followed by a margin of 265–2.

In their nationally syndicated column, journalists Joseph and Stewart Alsop described the Communist Control Act as "the most cleverly conceived, ruthlessly executed and politically adroit of all the sudden Democratic raids that have been such a feature of this session of Congress." The liberal Humphrey's sponsorship of such legislation was also a measure of the political hysteria that had arisen during the McCarthy era.

**Communist Party of the United States of America**   Established in 1920, the Communist Party of the United States of America (CPUSA) spent the first three years of its existence (its "First Period") struggling to build an organization and find an identity in the turbulent political atmosphere of the post-World War I era. By the end of 1922, the CPUSA was firmly under the control of the Communist International (Comintern), the Moscow-based organization that directed Communist Party activities outside the Soviet Union. Although CPUSA officials might claim that they were not directly subservient to Moscow, the party in the United States never deviated from the official Comintern line on policy matters. As part of a larger international organization, the Communist Party was and remains unique in American politics.

From 1923 to 1928 (its "Second Period," which the Comintern referred to as the "partial stabilization of capitalism"), the CPUSA attempted to work through American labor unions—to "bore from within"—to combine craft unions with the less-skilled industrial

**Top officials of the Communist Party of the United States: Gus Hall (left) and Ben Davis (right).**

unions, to obtain union recognition of the Soviet Union, and to organize workers who had not yet joined any union. Following the accession of Joseph STALIN to supreme power in the Soviet Union in 1928–29, the Sixth Congress of the Comintern inaugurated a far more severe and uncompromising line of opposition toward democracy and capitalism. Ostensibly, this shift was based upon the belief that the capitalist nations of the West were entering a time of crisis that provided an excellent opportunity for revolutionary Communist activity; in fact, the motivation for the change in policy could be discovered in the internal political requirements of the Stalinist regime, which wished to unify and enhance enthusiasm for revolution abroad while diverting attention from domestic difficulties.

During the period from 1928 to 1934, known as the "Third Period," the CPUSA dedicated itself to the goal of forceful, violent revolution under the leadership of William Z. FOSTER. Capitalism appeared to be on the verge of collapse, and it became the duty of the Communist functionary to prepare for the imminent seizure of power in the name of the people. The party therefore insisted upon iron discipline and centralized control in the interim.

In such an atmosphere, there could be no accommodation with traditional American liberalism; indeed, the party viewed liberals as the most dangerous enemies of Communist revolution because by ameliorating the worst abuses of the system, they would merely perpetuate its existence. Accordingly, the CPUSA denounced the staid American Federation of Labor as a fascist front and attempted to organize its own separate federation of trade unions. On a larger scale, the party had nothing but contempt for the New Deal programs of President Franklin Delano Roosevelt. According to party theorists, Roosevelt was nothing more than a capitalist stooge who had embarked upon a hypocritical mission to shore up the crumbling capitalist structure. As Foster noted, the New Deal "was calculated to preserve the capitalist system by relieving somewhat the economic and mass pressure. The center of it, the National Recovery Act (NRA), was contrived in Wall Street and was first enunciated by the U.S. Chamber of Commerce. Many capitalist theoreticians hailed it as the beginning of fascism. To call the New Deal socialistic or communistic is nonsense; it had nothing in common with either."

One interesting aspect of the CPUSA strategy during this period was its attempt to recruit African Americans in the southern states. The Sixth Congress of the Comintern declared that African Americans in the South had become an oppressed "nation" which needed to launch its own revolution and seek its own homeland within the United States. To demonstrate its commitment to the cause of African-American rights, the Communist Party took up the defense of the "Scottsboro Boys," a group of nine African-American men accused of raping two white women. After the first trial of the defendants ended in a mistrial, the CPUSA criticized the NATIONAL ASSOCIATION FOR THE ADVANCEMENT OF COLORED PEOPLE (NAACP) so violently that the NAACP withdrew from the case, giving the CPUSA a pulpit that it used to proclaim its solidarity with southern African Americans against the racist white oppressors.

The orientation of the CPUSA changed drastically in 1936, following the Seventh World Congress of the Comintern in 1935. Events in Europe—particularly the advent to power of Adolf Hitler and the National Socialist Party in Germany—led the Comintern to declare that Communists around the world needed to join other progressive and working-class elements in opposition to the rising theat of fascism. Clearly this shift toward cooperation with liberal elements in the Western democracies served the political ends of the Soviet Union, which feared that it would be left to stand alone against the European fascist powers.

In the United States, the CPUSA duly abandoned its harsh criticism of the New Deal and instead proclaimed its solidarity with liberal reformers in what came to be known as the POPULAR FRONT. Hard-liner William Z. Foster was forced out of the leadership and replaced by Earl BROWDER, who announced that "We Communists claim the revolutionary traditions of Americanism. . . . We are the Americans and Communism is the Americanism of the twentieth century." In labor affairs, the Communists celebrated the establishment of the CONGRESS OF INDUSTRIAL ORGANIZATIONS (CIO) under the leadership of John L. LEWIS and cooperated with the CIO and its member unions in organizing drives and strikes, lending the fledgling organization a significant measure of experience, toughness, and muscle.

During the early years of this new policy of accommodation—known as the "Fourth Period"—membership in the CPUSA rose from approximately 25,000 in 1934 to 55,000 in 1938. The growth in membership reflected both the appalling economic conditions of the Great Depression and the softening of the CPUSA's rhetoric. Yet, there remained little enthusiasm even among disaffected Americans to abandon the traditional domestic political party structure. When the CPUSA attempted in 1935–36 to establish a Workers and Farmers Party, it quickly abandoned that effort when it became clear that a third party had little chance of success. Instead, the CPUSA worked behind the scenes for the reelection of Franklin D. Roosevelt against Republican presidential nominee Alf Landon in 1936 on the theory that Landon was the representative of the forces of reaction and fascism.

The CPUSA appeared confused on such occasions because the premise that had produced the shift toward a Popular Front (that is, the need to combat fascism) did not apply in the United States. Another European event in 1939—the NAZI-SOVIET PACT of August 1939—led to yet another shift in policy. When Stalin consented to a nonaggression policy with Germany, American Communists suddenly found themselves forced to defend American isolationism and oppose U.S. entry into the European conflict that erupted following the German invasion of Poland in September 1939. Perhaps more than any other event, the Nazi-Soviet Pact disillusioned many Americans who had sympathized with the Communist Party and led numerous liberal American intellectuals to abandon their flirtation with Communism.

Following the German invasion of the Soviet Union in June 1941, the CPUSA performed another about-face and returned to a theme of solidarity with progressive/liberal elements under the slogan of "Everything for Victory." American Communists were instructed to work dutifully for the national-defense effort, forgoing strikes to increase production and ensure an Allied victory over the Axis Powers. Once the wartime emergency was over, however, the Comintern returned once again to a hard line, voiced by French Communist theorist Jacques Duclos in the spring of 1945. The CPUSA was ordered to return to the strategy of class warfare and to recognize that the United States and the

Soviet Union had become rival contestants for world power. In effect, this policy reflected the diplomatic realities of the post-1945 world, and the growing estrangement between the United States and the Soviet Union in the early years of the COLD WAR.

As the CPUSA obediently heeded the demands of Moscow and returned to a hard-line stance, the U.S. government began to increase its surveillance of party activities and, in 1948, launched a series of legal actions against the leaders of the CPUSA based upon the terms of the SMITH ACT. In July 1948, twelve leaders of the CPUSA were indicted for conspiracy to organize the Communist Party of the United States, an organization that purportedly taught and advocated "the overthrow and destruction of the Government of the United States by force and violence." The passage of the INTERNAL SECURITY ACT of 1950 and the COMMUNIST CONTROL ACT of 1954 further drove the party underground by requiring members of the Communist Party to register as subversives with the Attorney General of the United States. By the end of the 1950s, the CPUSA had been effectively eliminated as an independent force in American politics. Although it remains in existence, its membership in the 1990s has dwindled to approximately 20,000.

## Condon, Edward U. (1902–1974)

One of the foremost American experts in atomic physics in the postwar years, Edward U. Condon became a prominent target of the HOUSE COMMITTEE ON UN-AMERICAN ACTIVITIES (HUAC) under the chairmanship of Republican Congressman J. Parnell THOMAS in 1948.

Born in Alamagordo, New Mexico—not far from the site of the first American atomic test explosion several decades later—Condon was educated at the University of California at Berkeley, from which he received a B.A. in physics in 1924, and a Ph.D. two years later. Following the completion of his graduate work, Condon accepted a National Research Council

Fellowship, which permitted him to continue his studies in Europe at Gottingen and Munich. Upon his return to the United States in 1927, Condon was offered a teaching position at Princeton University, where he remained for most of the following decade.

At Princeton, Condon earned a reputation as one of the nation's foremost authorities in quantum mechanics and atomic structure. He also expressed his interest in applying the results of theoretical physics research to the industrial world. In 1937, Condon joined the Westinghouse Electrical and Manufacturing Company in Pittsburgh, Pennsylvania, where he enjoyed access to the only large atomic-fission equipment operated by an industrial research laboratory in the United States. As the nation edged closer toward war, Condon began to focus on military research, serving as a consultant to the National Defense Research Committee and leading Westinghouse's research into the relatively new field of radar. In 1942, Condon assisted fellow physicist J. Robert OPPENHEIMER in assembling the scientific team that subsequently developed the world's first nuclear weapons. The following year, Condon left Westinghouse to work full-time at the atomic research facility at the University of California on the problem of separation of the U-235 isotope from U-238.

Following the end of World War II, President Harry S. TRUMAN nominated Condon as director of the National Bureau of Standards, which at that time was the government's primary agency for fundamental scientific research. In November 1945, Condon was also appointed scientific adviser to the Senate Special Committee on Atomic Energy. Condon consistently urged Congress and the Truman administration to retain civilian control of atomic energy and nuclear research efforts. He criticized the intervention into scientific affairs of military officials who were, in his words, "without knowledge, and so without competence." "Any attempt to perpetuate into peacetime the restrictive practices which were used during the war will have disastrous consequences," Condon warned. "It spells death to our own activity."

Condon further alienated congressional conservatives and military officials by favoring communication between scientists of different nations and programs for international control of atomic weapons through the United Nations. "Prominent scientists are denied the privilege of traveling abroad," Condon complained in 1946. "Physicists are not allowed to discuss certain areas of their science with each other. . . . Information essential to understanding is being denied to students in our unvirsities, so that, if this situation were to continue, the young students . . . will get from their professors only a watered-down Army-approved version of the laws of nature." In an attempt to promote international scientific cooperation and decrease the dangers of nuclear war, Condon joined with other physicists, including Albert EINSTEIN, to form the Emergency Committee of Atomic Scientists in May 1946.

During 1947, Congressman Thomas wrote several articles that were published in ultraconservative magazines, that attacked Condon for his membership in the AMERICAN-SOVIET SCIENCE SOCIETY and that hinted that the scientist would soon be subpoenaed to testify before HUAC. On March 1, 1948, a subcommittee of HUAC that had purportedly been examining "groups and movements who are trying to dissipate our atomic bomb know-how for the benefit of a foreign power" released a report that stated that "from the evidence at hand, it appears that Dr. Condon is one of the weakest links in our atomic security." The report appears to have been prompted by a letter addressed to a member of the Congressional Joint Committee on Atomic Energy from an unnamed former security officer on the Manhattan Project, suggesting that Congress obtain the FEDERAL BUREAU OF INVESTIGATION's report on Condon, promising that "it would be enlightening."

The HUAC subcommittee's report on Condon consisted largely of innuendo, gossip, irrelevant facts, and unsubstantiated assertions. It began, for instance, with the statement that in 1922, Condon had "married Emilie Honzik, an American-born woman of Czechoslovakian descent." The report proceeded to point out that Condon had been appointed director of the National Bureau of Standards by liberal Secretary of Commerce Henry A. WALLACE, the former vice-president who had become a favorite target of congressional anti-Communist zealots. "In this country," the report stated, Communist subversives "haven't got as far as they have in Czechoslovakia, but they got pretty far, because they got a man as Vice President of the United States, and he is now their candidate for President, and he is the same man who recommended Dr. Condon as Director of the Bureau of Standards." The report then quoted a letter from FBI Director J. Edgar HOOVER in which Hoover noted that Condon had been observed in contact with an alleged Soviet espionage agent, though it omitted an explanation from Hoover that "there is no evidence to show that contacts between this individual and Dr. Condon were related to this individual's espionage activities."

In sum, the report contained no firm evidence that might have led an impartial observer to question Condon's loyalty. It seems to have arisen from the personal enmity of Congressman Thomas—who headed the subcommittee—toward Condon, which stemmed from the scientist's support of civilian control of atomic energy and from Condon's oft-stated opposition to military censorship of scientific information. Thomas appears to have acted on his own in releasing the report; indeed, the committee's chief investigator Robert STRIPLING later declared that he had objected to the release of the report without first providing Condon with an opportunity to appear in person and rebut the charges.

Within several hours after the release of the subcommittee's report, the Department of Commerce announced that its departmental loyalty board had unanimously issued Condon a clearance six days earlier, noting that "no reasonable grounds exist for believing that Dr. Condon is disloyal to the Government of the United States." Thomas replied that he found the department's defense of Condon incomprehensible and added that "the committee has no evidence that Dr. Condon is disloyal, but it has ample evidence that he had been at least indiscreet in a position in which indiscretion could have serious consequences." The congressman then ordered the committee to subpoena Condon's personal records from Commerce. Truman adminstration officials refused on the grounds that the executive department of the government had no obligation to share its files with Congress. Although the full House later passed a resolution requesting the Secretary of Commerce to surrender the relevant documents, Truman adamantly refused to comply and challenged the House to try to enforce its subpoena.

Condon, meanwhile, repeatedly demanded an opportunity to appear before HUAC and defend himself. On the day the subcommittee issued its report, he told reporters that "if it is true I am one of the weakest links in atomic security that is very gratifying and the country can feel absolutely safe for I am completely loyal, conscientious and devoted to the interests of my country, as my whole career and life clearly reveal." Although committee members occasionally made vague indications that Condon would be permitted to testify, no formal invitation was ever issued as long as Thomas remained chairman. The nation's scientific community backed Condon almost unanimously, sending letters, telegrams, and resolutions to Congress and the press in support of the beleaguered physicist. On July 15, 1948, the ATOMIC ENERGY COMMISSION declared that it had concluded following an exhaustive investigation (and two intensive FBI inquiries) that "Dr. Condon's continued clearance . . . 'will not adversely affect the common defense and security of the United States.' The Commission considers that his continued clearance is in the best interests of the atomic energy program."

Several months later, Truman himself publicly defended Condon at a meeting of the American Association for the Advancement of Science. With Condon seated behind him on the stage, Truman declared that scientific work for national security "may be made impossible by the creation of an atmosphere in which no man feels safe against the public airing of unfounded rumors, gossip, and vilification. . . . Such an atmosphere is un-American, the most un-American thing we have to contend with today. It is the climate of a totalitarian country in which scientists are expected to change their theories to match changes in the police state's propaganda line." As a result of the sudden and vicious assault upon Condon, Congressman Richard NIXON of California recommended in October 1948 that congressional committees should henceforth provide suspect individuals an opportunity to testify on their own behalf before they released information that casts doubt upon those individuals' loyalty. Condon, Nixon acknowledged, "should have been heard by the Committee before any statement about him was made public."

When Congressman John S. WOOD assumed the chairmanship of HUAC in 1949, he announced that he would be pleased to offer Condon a public hearing if he desired one, but by that time the furor had died down, and Condon appeared unwilling to reawaken the controversy. Nevertheless, in 1951 HUAC—prompted in large part by Congressman Harold VELDE— again assailed Condon's loyalty record, citing his continuing friendship with several former Berkeley colleagues who had previously belonged to Communist-front organizations. Following Condon's resignation from the Bureau of Standards in August 1951, Velde (a former FBI agent who had investigated security leaks at Berkeley during World War II), informed Condon that "while we do not want to cause you to be thought guilty by association with a lot of these Communists and espionage agents and so forth, it is a little peculiar that you seem to have hung around them like flies hanging around a pot of honey. . . ." In conclusion, the committee declared in late 1952 that it found Condon unfit for any government position requiring access to classified material because of his "propensity for associating with persons disloyal or of questionable loyalty and his contempt for necessary security arrangements."

From 1951 to 1954, Condon served as director of research at Corning Glass Corporation. Upon leaving Corning, he returned to the academic world by accepting an appointment as professor of physics at Washington University in St. Louis, where he remained for seven years. From 1963 until his death in 1974, Condon was a member of the faculty of the University of Colorado at Boulder.

## Congress of Industrial Organizations

Founded in October 1935, the Committee of Industrial Organizations—later renamed the Congress of Industrial Organizations (CIO)—was established by United Mine Worker president John L. LEWIS to represent the interests of unskilled and semiskilled American workers. Unlike the American Federation of Labor (AFL), whose local unions were organized on craft lines (for example, machinists, painters, carpenters), the CIO was organized on the basis of industrial unions that included all workers in each particular industry (for example, steel workers, auto workers, and coal miners). Lewis had grown disgusted with the conservative approach of the AFL—"The American Federation of Labor," he charged, "is standing still, with its face toward the dead past"—and from the start, the CIO adopted an aggressive approach toward organizing workers in the automobile and steel industries.

Although Lewis did not plan the wave of sitdown strikes that swept over the automobile industry in 1937, he decided to support the strikes unequivocally. His stance earned him the enmity of right-wing radio commentators who denounced him as "a Communist stooge." Nevertheless, the strikes succeeded in earning con-

cessions from every automobile manufacturer except the Ford Motor Company, and even Ford eventually signed a contract with the UNITED AUTO WORKERS in 1941. Moreover, the confrontation between the strikers and the automakers demonstrated that President Franklin D. Roosevelt, who refused to intervene to oust the strikers, had established at least an uneasy modus vivendi (a feasible arrangement) with the flamboyant Lewis and the CIO.

Lewis then turned his attention to the steel industry. For decades, United States Steel, by far the largest corporation in America, had resisted efforts to establish unions among its workers. The result was that the average steelworker in 1937 earned only $369 a year. Through adroit negotiations, Lewis was able to demonstrate to U.S. Steel's management that the CIO's Steel Workers Organizing Committee (SWOC), led by Philip MURRAY, had enlisted enough workers to stage a strike that would inflict severe damage on the company just as the economy was beginning to pull out of the Depression. To the surprise of virtually all observers, U.S. Steel consented to sign a contract with the SWOC that gave its workers substantial raises, shorter work weeks, and a variety of fringe benefits. Negotiations with the smaller steel companies were less amicable, however. The head of Republic Steel, Tom M. Girdler, refused to negotiate with the SWOC, claiming that they were Communists and "outside agitators." "I won't have a contract, verbal or written, with an irresponsible, racketeering, violent, communistic body like the CIO," declared Girdler, "and until they pass a law making me, I am not going to do it." A protest march sponsored by the union on Memorial Day, 1938, met with armed resistance by Chicago police, and ten marchers were killed by police gunfire. Although the conservative press blamed the violence on provocations by Communists among the workers, the National Labor Relations Board eventually forced Republic to negotiate with the SWOC.

By 1941, the CIO had resuscitated the nearly moribund American labor movement so successfully that the total union membership in the United States had risen to 10 million; by 1950, the figure had reached 15 million. But the CIO's impressive gains during the late 1930s had, in fact, been achieved through the assistance of Communists within the labor movement. Hardened, dedicated to their cause, and willing to risk violence, Communist labor officials provided the CIO with a core of experienced organizers. By 1939, however, moderate CIO officials such as Murray and Walter REUTHER had begun to turn against their Communist allies. The announcement of the NAZI-SOVIET PACT in August 1939—which led American Communists to advocate isolationism and abandon their dedication to their POPULAR FRONT antifascist alliances with liberals—further fueled the anti-Communist movement within the CIO.

At the CIO's annual convention in 1939, Murray succeeded in pushing through a resolution that condemned Communism. Fearful of shattering the fragile unity of the still-young organization, however, Murray hesitated to force an open break with the Communists in the CIO's member unions at that time. Certainly there remained substantial Communist elements within the CIO; although Congressman Martin DIES, chairman of the HOUSE COMMITTEE ON UN-AMERICAN ACTIVITIES (HUAC), was hardly an impartial observer, there was evidence to support his contention in 1941 that "Communists have obtained such a stranglehold on many of the unions in the CIO that it is now beyond the power of Mr. Philip Murray or anyone else in the organization's leadership to do anything about the matter." For his part, Lewis supported the antiinterventionist crusade and therefore established a working alliance with the Communists within the CIO in the months preceding Pearl Harbor.

In 1940, the CIO's annual convention ousted Lewis and elected Murray president of the organization, a post he would hold for the next twelve years. During World War II, the belligerent Lewis led his coal miners in work stoppages that infuriated Roosevelt; Murray, on the other hand, gave Roosevelt his pledge that the steel-

workers would not engage in strikes for the duration of the war. At the CIO's annual convention in 1946, Murray resumed his drive to oust Communists from the organization, as the delegates approved a resolution condemning Communist interference in the CIO's affairs. Meanwhile, Reuther was leading his own successful campaign to remove Communists from all positions of leadership within the United Auto Workers.

The presidential election of 1948 produced the climactic confrontation between the moderates and Communists in the CIO. At the CIO's convention that spring, Murray swung the organization behind the candidacy of President (and Democratic Party nominee) Harry S. TRUMAN despite the enthusiasm of radical elements within the CIO for the Progressive Party candidate, former Vice President Henry A. WALLACE. According to Murray, Wallace's candidacy could "only divide labor." Murray's task in swinging a majority of the CIO convention delegates behind the Truman candidacy was made considerably easier by the fact that the COMMUNIST PARTY OF THE UNITED STATES had returned to a hard-line, pro-Soviet stance in 1945, abandoning its prewar policy of collaboration with mainstream American liberalism. Murray was thus able to persuade the convention delegates that the Communists had betrayed "every decent movement into which they have infiltrated themselves." "Under no circumstances," he vowed, "am I going to permit Communistic infiltration into the national CIO movement."

The following year, the CIO expelled eleven Communist-led unions, including the UNITED ELECTRICAL WORKERS and the Farm Equipment Workers. The expulsion, combined with government persecution of Communist labor officials, served to break the power of Communists within the American labor movement.

**Connally, Tom** (1877–1963)   As chairman of the Senate Foreign Relations Committee from 1941 to 1947 and from 1949 to 1953, Democrat Tom Connally of Texas was one of the most powerful and well-respected members

Senator Tom Connally of Texas.

of the U.S. Senate and a consistent opponent of the extreme anti-Communist activities of Senator Joseph MCCARTHY of Wisconsin.

A native of western Texas, Connally graduated from Baylor University in 1896; following service in U.S. Army during the Spanish-American War, Connally completed his studies for his law degree at the University of Texas. After a brief stint in private practice, Connally entered politics as a member of the Texas state legislature in 1901. In 1917, Connally was elected to the U.S. House of Representatives from the Eleventh Congressional District of Texas. During his tenure in the House, Connally acquired a reputation as an internationalist, a staunch defender of President Woodrow Wilson's bid to establish a League of Nations.

In 1928, Connally won the Democratic nomination for the U.S. Senate, defeating in the primary a candidate who had the backing of the terrorist racist organization, the Ku Klux Klan. Connally was elected to the Senate in the general election of 1928 and won reelection in 1934, 1940, and 1946. In 1941, he became chairman of the Foreign Relations Committee and helped guide through the Senate President Franklin D. Roosevelt's initiatives to provide military assistance to Great Britain. Following the war, Connally served as a member of the first American delegation to the United Nations and as an adviser to Secretary of State James Byrne at the peace conference and the Council of Foreign Ministers Meetings of April–May 1946.

Although he frequently opposed the Truman administration's policies in domestic affairs, particularly in the field of civil rights, Connally was one of the administration's strongest defenders against the charges of Communist influence in the State Department. To provide closer senatorial oversight over the State Department's activities, Connally agreed to subdivide the Foreign Relations Committee into areas of geographic responsibility so that each group of senators could monitor a separate office within State. That, however, was the only significant concession Connally was willing to make to the growing hysteria over Communism in government. When Senator Joseph MCCARTHY of Wisconsin charged in February 1950 that there were "card-carrying Communists" in the State Department, Connally appointed a special subcommittee of the Foreign Relations Committee to investigate the charges and selected widely respected Millard TYDINGS of Maryland to chair the subcommittee.

McCarthy had accused an academic expert in Far East affairs, Owen LATTIMORE, of being the "top Russian espionage agent in America." Connally was present at the subcommittee's hearings when Lattimore testified and refuted McCarthy's allegations. During a break in the proceedings, Connally ostentatiously walked over to Lattimore, shook his hand as television cameras caught the gesture, and murmured a few harsh words about McCarthy's "conscienceless extremes."

Maintaining a consistent internationalist stand, Connally backed the Truman administration's efforts to contain Communism abroad and supported Truman's decision to commit American troops to fight Communist aggression in Korea. When Truman found it necessary to remove General Douglas MACARTHUR as commander of the United Nations troops in Korea in the spring of 1951, Connally moved to squelch senatorial criticism of the move, reminding his colleagues of the long-standing American tradition of civilian control over the military.

Connally chose not to run for reelection in 1952. His son, John Connally, served as governor of Texas during the 1960s and subsequently as secretary of the Treasury in the administration of President Richard M. NIXON.

## Cooke, Alistair (1908– )

A British-born journalist who became an American citizen in 1941, Alistair Cooke wrote one of the most complete and even-handed accounts of the perjury trials of Alger HISS, entitled *A Generation on Trial: U.S.A. v. Alger Hiss* (1950). During the Hiss trials, Cooke—who specialized in explaining American affairs to British audiences—served as the chief American correspondent of the *Manchester Guardian,* a venerable liberal British newspaper. Like many American observers, Cooke was perplexed by the complexities of the Hiss affair and the clash of conflicting (and occasionally bizarre) personalities; in fact, Cooke later admitted to a press colleague that he was glad he had not had to decide upon Hiss' guilt or innocence.

In *A Generation on Trial,* Cooke presented Hiss' trials as the story "of a man who was judged in one decade for what he was said to have done in another." In fact, Cooke claimed that the courtroom battle over Hiss' veracity was "the biggest trial in American history." His goal in writing *A Generation,* Cooke stated, was to make the reader feel as if he or she were actually on the jury. Because Cooke refused to reveal any bias for or against Hiss, reviewers praised the book as "a model of balance and lucidity" and "one of the most vivid and literate descriptions of an American political event that have ever been written." Following Hiss' eventual conviction and sentencing, Cooke continued to report on American affairs for British publications. In the 1960s and 1970s he became a familiar face on American television as the host of the Public Broadcasting Service series *Masterpiece Theatre.*

## Cooper, Gary (1901–1961)

A soft-spoken, laconic actor, Gary Cooper had starred in a number of popular films since his arrival in Hollywood in 1924. His best-known roles prior to 1947 were in *Pride of the Yankees* (Best Actor Oscar), *Saratoga Trunk,* and *Mr. Deeds Goes to Town.* Cooper was not intimately involved in political affairs at any point during his career, and the causes he did support tended to be slightly to the right of center. He had participated in one of the leading anti-Communist movements in the motion picture industry, as an organizer (along with fellow actor John WAYNE) of the MOTION PICTURE ALLIANCE in 1944.

In September 1947, the HOUSE COMMITTEE ON UN-AMERICAN ACTIVITIES (HUAC) subpoenaed Cooper to testify in its investigation of Communist influences in Hollywood. Because no one seriously believed Cooper was a Communist or a fellow traveler, observers were somewhat puzzled about the committee's motivation. When Cooper appeared before the committee on October 23, HUAC members appeared eager to clear his name of any taint of left-wing associations; indeed, it seemed that they had called him largely to generate publicity for their hearings.

Cooper—dressed in a double-breasted suit, a white shirt, and a light-blue silk necktie—certainly attracted a large crowd to the hearing room. In response to the committee's questions, he acknowledged that he had noticed some Communist prosyletizing in Hollywood, primarily at social gatherings, where he heard guests saying things like, "Perhaps this would be a more efficient Government without a Congress," or "Don't you think the Constitution is about a hundred and fifty years out of date?" Once, a fellow actor had tried to convince him that artists were treated better in the Soviet Union than in the United States. "From that time on," said Cooper, "I could never take any of this pinko mouthing very seriously because I didn't feel it was on the level."

Cooper also admitted that he had turned down "quite a few" scripts because he thought they were tainted with Communist ideas. But when the committee, its curiosity whetted, pressed him to reveal the titles of the scripts, Cooper said he couldn't recall any of them. "Most of the scripts I read at night," he explained, "and if they don't look good to me, I don't finish them, or if I do finish them I send them back as soon as possible to their author."

At the conclusion of his rather pointless testimony, Cooper observed that he had noticed far less open talk about Communism in Hollywood since 1945; when the committee sought to obtain his approval of legislation to outlaw the Communist Party, Cooper sidestepped the question. "I have never read Karl Marx and I don't know the basis of Communism, beyond what I have picked up from hearsay," he said. "From what I hear, I don't like it because it isn't on the level. So I couldn't possibly answer that question."

## Coplon, Judith (1920– )

A political analyst in the U.S. Department of Justice with access to secret FEDERAL BUREAU OF INVESTIGATION (FBI) reports, Judith Coplon came under suspicion by the FBI in late 1948 for allegedly passing counterintelligence data to Soviet agents. Several months later, Coplon's superiors in the Justice Department removed her from her job in the Internal Security Section and reassigned her to a less sensitive position.

At the same time, the FBI initiated its own probe of Coplon's activities. At the direction of Attorney General Tom CLARK, FBI agents placed wiretaps on Coplon's telephone lines, installed surveillance devices in her office, and trailed her to New York where Coplon met three times during the winter of 1948–49 with Valentin Gubitchev, an attaché with the Soviet Union's delegation to the United Nations. Coplon's transfer may have aroused her suspicions because an FBI report stated that she and Gubitchev spent their time together wandering "aimlessly about, meeting, separating, rejoining, going hither and yon, continually looking back, and in general giving every appearance of persons who thought they might be shadowed and wished to escape being trailed."

On March 4, 1949, Coplon traveled again to New York, carrying in her handbag summaries of classified FBI reports and a message—apparently intended for Gubitchev—explaining why she had been unable to obtain access to a "top secret" FBI report on Communist espionage in the United States. The FBI assigned twenty-four agents to follow her, and Attorney General Clark instructed the bureau to keep him personally informed of Coplon's movements. From their preparations—including the presence of a matron detailed to the New York City courthouse to take charge of Coplon—it seemed clear that the FBI intended to arrest her if agents witnessed an exchange of information between Coplon and Gubitchev. While leading agents on an erratic trek throughout the New York subway system, Coplon and Gubitchev never established contact that evening. When it appeared that Coplon would leave New York without handing over her material to Gubitchev, Attorney General Clark ordered the FBI to arrest her anyway. As suspected, agents discovered classified material in her purse.

When news of Coplon's arrest was released to the public, Congressman Richard M. NIXON of California demanded a congressional investigation of the affair. The fact that Coplon had been employed in a sensitive government position, Nixon charged, provided evidence that the Justice Department under the Truman administration "may be unfit and unqualified to carry out the responsibility of protecting the national security against Communist infiltration."

During her initial trial in Washington, D.C., on charges of espionage, Coplon claimed that Gubitchev was merely her lover and that she had appropriated secret documents only to help her write a spy novel entitled *Government Girl.* Neither of these arguments convinced a jury, and on June 30, Coplon was found guilty of stealing classified documents. Following the verdict, a member of the crowd that had gathered around the district courthouse muttered that "the hussy" deserved "a rope around her neck."

Defense counsel appealed the verdict, which was overturned when the Court of Appeals learned that the FBI had installed illegal wiretaps on Coplon's telephones and, during the trial, had falsely denied doing so. Further, the FBI had been unwilling to share with defense attorneys the contents of Coplon's purse. Coplon was therefore awarded a new trial.

Instead of retrying her immediately on the initial charge, the government decided to prosecute Coplon on a charge of conspiring to deliver classified documents to a foreign agent. Again, Coplon was convicted (on March 7, 1950), but again the verdict was overturned on appeal, largely because the FBI had arrested her without a warrant and because the bureau had destroyed the original tapes obtained from the wiretaps. This left the defense counsel with only edited versions of the original transcripts, with passages deleted, reportedly for reasons of national security. Writing for the Court of Appeals, Judge Learned Hand noted that the government's failure to confront Coplon with the evidence against her had subverted its case. "Few weapons in the arsenal of freedom," wrote Hand, "are more useful than the power to compel a government to disclose the evidence on which it seeks to forfeit the liberty of its citizens." Further, the FBI did not possess the authority to introduce in court evidence obtained through illegal wiretaps (that is, wiretaps installed without a warrant) in cases involving national security, a state of affairs which Attorney General Herbert BROWNELL

later sought to rectify during the first Eisenhower administration. Judge Hand consequently overturned Coplon's second conviction and ordered a new hearing on the first conviction. Both Coplon cases eventually made their way to the Supreme Court, and both appellate rulings in Coplon's favor were upheld. Although the indictments stood, Coplon never was retried.

Meanwhile, Gubitchev, who also had been convicted in Coplon's second trial, was released at the behest of the State Department and returned to the Soviet Union, apparently to avoid further persecution of American nationals in the Soviet satellite states of Eastern Europe.

Coplon's trials kept the issue of Communist espionage in the United States on the front pages of the nation's newspapers for two years. Her conviction on espionage charges in March 1950 also lent credence to the charges made by Senator Joseph MCCARTHY in his Wheeling speech of February 9, 1950, when he claimed to have evidence of more than 200 Soviet agents in the State Department.

***Counterattack***   A four-page weekly newsletter listing individuals suspected of belonging to the Communist Party or to Communist-front organizations, *Counterattack* was first published in 1947 by three former FBI agents as part of a business venture known as American Business Consultants (ABC). With financial aid from millionaire industrialist Alfred KOHLBERG and the CATHOLIC CHURCH, they first launched *Counterattack* and, three years later, a related publication called RED CHANNELS.

The premise behind *Counterattack* was simple: Its editors compiled a list of Communist-front organizations from reports issued by the federal government, congressional committees, state legislatures, and private organizations. (For the purposes of the editors, a *Communist-front group* was defined as any organization that "helped Communism." By 1948, they had identified 192 groups as fronts, far more than the 73 on the attorney general's official list of subversive organizations.) Individuals who were listed in a government source as belonging to any of these organizations were then identified in *Counterattack*, with no attempt to determine whether the original listing was accurate or not. Once an allegation of membership in a Communist front had been published in *Counterattack*, it took on an aura of veracity, forcing the accused to prove his or her innocence, an almost impossible task in the suspicion-laden atmosphere of the McCarthy era.

Originally intended as a guide for employers in all fields of business, *Counterattack* gradually came to focus on broadcasting as the most lucrative market. Beyond its $24 subscription fee, *Counterattack* charged producers for "vetting" performers before they were hired; that is, it ran names of actors or directors through its lists of front organizations to make sure the individual was "clean" before she or he was hired. Performers could also request a *Counterattack* clearance for themselves, although the fee for this service was considerably higher.

The power of *Counterattack* and *Red Channels* grew immensely in the years between 1950 and 1956. Along with AWARE, INC., another enterprise established by one of American Business Consultants' founders, they served as the arbiters of loyalty for the entertainment industry. One mention of a performer's name in either publication was sufficient to keep that performer off the radio and television networks for a decade or more. Folksinger Pete SEEGER was one of many whose careers were adversely affected by a listing in *Counterattack*. Although his group, the Weavers, was immensely popular in the early 1950s, Seeger's citation for contempt of Congress following his refusal to answer questions before the HOUSE COMMITTEE ON UN-AMERICAN ACTIVITIES in 1955 kept him off network television until 1967, when he finally made an appearance on the *Smothers Brothers Comedy Hour*.

**Cronin, Father John** (1908–1994)   Recognized as one of the leading experts on Com-

munism in the United States in the late 1940s, Cronin served as assistant director of social action for the National Catholic Welfare Conference. In that capacity, Cronin had spent twelve years compiling voluminous, detailed files on Communist subversion, with a special focus on Communist infiltration of American labor unions.

By the end of 1945, Cronin's research had led him to the conclusion that Alger HISS was "the most influential Communist" in the State Department. Thus when the HOUSE COMMITTEE ON UN-AMERICAN ACTIVITIES (HUAC) heard testimony from Whittaker CHAMBERS in the summer of 1948 that he had known Hiss in the 1930s as a member of the COMMUNIST PARTY, Cronin willingly became involved in the ensuing conflict between Hiss and Chambers. Cronin served as a liaison between the FBI and HUAC member Richard M. NIXON, leaking FBI material to Nixon prior to Hiss' appearance before the committee on August 5. Nixon, who disliked Hiss intensely, used Cronin's information to set up hostile confrontations between Hiss and Chambers.

While the Hiss case and the further investigations of HUAC stoked the anti-Communist fervor in the United States, Cronin believed that the critical threat from Communism had been curtailed by 1950, largely due to the change in the attitudes of the American public. In fact, Cronin's own investigation showed that there was not one known Communist Party member in the State Department in February 1950, precisely the time that Senator Joseph MCCARTHY claimed he knew of 205 Communists employed at State.

During the initial Senate investigation into McCarthy's charges, Cronin met with McCarthy to try to persuade him to curb his impulsive style, to stop making wild accusations, and to adopt instead a cautious, reasoned approach. Cronin even passed information from his files to McCarthy for the senator to use to support his charges, but McCarthy refused to even look at Cronin's data. Instead, McCarthy chose to go after bigger game, relying on his penchant for making headlines and keeping the opposition always on the defensive. "When he showed no improvement," said Cronin, "we gave up on him," and the priest publicly voiced his disillusionment with McCarthy. "It was unfortunate," Cronin observed later, "that Senator McCarthy went to such extremes."

Four years later, when McCarthy was facing censure charges in the Senate, he turned to Cronin for help, begging him for any material that would help him keep his enemies at bay. Recognizing that McCarthy was out of control, Cronin concluded that any attempt to help the senator was useless, and he refused to become involved in the fray.

***Crucible, The*** (1953)   Playwright Arthur MILLER's drama about the anti-Communist hysteria that gripped the United States during the McCarthy era, *The Crucible* recounted the story of the Salem witchcraft trials, an equally traumatic time of accusation and repression in colonial New England. Set in the 1690s, *The Crucible* focused on the character of John Proctor, who refused to give false evidence to save his own life. In words reminiscent of Miller's later testimony to the HOUSE COMMITTEE ON UN-AMERICAN ACTIVITIES (HUAC) in 1956, Proctor adamantly refused the prosecutor's demand that he name names: "I speak my own sins; I cannot judge another. I have no tongue for it. . . . I have three children—how may I teach them to walk like men in the world, and I sold my friends?"

Although Miller claimed that the idea for a play on the Salem witchcraft trials first occurred to him in 1938, he did not begin to write the play until 1952. By that time, Miller had become profoundly disturbed by the atmosphere created by HUAC, Senator Joseph MCCARTHY, and the rest of the anti-Communist zealots in the United States—what Miller called a "pall of suspicion" that victimized not only prominent public figures, but also thousands of ordinary Americans. Gradually, observed Miller, "A living connection between myself and Salem, and between Salem and Washington, was made in my mind—for whatever else they might be, I saw that the [HUAC] hearings in Washington were profoundly and even avowedly ritualistic."

> After all, in almost every case the Committee knew in advance what they wanted the witness to give them: the names of his comrades in the Party. The FBI had long since infiltrated the Party, and informers had long ago identified the participants in various meetings. The main point of the hearings, precisely as in seventeenth-century Salem, was that the accused make public confession, damn his confederates as well as his Devil master, and guarantee his sterling new allegiance by breaking disgusting old vows—whereupon he was let loose to rejoin the society of extremely decent people. In other words, the same spiritual nugget lay folded within both procedures—an act of contrition done not in solemn privacy but out in the public air.

Indeed, Miller claimed that the Salem witchcraft trials actually rested on more solid legal ground than the McCarthyite Red-hunts because Massachusetts Bay Colony did have laws against the practice of witchcraft. By contrast, those who were called before HUAC were, for the most part, accused only of "a spiritual crime, subservience to a political enemy's desires and ideology." Ironically, the day before Miller began his research into the original court records of the witch trials, he received a telephone call from Elia KAZAN, the director who had collaborated with Miller on several extremely successful productions, including *All My Sons* and *Death of a Salesman*. Kazan had been subpoenaed to testify before HUAC and wanted Miller to know that he intended to provide the committee with the names of his former associates.

Critics of *The Crucible* complained that the witchcraft trials were not analogous to HUAC's investigations; there had been no witches in Salem, but there were, in fact, Communists in the United States in the late 1940s and early

1950s, and the threat of Communist subversion appeared very real to some Americans in the postwar years. Miller responded by saying that his play took a broader view of the psychology behind witch hunts. "The playwriting part of me," he noted, "was drawn to what I felt was a tragic process underlying the political manifestation. . . . When irrational terror takes to itself the fiat of moral goodness somebody has to die. I thought that in terms of this process the witch hunts had something to say to the anti-Communist hysteria. No man lives who has not got a panic button and when it is pressed by the clean white hand of moral duty, a certain murderous train is set in motion." Other critics believed that Miller had written a defense of Julius and Ethel ROSENBERG, two alleged Soviet spies who were executed in 1953 for their role in an atomic espionage ring, but Miller denied that he had written the play with the Rosenbergs in mind.

When a Belgian theatrical company staged *The Crucible* in 1954, the American-Belgian Society invited Miller to travel to Belgium at its expense to attend the production. Because of Miller's past association with left-wing causes, the State Department refused to provide Miller with a passport. "It didn't harm me; it harmed the country," Miller said of the government's decision. "I didn't need any foreign relations." The playwright's continuing quest for a passport—and the State Department's refusal to provide one—was the issue which led HUAC to subpoena him to testify in the spring of 1956.

**Crusade for Freedom**   A privately funded international organization, the Crusade for Freedom was an operation of the National Committee for a Free Europe, Inc. (NCFE). Like Radio Free Europe, which also was sponsored by the NCFE, Crusade for Freedom was dedicated to keeping the Western democracies in contact with the inhabitants of Eastern Europe.

Recognizing that forthright appeals to revolution could backfire by provoking premature risings behind the Iron Curtain, the Crusade for Freedom employed a less threatening type of publicity and propaganda to achieve its goals. Its special province was the spectacular media event. In the autumn of 1950, for instance, it fashioned a 10-ton "freedom bell" and sent it on a tour across the United States prior to shipping it across the Atlantic to West Berlin. There the "freedom bell" was installed in the Rathaus Tower, just across the border from East Germany. On October 24—United Nations Day—the bell tolled for the first time, its "peals of peace" transmitted behind the Iron Curtain on Radio Free Europe. Close by the bell in the base of the Rathaus Tower were "freedom scrolls" bearing the signatures of millions of Americans. Contributions from each of the signatories were used to expand Radio Free Europe from a single station to a network of five stations.

In August 1951, the Crusade for Freedom sponsored another project, a propaganda balloon assault on Czechoslovakia. Led by crusade chairman Harold Stassen, the former governor of Minnesota, and columnist Drew PEARSON, an avid supporter of the Crusade for Freedom, officials of the organization stood in a wheatfield in Bavaria and released several thousand balloons filled with hydrogen gas and propaganda leaflets. The balloons ascended and floated across the border into Czechoslovakia until they reached a height of 30,000 feet. At that point they burst apart, releasing thousands of pamphlets bearing messages that promised Czechs that "there is no dungeon deep enough to hide truth, no wall high enough to keep out the message of freedom. Tyranny cannot control the winds, cannot enslave your hearts. Freedom will rise again." On the back of each leaflet was a list of wave lengths and schedules for Radio Free Europe broadcasts. At the United Nations, a Czech delegate protested the balloon attack, calling it "further proof of subversive activities by the U.S. Government."

# D

*Daily Worker*   Established in 1925, the *Daily Worker* was the official news publication of the COMMUNIST PARTY OF THE UNITED STATES OF AMERICA (CPUSA) and the primary American propaganda organ of the Communist International (Comintern). Readers of the *Daily Worker* could discern the latest shifts in the policy of the Soviet Union in the columns of the newspaper. In the early 1930s, for instance, the *Daily Worker* condemned President Franklin D. Roosevelt's liberal New Deal initiatives: it described the National Recovery Act as "a fascist slave program"; and the Wagner Act, which guaranteed the right of American workers to organize and bargain collectively, was defined by the *Daily Worker* as an "anti-strike" measure.

From 1935 to 1939, the *Daily Worker* altered its editorial views and promoted a POPULAR FRONT, collaborationist policy with American liberals, reflecting Moscow's concern with the growing power of fascism in Europe. The signing of the NAZI-SOVIET PACT in August 1939 produced another abrupt about-face in the newspaper's view of foreign affairs. Suddenly, it urged a policy of American isolationism, to keep the United States out of Europe while the Nazis and the Soviet Union divided Poland between themselves. With the Nazi invasion of the Soviet Union in June 1941 and the Japanese attack on Pearl Harbor six months later, the *Daily Worker*—under the supervision of managing editor Louis BUDENZ—enthusiastically supported an all-out war effort to defeat the Axis Powers. Following the successful conclusion of the war in Europe, the *Daily Worker* reprinted in May 1945 an article by Jacques Duclos, a French Communist theoretician, calling for an end to collaboration and a renewed dedication to the national interests of the Soviet Union. In 1948, the *Daily Worker* became one of only two newspapers in the United States to endorse the presidential bid of Progressive Party candidate Henry WALLACE.

Not surprisingly, the editors of the *Daily Worker* carried on a running war with the leaders of the American anti-Communist crusade. As early as 1930, Congress cited the *Daily Worker* in a resolution establishing a special committee to investigate Communist propaganda in the United States. The newspaper was a special target of the HOUSE COMMITTEE ON UN-AMERICAN ACTIVITIES, which the *Daily Worker* denounced in 1938 as an "outfit of storm troopers." Congressional anti-Communist investigators frequently employed the *Daily Worker* to compile their membership lists of allegedly subversive organizations. If an individual's name appeared in the pages of the *Daily Worker*, he or she was automatically regarded as suspect, even though the newspaper regularly used the

**An unidentified New Yorker scans the front page of the Communist publication the *Daily Worker*.**

names of individuals without their permission or even knowledge.

**Dartmouth College Speech** One of the actions of Senator Joseph MCCARTHY and his staff that most antagonized and embarrassed President Dwight David EISENHOWER in the early months of his first administration was the tour of McCarthy staffers Roy COHN and G. David SCHINE through State Department libraries in Europe, condemning books that they felt advocated subversive ideas. Pressed by his advisers to repair the damage to Europeans' image of the United States, Eisenhower chose the occasion of his commencement address at Dartmouth College on June 14, 1953, to respond to Cohn and Schine's censorship activities.

Speaking without notes, Eisenhower urged the audience of 10,000 to maintain the cause of intellectual freedom. "Don't join the book burners," the President said. "Don't think you are going to conceal faults by concealing evidence that they ever existed. Don't be afraid to go in your library and read every book as long as any document does not offend our own ideas of decency. That should be the only censorship."

Because Eisenhower deliberately refrained from mentioning McCarthy by name, the senator answered Eisenhower's jab with a shrug. "He couldn't very well have been referring to me," said McCarthy. "I have burned no books." One of McCarthy's allies, Senator Pat MCCARRAN of Nevada, was less charitable toward the President. Eisenhower, McCarran claimed, "showed no knowledge of his subject. It's bad a man in his position doesn't know more about it. Someone must have sold him a bill of goods."

When reporters pressed Eisenhower to expand upon the Dartmouth speech at a news conference on June 17, the President backtracked slightly by stating that he had not meant to approve of books that attempted to "persuade or propagandize America into communism." Presumably, he would not object to the removal of such volumes from U.S. libraries overseas.

("I think he has given a commendable clarification of the Dartmouth speech, which apparently has been misunderstood by many newsmen," observed McCarthy gleefully.) When a reporter asked the President if he had been referring to McCarthy as a "book-burner," Eisenhower again refused to confront McCarthy or even mention the senator by name. "I do not intend to be talking personally and in personalities with respect to anyone," he said.

In fact, Eisenhower backtracked so much from his Dartmouth remarks that he found it necessary to issue yet another statement clarifying his opposition to censorship in the form of a letter to the annual convention of the AMERICAN LIBRARY ASSOCIATION.

**Da Silva, Howard** (1909–1986) A prominent left-wing activist in the motion picture industry, actor Howard Da Silva was summoned to testify before the HOUSE COMMITTEE ON UN-AMERICAN ACTIVITIES (HUAC) in March 1951 during the committee's second investigation into Communist influence in Hollywood. Da Silva had been identified to HUAC as a possible subversive by actor Robert TAYLOR in October 1947; when asked if he knew of any Commu-

**Howard Da Silva, blacklisted from movies and television during the McCarthy era.**

nists in the Screen Actors Guild, Taylor replied that he was not certain that Da Silva was a Communist, but he certainly was disruptive, and "he always seems to have something to say at the wrong time." When the writers and directors known as the HOLLYWOOD TEN were indicted for contempt of Congress for their refusal to testify before HUAC, Da Silva signed a petition endorsing their appeal to the U.S. Supreme Court. Prior to that time, Da Silva had also supported efforts to abolish HUAC altogether.

Da Silva did not receive the same measure of support from the liberal community in Hollywood when he was called to testify before HUAC. By that time, the consequences of resistance had been made manifest through the appearance of BLACKLISTS throughout the entertainment industry, and few actors were willing to risk their careers to defend a colleague. Along with actress Gale SONDERGAARD, who had been summoned to testify on the same day, Da Silva took out a paid advertisement in *Variety* bitterly complaining about the noticeable silence that greeted the news of his subpoena.

Da Silva appeared before HUAC on the same day as actor Larry PARKS, who broke down on the stand and wept as the committee pressed him relentlessly to name his former associates in the Communist Party. By contrast, Da Silva obdurately refused to discuss his political background at all, citing his Fifth Amendment rights against self-incrimination. "He cried, so I shrieked," Da Silva later explained. "What else do you do?" For his recalcitrance, Da Silva was cited in *Hollywood Life* as "a commie member, and an active one."

Da Silva was the first uncooperative HUAC witness from the motion picture industry since the appearance of the Hollywood Ten. (Following the fiasco of the Ten's testimony, HUAC chairman J. Parnell THOMAS had adjourned the committee's investigation into the film industry and never resumed it.) During the four-year interval, the anti-Communist hysteria in the United States had increased markedly, and Da Silva's refusal to answer the committee's ques-

tions earned him a prominent place on the industry's unofficial blacklist. The producer of a film in which Da Silva was scheduled to appear promptly cut out his footage and replaced Da Silva with another actor. Fearing reprisals at the box office, no producer would hire Da Silva for any role, however minor. The HUAC incident so enraged Da Silva that he became obsessed with fighting the blacklist and denounced the insidious practice at every opportunity. "Even when he was talking to a group of Hadassah ladies," noted a friend, "he would work in a pitch against the blacklist."

Following the demise of the blacklist in the early 1960s, Da Silva once again obtained steady work. He became a regular on the short-lived television dramatic series *For the People* (1965) and in 1978 won an Emmy Award for his performance as a supporting actor in the PBS television drama "Verna: USO Girl."

## Daughters of the American Revolution

Founded in 1890, the Daughters of the American Revolution (DAR) became one of the nation's leading hereditary patriotic organizations in the midtwentieth century. For the first three decades of its existence, the DAR devoted itself to a number of progressive and humanitarian causes and was generally held in high esteem by the American public. Its first presidents were Caroline Harrison, wife of President Benjamin Harrison (1885–1889) and Mrs. Adlai E. Stevenson, wife of Grover Cleveland's vice president (1889–1893) and the grandmother of the Democratic presidential nominee of 1952 and 1956.

During the Spanish-American War, the DAR volunteered to screen nurses for the U.S. Army, thereby helping to establish the Army Nurse Corps. It subsequently campaigned for such progressive reform measures as restrictive child-labor laws, regulation of women's work hours, the improvement of sanitary conditions in stores and factories, compulsory education, universal marriage and divorce laws, tuberculosis control,

**Constitution Hall, headquarters of the staunchly anti-Communist Daughters of the American Revolution.**

the establishment of juvenile courts, prohibitions against the sale of liquor to minors, and tighter conservation regulations. In the "Red Scare" that followed World War I, however, the DAR veered from its concern with social welfare and focused its attention on the alleged threat of Bolshevik subversion in America. Not only did the DAR organize a committee on national defense to battle "Red internationalists" in 1925, it also prepared lists of speakers whose left-wing politics, in the opinion of the DAR's leaders, rendered them unsuitable for the organization's audiences. Because these blacklists included the names of numerous prominent Americans, including several husbands of DAR members, the affair earned the organization considerable public ridicule.

The advent of the Roosevelt administration's New Deal with its liberal reforms confirmed the

DAR in its belief that the United States was endangered by radical influences from abroad. In 1939, the DAR found itself in the headlines when it barred African-American singer Marian Anderson from performing at Constitution Hall, the organization's meeting place in Washington, D.C. Critics accused the DAR of promoting racism, and First Lady Eleanor ROOSEVELT withdrew her membership in the DAR in protest.

Not surprisingly, the DAR enthusiastically supported the investigations of the HOUSE COMMITTEE ON UN-AMERICAN ACTIVITIES (HUAC) from the time the committee came into existence in 1938. The DAR was one of only a handful of organizations that testified in favor of the committee's efforts to outlaw the COMMUNIST PARTY. In 1947 its leaders endorsed a bill sponsored by Congressman John RANKIN of Alabama that would have made it unlawful "in any course of instruction or teaching in any public or private school, college or university to advocate or to express or convey the impression of sympathy with or approval of, Communism or Communist ideology," or to send through the mails any publication which sympathized with or approved of Communism.

Officials of the DAR also opposed American participation in the United Nations, demanded the removal of Albert EINSTEIN's name from public-school textbooks because they considered the scientist a dangerous subversive, and campaigned against the fluoridation of the nation's water supply as a Communist plot. In 1956, the DAR opposed the Eisenhower administration's efforts to liberalize the McCarran-Walter Immigration Act, claiming that restricted immigration was essential to the security of the United States. Attempts to weaken the immigration law, claimed a DAR spokesperson who apparently ignored the President's support for reform, were led by "Communists and other left-wing groups."

## Davies, John Paton Jr. (1908– )   John Paton Davies, Jr., was born in China, the son of Baptist missionaries. He embarked upon a career in the United States foreign service and in 1942 was appointed to the staff of W. Averell Harriman, U.S. ambassador to the Soviet Union. The following year, General Joseph W. Stillwell, who was serving as chief of staff to Generalissimo CHIANG Kai-shek in Chungking, China, asked the State Department to second Davies to his staff as a political adviser.

Davies soon became convinced that the Chinese Communists were a far more effective foe of the Japanese invaders than Chiang's corrupt, inefficient Nationalist generals, who repeatedly refused to engage the Japanese in combat. Davies also believed that once the Japanese had been defeated, Chiang would launch a civil war against his Communist competitors. Chiang's only hope for success in such a struggle, Davies noted, lay in unlimited quantities of foreign military aid. In a series of notes to his superiors in Washington, Davies warned the U.S. government against granting Chiang a blank check and suggested instead that the nation make a strenuous attempt to reform and revitalize the Nationalist regime; if that approach failed, Davies urged cooperation with the Communists, whom he foresaw as the destined rulers of China due to their superior efficiency and popularity.

"The Communists have survived ten years of civil war and seven years of Japanese offensives," Davies wrote. "They have survived and they have grown. Communist growth since 1937 has been almost geometric in progression . . . and they will continue to grow. The reason for this phenomenal vitality and strength is simple and fundamental. It is mass support, mass participation. The Communist governments and armies are the first governments and armies in modern Chinese history to have positive and widespread popular support. They have this support because the governments and armies are genuinely of the people. . . . We may anticipate that Chiang Kai-shek will exert every effort and resort to every stratagem to involve us in active support of the Central Government. We will probably be told that if fresh American aid is not forthcoming all of China and eventually all of Asia will be swept by communism. It will be difficult for us to resist such appeals, especially in view of our moral commitments to continued assistance to China during the postwar period." If American policymakers did not hasten to influence the Communists in China into "an independent position friendly to the United States," Davies warned, "the Communists will be captured by the U.S.S.R. and become Soviet satellites."

Such candid comparisons of Nationalist and Communist prospects did not endear Davies to Chiang Kai-shek. Certainly, his characterization in 1945 of MAO Zedong's armies as "so-called Communists" who were committed to "agrarian reform, civil rights, [and] the establishment of democratic institutions" outraged the leaders of the CHINA LOBBY in the United States. Davies was subsequently recalled from China and reassigned to Moscow. There, he served as an assistant to Ambassador Walter Bedell Smith, who had been General Dwight David EISENHOWER's chief of staff during World War II.

In 1949, Davies proposed a highly confidential project to the State Department. Known as "Tawny Pippit," after a small English singing bird, the plan involved the use of liberals and disillusioned Marxists within China in ultrasecret psychological warfare against the Communist regime to prevent it from consolidating its power until the United States could gain more influence in its councils. The project was so vaguely described, however, that Davies' conservative critics claimed that he was actually proposing to send covert American aid to the Communist regime itself.

Such an interpretation of Davies' motives would have seemed ludicrous to those who knew of the diplomat's hard-line attitude toward the Soviet Union. Following the initial Soviet nuclear test blast in 1949, for instance, Davies had proposed "a preventive showdown with the Soviet Union." Nevertheless, in the atmosphere of suspicion that prevailed in the early 1950s, it was perhaps inevitable that Davies' oft-expressed admiration for the capabilities of the Chinese Communists would render him susceptible to questions concerning his loyalty. In June 1951, the State Department suspended Davies pending a security hearing. He was subsequently cleared, investigated again, and cleared once more, only to be subpoenaed by the Senate Internal Security Committee, chaired by Senator Patrick MCCARRAN. Unsatisfied with Davies' responses, McCarran threatened to indict Davies for perjury.

In an apparent effort to protect Davies from further controversy, the State Department transferred him to a position as counselor of the U.S. embassy in Lima, Peru. Yet, Davies' isolation in South America did not mollify Senator Joseph MCCARTHY. During the course of a nationwide television and radio broadcast on November 24, 1953, McCarthy assailed Davies as "part and parcel of the old ACHESON-LATTIMORE-VINCENT-WHITE-HISS group which did so much toward delivering our Chinese friends into Communist hands. Why," McCarthy asked, "is this man still a high official in our State Department after eleven months of Republican administration?"

Walter Bedell Smith, who had become undersecretary of state in the Eisenhower administration, publicly defended Davies as "a very loyal and capable officer." McCarthy thereupon rounded on Smith and questioned his loyalty, an action that appalled President Eisenhower and—as much as anything else McCarthy ever said or did—led him to regard the Wisconsin senator with revulsion. Secretary of State John Foster DULLES was less steadfast in his support of Davies. In an attempt to establish his own anti-Communist credentials, Dulles convened yet another security investigation into Davies' background, the ninth such inquiry since 1951. Like the previous eight, this board cleared Davies of all charges of disloyalty "in the sense of having any Communist affinity"; yet, it recommended his dismissal from the foreign service due to what it described as "a definite lack of judgment, discretion, and reliability." Dulles suggested that Davies retire before he was sacked; Davies refused. On November 24, 1954, Dulles personally informed Davies of the findings of the loyalty board, adding that he agreed with its recommendation for dismissal.

By that time, the ARMY-MCCARTHY HEARINGS and the Senate debate on a motion of censure against McCarthy had virtually finished the Wisconsin senator as an effective force in American politics. Yet, Dulles' action against Davies kept alive the spirit of McCarthy's assault upon the career officers of the State Department. "The message of the Davies decision was clear," wrote an observer in The New York Times. "Henceforth any Foreign Service officer who dared to question policy, who sent back reports that did not support policy or associated with individuals deemed questionable by the security office, ran the danger of being declared unreliable."

Following his dismissal from the foreign service, Davies entered the furniture-manufacturing business in Peru. So enduring were the effects of the McCarthy era upon the U.S. diplomatic establishment that Davies did not receive another security clearance until early 1969, in the final days of the administration of Lyndon B. JOHNSON.

**Davis, Robert Gorham** (1908– )   A professor of English at Smith College in the early 1950s, Robert Gorham Davis testified before the HOUSE COMMITTEE ON UN-AMERICAN ACTIVITIES (HUAC) on February 25, 1953, about the existence of an active Communist movement at Harvard College in the late 1930s. Davis had been subpoenaed by the committee largely because the influence of Communism on American higher education was an area of particular interest to Congressman Harold VELDE, who assumed the chairmanship of HUAC in January 1953.

Davis, who had received his undergraduate degree from Harvard in 1929 and returned to do graduate work and teach from 1933 to 1943, admitted that he had belonged to the COMMUNIST PARTY between 1937 and 1939. He had joined the party, he explained, because the Depression had left him disillusioned about the human cost of the capitalist system; at that time, David said, Marxism seemed to offer a more positive, hopeful solution to the nation's economic miseries. Further, Davis had been impressed by the willingness of the Communists to take a firm stand against Hitler and the growing menace of fascism in Europe.

Davis testified that Communist Party membership at Harvard was limited almost exclusively to faculty members. Students were considered bad security risks, and teachers felt uncomfortable indoctrinating their students (again, the open advocacy of a Communist point of view would have jeopardized the security of the party cell) or exerting pressure on their students to join the party. According to Davis, his own party section never numbered more than fifteen people who met once a week and spent their time discussing the establishment of Marxist study groups, fund-raising activities, and the policies of Communist-front organizations on campus.

Distressed by the signing of the NAZI-SOVIET PACT in August 1939, Davis broke with the party, as did fellow Harvard scholar Daniel J. BOORSTIN. By that time, Davis claimed, he already had grown disillusioned with the party and its methods. "I had had such experience of the intrigues and duplicity that are inseparable from Communist Party membership," he told HUAC at his hearing, "that as a person of morality and sincerity I could remain in that position no longer. I not only broke with the Party, but, increasingly in the years that have followed, have felt it necessary to fight the influence of the Communist Party in those areas where I could be most effective."

Davis concluded his testimony by reassuring the committee that the Communist presence on American university campuses was far less in 1953 than it had been during the POPULAR FRONT days of the 1930s. "The influence of Communists is very slight," he observed, "because the times have changed and because the teachers have been so shocked by the events in the Soviet Union in the last eight years. And among students at colleges like Smith any evidence of radical activity has disappeared entirely." At no point in his testimony did Davis attribute the lack of radical political activity on college campuses to the atmosphere of fear generated by the actions of HUAC and Senator Joseph MCCARTHY.

**Declaration of Conscience**   On June 1, 1950, freshman Republican Senator Margaret Chase SMITH of Maine, the only woman member of the U.S. Senate, rose to deliver a stinging rebuke to Senator Joseph MCCARTHY of Wisconsin that subsequently became known as the Declaration of Conscience.

Since McCarthy had launched his anti-Communist crusade with his speech in Wheeling,

West Virginia, nearly four months earlier, Smith had grown increasingly disturbed by the failure of the junior senator from Wisconsin to substantiate his accusations. She therefore drafted a declaration of her own, condemning McCarthy's use of innuendo and his appeal to the forces of intolerance. After reviewing the draft with veteran Senator George Aiken of Vermont, Smith decided to ask five other liberal Republicans—Wayne Morse of Oregon, Irving Ives of New York, Charles Tobey of New Hampshire, Robert Hendrickson of New Jersey, and Edward Thye of Minnesota—to join her protest. They all agreed to do so.

With McCarthy sitting just 3 feet behind her, Smith condemned the rising tide in America of "fear and frustration that could result in national suicide and the end of everything we Americans hold dear." The U.S. Senate, she said, had recently been "too often debased to the level of a forum of hate and character assassination sheltered by the shield of Congressional immunity." As the rest of the Senate listened in stunned silence, Smith charged that "freedom of speech is not what it used to be in America. It has been so abused by some that it is not exercised by others. . . . The American people are sick and tired of seeing innocent people smeared and guilty people whitewashed. . . . I don't want to see the Republican party ride to political victory on the four horsemen of calumny—Fear, Ignorance, Bigotry, and Smear."

Then Smith presented her "Declaration of Conscience," signed by herself and her six senatorial colleagues. It represented one of the few attempts by anyone in Congress to deal with the Communist threat in a rational, balanced manner.

"We are Republicans," began the declaration, "but we are Americans first. It is as Americans that we express our concern with the growing confusion that threatens the security and stability of our country." The declaration called for an end to "totalitarian techniques," and sought a new dedication to the cause of "national security based on individual freedom." It criticized the excesses of both Democrats and Republicans alike. Smith and her cosigners blamed the Truman administration for being overly sensitive to criticism, for failing to provide effective leadership, and for "complacency to the threat of Communism here at home and the leak of vital secrets to Russia through key officials of the administration," On the other hand, they charged that "certain elements of the Republican party have materially added to this confusion in the hopes of riding the Republican party to victory through the selfish political exploitation of fear, bigotry, ignorance, and introlerance."

When Smith concluded her speech, the only senator who rose to add his name to the declaration was H. Alexander Smith of New Jersey. McCarthy stalked out of the chamber without a word. President Harry S. TRUMAN privately praised Smith for her courage but wished that she had been even tougher on McCarthy.

The following day, McCarthy resumed his attack on the Truman adminstration for allegedly sheltering Communists in the federal government. With a passing sarcastic reference to "Snow White and the Seven Dwarfs"—Margaret Chase Smith and her six cosigners, plus Smith of New Jersey—McCarthy made it clear that "this fight against communism, this attempt to expose and neutralize the efforts of those who are attempting to betray this country, shall not stop, regardless of what any group in this Senate or in the administration might do. I hold myself accountable not to them, but first to the people of my state, and secondly to the people of the nation, and thirdly to civilization as a whole."

Before McCarthy was finally censured by the Senate four years later, all of the co-signers of the Declaration of Conscience except Margaret Chase Smith and Morse had either joined McCarthy's anti-Communist crusade or acquiesced in silence.

**Declaration of Conscience** (1953)   In the spring of 1953, twenty-eight actors and journalists signed a public manifesto which they called a "Declaration of Conscience," protesting what they considered the "unfair treatment" of Senator Joseph MCCARTHY in the press. The signers claimed that news reports had neglected the positive achievements of McCarthy's anti-Communist crusade and overemphasized the harmful effects. "What methods have his critics used," they asked, "to remove traitors and subversives and security risks from the govenment? How adequate is the substantiation of the charges that McCarthy has attacked and injured innocent people?" As further evidence of the media's bias against McCarthy, the signers—who included actors Adolphe MENJOU, Ward Bond, and Charles COBURN, along with writers Victor Lasky and William Loeb—noted that McCarthy's recent book, *McCarthyism,* had been virtually ignored by reviewers, while accused Communist spy Owen LATTIMORE's account of his perjury trial, *ORDEAL BY SLANDER*, had received the "most extravagant and uncritical praise" following its publication in 1950.

The declaration was dispatched to 700 newspapers across the United States, some of which already supported McCarthy's crusade through their editorial columns. Perhaps the most signficiant response to the declaration came from the national chairman of the AMERICANS FOR DEMOCRATIC ACTION (ADA), former Attorney General Francis Biddle, who claimed that—regardless of any journalistic bias—McCarthy had actually received preferential treatment by the Eisenhower administration, which had refused to launch a full-scale public investigation of the senator's personal financial affairs.

***Dennis v. U.S.***  As part of its effort to eliminate the COMMUNIST PARTY OF THE UNITED STATES OF AMERICA (CPUSA) from the American political scene, the Truman administration launched a prosecution in 1948 of CPUSA General Secretary, Eugene Dennis and ten other members of the CPUSA National Committee. The government charged Dennis and his codefendants with violations of the SMITH ACT of 1940, which made it a crime to teach or advocate the overthrow of the U.S. government or

to belong to an organization that taught or advocated the overthrow of the government.

The case began when Attorney General Tom CLARK ordered several Justice Department attorneys in early 1948 to look into the feasibility of prosecutions under the Smith Act. Without obtaining Clark's prior approval, the attorneys decided in June to request an indictment from the New York grand jury that had been hearing testimony from former Soviet espionage agent Elizabeth BENTLEY. Though the action caught President Harry S. TRUMAN by surprise, the President welcomed the indictments because they enabled him to defend his administration in the presidential election of 1948 against Republican charges that it had been "soft" on Communism.

The government launched its trial of Dennis and his codefendants in U. S. District Court in January 1949. To fulfill the requirements for conviction under the Smith Act, the indictment charged the defendants with (1) willfully and knowingly *conspiring* to organize a society or group (the CPUSA) that taught and advocated the overthrow of the American government and (2) knowingly and willfully advocating and teaching "the duty and necessity of overthrowing and destroying the Government of the United States by force and violence." Because the defendants had never made any public statements advocating violence or taken any action to foment revolution, the government was forced to rely upon the testimony of ex-Communists such as Louis BUDENZ, who identified militant passages in Marxist-Leninist literature and then linked those passages to the CPUSA. To strengthen its case and prove that the CPUSA represented a threat to forcibly overthrow the U.S. government, the prosecution emphasized the subservience of the CPUSA to the Soviet Union and described in dark terms the secretive, conspiratorial nature of the party's activities.

The outcome of the trial, which became extremely rancorous at times, was determined largely by the tactics adopted by defense counsel, who abjured the First and Fifth Amendments and relied instead on rousing the American working class to demand an acquittal. The trial was also influenced by the obvious bias of the trial judge, Harold Medina, who came to believe that the defendants and their attorneys were attempting to persecute him. Perhaps most important, the events of 1949—the Communist victory in the Chinese civil war, the Soviet Union's successful explosion of a nuclear device, the trial of Alger HISS (which proceeded simultaneously in the same New York courthouse), and continuing evidence of Soviet espionage activity in the United States—made it far easier to accept the government's contention that the CPUSA represented a danger to the security of the United States. In October, the jury returned a verdict of guilty for all eleven defendants, ten of whom received the maximum sentence of five years in prison.

Defense counsel—whom Medina had jailed for contempt immediately following the trial—appealed the verdict, but the U.S. Court of Appeals upheld the trial court. The appellate court decided that the Communist Party was "a highly disciplined organization, adept at infiltration into strategic positions, use of aliases, and double-meaning language"; that the party was rigidly controlled and tolerated no dissent from its policies; and that the party's literature demonstrated that its objective was "to achieve a successful overthrow of the existing order by force and violence." Therefore, the court accepted the argument that a position of leadership within the party was prima-facie evidence of intent to overthrow the government by force.

In 1951, the case reached the U.S. Supreme Court. On June 4, 1951, the Court handed down a 6–2 decision in favor of the prosecution. (Justices Hugo Black and William Douglas dissented; Justice Clark, who had been officially responsible as attorney general for the original indictments, disqualified himself from the case.) For Chief Justice Fred Vinson, who drafted the majority opinion, the outbreak of the KOREAN WAR had increased the threat from the CPUSA

sufficiently to meet the "clear and present danger" standard for suppression of First Amendment rights. The defendants, wrote Vinson, "intended to overthrow the Government of the United States as speedily as the circumstances would permit. Their conspiracy to organize the Communist Party and to teach and advocate the overthrow of the Government of the United States by force and violence created a 'clear and present danger' of an attempt to overthrow the Government by force and violence." In his dissent, Douglas scoffed at the notion that the CPUSA posed any threat to the government, dismissing it as "the best known, the most beset, and the least thriving of any fifth column in history."

The Supreme Court's ruling encouraged federal and state prosecutors to undertake scores of indictments of alleged Communist officials under the Smith Act. By the time any of those cases reached the Supreme Court, however, the effect of *Dennis v. U.S.* had been modified by the subsequent decision in 1957 by the Court (under the leadership of recently appointed Chief Justice Earl WARREN) in *YATES V. U.S.*

**Dien Bien Phu**   A French military stronghold in the northeastern part of Indochina which later became known as Vietnam, Dien Bien Phu was the center of international attention in the spring of 1954. Vietnamese guerrillas seeking independence from the French colonial government had surrounded the airstrip at Dien Bien Phu and cut the French supply lines.

To relieve the beleaguered garrison, the French government in Paris urgently requested American military aid, but President Dwight David EISENHOWER—who insisted that the United States maintain its tradition of anticolonialism—refused to dispatch American combat troops to Indochina unless a lengthy list of conditions were fulfilled. Eisenhower's conditions included a grant of independence for Indochina, prior congressional approval of the use of American troops, British participation in any military venture, and American direction of the

**Dien Bien Phu, site of the critical French defeat in Indochina, 1954.**

war effort. Most of all, Eisenhower opposed any American military involvement because "If we were to put one combat soldier into Indo China, then our entire prestige would be at stake, not only in that area, but throughout the world."

Dien Bien Phu surrendered on May 7, 1954. Because the fall of Dien Bien Phu occurred while Eisenhower—a Republican and the most respected American military leader of the twentieth century—was in the White House, the nation did not experience the same wrenching debate over blame and guilt that had followed the victory of the Communist forces in the Chinese civil war in 1949. At the Geneva conference on Indochina that followed the fall of Dien Bien Phu, U.S. Secretary of State John Foster DULLES consented to the temporary division of Vietnam into two separate states—one Communist, one democratic—that were scheduled to be reunited following elections in 1956.

**Dies, Martin** (1900–1972)   Martin Dies served as chairman of the HOUSE COMMITTEE ON UN-AMERICAN ACTIVITIES (HUAC) from its inception until 1945. The son of a Texas congressman, Dies practiced law briefly before win-

ning election to the House of Representatives in 1930 as a Democrat from Texas. In his first speech in the House, during the course of which he blamed the appalling problem of unemployment during the Depression upon the influx of immigrants, Dies revealed the distrust of foreign individuals and ideologies that would become one of the hallmarks of his political career.

On July 21, 1937, Dies introduced a resolution providing for a special committee to investigate un-American propaganda. Specifically, the bill authorized the House to establish a seven-member committee to investigate the extent, character, and objects of un-American propaganda activities in the United States and the diffusion of subversive and un-American propaganda from both domestic and foreign sources. After Dies told his colleagues that he expected the committee to conclude its investigation within seven months, the House overwhelmingly approved the resolution on June 7, 1938.

Dies assumed the chairmanship of the new committee; among its original members was J. Parnell THOMAS, a Republican congressman from New Jersey. Early in its life, however, the committee departed from its original mission and transformed itself into a vehicle to achieve the particular political goals of its individual members. Because a majority of the committee's members were bitterly opposed to most of the New Deal legislation that had been passed since 1933, it was not surprising that the committee attempted to equate the New Deal with Communism. "It seems," mused Representative Thomas during one hearing, "that the New Deal is working along hand in glove with the COMMUNIST PARTY. The New Deal is either for the Communist Party or is playing into the hands of the Communist Party."

Dies used the committee to label as *un-American* organizations or individuals of whom he disapproved, including the CONGRESS OF INDUSTRIAL ORGANIZATIONS (CIO) and labor union chieftain Harry BRIDGES. By 1939, Dies had come to focus on Communism as the most serious threat to American security, and he repeatedly sought to link the Roosevelt administration with the Soviet Union. In his book, *The Trojan Horse in America—A Report to the Nation,* published shortly before the 1940 presidential election, Dies charged that "Stalin baited his hook with a 'progressive' worm, and New Deal suckers swallowed bait, hook, line, and sinker." Eleanor ROOSEVELT, Dies wrote, "has been one of the most valuable assets which the Trojan Horse organizations of the Communist Party have possessed"; and "Following the lead of the White House, cabinet officers have done their part to add to the influence of some of the Communist Trojan Horses." Apparently Dies' rhetoric struck a responsive chord in certain segments of the American public, for he claimed to have received 2,800 invitations to speak to civic groups across the nation, and the *Washington Post* bestowed its "Americanism award for 1938" upon Dies for his "outstanding patriotic service."

Dies followed with a series of articles (with such titles as "More Snakes Than I Can Kill") and speeches warning of the threat from internal subversion, particularly from the Communist Party, which, Dies claimed, had infiltrated virtually every labor union and defense industry plant in the nation. As the United States edged closer toward war with Nazi Germany in 1940, Dies began to emphasize the similarities between Adolf Hitler and Joseph STALIN. Indeed, his speeches far more often denounced Communism ("The Soviet regime is utterly repugnant to the American people") than Nazism, even after the United States entered World War II with the Soviet Union as its ally. "I rise to protest against any effort in any quarter to dress the Soviet wolf in the sheep's clothing of the four freedoms," Dies wrote to Roosevelt during the war. "Believe me, Mr. President, we have not seen the end of Soviet and Communist double-dealing. The ever zig-zagging line of the party will zig-zag again."

Dies' vituperative attacks on his enemies did not go unchallenged. In 1942, the executive board of the CIO described the record of Dies

and HUAC as "one of the [most] sordid and reprehensible in the annals of the American Congress." The *St. Louis Post-Dispatch* described the HUAC investigations as "little better than a personal racket"; Vice President Henry WALLACE claimed that Dies could not have aided the Axis cause more effectively if he had been on Hitler's payroll; the NATIONAL LAWYERS GUILD charged that "Martin Dies and his committee is the secret weapon with which Adolf Hitler hopes to soften up our Nation for military conquest"; and columnists Drew PEARSON and Walter Winchell both denounced Dies in their nationwide radio broadcasts.

Nevertheless, throughout World War II, Dies continued to press the issue of Communism in government. He urged the administration to abandon its practice of dismissing federal employees only when there existed "reasonable doubt" of their loyalty. "It seems to me," Dies stated, "that if you . . . require any committee to prove beyond a reasonable doubt that a man is subversive or even to prove that he is a communist . . . you could never accomplish anything." Instead, Dies argued that if a federal employee "has knowingly or carelessly used his name and his influence to promote, to support, and to strengthen subversive movements in this country that fact, and that fact alone, ought to be sufficient to disqualify him from the Government service."

From 1941 to 1945, Dies ran HUAC as a one-man show, as the other members of the committee played virtually no role in its investigations. During 1944, the committee held few hearings, and by the end of that autumn Dies—under a steady drumbeat of criticism from the White House and the Democratic leadership in Congress—had decided not to seek reelection to Congress. He later decided to resume his political career and returned to the House of Representatives in 1953, claiming to possess "about a hundred thousand names of persons engaged in subversive activities." The Democratic leadership of the House, however, denied his request to resume his seat on HUAC.

Certainly, Dies pioneered many of the Red-baiting techniques employed by Senator Joseph MCCARTHY of Wisconsin, who once stated that "In my opinion [Dies] will go down in history as a heroic voice crying in the wilderness." Following Dies' return to Congress in 1953, he warned McCarthy to expect "abuse, ridicule, and every known device of 'character assassination' and mental torture" from his enemies. Dies continued to serve as a representative from Texas until 1959.

**Disney, Walter E.** (1901–1966)  One of Hollywood's foremost conservatives, Walt Disney participated actively in the movement to rid the motion picture industry of Communist influence in the 1940s. Disney first became involved in the anti-Communist crusade in 1940 when he reportedly consented to provide the FEDERAL BUREAU OF INVESTIGATION (FBI) with the names of writers, actors, technicians, and union leaders whom he suspected of subversion. The following year, after Disney—a longtime foe of organized labor—refused to bargain with

Hollywood executive Walt Disney served as an informant for the FBI.

the Cartoonists' Guild, the guild led a strike against Disney's studio. Disney characterized the strike as part of the Communist conspiracy to dominate Hollywood; "I am positively convinced that Communistic agitation, leadership, and activities have brought about this strike," Disney wrote in an advertisement in *Variety*. (There were, in fact, a number of Communists among the union's supporters, though the primary cause of the strike was Disney's intransigently paternalistic operation of his studio.) Shortly after the strike ended with a victory for the guild, Disney sent a message to Jack Tenney, chairman of the California state legislature's Committee for Un-American Activities, urging him to investigate the infiltration of "Reds in movies."

When a group of Hollywood's leading conservatives—including actors John WAYNE and Gary COOPER, and director Sam Wood—joined together in February 1944 to form the MOTION PICTURE ALLIANCE FOR THE PRESERVATION OF AMERICAN IDEALS, Disney agreed to serve as one of the organization's first vice presidents. In that capacity, he helped draft the alliance's "Statement of Principles," which pledged the organization to fight the motion picture industry's "domination by Communists, radicals, and crackpots." Disney also sent a letter to Senator Robert Reynolds of North Carolina, requesting a congressional investigation of "the flagrant manner in which the motion picture industrialists of Hollywood have been coddling Communists and totalitarian-minded groups working in the industry for the dissemination of un-American ideas and beliefs."

In 1947, the HOUSE COMMITTEE ON UN-AMERICAN ACTIVITIES (HUAC) did launch an investigation into Communist influence in the motion picture industry. Disney was one of the first "friendly" witnesses called by the committee. On October 24, he informed the committee that although he did not presently employ any Communists in his studio, he had encountered problems with Communists in the past; specifically, he claimed that the 1941 Cartoonists'

Guild strike was the result of "a communist group trying to take over my artists, and they did take them over." He named two of the guild's leaders, Herbert Sorrell and David Hilberman, as Communists. Hilberman seemed suspicious to Disney because "I found that, number one, he had no religion and that, number two, he had spent considerable time at the Moscow Art Theater studying art direction, or something." Both men were subsequently BLACKLISTED within the motion picture industry, and Sorrell died of a heart attack less than a year later.

Disney then proceeded to accuse the LEAGUE OF WOMEN VOTERS of being a Communist-front organization for its support of the guild's strike. (Actually, Disney had confused the League of Women Voters with the LEAGUE OF WOMEN SHOPPERS, and he had to issue a formal correction a month later after the League of Women Voters called upon American women to boycott Disney's movies.) Disney concluded his testimony before HUAC by calling upon the nation's unions to free themselves from all suspicion of Communist influence:

I don't believe [the Communist Party] is a political party. I believe it is an un-American thing. The thing that I resent most is that they are able to get into these unions, take them over and represent to the world that a group of people that are in my plant, that I know are good, 100 percent Americans, are trapped by this group, and they are represented to the world as supporting all of these ideologies, and it is not so, and I feel that they really ought to be smoked out and shown up for what they are, so that all of the good, free causes in this country, all the liberalisms that really are American, can go out without the taint of Communism. That is my sincere feeling on it.

Several years later, Disney himself suffered from the anti-Communist hysteria when an FBI memorandum questioned his loyalty, citing Disney as a sponsor of rallies staged by allegedly subversive organizations in 1943–44. The agent

who compiled the report apparently was unaware that Disney had been operating as an FBI informant at the time. Although FBI director J. Edgar HOOVER subsequently sent Disney a personal message praising his contributions to the nation and the motion picture industry, Disney was not mollified. Instead, he availed himself of several opportunities to portray the FBI in an unflattering manner in motion pictures produced by his studio during the 1960s.

**Dmytryk, Edward** (1908– )   A prominent motion picture director, Edward Dmytryk was the only member of the HOLLYWOOD TEN to denounce publicly his previous ties with Communism.

Born in Canada, Dmytryk left his home in British Columbia at the age of fourteen and traveled to Hollywood to begin a career in motion pictures. He obtained a part-time job as a messenger at Paramount Studios while attending Hollywood High School and subsequently attended the California Institute of Technology for one year before returning to the film industry. Working his way through a succession of jobs (including stints as a projectionist cutter and a film editor), Dmytryk made his directorial debut in 1939. For five years, Dmytryk directed grade "B" films, until the release of his first major feature films for RKO Studios, *Tender Comrade* (written by Dalton TRUMBO) and *Murder, My Sweet,* in 1944. By 1947, Dmytryk had earned a reputation as a brilliant craftsman; he was working 52 weeks a year, and making $2500 a week on a long-term contract with RKO. He had completed more than a dozen commercially successful and critically acclaimed films, including *Back to Bataan, Crossfire* (a fervent attack on anti-Semitism that earned Dmytryk an Academy Award nomination for Best Director in 1947), *Cornered, So Well Remembered,* and *Till the End of Time.*

Meanwhile, Dmytryk had become involved in left-wing political activities in Hollywood. In 1942–43, he served as a guest lecturer for the

Hollywood League of American Writers School and the left-wing Peoples' Education Center. According to Dmytryk, screenwriter Alvah BESSIE attempted to recruit him into the COMMUNIST PARTY in 1943, and by Dmytryk's own account, he decided to join the party in the spring of 1944. He later claimed that he left the party in the fall of 1945, although he continued to attend party meetings in Hollywood.

In September 1947, the HOUSE COMMITTEE ON UN-AMERICAN ACTIVITIES (HUAC) subpoenaed Dmytryk to testify about his reported Communist activities. Like the other members of the Hollywood Ten, Dmytryk initially failed to answer the questions of the committee and was convicted by a federal court for contempt of Congress. In November 1947, RKO fired Dmytryk for his defiance of HUAC and for political actions that the studio claimed had "offended the community."

While waiting for the Supreme Court to review his case, Dmytryk helped supervise the day-to-day affairs of his fellow members of the Hollywood Ten. He later claimed that he had decided even before his sentencing to announce his defection from the Communist ranks, but he decided to delay any announcement until he had served his prison term: "I knew that if I broke with the Ten before going to jail, everyone would think I was doing so to avoid prison, so I decided to postpone any move until I had served my sentence."

After the Court refused in April 1950 to hear the appeals of the Ten, Dmytryk entered a federal prison at Mill Point, West Virginia. After several months of incarceration, he decided to release a statement recanting his failure to testify before HUAC. In September 1950, Dmytryk openly declared that he was not then a member of the Communist Party, nor had he been a member at the time of the HUAC hearings in 1947. Even though he still opposed the inquisitorial methods of HUAC, Dmytryk acknowledged that the COLD WAR, Korea, and growing evidence of Soviet espionage in the United States had convinced him that there was indeed a Communist threat to the United States. He was also honest enough to admit that his change of heart was motivated in part by a desire to resume his directorial career. "I didn't want to be a martyr for a cause I didn't believe in," he later stated. "I believed that I was being forced to sacrifice my family and my career in defense of the Communist Party, from which I had long been separated and which I had grown to dislike and distrust."

On November 15, 1950, Dmytryk was released from prison. He subsequently commenced a series of meetings with the FBI and a group of prominent conservatives, including Ronald REAGAN, as part of a highly visible public effort to "rehabilitate" his reputation. The process also included further testimony before HUAC, and when Dmytryk appeared before the committee for a second time on April 25, 1951, he named twenty-six former Hollywood colleagues—virtually all of whom already had been named by previous witnesses—as Communist Party members or sympathizers. These, said Dmytryk, were the only Communists he knew because his experience as a party member had been "rather meager." He followed this testimony with an article in *The Saturday Evening Post,* in which he again renounced his past radical activities. Not surprisingly, Dmytryk's former colleagues reacted with shock and vituperation, and the major Hollywood studios hesitated before offering any films to someone who was still associated in the public mind with Communism.

Later that year, however, Dmytryk obtained a directing job on a modest-budget independent film. When conservative groups such as the AMERICAN LEGION failed to protest Dmytryk's employment, producer-director Stanley Kramer offered him a four-picture deal, and Dmytryk's career was finally back on track. His subsequent pictures included *The Caine Mutiny, The Young Lions, The Carpetbaggers,* and *Mirage.* Following his retirement, Dmytryk published his memoirs of Hollywood, entitled *It's a Hell of a Life But Not a Bad Living* (1978).

Congresswoman Helen Gahagan Douglas was defeated by Richard Nixon, who referred to her as
"the Pink Lady," in a race for the U.S. Senate in
1950.

## Douglas, Helen Gahagan (1902–1980)

As a Broadway star in the 1920s, Helen Gahagan
was considered one of the most beautiful
women in the world. She studied voice in Europe from 1928 to 1930, and made her debut
at the Metropolitan Opera in New York in 1930.
In 1931 Gahagan married actor Melvyn DOUG-
LAS, and together they participated in a wide
range of liberal and humanitarian causes in Hollywood during the decade-long Depression. Following a tour of Europe in 1937, during which
her husband and a member of her band suffered
from anti-Semitic discrimination at a music festival in Salzburg, Austria, Helen Douglas also
began devoting her energies to the cause of
antifascism.

In 1939, Douglas served as chairperson of the
John Steinbeck Committee to aid Agricultural
Organizations, a group that raised funds to support striking farm workers and wrote and distributed materials outlining the case of the unions
against California's agricultural corporations.
That same year, Douglas organized rallies in
favor of American aid to Great Britain in its
fight against Nazi Germany. "If Hitler couldn't
be stopped in Europe," Douglas warned, "it
wasn't likely that America would escape attack."
During the wartime Soviet-American alliance,
Douglas visited Moscow as a delegate to the
Soviet-American Women's Conference.

Douglas became vice-chairman of the California Democratic Party in 1941, and three years
later she won a seat in the U.S. House of Representatives. During her three terms in Congress,
Douglas established a record as a consistent
supporter of foreign aid, the United Nations,
civil liberties, and small family farms against
the huge California agricultural corporations. In
1946, she co-sponsored the McMahon-Douglas
bill, which sought to keep military officials off
the ATOMIC ENERGY COMMISSION

When the HOUSE COMMITTEE ON UN-AMERI-
CAN ACTIVITIES (HUAC), under the chairmanship of J. Parnell THOMAS, intensified its
investigations of Communist infiltration of
American industry in 1947, Douglas emerged
as one of the most consistent critics of the
committee. She was one of a handful of members of Congress to vote against the citations of
the HOLLYWOOD TEN for contempt, and she
opposed further appropriations for HUAC. Following the committee's relatively restrained activities in 1949, Douglas admitted that HUAC
had done "a fine job of what it had to do."
The following year, however, Douglas strongly
opposed the passage of the anti-Communist IN-
TERNAL SECURITY ACT (also known as the
MCCARRAN ACT).

In 1950, Douglas decided to give up her
House seat to run for the U.S. Senate. Her
voting record in Congress came under considerable attack during the primary campaign when
her conservative opponent attacked her for allegedly leading a "small, subversive clique of

'red-hots' " who sought to capture the state Democratic Party. Worse calumnies followed in the general election campaign against Congressman Richard M. NIXON. Nixon organized his campaign around the theme of Douglas as a Communist sympathizer. Calling her "the Pink Lady," he accused Douglas of following the Communist line "in voting time after time against measures that are for the security of this country." Had Douglas been responsible for investigating disloyalty, said Nixon, "the Communist conspiracy in the United States would never have been exposed." Nixon charged that Douglas was "pink down to her underwear" (to emphasize the point, his campaign workers distributed more than a half-million copies of Douglas' voting record printed on sheets of pink paper) and accused her of committing herself "to the State Department policy of appeasement toward Communism in the Far East."

Douglas sought to fight back by presenting herself as a more effective fighter against Communism than Nixon. She charged her opponent with adopting fascist tactics, calling Nixon and his supporters "a backwash of young men in dark shirts" (a reference to the Nazi "brown shirts"), and insisted that Senator Joseph MC-CARTHY was stumping California for Nixon, though "the Republican press is so ashamed of McCarthy that it doesn't publish a word about it." In fact, McCarthy only made one speech in California during the campaign, largely because Nixon preferred to keep control of the campaign in his own hands.

Although Democratic voters outnumbered Republicans by nearly a 2–1 majority on the state's registration rolls, Douglas lost the senatorial election by 700,000 votes. She had alienated many moderate Democrats with her votes in Congress and had allowed Nixon to seize the initiative and define the election as a referendum on anti-Communism. In the aftermath of the international shocks of 1949–50—evidence of Soviet espionage in America, the Communist victory in China, the first Soviet nuclear explosion, and the invasion of South Korea in June

1950—Douglas had no chance of winning such a contest. Embittered by the circumstances of her defeat, Douglas abandoned politics and returned with her husband to New York. For the remainder of her life, she appeared occasionally in public to support liberal causes. While at work on her memoirs, Douglas died of cancer in 1980.

**Douglas, Melvyn** (1901–1981)  A prominent Hollywood liberal and the husband of California Representative Helen Gahagan DOUGLAS, Melvyn Edouard Hesselberg changed his name to Melvyn Douglas when he embarked upon a stage career in 1919. In 1928, Douglas formed his own acting troupe in Madison, Wisconsin; later that year, he appeared for the first time on Broadway. There he starred opposite world-renowned beauty Helen Gahagan in *Tonight or Never,* and the two were married in 1931. They moved to Hollywood, where Douglas soon established himself as one of the American film industry's favorite romantic leading men.

Before his arrival in California, Douglas had given little thought to political affairs. During the mid-1930s, however, Douglas became one of the most tireless liberal activists in Hollywood and a leading supporters of President Franklin D. Roosevelt's New Deal reforms. His own experiences with anti-Semitism during a tour of Nazi Germany with his wife in 1936–37 created a passionate hatred of fascism. "We were terrified, traumatized, and profoundly shocked by what we saw and heard," Douglas later wrote. As the fascist threat mounted in Europe, Douglas willingly joined hands with American Communist leaders in POPULAR FRONT organizations such as the JOINT ANTI-FASCIST REFUGEE COMMITTEE and the Motion Picture Artists Committee to Aid Republican Spain.

Douglas had no illusions about collaborating with Communists; he later stated that he had always recognized their intentions and tactics, but used their support to achieve his own liberal goals. He resisted their attempts to recruit him into the COMMUNIST PARTY. "One night," Douglas recalled, "Lionel Stander kept me up till dawn trying to sell me the Russian brand of Marxism and to recruit me for the Communist Party. I resisted. I had always been condemnatory of totalitarianism and I made continual, critical references to the U.S.S.R. in my speeches."

When the NAZI-SOVIET PACT of August 1939 and the ensuing invasion of Poland destroyed the unity of the POPULAR FRONT, Douglas broke with the Communist community in Hollywood and became one of the film community's most militant anti-Communists. He condemned the Communist Party for its criticisms of Roosevelt and the New Deal and for its opposition to American intervention in the European conflict. A founding member of the Motion Picture Democratic Committee, which was devoted to the election of liberal Democratic candidates, Douglas resigned from that organization when it refused to support Roosevelt's foreign and domestic policies.

In 1940, Douglas became the first professional actor to serve as a delegate to the Democratic National Convention. Over the following decade, he fought to maintain a clear distinction in the public mind between liberalism and Communism. Douglas sponsored symposiums throughout California on Communist tactics, explaining how the party worked and how to combat it. As a reward for his support of the administration, Roosevelt appointed Douglas director of the Arts Council for the Office of Civilian Defense in 1942. When the AMERICAN LEGION denounced his appointment because of his past involvement in left-wing activities, Douglas replied that "I have as little regard for the Communists as I have for the Nazis, and I have been quick to condemn their influence wherever I have found it in operation." To strengthen his anti-Red credentials, Douglas cited his clearance of "Communistic tendencies" by former HUAC chairman Martin DIES, and he invited the FBI to run a security check on his past. The bureau declined the offer.

Following the war, Douglas joined with other anti-Communist liberals in 1947 to found the AMERICANS FOR DEMOCRATIC ACTION (ADA), an organization that barred Communists from membership. At the same time, he denounced the "careless and callous investigating methods" of the HOUSE COMMITTEE ON UN-AMERICAN ACTIVITIES (HUAC) and signed petitions condemning the committee for its treatment of the HOLLYWOOD TEN. Weary of reprising the same type-cast roles for films, Douglas temporarily deserted Hollywood in 1949 and returned to New York, where he spent the following decade writing, acting, and directing stage productions. His wife joined him in 1950 following her defeat in the California senatorial race against Congressman Richard M. NIXON.

Trapped between the extremes of Left and Right in the increasingly polarized political atmosphere of the McCarthy era, Douglas became a liberal casualty of the anti-Communist crusade. He curtailed his political activites and concentrated instead on his artistic career. Douglas won a Tony award in 1960 for his role as a presidential candidate in *The Best Man* and an Academy Award for Best Supporting Actor in 1963 for the film *Hud*. In 1981, Douglas died of pneumonia and heart failure.

**Douglas, William O.**   (1898–1980) Named to the U.S. Supreme Court in 1939 by President Franklin D. Roosevelt, William O. Douglas established a reputation as one of the Court's leading defenders of civil liberties. During the 1940s and 1950s, Douglas consistently voted against the conviction of known or suspected Communists for holding unpopular political beliefs.

In the case of *DENNIS V. UNITED STATES*, Douglas issued a strong dissenting opinion against the conviction of twelve leaders of the COMMUNIST PARTY OF THE UNITED STATES OF AMERICA for allegedly violating the SMITH ACT. Douglas argued that the prosecution had not introduced any evidence to prove that the defendants had been guilty of seditious conduct, nor

**U.S. Supreme Court Justice William O. Douglas, an outspoken defender of civil liberties.**

had the government proved that there was more than minuscule support for a Communist revolution among the American public. "Free speech—the glory of our system of government—should not be sacrificed on anything less than plain and objective proof of danger that the evil advocated is imminent," argued Douglas. "On this record no one can say that petitioners and their converts are in such a strategic position as to have even the slightest chance of achieving their aims."

Douglas also dissented in the case of YATES V. UNITED STATES, joining Justice Hugo Black in charging that "the present type of prosecutions [of Communists in the United States] are more in line with the philosophy of authoritarian government than with that expressed by our First Amendment." During the 1960s and 1970s, Douglas voiced his opposition to the American military role in the Vietnam War. In 1975,

Douglas resigned from the Supreme Court after having served longer than any other justice in the history of the court. An avid outdoorsman and advocate of protection of the environment, Douglas authored a number of books, including *Of Men and Mountains* (1950), *The Anatomy of Liberty* (1963), and *Points of Rebellion* (1970).

**Du Bois, William Edward Burghardt** (1868–1963)   The foremost radical African-American leader of the early twentieth century, W. E. B. Du Bois was born in Great Barrington, Massachusetts, and educated at Fisk University and Harvard University. After receiving an M.A. degree from Harvard in 1891, Du Bois spent several years studying at the University of Berlin. He returned to the United States to complete his doctoral thesis on the *Supression of the African Slave Trade* and received a Ph.D. from Harvard in 1895. Du Bois subsequently embarked upon an intensive research project into the status of African Americans in Philadelphia in the late nineteenth century. The experience, which resulted in his volume on *The Philadelphia Negro* (1899), provided Du Bois with insights into the practical difficulties facing urban African Americans in the northern United States.

As the product of a middle-class African-American family in the Northeast, Du Bois had little personal knowledge of the terrors of segregation in the South at the turn of the century. It was only after he accepted a position as professor of history and economics at Atlanta University in 1896 that Du Bois—who eventually became one of the nation's leading African-American sociologists—came to understand the depth of racial hatred that existed in the United States at that time. "I saw the race-hatred of the whites as I had never dreamed of it before—naked and unashamed," Du Bois wrote. "The faint discrimination of my hopes and desires paled into nothing before this great, red monster of cruel oppression. . . . I emerged into full manhood, with the ruins of some ideals about me, but with others planted above the stars . . .

determined, even unto stubbornness, to fight the good fight."

In 1905, Du Bois joined with twenty-eight other prominent African-American leaders to found the Niagara Movement, which was dedicated to the elimination of racial distinctions in the United States. Although the Niagara Movement itself did not last long, it served as the forerunner to the NATIONAL ASSOCIATION FOR THE ADVANCEMENT OF COLORED PEOPLE (NAACP), established in 1910 by a coalition of African and white Americans. Du Bois was named director of publicity and research for the fledgling organization, and for the next twenty-four years he served as editor of the NAACP's official journal, *The Crisis.* His uncompromising rhetoric won the journal a wide readership, increasing its circulation to 100,000 by 1918.

For Du Bois, the ultimate goal of African Americans had to be complete equality with all other groups within American society. Toward that end, he dedicated himself to "a fight to obtain without compromise such rights and privileges as belonged to members of the civilization of which he was a part." In 1919, he organized the Pan-African Congress, a move which helped earn him the sobriquet of "father of African liberation" among African Americans of a later generation. Frustrated by the unwillingness of mainstream American reform organizations to commit themselves to total racial equality and impressed by the accomplishments of the revolutionary Soviet regime during his visit to the USSR in 1926, Du Bois elected to join the COMMUNIST PARTY and subsequently participated in numerous Communist-front organizations in the 1940s and 1950s.

Not surprisingly, Du Bois supported the presidential candidacy of Progressive Party nominee Henry A. WALLACE in 1948. Although he recognized that Wallace had virtually no chance of winning the election, Du Bois selected him as "the one man worthy of [African-American] support." "At least," noted Du Bois, "we can let the country and the nations know that there are people in the U.S. who are not stupid, who

are not to be bought with graft and fooled with lies." Du Bois' outspoken support for Wallace cost him his position with the NAACP, which dismissed him for "insubordination." When Du Bois and another African-American Marxist, Paul ROBESON, subsequently joined an organization known as the Council on African Affairs, the attorney general promptly added the council—whose members did not all support the radical political philosophies of Du Bois and Robeson—to his list of subversive organizations.

By 1950, Du Bois had become one of the most outspoken critics within the African-American community of the anti-Communist crusade in the United States. For Du Bois, the root cause of the anti-Red hysteria lay in the desire of American industry for profits. "The basic cause of our insanity," he wrote, "is that in our unprecedented organization of industry with its marvelous technique, the vast majority of mankind are sick, ignorant and starved while a few have more income than they can use. . . . We think money-making is the great end of man; our whole ideology bows to this fantastic idea. War is a business immensely profitable to a few, but of measureless disaster and death of dreams to the many. In order to have war, big business must have hate, so its press asks you to hate Communists and, if not Communists, hate all who do not hate Communists."

In 1950, Du Bois accepted the chairmanship of an organization known as the Peace Information Center, dedicated to promulgating pacifist propaganda and obtaining petitions in favor of peace. He also continued his travels abroad, attending a peace assembly in Prague, Czechoslovakia, later that year. When the attorney general classified the Peace Information Center as an organization under the control of a foreign power, the government insisted that Du Bois register as a foreign agent under the terms of the SMITH ACT. Du Bois refused and was subsequently indicted for his failure to comply. Bereft of funds, Du Bois embarked upon a tour of the United States to raise money for his defense; among those who contributed were physicist

Albert EINSTEIN, novelist Thomas Mann, and poet Langston Hughes.

At his trial, Du Bois made no attempt to hide his Communist sympathies. "There is no path of human progress which a so-called 'free democracy' can advocate without adopting at least part of the program of socialists and Communists," he declared, adding that he believed in Communism "wherever and whenever men are wise and good enough to achieve it." When the prosecution failed to produce any witnesses or firm evidence proving that Du Bois was an agent of the Soviet Union, Judge James McGuire dismissed the charges.

Meanwhile, Du Bois had campaigned for a seat in the U.S. Senate as the Progressive Party candidate from New York and had won 4 percent of the vote, which he claimed was more than he had expected. Throughout the 1950s, Du Bois continued to speak out against the excesses of the McCarthy era. "A great silence has fallen upon the real soul of this nation," he declared. "We are smearing loyal citizens on the paid testimony of self-confessed liars, traitors and spies; we are making the voice of America the babble of cowards paid to travel." When he refused to state on his passport application whether he was a Communist or not ("It is none of your business what I believe so long as I transgress no law," Du Bois stated), the Department of State refused to grant him permission to travel abroad, a decision that was revoked only when the Supreme Court intervened in 1958.

In 1952, Du Bois was awarded the World Peace Council Prize. Seven years later, the Soviet Union awarded him its Lenin Peace Prize. He died on August 27, 1963, at the age of 95.

## Duggan, Lawrence (1905–1948)

A State Department official who served in the administration of President Franklin D. Roosevelt as an expert on Latin American affairs, Lawrence Duggan became one of the earliest casualties of the shoddy investigative practices of the HOUSE COMMITTEE ON UN-AMERICAN ACTIVITIES

(HUAC) when he jumped or fell to his death on December 20, 1948. The son of the founder of the Institute of International Education, an organization that facilitated the exchange of teachers and students between the United States and foreign nations, Duggan served briefly on the staff of the IIE in 1929–30 before joining the State Department. At State, Duggan rose to become chief of the Division of American Republics; he also renewed his acquaintance—first made during his undergraduate days at Harvard University—with Alger HISS. Together with six or seven of their colleagues, Duggan and Hiss met periodically to discuss foreign affairs, focusing particularly in the late 1930s on ways to combat the rising tide of fascism in Europe.

In 1946, Duggan rejoined the Institute of International Education as director. Two years later, HUAC investigators quizzed Alger Hiss about charges made by a former Communist journalist named Whittaker CHAMBERS to the effect that Hiss had been a member of the COMMUNIST PARTY during the 1930s. During his testimony before the Committee, Chambers also mentioned Duggan's name, though he apparently added that Duggan was not a Communist, at least "not to my direct knowledge." Chambers had, though, identified both Duggan and Hiss to Assistant Secretary of State Adolf BERLE in 1939 as suspects in the transmission of information from the State Department to foreign governments.

Hiss denied that he had ever been a member of the Communist Party, but on December 15, 1948, a grand jury in New York indicted Hiss for perjury. Five days later, at seven o'clock in the evening, Duggan fell to his death from his office on the sixteenth floor of an office building in midtown Manhattan. The official police report of the incident effectively ruled out any suggestion of foul play. There were no signs of a struggle within the room or on the window sill, and Duggan apparently had been alone in the room at the time, for there were no witnesses. "Unless other evidence develops that would indicate a necessity for reopening the case," the police stated, "we are concluding this investigation with the finding that Mr. Duggan either accidentally fell or jumped." Family members recalled that Duggan had been plagued by ulcers and back problems and theorized that he may have gone to open a window when he was seized by back spasms or an attack of nausea. A former colleague at the State Department, Undersecretary of State Sumner Welles, noted that Duggan had sent him a cheerful letter less than a day earlier and seemed to be in good spirits. On the other hand, a colleague at the institute claimed that Duggan had been "a very tired man and ill for some time."

Within five hours of Duggan's death, Representative Karl MUNDT, who was acting chairman of HUAC in the absence of J. Parnell THOMAS, held a hastily arranged press conference with fellow HUAC member Richard M. NIXON. Mundt informed reporters that a witness had identified Duggan as one of the suspects whose names had been forwarded from Chambers to Berle in 1939. When a reporter asked Mundt the following day for the names of the other men whom Chambers had named, Mundt replied flippantly, "We will give them out as they jump out of windows." He then added that "if foul play is involved it might lead directly to the Communist conspirators."

On December 24, Attorney General Tom CLARK angrily responded to Mundt's accusations by pointing out that an FBI investigation had produced no evidence of Duggan's connection with the Communist Party or with any other espionage activity. "On the contrary," noted Clark, "the evidence discloses that Mr. Duggan was a loyal employee of the United States Government." Numerous present and former members of the State Department, including Berle, Welles, and former Secretary of State Cordell Hull, also came to Duggan's defense by testifying to the excellent character, loyalty, and ability of their erstwhile colleague.

Mundt's decision to release testimony heard in executive session infuriated other members of the committee. Alabama Representative John

RANKIN described it as "atrocious" and "unfortunate." "I am sure if the full committee had been consulted it would not have been given out," said Rankin. "I would have tried to talk Mundt out of releasing it. Duggan was dead and nothing was accomplished by releasing it." Editorial comment in the nation's press—including right-wing journals—also was almost universally negative. As the *New York Herald Tribune* pointed out, Mundt's action had created wholesale revulsion with HUAC just when the committee had begun to improve its public image. "At a stroke," noted the *Herald Tribune*, "it has undone months of genuine effort on the part of the Un-American Activities Committee to correct past excesses and bring its procedures within the limits of reason and fairness." The *Washington Post*, which had long been a critic of HUAC, charged that "the trigger-happy legislators who are ready at any moment to abandon their own rules in order to strike at a helpless victim, without waiting to assemble all the pertinent facts, have once more demonstrated their unfitness for the task they are trying to do."

In short, members of the HUAC had publicly assailed the character of Duggan without ever holding hearings on the issue of his loyalty. Nor did the committee ever issue any formal report on the matter. If the episode left a shadow on Duggan's name, it left an even larger blot on the record of the committee.

**Dulles, Allen W.** (1893–1969)   Director of the CENTRAL INTELLIGENCE AGENCY (CIA) from 1953 to 1961, Allen W. Dulles was the younger brother of John Foster DULLES, secretary of state during the Eisenhower administration. The son of a Presbyterian minister and the grandson of John Watson Foster (President Rutherford B. Hayes' secretary of state), Dulles grew up in an affluent environment in New York City. After beginning his education in private academies in upstate New York and in Paris, France, Dulles attended Princeton University, graduating with a B.A. in 1914. Following a

**CIA director Allen Dulles.**

and from that post he provided advice to the Truman administration on occupation policies toward Germany in the immediate postwar period.

Returning to the United States, Dulles resumed his position with Sullivan and Cromwell, though he remained active in foreign affairs through his work with the Council on Foreign Relations, an organization which also included Dean ACHESON, secretary of state in President Harry S. TRUMAN's second administration. In 1948, Allen Dulles and his brother, John Foster, both served as foreign-policy advisers to Republican presidential candidate Thomas Dewey. Dulles' expertise in foreign policy and espionage, along with his ties to the eastern Republican establishment, involved him in the controversy between Alger HISS and Whittaker CHAMBERS in 1948. After hearing Chambers' allegations that Hiss had been an active member of the COMMUNIST PARTY in the late 1930s, Congressman Richard NIXON traveled to New York to ask Allen and John Foster Dulles for their opinions on Chambers' veracity. Upon reading the testimony, Allen Dulles concluded that Chambers unquestionably had known Hiss.

By that time, rising public concern among Americans about Soviet espionage had convinced the Truman administration to establish formally the CIA, with authority to conduct intelligence operations abroad. In 1950, President Truman named Allen Dulles deputy director of the CIA. With the inauguration of President Dwight David EISENHOWER in January 1953, Dulles was named director of the CIA. He soon became embroiled in a controversy with Senator Joseph MCCARTHY, who refused to slow the pace of his anti-Communist crusade with a Republican in the White House. Dulles' appointment of William Bundy to a post in the CIA infuriated McCarthy, partly because Bundy had contributed several hundred dollars to Alger Hiss' defense fund and partly because Bundy was the son-in-law of Dean Acheson, one of McCarthy's favorite targets. McCarthy demanded that Bundy appear to testify before

year-long tour in the Far East and India, he returned to Princeton to obtain his M.A. in 1916. Dulles subsequently entered the foreign service, rising to the position of chief of the Department of State's Division of Near East Affairs in 1922. Dissatisfied with the long-term prospects of life in the diplomatic corps, Dulles commenced the study of law, and received an LL.B. from George Washington University in 1926.

Joining his brother at the prestigious New York law firm of Sullivan and Cromwell, Dulles specialized in international law and finance. His extensive knowledge of European financial affairs persuaded William J. Donovan, head of the U.S. Office of Strategic Services (OSS) during World War II, to ask Dulles to serve as chief of the OSS in Switzerland, where he helped negotiate the surrender of Nazi troops in northern Italy in 1945. Near the end of the war, Dulles was named OSS director in Germany, the GOVERNMENT OPERATIONS COMMITTEE; Dulles adamantly refused to produce Bundy. When McCarthy vowed to launch an investigation of the CIA, Dulles threatened to resign if the Wisconsin senator were not silenced.

In the Senate, Oklahoma Democrat Mike Monroney observed on July 13, 1953, that McCarthy's proposed probe of the CIA "puts the Senate up to a choice of giving the distinguished Senator from Wisconsin carte blanche authority to fully explore . . . the innermost secrets of the nation's intelligence community." The result, Monroney contended, would be the public revelation of critical security information "that even the Kremlin's best spy apparatus could not get." Vice President Nixon eventually intervened in the dispute and convinced McCarthy to abandon his investigation of the CIA, but only at the cost of an extensive purge of the agency's personnel as a means of placating the Wisconsin senator.

Dulles remained director of the CIA until the advent of the administration of John F. KENNEDY in January 1961. Even after that time, however, Dulles stayed active as an unofficial consultant on intelligence affairs and served as a member of the Warren Commission, which investigated the assassination of Kennedy in November 1963.

## Dulles, John Foster (1888–1959)

Secretary of state during the first five years of the administration of Dwight David EISENHOWER, John Foster Dulles grew up in a family atmosphere that stressed Calvinist morality and a tradition of public service. Dulles' father and paternal grandfather were both Presbyterian ministers, and his maternal grandfather was John Watson Foster, who served for two years (1892–93) as President Benjamin Harrison's secretary of state. Dulles grew up in New York City and Watertown, New York, and entered Princeton University in 1905. He graduated at the top of his class and subsequently spent a year studying at the Sorbonne in Paris before returning to the

United States and receiving an LL.B. degree from the Law School of George Washington University.

Dulles accepted an offer to join the prestigious New York law firm of Sullivan and Cromwell, where he specialized in international law. During World War I, Dulles served in the military intelligence division of the U.S. Army General Staff. Following the armistice in November 1918, he joined his uncle, Secretary of State Robert Lansing, in the American delegation to the peace conference at Paris. Dulles' work in Paris made him an extremely valuable source of legal advice on international finance in the postwar period, and Dulles consequently completed numerous bond arrangements for the governments of France, Germany, Norway, Argentina, Poland, and Denmark, among others. In 1939, Dulles published his first book analyzing the international scene, *War, Peace and Change*. It was Dulles' contention that the Versailles settlement had collapsed largely because it did not contain sufficient provision for peaceful change.

Meanwhile, Dulles became involved in the work of the Federal Council of Churches of Christ in America, serving as chairman of the council's Commission on a Just and Durable Peace. He also became active in Republican Party affairs, particularly as a supporter of Governor Thomas E. Dewey of New York. In 1944, Dulles served as Dewey's foreign policy adviser; the following year, he joined Senator Arthur Vandenberg of Michigan as the leading Republican representatives on the American delegation to the San Francisco Conference that drafted the charter of the United Nations. Dulles later recalled that it was during the meeting in San Francisco that he first began to grow wary of Soviet objectives in the postwar world. "My troubles with the Russians started when I went to San Francisco," he stated. "Molotov and Gromyko were there and I soon learned they had ideas very different from the sweetness and light of the Atlantic Charter and the Four Freedoms."

Over the next four years, the TRUMAN administration—in a bid for bipartisan support for its foreign policy initiatives—frequently invited Dulles to accompany U.S. officials to important international conferences. In September 1945, Dulles attended the first meeting of the Council of Foreign Ministers in London; in 1946, he accepted Truman's request to serve as a member of the U.S. delegation to the first United Nations General Assembly. He again served as a U.N. delegate in 1947 and accompanied Secretary of State George Catlett MARSHALL to Moscow for another meeting of the Council of Foreign Ministers. Upon his return from the Kremlin, Dulles issued a warning to the American people to guard against the subversion of their democratic institutions. "It is up to us to show, in every available way," he declared in a radio address, "that free institutions are the means whereby men can save themselves from the sea of misery in which they find themselves." Reiterating the same theme he had sounded first in the late 1930s, Dulles also maintained that the United States could not afford to merely support the international status quo in the ongoing battle to stem the tide of Communist expansion. "The most important response to the Soviet challenge," he noted, "will be in effecting peacefully the reforms which Soviet leaders contend can only be effected by violent means."

During the presidential campaign of 1948, Dulles again acted as Republican candidate Governor Dewey's unofficial foreign-policy adviser. Following Dewey's defeat, Dulles accepted a nomination to serve as chairman of the Carnegie Endowment for International Peace. Upon the death of Senator Robert F. Wagner in the summer of 1949, Dewey appointed Dulles to fill Wagner's unexpired term in the U.S. Senate. Dulles, however, never seemed quite comfortable in the rough give-and-take of congressional politics. Certainly his Republican colleagues did not accept him enthusiastically and relegated him to committees on the civil service and post office. In the special election held to choose Wagner's successor, Dulles was defeated overwhelmingly by former Governor Herbert Lehman.

When Eisenhower restored control of the White House to the Republican Party in 1952, Dulles became his clear choice for the position of secretary of state. By that time, Dulles had grown convinced that the Truman policy of containment had failed and that the United States needed to exert constant pressure on the Soviet Union, seeking to roll back Communist gains in Eastern Europe and the Far East, and eventually to force the disintegration of the Soviet empire from within. Partly because of his strong Calvinist heritage, Dulles argued that the United States should employ the force of its spiritual superiority against the Soviet Union. "There is a moral or natural law not made by man which determines right and wrong," he wrote in May 1952, "and in the long run only those who conform to that law will escape disaster. This law has been trampled by the Soviet rulers, and for that violation they can and should be made to pay. This will happen when we ourselves keep faith with that law in our practical decisions of policy."

When discussing U.S. defense strategies, Dulles advocated a reliance upon the superiority of the American nuclear arsenal to deter further Soviet expansion. This policy, which came to be known as "massive retaliation," recommended that the United States and its allies "develop the will and organize the means to retaliate instantly against open aggression by Red armies, so that, if [Communist aggression] occurred anywhere, we could and would strike back where it hurts, by means of our choosing. . . ." Upon assuming office, the Eisenhower administration attempted to place this "new look" policy into effect, cutting spending for conventional military weapons and enhancing the nation's stockpile of nuclear weapons.

Secretary of State Dulles considered himself above the controversies of domestic politics; therefore, he refused to take a public stance either for or against the anti-Communist crusade of Senator Joseph MCCARTHY of Wisconsin and his allies. Yet Dulles certainly deferred to no one in his detestation of Communism, which provided with a certain measure of common ground with McCarthy. Moreover, Dulles agreed with McCarthy that the Democratic policy-making establishment had leaned too far to the left and had failed to provide adequate support to such anti-Communist stalwarts as Chinese Nationalist leader CHIANG Kai-shek.

Dulles also appears to have been frightened that McCarthy would continue the attacks upon the State Department that had virtually paralyzed U.S. foreign policy in the closing months of the Truman administration. Soon after assuming office at State, Dulles informed an aide that he wished "to find some basis for cooperation with McCarthy." His hopes for cooperation nearly vanished at once, however, when Eisenhower nominated Charles BOHLEN as U.S. ambassador to the Soviet Union. Bohlen's nomination was opposed vigorously by McCarthy and the conservative Republican coterie in the Senate, largely because Bohlen had served as an adviser to President Franklin Delano Roosevelt at the YALTA Conference in 1945. The Senate eventually approved Bohlen's nomination, but the scuffle over confirmation convinced Dulles that he could not afford to antagonize McCarthy unnecessarily. "So strong were [Dulles'] preoccupations with his job and staying in it," observed Bohlen, "that this affected his attitudes in actions" in virtually every area of the department's operations.

Dulles therefore deferred to the anti-Communist zealots in the area of employee security. The State Department had been ravaged by accusations of Communist sympathies during the Truman administration, and Dulles had no intention of shielding any Department officials whose loyalty was even slightly dubious. In this matter, Dulles followed the lead established by Eisenhower, who proclaimed in January 1953 that his administration intended to be sensitive to the "relationship between security problems and foreign relations." Besides, both Dulles and Eisenhower agreed that the United States was facing an extraordinary danger from abroad in the early 1950s, and in such circumstances prudence dictated that government set aside individual rights for the sake of increased security.

As an ideologue, Dulles had little interest in personnel affairs anyway; therefore, he was not reluctant to delegate responsibility to subordinates such as Scott MCLEOD, the State Department's chief security officer, despite the fact that McLeod subsequently ran amok in ferreting out alleged subversives. In the first two years of Dulles' tenure as secretary, investigations by McLeod and others led to the resignation of several hundred State Department employees.

Among the most celebrated cases were those of Far East experts John Carter VINCENT and John Paton DAVIES. Although Vincent, a former American consul in China who had criticized the Nationalist regime of Chiang Kai-shek for its corruption and inefficiency, had been cleared by both a special Senate subcommittee and a State Department loyalty review board, the Civil Service Commission's LOYALTY REVIEW BOARD claimed in December 1952 that there existed "reasonable doubt as to his loyalty to the Government of the United States." Shortly after taking office in January 1953, Dulles determined on his own initiative that Vincent—though not disloyal or a security risk—had been guilty of poor judgment and "a failure to meet the standard which is demanded of a Foreign Service Officer of his experience and responsibility at this critical time." Much to the dismay of Republican conservatives in Congress, Dulles allowed Vincent an opportunity to resign and keep his pension. From the Democratic side, Dulles' action in the Vincent case also outraged former Secretary of State Dean ACHESON, who claimed that "Mr. Dulles' six predecessors, under all of whom Mr. Vincent had served in the China field, did not find his judgment or services defective or substandard." Dulles' inflexible brand of anti-Communism, however, was far removed from Acheson's more realistic approach.

Davies, too, had grown disillusioned with Chiang Kai-shek and had urged that the United States seek an accommodation with the Chinese Communist regime of MAO Zhedong. In November 1953, McCarthy assailed Davies as "part and parcel of the old Acheson-LATTIMORE-Vincent-WHITE-HISS group which did so much toward delivering our Chinese friends into Communist hands." To validate his own anti-Communist credentials, Dulles convened a new security investigation into Davies' background. Although the board cleared Davies of all charges of disloyalty, it recommended his dismissal from the foreign service due to "a definite lack of judgment, discretion, and reliability." When Davies refused to resign voluntarily, Dulles abruptly dismissed him.

Dulles found himself embroiled in yet another controversy when he intervened in the dispute over the activities of the State Department's INTERNATIONAL INFORMATION AGENCY (IIA). McCarthy had assailed the State Department for including works by alleged Communists in the IIA libraries abroad, and two of McCarthy's leading subordinates, Roy COHN and G. David SCHINE, had taken a well-publicized tour of the department's libraries in Europe in 1953, during which they protested—with a maximum of publicity—the department's selection of reading matter. After initially attempting to distance himself from the entire brouhaha, Dulles attempted to follow a middle course in the matter, refusing to bow to the extreme demands of the McCarthyites while weeding out any volumes that he felt did not advance the diplomatic objectives of the United States. In March 1953, Dulles informed the head of the IIA that volumes by Communist authors should be used "only with great care" and that magazines "receptive to international Communist propaganda," along with any works critical of the United States, should be prohibited altogether. When some IIA librarians responded by actually burning a handful of allegedly anti-American books, Dulles accused them of deliberately overreacting in an effort "to discredit the anti-Communist policy by trying to make it appear absurd."

After McCarthy's censure by the Senate in 1954, Dulles continued to follow a moralistic and inflexible anti-Communist line in foreign policy. He steadfastly refused to acknowledge the Communist regime in China and twice threatened to use nuclear weapons to defend the Nationalist Chinese presence on the offshore islands of Quemoy and Matsu. Dulles also actively promoted the Eisenhower Doctrine, which provided the President with the authority to employ military force unilaterally to support American interests in the Middle East. As a result, Eisenhower dispatched U.S. Marines to the war-wracked state of Lebanon in the summer of 1958 to support the right-wing government of Camille Chamoun.

In December 1957, Dulles entered Walter Reed Hospital in Washington, D.C., suffering from intestinal difficulties. Doctors discovered that he had cancer, and in April 1958 Dulles resigned from the cabinet. He died in his sleep on May 24, 1959.

# E

**Eastland, James Oliver** (1904–1988) A conservative Democratic senator from Mississippi, James Eastland became one of the Senate's leading exponents of the theory that the civil rights movement in the United States was largely the product of Communist agitation. Born in Doddsville, Mississippi, Eastland grew up in a small town just outside the state capital of Jackson. Between 1922 and 1927, Eastland attended the University of Mississippi, Vanderbilt University, and the University of Alabama. In 1927, Eastland was admitted to the Mississippi bar and entered private practice in his home town of Forest, Mississippi. At the age of 24, he was elected to the Mississippi State House of Representatives, where he served for four

Senator James Eastland of Mississippi claimed to see Communist influences behind the civil rights movement in the South.

years before retiring to devote his time to supervising his cotton plantation in Ruleville.

When Senator Pat Harrison of Mississippi died unexpectedly in 1941, Governor Paul Johnson appointed Eastland to fill Harrison's seat until a special election could be held. With strong support from the state's agricultural community, Eastland subsequently won election to a full term in the U.S. Senate in 1942. In the Senate, he focused his attention on the interests of his state's farming constitutency and on obstructing all attempts to advance the cause of civil rights among the region's black community. In foreign affairs, Eastland generally followed an internationalist lead, though in the postwar period he emerged as a strong opponent of Soviet expansionism. In the autumn of 1948, Eastland broke with the Democratic Party over the issue of civil rights and refused to support the reelection of President Harry S. TRUMAN. Instead, Eastman supported the Dixiecrat ticket of Senators John Sparkman of Alabama and Strom Thurmond of South Carolina. Eastland himself won reelection to the Senate in 1948 as a "States Rights Democrat."

As the anti-Communist drive in the United States gathered momentum in the late 1940s, Eastland emerged as one of the leading southern supporters of the crusade. In 1950–51, he joined fellow renegade Democrat Senator Patrick MCCARRAN of Nevada in calling for the resignation of Secretary of State Dean ACHESON, whom Eastland accused of sympathizing with pro-Soviet advisers in the State Department. When the Senate formed the Internal Security Subcommittee in December 1950, Eastland was named one of the panel's original members. Although he refused to support Senator Joseph MCCARTHY during the Senate censure debate in the autumn of 1954, he did find common ideological ground with the Wisconsin senator in assailing those decisions of the U.S. Supreme Court that defended the civil rights and civil liberties of Americans. While McCarthy tended to ascribe the Court's decisions to incompetence, however, Eastland characterized the Court's record as "one pro-communist decision after another," and blamed its bias on "some secret, but very poweful Communist or pro-communist influence."

Eastland was particularly incensed by the Court's ruling in the case of *Brown v. Board of Education of Topeka, Kansas* in 1954, which paved the way for the desegregation of public schools in the United States. Chief Justice Earl WARREN's decision, claimed Eastland, cited experts with obvious ties to "the worldwide Communist conspiracy"; the fact that the Court had based its ruling upon "pro-communist" sources, Eastland argued, meant that the decision need not be obeyed.

In 1955, Eastland assumed the chairmanship of the Internal Security Subcommittee and embarked upon a crusade to seek out Communist influences behind such liberal organizations as the Southern Conference Education Fund (the successor to the SOUTHERN CONFERENCE ON HUMAN WELFARE) and the Highlander Folk School of Monteagle, Tennessee, an institution that attempted to promote the growth of labor unions throughout the South. In his testimony before the HOUSE COMMITTEE ON UN-AMERICAN ACTIVITIES (HUAC) in 1956, African-American singer and activist Paul ROBESON sought to point out the incongruence of Eastland's pursuit of subversive influences in America. Why, wondered Robeson, did not HUAC "investigate the truly 'un-American' activities of Eastland and his gang, to whom the Constitution is a scrap of paper when invoked by the Negro people and to whom defiance of the Supreme Court is a racial duty? And how can Eastland pretend concern over the internal security of our country while he supports the most brual assaults on 15 million Americans by the White Citizens' Councils and the Ku Klux Klan?"

As the anti-Communist hysteria subsided in the later years of the EISENHOWER administra-

tion, Eastland found it increasingly difficult to use the Communism issue in his fight to uphold white supremacy. In 1964–65, Congress passed a series of landmark civil rights measures initiated by President Lyndon B. JOHNSON, a former Senate colleague of Eastland. Eastland remained in the Senate for a total of six terms until his retirement in 1979. He died seven years later.

**Einstein, Albert** (1879–1955)  Probably the most famous scientist of the twentieth century, Albert Einstein was born in Ulm, Germany, and studied mathematics and physics at the Swiss Polytechnic Institute in Zurich. After his graduation in 1900, Einstein worked for seven years as an examiner at the Swiss patent office in Bern. It was during this time (1902–1909) that he published three papers in the German scientific periodical *Annalen der Physik* on quantum mechanics, relativity, and Brownian motion; together, these three articles helped lay the foundations for modern physics.

From 1909 to 1933, Einstein taught at several universities in Switzerland and Germany. While he was visiting England and the United States in 1933, the Nazi government of Germany revoked his citizenship, dismissed him from his teaching positions, and confiscated his property. Einstein promptly accepted an invitation to join the staff of the Institute for Advanced Study in Princeton, New Jersey, and spent the remainder of his life in Princeton. In 1940, Einstein became a U.S. citizen.

Although he had played a role in persuading the Roosevelt administration to pursue the development of an atomic bomb (in case the Nazis should obtain a similar weapon), Einstein never approved of the use of the bomb against the civilian populations of Hiroshima and Nagasaki, Japan. A lifelong socialist and pacifist and a convert to the cause of international cooperation, Einstein also witnessed with growing dismay the drift of postwar America toward confrontation with the Soviet Union. Reliance upon stockpiles of nuclear weapons, Einstein believed, could never bring lasting peace. He

**Albert Einstein answering questions at a news conference.**

feared that the United States was replacing Germany as the world's most powerful nation, dedicated to the search for "security through superior force, whatever the cost." His criticisms of American policy provoked a bitter reaction from conservatives in Congress, including the violently anti-Semitic John RANKIN of Alabama, who denounced Einstein in a House speech as a "foreign-born agitator" and suggested that "it's about time the American people got wise to Einstein."

Einstein did not hesitate to voice his opposition to the growing anti-Communist fervor in the United States in the late 1940s. He was one of the original sponsors of the Committee of One Thousand, the short-lived successor to the COMMITTEE FOR THE FIRST AMENDMENT, and along with writers such as E.B. White and Thomas Mann, Einstein signed statements in the fall of 1948 expressing his support for the HOLLYWOOD TEN in their legal battle against the HOUSE COMMITTEE ON UN-AMERICAN ACTIVITIES (HUAC). On February 1, 1950, Einstein joined fourteen other prominent scientists and authors in protesting the punishment meted out to several defense lawyers for the COMMUNIST PARTY leaders who had been convicted un-

der the first of the SMITH ACT trials. Such persecution of defense attorneys, Einstein pointed out, could eventually destroy the constitutional guarantees of a fair trial and adequate legal counsel.

Einstein was equally disturbed by the TRUMAN administration's commitment to the development of a hydrogen bomb. Following the first Soviet nuclear test explosion in 1949, Truman stepped up the pace of the United States' H-bomb project. Like fellow physicist J. Robert OPPENHEIMER, Einstein opposed the hydrogen-bomb research program and appeared on national television on February 12, 1950, to warn Americans that an uncontrolled arms race between the United States and the Soviet Union would likely lead to the complete destruction of civilization.

On the day following Einstein's televised appeal, FBI Director J. Edgar HOOVER asked his staff to compile a summary of all the information on Einstein in the bureau's files. Hoover received the file on February 15; in it, he found a wealth of accusations and hostile comments, including a report from an FBI informant in Phoenix, Arizona, that in the 1930s Einstein had been a "personal courier from Communist Party headquarters" who conveyed secret messages throughout the United States. The report charged that Einstein belonged to more than thirty organizations that had been cited by the attorney general or HUAC. "Einstein has made public statements lauding the scientific achievements of Russia," it continued, "and has indicated that it is the only country in which equality was not an empty phrase. He has opposed militarism and universal military training in the United States and has espoused world government. In 1948, he indicated to the Polish ambassador that the United States was not a free country and that his activities were carefully scrutinized."

FBI agents spent the next five years following up dozens of leads that cast doubt on Einstein's loyalty to the United States. Several informants attempted to place Einstein in Soviet espionage rings operating in Berlin in the 1920s and 1930s, but the sources for all these rumors proved to have grudges against Einstein for personal reasons. Finally, in March 1955, after assembling a file of more than 1,200 pages, the FBI concluded that there was no evidence that Einstein was a subversive and that additional investigation would not be warranted. Meanwhile, officials of the Immigration and Naturalization Service had been engaged in a similar search for information that might permit the agency to revoke the citizenship of Einstein and his secretary, Helen Dukas. They, too, failed to find anything more than hearsay from disgruntled individuals about Einstein's past activities.

Einstein further enraged anti-Communist zealots when he supported efforts to commute the death sentences of Ethel and Julius ROSENBERG, who had been judged guilty of passing atomic secrets to the Soviet Union. On December 23, 1952, Einstein dispatched a confidential plea for clemency to Judge Irving R. Kaufman, who had presided over the Rosenberg case; Kaufman promptly turned the letter over to the New York office of the FBI. Three weeks later, Einstein addressed a public appeal to President Harry S. TRUMAN, claiming that the Rosenbergs had been convicted in an atmosphere of political passion and that their punishment would be wholly disproportionate to their alleged crime— all to no avail: the Rosenbergs were executed on June 18, 1953.

Due to Einstein's repeated public stands in favor of civil liberties, numerous Americans facing inquiries by anti-Communist investigators turned to the famous physicist for support or advice. For the most part, Einstein demurred, primarily because of his advancing age and uncertain health. Einstein himself had never been subpoenaed by any congressional committees; he claimed half-jokingly that this was because he was "an incorrigible nonconformist whose nonconformism in a remote field of endeavor [i.e., theoretical physics] no Senatorial committee has as yet felt impelled to tackle."

In the spring of 1953, however, a New York schoolteacher named William Fruenglass who was under investigation by HUAC wrote to Einstein asking for advice and a public statement that might help rally the forces of academic freedom. Einstein replied with a letter that was published in *The New York Times* on June 12. In it, he noted that "reactionary politicians" were attempting "to suppress the freedom of teaching and to deprive of their positions all those who do not prove submissive, i.e., to starve them out."

> What ought the minority of intellectuals to do against this evil? Frankly, I can only see the revolutionary way of non-co-operation in the sense of Gandhi's. Every intellectual who is called before one of the committees ought to refuse to testify; i.e., he must be prepared for jail and economic ruin, in short, for the sacrifice of his personal welfare in the interest of the cultural welfare of his country.

Einstein urged that witnesses abjure the Fifth Amendment and take their stand instead "on the assertion that it is shameful for a blameless citizen to submit to such an inquisition and that this kind of inquisition violates the spirit of the Constitution. If enough people are ready to take this grave step they will be successful. If not, then the intellectuals of this country deserve nothing better than the slavery which is intended for them."

The publication of this letter produced a flood of newspaper editorials across the nation condemning Einstein. On June 22, Senator Joseph MCCARTHY compared Einstein's advice to the counsel provided by Communist lawyers to their clients when testifying before his subcommittee; that is, remain silent about espionage and sabotage. "I may say," McCarthy charged, "that any American, I don't care whether their name is Einstein or John Jones, who would advise American citizens to keep secret information which they may have about espionage and sabotage— that man is just a disloyal American."

Undaunted, Einstein continued to press the cause of academic freedom. In June 1954, he issued another statement supporting his Princeton colleague J. Robert Oppenheimer after the ATOMIC ENERGY COMMISSION voted to revoke Oppenheimer's security clearance. In the face of such arbitrary actions by the government, it seemed quite clear to Einstein that "America is incomparably less endangered by its own Communists than by the hysterical hunt for the few Communists there are here." Less than a year later, Einstein died of a heart ailment.

## Eisenhower, Dwight David (1890–1969)

President of the United States from 1953 to 1961—at the height of the controversy over Communism in America—Dwight David Eisenhower was one of the few career military officers who have succeeded at the highest levels of American politics. Born in Denison, Texas, Eisenhower was christened David Dwight Eisenhower, but his mother changed the order of his first two names to avoid confusion with his father, who was also named David. When Eisenhower was two years old, his family moved to Abilene, Kansas, where his father obtained a job in a creamery. The Eisenhower family also kept a two-and-a-half-acre farm that Eishenhower and his four brothers helped to maintain.

Following his graduation from high school in 1909, Eisenhower worked at a variety of odd jobs until he obtained an appointment to the U.S. Military Academy at West Point. Here, Eisenhower lettered in baseball and football but failed to distinguish himself academically, graduating 61st in a class of 164. He served in several different infantry posts as an instructor and commander in Texas, Georgia, and Kansas before and during World War I, and earned the Distinguished Service Medal in 1919. From 1920 to 1924, Eisenhower served as an executive officer at a U.S. military base in the Panama Canal Zone. Upon his return to the United States, he attended the Army's Command and General

President Dwight David Eisenhower, who sought to curb the power of Joe McCarthy while advancing the anti-Communist crusade.

Staff School at Fort Leavenworth, Kansas, from which he graduated first in his class a year later.

Following his graduation from the Army War College, Eisenhower was appointed assistant executive officer of the assistant secretary of war in Washington in 1929. The next year, he was chosen by General Douglas MACARTHUR, then Army chief of staff, to serve as one of his staff officers. Eisenhower served with MacArthur in Washington for five years and then accompanied MacArthur to the Philippines in 1935 when the general was appointed military adviser of the commonwealth government of those islands. Shortly after the outbreak of war in Europe in the autumn of 1939, Eisenhower returned to the United States. Upon the entrance of the United States into the war in December 1941, Eisenhower was appointed chief of the war plans division by Chief of Staff George Catlett MAR-SHALL.

Marshall continued to promote Eisenhower to a succession of increasingly responsible posts throughout the war. In March 1942, Eisenhower was named chief of operations for the Army and three months later became commanding general of the European Theater of Operations, with headquarters in London. In November of the same year, Eisenhower was appointed Allied commander in chief, North Africa. From that post, he directed the Allied victory over Nazi troops in North Africa in May 1943. Eisenhower then moved on to orchestrate the Allied invasion of Italy a month later. Not surprisingly, Roosevelt and Marshall selected Eisenhower to lead the Allied invasion of Europe in June 1944. In December of that year, Roosevelt named Eisenhower general of the Army. Following the German surrender in May 1945, Eisenhower also became the first non-Russian—and only the eighth man in history—to receive the highest military award of the Soviet Union, the jeweled Order of Victory.

In November 1945, President Harry S. TRUMAN recalled Eisenhower to Washington to serve as the Army's chief of staff, a position he held until February 1948. Three months later, Eisenhower retired from the Army and, in June 1948, accepted the position of president of Columbia University. He was recalled to the Army, however, in December 1950 when the twelve nations of the newly established North Atlantic Treaty Organization (NATO) asked President Truman to permit Eisenhower to command NATO forces. Eisenhower remained commander of NATO until May 1952 when he resigned to seek the nomination of the Republican Party as its presidential candidate.

During the campaign of 1952, Eisenhower expressed the frustration that millions of Americans felt over increasing government interference in their lives and the steady drumbeat of bad news in international affairs. After the sacrifices of the Great Depression and World War II, Americans hoped that they would be able to live in peace and security. The COLD WAR, continuing agitation for social reform, and evidence of Communist subversion at home dashed those hopes. As one observer noted, Eisenhower "may not always have had his facts quite right, but like his audiences he knew something had gone wrong for America, and it had put his dander up." Columnist Marquis Childs observed that Eisenhower represented "strength, triumph, unswerving confidence. Millions were happy to take him on faith, on his face, on his smile, on the image of American manhood, on the happy virtue of his family life."

As the standard-bearer of the Republican Party, Eisenhower inherited a significant element of conservatives who had long been frustrated by the perceived failures of the Democratic administrations of Franklin Roosevelt and Harry Truman. Eisenhower himself was a moderate Republican, and he displayed little affection for the more fanatical members of his party's right wing. When Senator William JENNER of Indiana attempted to embrace Eisenhower during a campaign appearance in Indianapolis, Eisenhower pulled away in disgust and threatened to "knock him right off the platform" if Jenner touched him again; "I felt dirty from the touch of the man," he explained later. When photographers asked him to pose with Senator Joseph MCCARTHY in Wisconsin, Eisenhower refused, saying that "the differences between me and Senator McCarthy are well known to him and to me, and we have discussed them." Much to the dismay of his admirers, however, Eisenhower refused to condemn McCarthy for the Wisconsin senator's violent and scurrilous attack upon George Marshall, Eisenhower's former mentor in the armed forces who had become secretary of state and subsequently secretary of defense in the Truman administration.

Eisenhower captured the White House in a landslide victory over Democratic nominee Adlai STEVENSON, but even as President he refused to confront or denounce McCarthy directly. "I will not get into the gutter with that guy," he told his advisers. The relationship between Eisenhower and McCarthy was captured succinctly by *Washington Post* editorial cartoonist Herbert BLOCK in a famous cartoon which portrayed Eisenhower brandishing a feather and warning, "Have a care, sir!" while McCarthy stood leering, carrying a bucket filled with the tar of slander and innuendo.

For his part, McCarthy refused to permit party loyalty to a Republican president to influence his choice of targets in his crusade against Communism. One of the Eisenhower administration's first diplomatic appointments in February 1953 was the nomination of Charles BOHLEN as ambassador to the Soviet Union. While most informed observers recognized Bohlen as one of the nation's leading authorities on the USSR, McCarthy, Jenner, and the rest of the Republican right wing in the Senate felt that he was tainted by his association with the Roosevelt administration. In particular, they were angry that Eisenhower would nominate a man who had served as a member of the American delegation to the YALTA conference in March 1945, where Roosevelt—according to the right-wing theory—virtually abandoned Eastern Europe to Soviet control in the postwar world. For several days, the nomination appeared to be in jeopardy as the Senate Foreign Relations Committee (SFRC) and Secretary of State John Foster DULLES wavered in their support of Bohlen, but Eisenhower insisted that the administration stand firmly behind its nominee. After Dulles told the committee that he was personally convinced of Bohlen's loyalty, the nomination received the preliminary approval of the SFRC. The Senate eventually approved Bohlen's nomination by an overwhelming margin of 74–13, but the long-term effects of the battle were less one sided. The incident demonstrated clearly that McCarthy and his allies would not refrain from attacking the administration on the issue of Communism in government.

McCarthy followed his assault upon the Bohlen nomination with a threat to investigate the CENTRAL INTELLIGENCE AGENCY (CIA) which he claimed had been infiltrated by Soviet spies. Once again Eisenhower stood firm, refusing McCarthy's request to open the agency's records for his inspection. Eisenhower did, however, permit the CIA to carry out an internal purge of its employees to remove any impression of subversion. Eisenhower proved less willing to resist McCarthy's investigation of the INTERNATIONAL INFORMATION AGENCY (IIA) a branch of the State Department that operated libraries overseas and supervised the activities of the VOICE OF AMERICA. In February 1953, McCarthy launched his inquiry into the IIA's activities and soon claimed to have discovered scores of books by Communist authors on the shelves of its overseas libraries. Eisenhower remained aloof from the controversy until June 14, when he delivered a speech at DARTMOUTH COLLEGE in which he urged his audience not to join "the book burners." "Don't think that you are going to conceal faults by concealing evidence that they ever existed," Eisenhower said. "Don't be afraid to go in your library and read every book as long as any document does not offend our own ideas of decency. That should be the only censorship." Within a week, however, Eisenhower had retreated from his Dartmouth stand. At a press conference three days after the speech, Eisenhower refused to discuss McCarthy by name, and explained that he had not meant to suggest that the U.S. government should subsidize or promote books that treated Communism in a sympathetic manner.

Throughout 1953, Eisenhower attempted to outflank McCarthy and the Republican right by establishing the credentials of his administration as an effective force against Communist subversion. Although Eisenhower resisted a suggestion by Vice President Richard NIXON that the White House reopen the case of Alger HISS, the President did allow Attorney General Herbert BROWNELL to intimate that the Truman administration had knowingly appointed a Communist agent named Harry Dexter WHITE as executive director of the International Monetary Fund. This foray backfired, however, when the resulting public outcry forced Eisenhower to admit in a press conference that he was unaware of the details of the White case.

In the sensitive area of federal employee loyalty programs, Eisenhower deferred to pressure from the Republican Party right wing when he issued EXECUTIVE ORDER 10450 on April 27, 1953. Far more stringent that the orders Truman had promulgated, EO 10450 declared that a federal employee's hiring and retention had to be "clearly consistent with the interests of national security." It further provided that investigations would be carried out on all new applicants for federal employment; that employees of "sensitive" agencies were required to undergo a full field investigation of the personal backgrounds and associates; that any information indicating that an employee might represent a security risk would result in the immediate suspension of that employee; and that all employees who had been cleared after full field investigations during the Truman administration would have to be investigated once again on the grounds that the Democrats' administration of the loyalty program had been either incompetent or deliberately misleading.

Yet, Eisenhower did attempt to ensure that the operation of the loyalty program did not violate the legitimate rights of government employees. In March 1954, the President issued a directive that instructed cabinet officials to "observe every requirement of law and ethics" in administering the new loyalty guidelines. Eisenhower also repeatedly recommended that individuals who had records of long service in the government and against whom there was "no clear finding of 'risk' " should be transferred to nonsensitive positions instead of being removed altogether from the federal payroll.

More than any other event, Joseph McCarthy's investigation of Communist infiltration of the United States Army convinced the President that the Wisconsin senator was a danger to American security. As the hearings on McCarthy's charges against the Army began in the spring of 1954, Eisenhower grew more willing to openly confront McCarthy. At one point, he apparently wished to issue a statement that the anti-Communist witch hunters were as dangerous as their Communist foes, but Nixon convinced him to withhold his criticism. On April 5, 1954, Eisenhower did remind a national television audience that Communists constituted only a tiny minority of the nation's population and that the continued use of unsubstantiated charges of disloyalty and subversion by senators and members of Congress were likely to produce "grave offenses" against the rights of individuals.

To protect White House officials from McCarthy's wide-ranging inquiries during the ARMY-MCCARTHY HEARINGS, Eisenhower issued an executive order on May 17 which forbade Defense Department officials from testifying about their conversations with other White House employees. When McCarthy publicly urged executive employees to ignore Eisenhower's directive, the President exploded in anger. Comparing McCarthy to Adolf Hitler, Eisenhower privately characterized McCarthy's statement as "the most disloyal act . . . [ever made] by anyone in the government of the United States." In an address at Columbia University several days later, Eisenhower delivered yet another warning against the tactics of "hysteria and intimidation" in the fight against subversion.

By the conclusion of the Army-McCarthy hearings in the summer of 1954, McCarthy had effectively destroyed himself as an effective political force. During the ensuing debate over the motion of censure against McCarthy offered by Republican Senator Ralph FLANDERS of Vermont, Eisenhower studiously refrained from taking a public stand on either side; any pressure from the White House, he feared, might shatter the Republican party irrevocably and create a backlash of support for the Wisconsin senator. Yet, after the Senate voted on December 2, 1954, to condemn McCarthy for contempt, Eisenhower invited Senator Arthur WATKINS of Utah—the chairman of the committee that had investigated the charges against McCarthy—to the White House and issued a statement commending Watkins' handling of the matter.

As public support for the anti-Communist crusade seemed to wane in the wake of McCarthy's fall, Eisenhower generally avoided any attempt to revive the issue. At most, the President paid lip service to the concerns of the ultraconservative right by promising (as in the State of the Union Address in 1956) that the White House would "not relax its efforts to deal forthrightly and vigorously in protection of this government and its citizens against subversion." In 1958, Eisenhower signed a congressional resolution establishing a national Loyalty Day. Yet, the administration also approved new regulations designed to afford greater legal protection to employees accused of disloyalty or subversion. The best indication of Eisenhower's lack of interest in the subject of employee loyalty was the fact that no government employee was suspended from the federal service under Executive Order 10450 during the President's second term (1957–1961).

After Eisenhower left the White House, his successor, President John F. KENNEDY, asked Congress to restore Eisenhower's rank as general of the Army. Congress agreed, and on March 22, 1961, Eisenhower once again became a general of the line. He spent the last eight years of his life in retirement with his wife, Mamie Doud Eisenhower, at their farm in Gettysburg, Pennsylvania.

**Eisler, Gerhart** (1897–1968)   One of the first Communist targets of the HOUSE COMMITTEE ON UN-AMERICAN ACTIVITIES (HUAC) in the post-World War II era, Gerhart Eisler was accused by several ex-Communist witnesses of being the leading representative of the Communist International (Comintern) in the United States. A native of Leipzig, Germany, Eisler joined the Communist Party after returning from the front at the end of World War I in November 1918. He moved to Berlin in 1920,

Gerhart Eisler (right), whom the House Committee on Un-American Activities identified as the leading Soviet agent in the United States.

where he helped organize the German Communist Party and disseminate propaganda. Following the death of Vladimir Lenin and the rise to power of Joseph STALIN in the late 1920s, Eisler fell into disgrace for a brief time because of his anti-Stalinist views. He was protected by the Soviet leader Nikolai Bukharin, however, and by 1931 Eisler had managed to rehabilitate himself through his work as an emissary to China, where he supervised the purge of rebellious members of the Chinese Communist Party.

According to the testimony of his sister, who recruited Eisler into the Communist Party and then broke with the party in 1926, Eisler first traveled to the United States in 1934. He returned to the United States in 1936 to help organize POPULAR FRONT activities at the behest of the Comintern. Eisler survived the Stalinist purges of the late 1930s (although his mentor Bukharin did not) and in 1941 came back to the United States, where he remained for the duration of World War II.

On October 13, 1946, Louis BUDENZ, a former member of the COMMUNIST PARTY OF THE UNITED STATES OF AMERICA, stated on a Detroit radio broadcast that there was a secret agent of the Kremlin in the United States from whom all American Communists took their orders. Budenz subsequently identified this agent as Eisler, whom he claimed had used the alias of Hans Berger. Eisler had, in fact, been under surveillance by the FBI for some time; the bureau had identified him as a liaison between the CPUSA and the Comintern and claimed that he had been receiving financial support from the JOINT ANTI-FASCIST REFUGEE COMMITTEE, an organization that was also under investigation for subversive activities. Eisler had been planning to leave the United States for Leipzig in late October, but Budenz's bombshell persuaded American authorities to cancel his exit permit. Subsequent testimony before HUAC by Budenz and other witnesses during the next two months provided committee investigators with sufficient evidence to issue a subpoena for Eisler's appearance.

Eisler duly appeared before HUAC on February 6, 1947, but he refused to answer any questions or even to be sworn in as a witness. "I am a political prisoner in the United States," he argued. "I have to do nothing. A political prisoner has to do nothing." Instead, Eisler asked permission to read a brief "three-minute" statement that turned out to be twenty legal pages long. Chairman J. Parnell THOMAS promised Eisler that he could read his statement after he was sworn in, but Eisler still refused. The committee thereupon voted to cite Eisler for contempt. On February 18, 1947, Congressman Richard NIXON, a member of HUAC, formally introduced a resolution to cite Eisler for contempt of Congress. (This was, incidentally, Nixon's first speech in the House.) The resolution passed almost unanimously, and Eisler was later found guilty of contempt, fined $1,000, and sentenced to one year in jail.

Insisting that he was "a victim of a witch-hunting hysteria in this country," Eisler jumped bail and stowed away aboard a Polish ocean liner on May 7, 1949. He was arrested when the ship reached Southampton, England, but British authorities decided to permit him to proceed to East Germany. He spent most of the remainder of his life in the German Democratic Republic.

**Eisler, Hanns** (1898–1962)  One of the most accomplished composers of the twentieth century, Hanns Eisler was born in Leipzig, Germany. He attended the Conservatory of the City of Vienna and studied under Arnold Schoenberg. Eisler fought in the Austrian Army in World War I and then returned to the conservatory in Vienna as a professor of music. In 1924 Eisler left Austria and moved to Berlin, where he collaborated with numerous lyricists—notably Bertolt BRECHT—in writing songs whose lyrics promoted the concept of a workers' revolution. Although he considered himself primarily an artist (and therefore ineffectual in political affairs), Eisler did join the Communist Party in Germany in 1926. By his own account, he never attended any party meetings, and within a year he had drifted away from the party. Because he never paid any dues, he assumed his membership had simply lapsed.

During the late 1920s and early 1930s, Eisler visited the Soviet Union three times, to lecture, give concerts, and compose scores for several Soviet films. Like Brecht, he found it necessary to flee Germany once the Nazi Party seized power in 1932. Eisler spent the next several years living in London and Paris, touring the United States once in 1935. In cooperation with other composers, he sought to organize a group of antifascist artists into an International Music Bureau, but the project fell through. Throughout this period, however, Eisler continued to write songs that praised the Soviet revolution and promoted the cause of the proletariat. "I think in music I can enlighten and help people in distress in their fight for their rights," Eisler explained. "The truth is songs cannot destroy Fascism, but they are necessary."

In 1940, Eisler applied for a visa to enter the United States. When the State Department hesitated because of Eisler's leftist background, a number of Hollywood artists, including author

Clifford ODETS and director George Cukor, wrote testimonials on his behalf. Eventually Eisler did receive his visa and settled in Hollywood, where he wrote the scores for numerous films, including *None But the Lonely Heart, Hangmen Also Die, Scandal in Paris, Deadline at Dawn,* and *So Well Remembered.* For a time, Eisler was also employed as professor of music at the New School for Social Research in Manhattan; while in New York, he received a Rockefeller grant to support him while continuing his creative efforts.

When the HOUSE COMMITTEE ON UN-AMERICAN ACTIVITIES (HUAC) embarked on its first full-scale investigation of Communism in the United States in late 1946, one of their prime targets was Gerhart EISLER, brother of Hanns. An ex-Communist witness, Louis BUDENZ, identified Gerhart Eisler as "the real head of Communism in America." HUAC questioned Gerhart in February 1947; not surprisingly, they subpoenaed his brother Hanns several months later. Hanns Eisler's ties to the Hollywood community also encouraged the committee to extend its investigation into Communist influence in the motion picture industry.

Hanns Eisler testified before HUAC on September 24, 1947. Eisler, who resented the rumors and leaks concerning his background that had emanated from the committee over the past year, asked permission to read a prepared statement. After glancing at the statement, HUAC Chairman J. Parnell THOMAS informed Eisler that he would not permit the witness to read it. The goal of the committee's chief investigator Robert STRIPLING was to prove that Eisler was, in his words, "the Karl Marx of Communism in the musical field." ("I would be flattered," was Eisler's response to the comparison.) Toward that end, Stripling cited numerous references to Eisler's revolutionary sympathies in articles from Communist publications such as the *DAILY WORKER* and *Soviet Music.* Stripling also listed a series of Communist-front gatherings which Eisler had attended—mostly in Europe, prior to 1940—and cited pro-Communist

songs that Eisler had cowritten with various lyricists, including "The Comintern March," "Fifty Thousand Strong," and "We're Marching, O Comrades."

Eisler acknowledged that he had written the music to the songs named by Stripling, but he reminded the committee that he had never written any lyrics. "Don't forget," he declared at one point, "this is music, and nothing else." After telling the committee point-blank that he was not a member of the Communist Party and had not been a member since 1926, Eisler noted that "I don't ask anybody is he a Communist or not when I go to a club and speak. I was in many clubs and in many concerts. I don't check up on them." As he warmed to his own defense, Eisler praised Joseph STALIN ("I think that Stalin is one of the greatest historical personalities of our time") and told the committee that he admired Communist revolutionaries of other nations. "I would be a swindler if I called myself a Communist," Eisler said. "I have no right. The Communist underground workers in every country have proven that they are heroes. I am not a hero. I am a composer."

At the conclusion of the hearing, Chairman Thomas instructed Eisler to remain in the United States until the committee gave him permission to leave. Meanwhile, actor Charlie CHAPLIN sent a telegram to Pablo Picasso in France, asking him to organize a committee in Eisler's defense; in November, a group of renowned European artists, including Picasso, Matisse, Jean Cocteau, and Louis Aragon, sent a strongly worded protest against HUAC's treatment of Eisler to the U.S. Embassy in Paris.

Late in 1948, the Department of Justice issued orders to deport Hanns Eisler and his wife. The government permitted the Eislers to leave the United States voluntarily on their pledge to never return. Eisler subsequently received a hero's welcome in the German Democratic Republic, for which he composed the national anthem. He was honored by the publication of his compositions in ten massive volumes, and Eisler's treatise on film scoring, entitled *Compos-*

*ing for the Films,* was published by Oxford University Press in 1947.

## Emergency Civil Liberties Committee

The Emergency Civil Liberties Committee (ECLC) was founded in 1951 by a coterie of academics, scientists, writers, and journalists who were alarmed by the assaults on American civil liberties by congressional investigating committees, particularly the HOUSE COMMITTEE ON UN-AMERICAN ACTIVITIES (HUAC). Many of the original sponsors of the ECLC—a group that included Albert EINSTEIN, columnist I. F. Stone, architect Frank Lloyd Wright, historian William Shirer, Carey McWilliams (editor of *The Nation*), and Thomas Emerson of Yale Law School—had previously counted on the AMERICAN CIVIL LIBERTIES UNION (ACLU) to uphold their cause. When the ACLU proved unwilling to defend Communists against the courts and congressional investigators, however, they abandoned that organization and formed the ECLC.

Early in its life, the ECLC passed through a crisis over the refusal of the more extreme members of the organization to disavow Communism. Although they were not Communists and did not defend the repressive Stalinist regime in the Soviet Union (in fact, they condemned Soviet anti-Semitism), they refused to publicly acknowledge their opposition to Marxism on the grounds that statements condemning Communism would only add fuel to the Red-hunting hysteria. As one speaker explained at the ECLC's founding conference, "The danger of political suppression is greater than the danger of political freedom. Repression is always foolish; freedom is always wise."

As one of the few groups of prominent Americans willing to defend the civil liberties of Communists, the ECLC found itself under attack from numerous right-wing groups, including the AMERICAN COMMITTEE FOR CULTURAL FREEDOM. Undaunted, it continued its struggle against HUAC and the courts, fighting contempt citations against its officers and providing legal support for those who resisted the anti-Communist crusade. It dedicated itself in the late 1950s to the abolition of HUAC, prompting the issuance of another investigation by HUAC. Despite the best efforts of both HUAC and the ECLC to put the other out of business, both survived and continued their struggle into the following decade.

## Executive Order 9835

In the late autumn of 1946, a combination of events persuaded President Harry S. TRUMAN to establish a comprehensive federal employee loyalty program. The repercussions from the *AMERASIA* affair, revelations of Soviet espionage in Canada, the success of anti-Communist Republican candidates (who charged the White House with harboring disloyal employees) in the congressional elections of November 1946, and pressure from his own Justice Department led Truman to appoint a Temporary Commission on Employee Loyalty to recommend changes in the existing program that had been fragmented among numerous agencies, each of which had its own loyalty standards and procedures. In establishing the temporary commission on November 25, Truman also hoped to seize the initiative on the loyalty issue from the HOUSE COMMITTEE ON UN-AMERICAN ACTIVITIES (HUAC), whose chairman, J. Parnell THOMAS, had threatened a thorough investigation of Communist influence in government and industry in 1947.

On February 27, 1947, the temporary commission submitted its report. After making a few minor changes, Truman implemented the report on March 22 as Executive Order 9835, establishing the nation's first comprehensive federal employee loyalty program. EO 9835 set up separate loyalty boards within each executive department and created a Civil Service Commission LOYALTY REVIEW BOARD—headed by a conservative Republican, Seth RICHARDSON—with appellate jurisdiction over the individual department boards.

Whenever information indicating disloyalty on the part of a federal employee came to the attention of the Civil Service Commission, it requested the FEDERAL BUREAU OF INVESTIGATION (FBI) to carry out a "full field investigation," a process that emphasized specific charges of "membership in subversive organizations, advocacy of revolution, or habitual contacts with known Communists." The attorney general was granted sole authority to determine which organizations would be listed as subversive or Communist fronts. Following its field investigation, the FBI forwarded its findings to the agency or department review board, which could recommend dismissal. Employees could then appeal dismissals to the head of the department, and finally to the Civil Service Loyalty Review Board.

It should be pointed out that this procedure was less concerned with past associations than with present indications of disloyalty. In the words of the executive order, it was designed to establish whether "on all the evidence, reasonable grounds exist for belief that the person involved is disloyal to the government of the United States." Membership in the COMMUNIST PARTY or Communist-front organizations in the past was not necessarily, in itself, sufficient grounds for dismissal. This reflected the theory—still tenable in 1947—that there were numerous loyal government employees who had belonged to Communist organizations during the period of the antifascist POPULAR FRONT of the 1930s or during World War II, when the Soviet Union was an ally of the United States. Employees who had been Communists in 1945 or later, however, were ruled unfit for government service.

In introducing the new program to the public, President Truman explained that it was not intended to set off a witch hunt. "Rumor, gossip or suspicion will not be sufficient to lead to the dismissal of any employee for disloyalty," Truman declared. "The Government, as the largest employer in the United States, must be the model of a fair employer. It must guarantee that the civil rights of all employees of the Government shall be protected properly and adequately. It is in this spirit that the loyalty program will be enforced." Privately, Truman

gave assurances that if injustices occurred he would modify EO 9835 or even repeal it if necessary.

By early 1951, the backgrounds of approximately 3,167,000 federal employees had been checked and their files cleared with the notation "no disloyal data." Fewer than one-half of 1 percent of government employees had been subjected to a full-scale investigation, and more than two-thirds of those were cleared. Most of the rest resigned before a final verdict was reached; slightly more than 200 were actually dismissed as disloyal. Loyalty Review Board chief Seth Richardson, who had previously alarmed civil libertarians by warning that the "first padlock" on disloyal speech might be placed on "the mouths of teachers and scientists," acknowledged that the loyalty program had uncovered "not one single case" of espionage in the government service.

It was precisely this failure to uncover widespread evidence of disloyalty that led MCCARTHY and his fellow anti-Communist crusaders to insist that the loyalty machinery was defective, and should be replaced by a more stringent program. The Truman administration granted their wish in April 1951 with the implementation of EXECUTIVE ORDER 10241.

**Executive Order 10241**   Issued by President Harry S. TRUMAN on April 28, 1951, Executive Order 10241 was designed to meet conservative criticisms of the administration by tightening the standards of the existing loyalty review program for federal employees as established in 1947 under EXECUTIVE ORDER 9835. Under the new guidelines (which actually represented a reversion to the standards employed during World War II), the government could dismiss any federal employees if there were a "reasonable doubt" of his or her loyalty at any time in the past. No longer did the government need to prove present disloyalty.

As interpreted by former Senator Hiram BINGHAM, whom Truman appointed to head the Civil Service Commission LOYALTY REVIEW

BOARD, Executive Order 10241 was also used to reopen security cases already decided under the previous standard. In 1955, the U.S. Supreme Court ruled that the board had exceeded its authority in taking this action.

If Truman had expected EO 10241 and the appointment of Bingham to assuage Republican critics of his loyalty program, he was disappointed. Instead, the new guidelines actually added to the power of Senator Joseph MCCARTHY's charges of Communist influence in government because all employees whose loyalty was called into question were now likely to be suspended pending further investigation. Further, Bingham's aggressive approach took control of the loyalty program away from the White House. In April 1953, EO 10241 was superseded by EXECUTIVE ORDER 10450.

**Executive Order 10450**   During the 1952 presidential campaign, Republican critics of the Truman administration obtained great political capital from charges that the White House had harbored disloyal federal employees. It was politically imperative, therefore, that President Dwight David EISENHOWER impose a far more stringent loyalty program after taking office in January 1953.

The result, Executive Order 10450, was promulgated on April 27, 1953 and was designed to assuage the concerns of Senator Joseph MCCARTHY and his associates. EO 10450 declared that a federal employees' hiring and retention had to be "clearly consistent with the interests of national security." It further provided that (1) investigations would be carried out on all new applicants for federal employment, whether they were candidates for sensitive or nonsensitive positions; (2) all employees of "sensitive" agencies must undergo a "full field investigation" which involved an FBI check of their personal backgrounds, associates, family relationships, and community activities; (3) all employees who had been cleared after full field investigations during the Truman administration would be investigated yet again; (4) all employees against whom adverse information of any type had been filed would be the subjects of full field investigations; (5) any information indicating that an employee might represent a security risk would result in immediate suspension; and (6) the administration of the order would be placed solely in the hands of government employees.

Critics complained that this program, which clearly placed the burden on an accused employee to prove his innocence, was far too draconian a measure. Former Republican Senator Hiram BINGHAM, a hard-line conservative who had administered the Civil Service Commission LOYALTY REVIEW BOARD under Truman, maintained that it was "just not the American way of doing things." The AMERICAN CIVIL LIBERTIES UNION (ACLU) agreed, noting that federal employees who sat in judgment on accused colleagues were hardly likely to clear anyone who seemed even slightly suspicious because that would bring their own loyalty into question.

The net effect of the order was to intensify the atmosphere of fear and suspicion within the federal bureaucracy and to encourage the public to believe that the problem of Communists in government was worse than it had imagined. Although Executive Order 10450 remained in effect through the end of the Eisenhower administration in January 1961, no federal employee was discharged or suspended under its terms during its final four years.

# F

**Fast, Howard** (1914– ) A prominent American author who achieved fame with his historical novels about the American Revolution and the white man's mistreatment of Native Americans, Howard Fast was also a left-wing activist who was accused of Communist sympathies by the HOUSE COMMITTEE ON UN-AMERICAN ACTIVITIES (HUAC) in 1950.

Born in New York, Fast received a public school education and, upon graduation from high school, spent several years hitchhiking around the country, working at a variety of odd jobs including stints as a butcher, lumberjack, delivery boy, tailor, and damworker. With the success of his novella, "The Children," in 1937, he began to write full-time.

In 1939, Fast published *Conceived in Liberty,* a novel of the Continental Army's experience at Valley Forge in the winter of 1777–78. He subsequently wrote a fictional treatment of the life of radical writer Thomas Paine, whose pamphlet *Common Sense* had helped crystalize American sentiment against Britain in 1776. In 1942 Fast published *The Unvanquished,* another tale of the American Revolution. His fascination with this period in American history reflected Fast's conviction that "the current of American history as expressed by the mass of American people is revolutionary."

During World War II, Fast served on the overseas staff of the Office of War Information (OWI), and as a special film advisor for the U.S. Army. In the aftermath of World War II, however, Fast's political activities came under the scrutiny of HUAC. Specifically, HUAC subpoenaed Fast to ask him questions about the JOINT ANTI-FASCIST REFUGEE COMMITTEE (JAFRC), a left-wing organization dedicated to helping political refugees from the Spanish Civil War and Nazi Germany. A member of the JAFRC board of directors, Fast refused to turn over the organization's records to HUAC, whereupon he was promptly accused of con-

Author Howard Fast, whose radical views led to the banning of his books from the U.S. State Department libraries abroad.

tempt of Congress, convicted of the same charge, and sentenced to three months in prison. Fast and his colleagues appealed the case to the U.S. Supreme Court, which refused to hear the case. The Supreme Court's decision, Fast concluded, marked "the beginning of fascism in America."

Fast ran afoul of the anti-Communist crusade once more in 1953, when investigators for the Senate Permanent Subcommittee on Investigations, headed by Senator Joseph MCCARTHY of Wisconsin, launched an investigation of the INTERNATIONAL INFORMATION AGENCY (IIA), the branch of the U.S. Department of State that operated overseas libraries. The subcommittee apparently was appalled to discover that the IIA's libraries included novels by Fast, whom one State Department official described as a "Soviet-endorsed author." When called to Washington to testify again about his political associations, Fast invoked the Fifth Amendment and refused to state whether he was a member of the COMMUNIST PARTY. Later that year, he received the Stalin Peace Prize from the Soviet Union.

Fast made one foray into domestic politics in 1952 when he ran unsuccessfully for Congress as the American Labor Party candidate. Following his defeat, he returned to writing as a full-time occupation. Fast's other novels include *Freedom Road* (1944), *My Glorious Brothers* (1948), and *April Morning* (1956).

## Faulk, John Henry (1913–1990)

Host of a New York-based talk show on the CBS network, homespun humorist John Henry Faulk was one of the nation's most popular radio performers in the early 1950s. In 1955, Faulk led a slate of "middle of the road" candidates to victory in the struggle for control of the local chapter of the American Federation of Television and Radio Artists (AFTRA). The following year, AFTRA passed a resolution condemning the entertainment industry's anti-Communist watchdog agency AWARE, INC. for its role in blacklisting performers. The head of AWARE, Vincent Hartnett, retaliated by making Faulk a prime target of his company's BLACKLIST. In its bulletin, AWARE cited numerous references to Faulk in the Communist publication, the *DAILY WORKER;* for instance, it noted that Faulk had been scheduled to appear "at Club 65, 13 Astor Pl., N.Y.C.—a favorite site of pro-Communist affairs." Hartnett was aided in his campaign against Faulk by amateur anti-Communist crusader Laurence Johnson, owner of a chain of supermarkets in Syracuse, N.Y., who had acquired influence with advertising agencies by threatening sponsors with boycotts of their products if they hired blacklisted producers (whom he referred to as "Stalin's little agents").

CBS buckled under the threats from the blacklisters and canceled Faulk's radio show in 1956. Faulk responded by filing a libel lawsuit against AWARE and Johnson. Represented by noted trial attorney Louis Nizer, Faulk persevered through six years of litigation, until in 1962 a jury found the defendants guilty, awarding Faulk a judgment of $3.5 million. Although the amount of the damages was subsequently reduced to $550,000, the jury's decision dealt the final blow to the blacklist procedure, which had already begun to disintegrate. Faulk's account of his ordeal, entitled *Fear on Trial*, was published in 1964. Eleven years later, CBS aired a dramatization of the incident under the same title.

## Federal Bureau of Investigation

See HOOVER, J. Edgar.

## Feller, Abraham (1905–1952)

In October 1952, American attorney Abraham Feller was appointed acting assistant secretary general of the United Nations (UN). Feller had an extensive background in education and government service, starting with various New Deal agencies in the early 1930s. During World War II, he served with the Office of War Information (OWI); when the United Nations staff was formed in London in 1946, Feller accepted a position as legal counsel and policy adviser to Secretary General Trygve Lie.

Feller became one of Lie's most trusted counselors, and when North Korea invaded South Korea in June 1950, Feller was one of two UN officials who persuaded Lie to recommend military intervention by the United Nations to help end the conflict. The inability of the UN to bring the KOREAN WAR to a satisfactory conclusion troubled Feller, but he recognized in his book, *United Nations and World Community* (published posthumously in 1953), that progress toward an effective world government would necessarily be slow, and must include efforts to promote economic and social progress and human rights, as well as collective security.

"No society can be stable unless it is founded on justice and the rule of law," Feller wrote. "We must build both together and the strengthening of one will progressively strengthen the other. If we try to take one alone, we shall lose out on both."

Even more troubling to Feller than the UN's failure to end the Korean conflict, however, was the investigation of the Senate Internal Security subcommittee, headed by Senator Pat MCCARRAN, into alleged Communist sympathies of the 2,000 American members of the United Nations staff. In 1950, the FBI launched an in-depth probe of suspected Communists among the Americans on Lie's staff. Bureau officials handed over their findings to the State Department, which passed the information on to the United Nations, where the inquiry apparently came to an end. Early in 1952, a federal grand jury called a number of the same individuals to testify in secret. When most of the witnesses invoked the Fifth Amendment and refused to testify about their involvement with the COMMUNIST PARTY, the UN again was notified, but apparently took no action.

McCarran's subcommittee entered the scene in October 1952. Seeking primarily to draw public attention to the presence of American Communists in the UN Secretariat, subcommittee investigators focused almost exclusively on the question, "Are you a member of the Communist Party?" Seventeen witnesses refused to answer. There were no indications that Feller himself was under suspicion by the subcommittee. As the UN's chief legal adviser, he reportedly had been negotiating with McCarran and his staff to find a solution to the difficulties caused by the investigation and the subsequent pleading of the Fifth Amendment; in fact, Feller had advised Lie to dismiss all American employees who refused to answer the subcommittee's questions.

Nevertheless, the strain of his work began to tell on Feller. His wife stated that she had "tried to cheer him up," but without success. "He was an idealist," she said, "and his whole life was

devoted to the United Nations. He thought he wasn't doing his job well. He was a perfectionist."

On November 13, 1952, Abraham Feller leaped to his death from the window of his twelfth-floor apartment overlooking New York's Central Park. Lie blamed Feller's suicide on the "prolonged and serious strain" of upholding "law and justice in the investigations against indiscriminate smears and exaggerated charges" by the McCarran subcommittee. In reply, McCarran called Lie's charge irresponsible and vowed to proceed with his investigation.

**Ferrer, Jose** (1912–1992)   A noted stage actor who made his breakthrough into motion pictures with the movie version of *Cyrano de Bergerac* (1950), Jose Ferrer saw his film career end almost immediately afterward when he was listed in RED CHANNELS, the entertainment industry's blacklisting bible. The effects of the listing were immediate: the right-wing MOTION PICTURE ALLIANCE FOR THE PRESERVATION OF AMERICAN IDEALS, headed by actor John WAYNE, campaigned strenuously to deny Ferrer an Academy Award for his work in *Cyrano*. The alliance's opposition forced Ferrer to take the extraordinarily step of paying for advertisements in the industry press to deny that he had ever been a member of the COMMUNIST PARTY.

At that time, the HOUSE COMMITTEE ON UN-AMERICAN ACTIVITIES (HUAC) offered a standing invitation to any persons who felt they had been wrongly accused to testify before the committee, and Ferrer availed himself of that opportunity. Accompanied by counsel Abe FORTAS, Ferrer appeared before the committee on May 22, 1951. Ferrer already had sent the committee a letter stating that "I am not, have never been, could not be, a member of the Communist Party, nor, specifically, am I a sympathizer with any Communist aim, a fellow traveler, or in any way an encourager of any Communist Party concept or objective."

Ferrer reiterated that statement at the start of his testimony. Committee investigators then sought to link Ferrer with organizations that had been defined—either by the attorney general or the committee itself—as Communist fronts, including the Artists' Front to Win the War, the JOINT ANTI-FASCIST REFUGEE COMMITTEE, the Spanish Refugee Appeal, and the Civil Rights Congress. Ferrer acknowledged that he had lent his name to several of those organizations or had appeared briefly at their rallies to introduce speakers, but he insisted that he had never knowingly endorsed any "Communist Party angle." Upon further questioning, Ferrer admitted that he had favored assistance to foreign-born immigrants, opposed the Franco regime in Spain, and voiced objections to the tactics employed by HUAC. At the end of his testimony, Ferrer defended his record by professing ignorance of any pro-Soviet activity on the part of any group to which he had belonged. "I have learned the hard way that there are agencies that inform you on these things," he told the committee, "and I intend to avail myself of them in the future."

Ferrer also emphatically stated that he favored the outlawing of the Communist Party in the United States. "I have been convinced and it has been pointed out to me irrefutably that the Communist Party of America is the instrument, definitely, of a foreign government," noted Ferrer, "that its aims are those of a foreign government, and have nothing to do with our own life or our own welfare. And the mere fact that it is un-American seems to me to make it ipso facto illegal."

Word of Ferrer's clearance did not spread as quickly as the news of his blacklisting, however. When Ferrer's next film, *Moulin Rouge,* was released in 1952, the AMERICAN LEGION called for a boycott of the movie because of Ferrer's questionable political background. The legion subsequently apologized for its error.

## Flanders, Ralph E. (1880–1970)

A moderate Republican from Vermont who was one of the earliest and strongest critics of Senator Joseph MCCARTHY, Ralph Flanders enjoyed an

Senator Ralph Flanders of Vermont (left) introduced the resolution of censure against Joseph McCarthy.

extremely successful career in industry before entering the political arena. He grew up in poverty in New England in the troubled, depression-laden years of the late nineteenth century. The eldest of nine children, Flanders was forced to go to work at the age of fifteen as an apprentice machinist (at a wage of four cents an hour) with the Brown and Sharpe Manufacturing Company in Providence, Rhode Island, to support his family. After completing correspondence courses in engineering, Flanders obtained employment as an engineer with several New England corporations, including the General Electric Company. Along the way, Flanders also published several articles on machine design which led to a position as associate editor of the industry journal, *Machinery,* and the publication of two books on the subject in 1909 and 1914.

In 1912, Flanders joined the Jones and Lamson Machine Company, one of the largest employers in Vermont. His technical and managerial innovations carried him up the corporate ladder, and in 1933 Flanders assumed the presidency of the company. Meanwhile, he had become active in management associations, serving as president of the National Machine Tool Builders Association and the American Society of Mechnical Engineers. He also turned his attention toward the study of national economic problems (Flanders concluded that most economists were sadly deficient in practical experience) and won appointments to the Rockefeller Foundation's social science research council and the Vermont State Planning Board. Despite Flanders' opposition to most New Deal legislation, President Franklin D. Roosevelt appointed him to the advisory board of several federal agencies, including the National Recovery Association and the Office of Price Management.

Flanders spent much of World War II as chairman of the machine tools committee of the Combined Production and Resources Board, a division of the War Production Board. In 1944, he accepted an appointment as president of the Federal Reserve Bank of Boston. During his two years in that post, he joined with financier Thomas Lamont and industrialist Paul Hoffman (a close associate of General Dwight David EISENHOWER) on the board of the privately financed, nonprofit, Republican-dominated organization known as the Committee for Economic Development.

Flanders first ventured into Vermont politics in 1940 when he lost a Senate primary contest to George Aiken. Six years later, Governor Warren Proctor of Vermont selected Flanders to fill the unexpired term of Senator Warren Austin. Aided by the support of the COMMITTEE OF INDUSTRIAL ORGANIZATIONS (CIO), who approved his enlightened attitude toward management-labor relations, Flanders rolled to victories in the primary and general elections that autumn. In his first term in the Senate, he established himself as one of the leading experts in the field of economic affairs. Following President Harry S. TRUMAN's upset victory in the presidential election of 1948, Flanders joined with several Republican colleagues in urging the defeated Republican Party to liberalize its policies.

Until 1954, Flanders—a mild-mannered, balding, bespectacled, unpretentious gentleman known in the Senate as "the quiet man"—had generally supported the anti-Communist crusade led by Senator Joseph MCCARTHY of Wisconsin and his allies. He had denounced the initial Senate investigation of McCarthy's charges of Communists in government as a highly partisan affair and had joined twenty-four other Republican senators in signing a petition in 1952 criticizing the Truman administration for allegedly running a "smear" campaign against McCarthy. McCarthy's savage treatment of General Ralph ZWICKER, however, appalled Flanders, who undoubtedly was one of the most decent men in the Senate. Further, it had become clear to Flanders that McCarthy did not discern any duty as a Republican to support the Eisenhower administration, particularly in the early months of Eisenhower's tenure in the White House.

On March 9, 1954—just before the start of the ARMY-MCCARTHY HEARINGS—Flanders suddenly rose on the Senate floor and launched a devastating attack upon McCarthy. The senator from Wisconsin, Flanders charged, was attempting to destroy the Republican Party "by intention or through ignorance" so that he could form his own "one-man party—MCCARTHYISM." The world outside the Senate chamber, Flanders claimed, was approaching a moment of crisis, "mobilizing for the great battle of Armageddon. Now is a crisis in the age-long warfare between God and the Devil for the souls of men." As the apocalypse neared, Flanders paused to describe to his audience the apparent inanity of McCarthy's recent behavior: "He dons his warpaint. He goes into his war dance. He emits his warwhoops. He goes forth to battle and proudly returns with the scalp of a pink Army dentist [Irving PERESS]. We may assume that this represents the depth and seriousness of Communist penetration at this time."

McCarthy brushed off Flanders' assault, telling reporters that "I am too busy to answer Republican heroes," and claiming that Flanders—whom he referred to as "one of the finest old gentlemen I've ever met"—had consistently voted against Republican programs in the Senate, a charge which the record did not substantiate. (In fact, Flanders supported the Republican leadership in the Senate far more regularly than the renegade McCarthy.) Eisenhower took the unusual step of commenting upon a Senate speech, declaring that Flanders had performed a "service" by chastising divisive elements within the party; privately, the President dispatched a note to Flanders conveying his appreciation for the speech.

The spectacle of McCarthy badgering distinguished military officials during his hearings into Communist influences in the United States Army disturbed Flanders even more deeply, and on June 1 Flanders again assailed McCarthy in a Senate speech. It was easily the strongest criticism of McCarthy yet uttered by a Republican senator. Flanders charged that McCarthy's crusade was spreading "division and confusion wherever he goes." The senator from Wisconsin and his allies were like some overgrown version of "Dennis the Menace," Flanders said, who blundered "into the most appalling situations as they ramble through the world of adults." In an even more damaging comparison, Flanders pointed out that Jews appeared particularly fearful of the anti-Red crusade and were justified in their concern because McCarthy's brand of anti-Communism "so completely parallels that of Adolf Hitler as to strike fear into the heart of any defenseless minority."

In a thinly veiled jab at McCarthy's sexual preferences, about which there had long been rumors on Capitol Hill, Flanders wondered aloud what the real relationship was between McCarthy and his two top assistants, Roy COHN and G. David SCHINE. Cohn, he said, "seems to have an almost passionate anxiety" to retain Schine on the staff of McCarthy's Goverment Operations Committee, while McCarthy seemed to alternate between keeping Schine and firing him. "Does the assistant have some hold on the Senator?" asked Flanders. "Can it be that our Dennis, so effective in making trouble for his elders, has at last gotten into trouble himself?" Flanders concluded by pointing out that McCarthy had never successfully prosecuted a single Communist in the federal government. Instead, he had only created dissension and disorder. "Were the junior Senator from Wisconsin in the pay of the Communists," Flanders observed, "he could not have done a better job for them."

Publicly, McCarthy dismissed the remarks of the seventy-three-year-old Flanders. "I wonder," he mused, "whether this has been a result of senility or viciousness." Privately, he was distressed by Flanders' comparison of himself to Hitler and the allegation of homosexual tendencies. Other Republican senators complained to Flanders that he should have given McCarthy warning of the attack. Accordingly, ten days later, Flanders walked into the committee room in which the final days of the Army-McCarthy hearings were being held and handed McCarthy a note which read, "This is to inform you that I plan to make another speech concerning your activities in the Senate this afternoon as soon after the morning hour as I can get the floor. If you desire, I would be glad to have you present." Because Flanders' invitation had been captured by the television cameras that were covering the hearings, he had created an aura of anticipation that paid off handsomely in publicity.

In his June 11 speech, Flanders offered a resolution recommending that the Senate strip McCarthy of his chairmanship of both the Permanent Subcommittee on Investigations and the Government Operations Committee if he refused to "purge himself of contempt" and respond to the charges of misconduct and financial impropriety leveled by the Hennings Committee in 1952. "It is no defense to call the charges a smear," Flanders told the Senate. "A smear is a most annoying thing and one which is perhaps—I would not speak definitely—not unknown to the junior senator from Wisconsin. But there is this about a smear: It can be removed by a dry-cleaning process which involves a vigorous application of the truth." McCarthy remained outwardly unconcerned over Flanders' attack. "I think," he suggested to reporters, "they should get a net and take him to a good quiet place."

Flanders followed his June 11 speech with an appearance on the NBC television program, *Meet the Press.* Displaying a determination to maintain his pressure on McCarthy, Flanders reiterated his objection to McCarthy's dangerous practice of setting himself up as the sole judge of an individual's guilt or innocence. McCarthy, Flanders claimed, "seeks to be the sole private eye, prosecutor, judge, jury and sentencer." Such tactics, Flanders noted, were "so clearly in the direction of fighting communism with Fascism that I am seriously disturbed." After the program, Flanders wrote to a friend that "I cannot conceive of wanting to live, or wanting my children or grandchildren to live, in an America fashioned in the image of the junior senator from Wisconsin."

By this time, Flanders was able to draw on increasing support from a recently established organization known as the Clearing House, a group of anti-McCarthy activists led by liberal Republican industrialist Paul G. Hoffman, who had served with Flanders previously on the Committee for Economic Development. Still, Flanders' criticisms of McCarthy appeared to draw little support from the White House. "I began to surmise," Flanders later wrote, "and still do wonder, whether he [President Eisenhower] did not find me an embarrassment as so many other rock-ribbed Republicans did." One cabinet officer—perhaps Secretary of State John Foster DULLES—visited Flanders and suggested that he desist from his attacks upon McCarthy for a time. "He talked very reasonably," Flanders recalled, "but I had to tell him that the strength of my position lay in being unreasonable." Democratic leaders in the Senate remained aloof from the fray, reluctant to oppose McCarthy openly, waiting to see how the Republican Party would resolve its internal dilemma.

When Flanders rose again in the Senate to speak against McCarthy on June 30, he substituted a different resolution for his previous motion. This time he suggested a straightforward motion of censure: "Resolved, That the conduct of the Senator from Wisconsin, Mr. McCarthy, is contrary to senatorial traditions, and tends to bring the Senate into disrepute, and such conduct is hereby condemned." The Senate delayed debate on the motion until July 30. As expected, conservative Republicans excoriated Flanders for his attack upon McCarthy. Everett Dirksen of Illinois, for one, pointed out that "the Senator from Vermont and the *DAILY WORKER* are on the same side of this issue." When critics complained that the motion was too vague, Flanders submitted a list of thirty-three particulars, many of which were actually drafted by the staff of the Clearing House.

To delay a vote on Flanders' motion, Senate Majority Leader William KNOWLAND recommended on August 2 that it be referred to a select committee of six senators, three from each party. Flanders and eleven other senators—most of whom favored immediate censure of McCarthy—opposed the proposal, but the Senate approved it and the select committee, headed by Utah Republican Arthur V. WATKINS, began hearings on August 31, 1954. McCarthy treated the inquiry with undisguised contempt. For his part, Flanders made clear to the committee precisely what was at stake. "We are faced," he noted in a letter to Watkins, "with conduct by a senator which I believe is unparalleled and unprecedented in the history of the United States Senate. If we fail to meet this challenge we leave the Senate debased and in the future unprotected from the vilest sort of demagogy and unprincipled attacks upon members of the Senate."

The Watkins Committee released its report on September 27, unanimously recommending that the Senate censure McCarthy. Following several months of debate, the Senate voted on December 2 to condemn McCarthy for contempt. Ralph Flanders voted in favor of the measure.

**Foreman, Carl** (1914–1984)   Best known for his work on the screenplays of *HIGH NOON* (1952) and *The Bridge Over the River Kwai* (1957), Carl Foreman was a Hollywood writer-producer who joined the COMMUNIST PARTY in the 1930s. He broke with the party in 1942, shortly after the United States entered World War II. Foreman spent the war years with legendary film director Frank Capra's unit in the Army Signal Corps; it was there, Foreman said later, that he learned how to make movies.

In 1946, Foreman joined with independent director Stanley Kramer to produce quality films on relatively low budgets, free from the bureaucratic interference of the studio system. Over the next six years, their partnership turned out such critically acclaimed films as *Champion* (1949), the anti-racist *Home of the Brave* (1949), *Cyrano de Bergerac* (1950), and *High Noon,* which won Foreman the prestigious Laurel Award from the SCREEN WRITERS GUILD.

During the filming of *High Noon,* however, Foreman was subpoenaed by the HOUSE COMMITTEE ON UN-AMERICAN ACTIVITIES (HUAC). Like many of his colleagues with a radical past, Foreman faced a quandary: he was willing to state publicly that he was not presently a member of the Communist Party, but he did not wish to discuss his past, and he especially did not want to give the committee the names of any of his former associates in the party. Foreman's own preference was to plead the First Amendment, which—based upon the precedent established by the HOLLYWOOD TEN—probably would have led to a citation for contempt of Congress, a fine, and a jail sentence of six to nine months. Instead, Foreman's lawyer, Sidney Cohn, recommended that Foreman tell the committee that he had not been a member of the party since 1942; if the committee asked him questions about his political activities before that time, he could still invoke the Fifth Amendment. (This strategy later became known as "taking the qualified Fifth.")

By making it clear that he had broken his ties with the Communist Party nearly a decade earlier, Foreman hoped that he could "ride out the storm." But another witness spoiled the strategy by naming Foreman as a former party member. At that point, Sidney Kramer—who was concerned that an investigation into Foreman's politics might spill over into his own liberal past—purchased Foreman's share of their production company so that they would no longer be business associates. It was not at all clear that Foreman's strategy would have succeeded anyway because HUAC Chairman Donald Jackson stated publicly that "the ultimate test of the credibility of a witness before the Committee, as far as I am concerned, is the extent to which he is willing to cooperate with the Committee in giving full details as to not only the place of activities, but also the names of those who participated with him in the activities of the Communist Party."

While Foreman was visiting England in 1952, the State Department revoked his passport. Effectively BLACKLISTED, Foreman was forced to write scripts without receiving credit for his work. He said that his treatment by the U.S. government made it difficult for him to concentrate on his writing. "Every time I sat down at the typewriter," complained Foreman, "bitter and aggrieved feelings intruded upon my screen work. I wanted to write angry letters rather than a script." His personal life, too, suffered. "When I joined him [in England]," noted Foreman's wife, Estelle, "he was a different man. He suffered terribly and I think he felt at that time that nothing was any use anymore, including loyalty to one's spouse. So he began leading a completely different life. We had a very happy marriage until then. It was quite the reverse afterward." While he was in England, Foreman wrote the original version of the screenplay for *The Bridge Over the River Kwai,* but he received no screen credit for the film. When the script won an Academy Award for best screenplay, Foreman could not accept the Oscar; indeed, his name was not on the award at all. "It hurt like hell not getting credits and accolades for the films I wrote," Foreman recalled years later.

In 1956, the head of Columbia Pictures, Harry Cohn, agreed to employ Foreman, but the contract was contingent upon Foreman testifying before HUAC without pleading the Fifth Amendment. Foreman's attorney, Cohn, convinced HUAC Chairman Francis WALTER that it would be a good public relations move for the committee to permit ex-Communists to renounce their past party membership without informing on their former comrades. Walter agreed, and the two men worked out an arrangement whereby Foreman could testify in executive session before Walter alone. The meeting took place on August 8, 1956. Foreman received criticism from some members of the Hollywood community who considered any compromise with the committee to be tantamount to dealing with the devil, but Foreman did not name any names, and soon after his appearance he returned to work. (Walter did not fare as well. The Pennsylvania congressman received so much criticism from his vigilant conservative supporters—who felt that Foreman had escaped too easily—that he abandoned the procedure after Foreman's appearance.)

By 1958, Foreman's name again appeared on the screen credits of his films. In 1969, the Screen Writers Guild gave him another Laurel Award; at the presentation ceremony, Foreman was recognized for having the courage "to stand up and risk his livelihood and his future in defense of a principle; to face exile from the country of his birth rather than compromise what he felt was his honor."

## Fortas, Abraham (1910–1982)

A partner with the law firm of Arnold, Fortas, & Porter during the McCarthy era, Abe Fortas served as defense counsel for several well-known individuals accused of Communist sympathies—including Owen LATTIMORE and Jose FERRER—when they were subpoenaed to testify before Congressional investigating committees. A native of Memphis, Tennessee, Fortas worked at numerous odd jobs as a boy to supplement his family's

Abe Fortas, the attorney who defended Owen Lattimore and Lillian Hellman.

income. Fortas then worked his way through Southwestern College by playing the fiddle at dances. Always a brilliant student, Fortas attended Yale University Law School, where he graduated first in his class and was named editor of the *Yale Law Journal*. From 1933 to 1937, Fortas served as an assistant professor of law at Yale, while working part-time at various New Deal government positions in Washington.

In 1937, Fortas accepted a full-time position as assistant director of the Securities and Exchange Commission. He subsequently served as general counsel to the Public Works Administration and as a special assistant to Secretary of the Interior Harold Ickes. In 1945, President Harry S. TRUMAN named Fortas as an adviser to the U.S. delegation at the United Nations conference in San Francisco. Shortly after the end of World War II, however, Fortas left government service and went into private practice in association with two other prominent New Deal attorneys, Paul Porter and Thurman Arnold.

A brilliant, tough adversary, Fortas entered the controversy over Communist influence in the United States in the spring of 1950 when he agreed to defend Owen LATTIMORE, the Far East expert whom Senator Joseph MCCARTHY claimed was the top Soviet spy in the United States. Through the skillful use of rebuttal witnesses who testified to Lattimore's patriotic character—and through the use of an affidavit from a former high-ranking COMMUNIST PARTY official who swore he had never heard of Lattimore—Fortas helped Lattimore defend himself successfully against McCarthy's allegations.

In 1951, Fortas appeared with actor Jose Ferrer when Ferrer was subpoenaed by the HOUSE COMMITTEE ON UN-AMERICAN ACTIVITIES (HUAC). He also consulted with counsel for playwright Lillian HELLMAN to develop a strategy whereby Hellman acknowledged her own radical past to HUAC but refused to testify about other individuals she had known. Fortas' willingness to defend accused Communist sympathizers earned him the enmity of McCarthy and other right-wing zealots, who privately branded him a Communist as well. Clearly the abuse of Congressional investigative powers during the McCarthy era bothered Fortas deeply. In 1953, he drafted a memorandum in which he stated that "the [Congressional] hearing has become a weapon of persecution, a useful tool to the demagogue, a device for the glory of the prosecutor and of shame for the accused."

Meanwhile, Fortas became a confidante of Senator Lyndon Baines JOHNSON of Texas. When Johnson became President following the assassination of John F. KENNEDY in November 1963, Fortas became one of Johnson's closest advisers. In July 1965, Johnson named Fortas to the U.S. Supreme Court. He resigned in 1969, following criticism of his association with the Wolfson Family Foundation at a time when financier Louis Wolfson, previously convicted of stock manipulation, was under further investigation by the federal government.

**Fort Monmouth**   See ARMY-MCCARTHY HEARINGS.

**Foster, William Z.** (1881–1961)   Chairman of the COMMUNIST PARTY OF THE UNITED STATES OF AMERICA during the late 1940s and early 1950s, William Z. Foster was an uncompromising Communist ideologue who rejected cooperation with mainstream liberalism in the United States.

Born in Taunton, Massachusetts, Foster went to work at the age of seven to supplement his family's meager income. During the next thirty years, he worked at more than a score of odd jobs, including stints as an engineer, steam fitter, laborer, fertilizer mixer, lumberjack, trolley motorman, merchant seaman, shepherd, and homesteader. In 1900, Foster joined the Socialist Party but resigned in disgust over its relatively moderate policies. Instead, he became active in the revolutionary (and frequently violent) labor organization known as the International Workers of the World (IWW).

Foster's travels around the country, organizing labor activities for the IWW and other unions, deepened his conviction that American workers could never gain independence or justice under the capitalist system. In 1920, he founded the Trade Union Education League, a propaganda organization designed to stimulate independent working-class political action. The following year, Foster accepted an invitation to the congress of the International of Labor Unions in Moscow, where he saw Soviet leader Vladimir Lenin for the first time. Upon his return from Moscow, Foster joined the Communist Party of the United States of America. In 1924, he served as the Communist Party's first nominee in a U.S. presidential election and was renominated in 1928 and 1932. (In the latter election, Foster gathered 55,000 votes.) During this period, the party adopted a hard line, emphasizing loyalty to the standard of worldwide Marxist revolution and tolerating little compromise with the forces of socialism or liberalism.

Foster's influence within the Communist Party of the United States declined in 1935 when the Party—following orders from Moscow—reversed its strategy and began to encourage the so-called POPULAR FRONT, an antifascist accommodation with liberals in Western Europe and the United States. Foster returned to leadership briefly in 1939 following the announcement of the NAZI-SOVIET PACT but was deposed once again after Germany attacked the Soviet Union in June 1941, an event that forced the International Communist movement (Comintern) to abjure isolation and seek compromise with the forces of democracy. For most of World War II, Foster remained in the background while Earl BROWDER, the representative of the Popular Front, dominated party affairs.

In April 1945, however, the Comintern reversed its position again and condemned Browder's "revisionist" wartime policies. Accordingly, Foster was once more returned to leadership of the American Communist movement with a mandate from Moscow to lead the party away from cooperation and toward a sharper struggle against the "class nature of bourgeois democracy." This shift in tactics and rhetoric alarmed many Americans and helped fuel the growing anti-Communist movement in the United States. During an appearance before the HOUSE COMMITTEE ON UN-AMERICAN ACTIVITIES (HUAC) in late 1945, Foster condemned President Harry S. TRUMAN for his policies of "aggressive imperialism" and denounced American aid to the Nationalist forces of CHIANG Kai-shek in the emerging Chinese civil war.

In 1948, Foster and eleven other top officials of the Communist Party of the United States were arrested and charged with violations of the SMITH ACT; that is, they were accused of advocating the violent overthrow of the U.S. government. Foster's case was severed from the other eleven, however, because doctors determined that his heart condition might not be able to withstand the strain of a trial. (In fact, Foster was never tried on this charge.) The gathering atmosphere of anti-Communist repression in the United States in the late 1940s and early 1950s seemed to justify Foster's predictions of inevitable conflict between capitalism and communism, and strengthened his position within the American Communist movement.

By 1956, however, the downfall of Senator Joseph MCCARTHY, the decline of public support for the anti-Communist crusade, and the emerging movement within the Soviet Union against the excesses of the Stalinist regime all combined to make Foster seem an aging and outmoded cold warrior whom time had passed by. His warnings that the thaw in U.S.–Soviet relations was nothing more than illusion and the resurrection of "collaborationist ideas cultivated by Browder" failed to move his colleagues, and Foster's influence in the party began to dwindle. His reputation revived briefly in the last years of the decade, just before his death in 1961.

**front**  During the McCarthy era, numerous screenwriters who had confessed to past membership in the COMMUNIST PARTY or Communist-front organizations or who had invoked the Fifth Amendment at Congressional hearings were BLACKLISTED; that is, they were refused employment by television and motion picture producers. In an attempt to continue to practice their craft and earn a living (albeit a reduced one), some writers wrote scripts and then hired another individual—often a struggling young writer looking for a way to establish her or his reputation—to act as a "front." Typically, the front would submit the script to producers under her or his name and then share the profits with the real author. There was a certain danger to the front, of course; had the arrangement been discovered and publicized, the front risked being blacklisted as well.

One prominent screenwriter who was forced to employ a front in the 1950s was Dalton TRUMBO. Following his release from prison where he had been serving a sentence for contempt of Congress, Trumbo contacted a former acquaintance who had published a biography of Lord Mountbatten and wished to break into fiction. Although Trumbo's "collaborator" originally offered his name to Trumbo at no cost, Trumbo insisted that he receive some compensation for the considerable risk he was running. Trumbo then completed a story treatment for a film and mailed it to the front, who sent it to the William Morris Agency. When the agency agreed to handle the story, a code was set up by which all communications were made through the front, and Trumbo remained in the background, referred to only as "Dr. John Abbott." The story was subsequently sold to Twentieth Century-Fox, and during the next several months Trumbo and his front consulted on this and other story ideas.

This entire process was satirized in Woody Allen's film *The Front,* in which Allen starred as a politically naive restaurant cashier and part-time bookmaker who became a front for blacklisted screenwriters, splitting the profits 50–50 between them.

***Front, The***   Actor-writer Woody Allen's tribute to the artists who were BLACKLISTED during the McCarthy era, *The Front* (1976) was written by Walter Bernstein and directed by Martin Ritt, both of whom were blacklisted during the 1950s. The film stars Allen (in his first appearance in a film he did not write) as a politically naive restaurant cashier and part-time bookie named Howie who becomes a "front" for blacklisted screenwriters. The writers give their film scripts to Howie, who passes them along to producers under his own name. As in real life, the profits are split 50–50 between the front and the blacklistees. As the plot proceeds, Howie comes to believe that he really does possess literary talent; more important, he also realizes that he must choose sides in the moral struggle between those who acquiesce in the blacklisting and their victims.

Besides Allen, *The Front* stars John Randolph, Herschel Bernardi, Lloyd Gough, and Joshua Shelley, all of whom had been blacklisted during the McCarthy era. So had Zero MOSTEL, who plays a blacklisted comic actor based in part upon actor Philip LOEB; like Loeb, Mostel's character commits suicide in a hotel room. In the credits at the end of the film, the names of the actors from the McCarthy era are accompanied by the dates on which they were blacklisted.

**Fuchs, Klaus** (1911–1988)   The key member of a Soviet atomic espionage ring that operated from 1943 to 1945, a ring which included Harry GOLD, David GREENGLASS, Morton SOBELL, and Julius ROSENBERG, Klaus Fuchs was a native of Germany and the son of a Protestant minister who was also a dedicated pacifist. He attended Kiel and Leipzig universities, where he studied mathematics and physics in the turbulent final years of the Weimar Republic. During his stay in Leipzig, Fuchs became active in Communist Party affairs.

When the Nationalist Socialist regime of Adolf Hitler came to power in early 1933, Fuchs' family—all of whom were actively opposed to the Nazis—was marked for retribution. His father was sentenced to nine months in a concentration camp, and one of his sisters committed suicide after assisting her husband to escape Germany. On the orders of German Communist Party officials, Fuchs himself fled first to France and then to Great Britain. "I was sent out by the Party," he recalled years later, "because they said that I must finish my studies because after the revolution in Germany people would be required with technical knowledge to take part in the building up of the Communist Germany."

Fuchs entered Bristol University to continue his graduate studies in theoretical physics (and, informally, Marxist philosophy). Five years later, having acquired an excellent reputation as a theoretician within the scientific community, he received a doctorate in physics from the University of Edinburgh, Scotland. The NAZI-SOVIET PACT of August 1939 caused Fuchs to doubt the sincerity of the Soviet Union's commitment to Communism, but "in the end I did accept that Russia had done it to gain time, that during the time she was expanding her own influence in the Balkans against the influence of Germany."

When the British government declared war on Germany following Hitler's invasion of Poland in August 1939, Fuchs was interned along with other German nationals in England. Sent first to the Isle of Man, he was subsequently transferred to Sherbrooke Camp in Canada, on the outskirts of Quebec, and returned to Britain in 1941.

Shortly after his release, Fuchs was invited by the British government to join a secret research project at Birmingham University, despite the fact that he made no secret of his sympathies for the Communist cause. Fuchs accepted the invitation without knowing the nature of the work; when he discovered that he would be working on a project to build an atomic bomb, he established contact with Soviet intelligence agents through an intermediary and alerted them to the nature of the research he was conducting at Birmingham. Fuchs initially believed that his only involvement as a spy would be to inform the Russians about the project, but when the Soviets asked for additional details, he agreed to supply them. "At this time," he observed, "I had complete confidence in Russian policy and I believed that the Western Allies deliberately allowed Russia and Germany to fight each other to the death. I had, therefore, no hesitation in giving all the information I had, even though occasionally I tried to concentrate mainly on giving information about the results of my own work." Indeed, Fuchs—who described himself as a "controlled schizophrenic"—maintained that he was able to separate the two halves of his psyche so that he could pass along secrets to the Soviet Union while maintaining his feelings of loyalty to his adopted country of Great Britain.

In November of the following year, the British government sent Fuchs to Los Alamos, New Mexico, as part of the British delegation to the Manhattan Project, the code name for the American research effort to develop an atomic bomb. Suspecting nothing, British intelligence officials assured their American counterparts of Fuchs' loyalty. At Los Alamos, Fuchs—who reportedly knew as much about the details of the bomb design as anyone on the Manhattan Project—made contact with other Soviet agents, including Julius Rosenberg. Through couriers such as Harry Gold, Fuchs passed to the Soviets vital data on the technical and theoretical design of the atomic bomb.

At the end of the war, Fuchs returned to England. Despite the appearance of his name on a list of possible espionage suspects compiled after the capture of a Russian spy ring in Canada in 1945, Fuchs was invited to join the British Atomic Research Centre at Harwell, Oxfordshire, in 1946 as head of theoretical physics. There he resumed his espionage activities, though he soon began to limit the data to less vital information. "I began to have doubts about the Russian policy," Fuchs later told British authorities. "During this time I was not sure I could go on giving the information I had. It became more and more evident that the time when Russia would expand her influence over Europe was far away. I had to decide for myself whether I could go on for many years continuing handing over information without being sure in my own mind whether I was doing right. I decided that I could not do so." By his own account, Fuchs ended his career as a Soviet agent in February or March 1949, and thereafter refused to pass along any additional material.

By that time, the Soviet Union was already far along in its own nuclear research effort. In August 1949, the Soviets successfully detonated a nuclear device for the first time. Caught completely by surprise, British and American authorities concluded that Soviet scientists must have received assistance from foreign sources. After consultations between the FBI and MI5, the British counterespionage agency, Fuchs was identified as a possible suspect and placed under surveillance. British authorities arrested Fuchs in early 1950; following extensive interrogation, he finally confessed on February 3 to a senior MI5 agent named James Skardon.

News of Fuchs' espionage activities stunned the American public. (As if the actual details were insufficiently dramatic, one enterprising newspaper claimed that Fuchs had betrayed the secret of a "hormone ray" that had the capacity to "feminize" enemy troops.) For many Republican critics in Congress, shaken by the domestic and international changes of the postwar years, the Fuchs revelations represented the climax of seventeen years of frustration with Democratic administrations. "How much more are we going to have to take?" asked Senate Homer Capehart of Indiana. "Fuchs and Acheson and Hiss and hydrogen bombs threatening outside and New Dealism eating away at the vitals of the nation. In the name of Heaven, is this the best America can do?" Six days after Fuchs' arrest was made public, Senator Joseph MCCARTHY delivered his Wheeling, West Virginia speech, charging that the U.S. Department of State harbored scores of "card-carrying Communists" among its employees.

Because the British government wished to keep the details of Fuchs' betrayal secret, his trial lasted only one day. In his brief statement, Fuchs defended his action on the grounds of "dialectical necessity of correct party behavior," which in his view allowed him to commit espionage "in the name of historical determinism." On March 1, 1950, Fuchs was sentenced to fourteen years in prison. Meanwhile, the FBI had embarked upon a frantic attempt to locate the courier who had passed Fuchs' data to the Soviets. Fuchs described his contact as a man about 40 years old, thickset, 5 feet 8 inches tall, 180 pounds, with a round face and a receding forehead. Agents showed photographs of Gold to Fuchs, but he denied that the man in the photos was his courier. Not until he saw photographs of Gold walking and doing chores around his house did Fuchs positively identify Gold. Only a few hours earlier, Gold had confessed to the FBI about his role in the affair. Gold's confession then led authorities to David Greenglass, who subsequently implicated the Rosenbergs. Unlike Fuchs, who received only a prison sentence for stealing atomic secrets, the Rosenbergs were sentenced to death and executed in May 1953.

A model prisoner who taught evening classes during his incarceration, Fuchs was released after serving nine years of his sentence. The British government deported him to East Germany, where he became a professor at Dresden University, deputy director of the Central Institute for Nuclear Research at Rossendorf, and a member of the Central Committee of East Germany's Communist Party. In its epitaph on the Fuchs affair, *The Times* of London concluded that "in the melancholy annals of incompetence which constitute the history of the British security service over the past 50 years, the story of Fuchs still has the power to astonish."

**Fulbright, James W.** (1905–1994) A leading Democratic opponent of Senator Joseph MCCARTHY in the Senate, James W. Fulbright was considered one of the most intellectual members of Congress during the 1940s and 1950s.

Born in Missouri and raised in Arkansas, Fulbright's father was a successful businessman and newspaper publisher. After graduating from the University of Arkansas (where he was senior class president and played varsity football), he spent six years in Great Britain studying history and political science at Oxford University on a Rhodes scholarship. Returning to the United States in 1931, he enrolled in the Law School of George Washington University, earning an LL.B. in 1934. Fulbright worked for one year as an attorney with the Department of Justice and then taught first at George Washington and subsequently at the University of Arkansas law school. In 1939, he was named president of the University of Arkansas, a post he left two years later to run for Congress.

Fulbright was first elected to the House of Representatives in 1942. Soon after, Fulbright introduced a resolution favoring the creation of—and American participation in—an international organization to preserve peace. Combined with a similar Senate resolution sponsored by Senator Tom CONNALLY, this legislation inaugurated the process by which the United Nations was formally established two years later.

After serving only one term in the House, Fulbright ran for a seat in the U.S. Senate in 1944 and easily defeated his two rivals. In De-

Senator William Fulbright of Arkansas, a leading opponent of Joseph McCarthy.

cember 1945, Fulbright introduced another piece of landmark legislation, providing federal funding for the exchange and support of teachers and students between the United States and foreign nations. Known as the Fulbright Act, the measure was designed to promote international understanding and is still in operation.

Given his interest in foreign affairs and international cooperation, it was not surprising that Fulbright was named to the Senate Foreign Relations Committee when a seat became available in 1949. By that time, Fulbright was convinced that the most serious long-range threat to American security lay not in military attack from the Soviet Union but in this nation's inability to live up to its ideals. "Democracy," Fulbright stated, "is more likely to be destroyed by the perversion of, or abandonment of, its true moral principles than by armed attack from Russia." Subsequently, Fulbright viewed the antics of the anti-Communist zealots in the United States with alarm and disgust; McCarthy, in particular, impressed Fulbright as an irresponsible and dangerous fanatic.

Elected to a second term with no opposition in 1950, Fulbright certainly had little reason to fear that McCarthy could damage his political career. In fact, Fulbright had no substantial contact with McCarthy until September 1951 when they clashed over McCarthy's opposition to the nomination of veteran State Department official Philip JESSUP as U.S. representative to the United Nations General Assembly. In dismissing McCarthy's flimsy allegations against Jessup, Fulbright commented that "a number of zeros doesn't make it amount to one if you put them all together." Despite his personal dislike of McCarthy, however, Fulbright generally followed the Democratic line in the Senate by treating McCarthy as a problem for the Republican majority to solve without Democratic interference.

As McCarthy's actions grew even more reckless in the summer of 1953, however, Fulbright began to move toward open opposition. Relations between the two men deteriorated after McCarthy disrupted a committee hearing on Fulbright's scholar-exchange program; McCarthy later claimed that his characterization of the operation as the "half-bright" program was not meant as an attack upon Fulbright himself. In January 1954, Fulbright cast the only vote in opposition to a $214,000 appropriation to McCarthy's permanent subcommittee on investigations.

When Senator Ralph FLANDERS of Vermont introduced a motion in June 1954 to remove McCarthy from the Senate GOVERNMENT OPERATIONS COMMITTEE chairmanship, Fulbright offered Flanders his support. On July 16, Flanders introduced a resolution calling upon the Senate to censure McCarthy; because this motion initially lacked specific charges, on August 1 Fulbright submitted six amendments that supplied detailed accusations against McCarthy. These included his appeal to government employees to circumvent their superiors and violate their employment contracts by supplying him with secret information; his vituperative attacks upon Secretary of State George Catlett MARSHALL and

General Ralph ZWICKER; his acceptance of a $10,000 fee from the Lustron Corporation for writing a brief pamphlet on the postwar housing shortage; and his contemptuous attitude toward the Hennings Committee that was established to investigate charges of misconduct leveled by Senator William BENTON of Connecticut. In introducing his amendment to Flanders' motion, Fulbright noted that McCarthy's "abuses have recalled to the minds of millions the most abhorrent tyrannies which our whole system of ordered liberty and balanced power was intended to abolish." Moreover, added Fulbright, McCarthy possessed "the most extraordinary talent for disruption and causing confusion . . . that I have ever seen." While Fulbright read the charges to the Senate, McCarthy sat seemingly unconcerned nearby, reading a newspaper.

Fulbright also was active behind the scenes, arranging a meeting between Flanders and the well-respected senior senator from Arkansas, Allen Ellender, whose support for the censure motion would virtually guarantee the backing of other southern Democrats. As the public became aware of Fulbright's campaign against McCarthy, the Wisconsin senator's adherents began to flood Fulbright's office with hate mail, calling him a "dirty Red," a "coward," and a "skunk," as well as other less complimentary epithets. Undaunted, Fulbright continued to press the censure effort.

The campaign to censure McCarthy reached its climax on December 2 when the Senate voted to approve Flanders' motion by a vote of 67–22. After the vote was announced, several of McCarthy's allies pointed out that because the resolution used the word *condemned* rather than *censure,* McCarthy still had not been formally censured. At that point, Fulbright rose and read aloud the definitions of *censure* and *condemn* from a dictionary to prove that they were more or less interchangeable. "Actually," Fulbright added, *"condemn,* as I read it, is a more severe term than *censure."*

Following the fall of McCarthy, Fulbright won reelection to the Senate for three more

terms. In 1959, he became chairman of the Senate Foreign Relations Committee. In that role, Fulbright served as one of the leading Congressional critics of American military involvement in Vietnam. The series of public hearings he held on U.S. policy toward Southeast Asia in 1964–67 played a significant role in stimulating domestic dissent on the war. Fulbright retired from the Senate in 1975, by which time the United States had withdrawn virtually all its troops from Vietnam.

**Fund for the Republic** Alarmed by the trend toward the curtailment of civil liberties in the United States, the Ford Foundation established the Fund for the Republic in 1951 to finance activities "directed toward the elimination of restrictions on freedom of thought, inquiry, and expression in the United States." Paul Hoffman, an internationalist Republican who had formerly headed the Marshall Plan, served as chairman of the fund.

The fund began its work by donating $25,000 to the American Bar Association for a study of congressional investigating committees, notably the HOUSE COMMITTEE ON UN-AMERICAN ACTIVITIES (HUAC) and Senator Joseph MCCARTHY'S PERMANENT SUBCOMMITTEE ON INVESTIGATIONS. The fund subsequently bestowed grants for studies of the effects of the government's loyalty program on individual rights; contributed $150,000 to the American Friends Service Committee for legal fees in cases that would "strengthen the right to freedom of conscience;" subsidized educational programs to encourage discussion of the country's "basic documents"; printed and distributed 35,000 copies of a study entitled *The Fifth Amendment Today,* written by Erwin Griswold, Dean of Harvard Law School; and supported efforts to promote racial tolerance. Once, the fund awarded $10,000 to an all-white Iowa community that managed to find housing for an African-American Air Force officer.

The fund's support of liberal causes soon aroused the ire of such conservative organizations as the AMERICAN LEGION, which accused it of attempting "to persuade Americans that communism is not and never has been a serious threat to the United States." Fearful of threatened customer boycotts of Ford Motor Company automobile showrooms, Henry Ford severed the Fund for the Republic from the Ford Foundation, although he provided the fund with $15 million to continue its work.

In 1954, the fund named Robert M. Hutchins as its president. As president of the University of Chicago, Hutchins had acquired a reputation as a critic of intolerance and a staunch defender of academic freedom. "I wouldn't hesitate to hire a Communist for a job he was qualified to do," observed Hutchins, "provided I was in a position to see that he did it." Under Hutchins' leadership, the fund pursued its goals even more aggressively. In 1955, it awarded a $5,000 grant to a Quaker organization known as the Plymouth Monthly Meeting. The meeting, located in southeastern Pennsylvania, had hired a librarian named Mary Knowles, who had been fired from her previous position in Massachusetts after FBI informant Herbert PHILBRICK had identified her as a Communist. Even though Knowles swore that she had not belonged to any subversive groups since 1947, her appointment outraged conservative elements in the local community. One group, Alerted Americans, claimed that Knowles' presence at the library "poses a possible future threat to our security." When the meeting resisted all pressure to fire Knowles, the fund decided to reward it with the $5,000 grant.

Perhaps the fund's most controversial project was a two-volume *Report on Blacklisting* compiled by former *Commonweal* editor John Cogley as part of a $300,000 fund grant to study "Communist influence in major segments of U.S. society." Cogley's report painted a picture of an entertainment industry terrorized by a handful of self-appointed anti-Communist vigilantes, notably the executives of AWARE, INC. and the editors of *RED CHANNELS* and *COUNTERATTACK*. The report so enraged the chair-

man of HUAC, Representative Francis WALTER of Pennsylvania, that he subpoenaed Cogley to testify before the committee. At the conclusion of Cogley's testimony, Walter—who had first achieved national prominence by sponsoring restrictive antiimmigration legislation—announced that "the Fund for the Republic report is a partisan, biased attack on all persons and organizations who are sincerely and patriotically concerned in ridding the movie industry and radio and television of Communists and Communist sympathizers."

As part of a counterattack against the fund, Walter then proceeded to summon Knowles, who invoked the Fifth Amendment and was cited for contempt. (Her conviction was later reversed on appeal.) Walter threatened to launch a full-scale probe of the fund's activities; because it was a tax-exempt organization, the fund was subject to a greater measure of congressional scrutiny (albeit from a committee other than HUAC) than a purely private organization. HUAC's investigation, however, never materialized.

McCarthy, too, struck back against the fund. The senator sarcastically referred to it as "the Ford Foundation Fund 'To Destroy the Republic' " and denounced its efforts "to reduce awareness of the Communist menace" and "destroy our security program." FBI Director J. Edgar HOOVER condemned the fund's activities as well, and at one point the Internal Revenue Service closely reviewed its status as a tax-exempt, nonprofit organization. But by this time the McCarthy era was coming to a close, and the fund was able to persevere in its activities reasonably free from right-wing interference. In fact, the fund itself helped signal an end to the anticommunist hysteria when it published the results of a 1954 public-opinion poll that revealed that "the number of people who said that they were worried either about the threat of Communists in the United States or about civil liberties was, even by the most generous interpretation of occasionally ambiguous responses, *less than 1 percent!*"

# G

**Garfield, John** (1913–1952) One of the leading liberals in Hollywood's motion picture industry, John Garfield (Julius Garfinkle) was born on New York's Lower East Side. After a rambunctious childhood during which he was frequently in trouble with school authorities, Garfield channeled his energies toward amateur boxing (he once was a semifinalist in a Golden Gloves tournament) and drama. Garfield attended the Hecksher Foundation drama school and also studied under Madame Maria Ouspenskaya and Eva Le Gallienne before taking several months off to travel across the country and back, hitchhiking and working at various odd jobs as a dishwasher, waiter, forest firefighter, and farm laborer.

In the early 1930s, Garfield joined the Group Theater Acting Company, a New York–based group of performers and writers who were dedicated to producing liberal, socially relevant drama. There Garfield appeared in such productions as *Counselor at Law* and Clifford ODETS' *Golden Boy*. "It seemed to me," Garfield later recalled, "that in the Group lay the future of American drama. We believed in what we were doing. I mean the social significance. We put on such plays as *Waiting for Lefty* [also by Odets], *Johnny Johnson, Awake and Sing, Weep for the Virgins,* and *Peace on Earth*".

Garfield signed a contract with Warner Bros. in 1938 and subsequently appeared in a number of popular and critically successful motion pictures, including *They Made Me a Criminal* (1939), *The Sea Wolf* (1941), *Out of the Fog* (1941), and John Steinbeck's *Tortilla Flat* (1942). During World War II, Garfield spent much of his time entertaining American troops overseas.

Meanwhile, Garfield had also become one of Hollywood's foremost liberal activists, serving on the executive board of the Screen Actors Guild and joining such organizations as the Motion Picture Artists Committee to Aid Republican Spain, the Motion Picture Guild, Inc., and the Independent Citizens Committee of the Arts, Sciences, and Professions. "I'm a fighting liberal, a progressive," Garfield once proudly declared. He demonstrated his liberal convictions by agreeing to appear in a featured role in the ground-breaking dramatic film, *Gentleman's Agreement* (1947), a powerful condemnation of anti-Semitism.

When the HOUSE COMMITTEE ON UN-AMERICAN ACTIVITIES (HUAC) launched its second investigation of Communist influence in Hollywood in 1951, however, Garfield was accused by informants of being a Communist sympathizer. At his own request, Garfield testified before the committee to clear his name. He acknowledged that he had naively supported numerous Communist front groups but insisted that he had not recognized them as Communist organizations. The members of the committee seemed to be unimpressed with Garfield's fervent declarations of anti-Communism. The actor was planning to return to Washington to testify a second time when he suffered a fatal heart attack.

*God That Failed, The (1949)* Edited by British Labour M.P. Richard Crossman and published in 1949, *The God That Failed* was a collection of essays written by six prominent ex-Communist intellectuals: Hungarian novelist Arthur KOESTLER, American journalist Louis Fischer, French essayist and novelist Andre Gide, African-American author Richard Wright, Italian journalist and playwright Ignazio Silone, and British poet Stephen Spender. In the essays, each author first explained why he had embraced Communism; each subsequently related his disillusionment with the party and/or Marxist ideology.

According to Crossman, the book grew out of a political discussion between himself and Koestler during which Koestler claimed that

"Anglo-Saxon anti-Communists" such as Crossman could not truly understand the appeal Communism held for a certain type of intellectual. The two men decided to limit the book to a half-dozen writers and journalists, most of whom had joined the Communist Party in the years between World War I and the NAZI-SOVIET PACT and who had subsequently discovered the gap between their own "vision of God and the reality of the Communist State," when "the conflict of conscience reached breaking point." "Our concern," noted Crossman, "was to study the state of mind of the communist convert, and the atmosphere of the period—from 1917 to 1939—when conversion was so common."

Crossman observed that all six authors had chosen Communism because they had lost faith in the ability of democracy to lead Western society further toward progress. The Depression of the 1930s and the ensuing policies of appeasement toward the Fascist powers of Germany, Italy, and Japan had appalled these men and opened their minds—along with many others like them—to the alternative faith of Communism. Crossman claimed that the conversion of these intellectuals was actually hastened by their deep Christian conscience. "The emotional appeal of Communism," he wrote, "lay precisely in the sacrifices—both material and spiritual—which it demanded of the convert." The notion of "an active comradeship of struggle" that required personal sacrifice and a leveling of class distinctions appealed to intellectual personalities searching for a higher and unquestioned purpose.

For these intellectuals, the Spanish Civil War of 1936–39 and the accompanying concept of a POPULAR FRONT embodied the struggle against Fascism. The conflict in Spain also brought a new generation of converts into the party while delaying the departure of others who had already glimpsed the reality of Communism. "To denounce Communism now," explained Crossman, "seemed tantamount to supporting Hitler and [British Prime Minister Neville] Chamberlain." The Nazi-Soviet Pact of August 1939,

however, aligned Moscow clearly on the side of the fascist states and therefore inaugurated a mass exodus of left-wing activists from the party in Europe and the United States.

Contributing to the disillusionment of each of these authors was the hostility felt by working-class members of the Communist Party toward intellectuals who joined the movement. The workers appear to have believed that writers and artists were merely playing at radical activism. Certainly, the commitment of the rank-and-file members of the party was based less on a need for spiritual fulfillment than for tangible economic and social rewards. Richard Wright's essay also provided a glimpse into the role of racial prejudice in the American Communist movement.

The appearance of *The God That Failed* provided a significant intellectual underpinning to the anti-Communist crusade in the United States, although it did not generate the sort of widespread publicity provided by more flamboyant former Communists such as Louis BUDENZ and Whittaker CHAMBERS.

**Gold, Harry** (1911– )   During World War II, American-born chemist Harry Gold served as a vital link in a Soviet espionage ring that also included Klaus FUCHS, David GREENGLASS, Morton SOBELL, Julius ROSENBERG, and possibly Ethel ROSENBERG.

Gold had grown up an intellectual loner in the slums of Philadelphia and graduated with distinction from Xavier University. When he entered the workforce during the depths of the Great Depression, Gold found it difficult to obtain a position in his chosen field until another chemist offered him a job along with an opportunity to join the COMMUNIST PARTY. According to Gold, he initially refused to become involved in left-wing political activities, believing that Communists were "a lot of whacked-up Bohemians."

By November 1935, however, Gold apparently had changed his mind, for he began to pass industrial secrets to Soviet agents. "I

Harry Gold (left), convicted of espionage as part of the Fuchs-Rosenberg spy ring.

thought that I would be helping a nation whose final aims I approved, along the road to industrial strength," Gold later told the FBI. "Particularly was I taken with the idea that whatever I did would go to help make living conditions far more advanced along the road as we know them here in the United States."

Gold claimed that he tried to make a break with his Soviet handlers in 1938 but agreed to continue passing along secrets when they threatened to expose him as a spy. During World War II, Gold advanced to a far more significant assignment. Under the direction of Soviet Vice Consul Anatoli Yakovlev in New York, Gold became the courier for atomic secrets obtained by British physicist Klaus Fuchs, who was working on the Manhattan Project's laboratory at Los Alamos, New Mexico. "I felt," explained Gold, "that as an ally I was only helping the Soviet Union obtain certain information that I thought it was entitled to." The two men met nearly a dozen times, at locations from New York's East Side to Santa Fe, New Mexico. Specifically, Fuchs gave Gold information on the application of theoretical fission to the building of a nuclear bomb. Gold also transferred information to the Soviets from David Greenglass, an Army technician stationed at Los Alamos. Greenglass' contribution was schematic drawings of a specialized lens mold for detonating an atomic weapon. The means used by Greenglass to identify Gold as the courier would later become famous: a third member of the espionage ring—allegedly Greenglass' brother-in-law, Julius Rosenberg—tore the top of a Jell-O package in two and gave half to Greenglass and the other half to Gold. When Gold appeared at Greenglass' apartment in Albuquerque and produced his torn half of the Jell-O package, Greenglass handed over the data.

In August 1949, the Soviet Union detonated its first nuclear device. U.S. military-intelligence officials, who had been caught by surprise, doubted that Soviet scientists could have built a bomb on their own in such a short time. Convinced that the Soviet Union must have received assistance from spies close to the U.S. nuclear-research effort, military officials and the FBI launched a search for Russian espionage agents in the United States.

In February 1950, the British government arrested Fuchs, who confessed to passing information to the Soviets during and after the war. Fuchs admitted that he had had an American contact, but he swore that he had never learned the man's name. Following a frantic search among possible suspects, the FBI finally narrowed the list down to three men including Harry Gold, who had been identified by ex-Communist Elizabeth BENTLEY in 1947 as one of her colleagues in another Soviet espionage network. At that time, a federal grand jury in New York had called Gold to testify, but because he succeeded in convincing the grand jury that he had never committed an overt act and was, in fact, "completely aghast at what he was on the brink of," no charges were filed against him at that time.

When British authorities first showed Gold's photograph to Fuchs, he denied that Gold had been his contact. Nevertheless, in May 1950 the FBI began to interrogate Gold, who was then working as a biochemist at Philadelphia General Hospital, specializing in research into the causes of heart disease. Gold denied any involvement in the Fuchs espionage ring and swore that he had never even been west of the Mississippi. When a search of Gold's apartment uncovered a pamphlet from the Santa Fe Chamber of Commerce, Gold broke down and confessed to having served as Fuchs' courier. Later that same day, Fuchs positively identified Gold from a new set of photographs provided by American authorities.

Gold proceeded to cooperate fully with the FBI. "When I went into custody," he later stated, "it was as if a mountain was in front of me. The mountain began to disappear after I talked to my father and brother, and disappeared completely after I pleaded guilty." The first name he gave the FBI was that of David Greenglass, who was arrested before he could flee the country. Greenglass subsequently informed the FBI that his contact had been his brother-in-law, Julius Rosenberg. Through adroit questioning, the FBI was able to corroborate Greenglass' testimony against Rosenberg by leading Gold to confess that one of his contacts, whom he had first identified as "Ben," actually employed the name "Julius."

Three days after the FBI arrested Julius Rosenberg, Gold was brought into court for sentencing. Although Gold had confessed before Fuchs provided positive identification of him as his courier and had cooperated fully with federal investigators, Judge James P. McGranery (who later became attorney general in the waning years of the Truman administration) sentenced Gold to thirty years in prison—five years more than the amount demanded by the prosecution. By handing down such a severe sentence,

McGranery claimed that he hoped to "deter others in the future from the commission of similar offenses." Gold eventually was released after serving fifteen years of his sentence.

**Goldwyn, Samuel** (1879–1974)   One of the few Hollywood film-studio executives who was willing to take a stand against the HOUSE COMMITTEE ON UN-AMERICAN ACTIVITIES (HUAC), Samuel Goldwyn—whose original name was Schmurl Gelbfisz—was born in Warsaw, Poland, and emigrated to the United States in 1895. Goldwyn worked his way up from a job as a floor sweeper in a glove factory in Gloversville, New York, to become one of the pioneers of the motion picture industry in Hollywood, California. During the next thirty years, Goldwyn helped organize several major studios—United Artists, Paramount, and Metro-Goldwyn-Mayer—but left each company in turn, always perferring to operate as an independent.

Operating outside the traditional studio system, Goldwyn acquired a well-deserved reputation for unpredictability. In September 1947, HUAC subpoenaed Goldwyn as part of its initial full-scale investigation into Communist influence in Hollywood, but the committee—unable to predict Goldwyn's stance toward the investigation—never called him to testify. As writer Lillian HELLMAN later explained, Goldwyn was "too much of a wild card. You never knew what was going to come out of his mouth, and he probably wouldn't have gone along with the committee's script." While waiting to be called by the committee, Goldwyn expressed his frustration to a reporter from *The New York Times*. "What is the matter?" Goldwyn asked. "Are they afraid to call me?"

When the committee continued to ignore him, an angry Goldwyn released his own public statement castigating the committee's investigation at the end of October. "As an American," he declared, "I have been astounded and outraged at the manner in which the committee has permitted our industry to be vilified by gossip, innuendo and hearsay. . . . The most un-American activity which I have observed in connection with the hearings has been the activity of the Committee itself. The purpose of these hearings seems to have been to try to dictate and control what goes on the screens of America. I resent and abhor censorship of thought. I assure you that as long as I live no one will ever be able to dictate what I put on the screen so long as I continue to honor and obey the laws of our country."

The following month, Goldwyn met with President Harry S. TRUMAN and assured Truman that "there never has been, and there never will be, any Communism in our pictures." He reiterated his charge that HUAC "has been un-American in the way it has handled this," and he suggested that HUAC Chairman J. Parnell THOMAS "is seeing this through pink-colored glasses." When he received a letter from an outraged patron who claimed to have walked out of a performance of a film starring Danny Kaye, a leading Hollywood liberal and a member of the COMMITTEE FOR THE FIRST AMENDMENT (an ad hoc organization established to protect the rights of motion-picture witnesses called to testify before HUAC), Goldwyn defended Kaye by reviewing his war record and citing Kaye's "old-fashioned and fundamental American right of expressing his opinion to the elected representatives of the people."

Following the refusal of a group of left-wing actors and directors—who became known as the HOLLYWOOD TEN—to answer HUAC's questions about their past political activities and associations, executives from the major Hollywood studios gathered at the Waldorf-Astoria Hotel in New York on November 25, 1947, to determine their course of action. Most of the studio heads wished to abandon the Ten to their fate (that is, prison) and refuse to hire them until they had purged themselves of contempt charges. The executives also hoped to forestall further government interference in the motion picture industry by announcing that they would not knowingly hire anyone who was a Communist or a Communist sympathizer.

Goldwyn, who attended the Waldorf conference, was appalled by the willingness of his colleagues to submit to pressure from the anti-Communist zealots. Since the Hollywood Ten were appealing their convictions for contempt, Goldwyn suggested that the studios await the verdict of the U.S. Supreme Court instead of immediately declaring the Hollywood Ten unsuitable for employment. "After the Supreme Court has spoken," Goldwyn explained, "we will know definitely whether they were within their rights or not, in acting as they did. Until then we are reserving judgment and suspending action." When it became clear that the majority of studio executives, led by Eric Johnston, favored immediate action, Goldwyn announced that he "would not be allied to any such nonsense." In the end, however, Goldwyn relented and signed the WALDORF STATEMENT.

Despite his misgivings about the implications of the Waldorf declaration, which played a crucial role in the establishment of a BLACKLIST in Hollywood, Goldwyn refused to relent and hire one of the Ten, even when director William Wyler implored him to change his mind. "I'm sorry," the veteran producer told Wyler. "It would be a dishonorable thing to do." Having signed the statement, Goldwyn said, "I couldn't go back on it."

**Gouzenko, Igor** (1915–1982)  A cipher clerk in the Soviet embassy in Ottawa, Canada, who defected in September 1945, Igor Gouzenko brought with him a bundle of coded documents that he claimed provided evidence of a spy ring consisting of prominent leaders in the Canadian political and scientific communities. Partly to avoid a confrontation with the Soviet Union at a time when Soviet-Western relations were deteriorating badly, the Canadian government did not move against the espionage ring for several months, until reports in the American press forced its hand. Canadian offi-

Igor Gouzenko (with hood), the Soviet diplomat who defected to Canada and subsequently made allegations of Soviet espionage in North America.

cials subsequently established a special commission to investigate Gouzenko's charges, and a number of individuals were eventually accused of espionage.

Nearly five years later, Gouzenko's testimony helped lead British authorities to atomic spy Klaus FUCHS. Gouzenko also reportedly told investigators that Soviet officials had told him that a Soviet agent had obtained a position near the top of the U.S. State Department, with access to the secretary of state himself. Evidence to support Gouzenko's allegations was noticeably thin. Nevertheless, the FEDERAL BUREAU OF INVESTIGATION (FBI) combined Gouzenko's testimony with statements previously made by an ex-Communist journalist named Whittaker CHAMBERS and concluded that the purported Soviet agent probably was a young State Department official named Alger HISS. FBI agents subsequently began to trail Hiss and placed a wiretap on his phone. In 1948, Hiss became the subject of a grand-jury investigation into his past political activities and associations.

Gouzenko's revelations represented the first evidence, however tenuous, to support the belief of FBI officials and conservatives in Congress that there were Soviet espionage agents in the federal government and that members of the COMMUNIST PARTY OF THE UNITED STATES were still operating under the direction of Moscow, thereby rendering them a threat to the security of the United States.

## Government Operations Committee

Originally known as the Committee on Expenditures in the Executive Department, the Senate Committee on Government Operations was established in 1946 by the Legislative Reorganization Act. Before its powers were expanded by Senator Joseph MCCARTHY of Wisconsin, the Government Operations Committee was generally regarded as one of the two least influential committees in the Senate, along with the District of Columbia Committee. Upon McCarthy's election to the Senate in 1946, the Republican leadership in the Senate had placed him on the Government Operations Committee largely because it had such little respect for his abilities. By 1949, when Senator Clyde HOEY of North Carolina became chairman of the committee, McCarthy was the ranking Republican member and as such enjoyed the authority to make all Republican assignments on the Government Operations subcommittees. One of his first actions in that role was the assignment of Senator Richard M. NIXON to the PERMANENT SUBCOMMITTEE ON INVESTIGATIONS when Nixon took his seat in the Senate in 1951.

McCarthy employed the power of the Government Operations Committee to conduct investigations into Communist influence in the State Department during the TRUMAN administration. When the Republicans gained control of Congress following the elections of 1952, McCarthy had the option of chairing either the Senate Appropriations Committee or the Government Operations Committee. Much to the surprise of veteran Washington observers, McCarthy chose to remain with the traditionally less prestigious Operations committee. McCarthy's decision pleased Senate Majority Leader

Robert TAFT, who believed that "he can't do any harm" in that role.

Taft was badly mistaken. McCarthy continued to use the investigatory authority of the committee to harass the EISENHOWER administration, conducting inquiries into Communist infiltration of the CENTRAL INTELLIGENCE AGENCY (CIA), the INTERNATIONAL INFORMATION AGENCY (IIA), the Government Printing Office, and, finally, the U.S. Army. During the next two years, the Government Operations Committee became one of the three leading anti-Communist investigative bodies in Congress, rivaled only by the SENATE INTERNAL SECURITY SUB-COMMITTEE and the HOUSE COMMITTEE ON UN-AMERICAN ACTIVITIES (HUAC). During McCarthy's chairmanship in 1953–54, the committee's Republican membership included Karl MUNDT, Everett Dirksen, Henry Dworshak, John M. Butler, Margaret Chase SMITH, and Charles Potter; Democratic members of the committee were Hoey, John L. MCCLELLAN of Arkansas, Hubert HUMPHREY, and freshmen senators John F. KENNEDY, Stuart SYMINGTON, and Henry Jackson of Washington. The latter three Democratic members had been appointed to Government Operations by Senate Minority Leader Lyndon Baines JOHNSON largely because they would not face reelection for another six years and presumably would be more willing to confront McCarthy if necessary.

## Greenglass, David (1922– )

An Army technician stationed at Los Alamos, New Mexico, during World War II, David Greenglass was part of a Soviet atomic espionage ring that also included Harry GOLD, Klaus FUCHS, Julius ROSENBERG, and perhaps Ethel ROSENBERG, who was Greenglass' sister. According to Greenglass' testimony to federal authorities, he was recruited as a spy by Julius Rosenberg. Although Greenglass was only a sergeant and a machinist at Los Alamos, New Mexico—the site of the Manhattan Project, which produced the nuclear weapons used against Japan in August 1945—

he enjoyed access to highly classified research data. Rosenberg allegedly described to Greenglass the atomic bomb the Manhattan Project scientists were constructing and gave Greenglass detailed instructions on the sort of data the Soviet Union wanted him to provide. Rosenberg also gave Greenglass half of a raspberry Jell-O box that he had torn in two and gave the other half to a Soviet courier—Harry Gold—as a means of identification to Greenglass.

As instructed, Greenglass obtained copies of drawings of a specialized lens mold that produced a vital component for detonating the bomb. When Gold appeared at the Greenglass' apartment at 209 North High Street in Albuquerque in June 1945 with the second half of the torn Jell-O box, Greenglass handed him the information, and Gold turned over $500 to Greenglass. The transaction apparently upset Greenglass' wife, who had assumed her husband was betraying his country for idealistic reasons. "Now I see how it is," she cried. "You turn over the information and you get paid. Why, it's just—it's just like C.O.D.!"

Four months later, Greenglass provided Rosenberg with additional sketches of the trigger mechanism that had been employed in the bomb dropped upon Nagasaki. He also reportedly gave Rosenberg information about a highly classified American satellite research project.

When the Soviet Union successfully detonated its first nuclear device in August 1949, U.S. military-intelligence officials—who were convinced that the Soviets could not have produced such a device in so short a time without outside assistance—joined the FBI in a search for Russian espionage agents in the United States. In February 1950, the British government arrested Klaus Fuchs, a former member of the Los Alamos laboratory team, who promptly confessed to his part in the espionage ring. Using Fuchs' testimony, FBI agents were able to track down Harry Gold, who had carried information from Fuchs to the Soviet vice consul in New York. Gold, too, confessed, and told authorities that he had another contact—Greenglass—at Los Alamos besides Fuchs.

When Julius Rosenberg learned that Gold had been arrested on May 23, 1950, he gave Greenglass $1,000 in cash and instructed him to flee the country and report to the Soviet Embassy in Prague, Czechoslovakia, where he would meet the Rosenbergs before continuing their journey to Moscow. Greenglass, however, hesitated. His wife refused to leave the country because she did not want to subject their ten-day-old infant to the rigors of travel. Unwilling to abandon his wife and two children, Greenglass briefly considered suicide. Instead, he remained in Albuquerque and was subsequently arrested and charged with conspiracy to commit espionage. Perhaps to prevent the implication of his wife in the affair, Greenglass cooperated fully with federal authorities. On June 15, he signed a statement admitting that Julius Rosenberg had recruited him as a Soviet agent. He told prosecutors of the torn Jell-O box and the payments from Gold and Rosenberg.

It was Greenglass' testimony that directly linked Julius Rosenberg to the spy ring. Gold had told the FBI that he had identified himself to Greenglass with the message, "Greetings from Ben," but Greenglass adamantly insisted that if Gold had brought greetings from anyone, the name "Ben" would not have been used as a code word because it meant nothing to him. Rather, Greenglass suggested that Gold had used the phrase, "Greetings from Julius," meaning Julius Rosenberg. When investigators suggested to Gold that the name he had used was "Julius" instead of "Ben," Gold—after considerable reflection—agreed that Julius was, indeed, the name he probably had used on the instructions of the Soviet vice consul.

Defenders of the Rosenbergs, who were convicted of conspiracy to commit espionage and executed in June 1953, later claimed that Greenglass perjured himself by implicating his own sister and her husband in the espionage ring. An analysis of the available evidence does not support that contention. For his role in the atomic espionage affair, Greenglass was sentenced to fifteen years in prison. He was subsequently released after serving ten years.

# H

**Hammett, Samuel Dashiell** (1894–1961)
Best-known for his hard-boiled detective novels, Samuel Dashiell Hammett was also a dedicated Marxist who supported numerous radical political and educational causes in the United States.

A native of southern Maryland, Hammett left school at the age of 14 to help support his family as a messenger for the Baltimore and Ohio Railroad. He worked at a variety of odd jobs for the next seven years, until he obtained a job in 1915 as an operative with the Pinkerton National Detective Agency. Hammett's experiences as a detective formed the basis for his detective stories, many of which were first published in the 1920s in *The Black Mask* mystery magazine.

By 1927, when Hammett completed his first novel—*Red Harvest*—he was writing detective fiction on a full-time basis. He followed the success of *Red Harvest* with *The Dain Curse, The Maltese Falcon,* and *The Glass Key.* In 1930, Hammett moved to Hollywood, where he wrote a series of screenplays for Paramount and Warner Bros. studios and began a lifelong relationship with aspiring author Lillian HELLMAN.

Hammett produced virtually no significant works of prose fiction after 1934; instead, he continued to write screenplays while becoming deeply involved in left-wing political activities in Hollywood. Disturbed by what he called "a rising tide of anti-Semitism and Fascism," Hammett joined a number of POPULAR FRONT organizations. With Hellman, Lester COLE, Melvyn DOUGLAS, John GARFIELD, Fredric MARCH, and director John Ford, Hammett helped establish the Motion Pictures Arts Committee to Aid Republican Spain. He also served as cofounder of the League of American Writers, another group dedicated to supporting the Loyalist cause in the Spanish Civil War. In 1938, Hammett was elected chairman of the Motion Picture Democratic Committee, a campaign organization devoted to the election of Democratic candidates in California.

Although Hammett never joined the COMMUNIST PARTY—he was far too independent to submit to party discipline—he did consider himself a Marxist and in 1940 worked unsuccessfully to defeat the passage of the SMITH ACT, which sought to make membership in the Communist Party a crime. That same year, Hammett led an equally unsuccessful effort to force states to include Communist Party candidates on their ballots. As Hammett's name appeared frequently on antifascist notices in the Communist publications *New Masses* and the *DAILY WORKER,* FBI agents began to compile a dossier on him.

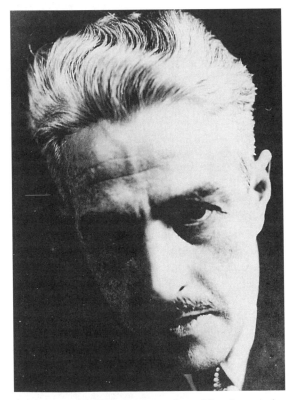

Author Dashiell Hammett, whose Marxist convictions helped earn him a jail sentence for contempt of court.

Hammett served in the U.S. Army Signal Corps during World War II. Following his discharge, he resumed his radical activities. In June 1946, the Civil Rights Congress (CRC) (cited by the federal government as a Communist-front organization) elected Hammett its president and made him one of the trustees of the bail-bond fund established for the use of members who encountered legal difficulties. Hammett also began to teach that year at the Jefferson School of Social Science in New York, a shabby institution with an admittedly Marxist philosophy. (The Jefferson School was also on the government's list of subversive organizations.) As the anti-Communist crusade in the United States gathered momentum, Hammett joined sixty-five other prominent celebrities in questioning the legality of the tactics employed by the HOUSE COMMITTEE ON UN-AMERICAN ACTIVITIES (HUAC). Still, Hammett remained contemptuous of both the Soviet Union and the American Communist Party.

By the end of 1950, the FBI had compiled a voluminous dossier on Hammett. An article by a columnist in the tabloid *Hollywood Life,* clearly written with access to FBI files, referred rather ungrammatically to Hammett as "one of the most dangerous (if not *the*) influential communists in America." The column cited several of the more than thirty-five Communist-front organizations to which Hammett allegedly belonged, according to FBI files; the list included the Hollywood Writers' Congress, the Citizens Committee for Harry Bridges, the Civil Rights Congress, the American Committee for the Protection of the Foreign Born, and the Motion Picture Artists' Committee.

In June 1951, four American Communist leaders who had been convicted of violations of the Smith Act jumped bail and disappeared. Because the Civil Rights Congress had secured the defendants' bail bonds, government prosecutors decided to question Hammett—as a trustee of the CRC bail-bond fund—to help them track down the vanished defendants. Hammett's position in the organization, however, had been purely honorary; he had never been in the offices of the CRC, and he did not know the name of a single contributor to the bail-bond fund. Instead of pleading ignorance, which he would have been justified in doing, Hammett invoked the Fifth Amendment more than eighty times during his interrogation by the district attorney, refusing to answer any questions about the CRC or its membership. "I guess," he explained to Hellman, "it has something to do with keeping my word."

For his silence, Hammett was sentenced to six months in federal prison. After his release in December 1951, Hammett discovered he had been BLACKLISTED from radio, television, and films. NBC canceled his Sam Spade radio series, and Universal Studios removed his name from the credits of the movie version of Hammett's *The Fat Man.* Following an audit by the IRS, Hammett received a bill for more than $100,000 in back taxes. In March 1953, Senator Joseph MCCARTHY summoned Hammett to testify before his subcommittee. Asked if he had ever been involved in espionage or sabotage against the United States, Hammett answered with an unequivocal "No." He added that he did not think Russian Communism would be better for the United States than the present democracy; besides, he added, "it would seem to me impractical if most people didn't want it."

Several months later, McCarthy's aides, Roy COHN and G. David SCHINE, toured State Department libraries overseas and insisted that all works by Communists or Communist sympathizers be removed from the libraries' shelves. Among the books they identified as subversive were Hammett's mystery novels. This action struck President Dwight David EISENHOWER as somewhat excessive, and he ordered Hammett's works restored.

Impoverished and in failing health, Hammett spent the remaining years of his life living alone in New York, visited occasionally by Lillian Hellman. He died of lung cancer on January 10, 1961.

**Actor Sterling Hayden recanted his Communist beliefs in testimony before HUAC.**

## Hayden, Sterling (1916–1986)

A Hollywood actor who vaulted to stardom with his role in *The Asphalt Jungle* (1950), Hayden was subpoenaed to testify in April 1951 before the HOUSE COMMITTEE ON UN-AMERICAN ACTIVITIES (HUAC) about his alleged involvement with the Communist Party. Afraid that a refusal to comply might jeopardize his career, Hayden temporized but finally agreed to appear before the committee. In his testimony, Hayden admitted that he had first become interested in left-wing politics during World War II while serving as a Marine officer attached to the U.S. Office of Strategic Services (OSS). Hayden had been assigned to help smuggle arms to the partisan forces of Marshal Tito in their struggle against German troops in Yugoslavia, and Hayden informed the House committee that he had been "tremendously impressed" and "deeply affected" by the dedication displayed by Tito's

Communist guerrillas. As a result, Hayden decided to become involved in politics when he returned to the United States at the end of the war. Hayden joined the COMMUNIST PARTY in 1946 but left, disillusioned, approximately six months later. He told the House committee at the end of his prepared statement that the whole affair seemed "the stupidest, most ignorant thing I've ever done."

When the committee pressed him to reveal the names of other members of the Communist Party, Hayden claimed that he had known most of them only by their first names. Nevertheless, he did provide the committee with the full names of seven alleged members, including his former mistress (who was also his agent's secretary), whom Hayden claimed had recruited him into the party. After he had completed his testimony, Hayden was stricken with remorse and came to consider himself a coward for having informed on his former associates. He subsequently went on a speaking tour across the United States, renouncing his decision to act as an informer and candidly explaining that he had told the committee what it wanted to know solely to save his acting career. In so doing, Hayden became one of the few Hollywood celebrities who cooperated with HUAC and then recanted their testimony. Hayden's career did, in fact, prosper throughout the 1950s until he left Hollywood to devote himself to sailing and writing.

## Hays, Arthur Garfield (1881–1954)

Counsel to the AMERICAN CIVIL LIBERTIES UNION (ACLU), Arthur Garfield Hays was a leading liberal opponent of efforts to outlaw the COMMUNIST PARTY in the United States.

A graduate of Columbia College, Hays received his law degrees from Columbia Law School in 1905 and entered private practice. After spending several years in England during World War I, he returned to the United States and became interested in the work of the ACLU, accepting a position as counsel for the organization in the early 1920s. Hays—who had been an active supporter of Theodore Roosevelt's Progressive Party candidacy in 1912—joined the left-wing Farmer-Labor Party in 1920, and acted as New York state chairman of the Progressive Party during the presidential candidacy of Robert La Follette in 1924. Following that campaign he joined the Democratic Party, to which he belonged for the remainder of his life.

On February 10, 1948, Hays testified before the HOUSE COMMITTEE ON UN-AMERICAN ACTIVITIES (HUAC) to urge the committee to reject proposed measures to make membership in the Communist Party illegal in the United States. In taking this stand, Hays distanced himself from numerous other officials of the American Civil Liberties Union who supported such legislation in an attempt to establish their credentials as anti-Communist liberals. To Hays, legislation outlawing the Communist Party was equivalent to substituting "totalitarian practices for democratic principles." In the first place, Hays argued that the Communist Party could easily evade such a law merely by changing its name. Moreover, Hays echoed the criticism of FBI director J. Edgar HOOVER to such legislation, on the grounds that it would actually promote the growth of the Communist movement in the United States. "Experience," noted Hays, "shows that laws of this kind would merely drive the movement underground, give it the advantage of the emotionalism that arises from secrecy, and lend to its members the halo of martyrdom."

In observing that the Communists had made little headway in the United States during the past twenty-five years, Hays wondered why the members of HUAC were so alarmed about the potential future growth of Communism in America. "I cannot understand you men," Hays told the committee. "You say you are Americans. You are so little American; you have so little faith in our institutions. The idea of being afraid of Communists is ridiculous."

Hays' primary objections to the proposed legislation, however, were philosophical rather than practical. "This kind of legislation," he stated,

"seems to me to be wholly un-American, indicates lack of faith in our institutions, would arouse fear and timidity, and invite attacks upon sincere liberal thought." To Hays, HUAC's proposals bore a frightening resemblance to measures passed in the 1920s and 1930s in fascist nations abroad. "Freedom," Hays concluded, "is the right to hear an opinion, and the idea of passing laws to keep people's names off the ballot—those are the views of the totalitarians, and if those views are contrary to Americanism, if that is Communistic, then I am a Communist."

## Hellman, Lillian (1905–1984)

An award-winning playwright and former member of the COMMUNIST PARTY, Lillian Hellman was born in New Orleans and grew up in New York City. An only child—and an unusually inquisitive one—in an affluent family, Hellman admittedly was spoiled by her parents in her youth. "I must have been a prize nuisance child," she recalled years later. "I formed everything in the form of a question. And I would pull at everybody's coats or dresses to tell me what I wanted to know along a street." Following her graduation from high school, Hellman attended New York University and Columbia University but never distinguished herself by her scholarship. Instead, she obtained a position with a New York publishing firm in 1924, doing "a little advertising work, a little publicity, and a lot of manuscript reading." By 1926, Hellman had begun to write short stories, as well as book reviews for the New York *Herald Tribune*.

In 1930, Hellman met Dashiell HAMMETT, the author of a number of well-received hard-boiled detective novels (*The Maltese Falcon* and *The Thin Man,* among others); although Hellman was already married when they met (she received a divorce in 1932), the two soon began a relationship that continued for three decades. Hammett encouraged Hellman to continue her writing, and in 1934 she completed her first play, *The Children's Hour.* The play proved a hit on Broadway, earning praise from reviewers for its originality and dramatic force. (It also earned Hellman more than $125,000 in profits.) Near the end of 1934, Hellman moved to Hollywood and subsequently accepted an offer from film producer Samuel GOLDWYN to write screenplays at a salary of $2,500 a week. For the next decade, Hellman moved back and forth between Hollywood and New York, seldom staying in one place for more than four or five months at a time.

During this time, she became actively involved in radical political activities. Hammett had long been a dedicated Marxist, and in 1938 Hellman—already well-known as a prominent member of antifascist organizations and a leading supporter of the Loyalist cause in the Spanish Civil War—appears to have joined the Communist Party. "I was late [in joining the radical movement]," she later wrote; "by that period many intellectuals had made the turn. So many, in fact, that some were even turning another way."

Hellman began a rigorous study of political texts: "I put aside most other books for Marx and Engels, Lenin, Saint-Simon, Hegel, Feuerbach. Certainly I did not study with the dedication of a scholar, but I did read with the attention of a good student, and Marx as a man and Engels and his wife Mary became, for a while, more real to me than my friends."

Her decision to join the party, Hellman claimed, was motivated by a conviction that the party's "ultimate aims were humanitarian and idealistic." In June 1939, Hellman attended the Third National Congress of the League of American Writers and signed the congress' resolution calling for "cooperation of this country with other nations and people opposed to Fascism, including the Soviet Union, which has been the most constant defender of the people." Unlike many of her fellow left-wing writers and artists, Hellman did not abandon the cause of the Soviet Union following the announcement of the NAZI-SOVIET PACT in August 1939; loyally adopting the Communist line, Hellman opposed American involvement in the European

war. In June 1941, for instance, Hellman and Hammett both publicly backed the decision of the Fourth National Congress of the League of American Writers urging that America stay out of the conflict.

Yet in her strongly antifascist play, *Watch on the Rhine,* which made its debut in April 1941, Hellman clearly appeared to be moving toward acceptance of the need for American intervention. The German invasion of the Soviet Union in June 1941 led Hellman to complete the transition. Less than a month after the invasion, Hellman signed a resolution by the League of American Writers calling upon "all creative workers" in the United States to "demand full support to Great Britain and the Soviet Union in their struggle for the 'demolition of Fascism.' "

Hellman later acknowledged that she had, in fact, left the Communist Party in 1940. She claimed that she had originally joined the party without "any real information about the nature of the party." Besides, she added, she had never been a very active party member, partly because she chafed under the restrictions of party discipline. In her memoir, *An Unfinished Woman* (1969), Hellman noted that "my political convictions were never very radical, in the true, best, serious sense. Rebels seldom make good revolutionaries, perhaps because organized action, even union with other people, is not possible for them."

During World War II, Hellman worked with Goldwyn on a script for the film NORTH STAR. According to Hellman, the film originally was intended to be a semidocumentary but evolved instead into a rather soggy melodrama that portrayed the Russian peasantry as simple, noble-hearted victims of Nazi tyranny. Nevertheless, the film earned Hellman an invitation from the Soviet Union to discuss cultural affairs in 1944. President Franklin Delano Roosevelt approved Hellman's mission to Moscow, though he did not endorse it as an official trip.

Hellman's radical activities also earned her an invitation from the HOUSE COMMITTEE ON UN-AMERICAN ACTIVITIES (HUAC) to testify on

May 21, 1952 about her past. By that time, numerous witnesses had invoked the protection of the Fifth Amendment in their appearances before HUAC to avoid incriminating themselves; some had also attempted to employ the Fifth Amendment to avoid implicating their former associates, although the amendment did not provide a witness with the right to avoid incriminating anyone except himself or herself. In any event, Hellman wrote a letter to HUAC Chairman John S. WOOD on May 19, in which she expressed a willingness to testify about her own beliefs and activities but not about anyone else. This position actually represented a sort of mirror image of the Fifth Amendment's protection against self-incrimination. Hellman's counsel informed her, however, that she could not even testify freely about herself, for—as the Supreme Court had decided in 1951—once a witness had disclosed a fact, that witness had waived the privilege of Fifth Amendment protection as to details. If one admitted that one had been a Communist Party member, one could not employ the Fifth Amendment to avoid testifying about the details of one's membership, that is, fellow members, details of meetings, and so forth.

Hellman therefore wrote to Chairman Wood that "I am most willing to answer all questions about myself. I have nothing to hide from your Committee and there is nothing in my life of which I am ashamed. . . . But I am advised by counsel that if I answer the Committee's questions about myself, I must also answer questions about other people and that if I refuse to do so, I can be cited for contempt. . . . This is very difficult for a layman to understand. But there is one principle that I do understand: I am not willing, now or in the future, to bring bad trouble to people who, in my past association with them, were completely innocent of any talk or any action that was disloyal or subversive. I do not like subversion or disloyalty in any form, and if I had ever seen any, I would have considered it my duty to have reported it to the proper authorities. But to hurt innocent people

whom I knew many years ago in order to save myself is, to me, inhuman and indecent and dishonorable. I cannot and will not cut my conscience to fit this year's fashions, even though I long ago came to the conclusion that I was not a political person and could have no comfortable place in any political group."

Wood refused to accept Hellman's letter, explaining that "the Committee cannot permit witnesses to set forth the terms under which they will testify." The committee, he noted, understood that there were many people who had belonged to the Communist Party under the assumption that it was not a subversive organization. Yet, Wood pointed out, the contributions of such individuals had made it possible for the true subversives in the party to carry on their insidious work. Wood closed with a promise that anyone whom Hellman named in her testimony would receive an opportunity to testify before HUAC and clear his or her name.

A day before she was scheduled to testify, Hellman received a call from her attorney, Joseph Rauh, who informed her that another lawyer with extensive experience in dealing with HUAC (Thurman Arnold, a partner of Abe FORTAS) had advised him that if Hellman did not retract her letter, she likely would be cited for contempt and convicted. Nevertheless, Hellman refused to retract the note, and on the morning of May 21 she appeared at the appointed committee hearing room. The committee appeared most interested in obtaining Hellman's confirmation of the testimony of Martin Berkeley, a previous witness who had supplied HUAC with extensive details about Communist infiltration of the motion picture industry in Hollywood. Hellman refused to answer, and after several more questions on the matter, Rauh began passing copies of Hellman's and Wood's letters to reporters in attendance. Several minutes later, after the press had an opportunity to read Hellman's note, Hellman heard a voice from the audience saying, "Thank God somebody finally had the guts to do it." She later wrote that that moment had been one of the best times of her life and that "that unknown voice made the words that helped to save me" because Hellman had been seriously considering launching into a verbal attack upon the committee for its arrogance.

After a few additional perfunctory questions, Wood dismissed Hellman, and her ordeal was over. Hammett, however, was later convicted for contempt following his refusal to testify before the Senate INTERNAL SECURITY SUBCOMMITTEE. Like most witnesses from the motion picture industry who invoked the Fifth Amendment, Hellman found herself BLACKLISTED for several years on the assumption that she was or had been a Communist. By 1958, Hellman began to receive screenwriting offers once again, but she declined to return to Hollywood. Hellman subsequently wrote a personal account of the era of anti-Communist hysteria in the United States, entitled SCOUNDREL TIME. (1976), in which she concluded that the anti-Communist zealots did far more harm to the United States than she and her fellow radicals. "They went to too many respectable conferences that turned out not to be under respectable auspices, contributed to and published too many CIA magazines," she wrote. "The step from such capers was straight into the Vietnam War and the days of Nixon. Many of the anti-Communists were, of course, honest men. But none of them, as far as I know, has stepped forward to admit a mistake."

## Hepburn, Katharine (1907– )

A leading Hollywood film star from the 1930s, Katharine Hepburn became a target of anti-Communist zealots in 1947 due to her outspoken support of liberal causes. Although she once claimed that "I'm not very political. I just believe in being liberal and affirmative," Hepburn became active in national political affairs in the postwar years due to her disillusionment with President Harry S. TRUMAN as leader of the Democratic Party. When former Vice President Henry WALLACE announced his intention to run for the presidency in 1948 on the Progressive Party

Actress Katharine Hepburn, an outspoken Hollywood liberal and supporter of the First Amendment.

ticket, Hepburn supported him enthusiastically. At a pro-Wallace and anticensorship rally in Los Angeles in May 1947, Hepburn delivered a stinging rebuke to the HOUSE COMMITTEE ON UN-AMERICAN ACTIVITIES (HUAC)—and particularly committee chairman J. Parnell THOMAS—for the committee's recent decision to launch an investigation of Communist influences in the motion picture industry: "J. Parnell Thomas is engaged in a personally conducted smear campaign of the motion picture industry," Hepburn declared. "He is aided and abetted in his efforts by a group of super patriots who call themselves the MOTION PICTURE ALLIANCE FOR THE PRESERVATION OF AMERICAN IDEALS. For myself, I want no part of their ideals or those of Mr. Thomas. The artist since the beginning of time has always expressed the aspirations and dreams of his people. Silence the artist and you have silenced the most articulate voice the people have." Unfortunately for Hepburn, she chose (apparently innocently) to wear a pink dress to the Wallace rally, a color which Wallace's enemies had long associated with the ultraliberal politician.

Hepburn's name surfaced several times during the ensuing HUAC hearings in Washington. At one point, director Leo McCarey, one of the "friendly" witnesses the committee imported from Hollywood, pointed out that Hepburn had helped raise nearly $90,000 for a "very special" radical political cause that, McCarey pointed out, "certainly wasn't the Boy Scouts."

When a group of left-wing actors and directors who subsequently became known as the HOLLYWOOD TEN were summoned to answer the committee's questions about their past political activities and associations, Hepburn joined with several hundred other liberals in the motion picture community—including William Wyler, John Huston, Humphrey BOGART, and Frank SINATRA—in supporting the COMMITTEE FOR THE FIRST AMENDMENT to protest HUAC's invasion of their right of free speech. When the Hollywood Ten refused to answer the committee's questions, they were cited for contempt of Congress and subsequently fined and sentenced to prison.

Fearful that Congress might attempt to impose further control over the motion picture industry, a conference of leading studio executives formulated the WALDORF STATEMENT, in which they pledged not to employ any members of the Ten until they had purged themselves of contempt. The studios also vowed to refrain from hiring anyone whom they suspected of aiding the Communist cause, in part because they feared adverse public reaction to films featuring alleged Communists sympathizers. Already, the executives pointed out, a film starring Hepburn had been stoned by an angry audience in North Carolina. Hepburn was consequently BLACKLISTED from films for several months. She returned to work only when Spencer Tracy, with whom she had starred in *Woman of the Year* (with a screenplay written by Ring LARDNER, Jr., a member of the Hollywood Ten), recommended that she replace Claudette Colbert in the movie *State of the Union* in 1949. One of Hepburn's co-stars in *State of the Union* was Adolphe MENJOU, a leading Hollywood conservative who had cooperated enthusiastically with HUAC investigators. At one point during the filming, Menjou muttered, "Scratch a do-

gooder like Hepburn, and they'll yell '*Pravda*,' " a reference to the Soviet Union's leading daily newspaper. Thereafter, director Frank Capra kept the set closed to reporters to reduce the risk of further public confrontations between the two stars.

## Hicks, Granville (1901–1982)

A prominent historian and literary critic, Granville Hicks was a former COMMUNIST PARTY member who was subpoenaed by the HOUSE COMMITTEE ON UN-AMERICAN ACTIVITIES (HUAC) as part of its investigation of Communist influence in American colleges and universities. Hicks had joined the Communist Party in 1934–35, while an assistant professor of English at Rensselaer Polytechnic Institute in Troy, New York. Prior to that time, he had served for a year as literary editor of the Communist publication *New Masses*. (" 'Employed' is not the right word," noted Hicks, "since the *New Masses* never paid anything.").

Hicks made no secret of his party membership, believing that Communism represented the world's best hope in the struggle against fascism. Six months after he joined the party, he was fired by Rensselaer, presumably for his political convictions. Hicks spent the next few years as a freelance writer, speaking at Communist Party meetings, helping to organize the League of American Writers, and broadcasting for the party on the radio. At that time, Hicks later testified, the party's strategy was designed to achieve two fundamental objectives: "One was to carry out the existing [POPULAR FRONT] line which they wanted to make a show of advancing, and then, of course, the other was to try to have a corps of disciplined revolutionaries whom they could use for other purposes when the time came."

In 1938, Hicks was hired by Harvard as a counselor in the American Studies program, where he came in contact with Daniel J. BOOR-STIN. Perhaps because of his membership in the Communist Party, the college declined to extend Hicks' contract past the initial term of one year. Like numerous other radical intellectuals who had joined the Party as part of the Popular Front movement against fascism, Hicks was disillusioned by the announcement of the NAZI-SOVIET PACT in August 1939. "It made clear to me what should have been clear to me earlier," noted Hicks, "and that is that the Communist Party in the United States was wholly under the domination of the Soviet Union." He left the party, and began to write articles critical of the Communist movement for American journals. In the late 1940s, Hicks also became an active participant in the militantly anti-Communist AMERICANS FOR DEMOCRATIC ACTION (ADA).

Unlike Boorstin, Hicks refused to join HUAC in its attempt to deny employment in American universities to anyone who was a member of the Communist Party. Arguing that "you cannot protect all college students a hundred per cent," either from the evils of drink or Communism, Hicks maintained that "there are situations in which it would be better to let a Communist keep his job than to disrupt the whole fabric of academic freedom."

In his testimony before HUAC, Hicks provided the committee with the names of his former comrades in the Communist Party at Harvard. Eight were later subpoenaed by the committee; one of those who appeared but refused to testify, claiming immunity under the Fifth Amendment, subsequently lost his job. In his account of the travels and tribulations of his generation of American liberals, entitled *Where We Came Out* (1954), Hicks delivered judgment on his testimony before HUAC and the committee's investigation into academia. "It appears," concluded Hicks, "that little damage was done, and I am happy that this is so. On the other hand, as I have already said, I cannot see that Communism was appreciably weakened by this particular inquiry. No conspiracy was exposed; no spies or saboteurs were apprehended. No record of current Communist activity of any sort was brought to light. Even as a piece of historical research, a study of Communism at

Harvard fifteen years ago, the investigation produced no impressive results."

***High Noon***   Produced by independent filmmaker Stanley Kramer, with a script written by soon-to-be-BLACKLISTED Carl FOREMAN, *High Noon* (1952) represented a veiled attack on McCarthyism and the American public's cowardice in the face of evil. On the surface, the film is a taut western drama starring Gary COOPER as Will Kane, the ex-marshal of a peaceful town called Hadleyville, a role for which Cooper won the Oscar as Best Actor. At the outset of the movie, Cooper is preparing to leave town with his new wife, a Quaker (played by Grace Kelly), when he learns that the feared outlaw Frank Miller is coming into town on the noon train. Miller intends to reunite with his gang and take revenge on Kane for sending him to prison five years earlier. Despite the pleas of his violence-hating wife, who wants him simply to leave town and save himself, Kane decides to stay and fight Miller. But when Kane appeals to the town to join him in the fight against Miller and his gang, no one steps forward; the nervous, beleaguered townspeople all claim that the fights is Kane's and not theirs.

During the filming of *High Noon*, screenwriter Foreman received a summons to testify before the HOUSE COMMITTEE ON UN-AMERICAN ACTIVITIES (HUAC). Foreman, a former member of the COMMUNIST PARTY (he and his wife had broken with the party in 1942), was willing to state that he was not a Communist and had not been one since 1942. He refused, however, to inform on his former associates. The character of Will Kane in the film may be seen as Foreman or any witness willing to stand up against McCarthy and HUAC. With his surly manner and leering smile, Frank Miller resembles no one as much as McCarthy himself. In an interesting turn of casting, Lloyd Bridges—who himself possessed a radical past—played Kane's deputy who urged the marshal to run away from the confrontation.

Foreman received a prestigious award from the SCREEN WRITERS' GUILD for the script of *High Noon,* but it was the last screen credit he would receive for six years. Blacklisted after another witness named him in testimony before HUAC as a former member of the Communist Party, Foreman was forced to write without receiving credit for his work. Foreman co-authored the Academy Award–winning screenplay for *The Bridge Over the River Kwai* (1957), but his name appeared on neither the screen nor the award.

**Hiss, Alger** (1904– )   One of the most controversial figures of the McCarthy era, Alger Hiss was a prominent member of the U.S. State Department establishment who was convicted of perjury in 1950 for denying that he had ever been a member of the COMMUNIST PARTY.

The son of a business executive who committed suicide in 1907, Hiss grew up in Baltimore and attended high school at Baltimore City College. He was graduated with a B.A. in political science in 1926 from John Hopkins University and continued his studies at Harvard University Law School, where his favorite professor was Felix Frankfurter; this iconoclastic liberal legal scholar was engaged at that time in the defense of the immigrant anarchists Nicola Sacco and Bartolomeo Vanzetti. Frankfurter was appointed to the Supreme Court during the administration of President Franklin Delano Roosevelt.

Through Frankfurter, Hiss became acquainted with U.S. Supreme Court Justice Oliver Wendell Holmes, for whom he clerked for one year following graduation from law school.

Following his clerkship with Holmes, he entered private practice with a Boston law firm. In 1932, Hiss joined the prestigious Wall Street law firm of Cotton, Franklin, Wright & Gordon. He rejected an appointment to the Department of Justice during the Hoover administration, but in 1933, Frankfurter prevailed upon him to accept a post with the newly formed Agricultural Adjustment Administration.

Until that time of his life, Hiss had not been deeply involved in political affairs. "During my college years at Johns Hopkins," he later wrote, "I had scorned politics as the necessary but demeaning scut work that in a wasteful and corrupt way had kept the essential, minimum machinery of government running since Andrew Jackson's day. That machinery . . . needed little learning and less dedication to operate. The operation was, I thought smugly, performed by a low, parasitic class of citizen-politicians." His association with Frankfurter at Harvard, however, had awakened in Hiss an interest in public service, and his acceptance of the position at Agriculture represented for Hiss another step in the evolution of his social and political attitudes.

As a young attorney in Washington during the early days of the New Deal, Hiss became friends with other zealous reformers of his age, including Tommy Corcoran, Harold Rosenwald, and Lee PRESSMAN, a former classmate at Harvard Law School. Discontented with the pace of change at the Department of Agriculture under Secretary Henry A. WALLACE, Hiss accepted a position in 1934 as counsel to the Senate Committee to Investigate the Munitions Industry. This committee, popularly known as the Nye Committee after its chairman, Republican Senator Gerald P. Nye of North Dakota, had been formed to investigate the connection between the munitions industry and U.S. entry into World War I in 1917. Hiss resigned from the committee's staff in the fall of 1935 because he feared that its work might encourage a passive, or at least neutral, American attitude toward the expansion of Nazi Germany in Europe.

In the autumn of 1936, Hiss joined the Department of State as an aide to Assistant Secretary of State Francis B. Sayre, a former professor at Harvard Law School, and three years later, Hiss became an assistant to Stanley K. Hornbeck, the department's adviser on political relations. Following the Japanese attack upon Pearl Harbor, Hiss attempted to join the U.S. Army, although State Department officials were exempt from the military draft. The State Department refused his request to enlist, and he remained in his post as Hornbeck's assistant for two more years.

During that time, Hiss was one of the officials responsible for monitoring the morale of the Chinese regime of CHIANG Kai-shek and for attempting to obtain as much aid for Chiang as possible in his battle against the Japanese invaders. One of the more pressing issues facing Hiss and his colleagues during the war years was the question of whether the United States should also support the efforts of the Chinese Communist forces under MAO Zedong in their guerrilla campaign of resistance against Japanese forces. "There were vigorous debates among those of us engaged in Far Eastern matters about the role of the Chinese Communists," noted Hiss. "It seemed to me unproductive to weaken our support of Chiang, but at the same time it was vitally important to encourage all forces that were actively resisting the Japanese invaders. I therefore hoped continually for compromise between the two contending factions—and there were certainly many moments when such compromise seemed feasible."

As the tide of war shifted in favor of the Allies, Hiss became increasingly involved in the planning of a postwar international organization. In May 1944, Hiss joined the Office of Special Political Affairs, and from August to October that year he served as executive secretary of the Dumbarton Oaks Conversations in Washington, during which the United States, Great Britain, and the Soviet Union began the initial planning for the proposed United Nations (UN). In early 1945, Hiss was named director of the Office of Special Political Affairs, and in that capacity he attended the YALTA conference in February as one of President Roosevelt's advisers. Hiss also represented the United States at the United Nations Conference in San Francisco in April 1945 and served as temporary secretary general of the UN during its formative stages. In June 1945, Hiss brought the UN charter from San Francisco to Washington so that it could be ratified by the U.S. Senate.

From January to March 1946, Hiss served as one of the principal advisers to the U.S. delegation to the UN General Assembly during its meetings in London.

Upon his return to the United States, Hiss was informed by Secretary of State James Byrnes that several Republican congressmen were charging that Hiss was a Communist. According to Hiss, the rumors had originated with Whittaker CHAMBERS, an admitted ex-Communist who claimed to have known Hiss during his days in the Communist Party. Chambers had first mentioned Hiss to the FBI in 1942, and FBI director J. Edgar HOOVER had subsequently leaked the charges to Republican allies in Congress. "The rumor that I was a Communist," noted Hiss several decades later, "led me to stay on in my State Department post longer than I had planned. I did not wish to appear to be leaving under fire." He met with an FBI official who asked him a few perfunctory questions, and Hiss believed that the matter had been laid to rest.

In December 1946, the Carnegie Endowment for International Peace—which had spent the past thirty-six years studying ways to abolish war—elected Hiss to serve as its president. The recommendation to elect Hiss had originally come from the chairman of the Endowment's Board of Trustees, John Foster DULLES, later secretary of state in President Dwight David EISENHOWER's administration. When the endowment's trustees held their annual meeting the following May, Hiss urged that the organization could best achieve its objectives by focusing its efforts upon supporting the UN.

On August 3, 1948, Chambers told the HOUSE COMMITTEE ON UN-AMERICAN ACTIVITIES (HUAC) that he had known Hiss in 1934–35 as a member of a small Communist group in Washington that also had included Lee Pressman. On August 4, Hiss sent the committee a telegram from New York, insisting that he be allowed to testify in person to rebut Chambers' charges. Meanwhile, Chambers' allegations had created a furor in the nation's press. President

Harry S. TRUMAN responded to the accusations against Hiss by claiming that they were nothing more than a "red herring" designed to deflect the public's attention from the obstructionist tactics of the Republican-controlled Congress. The following day, Hiss appeared before the committee and persuasively denied Chambers' allegations. Indeed, he denied ever knowing Whittaker Chambers at all. Certainly Hiss—tall, lean, polished, and eloquent—made a far more impressive witness than the rumpled, mumbling Chambers. When Hiss concluded his defense, even such a devout anti-Communist crusader as Karl MUNDT, acting chairman of the committee, complimented Hiss on his "very cooperative attitude" and "forthright statements."

In a closed meeting after Hiss' appearance, the committee seemed predisposed to turn the matter over to the Justice Department. Chambers and fellow ex-Communist Elizabeth BENTLEY had accused numerous individuals of membership in the Communist Party during their testimony before HUAC, but the committee had not yet uncovered evidence to corroborate their accusations. The only member of HUAC who favored further investigation of Hiss was Richard M. NIXON, who had developed a personal dislike for the urbane Hiss. With the assistance of committee counsel Robert STRIPLING, Nixon managed to persuade his colleagues to permit him to question Chambers once again. On August 7, Nixon and two other members of HUAC met Chambers in a secret session in a New York federal courtroom. During the session, Chambers revealed an encyclopedic knowledge of Hiss' personal life and habits. He knew the family's nicknames for one another, for instance, and minor details about their furniture, servants, books, and hobbies.

This information convinced the committee that Chambers had, in fact, been closely acquainted with Hiss. If Hiss had lied about knowing Chambers, perhaps he also had lied about his former political activities and associations. Therefore, the committee again questioned Hiss, this time in executive session in Washington on August 16. During the interview, Hiss stated that during his tenure with the Nye Committee, he had known a free-lance magazine writer named George Crosley who seemed to resemble Chambers. This admission convinced Nixon that Hiss might buckle under further pressure. He therefore arranged a confrontation between Hiss and Chambers in a New York hotel room on August 25. At the meeting, Hiss grew flustered by Nixon's persistent questioning and at one point nearly struck Chambers. Hiss also stated that he "would like to invite Mr. Whittaker Chambers to make those same statements [about his activities as a member of the Communist Party] out of the presence of this committee without their being privileged for suit for libel. I challenge you to do it, and I hope you will do it damned quickly."

Hiss testified before HUAC yet again on September 2, 1948. At that time, he acknowledged that he might have given Crosley/Chambers one of his automobiles—a 1929 Model A Ford—to use; he also admitted that he may have allowed Crosley/Chambers to use the Hiss apartment on occasion. Throughout the session, Hiss prefaced his answers with qualifications ("To the best of my recollection . . .") and generally presented the appearance of a man who was either frightened or unsure of himself. Nixon pounced on Hiss' equivocations, pointing out that Hiss was claiming that he had gone to New York with Chambers in 1934–35, "stayed in a house with him, loaned him money and a car, and he didn't know he was a Communist."

Chambers also testified at the August 25 hearing; this time, he seemed far more self-assured than Hiss. When asked why he was attacking a man of Hiss' stature, Chambers replied that "Mr. Hiss represents the concealed enemy we are all fighting. I am testifying against him with remorse and pity. But in this moment of historic jeopardy at which this nation now stands, so help me God, I could not do otherwise."

On September 4, Chambers appeared on the radio news interview program *Meet the Press* and asserted that Hiss "was a Communist and may be one now." Nearly a month later, Hiss sued Chambers for defamation of character. To defend himself, Chambers had to produce evidence that Hiss had been a Communist. He thereupon charged that Hiss had not only been a member of the Communist Party but had passed along to him scores of classified documents, cables, and reports. The documents, Chambers said, had either been passed along as summaries in Hiss' own handwriting, as originals—in which case Chambers had microfilmed them and returned them to Hiss—or as copies that Hiss' wife had typed on an old Woodstock typewriter at their home. On November 17, Chambers produced eighty-four of the documents that he claimed Hiss had transmitted to him; forty-three had been copied on the typewriter, and forty-one were in Hiss' handwriting. Several weeks later, Chambers also took members of HUAC to his Maryland farm where he showed them a hollowed-out pumpkin in which he had placed three strips of microfilmed documents that Hiss allegedly had passed along to him. Although many of the documents concerned trivial subjects, they had all been written in the State Department's classified code.

At that point, the Justice Department issued subpoenas for Hiss, his wife, and Chambers. A grand jury examined the evidence and, on December 15, indicted Hiss on two counts of perjury for denying under oath—during his testimony before HUAC—that he had ever been a member of the Communist Party and for denying that he had given Chambers State Department documents in 1938 for transmission to the Soviet Union. Hiss' first trial ended in a hung jury on July 8, 1949, with four jurors voting for acquittal and eight for conviction. The government subsequently tried Hiss a second time; in January 1950, the jury returned a verdict of guilty, and Hiss was sentenced to a term of five years in the Lewisburg Federal Penitentiary.

Some observers have noted that the period between Hiss' two trials was filled with evidence of Communist aggression abroad and Communist subversion in the United States. In China, the Communist forces of Mao Zedong defeated the Nationalist armies of Chiang Kai-shek in the autumn of 1949; in August 1949, the Soviet Union exploded its first nuclear device; and the Red Army was extending its dominion over one nation after another in Eastern Europe. At home, the FBI arrested Judith COPLON on espionage charges (as was Klaus FUCHS in Britain), and federal prosecutors had launched their attack upon the leaders of the Communist Party of the United States through the use of the SMITH ACT. Clearly the American public was growing increasingly concerned over the Communist threat and was in no mood to tolerate evidence of divided loyalties or subversive activities among government officials, no matter how prestigious their background.

Hiss himself blamed his conviction partly on the activities of Nixon and his fellow anti-Communist crusaders outside the courtroom. "As the second trial wore on," Hiss wrote later, "I realized that it was no ordinary one. The entire jury of public opinion, all of those from whom my juries had been selected, had been tampered with. Richard Nixon, my unofficial prosecutor, seeking to build his career on getting a conviction in my case, had from the days of the congressional committee hearings constantly issued public statements and leaks to the press against me." As far as Hiss was concerned, Chambers' animosity toward him stemmed from a desire for personal revenge. "Years later," Hiss explained, "I learned that in the mid-1930s, when I knew him as Crosley, Chambers was a closet homosexual. I now believe that my rebuff to him wounded him in a way that I did not realize at the time. I think the rebuff, coupled with his political paranoia, inspired his later machinations against me."

Secretary of State Dean ACHESON, however, refused to abandon Hiss following Hiss' conviction. At a press conference several days after the second trial ended, Acheson noted that "whatever the outcome of any appeal which Mr. Hiss or his lawyers may take in this case, I do not intend to turn my back on Alger Hiss." Acheson's defense of Hiss earned him the excoriation of Republican critics. Nixon termed it "disgusting," and Congressman Walter Judd, one of the leading members of the pro-Chiang CHINA LOBBY, suggested that Truman should turn his back on Acheson. For his part, Republican Senator Homer Capehart of Indiana wondered aloud in the Senate, "How much more are we going to take? Fuchs and Acheson and Hiss and hydrogen bombs threatening outside and New Dealism eating away the vitals of the nation. In the name of heaven, is this the best America can do?"

After the U.S. Supreme Court declined to review his case, Hiss spent forty-four months in prison, from March 1951 to November 1954. He subsequently wrote an account of his trial, which earned poor sales and only lukewarm reviews. To his dismay, Hiss found that he was virtually unemployable at the height of the anti-Communist fervor in the United States. To earn a living, Hiss attempted to teach himself to type but failed abysmally. He eventually accepted a position as an executive assistant in a company that sold combs and women's barrettes. When the company suffered financial reverses, Hiss was fired. For most of 1959 and part of 1960, he lived on unemployment-insurance benefits. In 1960, Hiss obtained a job as a salesman with a printing firm in New York, a position he retained until he retired in the late 1970s. During that time, as the COLD WAR thawed, Hiss occasionally lectured to college audiences on such topics as Far East policy, the McCarthy era, and the UN.

In 1979, Hiss filed a petition for a writ of error *coram nobis,* a legal procedure that requests the court to review a case—no matter how old— that allegedly contained errors so egregious that such a review would be warranted. Four years later, his petition was denied, and once again the Supreme Court refused to hear his case. In 1988, Hiss published a memoir, *Recollections of a Life,* in which he briefly reviewed his past and presented a detailed refutation of the evidence

used against him at his trials. "My public life," he concluded, "has been deeply rewarding. In the New Deal, in the wartime State Department, for the nascent United Nations, I did what I could toward the common goal of a better world. Since the war, in my adverse circumstances, the fact that I fought for my beliefs has been more than just a private good for me alone—I continue to meet people who take heart from what I stood for. I count as successful my efforts to live according to my goals and principles, and so I have no cause for bitterness or regret, nor have I ever felt any."

**Hoey, Clyde** (1877–1954) A United States senator from North Carolina, Clyde Hoey was a member of the anti-Communist coalition in Congress from 1944 until his death in 1954.

The son of a Confederate Army captain, Hoey was born in Shelby, North Carolina. He left school at the age of twelve to begin an apprenticeship in a local print shop and subsequently embarked upon a successful career as a newspaper publisher and editor. Hoey began his political career at the age of twenty, when he was first elected to the North Carolina state legislature. He studied law at the University of North Carolina during the summers, and was admitted to the bar in 1899. In 1913, President Woodrow Wilson appointed Hoey U.S. attorney for the Western District of North Carolina.

During the 1920s and early 1930s, Hoey gave most of his attention to his private law practice, but he reentered the political arena in 1936 when he was elected governor of North Carolina. Eight years later, he was elected to the Senate by a substantial majority.

Hoey displayed an animus toward Communists even before he arrived in Congress. In 1935, he successfully defended a group of deputy sheriffs who had been accused of killing six people during a Communist rally in Marion, North Carolina, and he later won the conviction of several Communists for the murder of a local police chief.

As a member of the U.S. Senate, Hoey was assigned to the GOVERNMENT OPERATIONS COMMITTEE, serving as chairman from 1949–53. In June 1950, Hoey initiated an investigation of homosexuality among federal employees. He justified this inquiry on the grounds that homosexuals represented an increased security risk because (according to Hoey) they would be vulnerable to blackmail by Communist agents. Despite the rising public concern over Communist espionage activities in the United States, Hoey conducted the investigation with considerable restraint, holding most of the hearings in executive session.

When Senator Joseph MCCARTHY assumed chairmanship of the Government Operations Committee in the wake of the Republican victories in the congressional elections of 1952, Hoey remained the ranking Democratic member of the committee. Before he could complete his second term in the Senate, however, Hoey passed away in 1954.

## Holliday, Judy (1922–1965)

An actress who gained fame by playing the role of a "dumb blonde" on Broadway and in motion pictures, Judy Holliday was accused in 1951 by anti-Communist crusaders and right-wing columnists in Hollywood of having Communist sympathies.

Originally named Judith Tuvim, Holliday changed her name when she began her stage career; she chose *Holliday* because the word *holiday* was the English equivalent of the Hebrew *tuvim*. A precocious child, Holliday reportedly once scored 172 on an I.Q. test, and attended the prestigious Julia Richman High School in Manhattan. After she failed to gain entrance to the Yale Drama School, Holliday joined a troupe of performers who called themselves the Revuers. Near the start of World War II, the Revuers moved to Hollywood, where they performed in night clubs and obtained bit parts in several motion pictures.

Holliday received her big break in January 1946, when she was chosen to play the lead role as a wisecracking ex-chorus girl in a theatrical production of Garson Kanin's comedy, *Born Yesterday*. Holliday's success in that role led to a part in the film comedy *Adam's Rib*, starring Katharine HEPBURN and Spencer Tracy. In 1950, Holliday was signed to play in the movie version of *Born Yesterday*, and her performance won her the Academy Award as Best Actress.

In the spring of 1951 a columnist in *Hollywood Life* accused Holliday of harboring Communist sympathies. "Judy only acts dumb," claimed the columnist. "She's a smart cookie. . . . The Commies got her a long time ago." Among other allegations, *Hollywood Life* charged that Holliday had been a guest speaker, sponsor, and performer for several Communist-front organizations, including the Civil Rights Congress and the World Federation of Democratic Youth.

To keep her name off the BLACKLISTS of suspected performers, Holliday voluntarily testified before the Senate INTERNAL SECURITY COMMITTEE. When her appearance before the committee failed to stop the rumors, Holliday took the extraordinary step of hiring a researcher to dig into her past and then issue a report clearing her of any subversive inclinations. Yet, the damage had been done, and Holliday's career never fully recovered.

## Hollywood Ten

The Hollywood Ten were a group of ten motion picture screenwriters and directors who were convicted of contempt of Congress for their refusal to answer questions about their political beliefs before the HOUSE COMMITTEE ON UN-AMERICAN ACTIVITIES (HUAC).

In May 1947, HUAC held a series of closed hearings in Los Angeles as part of its investigation of Communist influence in the motion picture industry. Using the information it obtained from cooperative witnesses, the committee issued subpoenas in September 1947 to several dozen screenwriters, directors, and producers to appear before the committee in Washington in October. Nineteen of the scheduled witnesses were designated by the *Hollywood Reporter* as "unfriendly," based upon the hostile attitude they had displayed toward the committee in their speeches and writings.

Only eleven of the "unfriendly" nineteen—all of whom had been active in left-wing causes in Hollywood—were actually called by HUAC to testify in October: Alvah BESSIE, Bertolt BRECHT, Howard BIBERMAN, Lester COLE, Edward DMYTRYK, Ring LARDNER, Jr., John Howard LAWSON, Albert MALTZ, Samuel ORNITZ, Robert Adrian SCOTT, and Dalton TRUMBO. Before the hearings began, a coalition of prominent Hollywood personalities formed the COMMITTEE FOR THE FIRST AMENDMENT to generate public support for the witnesses in particular and the cause of freedom of political expression in the motion picture industry in general.

Ten of the eleven witnesses (excluding Brecht) had joined the COMMUNIST PARTY in Hollywood, and all but Dmytryk were still Party members in 1947. In discussions among themselves and their defense counsel—including Robert Kenney, a former California state attorney general, Bartley Crum, a prominent Republican corporate attorney, and two charter members of the NATIONAL LAWYERS GUILD— these ten decided to refuse to answer any of the committee's questions regarding their political affiliations or activities. They planned to justify their silence by citing their rights under the First Amendment, with its protection of free speech, instead of taking the Fifth Amendment, which likely would have provided them with a more reliable defense against self-incrimination.

From the appearance of the first "unfriendly" witness, John Howard Lawson, on October 27, the Hollywood Ten—as the witnesses were dubbed by the press—displayed an openly hostile attitude toward the committee. The attitude was reciprocated by the committee chairman, J. Parnell THOMAS. With the exception of Maltz, Thomas refused to allow the witnesses to read their prepared statements into the record. One by one, each of the witnesses was asked what

Parnell referred to as "the $64 question": "Are you now, or have you ever been, a member of the Communist Party?" (Most of the witnesses were also asked whether they were or had been members of the SCREEN WRITERS' GUILD, which HUAC believed was a stronghold of Communist influence in Hollywood.) Although the Ten did not formally refuse point-blank to answer the question, they all attempted to preface their response with explanations or attacks upon the committee's authority. At one point, Alvah Bessie shouted that "General Eisenhower has refused to reveal his political party affiliation and what's good enough for General Eisenhower is good enough for me." Thomas cut them all off curtly, pounding his gavel as he dismissed them from the stand. Several of the witnesses, including Lardner, Trumbo, and Lawson, had to be forcibly evicted from the hearing room.

For their failure to answer the committee's questions, the Ten were cited in November for contempt of Congress. Their truculence before HUAC had alienated public opinion and discouraged further displays of sympathy from the Committee for the First Amendment. Support within Hollywood eroded further following the release of the WALDORF STATEMENT by the major film studios in the first week of December. The five members of the Ten who were then under contract to the studios were promptly suspended or dismissed, and studio executives agreed not to hire any of the Ten until they had cleared themselves of the contempt charge and cooperated with HUAC.

Confident of their First Amendment defense, all of the Ten waived their right to a trial by jury. On April 19, 1948, a federal judge found Lawson guilty of contempt of Congress and sentenced him to one year in jail and a fine of $1,000. On May 5, Trumbo received an identical sentence. Both men appealed their cases, and the remaining eight—facing an uncertain future with dwindling financial resources—entered into an agreement with the federal government which stipulated that the outcome of the Trumbo and Lawson appeals would govern all their cases. On June 13, 1949, a Circuit Court of Appeals judge ruled against Lawson and Trumbo, stating that "we expressly hold herein that the House Committee on Un-American Activities, or a properly appointed subcomittee thereof, has the *power* to inquire whether a witness subpoenaed by it is or is not a member of the Communist Party or a believer in communism and that this power carries with it necessarily the power to effect criminal punishment for failure or refusal to answer that question."

The Ten then pinned their hopes on the U.S. Supreme Court, where they predicted a majority of five sympathetic justices. But the deaths of two justices in the summer of 1949 and their replacement by more conservative jurists altered the character of the Court, and on April 10, 1950, the Supreme Court officially refused to review the constitutional issues involved in the Lawson and Trumbo cases. The other members of the Ten were subsequently convicted of contempt charges and received identical sentences of one year in jail and a $1,000 fine (except for Biberman and Dmytryk, who were sentenced to only six months in prison solely because their cases were heard by a more lenient judge).

Only one member of the Ten—Edward Dmytryk—ever recanted his failure to testify and publicly declared that he had abandoned his membership in the Communist Party. He was subsequently allowed to resume his directing career.

Following their release from prison, the other nine men found it impossible to obtain work with the major studios in Hollywood because an informal BLACKLIST was in effect. Several went to Mexico, others journeyed to Europe, and the rest remained in America, working at odd jobs or writing screenplays under assumed names. It was not until 1961, when Otto Preminger openly hired Trumbo to write the screenplay for the film *Exodus,* that the blacklist was finally broken.

In the end, it seemed that the Ten had overestimated both the support they would receive from members of the liberal community in the United States (and in Hollywood in particular) and their own importance to the motion picture industry. The tragedy of the Hollywood Ten, wrote columnist Murray Kempton, was "a failure of promise: first, of the promise in themselves, and last, of the promise of the Hollywood which was so kind to them until they became an embarrassment and then turned them out. . . . They were entombed, most of them, not for being true to themselves, but for sitting up too long with their own press releases."

**Hoover, J. Edgar** (1895–1973)   Director of the FEDERAL BUREAU OF INVESTIGATION (FBI) for forty-nine years, J. Edgar Hoover was one of the guiding forces behind the anti-Communist crusade in the United States during the McCarthy era.

Born in Washington, D.C., Hoover grew up as a bookish child who earned the nickname "Speed" for his quick mind and rapid speech. As a senior at Washington's Central High School, he became captain of the school's military drill team, early evidence of the intense self-discipline that formed such an important part of his character. Although he was offered a scholarship to the University of Virginia, Hoover chose to remain in Washington to work his way through college to ease the strain on his family's finances. In 1916, he received a law degree from George Washington University; the following year, Hoover passed the bar exam and obtained a position with the Department of Justice as an aide to the special assistant to the attorney general for war work.

At Justice, Hoover impressed his superiors with his single-minded dedication to his work. He was initially placed in charge of a section in the alien registration division; in 1919, however, Hoover was named to head the department's new General Intelligence Division. Under the direction of politically ambitious Attorney General A. Mitchell Palmer, who wished to use the post-World War I fear of Bolshevik subversion in the United States to boost his own presidential aspirations, Hoover compiled a card file on

FBI director J. Edgar Hoover (left), one of the leaders in the crusade against Communism in the United States.

450,000 purported radicals, assembled an impressive network of informants across the country, and drafted a brief on the goals and activities of the recently established COMMUNIST PARTY OF THE UNITED STATES. "These [Communist] doctrines," noted Hoover, "threaten the happiness of the community, the safety of every individual, and the continuance of every home and fireside. They would destroy the peace of the country and thrust it into a condition of anarchy and lawlessness and immorality that passes imagination." Over the following four decades, this conclusion formed the basis for Hoover's relentless assaults upon the Communist movement in the United States. As head of the General Intelligence Division, Hoover played an integral role in planning the so-called "Palmer Raids," which rounded up hundreds of alleged radicals and held them for deportation without benefit of legal counsel or hearings.

In 1924, Attorney General Harlan Fiske Stone named Hoover to head the Bureau of Investigation within the Department of Justice. During the administration of President Warren G. Harding, the bureau had deteriorated into an agency of corruption and partisan politics, but Hoover insisted upon separating it from all outside political pressures. Stone granted him

that freedom, and Hoover used it to rule the bureau—which was renamed the Federal Bureau of Investigation in 1935—with an iron hand for nearly fifty years.

Hoover combined a flair for self-promotion with a commitment to modern, scientific police procedures. Under his leadership, the bureau established a national centralized fingerprint file, the National Police Academy to train leaders of local police forces across the country, and the National Crime Information Center. During the 1930s, the FBI focused its efforts on the arrest of gangsters such as John Dillinger who had flourished in the days of prohibition; following the capture of Bruno Hauptmann, the accused kidnapper of the child of Charles and Anne Lindbergh, the bureau also moved to eliminate effectively the crime of kidnapping in the United States. Meanwhile, Hoover publicized the work of the bureau by issuing its "ten most-wanted" lists, promoting "junior G-man" clubs for boys, and approving radio shows celebrating the exploits of FBI agents.

Hoover also undertook to educate Americans about the dangers of Communist subversion. Besides publishing volumes such as "Masters of Deceit" to alert the public to the methods employed by Communist propagandists, Hoover ordered a select group of FBI agents in the late 1930s to begin compiling data on subversive groups and activities in the United States. This intelligence operation, quite unrelated to the enforcement of any existing federal criminal statutes, grew by 1939 into a full-scale investigation of the Communist Party in the United States, aided by the development by the FBI of a network of thousands of informants in defense plants across the nation. As U.S. entry into World War II grew nearer, the pace of Hoover's campaign against Communist espionage and sabotage intensified. Although President Franklin Delano Roosevelt provided the FBI with federal jurisdiction in this area, Hoover moved beyond Roosevelt's instructions by ordering his agents to compile the "Custodial Detention List" of citizens and aliens "on whom there is information available to indicate that their presence at liberty in this country in time of war or national emergency would be dangerous to the public peace and the safety of the United States Government." To help ensure that the bureau's list was as comprehensive as possible, Hoover's agents encouraged private citizens to gather information on any suspected subversives in their communities on the grounds that "this job is essential to the internal security of the United States." One citizen who accepted the FBI's invitation to serve as an informant was Herbert PHILBRICK, who later became famous when he published his account of his undercover activities under the title, *I LED THREE LIVES*. In Hollywood, studio executive Walt DISNEY also became an FBI informant, as did actor Ronald REAGAN.

In 1943, Attorney General Francis Biddle directed Hoover to discontinue the Custodial Detention List, claiming that it was both illegal and "inherently unreliable," but Hoover effectively circumvented Biddle's order by replacing the list with a "Security Index"; by the beginning of 1946, this included the names of more than 10,000 individuals, most of whom were accused of Communist sympathies. Hoover maintained close control over the Security Index—it was not at all clear whether Attorney General Tom CLARK understood precisely how extensive a network of informants Hoover had established, or to what end—and continued to jealously guard the FBI's prerogatives in the battle against domestic subversion. As the TRUMAN administration moved to establish a comprehensive federal loyalty-review program, Hoover vehemently objected to any attempts to dilute the bureau's authority in this area.

At the same time, Hoover began to send numerous memoranda to the White House, insisting that certain federal employees—particularly scientists with access to atomic research data—were involved in Communist espionage networks. Hoover also started to leak information on suspected subversives to sympathetic members of Congress, and established an effec-tive working relationship with the HOUSE COMMITTEE ON UN-AMERICAN ACTIVITIES (HUAC), providing the committee with material to further its investigations into Communist activities in the United States. (Although Hoover certainly helped fuel the anti-Communist movement in the United States during the postwar years, the FBI generally insisted upon far more rigorous standards of evidence in publicly identifying individuals as subversives than did congressional committees such as HUAC.) On March 28, 1947, Hoover testified before the committee, delivering a dire warning about the threat to American liberties posed by the "Red Menace." "The Communist party of the United States is a fifth column if there ever was one," declared Hoover. "It is far better organized than were the Nazis in occupied countries prior to their capitulation. They are seeking to weaken America just as they did in their era of obstruction when they alined [sic] with the Nazis. Their goal is the overthrow of our Government."

Hoover appears to have overestimated consistently the strength of the Communist Party within the United States. In 1950, for instance, he claimed that there were 54,000 Communist Party members in the United States; combined with an estimated 10 fellow travelers for every actual Party member, Hoover's figure would have placed the total strength of the pro-Soviet movement in the United States at approximately 600,000 individuals, a number that seems vastly overinflated, considering the few convictions of American Communists for subversive activities—or even the dismissal of suspected Communist sympathizers from federal employment—during the height of the anti-Communist hysteria.

Throughout the late 1940s and early 1950s, Hoover consistently opposed legislation to make membership in the Communist Party illegal, fearing that such measures would drive the party underground and make it far more difficult for the FBI to maintain its surveillance of Communist actions. Nevertheless, that appears to have been precisely the effect of the Truman administration's prosecution of Communists from 1946 to 1950. In February 1950, Hoover declared that the Communist Party had, for all practical purposes, become a clandestine operation. "To counteract the FBI's penetration of the Communist Party," he said, "its leaders have established a far-reaching and vigorous loyalty program of their own. . . . Public meetings are at an absolute minimum. Party records have been destroyed or removed to clandestine hiding places. Secret printing facilities and supplies have been secreted for future underground operations. Transfers of party members from one district to another are now controlled through the use of an elaborate identification system."

In the same month that Hoover made the above statement, Senator Joseph MCCARTHY of Wisconsin delivered a speech in Wheeling, West Virginia, in which he accused the State Department of harboring a number of "card-carrying Communists" among its employees. Hoover and McCarthy had been friends since McCarthy first was elected to Congress; they often ate dinner together at Harvey's Restaurant in downtown Washington, and McCarthy regularly was seen with Hoover at the FBI director's private box at a local race track. Yet, Hoover reportedly was furious with McCarthy for making his speech at Wheeling. Hoover feared that such reckless allegations about Communism in government—which were supported by little or no evidence—could discredit the entire anti-Communist crusade. Still, after he gave McCarthy "unshirted hell" for the Wheeling speech, Hoover ordered his subordinates to provide McCarthy with any material from FBI files that might prove helpful to the senator in defending his charges and avoiding further embarrassment. Moreover, Hoover dispatched former FBI investigator Donald A. Surine to McCarthy to help McCarthy gather incriminating data on possible subversives in the State Department. For the next few years, Surine served as a link between Hoover and McCarthy; according to Surine, he and McCarthy met secretly with Hoover nearly every week to exchange information.

Hoover refused, however, to tie the FBI's

reputation too closely to the unpredictable McCarthy. In fact, as the senator's behavior became increasingly reckless in 1953–54, Hoover moved to distance himself and the bureau from McCarthy. During the ARMY-MCCARTHY HEARINGS in the spring of 1954, McCarthy attempted to introduce a document which purported to be a memorandum from Hoover to an Army general, alerting military officials to security problems at several Army scientific installations. When a controversy arose over the origins of the document, Hoover was quick to point out that the memorandum introduced by McCarthy was not a copy of his original memo; that the original memo was still highly classified and hence should not have been in McCarthy's possession; and that the memo did not discuss the question of Soviet espionage, as McCarthy had claimed. Privately, Hoover informed President Dwight David EISENHOWER that McCarthy's well-publicized investigations were actually hampering the government's efforts to uncover evidence of Communist subversion.

Hoover continued to pursue his own crusade against Communists long after the United States Senate voted to censure McCarthy in December 1954. Despite Hoover's willingness to provide the Eisenhower administration with information that proved politically valuable, the Democratic administrations of John F. KENNEDY and Lyndon B. JOHNSON retained him as FBI director. During the waning years of his directorship, Hoover increasingly came under attack for the bureau's violations of civil liberties and for his own personal feuds with liberal activists such as Martin Luther King, Jr., and Attorney General Ramsay Clark. Because he remained politically unassailable, however, Hoover retained the directorship of the FBI until his death in 1972.

**House Committee on Un-American Activities**   On June 7, 1938, the U.S. Congress created the House Committee on Un-American Activities (HUAC) as a temporary investigating committee. The primary motivating force behind the establishment of the committee was

(HUAC) Hearings before the House Committee on Un-American Activities. The witness, Under Secretary of State Summer Wells, is at the center of the photo.

the growing concern over propaganda activities of both Nazi and Communist sympathizers in the United States in the late 1930s. According to the resolution that created it, the committee consisted of seven members and had a charge to investigate "(1) the extent, character, and objects of un-American propaganda activities in the United States, (2) the diffusion within the United States of subversive and un-American propaganda that is instigated from foreign countries or of a domestic origin and attacks the principle of the form of government as guaranteed by our Constitution, and (3) all other questions in relation thereto that would aid Congress in any necessary remedial legislation."

The first chairman of the committee was Martin DIES, a Democratic representative from Texas, who originally promised that he would conduct his inquiries with respect "for the undisputed right of every citizen in the United States to express his honest convictions and enjoy freedom of speech." Despite this pledge,

Dies employed the committee as a weapon with which he bashed the liberal New Deal programs of the administration of President Franklin D. Roosevelt. In 1940, Dies wrote that Soviet dictator Joseph STALIN had "baited his hook with a 'progressive' worm, and New Deal suckers swallowed bait, hook, line, and sinker." Dies also used the committee to brand as "un-American" individuals or organizations of whom he disapproved, including radical labor-union leader Harry BRIDGES and the CONGRESS OF INDUSTRIAL ORGANIZATIONS (CIO).

Other members of the committee followed Dies' lead. In one hearing in 1939, for instance, Representative J. Parnell THOMAS of New Jersey noted that "it seems to me that the New Deal is working hand in glove with the COMMUNIST PARTY. The New Deal is either for the Communist Party, or is playing into the hands of the Communist Party." Following the entry of the United States into World War II in December 1941, however, Dies and the rest of HUAC virtually abandoned their investigatory activities for the duration of the conflict. Nonetheless, critics of the committee continued to denounce the bias that had marked its previous inquiries. In 1942, the executive board of the CIO described the record of the committee as "one of the [most] sordid and reprehensible in the annals of the American Congress," and the NATIONAL LAWYERS GUILD charged that "Martin Dies and his committee is the secret weapon with which Adolph Hitler hopes to soften up our Nation for military conquest."

On the first day of the seventy-ninth Congress—January 3, 1945—Democratic Congressman John RANKIN of Alabama took his colleagues by surprise when he offered a resolution establishing HUAC as a permanent committee. Although the initial vote went against Rankin, a second vote produced an sizable majority in favor of the resolution. The committee was thereby made a standing committee of Congress with a membership of nine representatives, far fewer than the average committee's total of twenty-five members. Rankin's resolution used virtually the same language as Dies' original motion in describing the responsibility of the committee and further provided it with authority "to hold such hearings, to require the attendance of such witnesses and the production of such books, papers, and documents, and to take such testimony, as it deems necessary to fulfill its mission."

Unlike other congressional committees, HUAC never was much concerned with producing legislation. Rather, its function was almost exclusively investigative. Moreover, the members of the committee were exempted from the restriction that prohibited representatives from sitting on more than one standing committee. Service on HUAC always was considered the secondary assignment of a member of Congress, although a number of particularly zealous HUAC members neglected their "primary" assignments to focus on their work with HUAC. Other members viewed their service with the committee as a burden which they undertook

only as a matter of party responsibility; therefore, turnover among the committee's members was fairly frequent.

When HUAC was established as a standing committee in January 1945, Representative Edward J. Hart of New Jersey was named as its chairman, primarily on the basis of his loyal service to the Roosevelt administration. Hart had little interest in the proceedings of the committee and consequently permitted Rankin, a noted bigot and racist, to dominate HUAC's investigations in the seventy-ninth Congress. In fact, Hart resigned from the chairmanship and the committee in July 1945 and was replaced by Georgia Democrat John S. WOOD, who proved equally unwilling or unable to control Rankin. (Rankin, who was vitally interested in veterans' affairs, chose not to seek the chairmanship because it would have required him to give up his position of leadership on the influential Armed Services Committee.) During the seventy-ninth Congress, HUAC conducted only two investigations: an inquiry into the operations of the Office of Price Administration (which conservatives on the committee denounced as the sort of government intervention in the economy that was likely to lead to a Communist takeover in the United States) and a brief look into the activities of the Communist Party in the United States, during which the committee heard testimony from Communist Party leaders Earl BROWDER and William Z. FOSTER.

When the Republican Party gained control of Congress in the 1946 elections, the chairmanship of HUAC passed to J. Parnell Thomas, who had been a member of the original committee in 1938. Although he initially claimed that HUAC had been "too melodramatic" in the past, Thomas proceeded to conduct hearings in an even more flamboyant fashion, interjecting his own prejudices into the proceedings and stating before an investigation began that he was certain that the committee would uncover un-American activity. Confronted with hostile witnesses, Thomas reacted petulantly, pounding his gavel and matching the truculence of the witnesses with vituperative responses of his own. He refused to acknowledge that any witness had a constitutional right to refuse to cooperate with HUAC; such a defense, he told his colleagues in the House, was nothing more than "a concerted effort on the part of the Communists, their fellow travelers, their dupes, and paid apologists to create a lot of fog about constitutional rights, the First Amendment, and so forth."

Under Thomas' leadership in the eightieth Congress (1947–49), HUAC began by conducting investigations of alleged Soviet espionage agent Gerhart EISLER and his brother, noted composer Hanns EISLER. The inquiry into Hanns Eiseler's activities as a film composer persuaded Thomas to launch an inquiry in the spring of 1948 into Communist influence in the American motion picture industry. The investigation of Hollywood gathered momentum in October of the same year when the committee summoned more than a score of actors, directors, and writers to testify in Washington. The dramatic highlight of the proceedings was the appearance of the unfriendly witnesses known as the HOLLYWOOD TEN, all of whom refused to answer the committee's questions about their past political activities and associations. As a result, members of the committee charged the witnesses with contempt of Congress, and all ten were subsequently convicted and imprisoned for terms of six to twelve months.

In 1947–48, HUAC also heard extensive testimony about Communist infiltration of the Roosevelt and Truman administrations. The star witnesses before the committee were a trio of ex-Communists: Elizabeth BENTLEY, Louis BUDENZ, and Whittaker CHAMBERS. Both Bentley and Chambers identified former State Department official Alger HISS as having been a Soviet agent during the 1930s. Although Hiss answered the allegations to the satisfaction of most of the committee members, Republican Congressman Richard M. NIXON, who had joined the committee shortly after taking his seat in January 1947, believed that Hiss was lying. It was Nixon's relentless pressure upon Hiss that

led to the latter's conviction on perjury charges in 1950, and it was the Hiss case—along with his work on other HUAC investigations—that vaulted Nixon into national prominence.

In 1947, the committee also conducted investigations into such reputed Communist-front organizations as the AMERICAN YOUTH FOR DEMOCRACY, the SOUTHERN CONFERENCE FOR HUMAN WELFARE, and the Civil Rights Congress. The committee's report on the Southern Conference for Human Welfare stands as a model of HUAC's use of innuendo and insubstantial evidence to smear liberal organizations. After studying HUAC's report in depth, Professor Lawrence Gellhorn of the Columbia University Law School concluded that "the report demonstrates not that the Southern Conference is a corrupt organization, but that the Committee has been either intolerably incompetent or designedly intent upon publicizing misinformation."

Nor did this exhaust the list of the committee's activities in 1947. Thomas also led HUAC into an investigation of Communist infiltration of labor unions, including such radical unions as the UNITED ELECTRICAL, RADIO AND MACHINE WORKERS (UE). The inquiry revealed that Communists had, in fact, gained control of the union at the national level; following an unsuccessful strike in 1948 and the decertification of the union under the terms of the TAFT-HARTLEY ACT, the UE was expelled by the CIO at its national convention in November 1949. Once again, it was Richard Nixon who led HUAC's successful prosecution of the union.

Thomas remained chairman until the Democrats regained control of Congress in January 1949. In January 1950, however, he was forced to resign from Congress after he was convicted of accepting kickbacks from members of his congressional staff. Not surprisingly, Thomas' legal problems did not enhance the stature of HUAC. To add to the committee's troubles, President Harry S. TRUMAN—who considered the committee's inquiries to be little more than thinly veiled witch hunts against liberals and

Democrats—seemed prepared to ask Congress to cut off funding to HUAC. In an attempt to rehabilitate the public image of the committee, HUAC issued a series of pamphlets known collectively as ONE HUNDRED THINGS YOU SHOULD KNOW ABOUT COMMUNISM. Written largely by a Washington journalist named Frank Waldrop, a steadfast supporter of the committee, the pamphlets were cast in a question-and-answer format that reduced complex issues to simplistic formulas. As one example, the question "What is Communism?" received a one-sentence answer: "A system by which one small group seeks to rule the world." Nevertheless, the public greeted the pamphlets with enthusiasm. In little more than 12 months, the committee distributed approximately 850,000 copies of the pamphlets free of charge. They proved so popular that another 320,000 copies were subsequently sold by the Government Printing office at a cost of 10 cents apiece.

In 1949, the committee's chief investigator, Robert STRIPLING, also published a book entitled THE RED PLOT AGAINST AMERICA, which purported to be an expose of "the Communist conspiracy against the Government and people of the United States." Stripling's prose reveals the defensive attitude that frequently characterized the committee. Responding to criticism from the Left, Stripling noted that "apparently it is in bad taste to expose the fact that Government documents of great importance are being stolen; . . . that a number of Government officials, by their admission or refusal to answer, have been mixed up with a gang of cold-blooded subversives; that choice military secrets, including A-bomb data, have been passed on to the leaders of a country which since V-E day has overrun Poland, Hungary, Bulgaria, Romania Czechoslovakia, Finland, Albania and most of China."

Following the Democratic victories in the elections of 1948, John Wood of Georgia once again assumed the chairmanship and made a sincere attempt to operate the committee with a far greater measure of civility and decorum than had Thomas. Under Wood's leadership, HUAC returned in 1951–52 to Hollywood, hearing such witnesses as Larry PARKS, Elia KAZAN, Lillian HELLMAN, Clifford ODETS, Budd SCHULBERG, and Edward DMYTRYK, the only member of the Hollywood Ten who recanted his earlier refusal to answer the committee's questions.

From 1953–54, HUAC was chaired by Harold VELDE, an ex-FBI agent from Illinois who had first won election to the House in 1948. Velde, considered an intellectual lightweight, established a record for the number of HUAC investigations in a single session, leading the committee into such ultimately fruitless areas as Communist infiltration of the nation's churches and Communist study cadres at Harvard University in the 1930s. In 1955, Democrat Francis WALTER of Pennsylvania assumed the chairmanship of HUAC. Despite attempts early in his tenure to modify the harsh rhetoric which Velde had employed, Walter grew increasingly nettlesome in his role as chairman. The transformation was undoubtedly caused in part by the increasing criticism which the committee received in the late 1950s as the anti-Communist fervor of the McCarthy era subsided. Walter, moreover, was a devoted opponent of liberal immigration policies, and any harsh criticism of his legislative initiatives to curb immigration led him to accuse his critics of Communist sympathies.

By the time Walter retired from Congress in 1963 and relinquished the chairmanship of HUAC to Democrat Edwin Willis of Louisiana, the committee's power had virtually disappeared. It returned to the nation's headlines during the Vietnam War, as it investigated the activities of antiwar protesters, but it never regained the prominence it had achieved during the height of the McCarthy era. In 1969, the House changed the name of HUAC to the Committee on Internal Security, and in 1975 the committee was abolished altogether.

**Hughes, Howard** (1905–1975)  Known as America's most reclusive billionaire, Howard

Hughes earned most of his fortune in the aircraft industry. In the late 1920s, Hughes dabbled in motion pictures as a producer but left Hollywood when he felt its censorship restrictions were becoming too rigid. Hughes returned to Hollywood in 1948 with his purchase of RKO Studios.

When he learned that some of RKO's writers and directors had been linked to Communist front activities, Hughes launched a determined effort to clean house. He decided that a film called *The Boy with Green Hair,* an impassioned plea for tolerance of human diversity, was actually a thinly disguised piece of Communist propaganda, and he rewrote the script, injecting anti-Marxist lines into the dialogue himself. Hughes then rid himself of the film's director, Joseph Losey, by offering him the opporunity to direct Hughes' pet movie project, I MARRIED A COMMUNIST. Losey later claimed that Hughes used the screenplay as a sort of loyalty check on prospective directors. "It was a touchstone for establishing who was a 'red,' " said Losey. "You offered *I Married a Communist* to anybody you thought was a Communist, and if they turned it down, they were. It was turned down by thirteen directors before it was made [in April–May 1949]."

Six months later, Hughes produced another anti-Communist film, *Jet Pilot,* in which Janet Leigh played a Soviet defector controlled by John WAYNE. During the course of the film, Wayne and Leigh flew to Russia, obtained secret information, and fled back to the United States with Soviet jets in hot pursuit. As art and propaganda, *Jet Pilot* received even worse critical reviews than *I Married a Communist.*

Determined to rid RKO of any lingering vestiges of Communist sympathies, Hughes moved in 1951 to deny screenwriting credit to Paul Jarrico for *The Las Vegas Story.* Jarrico had completed the screenplay for the film prior to his appearance as a witness before the HOUSE COMMITTEE ON UN-AMERICAN ACTIVITIES (HUAC). When Jarrico refused to answer the committee's questions and pleaded the Fifth Amendment,

Hughes claimed that he had violated the morals clause of his contract and removed Jarrico's name from the film's credits. Jarrico sued, but the courts (and eventually the U.S. Supreme Court) ruled in Hughes' favor.

## Humphrey, Hubert H. Jr. (1912–1978)

A leading anti-Communist liberal in the United States Senate, Hubert H. Humphrey was born and raised in South Dakota. In 1939, Humphrey graduated from the University of Minnesota after only two years of study, and earned a master's degree in political science in 1940 from Louisiana State University. Humphrey also held a degree from the Denver College of Pharmacy, and during the Great Depression of the 1930s he worked as a pharmacist in his father's drugstore to help support his family. After teaching briefly at the University of Minnesota while

Senator Hubert Humphrey of Minnesota, a leading anti-Communist liberal.

pursuing his doctorate in 1941, Humphrey accepted a job with the Workers Education Service of the Works Progress Administration. During World War II, Humphrey headed the Minnesota branch of the War Production Administration and taught from 1943 to 1944 in the Army Air Force training program at Macalester College.

In the presidential election of 1944, Humphrey served as President Franklin D. Roosevelt's Minnesota campaign manager. The following year, he was elected mayor of Minneapolis as the candidate of the merged Democratic and Farmer-Labor parties. He earned a national reputation for his attacks on organized crime and racial prejudice, and established the first municipal fair-employment-practices commission. At the 1948 Democratic National Convention, Humphrey led a successful battle for the strongest civil-rights platform in the party's history.

Humphrey won election to the U.S. Senate in 1948, where he continued to campaign for civil-rights and social-welfare legislation. He also served as head of the Minnesota chapter of the AMERICANS FOR DEMOCRATIC ACTION (ADA), organized by American liberals in 1946 as part of their drive to distance themselves from Communism. From 1946 to 1948, Humphrey battled Communists and their allies for control of the Democratic-Farmer-Labor Party in Minnesota, a confrontation that awakened him to the presence—and resourcefulness—of Communists in left-wing political and labor organizations. "Many liberals in this country have failed to face up to this issue," Humphrey wrote. Aggressive Communism, he believed, was a major threat to American security, "and liberals should be in the forefront of the fight against it, not in the rear."

Like numerous other liberals within the Democratic Party, Humphrey was sensitive to criticism that he was "soft" on Communism. Thus when Senator Patrick MCCARRAN of Nevada introduced an internal security bill in 1950 which (1) required the registration of Communist-action and Communist-front organizations, (2)

gave the government authority to detain persons whom it believed likely to commit espionage or sabotage, and (3) prohibited Communists from holding government or defense jobs, Humphrey decided that he could not oppose the measure without offering an alternative. He therefore joined with fellow Senate liberals Paul Douglas of Illinois and Harley Kilgore of West Virginia to propose a Democratic version of an internal security bill. After flexing his anti-Communist muscles by referring to the McCarran bill as a "cream-puff special," Humphrey and his colleagues met with President Harry S. TRUMAN on September 5, 1950, to explain that "they had to make a move of this sort as the only possible way of beating the McCarran bill." The liberal Democrats reasoned that the best way to prevent anti-Communist fanatics from wreaking further havoc was to assume leadership of the crusade themselves and ensure that it was run in a responsible fashion.

Nevertheless, the Senate leadership brought the McCarran version of the INTERNAL SECURITY ACT OF 1950 to the floor, and Humphrey—fearful that a negative vote would damage his chances for reelection in 1954—voted in favor of the measure, much to his subsequent regret. "I was very proud of you and your vote on the McCarran bill," he wrote to Senator Estes Kefauver of Tennessee, who had opposed the measure. "I wish I could say the same for myself." Humphrey privately urged Truman to veto the bill (which the President did), and when the Senate reconsidered it, Humphrey led a filibuster in an attempt to sustain the veto. In the end, the Senate overrode Truman's veto, though this time Humphrey was one of ten senators who voted against the bill.

For the next four years, Humphrey alternated between attacking Communists and the ultra-conservative followers of Senator Joseph MC-CARTHY of Wisconsin, many of whom felt that Humphrey's support of civil-rights and social-welfare legislation made his loyalty suspect. In 1952, Humphrey conducted hearings into Communist infiltration of labor unions. His investigation started, he said, from the assumption that "there are certain Communist-dominated unions in the United States operating in defense industries," and that "Communists seek to use the unions as systems of power to promote Soviet Russia's foreign policies." Yet, Humphrey also rose in the Senate later that year to lament the deleterious effects of the mounting anti-Communist hysteria. "Something terrible has happened to us," Humphrey declared. "We go around accusing people day after day and demanding they prove their innocence. That is totalitarian law, not democratic law. I think it is time we stated that we are not going to let people be ruined, their reputations destroyed, and their names defiled because we happen to be in the great game of American politics." Further, Humphrey argued that the atmosphere of political paranoia in the United States was diverting the attention of Congress from social problems which desperately required solutions.

To his later regret, Humphrey, who was a member of McCarthy's GOVERMENT OPERATIONS COMMITTEE, seldom criticized the Wisconsin senator directly. In 1968, Humphrey explained his reluctance: "I felt that America was going through a very unwholesome, degrading experience, and sometimes I feel that I should have stood up more strongly against [McCarthy], but I was literally fighting for political survival and even though I voted against him and I took my knocks from him and his supporters, I think I could have been a little braver during that time."

In the summer of 1954, Humphrey moved to wrest control of the anti-Communist crusade from McCarthy. On August 11, Humphrey introduced a bill that became known as the COMMUNIST CONTROL ACT OF 1954. Designed to replace the Internal Security Act of 1950, Humphrey's bill declared the COMMUNIST PARTY illegal and provided criminal penalties for anyone who "knowingly and willfully" joined the Party. It was time, Humphrey insisted, "to quit 'horsing around' "; he claimed that he also wanted to take the issue of Communism out of politics

and leave it to the courts, where it belonged. "I am tired of reading headlines about being 'soft' toward communism," Humphrey told the Senate. "I am tired of having people play the communist issue as though it were a great overture which has lasted for years. . . . I want Senators to stand up and to answer whether they are for the Communist Party, or are against it." Not surprisingly, the measure passed the Senate by a margin of 85–1.

When the chamber considered Senator Ralph FLANDERS' motion of censure against McCarthy, Humphrey spoke strongly in favor of the measure. At one point, he pointedly suggested to Senate Majority Leader Lyndon B. JOHNSON—who hesitated to openly support the motion—that it was the duty and responsibility of the Democratic Party to line up solidly behind Flanders.

Humphrey campaigned unsuccessfully for the Democratic vice presidential nomination in 1956, and lost the 1960 presidential nomination to Massachusetts Senator John F. KENNEDY. In 1964, President Lyndon Johnson selected Humphrey as his vice-presidential running mate. After Johnson decided not to seek reelection in 1968, Humphrey won the Democratic presidential nomination but lost to Republican Richard M. NIXON in one of the closest presidential elections in American history. Humphrey died of cancer in 1978.

**hydrogen bomb**   A weapon that derives its explosive power from the fusion of hydrogen atoms, the hydrogen bomb was developed in the United States in 1950–52 largely as a response to the first successful atomic-weapon test by the Soviet Union in 1949. Although some American scientists had proposed research into fusion (thermonuclear) weapons during World War II, the federal government decided to focus its efforts on fission weapons instead. (The two atomic bombs dropped on the Japanese cities of Hiroshima and Nagasaki in August 1945 were nuclear-fission weapons; that is, they derived their energy from the splitting of uranium

A test explosion of a hydrogen bomb, the "super weapon" whose development was opposed by physicist J. Robert Oppenheimer.

atoms.) Following the announcement of the first Soviet nuclear test in September 1949, however, momentum began to build within the American military and scientific community for research on a fusion weapon. The leading advocates of the development of a hydrogen bomb included physicist Edward Teller and ATOMIC ENERGY COMMISSION director Lewis A. STRAUSS.

In January, 1950, Chairman of the Joint Chiefs of Staff Omar Bradley endorsed a program of nuclear-fusion-weapon research. Several days later, the American public was stunned by news of the arrest in Britain of atomic spy Klaus FUCHS. Fears that Fuchs and his colleagues in a Soviet spy ring had compromised U.S. atomic secrets helped persuade President Harry S. TRUMAN to approve a full-scale hydrogen-bomb research project on January 31, 1950.

For anti-Communist zealots in the United States, support for the hydrogen-bomb project became a touchstone for determining the loyalty of scientists. The opposition of Albert EINSTEIN and J. Robert OPPENHEIMER to further research

on thermonuclear weapons cost them public support. In Oppenheimer's case, his stand against the hydrogen bomb eventually led to the revocation of his security clearance. On June 1, 1954, a special Personnel Security Board ruled that "Dr. Oppenheimer's continuing conduct and associations have reflected a serious disregard for the requirements of the security system," and that "we find his conduct in the hydrogen-bomb program sufficiently disturbing as to raise a doubt as to whether his future participation . . . would be clearly consistent with the best interests of security."

By that time, the hydrogen bomb was a reality. On the morning of November 1, 1952, a team of American experts detonated a thermonuclear weapon on the Pacific island of Elugelab in the Marshall Islands. The fireball from the explosion rose 5 miles into the sky, followed by a gigantic multicolored, mushroom-shaped cloud that spread 25 miles into the stratosphere. The following summer, the Soviet Union conducted its first successful hydrogen-bomb test.

# I

**I Led Three Lives**   A television show based upon the best-selling book by ex-Communist and FBI informant Herbert PHILBRICK, *I Led Three Lives* made its debut on the NBC network in September 1953. The part of Philbrick was played by Richard Carlson; other regulars included Virginia Stefan as his wife, Eva Philbrick, and John Zaremba and Ed Hinton as special FBI agents Dressler and Henderson, respectively. Because most of the Communists in the series were quickly arrested due to the vigilance of Philbrick and his associates in the FBI, none of them lasted long enough to become regulars.

To provide the series with an authentic documentary atmosphere, each episode began with an announcer declaring that "this is the fantastically true story of Herbert A. Philbrick, who for nine frightening years did lead three lives—average citizen, member of the COMMUNIST PARTY, and counterspy for the FBI. For obvious reasons the names, dates, and places have been changed, but the story is based on fact." The series provided viewers with tense, well-written scripts and gritty urban locations, complete with the requisite dark alleys and secret party meetings. Philbrick himself served as technical consultant and narrator for the series, always referring to himself on screen in the third person. ("This could be a trap, Philbrick," he warned himself in moments of danger, of which there was at least one each week.) In a typical episode, the mother of a teenaged girl contacted the FBI because her daughter had suddenly started spouting antiwar propaganda; "Where," the distraught mother wondered, "did my daughter get the outrageous ideas she's been expressing?" Although the mother identified the girl's boyfriend as the source of her radical notions, Philbrick tracked down the real Communist, an art dealer whom the girl had come to know and trust. By the end of the half-hour, the girl was "not only safe and sound, but cured of her Communist infection."

Each week's script was reviewed by the FBI, which officially endorsed the series. Still, the producers claimed that they were not attempting to deliver any political message. "That's not our field," they explained. "Our chief purpose is to find good story properties, turn them into good films, and sell them." But as the series entered its third year, scripts drifted ludicrously far from Philbrick's actual adventures. For instance, one episode detailed a purported Communist plot to convert vacuum cleaners into guided-missile launchers. Despite the ludicrous nature of such conspiracies, many viewers took the series seriously, either because of its realistic atmosphere or the hysteria created by the anti-Communist crusade. "It's hard to believe," said Stefan, "but people actually write us and ask us to investigate Communists in their neighborhood." The series ended its run of original episodes in 1956, though reruns continued into the mid-1960s.

**I Married a Communist**   A film starring Laraine Day as a woman who, as the title indicates, marries a comparative stranger who turns out to be a Communist—a San Francisco shipping executive played by Robert Ryan. *I Married a Communist* appeared briefly in American movie theaters in November 1949. As the plot of the film unfolds, Day realizes that Ryan formerly worked for the COMMUNIST PARTY as a strong-arm thug. Ryan has had a change of heart, however, and wants to leave the party. The party refuses to let him go and eventually murders him, just as it kills Day's brother (by running over him with a convertible sports car) and her sister-in-law (who is pushed out of a window).

A low-budget film from RKO Radio, *I Married a Communist* refrained from treating its theme with subtlety. Communist characters were portrayed as ruthless gangsters or psycopathic killers. Critics admired the pace of the movie ("It is well loaded with scary sequences

# Institute for Pacific Relations 193

photographed in frightening semi-darkness," noted *Commonweal*), but they decried the use of characters who were nothing more than caricatures. Along with *I WAS A COMMUNIST FOR THE FBI* (1951), the film represented an attempt by the major Hollywood studios both to profit from the prevailing anti-Communist fervor and to establish their loyalty to avoid further investigation by the House Committee on Un-American Activities or Joseph MCCARTHY.

**Institute for Pacific Relations** Founded in 1925 by officials of the Young Men's Christian Association, the Institute for Pacific Relations (IPR) was a privately financed international organization dedicated to the study of Far East affairs. Originally, the institute had branches in ten separate nations, including the United States and the Soviet Union. Supported by funds from a number of corporations and major foundations, the Institute published *Pacific Affairs*, a quarterly journal written primarily by and for scholars on such subjects as Asian contemporary events, history, economics, and agriculture. Between 1934 and 1941, *Pacific Affairs* was edited by Owen LATTIMORE, whom Senator Joseph MCCARTHY identified in March 1950 as "the top Russian espionage agent" in the United States.

Although many of the articles published in *Pacific Affairs* tended to reflect a definite leftist political orientation, the journal could not fairly be described as a pro-Communist publication. There were, however, Communists on the institute's staff, and its activities in the 1930s appeared to be sufficiently suspicious to warrant an investigation by U.S. Army Intelligence.

The institute's affinity for the Communist cause in the Chinese civil war (1945–49) made it a favorite target of the CHINA LOBBY, under the direction of millionaire industrialist Alfred KOHLBERG, a longtime admirer of CHIANG Kai-shek. The IPR made headlines again in the spring of 1950, when McCarthy first attacked Lattimore. McCarthy's charges prompted another investigation of the IPR by U.S. Army

Intelligence in the person of retired Brigadier General Elliott R. Thorpe. In his testimony to a Senate subcommittee, Thorpe stated that "it is my personal belief that this organization contains within its membership highly respectable citizens interested in the Pacific basin and the furthering of peace in that part of the world. It also has associated with it educators interested in using its facilities in their education work. Finally it has, as have apparently all such organizations, the usual collection of intellectual panhandlers and screwballs. From my limited examination in recent years, I doubt the value of these latter characters to any intelligence-seeking organization." "I believe the Institute of Pacific Relations could profitably part with some of their people," concluded Thorpe, "but I doubt the capacity of such people to do any serious harm to the United States should they be so inclined."

There the matter might have rested had not a schoolteacher visiting his aunt at a farm in Massachusetts discovered several steel file cabinets, filled with thousands of documents from the IPR's files in a barn owned by the institute's former secretary-general. There was nothing sinister or mysterious about these files. The documents had been moved to the barn to save space in the institute's New York office, and a team of FBI agents had, in fact, already examined the material at considerable length at the invitation of the Institute.

Nevertheless, such was the atmosphere of intrigue and hysteria encouraged by McCarthy and his associates that the schoolteacher, believing he had stumbled across evidence of subversion, hurriedly telephoned McCarthy's Washington office. McCarthy's staff engaged in a brief battle of subpoenaes for custody of the IPR documents with investigators from the House Committee on Un-American Activities, who wanted to seize the files and the headlines for themselves. McCarthy's staff emerged victorious, and after McCarthy milked the incident for its publicity value—he described the barn as a center for Soviet espionage activity—the files were passed on to Senator Patrick MCCARRAN's Internal Security Subcommittee.

McCarran's subcommittee held hearings on the IPR cache from July 1951 to June 1952, using selections from the documents to bolster Republican charges of treason and espionage. Essentially, the McCarran subcommittee attempted to prove a connection between the IPR, the State Department, and the victory of MAO Zedong's Communist forces in China. The fact that a number of IPR witnesses pleaded the Fifth Amendment before McCarran's subcommittee and that one of the IPR's executives, Frederick Vanderbilt Field, already had been sentenced to prison for contempt of Congress in the AMERASIA affair, bolstered the linkage in the eyes of McCarthy and McCarran. Further, many veteran members of the State Department's Far Eastern desk had ties to the IPR, as did some of the individuals whom Elizabeth BENTLEY had named before congressional committees as Communists or Communist sympathizers.

As part of the IPR hearings, the Senate Internal Security subcommittee called Owen Lattimore to testify. It kept him on the stand for twelve days. Although the veracity of Lattimore's chief accusers—Louis BUDENZ and Harvey Matusow—had been questioned even by the FBI (Matusow eventually pleaded guilty to perjury), Lattimore's own memory about his activities and writings proved sufficiently faulty to encourage suspicions in the minds of the IPR's detractors.

At the conclusion of its hearings on the Institute for Pacific Relations, the Republican majority of the McCarran subcommittee issued a report that claimed that the IPR's activities had helped "to serve international Communist interests and to affect adversely the interests of the United States." Save for the work of the IPR, said McCarran in a grossly exaggerated statement, "China today would be free and a bulwark against the further advance of the Red hordes into the Far East." The IPR, McCarran charged, had helped infiltrate Soviet sympathizers into government offices, placed Communist professors on university faculties, and filled textbooks with Communist propaganda. McCarran also singled out Owen Lattimore as "a conscious and articulate instrument of the Soviet conspiracy."

McCarran's charges clearly overestimated the influence of the IPR on the formulation of American foreign policy. Nevertheless, McCarran was able to persuade U.S. Attorney General James McGranery to indict Lattimore in December 1952 on seven counts of perjury stemming from his testimony in the IPR hearings. The government's case was so insubstantial that the trial judge dismissed most of the counts, and by the summer of 1955 the government had abandoned the case. Yet, the institute proved unable to survive under the relentless harassment of congressional conservatives, and the IPR—discredited in the public view and bereft of effective leadership—subsequently was disbanded.

**Internal Security Act of 1950**   Known familiarly as the MCCARRAN ACT, after Senate Judiciary Committee Chairman Senator Patrick MCCARRAN of Nevada, the Internal Security Act of 1950 was the result of mounting pressure within Congress in the early days of the KOREAN WAR for antisubversive legislation. A similar measure, known as the Mundt-Nixon bill (for Representatives Karl MUNDT and Richard M. NIXON), had passed the House of Representatives in 1948 but expired in the Senate. A slightly revised version—the Mundt-Ferguson-Johnston bill—was introduced in early 1950, but the measure made little headway in the Senate until the outbreak of the Korean conflict in June 1950 significantly altered the political environment. Sensing the rising consensus for action, President Harry S. TRUMAN attempted to preempt Congress by proposing his own measure to strengthen laws against espionage activities and subversive aliens, but the administration's bill was far too mild for a majority of members of Congress in both parties.

On August 10, 1950, McCarran introduced Senate Bill 4037, which combined the Mundt-Ferguson-Johnston bill with several provisions of his own. The bill was essential, McCarran argued, to "fortify the home front even as we are today fortifying our boys on the battlefield of Korea." Fundamentally, S.4037 was designed to eliminate any threat from Communists in the United States by requiring the COMMUNIST PARTY and members of Communist-front organizations to register with a newly established five-person Subversive Activities Control Board (SACB). The bill posited the existence of "a world Communist movement which, in its origins, its development, and its present practice, is a world-wide revolutionary movement whose purpose it is, by treachery, deceit, infiltration into other groups (governmental and otherwise), espionage, sabotage, terrorism, and any other means deemed necessary, to establish a Communist totalitarian dictatorship in the countries throughout the world." The international Communist movement, it claimed, was directed by the Soviet dictatorship that supervised "clever and ruthless espionage and sabotage tactics" designed to subvert democratic governments.

Specifically, the bill claimed that the Communist movement in the United States consisted of "thousands of adherents, rigidly and ruthlessly disciplined" who were "awaiting and seeking to advance a moment when the United States may be so far extended by foreign engagements, so far divided in counsel, or so far in industrial or financial straits, that overthrow of the Government of the United States by force and violence may seem possible of achievement." The threat of Communist domination, the bill stated, represented "a clear and present danger to the security of the United States and to the existence of free American institutions." The Communist Party and all Communist-action and Communist-front organizations would therefore be required to register with the SACB, on the theory that the resulting publicity would destroy the political effectiveness of all such groups. The

Communist Party was not declared illegal, however. FBI director J. Edgar HOOVER had long opposed outlawing the Communist Party, for he feared that such an action would drive the party underground and make it more difficult for the Justice Department to maintain its surveillance of party activities.

By the summer of 1950, many Democratic liberals in Congress had grown weary of Republican charges that they were "soft" on Communism. Fearing for their political future and angry that anti-Communist zealots had succeeded in linking traditional American liberalism with Communism in the minds of many Americans, a group of liberal Democratic senators—including Harley Kilgore of West Virginia and Paul Douglas of Illinois—proposed their own alternative to McCarran's bill. The Democratic measure was even more extreme than S.4037, for it provided the federal government with authority in a national emergency to detain anyone whom it deemed likely to engage in espionage or sabotage. As the Democrats sought to substitute their measure for the McCarran bill, prominent liberal Hubert HUMPHREY of Minnesota dismissed S.4037 as a "creampuff special." McCarran, whose record on civil liberties was far more conservative than Humphrey's, replied that the liberals' proposal—which critics derided as a "concentration camp bill"—violated the Fifth and Sixth Amendments—and possibly the Thirteenth Amendment as well—and was clearly "not workable under any of the accepted standards of Americanism." In the House, Karl Mundt also opposed the drastic Democratic measure. "Let us not tear the Constitution to shreds," Mundt pleaded. "Let us not out-Hitler Hitler; let us not out-Stalin Stalin; let us not establish concentration camps in America."

In the end, the Senate combined the detention provisions of the Democrats' bill with S.4037 to form the Internal Security Act. The omnibus measure passed the Senate easily, by a margin of 70–7. President Truman promptly vetoed the bill. On September 22, he returned the McCarran Act to Congress, claiming that it would help rather than hurt the Communist cause. "It would actually weaken our existing internal security measures," Truman argued, "and would seriously hamper the Federal Bureau of Investigation and our other security agencies. It would help the Communists in their efforts to create dissension and confusion within our borders. It would help the Communist propagandists throughout the world who are trying to undermine freedom by discrediting as hypocrisy the efforts of the United States on behalf of freedom." The notion of requiring Communist organizations to divulge information about themselves, said Truman, was "about as practical as requiring thieves to register with the sheriff."

Moreover, Truman saw the application of the registration requirements to alleged Communist-front organizations as "the greatest danger to freedom of speech, press, and assembly, since the Alien and Sedition Laws of 1798" because any group that happened to advocate policies that coincided with Communist Party objectives—the example Truman employed was low-cost housing—could be branded as a Communist-front organization. In urging Congress to allow existing legislation and the courts to deal effectively with the Communist threat, Truman concluded that "this is a time when we must marshall all our resources and all the moral strength of our free system in self-defense against the threat of Communist aggression. We will fail in this, and we will destroy all that we seek to preserve, if we sacrifice the liberties of our citizens in a misguided attempt to achieve national security."

All to no avail. The House of Representatives overrode Truman's veto, 248–48, and the Senate followed suit by a margin of 57–10, despite a filibuster led by Humphrey and Republican William Langer of North Dakota, who fainted from exhaustion during his speech. On November 22, the attorney general petitioned the SACB to force the Communist Party to register under the terms of the McCarran Act. The SACB hearings lasted from November 1950

to 1953; finally the board concluded that the Communist Party was required to register. Communist Party officials appealed the decision, but the Court of Appeals for the District of Columbia affirmed the board's registration order.

The case, known as *Communist Party v. Subversive Activities Control Board,* reached the Supreme Court in 1961. By a 5–4 majority, the Court upheld the ruling of the board, though the narrowly focused majority opinon, written by Justice Felix Frankfurter, avoided the broader question of the constitutionality of the registration provisions. Instead, the Court restricted itself to confirming that the Communist Party was substantially controlled by a foreign government and that the party did engage in activities which were proscribed by the McCarran Act. "There is no attempt here," wrote Frankfurter, "to impose stifling obligations upon the proponents of a particular creed as such, or even to check the importation of particular political ideas from abroad for propagation here." Instead, the act compelled the registration of organized groups "which have been made the instruments of a long-continued, systematic, disciplined activity directed by a foreign power and purposing to overthrow existing government in this country."

Chief Justice Earl WARREN and Associate Justices Hugo Black, William DOUGLAS, and William Brennan dissented, largely on grounds that the Internal Security Act violated the First and Fifth Amendments. "This whole Act, with its pains and penalties," noted Black, "embarks this country, for the first time, on the dangerous adventure of outlawing groups that preach doctrines nearly all Americans detest. . . . The same arguments that are used to justify the outlawry of Communist ideas here could be used to justify an outlawry of the ideas of democracy in other countries."

When the Supreme Court addressed the broader issue of the constitutionality of the Internal Security Act several years later, it ruled

International Information Agency: a typical library in Dakar.

that the act violated the defendants' rights to avoid self-incrimination under the Fifth Amendment.

**International Information Agency**   A division of the Department of State, the International Information Agency (IIA) sponsored the short-wave radio broadcasts of the VOICE OF AMERICA (VOA) to the populations of Communist nations in Europe and the Far East, and maintained nearly 200 libraries in more than 60 nations around the world. By 1953, the IIA had grown to employ 10,000 people and was supported by an annual budget of $100 million. Conservatives in Congress objected to the agency in part because of its huge size—they considered it poorly run and bloated with unnecessary administrative personnel—and partly because they believed the agency's libraries in-

cluded works by authors whom, they suspected, harbored Communist sympathies. At one point, the chairman of the House Appropriations Committee announced that he felt the IIA was "decidedly pinko," and Senator Robert TAFT of Ohio argued that "it should have been cleaned out or abolished long ago."

The agency thus represented an ideal target for Senator Joseph MCCARTHY, who launched a full-scale investigation of the IIA in February 1953. Declaring that his inquiry would seek evidence of "mismanagement, waste and subversion," McCarthy issued subpoenas to more than 50 present and former employees of the VOA and predicted that his investigation might continue for months. "Some persons in the Voice of America are doing a rather effective job of sabotaging Dulles' and Eisenhower's foreign policy," McCarthy charged. In fact, President

Dwight David EISENHOWER, who had taken office only a month earlier, already had launched his own investigation of the agency. When the White House learned that a VOA official had issued a memorandum approving the use of excerpts from the works of Communists or "Soviet-endorsed" authors, Secretary of State John Foster DULLES immediately rescinded the order, insisting that no "controversial" material—that is, material that might be construed as anti-American—could be employed on VOA broadcasts.

McCarthy began his hearings in New York City on February 16. As millions watched on live network television, McCarthy accused the VOA of stationing its two main transmitters in sites that did not provide for maximum penetration of the Iron Curtain. Such a decision, McCarthy argued, represented a deliberate attempt by Communist sympathizers within the IIA to sabotage the agency's activities. Witnesses testified to other alleged instances of pro-Soviet actions: VOA writers claimed that anti-Communist comments had been excised from broadcasts to Latin American countries; another writer claimed that she had been dismissed after she wrote a complimentary review of *Witness*, ex-Communist Whittaker CHAMBERS' account of his confrontation with Alger HISS; and a technician complained that the VOA had reduced the size of its radio tower in Vienna by half so that its broadcasts could no longer reach behind the Soviet border.

Rejecting complaints from VOA officials that he was dealing in gossip and innuendo, McCarthy soon expanded his inquiry to include the IIA's overseas libraries. Someone in the Truman administration, he charged, had used American taxpayers' money to purchase books with a pronounced pro-Communist bent. Among the authors to whom McCarthy objected were hard-boiled detective writer Dashiell HAMMETT, whose novels included *The Maltese Falcon* and *The Thin Man*, black poet Langston Hughes, and novelist Howard FAST, all of whom had been accused of Communist sympathies. Complaining that his discussions on this matter with former Secretary of State Dean ACHESON's assistants had resulted only in "bad memories, evasion, and no cooperation whatever," McCarthy insisted that Dulles meet privately with him to discover who had authorized the purchase of these objectionable works.

Meanwhile, McCarthy dispatched his two top subordinates, Roy COHN and G. David SCHINE, on a nineteen-day "fact-finding tour" of IIA libraries in Europe. The Cohn-Schine tour quickly degenerated into a farce, as the two young men created disturbances in one European city after another with their childish antics (at one point, Schine allegedly chased Cohn through a hotel lobby, whacking him on the head with a rolled-up newspaper) and their petulant diatribes about "Communist-slanted" literature. American newspapers dismissed Cohn and Schine as "the Rover Boys," but European observers—who used such epithets as "Mr. McCarthy's distempered jackals" and "latter-day fascists"—viewed their progress with considerable concern, comparing their crusade to the book-burning that occurred under the Nazi regime of Adolf Hitler twenty years earlier. "Their limited vocabulary, their self-complacency, and their paucity of ideas," complained the *Manchester Guardian*, "coupled with the immense power they wield, had the effect of drawing sympathy for all ranks of the United States diplomatic service who have to submit to this sort of thing." After returning to the United States in late April with three briefcases full of documentary evidence for McCarthy, even Cohn came to view the junket as a blunder. "It turned out to be one of the most publicized trips of the decade," he wrote. "We soon realized, although neither of us could admit to the distressing fact, that it was a colossal mistake."

In an attempt to deflect McCarthy's criticism of the IIA, the Eisenhower administration forced the resignation of the deputy director of the agency, a move McCarthy claimed was "the best thing that has happened in a long time," though he pointedly suggested that many other employees of the agency also deserved to be dismissed. The administration quickly complied. On April 23, the VOA announced that 830 employees had been fired in what it termed a "retrenchment program." Less than three weeks later, Theodore Kaghan, acting deputy director of the Office of Public Affairs in the American High Commission in Germany—who had feuded with Cohn and Schine during their tour—also resigned after receiving a warning from a State Department security official that "when you cross swords openly with Senator McCarthy, you can't expect to stay in the State Department."

To counter press speculation that the White House had knuckled under altogether to McCarthy and his fellow anti-Communist zealots, President Eisenhower used the occasion of a commencement address at DARTMOUTH COLLEGE on June 14, 1953, to deliver an unusually strong defense of intellectual freedom. "Don't join the book burners!" Eisenhower told an audience of nearly 10,000. "Don't think you are going to conceal faults by concealing evidence that they ever existed. Don't be afraid to go in your library and read every book as long as any document does not offend our own ideas of decency. That should be the only censorship." McCarthy replied with a shrug, stating that "he couldn't very well have been referring to me. I have burned no books." Yet, Eisenhower still chose to retreat from his Dartmouth speech at a press conference three days later. "By no means," he explained—"am I talking, when I talk about books or the right of dissemination of knowledge, am I talking about any document or any kind of thing that attempts to persuade or propagandize America into communism. . . . I just do not believe in suppressing ideas. I believe in dragging them out in the open and taking a look at them. That is what I meant, and I do not intend to be talking personally and in personalities with respect to anyone"—including, of course, McCarthy.

For his part, McCarthy continued to assail the IIA throughout the summer of 1953. According to the Wisconsin senator, IIA libraries sheltered 30,000 books written by pro-Communist authors. "When the State Department purchases a book by a Communist author," McCarthy charged, "it is . . . placing its stamp of approval upon his writings." By September, McCarthy had moved on to other targets, and the investigation stumbled to a close with no conclusive findings. In the end, few books were actually removed permanently from the IIA's shelves, though the State Department did drastically reduce its purchase of books to stock its overseas libraries. In the atmosphere of fear and suspicion that characterized the McCarthy era, few government officials (particularly in the State Department) wished to risk their careers in the cause of artistic or intellectual freedom. The incident served primarily to demoralize the staff of the IIA, and to affect American prestige abroad adversely.

***I Was a Communist for the FBI***   Released in the spring of 1951, *I Was a Communist for the FBI* was a melodramatic film from the Warner Bros. studio based on the true story of a Pittsburgh steelworker named Matt Cvetic who served the FBI for nine years as an undercover agent in the COMMUNIST PARTY. Cvetic's story had previously been serialized in *The Saturday Evening Post,* and producer Brian Foy admitted that he had mixed 85 percent fact with 15 percent fiction to enhance the plot of the film. Frank Lovejoy starred as Cvetic, and Dorothy Hart played a Communist schoolteacher who escaped from the party in the nick of time.

Among the characters portrayed in the film were Gerhard EISLER, one of the leading Communist Party functionaries in the United States, and the members of the HOUSE COMMITTEE ON UN-AMERICAN ACTIVITIES (HUAC)—Cvetic did testify before the committee in 1949. Although critics admired the pace of the plot, they generally considered the film a heavy-handed attempt to exploit the rising tide of anti-Communist sentiment. "The picture represents Communists as simple gangsters, cynically out for a fast buck and the ultimate spoils of power," complained *Time* magazine. "Real-life Communists are not so simple. They are after the spoils of power all right, and have been known to welcome a fast buck, but their cynical opportunism is rooted in a warped but zealous idealism, which makes them more formidable foes—and better material for dramatic treatment."

# J

**Jenkins, Ray Howard** (1897–1975) Special counsel to the U.S. Senate subcommittee formed to investigate Senator Joseph MCCARTHY's charges of Communist infiltration of the U.S. Army, Ray Jenkins was a flamboyant criminal attorney who gained notoriety by his courtroom theatrics and his almost unbroken record of success in defending clients whose cases had appeared hopeless. Born in the mountains of North Carolina and raised in the small town of Tellico Plains, Tennessee, Jenkins turned down a career as a professional baseball player (he reputedly threw a particularly nasty spitball in the days when that pitch was still legal) to attend the University of Tennessee Law School. A large, rawboned man with close-cropped hair, Jenkins quickly earned a reputation for his ability to cajole juries into sympathizing with his clients. "You can always defend a man who kills a bully," he once explained. "You make the jury so damned mad that they want to dig up the body and kill the s.o.b. all over again."

Although he had little previous experience in matters of Communist espionage or subversion, Jenkins was selected (on the advice of Senator Everett Dirksen of Illinois) to act as special counsel to the Senate subcommittee investigating McCarthy's charges against the Army. Before the ARMY-MCCARTHY HEARINGS began in the spring of 1954, Jenkins claimed that he had not formed any opinion of McCarthy or his anti-Communist crusade. "I have no record, publicly or otherwise, with regard to Senator McCarthy or what has come to be called MCCARTHYISM," stated Jenkins. "I have no prejudice, and no bias."

Indeed, it seemed clear that Jenkins had not thought deeply about the issues involved in the confrontation between McCarthy and the Army, nor had he understood McCarthy's willingness to fabricate or twist evidence to support his contentions. At the outset of the hearings, Jenkins accepted without question the notion that McCarthy's inquiry into Communist infiltration of the Army base at FORT MONMOUTH, New Jersey, had been an unqualified public service; later, indications that McCarthy had misrepresented vital pieces of evidence caused Jenkins to retreat into a more impartial position. Jenkins also initially accepted as authentic the photograph supplied by McCarthy of Secretary of the Army Robert T. STEVENS beaming proudly at McCarthy's associate, G. David SCHINE, though the picture was soon revealed to be a composite photo.

Because the subcommittee's goals were open-ended, Jenkins' role in the hearings was not particularly well defined. Circumstances forced him to alternate between acting as defense counsel for the Army, defending it from McCarthy's assaults; as counsel for the subcommittee, pressing the Army for further information; and as an impartial judge ruling on legal questions. Typically, Jenkins examined each witness first, leading the witness through a lengthy direct examination, allowing the witness to state his or her case before launching into an equally lengthy cross-examination. At one point, Jenkins pressed Secretary Stevens so rigorously that the Army's counsel, Joseph WELCH, protested that "This is not a murder trial. . . . This witness is entitled to at least ordinary courtesy." Yet, a few hours later, Jenkins' treatment of Schine led McCarthy to object, stating that Jenkins' cross-examination was "the most improper exhibition I have ever seen. You have a lawyer here who brags about being one of the greatest criminal lawyers in the country, badgering this private. . . . He can't gain anything further by badgering this Army private. I think it is indecent, and I think the Chair should comdemn it."

Jenkins received high marks from observers for the impartial manner in which he conducted the inquiry, but the constraints of a congressional hearing prevented him from employing the sort of theatrics that had made him a successful criminal attorney. Further, he was upstaged by Welch, whose low-key style and wry humor made him the favorite of the television cameras. At the end of the hearings, Jenkins conducted a particularly unenlightening examination of McCarthy himself; even that event was eclipsed by the appearance in the hearing room of Senator Ralph FLANDERS of Vermont, who handed to McCarthy a message informing him that Flanders planned to deliver on the following day a speech denouncing McCarthy and his irresponsible methods.

**Jenner, William** (1908–1985)  A staunch political ally of Senator Joseph MCCARTHY of Wisconsin, William Jenner was first elected to the U.S. Senate in 1946. Having served in the U.S. Army Air Corps during World War II, Jenner thus became the first veteran of the war to be elected to the Senate; at the time, he was also the youngest member of that chamber.

Although he began his term as a moderate Republican, Jenner soon turned toward the right, favoring the antilabor-union bill known as the TAFT-HARTLEY ACT, and opposing the Marshall Plan, which sought to rebuild the shattered economies of the nations of Western and Southern Europe. It would "please Stalin," Jenner claimed, if the United States decided to "spend itself into bankruptcy." Jenner also opposed American entry into the North Atlantic Security Pact, fearing that its arms program might also bankrupt the nation. Although he rarely had any kind words to say for any member of the administration of President Harry S. TRUMAN, Jenner was particularly violent in his denunciations of Secretary of State Dean ACHESON. Jenner also appeared to detest George Catlett MARSHALL, who preceded Acheson as secretary of state and subsequently served as secretary of defense. In September 1949, Jenner excoriated Marshall—who had also served as U.S. Army chief of staff during World War II—in a Senate speech that was notorious for its viciousness. In charging that the Truman administration would go down in

Senator William Jenner of Indiana, a leading anti-Communist crusader, launched a vicious attack on General George C. Marshall.

history as "America's greatest criminals in peace and war," Jenner shouted that "General Marshall is not only willing, he is eager to play the role of a front man for traitors. The truth is this is no new role for him, for General George C. Marshall is a living lie."

Outraged when Truman dismissed General Douglas MACARTHUR as commander of the United Nations forces in Korea, Jenner took the opportunity to again denounce the Truman administration. "This country today," he declared, "is in the hands of a secret inner coterie which is directed by agents of the Soviet Union. We must cut this whole cancerous conspiracy out of our Government at once. Our only recourse is to impeach President Truman and find out who is the secret invisible government which has so cleverly led our country down the road to destruction."

When Senator Joseph McCarthy launched his anti-Communist crusade by accusing the State Department of harboring "card-carrying Communists" in its ranks, Jenner became one of McCarthy's most devout supporters. The Senate appointed a subcommittee headed by Maryland Democrat Millard TYDINGS to investigate McCarthy's charges; following the subcommittee's conclusion that McCarthy's accusations were "a fraud and a hoax," Jenner retaliated by describing Tydings as a "trained seal" who had led "the most scandalous and brazen whitewash of treasonable conspiracy in our history."

Although Jenner had originally supported the presidential candidacy of Ohio Senator Robert TAFT in 1952, he readily accepted assistance for his own reelection campaign from the eventual Republican nominee, General Dwight David EISENHOWER. Eisenhower, however, detested Jenner for his savage attack on George Marshall, who had personally selected Eisenhower to lead the Allied command in Europe during World War II. When Eisenhower and Jenner appeared together at a rally in Indianapolis during the 1952 campaign, Eisenhower pointedly refused to mention Jenner by name in his speech. After Jenner attempted to maneuver Eisenhower into a public embrace—captured by news cameras—Eisenhower confided to his associates that "he felt dirty from the touch of the man."

After the 1952 election results provided the Republican Party with control of the White House and both houses of Congress, Jenner was named chairman of the Senate Internal Security Subcommittee, which previously had been chaired by the equally zealous anti-Communist Patrick MCCARRAN of Nevada. The Eisenhower administration hoped that Jenner, who had a reputation as a loyal Republican partisan, would restrain the subcommittee's excesses and even act as a check on McCarthy, but Jenner proved as unmanageable as the obstreperous McCarthy. He launched investigations into Communist in-

fluence in the nation's churches, schools, and military forces, all of which embarrassed White House officials. When rulings of the U.S. Supreme Court, headed by Chief Justice Earl WARREN, threatened to restrain the freedom of congressional investigations, Jenner struck back by introducing legislation to reduce the Court's authority to oversee Congress.

Meanwhile, Jenner had turned against Eisenhower's moderate policies, claiming that the President had "ruined" the Republican Party. A dedicated member of the CHINA LOBBY, Jenner consistently urged the White House to "unleash" Nationalist Chinese leader CHIANG Kaishek and aid his efforts to recapture the mainland from the Communist Chinese regime of MAO Zedong.

Jenner elected not to run for a third term in 1958, perhaps because the anti-Communist crusade was faltering in the face of McCarthy's censure by the Senate, along with revelations that the hysteria of the late 1940s and 1950s had recklessly damaged the reputations of innocent individuals. Upon the expiration of his term in 1959, Jenner returned to Indiana, where he practiced law and later became an executive for the Seaway Corporation.

**Jessup, Philip C.** (1897–1986)   An early target of the HOUSE COMMITTEE ON UN-AMERICAN ACTIVITIES (HUAC) and Senator Joseph MCCARTHY of Wisconsin, Philip Jessup was a veteran American diplomat and one of the highest-ranking officials in the U.S. foreign service.

Born in New York City, Jessup attended a prestigious private school in Connecticut before enrolling at Hamilton College in 1914. His studies were interrupted by the American entry into World War I in February 1917. Jessup enlisted in the Army and served overseas in Belgium and France, until he was ordered in October 1918 to enroll in the U.S. Military Academy at West Point. The following year, Jessup returned to Hamilton and completed the work for his B.A. degree. He obtained a Carnegie Fellowship to study law and received both

Former ambassador-at-large Philip Jessup, a target of Senator Joseph McCarthy and his allies.

an LL.B. from Yale and an M.A. from Columbia in 1924. After a brief stint in the banking business, Jessup joined the Department of State as an assistant solicitor. In 1927, Jessup returned to private practice as a member of the New York law firm of Parker and Duryee. That same year, he received his Ph.D. and—while remaining a member of the law firm—embarked upon a teaching career at Columbia University.

Beginning in 1929, Jessup accepted a series of appointments to diplomatic and military government positions. He served as assistant to Elihu Root at the Conference of Jurists on the Permanent Court of International Justice in Geneva and, in 1930, was appointed legal adviser to the American ambassador in Cuba. From 1942 to 1944, Jessup served as an instructor and assistant director of the Naval School of Military Government and Education at Columbia University and as a lecturer at the U.S. Army School of Military Government at the University of Virginia. In January 1943, Jessup was also appointed division chief of the United Nations (UN) Refugee and Rehabilitation Administration. Following the end of the war, Jessup accepted a position as a judicial expert with the U.S. delegation to the UNITED NATIONS Conference in San Francisco.

On January 3, 1948, President Harry S. TRUMAN named Jessup deputy representative of the United States to the UN General Assembly; several months later, Jessup became deputy representative to the UN Security Council. He took an especially active role in the UN negotiations on the Middle East, proposing the admission of the newly established state of Israel to the UN in December 1948. Jessup also denounced the Soviet blockade of Berlin in 1948, claiming that negotiations with the Soviets were futile so long as "there is no evidence that the Russians desire to reach an agreement on the Berlin issue."

From 1948 to 1952, Jessup served the Truman administration as an ambassador-at-large, and specifically as a source of expert advice on Far East policy. He helped Secretary of State Dean ACHESON edit the State Department's CHINA WHITE PAPER in 1949, which attempted to place the blame for the Communist victory in China on the corruption and inefficiency of the Nationalist regime of CHIANG Kai-shek; he testified on behalf of Alger HISS at the latter's trial for perjury in 1950; he participated in the decision to commit U.S. military forces to Korea following the surprise attack by the North Korean forces in June 1950; and he attended the conference between Truman and General Douglas MACARTHUR at Wake Island in early 1951 that ultimately resulted in MacArthur's dismissal as commander-in-chief of the UN forces in Korea.

From 1933 to 1946, Jessup had served on the board of trustees of the INSTITUTE OF PACIFIC RELATIONS, and it was primarily this connection that brought him to the attention of Senator McCarthy and his fellow anti-Communist crusaders. Members of the CHINA LOBBY, an ultraconservative coalition of businessmen and politicians who supported the Nationalist cause in China, had long considered the Institute of Pacific Relations a shelter for Communist sympathizers, and in 1950—just several months after the Communists overthrew Chiang and forced the Nationalists off the mainland—several pro-Chiang members of Congress (including

Richard M. NIXON, Styles BRIDGES, and Karl MUNDT) began to attack Jessup. In February 1950, McCarthy named Jessup as one of a group of purported Communist sympathizers within the State Department. Without directly accusing Jessup of being a member of the COMMUNIST PARTY, McCarthy claimed that Jessup appeared to have "an unusual affinity for Communist causes." The ambassador, in McCarthy's opinion, was "a well-meaning dupe of the Lattimore crowd," a reference to Far East expert Owen LATTIMORE, whom McCarthy had earlier identified as the top Soviet espionage agent in the United States.

McCarthy subsequently claimed that Jessup had been associated with six Communist-front organizations. Despite the State Department's refutation of these charges—several of the organizations were not Communist fronts at all, and Jessup was not affiliated with the others—McCarthy refused to abandon his attack. In the autumn of 1951, McCarthy distributed a lengthy brochure entitled *The Case of Ambassador-At-Large Philip C. Jessup,* which accused Jessup of complicity in the Communist victory in China. Against the advice of numerous advisers within the Democratic Party who recognized the political force of McCarthy's allegations, Truman again nominated Jessup as a member of the American delegation to the UN in September 1951.

During the ensuing Senate hearings on the nomination, McCarthy appeared as a witness, repeating his claims that Jessup had belonged to six separate Communist-front groups. When Senator William FULBRIGHT produced the State Department's evidence exonerating Jessup, McCarthy flew into a rage and declared that he intended "to bring this story to the American people, from the Atlantic to the Pacific, from New Orleans to St. Paul, because it appears now . . . the only way we can get a housecleaning." McCarthy added that even if each case appeared weak on its own merits, the cumulative effect produced a pattern that appeared to indicate that Jessup was sympathetic to the Communist

cause. Fulbright snapped back that McCarthy's purported evidence against Jessup was wholly unsubstantiated. "There has to be something in each one of these cases, it seems to me—active participation in the organizations that were subversive," observed Fulbright. "The fact that there were a number of zeros doesn't make it amount to one if you put them all together." Fulbright later declared that he had never seen "a more arrogant or rude witnesses" than McCarthy before any Senate committee.

Jessup appeared several times before a Senate subcommittee to defend his record. Besides refuting McCarthy's specific charges, Jessup attempted to prove—as did many of McCarthy's victims—that he was as devoted an enemy of Communism as his persecutors. In his testimony, Jessup noted that "the Communists have attacked me with a violence equal to that displayed by the senator from Wisconsin, and with far greater justification." Jessup's defense was bolstered by a report from the U.S. Civil Service Commission LOYALTY REVIEW BOARD announcing that it had found "no reasonable doubt" of Jessup's loyalty.

Nevertheless, the Senate subcommittee assigned to report on Jessup's nomination voted 3–2 against Jessup. The decisive vote was cast by New Jersey Republican H. Alexander Smith, who explained that he saw Jessup as too controversial and "the symbol of a group attitude toward Asia"—that is, an unwillingness to support the Chinese Nationalist cause unequivocally—"which seems to have been proven completely unsound." Stung by the Senate's action, Truman waited until Congress had adjourned in the autumn of 1951 and then named Jessup as a recess appointment. "The record of the hearings," Truman noted, "shows that charges to the effect that [Jessup] was sympathetic to Communist causes were utterly without foundation." Not surprisingly, McCarthy denounced Truman's action, claiming that Jessup was "unfit to represent this country." President Dwight David EISENHOWER did not renew Jessup's appointment.

## Johnson, Lyndon Baines (1908–1973)

Minority Leader of the U.S. Senate when Senator Joseph MCCARTHY was censured in December 1954, Lyndon Baines Johnson began his political career at the age of 29, when he was nominated to fill an unexpired term of the late Congressman James F. Buchanan. Johnson was born in central Texas, outside the town of Stonewall, and grew up in Johnson City, a small town in Blanco County, Texas. He worked his way through Southwest Texas State Teachers College and spent several years as a public school teacher before moving to Washington, D.C., as secretary to Representative Richard M. Kleberg in 1932. Four years later, Johnson was named director of the National Youth Administration of Texas. He resigned that post in 1937 to run for Congress following the death of Representative Buchanan.

Johnson won election to the House by promising to support the New Deal initiatives of President Franklin D. Roosevelt—his campaign slogan was "Johnson and Roosevelt"—and he continued to act as one of Roosevelt's staunchest backers (becoming a member of the "Young Guard" of FDR supporters in the House) during his next four terms in Congress. Three days after the Japanese attack on Pearl Harbor, Johnson enlisted in the U.S. Navy, but returned to Washington in the summer of 1942 when Roosevelt insisted that members of Congress could not serve in the armed forces. Johnson spent the remainder of the war as chairman of an investigative subcommittee of the House Naval Affairs Committee. He proved one of the most regular Democratic Party members in the House, voting with the party leadership 95 percent of the time. During his tenure in the House, Johnson never was intimately involved in the growing anti-Communist fervor; at one point, he even took the politically risky step of voting against further appropriations for the HOUSE COMMITTEE ON UN-AMERICAN ACTIVITIES (HUAC).

In 1948, Johnson ran for the U.S. Senate and narrowly won a bitterly contested primary election against Governor Coke Stevenson of

Lyndon B. Johnson, leader in the U.S. Senate.

Texas. Stevenson later challenged the results of the election in the courts, charging irregularities in the counting of several hundred disputed votes which would have been sufficient to change the result. The U.S. Supreme Court eventually ruled against Stevenson, and the Senate Rules Committee voted unanimously to seat Johnson. Although Johnson continued to serve the Democratic administration of President Harry S. TRUMAN loyally, he occasionally broke ranks on the issue of military preparedness, arguing that the administration needed to enhance the fighting strength of the nation. "Our armed strength looks better in terms of bookkeeping," Johnson argued in July 1950, "than it does in performance."

Once McCarthy vaulted himself into prominence by his charge in February 1950 that the Truman administration, and specifically the State Department, was harboring Communists within the federal government, Johnson preferred to remain on the sidelines, refusing to confront the Wisconsin senator directly until he was certain he could do so successfully. Following the election of Dwight David EISENHOWER as president in 1952, Johnson repeatedly declared that McCarthy had become a Republican problem, one which he and his fellow Democrats had no intention of resolving for the White House. "I will not commit my party," announced Johnson, "to some high school debate on the subject, 'Resolved that Communism is good for the United States,' with my party taking the affirmative." Early in 1953, Johnson—who was elected minority leader of the Democrats at the start of the eighty-third Congress—derided the Republican Party's inability to force McCarthy to follow the lead of the White House. "They have the Republican Party of President Eisenhower," observed Johnson. "They have the Republican Party of Senator [Robert] Taft. . . . And somewhere—way out behind the *Chicago Tribune* tower—is the Republican Party of Senator McCarthy with one foot heavy in Greece and the other foot in Secretary Dulles' security files. It makes bipartisanship right difficult. We Democrats need to know which one of the Republican parties to be bipartisan *with*; and which one of the Republican parties to be bipartisan *against*."

Johnson did, however, attempt to weaken McCarthy at the outset of the eighty-third Congress by placing three relatively secure Democrats on McCarthy's GOVERNMENT OPERATIONS COMMITTEE: W. Stuart SYMINGTON of Missouri, John F. KENNEDY of Massachusetts, and Henry M. Jackson of Washington, none of whom would face reelection until 1958. Johnson also missed no opportunity to heighten the Republican Party's embarrassment over McCarthy's reckless activities. When the Wisconsin senator became embroiled in a controversy with the U.S. Army, Johnson insisted that the resulting hearings be televised live across the nation.

Following the conclusion of the ARMY-MC-CARTHY HEARINGS, Republican Senator Ralph

FLANDERS of Vermont introduced a motion of censure against McCarthy. Again Johnson—who despised McCarthy's disregard for Senate tradition and decorum—refused to commit himself or his party at the outset of debate, allowing Republican foes of the senator to take the lead, preferring instead to work behind the scenes to ensure McCarthy's defeat. When the Senate formed a special subcommittee (chaired by Republican Arthur V. WATKINS of Vermont) to hold hearings on Flanders' motion, Johnson packed the subcommittee with Democrats who were both conservative and relatively immune from McCarthyite pressure; all of them, Johnson declared, were "men who are symbols for patriotism, integrity, and judicial temperament."

As the issue moved closer to a vote, Johnson insisted publicly that the Democratic Party would allow each senator to vote his conscience on the issue; yet, no Senate Democrat delivered a single speech in favor of McCarthy throughout the debate. At the same time, the minority leader persuaded his colleagues to refrain from direct personal attacks on McCarthy, fearing that partisan rhetoric might shatter the fragile anti-McCarthy consensus that had been building since the conclusion of the Army hearings. Instead, Johnson preferred to focus the debate on the official report of the Watkins subcommittee. "Lyndon Johnson and others are literally demanding that we refrain from rocking the boat," complained one liberal Democratic staffer. "I hate to see the entire issue decided on as narrow base as the Watkins report establishes, but I am pretty well convinced that the size of the vote is more important than the arguments that are made."

On November 30, 1954, Johnson finally made his sentiments on the censure motion known to the full Senate. "In my mind," he announced, "there is only one issue here—morality and conduct. Each of us must decide whether we approve or disapprove of certain actions as standards of Senatorial integrity. I have made my decision." McCarthy's vicious denunciations of his Senate colleagues, Johnson declared, belonged not in the pages of the *Congressional Record*, but would "more fittingly [be] inscribed on the wall of a men's room." When the Senate voted on the censure motion two days later, every Democrat present voted for the motion. The size of the majority against McCarthy has been attributed by historians in large measure to Johnson's skill in forging the bipartisan anti-McCarthy coalition.

When the Democrats recaptured control of Congress in the 1954 elections, Johnson became majority leader, a post he held until 1961. In the spring of 1960, Johnson entered the contest for the Democratic nomination for President. His reputation among the nation's voters was never as high as it was among his Senate colleagues, however, and Johnson reluctantly accepted the vice presidential nomination. He served as vice president in the administration of President John F. KENNEDY from 1961 to 1963, succeeding to the presidency upon Kennedy's assassination in November 1963. The following year, Johnson rolled to a landslide reelection victory over archconservative Republican candidate Senator Barry Goldwater of Arizona. Although Johnson succeeded in persuading Congress to pass a significant number of domestic social reform measures—known collectively as the Great Society—the escalating American military involvement in Vietnam aroused such passionate opposition that Johnson decided not to run for reelection in 1968. Upon the conclusion of his second term in the White House, Johnson returned to Texas, where he died of a heart attack in 1973.

## Joint Anti-Fascist Refugee Committee

Organized in 1939 by veterans of the Abraham Lincoln International Brigade following the victory of General Francisco Franco's Nationalist forces in the Spanish Civil War, the Joint Anti-Fascist Refugee Committee (JAFRC) represented the consolidation of three separate groups: The American Committee to Save Refugees, the United American Spanish Aid Committee, and the League of American Writers. The chairman of the JAFRC was Dr. Edward K. Barsky, who had supervised the operation of American hospital units in the Spanish Civil War.

Originally dedicated to providing medical and financial assistance to Spanish refugees in French relocation camps and in South America, the JAFRC gradually expanded its activities to include aid to refugees from Nazi Germany and fascist Italy. To the HOUSE COMMITTEE ON UN-AMERICAN ACTIVITIES (HUAC), the JAFRC also appeared to serve as a clearinghouse for funds for various Communist-front organizations. (For instance, the JAFRC was accused of providing International Communist (Comintern) representative Gerhart EISLER, posing under one of his many aliases, with a stipend of $150 per month while he was in the United States.)

At a massive rally at Madison Square Garden in December 1945, the JAFRC called upon the Truman administration to sever diplomatic relations with the Franco regime. One of the speakers at the gathering was Nikolai Novikov, acting head of the Soviet embassy in the United States, who informed his audience that "now as before the Soviet Union is the leading power in the task of protection of democracy in the whole world." In the heightening tensions between the United States and the USSR in late 1945, such rhetoric was certain to capture the attention of the members of HUAC, who promptly accused the JAFRC of engaging "in political activity in behalf of Communists" and distributing propaganda "of a subversive character."

In February 1946, HUAC subpoenaed Barsky and directed him to bring the committee's correspondence files and financial records to the hearing so that they could determine whether the organization was, in fact, disbursing funds to COMMUNIST PARTY officials or Communist-front groups. Barsky appeared at the appointed hour, but he arrived empty-handed; the JAFRC board, he informed HUAC, had told him not to produce the records. At the request of HUAC, the House of Representatives thereupon cited Barsky for contempt by a vote of 339–4.

This action, however gratifying to the committee, did not move HUAC further toward the possession of JAFRC's records, and so it directed the sixteen members of the JAFRC board to appear on April 4, 1946, bringing with them the previously requested documents. Again the committee was disappointed, as the JAFRC board members appeared without their records; their executive secretary, they said, had official custody of the organization's files. Anticipating such a response, HUAC had also subpoenaed the executive secretary, Helen R. Bryan, who refused to turn over the documents on the advice of counsel. HUAC subsequently cited all sixteen board members and Bryan for contempt; all were sentenced to three months in prison, except Barsky, who received six months and a fine of $500. Five members of the board then recanted and were dismissed with suspended sentences.

The remaining defendants appealed their case, but the Court of Appeals upheld the verdict. In *Barsky et al. v. United States,* the court affirmed the right of Congress to investigate potential threats to the national security, even if that threat did not meet the historic criteria of a "clear and present danger." The Supreme Court declined to review the case. On his way to prison, JAFRC board member Howard FAST declared, with more than a touch of martyrdom, that the persecution of the JAFRC marked "the beginning of fascism in America." More accurately, the encounter marked the first time HUAC had been confronted by obdurate witnesses and set a precedent for the committee's strategy in dealing with such recalcitrance.

### Joseph Julian v. American Business Consultants

In 1950, popular radio actor Joseph Julian brought suit for libel against American Business Consultants (ABC), the firm founded by three former FBI agents in 1947 to publish the anti-Communist newsletter *COUNTER-ATTACK.* In 1950, ABC also began to publish *RED CHANNELS,* a periodical that quickly became the BLACKLISTING bible for the entertainment industry. Julian had been cited in *Red Channels* in 1950 for his appearance eight years earlier at a Carnegie Hall program sponsored by an organization known as Artists Front to Win the War, and for his attendance at a rally in 1949 of dedicated opponents of the HOUSE COMMITTEE ON UN-AMERICAN ACTIVITIES (HUAC).

Julian's promising career had promptly disintegrated, for once *Red Channels* listed an artist's name as an alleged member of the COMMUNIST PARTY or Communist-front organizations, the artist was virtually excluded from all employment in radio, television, or motion pictures. By 1953, Julian was earning only $1,630 a year. Julian subsequently filed suit against the publishers of *Red Channels* for libel and $150,000 damages. When he approached the executives of the CBS radio network for support, Julian was told that he could go far toward resuscitating his career by appearing at rallies of prominent anti-Communist groups and by dropping the suit against *Red Channels.* Julian refused and subsequently persuaded television newsman Edward R. MURROW to testify on his behalf in his action against American Business Consultants.

Julian's suit was heard in New York State Supreme Court in May 1954. Arthur Garfield HAYS, counsel for the AMERICAN CIVIL LIBERTIES UNION (ACLU), described the case as a crucial battle in the war against the blacklist. "I need hardly tell you the importance of these cases to the general cause," noted Hays at the outset of the hearing. "If we can get a substantial judgment against these people, we will put them out of business." Unfortunately for Julian, the case was heard by Judge Irving Saypol, a former prosecutor in the atomic espionage trial of Julius and Ethel ROSENBERG. Saypol refused to acknowledge the existence of a blacklist, or admit that a listing in *Red Channels* would necessarily damage an actor's career. In the end, Saypol ruled that because the officials of American Business Consultants did not actually engage in hiring artists themselves, any discussion of a blacklist was irrelevant.

Saypol consequently dismissed the charges for lack of evidence. The case never even made it to the jury. After the trial, one juror reportedly told Julian that he, at least, had been prepared to bring in a verdict against the defendants.

# K

**Kazan, Elia** (1909– ) One of America's most prestigious directors of films and stage plays, Elia Kazan earned the enmity of many of his former radical colleagues by cooperating with anti-Communist investigators. Kazan (nee Kazanjoglous) was born in Istanbul, Turkey, the son of a Greek rug merchant. When he was four years old, his family emigrated to the United States and soon settled in New Rochelle, New York. Kazan attended Williams College, where—in an effort "to stay out of my father's business"—he decided to major in English. He found the social atmosphere at Williams stifling, however, and the fact that he had to work his way through school as a waiter did nothing to lessen his antagonism toward his classmates. "I think the reason why I later joined the COMMU-NIST PARTY and turned against everybody," Kazan once noted, "was born at Williams. I had this antagonism to privilege, to good looks, to Americans, to Wasps."

Kazan briefly attended Yale Drama School and then joined the Group Theatre in New York, which had been founded in 1933 to perform plays with socially relevant themes. In 1935, Kazan played the role of taxi driver Agate Keller in the Group Theatre's production of Clifford ODETS' *Waiting for Lefty;* during the next year and a half, he also appeared in featured roles in Odets' *Paradise Lost* and *Golden Boy.* Despite the glowing critical notices he received for his performances, Kazan preferred to direct rather than act. His breakthrough as a director came in 1942, when he staged Thornton Wilder's *The Skin of Our Teeth,* which won Kazan the New York Drama Critics Award for direction. He won the Drama Critics Award a second time in 1947 for his direction of *All My Sons,* written by Arthur MILLER. Miller and Kazan subsequently formed an artistic partnership that continued through their productions of *Death of a Salesman* and AFTER THE FALL.

Meanwhile, Kazan had also ventured into the motion picture industry. Many of his early films, like his plays, dealt with contemporary social and political themes. In 1945, he directed his first major film, *A Tree Grows in Brooklyn.* He followed this with *Gentleman's Agreement,* based upon the powerful anti-Semitic novel by Laura Hobson and for which he won the Best Director Oscar, and *Pinky,* a story of racial prejudice in the southern United States.

In 1952, Kazan was subpoenaed by the HOUSE COMMITTEE ON UN-AMERICAN ACTIVITIES (HUAC) as part of its investigation into Communist infiltration of the motion picture

Director Elia Kazan "named names" of former political associates in his testimony before HUAC.

211

industry. Such was Kazan's stature within the theatrical and film communities that some observers felt he could have defied the committee and broken the power of the BLACKLIST. Initially, Kazan apparently intended to provide the committee with a full account of his own background, without naming any other names. Kazan had, in fact, belonged to the Communist Party from 1934 to 1936, during the time he was part of the Group Theatre project. His party unit was made up of other Communist members of the Group Theatre (including Odets), and his duties consisted of (1) purchasing and reading Marxist pamphlets and books; (2) supporting the party's efforts to gain a foothold in the Actors Equity Association; (3) supporting Communist-front organizations by writing and performing in dramas and teaching a school run by the League of Workers Theaters; and (4) attempting to convert the Group Theatre into an instrument of Communist propaganda.

The order to subvert the Group Theatre led directly to Kazan's departure from the Communist Party. "I had enough regimentation," he later stated, "enough of being told what to think and say and do, enough of their habitual violation of the daily practices of democracy to which I was accustomed." When a party official who claimed to be a member of the UNITED AUTO WORKERS from Detroit ordered Kazan to repent for his resistance to the party's directives, Kazan decided to quit. "I had found that I was being used to put power in the hands of people for whom, individually and as a group, I felt nothing but contempt, and for whose standard of conduct I felt a genuine horror." During the rest of the 1930s, Kazan later claimed that he tried to avoid POPULAR FRONT organizations that included Communists, although he occasionally found it necessary to join forces with them in the battle to obtain domestic social reforms and fight fascism abroad.

Despite Kazan's initial resolve not to discuss other individuals with HUAC, discussions with FBI Director J. Edgar HOOVER and Spyros Skouras, head of the Twentieth Century-Fox studio, led him to change his mind. Kazan first appeared before HUAC on January 14, 1952. At that time, he spoke freely about his own activities but refused to discuss others whom he knew as members of the Communist Party during his period of party membership. On April 9, Kazan sent the committee a note that expressed his wish to amend his testimony. "I have come to the conclusion," he wrote, "that I did wrong to withhold these names before, because secrecy serves the Communists, and is exactly what they want. The American people need the facts and all the facts about all aspects of Communism in order to deal with it wisely and effectively. It is my obligation as a citizen to tell everything that I know."

In an executive session with the committee on April 10, Kazan proceeded to provide HUAC with the names of the other members of his party cell in the Group Theatre, along with several party functionaries. "I think it is useful that certain of us had this kind of experience with the Communists, for if we had not, we should not know them so well," said Kazan, in an effort to put a positive gloss on his former radical activities. "Today, when all the world fears war and they scream peace, we know how much their professions are worth. . . . First hand experience of dictatorship and thought control left me with an abiding hatred of these. . . . It also left me with the passionate conviction that we must never let the Communists get away with the pretense that they stand for the very things which they kill in their own countries." Kazan appended to his testimony a list of the motion pictures he had directed, accompanied by his personal analysis of the ways in which they served the cause of anti-Communism.

On April 13, the day following the release of his testimony, Kazan took out an ad in *The New York Times* explaining his reasons for cooperating with HUAC and urging other ex-Communists to follow his lead. "Secrecy serves the Communists. At the other pole, it serves those who are interested in silencing liberal voices. The employment of a lot of good liberals is threatened because they have allowed themselves to become associated with or silenced by the Communists."

Following his testimony before HUAC, Kazan directed several pictures with anti-Communist themes: *Man on a Tightrope* (1953) and *On the Waterfront*, in which a young dockworker discovers the virtue of informing on representatives of organized crime who had infiltrated his labor union. With a script written by Budd SCHULBERG, another ex-Communist who cooperated with HUAC, *On the Waterfront* won Kazan his second Academy Award as Best Director. Nevertheless, Kazan's testimony ruined his reputation among certain left-wing elements of the Hollywood community who regarded any cooperation with HUAC as a total betrayal of liberal ideals. (For years afterward, actor Zero MOSTEL invariably referred to Kazan as "Looselips.") Certainly it shattered Kazan's relationship with Arthur Miller, who was called to testify and talked freely about his own political past but refused to name any other names. After Kazan testified, Miller wrote the anti-McCarthy drama, THE CRUCIBLE, which excoriated informers and extolled the virtues of unyielding resistance to evil. The two men established an uneasy reconciliation in 1963 when Kazan directed Miller's play *After the Fall* despite its unflattering portrayal of an informer partly based upon Kazan himself.

Following the initial furor over his testimony, Kazan, who decided in the 1960s to devote himself to writing novels, steadfastly refused to discuss his decision to cooperate with HUAC. He broke his silence in 1971 in an interview with a French film critic. "I don't think there's anything in my life toward which I have more ambivalence," Kazan admitted, "because, obviously, there's something disgusting about giving other people's names. On the other hand . . . at that time I was convinced that the Soviet empire was monolithic. . . . I also felt that their behavior over Korea was aggressive and essentially imperialistic. . . . Since then, I've had two feelings. One feeling is that what I did

was repulsive, and the opposite feeling, when I see what the Soviet Union has done to its writers, and their death camps, and the Nazi pact and the Polish and Czech repression. . . . It revived in me the feeling I had at the time, that it was essentially a symbolic act, not a personal act. . . .

"I've often, since then, felt on a personal level that it's a shame that I named people, although they were all known, it's not as if I were turning them over to the police; everybody knew who they were, it was obvious and clear. It was a token act to me, and expressed what I thought at the time."

In 1988, Kazan published his autobiography, entitled *A Life*.

**Kennedy, John F.** (1917–1963) Throughout the early 1950s, freshman Senator John F. "Jack" Kennedy refused to become involved in the controversies surrounding the actions of Senator Joseph MCCARTHY. Kennedy's father, millionaire and former Ambassador to Great Britain Joseph P. Kennedy, was an enthusiastic supporter of McCarthy's anti-Communist crusade and had contributed substantial sums to McCarthy's campaign chests.

Jack Kennedy appeared to share McCarthy's militantly anti-Communist sentiments, though he never adopted McCarthy's flamboyant tactics. In his first term in the House of Representatives (1946–48), Kennedy became the first congressman to win a citation against a Communist for perjury, as part of an investigation into the UNITED AUTO WORKERS. In November 1950, Kennedy wrote to a friend expressing his pleasure at Richard NIXON's victory in the California Senate campaign against Helen Gahagan DOUGLAS, and one month later, Kennedy attacked the Truman administration—and State Department official Owen LATTIMORE in particular—for its role in allowing the victory of Communist forces in China.

When Kennedy ran for the Senate seat held by Henry Cabot Lodge in 1952, his campaign literature described him as an enemy of "atheis-

John F. Kennedy (left) was absent from the Senate on the day motion to censure Joseph McCarthy came to the floor for a vote.

tic Communism," and it criticized Lodge for not doing more to rid the federal government of Communist influences. To help his son's campaign, Joseph Kennedy convinced McCarthy to stay out of Massachusetts; McCarthy was tremendously popular among the Irish-American Catholic population of Boston, and his failure to speak on behalf of his Republican colleague Lodge played a critical role in Kennedy's victory.

Although Senate Democratic leader Lyndon B. JOHNSON assigned Kennedy one of the party's three seats on McCarthy's PERMANENT SUBCOMMITTEE ON INVESTIGATIONS in hopes of providing a check on the Wisconsin senator, Kennedy failed to take an active role in restraining or criticizing McCarthy's excesses. For the most part, Kennedy remained aloof from the growing controversy over McCarthy's activities, although he did remain a personal friend of McCarthy. When a reporter asked him in the spring of 1954 what he thought about McCarthy, Kennedy replied, "Not much. But I get along with him."

Kennedy did, however, join enthusiastically with Minnesota Senator Hubert H. HUMPHREY in cosponsoring the COMMUNIST CONTROL ACT of 1954, which made membership in the COM-

MUNIST PARTY punishable by fine and imprisonment. Kennedy also voted for full appropriations for McCarthy's subcommittee and for McCarthy's amendment to reduce U.S. aid to nations trading with Communists. Throughout the early 1950s, Kennedy refused to condemn McCarthy's investigation of Communist subversion.

When the Senate considered a motion of censure against McCarthy in December 1954, Kennedy reportedly was suffering from a back ailment that had kept him hospitalized. Before he entered the hospital in October, Kennedy had refused to take a stand on the issue, preferring instead to wait until Lyndon Johnson and Democratic elder statesman Senator John J. McClellan committed themselves. Although Kennedy could have made his position on the censure motion known, he failed to do so. In a speech he prepared but never delivered, Kennedy acknowledged that his ambivalence on the issue was due in large part to the support McCarthy enjoyed among Kennedy's Massachusetts constituency. "I am not insensitive," Kennedy stated, "to the fact that my constitutents perhaps contain a greater proportion of devotees on each side of this matter than the constituency of any other Senator."

Not until the summer of 1956, when Kennedy was an aspirant for the Democratic presidential nomination, did he publicly endorse the Senate's censure of McCarthy. It is likely that Kennedy's memories of the criticism which the Democrats endured in the 1950s for their failure to take a stronger stand against Communism abroad, contributed to his administration's hard-line COLD WAR policies in Indochina, Berlin, and Cuba between 1961 and 1963.

**Kennedy, Robert F.** (1925–1968) A younger brother of John F. KENNEDY, Robert F. Kennedy served from 1952 to 1955 as an aide and counsel to the U.S. Senate's PERMANENT SUBCOMMITTEE ON INVESTIGATIONS, the subcommittee of the GOVERNMENT OPERATIONS COMMITTEE that provided Senator Joseph McCARTHY with his vehicle for investigating Communist influence in government. Kennedy first acquired a position on the subcommittee when his father, Joseph P. Kennedy, who had contributed to McCarthy's campaigns, asked the Wisconsin senator in the autumn of 1952 if he would appoint the twenty-six-year-old Robert Kennedy as chief counsel. McCarthy had previously met Robert Kennedy when he accepted Kennedy's invitation to speak at a forum at the University of Virginia Law School. Kennedy was certainly willing and eager to work for McCarthy, though his brother advised him not to take the job.

"At that time," Kennedy later explained, "I thought there was a serious internal security threat to the United States; I felt at that time that Joe McCarthy seemed to be the only one who was doing anything about it." McCarthy, however, had already decided to appoint Roy COHN as chief counsel; he gave Kennedy a lower-ranking position as an aide to the subcommittee's general counsel.

From that post, Kennedy supervised an investigation of trade between the U.S.' allies and Communist nations during the KOREAN WAR. Because Great Britain was involved in a large share of that trade, McCarthy was able to employ Kennedy's findings to condemn the British Labour government of Clement Attlee. Kennedy, though, found McCarthy's investigative style too chaotic; besides, Kennedy resented McCarthy's decision to relegate him to poring over trade statistics while Cohn grabbed headlines with his highly publicized search for Communist literature in State Department libraries abroad.

Kennedy resigned his position with the subcommittee in July 1953, though he retained his personal affection for McCarthy. "He was a very complicated character," recalled Kennedy. "His whole method of operation was complicated because he would get a guilty feeling and get hurt after he had blasted somebody. . . . He didn't anticipate the results of what he was doing. He was very thoughtful of his friends, and yet he could be so cruel to others."

In January 1954, Kennedy returned to the subcommittee as counsel to the Democratic minority. During the ARMY-MCCARTHY HEARINGS, Kennedy clashed bitterly with Cohn over the latter's threat to "get" Senator Henry Jackson of Washington in retaliation for Jackson's mocking attack on Cohn's friend, G. David SCHINE. When the Democrats regained control of the Senate in the elections of 1954, Kennedy became chief counsel of the subcommittee. He remained with the subcommittee for another year, continuing his investigation of Communism in the U.S. government, albeit in a far more orderly and less spectacular manner than McCarthy had done. In an effort to understand the appeal of Communism, Kennedy once went so far as to hold a lengthy one-on-one discussion with Earl BROWDER, former executive secretary of the Communist Party in the United States.

Kennedy subsequently served as attorney general of the United States in his brother's presidential administration (1961–63). He mounted his own campaign for the presidency in 1968 and was assassinated in June of that year, following his victory in the California Democratic primary election.

**Kent, Morton** (1901–1949)   A former official in the U.S. Department of State, the Department of Labor, and the Bureau of Economic Warfare, Morton Kent apparently committed suicide in June 1949 after the FEDERAL BUREAU OF INVESTIGATION (FBI) linked him to the espionage activities of Judith COPLON. According to published FBI reports, Kent acted as a contact between suspected Communist agents and various foreign embassies. In particular, Kent was accused by FBI officials of attempting to contact in 1948 a Bulgarian diplomatic official whom they suspected of being a Soviet spy. The FBI also attempted to link Kent with its case against Dr. Edward U. CONDON, director of the National Bureau of Standards, by claiming that in October 1948 Dr. Condon's wife had given Kent the new address of the Bulgarian diplomat.

Depressed after losing his job with the private Washington commercial firm that he had joined after leaving government service in 1944, Kent rented a canoe, rowed alone up the Potomac River, and then reportedly slashed his throat with a kitchen knife. District of Columbia police ruled his death a suicide.

**Kenyon, Dorothy** (1888–1972)  A New York attorney and former municipal judge, Dorothy Kenyon was the first person cited by name by Senator Joseph MCCARTHY following his Wheeling, West Virginia, speech on February 9, 1950, in which he charged that there were numerous Communists in the U.S. State Department. Kenyon's name entered the McCarthy controversy on the afternoon of March 8 at the close of the initial day of hearings held by the subcommittee (chaired by Senator Millard TYD-INGS) established by the Senate to investigate McCarthy's charges. Brandishing copies of government documents and newspaper articles, McCarthy informed the Senate that Kenyon was "in a high State Department position" and that she belonged to twenty-eight separate organizations listed as "subversive and disloyal" by either the attorney general or congressional committees. "I might say that I personally would not be caught dead belonging to any one of the twenty-eight," said McCarthy. He urged the State Department to fire Kenyon as "an extremely bad security risk" before the end of the day.

When Kenyon held her own press conference that same afternoon, she began by saying that "Senator McCarthy is a liar." Kenyon was not, in fact, an employee of the State Department or any other government agency. She had served for three years as an American representative on the United Nations Commission on the Status of Women (her term had expired in December 1949), where she had frequently engaged in heated debate with the Soviet representative on the commission. Moreover, only four of the twenty-eight allegedly pro-Communist organizations mentioned by McCarthy had been cited

by the attorney general as subversive organizations, and Kenyon had resigned from three of the four before they were placed on the attorney general's list. She had never belonged at all to a number of other groups on McCarthy's list.

Kenyon subsequently appeared before the Tydings subcommittee on March 14 to defend herself against McCarthy's accusations. She denied that she had ever been a Communist or a Communist sympathizer, and she said she had never belonged to any group which she knew to be "even slightly subversive." "I am, and always have been, an independent, liberal Rooseveltian Democrat," Kenyon declared, "devoted to and actively working for such causes as the improvement of the living and working conditions of labor and the preservation of civil liberties." Kenyon acknowledged with considerable pride that she was currently active in the AMERICAN CIVIL LIBERTIES UNION, AMERICANS FOR DEMOCRATIC ACTION, the League of Women Voters, the Association for the Aid of Crippled Children, and the Association of University Women, among other groups.

By the end of Kenyon's testimony, archconservative Iowa Republican Senator Bourke Hickenlooper, McCarthy's staunchest ally on the Tydings subcommittee, stated that he had found no evidence that Kenyon was "subversive in any way." Kenyon closed the hearing with an indictment of McCarthy's technique of guilt by association, particularly when the organizations named by the senator "have never been found subversive by a court of law or by any process other than an administrative edict; and administrative edicts or fiats or whatever you call them sound to me like Mr. Hitler and Mr. Stalin; therefore, I think that the terming of an organization subversive is in itself a violation of civil liberty."

And then from that to jump to the fact that a person who is a sponsor or a member or participates in one tiny little project for a short period of time is therefore tarred with the same brush and is therefore himself or herself subversive seems to me a non sequitur. Very frequently it just is not true.

In its report of July 17, 1950, the Tydings subcommittee exonerated Kenyon of all McCarthy's accusations.

**Khrushchev, Nikita** (1894–1971) Premier of the Union of Soviet Socialist Republics from 1958 to 1964, Nikita Khrushchev inaugurated a policy of accommodation with the United States that reduced tensions between the two nations and helped allay American fears of an aggressive international Communist movement. Khrushchev grew up in southwestern Russia, the son of a peasant family. He joined the Bolshevik movement in 1918, a year after the overthrow of Czar Nicholas II. He rose steadily through the Communist Party hierarchy, surviving the purges of the mid-1930s to become a member of the ruling Politburo by 1939.

Following the death of Joseph STALIN in 1953, Khrushchev was named to the critical post of first secretary of the party. Three years later, Khrushchev bitterly denounced the crimes of the Stalinist regime; this earned him a reputation in the United States as a moderate Soviet leader, and his tour of America in 1958 reinforced the public's impression of Khrushchev as a moderate with whom the United States could safely negotiate. In short, Khrushchev helped make Soviet Communism appear less threatening at a time when the anti-Communist crusade in the United States already had begun to wane. There were continuing clashes between the United States and the Soviet Union during the remainder of Khrushchev's regime, including the U-2 spy plane incident in 1960 and the Cuban missile crisis in 1963, and there remained considerable suspicion of the Soviet Union among anti-Communist zealots in the United States, such as conservative columnist William BUCKLEY and HOUSE COMMITTEE ON UN-AMERICAN ACTIVITIES chairman Francis WALTER, but American-Soviet relations clearly had improved

Nikita Khrushchev (left), Soviet premier whose moderate stance toward the United States helped ease tensions and hasten the end of the McCarthy era.

by the time Khrushchev was ousted from power in 1964. Khrushchev spent part of the last seven years of his life writing his memoirs, entitled *Khrushchev Remembers,* which were published in the United States in 1972.

**Kinsey, Alfred C.** (1894–1956) Originally a professor of zoology whose first major scientific research project was a monumental study on the behavior of gall wasps, Alfred C. Kinsey earned a national reputation in 1948 with the publication of his ground-breaking work on human sexuality, *Sexual Behavior in the Human Male.* Kinsey had begun his research into human sexual habits in 1938 when he was teaching a course on marriage at Indiana University. Shocked by the dearth of scientific data on the subject, Kinsey embarked upon a massive research project that eventually included more than 16,500 case histories. The primary sponsor of his research during the 1940s and early 1950s was the Rockefeller Foundation.

Within ten days of its publication, *Sexual Behavior in the Human Male* was already on *The New York Times* bestseller list, with 185,000 copies in print. Some critics disputed Kinsey's findings, which revealed generally that "healthy sex led to a healthy marriage"; that premarital sex, extramarital sex, and homosexuality were more common in the United States than many people had believed; and that man was an animal of "extremely versatile sexuality." More serious for the future of Kinsey's research were the religious leaders and politicians who denounced Kinsey for his failure to condemn the allegedly aberrant practices he discussed.

When Kinsey's second book, *Sexual Behavior in the Human Female* (which Kinsey said was "double the work" because women's sex habits were harder to tabulate than men's) was published in 1953, the outcry grew louder. Henry Pitney Van Dusen, president of Union Theological Seminary—and an influential member of the board of the Rockefeller Foundation—declared that Kinsey's findings revealed "a prevailing degradation in American morality approximating the worst decadence of the Roman Empire." By this time, the crusade against Communism as an alien, anti-American ideology had spilled over into other areas of the nation's life, and practices that called traditional American social norms into question were subject to attack. Clerics linked Kinsey's statistics about extramarital sex with Communism; his books, charged one Catholic newspaper, "pave the way for people to believe in communism and to act like Communists." Conservative Congressman B. Carroll Reece of Tennessee, national chairman of the Republican Party, threatened to investigate the Rockefeller Foundation for its support of Kinsey's research.

The director of the Rockefeller Foundation at that time was Dean Rusk, formerly assistant secretary of State for Far East Affairs. Unwilling to expose the Rockefeller Foundation to the same type of congressional pressure that had damaged the State Department, Rusk declined Kinsey's request for additional funding. Kinsey subsequently threw himself into his work even more assiduously. Suffering from heart trouble and insomnia, he was hospitalized several times

William Knowland of California, Republican leader in the United States Senate.

over the next two years. He died on August 25, 1956, at the age of sixty-two,

**Knowland, William F.** (1908–1965)   Senate majority leader from 1953 to 1955 and minority leader from 1955 to 1959, William F. Knowland played an integral role in the censure of Senator Joseph MCCARTHY in December 1954.

The son of a newspaper publisher and politician who served six terms in the U.S. House of Representatives, Knowland graduated from the University of California in 1933 and obtained a position on his father's newspaper, the Oakland *Tribune,* began his political career that same year as the youngest member of the California state legislature, and moved into national politics in 1938 when he was elected to the Republican National Committee. Three years later, he became the youngest man ever to serve as chairman of the Republican National Committee's executive committee.

During World War II, Knowland served as an officer with the U.S. Army historical section. Following his discharge in August 1945, he was appointed by California Governor Earl WARREN to fill the unexpired U.S. Senate term of the late Hiram W. Johnson. From the start of his Senate career, Knowland established a reputation as a moderate in domestic affairs, favoring such antilabor measures as the TAFT-HARTLEY ACT and antistrike legislation, while declaring himself firmly in favor of civil-rights measures and the establishment of a permanent Fair Employment Practices Commission. In foreign affairs, Knowland generally adopted an internationalist approach, supporting a continued American presence abroad in the postwar world. Soon after his election to a full term in 1946, Knowland emerged as a leading member of the CHINA LOBBY, the coalition of conservative businessmen and politicians who supported the Nationalist Chinese government of CHIANG Kai-shek. His support for the Nationalists was so fervent that one critic (Far East expert Owen LATTIMORE) referred to him as "the Senator from Formosa," a reference to the island where Chiang sought refuge following his defeat by the Communist forces on the Chinese mainland in 1949.

Throughout his Senate career, Knowland was known as a conciliator who sought to unite the frequently fractious members of the Republican Party in the upper chamber. "We don't want the nation to swing too far to the Left or too far to the Right," he declared in the aftermath of the 1946 congressional elections. "We want to keep it on an even keel." The same moderate attitude marked his approach to the issue of Communist subversion in the United States. Given his commitment to the Nationalist cause in China, it was not surprising that Knowland supported the investigation into the activities of the INSTITUTE FOR PACIFIC RELATIONS. Knowland also gave McCarthy his backing when the Wisconsin senator sought to quash any attempt to open trade channels between the United States and Communist China. Yet, when Senator McCarthy challenged President Dwight David EISENHOWER's nomination of Charles BOHLEN as U.S. ambassador to the Soviet Union, Knowland reacted angrily and rejected McCarthy's assertion that the White House had somehow fabricated evidence in support of Bohlen's nomination. When McCarthy and his fellow right-wing Republicans in the Senate launched their investigation of Communist influences in the U.S. Army, Knowland strove (albeit unsuccessfully) to limit their inquiry and to soften the virulence of their rhetoric against the armed services.

Following Senator Ralph FLANDERS' introduction of a motion of censure against McCarthy in August 1954, Knowland referred the motion to a special six-man committee appointed by Vice President Richard M. NIXON. During the ensuing debate over McCarthy's activities, Knowland steadfastly refused to commit himself or to pressure Republican senators to adopt a uniform course of action. Shortly before the Senate voted on the censure motion, however, Knowland—apparently acting at the request of the White House—declared himself in favor of the resolution. His action persuaded Senate Minority Leader Lyndon B. JOHNSON of Texas to publicly declare his own support of the measure; Johnson's support, in turn, convinced other Democrats to vote for censure. Despite Knowland's vote on the censure motion, McCarthy indicated in 1955 that he would support Knowland's candidacy for the presidency in 1956 should the California senator choose to run for the White House. "Then," claimed McCarthy, in a swipe at Eisenhower, "we'd have a real anti-Communist President in the White House for a change."

In 1958, Knowland decided not to run for reelection to the Senate. Instead, he returned to his family's newspaper business, serving as publisher of the Oakland *Tribune* until 1965, when he died from a self-inflicted gunshot wound to the head.

## Koestler, Arthur (1905–1983)

A prominent author and former Communist, Arthur Koestler provided an intellectual critique of Marxism that helped buttress the conservative anti-Communist crusade in the United States in the 1940s and 1950s.

Born in Budapest, Koestler grew up in Vienna and became interested in Zionism at an early age. At the age of 21, he went to Palestine to try life in a kibbutz but did not stay long; instead, Koestler obtained a job as the Middle East correspondent for a prestigious chain of German newspapers, and upon his return to Europe in 1930, he became the foreign editor of Germany's largest daily newspaper.

On December 31, 1931—at the start of what Koestler later called the "Pink Decade" because of its fascination with radical and antifascist causes—Koestler joined the Communist Party. He spent a year touring the Soviet Union so that he could witness the Marxist experiment firsthand. When he returned to Berlin, Koestler began to write propaganda tracts for the party. In 1936, he went to Spain to cover the Civil War as a journalist. Captured by General Franco's Nationalist forces and sentenced to death as a Communist, he spent three months in solitary confinement, waking each morning expecting to be executed before nightfall. Much to his surprise, diplomatic protests in London secured his release. Koestler then resumed the fight against fascism by joining the French Foreign Legion after the fall of France in 1940. Again he was captured (this time by the Vichy government); he escaped and fled to England, where he worked as a reporter for the British Broadcasting Corporation and published two novels, *The Gladiators* and *Darkness at Noon.*

During his imprisonment in Spain, Koestler underwent a mystical experience, almost a religious conversion, which led directly to his disillusionment with Marxism. As he recalled it,

Koestler felt himself losing his identity as an individual, melting into the "universal pool," experiencing what he termed "the oceanic feeling." Realizing how inadequate communism was because of its reliance on purely utilitarian ethics, he made a definitive break with the party in 1938. "I went to Communism as one goes to a spring of fresh water," Koestler wrote in his autobiography, "and I left Communism as one clambers out of a poisoned river strewn with the wreckage of flooded cities and the corpses of the drowned."

Koestler's personal experience was mirrored by the fate of his character Nikolai Rubashov in *Darkness at Noon,* a work which represented a landmark in international politics because it exposed the cruelties of the Stalinist regime and provided insights into the Moscow purge trials of the 1930s. Published in 1944, the novel also projected him into the ideological debate over communism in the postwar world, particularly in Europe.

In 1949, Koestler recounted and explained his renunciation of communism in a volume entitled THE GOD THAT FAILED. This book, along with *Darkness at Noon,* provided ammunition for the anti-communist crusade in the United States. On the other hand, the stage version of *Darkness* provided several actors—including Edward G. ROBINSON—with evidence of their anti-Communist credentials when they appeared before the HOUSE COMMITTEE ON UN-AMERICAN ACTIVITIES; they reasoned that no one who took part in a dramatic production so biased against Communism could possibly be a member of the COMMUNIST PARTY.

The story of Rubashov's disillusionment with Marxism in *Darkness at Noon* was also cited by a number of witnesses before congressional investigating committees who claimed to have undergone similar awakenings; one witness, for instance, quoted with approval the line from the novel, "In the life of every Communist there comes a moment when he hears the screams." Further, Koestler's essay in *The God That Failed* explained why ex-Communists such as Elizabeth

BENTLEY and Whittaker CHAMBERS often proved the most enthusiastic informers against their former comrades. "When one has renounced a creed or been betrayed by a friend," wrote Koestler, "the original experience loses its innocence, becomes tainted and rancid in recollection. . . . Those who were caught in the great illusion of our time, and have lived through its moral and intellectual debauch, either give themselves up to a new addiction of the opposite type, or are condemned to pay with a life-long hangover."

Koestler himself visited the United States for two years in the early 1950s, but it required an act of Congress to allow him to stay in the country at all. Specifically, he needed an exemption from the INTERNAL SECURITY ACT OF 1950 (also known as the MCCARRAN ACT), which denied access to U.S. territory to anyone who had ever belonged to the Communist Party. While in the United States, Koestler purportedly helped those who had renounced Communism understand the emotions they were experiencing and taught them to distinguish between liberal activism and Communism. When screenwriter Budd SCHULBERG said to Koestler that he hated the Communists but didn't want to attack the Left, Koestler replied, "You've got to get over that. They're not Left; they're East."

In an attempt to support the independence of writers trapped in totalitarian countries, Koestler cofounded Friends for Intellectual Freedom, an organization devoted to providing political and financial support to persecuted artists. Koestler himself provided 10 percent of his income to the cause.

**Kohlberg, Alfred** (1886–1960)   A millionaire businessman, Alfred Kohlberg was the unofficial head of the CHINA LOBBY, the coalition of anti-Communist conservatives who vociferously supported the Nationalist China regime of CHIANG Kai-shek. A graduate of the University of California, Kohlberg had made his fortune in the linen-and-lace business; he imported cloth from Ireland and then shipped it to China where workers embroidered the lace for bare subsistence wages. Kohlberg then brought the lace and linen into the United States where he marketed it under European names, a deceptive practice which the Federal Trade Commission ordered Kohlberg to cease in 1943. At its zenith, the Chinese textile business brought Kohlberg $1.5 million a year.

Kohlberg's interest in China extended beyond his company's economic involvement, however. Following his first visit to the Far East in 1916, Kohlberg became an avid student of Chinese affairs. He traveled to China frequently, though he never learned to speak the language. Convinced that Chiang Kai-shek was the savior of modern China (and a guarantee of continued profits for his own firm), Kohlberg began to promote Chiang's cause tirelessly in the United States. At the same time, he excoriated the Chinese Communists, who represented the primary domestic threat to Chiang's supremacy in China.

During World War II, when American policymakers attempted to persuade Chiang and the Communists to form a common front against the Japanese invaders, Kohlberg became convinced that the U.S. Department of State harbored officials who favored the Communist cause in China. After reviewing hundreds of documents in the files of the INSTITUTE FOR PACIFIC RELATIONS (IPR), a privately operated research agency on whose board he served as a director, Kohlberg also discerned a strong similarity between the positions taken by the Institute's publications and that of the DAILY WORKER, a Communist newspaper. The Institute, he charged, was being "used by the Reds to orientate American Far Eastern policies toward Communist objectives." In 1945, Kohlberg attempted to turn the IPR toward the right. When he failed, he withdrew from the IPR and helped found another research organization on Chinese affairs, the American China Policy Association, which subsequently attracted support from other members of the China Lobby, including editor William Loeb and Clare Boothe Luce, wife of publisher Henry LUCE. To disseminate the views of the China Lobby, Kohlberg provided financial support to a journal called *China Monthly*, to which he frequently contributed articles. (*China Monthly* also had ties to the Chinese Catholic establishment.)

As Chiang's fortunes deteriorated in the postwar years, Kohlberg decided that the Nationalists were being sold out by the State Department. In 1946, Kohlberg bitterly opposed the nomination of longtime Far East specialist John Carter VINCENT for the foreign-service rank of career minister. Three years later, he denounced Ambassador-at-Large Philip JESSUP as "the initiator of the smear campaign against Nationalist China and Chiang Kai-shek, and the originator of the myth of the democratic Chinese Communists." When the Truman administration sought to defuse the controversy over Chiang's impending defeat by publishing a massive account of U.S.-Chinese relations known as the CHINA WHITE PAPER, Kohlberg concluded that "the real purpose of the White Paper seems . . . to be to reveal to the chancellories of the world the story of the American betrayal of the Republic of China. What could be of greater aid to the Soviet Union than this?"

Kohlberg did not limit his anti-Communist activities to the Chinese front, however. In 1947, he founded another publication, *Plain Talk*, which promulgated right-wing theories about Communist influence in American society. He provided financial support to three ex-FBI agents who launched *COUNTERATTACK*, a weekly expose of Communist infiltration of American industry, and *RED CHANNELS*, the anti-Red BLACKLISTING bible of the entertainment business. In 1950, Kohlberg became a member of the New York-based Joint Committee against Communism's special committee on television and radio, a body that provided information on suspected subversives to *Red Channels*.

When Kohlberg learned of Senator Joseph MCCARTHY's Lincoln Day speech of February 9, 1950, in Wheeling, West Virginia, he promptly set up a meeting with the Wisconsin senator. He supplied McCarthy with material against the enemies of the China Lobby, including Owen LATTIMORE, Jessup, Vincent, and John Stewart SERVICE, and helped persuade McCarthy to reopen the *AMERASIA* affair. Their association continued over the next several years; according to one congressional inquiry into McCarthy's affairs, there was contact between Kohlberg and McCarthy's office on nine separate occasions between April and September 1952. When McCarthy's investigative methods came under attack in the spring of 1952, Kohlberg sponsored the distribution of a ten-page pamphlet entitled *Senator McCarthy* that defended the senator from the criticisms of his opponents, describing him as the victim of "one of the most vicious smear campaigns in American history." On December 10, 1952, Kohlberg arranged a dinner in McCarthy's honor in New York City, at which McCarthy promised that his crusade against Communism would not abate "until we've won this war or our civilization has been destroyed."

The indefatigable Kohlberg also subsidized the ultraconservative periodical *The Freeman* and worked as an adviser to the Committee for Constitutional Government, one of the most active propaganda machines of the anti-Communist crusade. In 1955, Kohlberg served as head of the American Jewish League against Communism; his successor in that position was Roy M. COHN, who had been McCarthy's chief assistant during the ARMY-MCCARTHY HEARINGS. To keep all his ventures supplied with information about alleged subversives, Kohlberg employed material obtained from the files of the Chinese Nationalist secret police, and—surreptitiously, through a sympathetic government clerk—from the records of the Civil Service Commission's LOYALTY REVIEW BOARD. Kohlberg also contributed liberally to the campaigns of right-wing Republican candidates, although McCarthy once returned with considerable publicity a $500 contribution from Kohlberg.

Ironically, the ban on trade with mainland China which the China Lobby assiduously promoted worked to Kohlberg's disadvantage in 1956, when the Treasury Department refused to allow him to import $90,000 worth of Chinese handkerchiefs because it feared they had been made in Communist China. (Kohlberg insisted that the lace had come from Hong Kong.) On April 7, 1960, Kohlberg died of a heart attack at his home in New York City.

**Korean War** Shortly after 4 A.M. on the morning of June 24, 1950, batteries of North Korean People's Army (NKPA) artillery, stationed along the 38th parallel, which divided North and South Korea, began to shell targets in the Republic of Korea (ROK). Within several hours, more than 90,000 NKPA troops had crossed the border into South Korea. The attack caught the Truman administration and U.S. military officials completely by surprise. It was not at all certain what the American reseponse would be, for six months earlier, Secretary of State Dean ACHESON had publicly defined an American perimeter of strategic interest in Asia that excluded Korea.

As White House officials and the Joint Chiefs of Staff considered their options, and the United Nations (UN) Security Council deliberated over its response, the North Korean advance continued, driving ROK troops and terrified civilians before it. The capital of South Korea, Seoul, fell on June 28. By that time, ROK casualties surpassed 30,000, nearly half of the nation's armed forces. U.S. General Douglas MACARTHUR, who had flown into Korea to obtain a firsthand view of the debacle, reported to Washington that "the only assurance for holding the present line and the ability to regain later the lost ground is through the introduction of United States ground combat forces into the Korean battle area."

On the morning of June 30, President Harry S. TRUMAN authorized the commitment of U.S. troops to combat in Korea. Three days earlier, the UN had approved a resolution authorizing armed resistance to the NKPA aggression. Truman insisted to reporters that the United States was "not at war"; instead, he termed the American involvement "a police action under the United Nations." For the next six weeks, it was called a "retreat." Inexperienced and vastly outnumbered, American troops failed to stem the North Korean advance. On August 6, the nightmare finally ended as U.S. and ROK troops held their ground outside the American base at Taegu.

Reinforced by fresh American troops—the Truman administration had called up National Guard units and increased draft quotas—MacArthur organized a brilliant and unconventional amphibious assault at Inchon, 150 miles behind enemy lines. The landing, on September 15, caught the North Korean military command completely by surprise. By October 1, UN troops under MacArthur's command had recaptured Seoul and regained virtually all the territory south of the 38th parallel. The North Korean army had been shattered; but across the Yalu River in Manchuria, 850,000 troops of the Chinese Communist government (which had defeated the Nationalist Chinese forces of CHIANG Kai-shek in a civil war less than a year earlier) were gathering in preparation for an invasion in the event the UN forces moved north of the 38th parallel.

Most of the top officials in the Truman administration would have been content with nothing more than the restoration of the status quo ante bellum in Korea. MacArthur, however, viewed the situation as an opportunity to forge a stronger alliance with Chiang Kai-shek and to reestablish the Nationalist government in China. The general's call for "aggressive, resolute and dynamic leadership" was greeted with great enthusiasm by members of the CHINA LOBBY (the coalition of American politicians, military officials, and businessmen who supported Chiang), and the Lobby joined with MacArthur in denouncing what they considered the defeatist attitude of the State Department.

Meanwhile, the outbreak of the Korean conflict—and the heightened danger to American security interests that accompanied it—provided

**Korean War: General Douglas MacArthur (sunglasses) discussing strategy with General Matthew B. Ridgway.**

impetus to the demands of anti-Communist crusaders for stronger legislation against domestic subversion. Two years earlier, the House of Representatives had passed a bill sponsored by Representatives Karl MUNDT and Richard M. NIXON that required the COMMUNIST PARTY and members of Communist-front organizations to register with the federal government. The mea-

sure had died in the Senate, but in the summer of 1950 the issue assumed added urgency, and in August Senator Patrick MCCARRAN, chairman of the Senate Judiciary Committee, reported a bill that adopted many of the Mundt-Nixon recommendations while adding provisions barring Communists from employment in the federal government and the defense industry.

Fearing charges that they were "soft" on Communism during a military crisis, liberal Democrats in the Senate proposed an even stronger measure that authorized the federal government to detain suspected subversives in detention camps in times of national emergency. The two measures were eventually combined in a bill known as the INTERNAL SECURITY ACT OF 1950. The legislation easily passed both houses of Congress. President Truman vetoed the measure, but Congress overrode his veto.

Persuaded by MacArthur that neither the Soviet Union nor the Communist Chinese government would intervene in Korea, Truman gave the general permission to cross the 38th parallel in pursuit of the enemy. The UN General Assembly subsequently authorized "the establishment of a unified, independent, and democratic Korea." For a while, MacArthur's strategy appeared to pay dividends. On October 20, UN troops entered the North Korean capital of Pyongyang. MacArthur then directed his officers to lead a two-pronged advance to the north over mountainous and largely uninhabited terrain. When the two ends of the pincers rejoined forces, MacArthur predicted, the war would "for all practical purposes" be over. He promised U.S. soldiers that "they will eat Christmas dinner at home."

In the first week of November, Truman received ominous reports of confrontations between UN troops and scattered units of Chinese Communist forces. At the end of November, Communist China suddenly sent 300,000 troops across the Yalu River into Korea. "The Chinese," reported a stunned MacArthur, "have come in with both feet." The UN lines collapsed, forcing a retreat along the entire front. American casualties were appalling. *Time* magazine termed the defeat "the worst the United States has ever suffered." MacArthur recommended that Truman consider the use of nuclear weapons against the Chinese, but the President demurred. At Christmas 1950, the UN troops' retreat was still in full force. "Conference after conference on the jittery situation facing the country," Truman wrote in a bleak memorandum to himself. "Formosa, Communist China, Chiang Kai-shek, Japan, Germany, France, India, etc. I have worked for peace for five years and six months and it looks like World War III is near."

Seoul fell to the Chinese on January 4, 1951, but in mid-January the UN troops reformed their lines and launched a counterattack. By the end of March, the two sides had once again reestablished the preinvasion border along the 38th parallel. Truman and his advisers elected not to initiate a second major offensive across the border. Their restraint was greeted with cries of appeasement and treason from the right wing of the Republican Party.

MacArthur, too, wished to attempt another offensive, and in March he deliberately sabotaged a Truman peace initiative. Unwilling to tolerate the general's insubordination, Truman fired MacArthur on the grounds that the general was "unable to give his wholehearted support to the policies of the United States and of the United Nations." Public reaction was swift. The state legislatures of Florida, California, and Michigan passed resolutions condemning Truman. Senator William JENNER of Indiana declared that "this country today is in the hands of a secret coterie which is directed by agents of the Soviet Union." "Our only choice," said Jenner, "is to impeach President Truman and find out who is the secret invisible government which has so cleverly led our country down the road to destruction." In Milwaukee, Senator Joseph MCCARTHY informed a gathering that Truman was "a son of a bitch." House Republican Minority Leader Joe MARTIN told reporters that the House GOP caucus had discussed the question of impeachment of Truman and perhaps Acheson and other administration officials as well. MacArthur fed the controversy by denouncing the Truman administration's policy of "appeasement on the battlefield" and accused the State Department of harboring secret plans to abandon Chiang Kai-shek and the Nationalist regime on Taiwan to the Communists.

The immediate furor died down after a parade of U.S. Army commanders, including MacArthur's successor in Korea, General Matthew B. Ridgway, testified that MacArthur's strategy would have led the United States into a disastrously expensive land war in Asia. Nevertheless, the American public, accustomed to total victory in wartime, found a policy of stalemate unappealing, and the nation's mounting frustration while fighting continued for two more years provided fertile ground for Senator Joseph McCarthy's accusations of disloyalty and subversion within the Truman administration. If Americans could not strike directly at the enemy in the Far East, they could relieve the tension by searching for enemies at home. Tolerance for dissent declined; the atmosphere of repression grew harsher. Consequently, the HOUSE COMMITTEE ON UN-AMERICAN ACTIVITIES (HUAC) redoubled its efforts to uncover Communists in the federal government. "While our boys are being killed or freezing to death in Korea," declared HUAC member John RANKIN of Alabama, "these Reds ought not to be permitted to undermine their country." Even the Truman administration was not immune from the pressure. In April 1951, the President issued EXECUTIVE ORDER 10241, which tightened the standards of the existing loyalty review program for federal employees. Under the new guidelines, the government could dismiss any federal employee if there existed a "reasonable doubt" of his or her loyalty at any time in the past. No longer did prosecutors need to prove present disloyalty.

State legislatures and local governments across the nation rushed to pass anti-Communist measures of varying degrees of irrationality. Ohio established its own un-American activities committee. Indiana insisted that its state employees take "voluntary" LOYALTY OATHS, and barred subversives from state employment. Michigan—along with numerous cities and small towns—passed its own version of the INTERNAL SECURITY ACT OF 1950, requiring Communists to register with the state government, and approved another bill that nullified any will that included bequests to subversive causes. The city council of Birmingham, Alabama, ordered Communists and fellow travelers to leave town within 48 hours. Public school systems, private employers, movie studios, newspapers, and universities throughout the United States adopted procedures to remove politically suspect individuals from their payrolls.

Even the U.S. court system was affected. In the atomic espionage trial of alleged Soviet spies Julius and Ethel ROSENBERG, Judge Irving Kaufman declared that the Rosenbergs' betrayal of nuclear secrets "has already caused . . . the Communist aggression in Korea." The Korean conflict persuaded Judge Learned Hand of the U.S. Court of Appeals, hitherto a staunch defender of civil liberties, that a "clear and present danger" to the nation's security existed. In his ruling in the case known as DENNIS V. UNITED STATES, Hand consequently upheld the conviction of leaders of the COMMUNIST PARTY OF THE UNITED STATES under the SMITH ACT. In 1951, the U.S. Supreme Court also refused to overturn the original verdict against the defendants. The decisions led the Justice Department to pursue additional indictments against Communist Party officials. In his dissent in *Dennis,* Associate Supreme Court Justice Hugo Black expressed his hope that "in calmer times, when present pressures, passions and fears subside, this or some later Court will restore the First Amendment liberties to the high preferred place where they belong in a free society."

As the Korean conflict dragged on into 1953, critics of American policy found themselves compelled to criticize President Dwight David EISENHOWER, who had easily defeated Democratic nominee Adlai STEVENSON in the 1952 election. Shortly after he assumed the presidency, Eisenhower indicated that he was willing to conclude a peace treaty that left Korea divided along the 38th parallel; he also threatened to consider the use of nuclear weapons if the People's Republic of China refused to negotiate in good faith. Conservative Republican senators denounced Eisenhower's policy of "appeasement." Senator Knowland, now majority leader, argued that any treaty that left part of Korea in Communist hands would not be a truce with honor. Under such an arrangement, Knowland predicted, "Inevitably we will lose the balance of Asia."

On the morning of July 27, 1953, UN and North Korean representatives signed an armistice agreement at the town of Panmunjon. The United States had lost nearly 54,000 soldiers during thirty-seven months of fighting. The truce settlement left the boundaries almost precisely where they had been at the beginning of June 1950. Eisenhower observed that the United States had "won an armistice on a single battlefield, not peace in the world," and he voiced a hope that the events of the past three years in Korea would convince the peoples of the world to resolve their differences through negotiation rather than "futile battle."

# L

**Lardner, Ring Jr.** (1915–1983)   Lardner, the son of noted American humorist Ring Lardner, was the youngest member of the HOLLYWOOD TEN, a group of motion picture screenwriters and directors suspected of Communist sympathies. Born in New York, Lardner worked briefly as a reporter for the *New York Daily Mirror* before moving to Hollywood, where he became a screenwriter at the age of 21. His early work included the scripts for *Cloak and Dagger* and *Forever Amber,* and in 1942 he won an Academy Award for his original screenplay for *Woman of the Year,* starring Katharine HEPBURN and Spencer Tracy. By the time the HOUSE COMMITTEE ON UN-AMERICAN ACTIVITIES (HUAC) summoned him to testify in 1947, Lardner was under contract with 20th Century-Fox, earning $2,000 a week and working on two major film projects.

Beyond his professional accomplishments, Lardner had also participated in the activities of numerous radical organizations in Hollywood. He joined the left-wing Anti-Nazi League in 1936 and worked for the American Peace Mobilization effort after the signing of the NAZI-SOVIET PACT. Along with fellow screenwriter John Howard LAWSON, Lardner operated the Writers' Clinic, which analyzed movie scripts from a Marxist viewpoint, and served several terms on the executive board of the SCREEN WRITERS' GUILD.

Lardner claimed to be an intellectual convert to Marxism, frequently holding discussions with other young Hollywood authors on ways to communicate Marxist ideology through films, and in the late 1930s he visited the USSR to see firsthand the progress of the Soviet experiment.

In 1939, Lardner joined the Motion Picture Guild, Inc., a group dedicated to the production of politically progressive movies. As a member of the guild, Lardner wrote a script for a documentary funded by the UNITED AUTO WORKERS on the subject of racism. When he tried to join the U.S. armed services in World War II, however, Lardner was informed that his past radical activities rendered him unacceptable.

At the end of the war, Lardner realized that the prevailing political climate would make the production of socially relevant movies far more difficult than in the 1930s. He later acknowledged that he was "despondent about the chances of getting anywhere with significant content. . . . I began the postwar period with a less optimistic attitude about 'political' films, accepted more commercial assignments, and started brooding about getting out of Hollywood."

In September 1947, HUAC subpoenaed Lardner to testify in Washington as part of its investigation into Communist influence in the motion picture industry. When he appeared as a witness on October 30, the committee chairman, J. Parnell THOMAS asked Lardner whether he was or had ever been a member of the COMMUNIST PARTY. Lardner replied that he could answer that question, "but if I did, I would hate myself in the morning." His attempts to preface his answer with an explanation were denied by the gavel-pounding Thomas, and Lardner was forcibly evicted from the stand. Several weeks later, Lardner—along with the nine other uncooperative witnesses who made up the Hollywood Ten—was cited for contempt of Congress for his refusal to answer Thomas' question. He was subsequently convicted and sentenced to one year in prison and a fine of $1,000.

At that time, Lardner already had begun to withdraw from active participation in the Communist Party, but he decided to maintain his membership in the party until his case had been resolved. In the meantime, however, he would not be able to work for a major American movie studio. On December 3, 1947, the top executives of Hollywood's major studios issued the WALDORF STATEMENT, in which they pledged not to hire any member of the Hollywood Ten. Lardner was dismissed from his position at 20th Century-Fox and given only two hours to vacate the premises. (Darryl Zanuck, the head of the studio, could not bring himself to fire Lardner in person and ordered an assistant to bear the bad news.) For the next two-and-a-half years, Lardner tried to earn a living by writing anonymously or under assumed names. In April 1950, the U.S. Supreme Court announced that it would not hear the appeals of the Ten, and soon thereafter Lardner entered the Federal Correctional Institution in Danbury, Connecticut, to serve his prison sentence.

Following his release nearly ten months later (with time off for good behavior), Lardner lived in Mexico for a brief time but soon moved back to the United States. During the 1950s, he wrote scripts for television shows—notably *The Adventures of Robin Hood* series, which was produced in Britain—under a pseudonym because no major studio would hire him while he was still on the BLACKLIST. Lardner's novel, *The Ecstasy of Owen Muir,* could not find an American publisher until the 1960s; in the meanwhile, it was published in Britain to considerable critical acclaim.

In an article for *The Saturday Evening Post* in 1961, Lardner became the first member of the Hollywood Ten to acknowledge publicly that he had been a Communist at the time of the HUAC hearings in 1947. Following the demise of the blacklist in the early 1960s, he returned to Hollywood, and won another Academy Award for his work on the screenplay of the movie *M\*A\*S\*H.*

**Lattimore, Owen** (1900–1988)  An expert on Far East affairs who was once identified by Senator Joseph MCCARTHY as the leading Soviet espionage agent in the United States, Owen Lattimore was the son of a Dartmouth College professor of foreign languages. Born in the United States, Lattimore spent most of his boyhood in China, where his father taught classes in French and German. Lattimore received his

Owen Lattimore, the expert in Far East affairs whom Joseph McCarthy identified as the leading Soviet spy in the United States.

formal schooling in Switzerland and Britain, and upon graduation from St. Bees School in Cumberland, England, he returned to China to clerk for a British firm at Tientsin. He worked briefly as a reporter for the *Peking and Tientsin Times* before joining a company that exported produce from western China. In 1925, Lattimore joined a Mongolian caravan and spent the following two years traveling by camel across the Sinkiang to Siberia and back to Kahmir.

Upon his return to the United States in 1928, Lattimore recounted his travel experiences in his first published work, *Desert Road to Turkestan* (1929), followed by *High Tartary* (1930). He resumed his studies at Harvard University and in 1929 received a series of grants from Harvard and the Guggenheim Foundation that enabled him to go back to Peking to continue his research into Chinese studies, with a particular emphasis upon Manchuria. Four years later, Lattimore accepted a position as editor of *Pacific Affairs,* the scholarly journal published by the INSTITUTE FOR PACIFIC RELATIONS (IPR). In 1938, he became director of the Walter Hines Page School of International Relations at Johns Hopkins University. Meanwhile, Lattimore published four more books, primarily studies of Manchurian history and geography.

Shortly before the United States entered World War II, Chinese Nationalist leader CHIANG Kai-shek named Lattimore as his personal political American adviser. One year later, in 1942, Lattimore returned again to the United States to serve as deputy director of Pacific operations for the Office of War Information (OWI). In 1944, he participated in the mission headed by Vice President Henry WALLACE to China to attempt to persuade the Nationalists and the Communist forces under MAO Zedong to establish a united Chinese front against Japan. Although the mission failed, Lattimore subsequently served on the first United States Reparations Commission in Japan in 1945. He then resumed his teaching career at the Page School on a full-time basis.

In his study of the emerging postwar Chinese situation, *Solution in Asia* (1945), Lattimore warned that U.S. policy in the Far East would be doomed to failure if the nation allowed its fear of change to lead it to support reactionary regimes without popular support. The fall of Chiang's increasingly corrupt and ineffectual regime—which Lattimore claimed was far from democratic—to the Communist armies in 1949 fulfilled Lattimore's prophecy. In his subsequent book, *The Situation in Asia,* Lattimore urged American policymakers to accept that Asia was no longer under the control of the West. "Where we do not have the power to get exactly what we want," Lattimore suggested, "we must negotiate and combine our interests with those of others in order to get as much as possible of what we need." On the other hand, Lattimore argued that the Soviet Union would not be able to dominate China either. He applauded the

Truman administration's commitment to foreign aid, but he warned that the United States would not succeed in obtaining its objectives in the Far East if it demanded "bad political relations with Russia as the price of good economic relations with America."

Lattimore's denunciation of Chiang Kai-shek and his suggestion that the Chinese Communists were better described as agrarian reformers than Marxists infuriated the pro-Chiang CHINA LOBBY in the United States, and particularly millionaire industrialist Alfred KOHLBERG, who was establishing increasingly close ties with Senator Joseph McCarthy in the early months of 1950. On February 9, 1950, McCarthy delivered his Wheeling, West Virginia, speech accusing the Truman administration of harboring a number of Communists in the State Department. The Senate subsequently established a subcommittee under the leadership of Maryland Democrat Millard TYDINGS to investigate McCarthy's charges.

On March 13, the third day of hearings, McCarthy suddenly introduced Owen Lattimore's name into the controversy when he informed the Tydings subcommittee that Lattimore was "one of the principal architects of our Far Eastern policy." Lattimore, claimed McCarthy, was "pro-Communist" and "an extremely bad security risk." Eight days later, McCarthy elaborated on his charges when he told the subcommittee in executive session that Lattimore was "the top Russian espionage agent in the country." "If you crack this case," McCarthy urged his colleagues, "it will be the biggest espionage case in the history of this country." At that time, the American public knew only that McCarthy had singled out one individual as the foremost Soviet spy; newspapers refused to print Lattimore's name for fear of a libel suit. Nevertheless, McCarthy told reporters off the record that he was speaking of Lattimore, and he insisted that "I am willing to stand or fall on this one." Having staked his credibility on the Lattimore case, McCarthy and his staff started poring over Lattimore's files, searching for evidence of disloyalty. When he found no conclusive proof, McCarthy blamed his failure on the Truman administration's reluctance to turn over material on Lattimore's past activities, and he fired off a telegram to President Truman: "I feel that your delay of this investigation by your arrogant refusal to release all necessary files is inexcusable and is endangering the security of this nation." McCarthy told reporters, "It is up to the President to put up or shut up. Unless the President is afraid of what the files would disclose, he should hand them over."

McCarthy's request touched upon the sensitive issue of executive-legislative prerogatives, but Truman agreed to allow FBI Director J. Edgar HOOVER present a summary of Lattimore's FBI file to the Tydings subcommittee. Presented with Hoover's evidence, the senators and Hoover agreed there was nothing in the file to suggest that Lattimore had ever been a Communist or had ever been connected with an espionage ring. Further, Tydings pointed out that Lattimore was not even a State Department employee. Undaunted, McCarthy insisted that Lattimore (whom he still referred to publicly only as Russia's "top espionage agent") had a desk at the State Department, "or at least he did until three or four months ago," and the senator shook off the news that Lattimore was not employed by State. "He is one of their top advisers on Far Eastern affairs," McCarthy said, "or at least he was until three or four weeks ago."

On March 26, columnist Drew PEARSON leaked Lattimore's name on his weekly national radio broadcast. "I happen to know Owen Lattimore personally," observed Pearson, "and I only wish this country had more patriots like him." Once his name had been revealed, Lattimore received news of McCarthy's charges via telegram in Afghanistan, where he was serving as an adviser on a United Nations commission. Lattimore replied by terming McCarthy's accusations "pure moonshine," and he predicted that the senator would "fall flat on [his] face." As Lattimore prepared to return to the United States to answer the charges before the Tydings committee, McCarthy's staff met with ex-Communist informer Louis BUDENZ, who had already testified at length before the HOUSE COMMITTEE ON UN-AMERICAN ACTIVITIES (HUAC), accusing dozens of individuals of membership in the COMMUNIST PARTY. Budenz claimed that Lattimore had been a member of the party; in fact, Budenz stated that Lattimore had been the party's expert on Asian affairs and even possessed a code name so that writers of the Communist publication, the DAILY WORKER, would recognize as authentic material that came from Lattimore.

Bolstered by Budenz' testimony, McCarthy continued to hammer at Lattimore. In a speech on March 30, McCarthy again identified Lattimore as a Soviet espionage agent. "He either is, or at least has been, a member of the Communist Party," noted the senator. According to McCarthy, Lattimore had exerted "a dominant influence over the formulation and implementation of the policy which has delivered China to the Communists." Secretary of State Dean ACHESON, added the senator, was merely "the voice for the mind of Lattimore." In a press conference held within hours of McCarthy's statement, Truman labeled the latest allegations "silly," and administration spokesmen scoffed at the notion that there were any "card-carrying Communists in the State Department."

On April 6, Lattimore—accompanied by attorney Abe FORTAS—appeared before the Tydings subcommittee to answer McCarthy's charges. In a prepared statement that took him one hour forty-five minutes to read, Lattimore characterized McCarthy's accusations as "base and contemptible lies." By identifying him as a Soviet spy and the guiding hand behind U.S. Far East policy, Lattimore claimed that McCarthy had made "the Government of the United States an object of suspicion in the eyes of the anti-Communist world, and undoubtedly the laughing stock of the Communist governments." Lattimore proceeded to charge McCarthy with "instituting a reign of terror among officials and employees in the United States government," using classified documents without authorization, accusing American citizens of treason and disloyalty without giving them an opportunity to defend themselves, and refusing to submit "alleged documentary evidence" of espionage and treason to the Tydings subcommittee. Lattimore then dealt with McCarthy's allegations against him in detail, pointing out dozens of factual inaccuracies in the senator's statements. Lattimore dismissed the notion that he possessed extensive influence over U.S. policy in Asia, though he added that "I wish that I had in fact had more influence. If I had, I think that the Communists would not now control China." He concluded with a warning that "The sure way to destroy freedom of speech and the free expression of ideas and views is to attach to that freedom the penalty of abuse and vilification."

McCarthy, however, persisted in his attempt to tie Lattimore to a Soviet espionage ring. On April 20, the Tydings subcommittee heard the testimony of Louis BUDENZ, whose credibility in other cases had recently been questioned by the FBI. Budenz repeated his allegation that Communist Party leaders had informed him in 1937 that Lattimore was part of a party cell centered in the Institute for Pacific Relations, though he acknowledged under questioning that he had no personal knowledge of Lattimore's membership in the party. Perhaps, Budenz added, Lattimore might not actually be the foremost Soviet spy in the United States: "Well, to my knowledge, that statement is technically not accurate. I do not know, of course, the whole story, what other evidence there is, but from my own knowledge I would not say he was a top Soviet agent." The subcommittee then called to the stand Brigadier General Elliott R. Thorpe, a retired Army intelligence expert and former member of General Douglas MACARTHUR's staff who had conducted previous security investigations into Lattimore's background. The end result of all his inquiries, claimed Thorpe, was that he had never "heard a man so

frequently referred to as a Communist with so little basis in fact."

Meanwhile, Tydings contacted Secretary of State Acheson and three of his predecessors (Cordell Hull, James Byrnes, and George MARSHALL), and asked them whether Lattimore had exercised any significant influence over U.S. Far East policy during their terms at the State Department. Each of the four denied consulting with Lattimore on any policy issue at any time.

In its final report on the matter, the Tydings subcommittee exonerated Lattimore of all of McCarthy's charges. "We have seen a distortion of the facts," it announced, "on such a magnitude as to be truly alarming." Yet McCarthy's allegations had struck a nerve with the American public; in a poll taken in April 1950, respondents sided with McCarthy against Lattimore by a margin of 4–3. Although he never proved his case against Lattimore, the affair brought McCarthy invaluable publicity, and contributions from citizens across the nation who were frightened about Communist influence in the federal government began to flow into his Senate office. There were, in fact, repeated instances of pro-Communist leanings in Lattimore's writings on Chinese and Soviet affairs, and in the increasingly hysterical atmosphere of the McCarthy era, these could be (and were) viewed as evidence of disloyalty. State Department spokesman John Peurifoy, who supervised the department's security affairs, ventured his guess that "Lattimore is guilty, but McCarthy can't prove it, anymore than we can."

The dramatic discovery in a Massachusetts barn in February 1951 of files belonging to the Institute of Public Relations brought Lattimore back into the spotlight. McCarthy claimed that these files proved that the IPR was a thinly disguised Soviet espionage ring, and in the ensuing investigation, the Senate Internal Security subcommittee, headed by Senator Patrick MCCARRAN, recalled Lattimore to testify. For twelve days, Lattimore was examined about his role in the formulation of U.S. foreign policy during the Roosevelt and Truman administrations. Lattimore was openly hostile to certain members of the subcommittee, accusing them of suborning perjury from witnesses against him. McCarran reciprocated by provoking Lattimore and then complaining that Lattimore was "flagrantly defiant." The subcommittee's questions revealed that Lattimore had, in fact, met with Truman to discuss Far East affairs once in 1945 and had written the President at least one memorandum on the subject. But evidence of Lattimore's involvement was so thin that the subcommittee was reduced to asking the witness to prove "that the IPR and you had no influence upon the far-eastern experts of the State Department."

Nevertheless, the subcommittee's final report characterized Lattimore as a "conscious articulate instrument of the Soviet conspiracy," and it accused Lattimore of lying under oath during his testimony. McCarran pressured Attorney General James McGranery into bringing charges against Lattimore. In December 1952, a Washington grand jury indicted Lattimore on seven counts of perjury. Six of the charges involved specific answers Lattimore had given to the Senate Internal Security subcommittee; the seventh accused Lattimore of lying when he swore that he had "never been a sympathizer or . . . promoter of Communism or Communist interests."

That final charge, along with three others, were dismissed almost immediately by federal District Court Judge Luther Youngdahl for lack of evidence. The accusations were so "formless and obscure," noted Youngdahl, that they would make a "sham of the Sixth Amendment." The government's case against Lattimore suffered another blow when one of its witnesses, Harvey Matusow, admitted that he had perjured himself during his testimony before the Senate Internal Security subcommittee. In 1955, the Justice Department finally dropped the case altogether.

Lattimore returned to his position at Johns Hopkins University. He taught at the Hopkins until 1963 when he became head of the department of Chinese studies at Leeds University in Britain. He remained at Leeds until he retired in 1975. In later years, Lattimore said that his confrontation with McCarthy had been "but a small chapter in my life." On May 31, 1988, Lattimore died in his sleep at a hospital near his home in Pawtucket, Rhode Island.

**Lavery, Emmet** (1902–1986)  Three-time president of the SCREEN WRITERS' GUILD (SWG), Emmet Lavery was an outspoken liberal screenwriter who denounced both Communists and the demagogic tactics of the HOUSE COMMITTEE ON UN-AMERICAN ACTIVITIES (HUAC).

Trained as an attorney with an LL.B. from Fordham University, Lavery first began to act and write as a hobby in 1927. Seven years later, his play *First Legion* was produced on Broadway. After spending two years in Hollywood as a scenario writer, Lavery served as a director of the Federal Theater Project from 1937 to 1939. By that time, the Federal Theater Project had acquired a reputation among conservatives as a Communist-dominated organization; Congressman J. Parnell THOMAS, for instance, insisted that "The Federal Theater Project produced plays which were nothing but straight Communist propaganda." Lavery, a devout Catholic, rejected such accusations and attempted to defend the project from congressional attacks. Despite his best efforts, the Roosevelt administration elected to discontinue its support of the Federal Theater Project in 1939.

During World War II, Lavery served as a screenwriter for RKO studios, where he wrote scripts for such films as *Hitler's Children* and *Behind the Rising Sun,* in an attempt to depict what he considered "the true nature of the enemy without arousing race hatred." Lavery's most famous work, however, was *The Magnificent Yankee,* a dramatic biography of Supreme Court Justice Oliver Wendell Holmes, which was first produced on the stage in 1946.

In 1944, Lavery was elected president of the Screen Writers' Guild and was subsequently reelected for two additional one-year terms. As president of the SWG, Lavery responded angrily to accusations from right-wing zealots in Washington and Hollywood that the guild was dominated by Communists. First, in the fall of 1947 he filed a libel suit against Lela Rogers—the mother of actress Ginger Rogers—for implying on a nationwide radio program that Lavery was a Communist. (The suit was later settled in Lavery's favor.) Then, on October 29, 1947, Lavery appeared before HUAC to defend the guild and himself from such allegations. Lavery's testimony followed close upon that of the HOLLYWOOD TEN, several of whom had preceded him to the witness stand that morning.

In his defense, Lavery cited the conclusions of the Tenney Committee—the California state legislature's version of HUAC—that in the opinion of the committee chairman, Jack Tenney, Lavery was not a Communist and that the guild was not controlled by Communists. After further reminding the members of HUAC that he had voluntarily offered to cooperate with the Los Angeles office of the FEDERAL BUREAU OF INVESTIGATION, Lavery willingly declared that "I am not a Communist. I never have been. I don't intend to be. I will," he added wryly, "make open confession and admit that I am a Democrat, who in my youth was a Republican." Coming upon the heels of the Hollywood Ten's refusal to declare whether they were Communists or not, Lavery's statement was greeted with approbation by the chairman of HUAC, the same J. Parnell Thomas who had denounced the Federal Theater Project a decade earlier.

Asked whether the Screen Writers' Guild included Communists among its membership, Lavery openly acknowledged that "I am willing to make the assumption that there are Communists in the Screen Writers' Guild." He subsequently chastised the committee, however, for its assumption that Communist members of the guild held any significant influence upon the policies of that organization. Citing three members of the Hollywood Ten, Lavery stated that he did not understand "why you rate so highly the influence of Mr. [Albert] MALTZ, Mr. [John Howard] LAWSON, Mr. [Dalton] TRUMBO. They are able men. They are articulate men. And they are competent screen writers. But they are only a few of a membership of nine hundred some. We have often had our arguments within the family. I think so far I have had the upper hand. I have nothing to complain about. And when Mr. [Robert] STRIPLING [chief investigator of HUAC] says, 'Aren't you worried about Mr. Maltz,' I say, 'Not particularly.' "

As Lavery continued his testimony, it became clear that the members of HUAC were not quite certain how to deal with a witness who boasted of being a liberal, a Catholic, and an anti-Communist. For his part, Lavery delivered a ringing denunciation of the committee's tactics before he left the stand. "If we are to keep harping on the note of fear," Lavery informed the committee, "it is like the old-fashioned revival or the old-fashioned mission, where you scare the devil out of the parishioners for a week, and after that they are rather accustomed to the notion of fear. I don't think it is enough to make people afraid. It is very easy to make them afraid. I think the problem is how to make people aware of the active love that they have. . . . The challenge of the theater and the screen is to project an American way of life, particularly an historical drama, that vitalizes the whole tradition of which we are a part. Believe me, I am much more interested, as a playwright and a screen writer, in trying to show, for instance, what Mr. Justice Holmes would be like than showing how bad Mr. STALIN is. It would be very easy to show how bad Mr. Stalin is, but the positive virtues of our great American leaders are the thing that the screen should be showing at this time."

In 1955, Lavery earned an Academy Award nomination for his screenplay for the film *The Court Martial of Billy Mitchell,* an account of the iconoclastic Mitchell's battle against a conservative U.S. Army establishment. Lavery subsequently died of a heart attack in Poughkeepsie, New York.

**Lawson, John Howard** (1894–1977)
Generally regarded as the dean of Communists in the motion picture industry, Lawson was a successful playwright on Broadway before moving to Hollywood.

He became interested in radical causes early in his career. After graduating from Williams College, Lawson served as a volunteer ambulance driver in World War I, and his experiences during the war apparently stimulated his interest in social reform. He remained in Paris for a brief time after the war but returned to the United States to author two successful expressionist plays.

In 1926, Lawson co-founded the New Playwrights Theater, a left-wing venture which, in Lawson's own words, was intended to "have some contact with workers and reflect realities of American life." Like many American radicals in the 1920s, Lawson demonstrated against the execution of anarchists Niccola Sacco and Bartolomeo Vanzetti in 1927. Shortly thereafter, he moved to Hollywood to write for Metro-Goldwyn-Mayer. Disillusioned by the studio's obsession with profits, however, he left MGM in 1930 to join a left-wing ensemble known as the Group Theatre.

After being elected the first president of the SCREEN WRITERS' GUILD in 1933, Lawson joined the COMMUNIST PARTY the following year and became a contributing editor to *New Masses,* the leading Communist cultural publication in the United States. Along with his colleagues in the party, Lawson joined with American liberals in promoting the cause of civil rights and the labor movement. Outraged by what he perceived as a gross miscarriage of justice in the case of the Scottsboro Boys, a group of black men accused of rape in Alabama, Lawson wrote a series of newspaper articles in the 1930s attacking the state of Alabama and the Ku Klux Klan for their roles in railroading through a guilty verdict. Through his writings and his participation in leftist organizations in Hollywood, he soon earned a reputation as the most doctri-

naire, enthusiastic, and inflexible Communist within the motion picture screenwriter community.

During World War II, Lawson's film credits included *Sahara, Action in the North Atlantic, Counterattack, Blockade, Algiers, Smash-Up,* and *Four Sons.* But his radical statements rendered him unpopular among film-studio executives in the tensions of the postwar period, and after the end of the war in 1945 Lawson found it virtually impossible to obtain work as a screenwriter. On September 21, 1947, the HOUSE COMMITTEE ON UN-AMERICAN ACTIVITIES (HUAC) subpoenaed Lawson, along with eighteen other allegedly subversive Hollywood writers, directors, and actors, to testify in Washington about his pro-Soviet sympathies. With the exception of Bertolt BRECHT, who adamantly denied that he was a Communist, Lawson and the other nine unfriendly witnesses who were called to testify in Washington adopted an uncooperative and occasionally hostile attitude toward the committee's inquiries and were subsequently dubbed "the HOLLYWOOD TEN" by the press. Lawson, however, was the only member of the Ten who had meaningful ties with the leaders of the Communist Party of the United States in New York.

Lawson was the first of the Hollywood Ten witnesses to appear before the committee. From the time he took the stand on October 27, 1947, Lawson challenged the committee's authority to investigate his political activities. He attempted to deliver an opening statement into the record, but after glancing at the first line of Lawson's statement, HUAC chairman J. Parnell THOMAS refused to allow him to read it. When a committee investigator asked him "Are you now or have you ever been a member of the Communist Party of the United States?" Lawson refused to answer directly. Instead, he replied that "The question of communism is in no way related to this inquiry, which is an attempt to get control of the screen and to invade the basic rights of American citizens in all fields. . . . The question here relates not only to the question of my membership in any political organization, but this committee is attempting to establish the right which has been historically denied to any committee of this sort, to invade the rights and privileges and immunity of American citizens, whether they be Protestants, Methodist, Jewish or Catholic, whether they be Republicans or Democrats or anything else."

For his failure to answer the questions of the committee, Lawson was forcibly evicted from the hearing room. An investigator for HUAC then took the stand and read into the record a detailed dossier of more than 100 exhibits which the committee had compiled on Lawson, including a purported Communist Party "registration card" in his name. Lawson's combative attitude and aggressive rhetoric—he compared HUAC's tactics to those of the Nazi regime in Germany—lent credence to the committee's accusations and cost Lawson (and the rest of the Hollywood Ten) public support and the sympathy of moderate liberals who might have been willing to support him and his colleagues on First Amendment grounds.

No major studio would employ Lawson after his turbulent appearance before HUAC. On December 5, 1947, he was indicted for contempt of Congress and was tried and convicted in April 1948. He continued to speak out against the rising anti-Communist fervor, declaring in a speech to the Progressive Citizens of America that "The attack on the motion picture industry marks an entirely new phase of the drive toward thought control in the United States." But Lawson's militancy earned him little public sympathy, and the Supreme Court refused to hear his appeal. On June 11, Lawson and another member of the Hollywood Ten, Dalton TRUMBO, entered the federal prison at Ashland, Kentucky, to begin their one-year sentence. After his release, Lawson found it necessary to write screenplays under an assumed name. Nevertheless, he refused to indulge in self-pity. "I'm much more completely blacklisted than the others," he once told a reporter. "I'm much more notorious, and I'm very proud

of that. It had much to do with the fact that I helped to organize the guild and played a leading role in progressive attitudes after 1947." Lawson continued to speak out against the BLACKLIST, but found little public support. He never wrote another successful motion picture screenplay.

**League of Women Shoppers**    A consumer activist organization with left-wing sympathies, the League of Women Shoppers was founded, according to its constitution, upon the principle that "working conditions are important considerations in the purchase of goods." In other words, the league urged consumer boycotts of companies whose labor-management policies did not meet its standards. In 1941, for instance, the League recommended that the American public refuse to patronize theaters that featured movies from Walt DISNEY Studios because the studio was locked in a bitter strike dispute with the Cartoonists Guild.

As part of an investigation into consumer organizations in 1939, the HOUSE COMMITTEE ON UN-AMERICAN ACTIVITIES (HUAC) cited the League of Women Shoppers as a Communist-front organization, part of a plot "to sabotage and destroy advertising, and through its destruction to undermine and help destroy the capitalist system of free enterprise." The committee cited the league again in 1944, and the California Committee on Un-American Activities issued its own report on the league in 1943. In response, the league condemned HUAC's smear tactics.

The League made national headlines in 1947, when Walt Disney confused it with the League of Women Voters in his testimony before HUAC. In an obvious reference to the League of Women Shoppers' action against his films in 1941, Disney described the League of Women Voters as an organization of Communist sympathizers. Not until the League of Women Voters called upon all American women to boycott Disney's films did he correct his statement.

**League of Women Voters**   See LEAGUE OF WOMEN SHOPPERS.

**Lennart, Isobel** (1915–1971)   A native of New York, Isobel Lennart joined the Young Communist League (YCL) when she was sixteen years old. Shortly thereafter, Lennart moved to Hollywood, where she obtained a job in the mail room of Metro-Goldwyn-Mayer studio. She was fired when she attempted to organize a union to represent the studio's workers. Two years later, however, Lennart returned to MGM—presumably older and wiser—as a script girl. She remained with the studio for the remainder of her career.

Lennart also retained her interest in left-wing political activities. In 1938, she joined one of the numerous Marxist study groups in Hollywood that were often thinly disguised meetings of the YCL. Lennart joined the COMMUNIST PARTY the following year, but she broke with the party following her marriage in 1944 to actor-writer John Harding, a socialist who strongly opposed Communism. By the time the HOUSE COMMITTEE ON UN-AMERICAN ACTIVITIES (HUAC) launched its second investigation of Communist influence in the motion picture industry in 1951, Lennart had authored screenplays for such popular and critically acclaimed films as the musical *Anchors Aweigh* and *East Side, West Side.*

Before HUAC subpoenaed her to testify, several of the committee's investigators visited Lennart to determine whether she would cooperate and provide the committee with the names of her former associates in the Communist Party. "I told them," Lennart later recalled, "that since I was out of the Party, I didn't know who else was out of the Party." She promised to answer all questions about her own activities, but none about anyone else. According to Lennart, the investigators warned that such recalcitrance would probably earn her a prison sentence for contempt, but she refused to change her mind. A week later, the investigators returned. In the interim, they had learned that she was pregnant and that her obstetrician refused to sign an affidavit stating that she could testify without endangering her health. The committee consequently withdrew its subpoena.

The following year, after the delivery of her child, the FBI visited Lennart and asked her numerous questions about radical activists she had known in the theater. "I answered quite honestly," she said, "that I had a different feeling about the FBI than I did about the Un-American Activities Committee." When MGM executives informed her that they could not protect her any longer from a subpoena from HUAC, Lennart—under pressure from Harding and her attorney—decided to testify. "I had, I must say, a tremendous reversal of feelings about the Party at that time," she said. "My father had died, which made me know I would now be responsible for my stepmother and my brother. . . . On a personal level, I had come to feel that people don't sustain you; your work sustains you, and I knew how to do absolutely nothing else but screenwrite. I didn't know how to live if I couldn't work."

Lennart insisted, however, that she would provide the committee only names that had already been mentioned at least ten times by other witnesses. "We made a stopping place," she said, "and I felt I could live with this. I couldn't live beyond that. I don't think anything would have made me mention a group of new names. It's a small device, but at least there's nobody who was ruined and informed on because of me, and that made it at least tolerable for me." Despite HUAC pressure to implicate a prominent actor, Lennart refused, claiming that if the committee insisted on asking her about that individual, she would plead the Fifth Amendment. The committee retreated, and she was permitted to continue her work at MGM.

Following Lennart's death in an automobile accident in 1971, Harding revealed that she had regretted for the rest of her life her decision to cooperate with HUAC. Before she died, Lennart expressed that regret to an interviewer:

I believe with all my heart that it was wrong to cooperate with this terrible Committee in any way, and I believe that I was wrong. I believe I did a minimum of damage, but I still believe I was wrong. I had a much bigger reaction to it than I thought I would. . . . It was shame and guilt and nothing else. I've never gotten over it. I've always felt like an inferior citizen because of this. But it was a consensus decision. . . . I am able to comfort myself by saying I hurt nobody, but I'm aware that this is a comfort device. . . .

CIO chief John L. Lewis (right) receiving an award from the American Red Cross.

## Lewis, John L. (1880–1969)

The son of a Welsh miner, John L. Lewis became the most famous and controversial American labor-union leader during the 1930s. Elected president of the UNITED MINE WORKERS (UMM) in 1919, Lewis eventually grew disenchanted with the conservative, subservient approach of the nation's largest labor organization, the American Federation of Labor; the AFL, Lewis charged, "is standing still, with its face toward the dead past." At the AFL's stormy annual convention in 1935, he led a walkout of discontented delegates and subsequently formed the Committee of Industrial Organizations, which later was renamed the CONGRESS OF INDUSTRIAL ORGANIZATIONS (CIO).

For the remainder of the decade, Lewis freely accepted the assistance of Communist labor organizers in battling management in the automobile and steel industries. At that time, the international Communist (Comintern) movement was attempting to establish a coalition—known as the POPULAR FRONT—with liberal elements in the democracies of Western Europe and North America to provide additional protection against the growing fascist movements in Germany and Italy. Communist organizers provided Lewis and his colleagues with tough, experienced associates, although the expedient alliance also earned Lewis the enmity of right-wing commentators, who denounced him as "a Communist stooge." At least one steelmaker refused to negotiate with Lewis, claiming that the CIO was "an irresponsible, racketeering, violent, communistic body." Nevertheless, the CIO managed to revive the nearly moribund American labor movement, and by 1941 union membership in the United States had risen to 10 million.

Meanwhile, anti-Communist liberals within the CIO—such as Walter REUTHER and Philip MURRAY—decided to break with their Communist allies, in large measure, as a reaction against the announcement of the NAZI-SOVIET PACT in August 1939. The pact swung Communists over to the isolationist movement in the United States, and Lewis joined them by becoming one of the leading spokesmen of the "America First" noninterventionist crusade. At the CIO's annual convention of 1939, Murray captured leadership of the organization from Lewis at the same time that he pushed through a resolution that condemned Communism.

Lewis remained head of the United Mine Workers, however, and in 1942 he withdrew the UMW from the CIO and, during World War II, led his miners on several dramatic work stoppages that infuriated President Franklin Delano Roosevelt. In 1946, the UMW rejoined the AFL but withdrew again the following year. For the remainder of his career with the union,

Lewis focused his attention on such concrete, limited goals as the acquisition of health and unemployment benefits.

**Loeb, Philip** See BLACKLIST.

**loyalty oaths** As the American public grew more concerned over Communist infiltration of the United States in the late 1940s and early 1950s, many local and state governments, educational institutions, and corporations adopted loyalty oaths. Typically, such oaths required an individual to swear that he or she was not a member of any organization that sought to overthrow the state or national government by force and to declare his or her loyalty to the U.S. Constitution (and possibly a state constitution as well). The ostensible purpose of the oaths were to deny employment to Communists, though the organizations failed to take into account the possibility—indeed, the likelihood—that true Communists would readily swear a false oath to keep their identity secret. Many of the individuals who refused to take loyalty oaths did so because they opposed the oaths on moral or religious principles.

State universities, which were often accused by right-wing zealots of harboring Communist intellectuals, frequently employed loyalty oaths during the late 1940s and early 1950s. One of the most widely publicized incidents of this occurred in California in 1949 when members of the University of California faculty were required to pledge their loyalty to the state government. Although the university's regents attempted—against the advice of Governor Earl WARREN—to dismiss the numerous professors who refused, the oath was subsequently declared unconstitutional by the California State Supreme Court. Still, one observer noted that the vigorous attempt to impose the loyalty oath at the university led to widespread demoralization among the faculty, along with "worry, depression, fatigue, fear, insomnia, drinking . . . wors-

ening of relations to colleagues, suspicion, distrust, loss of self-respect."

On a national level, the TAFT-HARTLEY ACT of 1947 required all labor union officials in the United States to take a loyalty oath; if they refused, their union risked decertification by the National Labor Relations Board. In Hollywood, the Screen Directors Guild passed a measure in 1950 requiring its members to take an oath declaring their loyalty to the U.S. Constitution and swearing that they were not members of the COMMUNIST PARTY. This measure established a precedent which anti-Communists used to inaugurate similar requirements throughout the entertainment industry; combined with the use of the BLACKLIST, loyalty oaths instilled an atmosphere of fear and paranoia throughout the industry for the remainder of the decade.

**Loyalty Review Board** On March 21, 1947, President Harry S. TRUMAN issued EXECUTIVE ORDER 9835 that established the first peacetime federal-employment loyalty program in the history of the United States. As part of Executive Order 9835, the government established a Loyalty Review Board under the aegis of the Civil Service Commission. Although Truman himself privately expressed doubts that there was any substantive danger of subversion within the federal government, he agreed to support the establishment of a loyalty board in response to growing political pressure from the Right.

The purpose of the board purportedly was to investigate the backgrounds of current and prospective federal employees; those who were deemed security risks would be dismissed or rejected. Over the next several years, many government departments also established their own security and loyalty review boards to investigate employees' political activities and beliefs. Any employee who received an adverse ruling from his departmental board could appeal to the Civil Service Commission's Loyalty Review Board for a final determination.

In the first four years of its existence, the Loyalty Review Board investigated and cleared nearly 3 million federal employees. Over this same period, only 212 employees were dismissed as potentially disloyal or security risks. Following the inauguration of President Dwight David EISENHOWER in 1953, the Loyalty Review Board was afforded increased discretion to dismiss employees whose record indicated that they might have been security risks at any time in the past. In January 1954, Eisenhower reported that approximately 2,200 federal employees had either resigned or been dismissed from their jobs as security risks. On the other hand, a later Senate study discovered that only 343 federal employees had actually been dismissed as security risks by the Eisenhower administration between May 1953 and June 1955, and another 662 had resigned after being informed that they were considered disloyal. (See also EXECUTIVE ORDER 10450; Hiram BINGHAM.)

**Luce, Henry R.** (1898–1967)  Founder of the Time, Inc., publishing empire, Henry R. Luce was also a dedicated anti-Communist and member of the CHINA LOBBY.

The son of a Presbyterian missionary, Luce was born in China and spent the first thirteen years of his life in the Far East. He arrived in the United States at age fifteen and subsequently attended Yale University, where his classmates voted him the "most brilliant" member of their senior class. Following a brief career as a reporter for the Chicago *Daily News* and the Baltimore *News,* Luce joined a former Yale classmate to found *Time* magazine. From the publication of its first issue in March 1923, *Time* was a major success. In 1930, Luce introduced a business news magazine called *Fortune;* during the following three decades, he also introduced *Life* (the magazine that wrought a revolution in photojournalism) and *Sports Illustrated.* By the end of the 1950s, Luce's Time-Life empire was earning over $270 million in revenues annually.

Partly because of the circumstances of his youth in China, Luce was a dedicated supporter of Chinese Nationalist leader CHIANG Kai-shek; For Luce, Chiang—who had joined the Methodist church in 1931—represented the best hope of christianizing China. He used the resources of his publishing empire to promote the Nationalist cause in the United States; for instance, he featured Chiang on the cover of *Time* magazine seven times, more than any other individual to date. Luce also contributed financially to the activities of the China Lobby and supported his wife's decision to serve as head of the conservative American China Policy Association.

While he avidly encouraged the anti-Communist crusade in the United States in the postwar years, Luce remained suspicious of the motives of Senator Joseph MCCARTHY of Wisconsin and refused to support McCarthy's reckless methods of seeking out Communist influence in America. In fact, Luce—who could never be accused of pro-Communist behavior by any rational observer—used *Time* and *Life* to attack McCarthy. In October 1951, for instance, as McCarthy's fortunes were ascending, *Time* ran a story that stated that "experience proves . . . that what the anti-Communist fight needs is truth, carefully arrived at and presented with all the scrupulous regard for decency and the rights of man of which the democratic world is capable. This is the Western world's greatest asset in the struggle against Communism, and those who condone McCarthy are throwing that asset away." McCarthy responded by pressuring *Time*'s advertisers to withdraw their support of the magazine, to little avail.

Throughout the 1950s, however, Luce steadily grew more conservative, opposing the thaw in relations between the United States and the Soviet Union. By 1960, Luce was publicly advocating all-out victory in the Cold War, even at the risk of a shooting war with the Soviets.

# M

**MacArthur, Douglas** (1880–1964) A flamboyant and controversial military figure, General Douglas MacArthur was fired by President Harry S. TRUMAN as commander of United Nations (UN) troops in Korea in 1951, thereby precipitating a bitter confrontation between Truman and conservative Republicans in the U.S. Congress. In the ensuing exchange of violent rhetoric, Senator Joseph MCCARTHY called Truman a "son of a bitch" for dismissing MacArthur, and a number of right-wing Republicans, including Senator William JENNER of Indiana and House Minority Leader Joseph MARTIN, called for the impeachment of the President.

The son of General Arthur MacArthur, Douglas MacArthur grew up in Texas and attended Texas Military Academy before entering the U.S. Military Academy in 1899. At West Point, MacArthur achieved the highest grade-point average in the history of the academy. Following his graduation, he served at a series of overseas posts in the Philippines, Japan, and the Canal Zone in Panama. After the United States entered World War I, MacArthur helped organize and train the famous Rainbow Division, which consisted of National Guard units from twenty-seven states. His personal bravery in combat won him both the Distinguished Service Cross and the Oak Leaf Cluster.

Once the war was over, he returned to the United States to become superintendent of the U.S. Military Academy. During the following three years, he helped modernize the academy's military training, broadening the curriculum while relaxing discipline and introducing compulsory intramural athletics.

In 1922, MacArthur was detailed to the Philippines and three years later returned again to the United States to take command of a corps area in Baltimore, Maryland. In November 1930, he was named chief of the General Staff, from which position he worked to modernize the Army by promoting the twin trends of mechanization and motorization, while encouraging the development of new ideas through the advancement of young junior officers.

MacArthur himself retired from the service for the first time in 1937, "in order to accelerate the promotion of junior officers." As the United States drifted closer to war, however, he was recalled to active duty in July 1941 to command American forces in the Far East, and following America's entry into the war, he was named supreme commander of the Southwest Pacific. Although ordered to retreat from his Philippines base in January 1942, MacArthur returned and led a successful invasion of the islands in October 1944. Promoted to General of the Army MacArthur in December 1944 and named in April 1945 to command all U.S. Army forces in the Pacific, MacArthur—by presidential appointment—received the Japanese surrender on August 14, 1945, the use of atomic weapons against Japan having made an invasion of the Japanese home islands unnecessary. Truman subsequently ordered MacArthur to remain in Japan as commander of the occupation forces, and during the following three years, MacArthur supervised the wholesale revision of the Japanese constitution.

Although some conservative Republican leaders nominated MacArthur as the party's presidential candidate in 1948, he did not actively campaign for the honor. Instead, he was activated in June 1950 to command UN military forces in Korea, following the invasion of South Korea by North Korean forces on June 24: MacArthur had helped convince Truman that "the only assurance for holding the present line and the ability to regain later the lost ground is through the introduction of United States ground combat forces into the Korean battle area." On September 15, MacArthur led a bril-

General Douglas MacArthur (left), hero of the anti-Communist China lobby.

liant amphibious assault at Inchon, 150 miles behind enemy lines. The attack caught the North Korean command entirely by surprise. By October 1, UN troops had recaptured the capital city of Seoul and regained virtually all the territory lost at the outset of the conflict.

Truman and his civilian advisers favored a return to the status quo ante bellum, but MacArthur—along with members of the zealously anti-Communist CHINA LOBBY—saw the Korean conflict as an opportunity to commit the United States to the return of Chinese Nationalist leader CHIANG Kai-shek to power on the mainland. Persuaded by MacArthur that neither the Soviet Union nor the Communist Chinese government would intervene in Korea, Truman gave MacArthur permission to cross the 38th parallel in pursuit of the enemy. MacArthur thereupon predicted that the war would "for all practical purposes" be over within a few weeks, and that

U.S. soldiers would "eat Christmas dinner at home." Much to MacArthur's chagrin, Communist China suddenly sent 300,000 troops across the Yalu River into Korea on November 30, precipitating a headlong retreat by UN forces.

MacArthur recommended the use of nuclear weapons against the Chinese, but Truman demurred. The UN lines finally stabilized in mid-January, and by March the two sides had once again reestablished the preinvasion border along the 38th parallel. Unwilling to consider the war a stalemate, however, MacArthur deliberately sabotaged Truman's peace initiative. In the face of his blatant insubordination, Truman dismissed the general on the grounds that MacArthur was "unable to give his wholehearted support to the policies of the United States and of the United Nations." Public reaction in the United States sided overwhelmingly—by an estimated 2–1 margin—with MacArthur. The state legislatures of California, Florida, and Michigan passed resolutions condemning Truman.

For his part, Joseph McCarthy warned that he intended to uncover the "efforts to aid the Communists that are behind our activities in Asia." In a speech in Wisconsin, McCarthy blamed Truman's dismissal of MacArthur on the influence of alcohol and pro-Communist advisers. The President, McCarthy charged, "is surrounded by the JESSUPS, the ACHESONS, the old HISS crowd. These men have no hypnotic influence; most of the tragic things are done at 1:30 and 2 o'clock in the morning when they've had time to get the president cheerful." Jenner, meanwhile, was so incensed by the administration's treatment of MacArthur that he told his colleagues in the Senate that "our only choice is to impeach President Truman and find out who is the secret invisible government which has so cleverly led our country down the road to destruction."

When MacArthur returned to the United States, he was treated like a hero. Admirers gave him a ticker-tape parade through New York City, and—in a remarkable display of congressional disrespect toward President Truman—MacArthur was invited to deliver an address to a joint session of Congress. (It was during this speech that he quoted the famous line from a British army song, "Old soldiers never die. They just fade away.") In numerous interviews that followed his appearance before Congress, MacArthur insisted that the United States could never compromise with the forces of "atheistic Communism." "I believe we should defend every place from Communism," MacArthur insisted. "I believe we can. I believe we are able to."

MacArthur spent much of the next year traveling across the United States, speaking out against what he perceived as a Communist conspiracy abroad and at home. As time went on, he came to place greater emphasis on the domestic threat of subversion. "If this nation is ever de-stroyed," he warned the Michigan state legislature, "it will be from within, not from without." In March 1952, he accused the Truman administration of leading the nation along a course that could only end in Communist domination. Truman's policies, MacArthur said, were "leading toward a Communist state with as dreadful certainty as though the leaders of the Kremlin were charting the course."

MacArthur mounted a challenge for the Republican presidential nomination in the summer of 1952, but he was outmaneuvered by the forces of General Dwight David EISENHOWER, who had served as MacArthur's subordinate in Washington and the Philippines in the early 1930s. Not surprisingly, MacArthur opposed Eisenhower's decision to negotiate a peace treaty with North Korea that restored the status quo ante bellum. When the Eisenhower administration signed an armistice that left Korea divided at the 38th parallel, MacArthur warned that the treaty would inevitably lead to a Communist takeover of Southeast Asia. "This," he said, "is the death warrant for Indochina." But his criticisms of Eisenhower—an even more popular American military hero—carried far less weight than his complaints against Truman, and MacArthur soon discovered that the public spotlight had turned away from him.

In late 1952, he accepted the chairmanship of the Remington Rand Corporation. Although he received a handsome salary, his functions in that position were largely ceremonial. He was consulted frequently on a variety of domestic and diplomatic topics by President John F. KENNEDY, who considered MacArthur a genuine hero. On April 3, 1964, following a series of difficult operations, MacArthur died of acute kidney and liver failure.

**Maltz, Albert** (1908–1985)  A screenwriter and member of the HOLLYWOOD TEN, Albert Maltz was the son of immigrant parents from Lithuania. Maltz grew up in Brooklyn and graduated from Columbia College in 1930. He then enrolled at Yale University's School of Drama to study with George Pierce Baker; while at Yale, he completed his first play, *Merry Go Round,* which played in New York in 1932.

In 1933, Maltz joined the executive board of the newly organized Theatre Union, a workers' theater whose purpose, according to its founders, was "to produce plays about the working class, written from the point of view of the interests of the working class—where workers can attend plays at prices they can afford and where the theatre is not a form of titillation but is a moving cultural force, dramatic and alive." Maltz collaborated with a fellow student to write the Theatre Union's first production, *Peace on Earth,* which won an award in 1934 as "the outstanding American work of art contributing most to the cause of peace."

During the 1930s, Maltz also provided articles on American labor affairs for the Communist publication *New Masses* and authored numerous critically acclaimed short stories, winning the O. Henry Memorial Award for the best American short story in 1938. From 1937 to 1941, he instructed in playwriting at New York University's School of Adult Education.

In 1941, Maltz abandoned his academic career to move to Hollywood, where he wrote the screenplays for such highly regarded films as *This Gun for Hire, Destination Tokyo* (which was also used as a training film by the U.S. Navy), *Pride of the Marines,* and *Moscow Strikes Back.* He won Academy Awards for two documentaries, *The Defeat of the German Armies Near Moscow* (1942) and *The House I Live In* (1945).

His success in the motion picture industry did not diminish Maltz's devotion to left-wing causes. He belonged to both the New York and Hollywood branches of the COMMUNIST PARTY and once declared that "Marxist literature seemed to me the noblest body of literature ever penned by man." Unlike some of his Communist colleagues, however, Maltz believed that all art did not necessarily have to serve social purposes. In 1946, he wrote an article for *New Masses* that called for more Communist toleration of non-Marxist writers. He was excoriated by party leaders for this stance, and abjectly retracted his opinions in a subsequent article.

Early in 1947, Maltz roundly criticized the HOUSE COMMITTEE ON UN-AMERICAN ACTIVITIES (HUAC) for its attempts to intimidate leftist organizations in the United States, so it was not surprising that the committee subpoenaed Maltz as one of nineteen unfriendly witnesses when it launched its investigation of Hollywood in the autumn of 1947. Like nine of the other unfriendly witnesses who were actually called before the committee, Maltz refused to answer questions about his political beliefs or activities, although he was the only member of the Hollywood Ten who was allowed to read his prepared statement into the record: "I insist upon my right," Maltz informed the committee, "to join the Republican Party or the Communist Party . . . to publish whatever I please; to fix my mind or change my mind without dictation from anyone. . . . Above all, I challenge the right of this Committee to inquire into my political or religious beliefs, in any manner or degree, and I assert that not only the conduct of the Committee but its very existence are a subversion of the Bill of Rights."

For his protest, Maltz was selected as the first of the Hollywood Ten to be cited by Congress for contempt; he was described on the floor of the House of Representatives as "the most arrogant, the most contemptible, the most bitter of all of these people who do not believe in their own country." He was convicted by a federal court in 1948 and sentenced to one year in prison and a $1,000 fine. After the U.S. Supreme Court refused to overturn the verdict, Maltz served his term at the federal prison in Mill Point, West Virginia.

Following his release from prison in April 1951, Maltz moved to Mexico to continue his writing career. Like the other members of the Ten, he had been blacklisted from the motion picture industry, and the effects of the BLACKLIST lasted long after the original outburst of anti-Communist hysteria had abated. For the rest of the decade, Maltz remained in Mexico, occasionally drafting a screenplay under a pseudonym.

In March 1960, actor-singer Frank SINATRA announced that he had hired Maltz to write the script for a film version of *The Execution of Private Slovik*, the World War II GI who was the only American soldier to be executed for desertion since the Civil War. Sinatra's choice of Maltz was greeted with violent denunciations from the AMERICAN LEGION and other veterans' organizations who threatened to boycott the film, as well as from newspapers in the Hearst chain, and Sinatra was forced to terminate his arrangement with Maltz. Finally, in 1967, Universal Studios hired Maltz to write a screenplay for the movie *Two Mules for Sister Sara*. It was the last film Maltz ever wrote.

In 1970, a collection of Maltz's short stories (*Afternoon in the Jungle*) was published. It was the first time since the late 1930s that any of his written works had been available to the public, and the publication of *Afternoon* stimulated a brief revival in Maltz's literary contributions. *The Execution of Private Slovik* was later filmed as a made-for-television movie, starring Martin Sheen.

## Mao Zedong (1893–1976)

The leader of the Communist forces that overthrew the Chinese Nationalist government of CHIANG Kai-shek in 1949, Mao Zedong was born into a peasant family in Hunan Province in the waning years of the Manchu government. While a student at the National University in Peking (Beijing) in 1918, Mao was converted to the Communist cause. Three years later, he joined with eleven other radicals in Shanghai to establish the Chinese Communist Party. Although the Communists cooperated with the Nationalists in the early 1920s, the coalition fell apart following the death of Kuomintang leader Sun Yat-sen in 1925. Open warfare erupted between the two groups, and in 1934, Mao was forced to lead his followers to remote Shaanxi Province

Mao Zedong (right), leader of the Communist forces in the Chinese civil war (1946–1949).

to escape extermination at the hands of the Nationalists.

Japan's invasion of China in 1931 introduced a third element into the equation. As Mao's troops waged a guerrilla campaign against the Japanese, the Communists gradually consolidated their control over much of northern China. By the end of World War II in August 1945, the Chinese Communists had become the most effective political and military force on the mainland. In the ensuing civil war, Mao's forces defeated the corrupt, demoralized Nationalist armies, and by December 1949 they had emerged victorious, driving Chiang and his advisers to the offshore island of Formosa.

The Communist victory in China appalled Republican conservatives in Congress, particularly those who were members of the CHINA LOBBY, an informal coalition of politicians and businessmen who supported the Nationalist cause. The question of "who lost China" became an explosive political issue in the United States. Anti-Communist zealots assumed that Mao could never have won the Chinese civil war without the active assistance of Communist sympathizers in the U.S. Department of State who had betrayed the Nationalist cause. In the subsequent search for scapegoats, career Far East experts such as Owen LATTIMORE, John Carter VINCENT, Alger HISS, and John Stewart SERVICE came under suspicion of disloyalty. The Truman administration's release of the CHINA WHITE PAPER, a voluminous study of U.S.-Chinese relations from 1939 to 1949, did nothing to end the controversy.

For his part, Mao continued to govern China until his death in 1976. During the late 1950s and early 1960s, ideological and nationalistic differences between China and the Soviet Union widened and intensified into open hostility. Mao's later years were marred by the excesses of the Cultural Revolution, in part an attempt to recapture the zeal of the original revolutionary generation. In 1972, China reopened diplomatic relations with the United States. The historic occasion was highlighted by a meeting between Mao and President Richard NIXON, one of the most vocal anti-Communist crusaders of the McCarthy era.

**March, Fredric** (1897–1975) An extremely successful film actor, Fredric March (born Frederick McIntyre Bickel) was accused by right-wing Congressman Martin DIES in 1939 of promoting the cause of Communism in the United States.

After a moderately successful career on the stage, March appeared in his first motion picture in 1928 and subsequently won Best Actor Oscars in *Dr. Jekyll and Mr. Hyde* and *The Best Years of Our Lives.* He proved so popular at the box office that by 1937, he was listed by the Treasury Department as having the fifth-highest income of any individual in the United States.

In 1939, Representative Dies—then chairman of the HOUSE COMMITTEE ON UN-AMERICAN ACTIVITIES (HUAC)—investigated allegations of Communist influence in Hollywood. Because March had been one of the leading liberals in the motion picture industry during the 1930s, belonging to prolabor and civil-rights groups such as the short-lived Films for Democracy (established "to safeguard and extend American democracy"), the actor became one of Dies' primary targets. In an article that appeared in *Liberty* magazine on May 4, 1940, March re-

sponded to Dies' accusations of radicalism in the film community. "There are men of intelligence and good will everywhere," he wrote. "Perhaps Hollywood has a few more than her share. . . . It may be that some of us more guillible, 'highly overpaid' pariahs made a great mistake several years ago in joining an organization that set itself up to fight Nazism—and did fight it. It may be that its officers are in the pay of Moscow and get their orders directly from the Kremlin. Until proved 100 per cent wrong, I shall stand by my conviction that that is complete and utter bunk." Responding to the increasing pressure from anti-Communist crusaders in Congress in the late 1930s, March expressed his satisfaction that "there are a few of us dim-witted liberals who continue to put our necks out for what we hope will prove to be the Right—the side that the Men of Good Will are on." Dies later acknowledged that he had no evidence connecting March with Communist activities but reiterated his charge that March had contributed money and the use of his name to Communist-front organizations.

When HUAC returned to investigate Hollywood once again in 1947–48, March again took an outspoken position against the committee's work. He joined the COMMITTEE FOR THE FIRST AMENDMENT (CFA), formed to protest HUAC's decision to subpoena ten unfriendly witnesses in the fall of 1947, and later supported the Committee of One Thousand, the successor organization to the CFA.

March's career prospered despite his liberal convictions, however. In 1957, March won a Tony award for his portrayal of the alcoholic, tortured James Tyrone in Eugene O'Neill's play, *Long Day's Journey Into Night.*

**Marshall, George Catlett** (1880–1951) The first career U.S. Army officer to serve as secretary of state, George C. Marshall accumulated an extraordinary record of public service in both the military and civilian spheres. A descendant of Supreme Court Chief Justice John

Secretary of State George C. Marshall, a frequent target of anti-Communist zealots in the U.S. Congress.

Marshall, he was born in Uniontown, Pennsylvania. Although he knew from an early age that he wished to pursue a military career, Marshall was unable to obtain an appointment to the U.S. Military Academy at West Point primarily because his father, a coal industry executive, was a transplanted Kentucky Democrat in a Pennsylvania Republican district. Instead, he attended the Virginia Military Institute (VMI), where he graduated as senior first captain of the corps of cadets, while receiving all-conference honors as a tackle on the VMI football team.

Commissioned a second lieutenant in the Army in 1902, Marshall found the road to career advancement difficult because he had not attended West Point. He spent the next fifteen years in a variety of military posts: studying and subsequently serving as an instructor at the Army Staff College in Fort Leavenworth, Kansas; serving as a commander of U.S. forces

in the Philippines during the native rebellion of 1913–16; and as a staff officer at the Civilian Training Camp at Fort Douglas, Utah. During World War I, Marshall served as chief of operations of the First Army, which witnessed combat in the Meuse-Argonne sector, and as chief of staff of the Eighth Army Corps. Appointed aide-de-camp in May 1919 to General John J. "Black Jack" Pershing, who was sufficiently impressed that he described Marshall as "a man who understands military," Marshall helped design and obtain legislative approval of the National Defense Act, which was designed to prevent a recurrence of the woeful unpreparedness which had hampered the United States during the early months of World War I.

From 1924 to 1927, Marshall was assigned to the Fifteenth U.S. Infantry stationed in Tientsin, China. Upon his return to the United States, he became assistant commandant of the Infantry School at Fort Benning, Georgia, where he reorganized and modernized the antiquated curriculum. In 1938, Marshall—by that time a brigadier general—became assistant chief of staff in the War Plans Division, stationed in Washington, D.C. Promoted to the rank of general in September 1939, he was appointed chief of staff of the Army.

As the nation moved closer toward involvement in the European conflict that had erupted with the German occupation of Poland in September 1939, Marshall assisted President Franklin D. Roosevelt in guiding military preparedness legislation through Congress. During World War II, he served as the professional head of the U.S. military establishment, responsible only to the commander-in-chief. He also helped reorganize the Army into ground, air, and service forces; acted as Roosevelt's military adviser at conferences with allied leaders at Casablanca, Quebec, Cairo, Teheran, YALTA, and (with President Harry S. TRUMAN) Potsdam; served on the policy committee that supervised the atomic-weapons research at Los Alamos, New Mexico; and selected and promoted the field officers—including General Dwight David EISEN-

HOWER—who led the Allied armies to victory in 1945.

At his request, Marshall was released from duty as chief of staff in November 1945 and was subsequently appointed by Truman as special representative of the President to China with the personal rank of ambassador. In that role, he attempted to persuade the warring forces of Nationalist Chinese president CHIANG Kai-shek and Communist Chinese commander MAO Ze-dong to cease the civil war that had broken out in China following the defeat of the Japanese invaders in August 1945. "War," he noted, "is the most terrible tragedy of the human race and it should not be prolonged an hour longer than is absolutely necessary." Through the judicious use of threats and promises of American military and economic assistance, Marshall was able to obtain a brief cease-fire, but the truce was broken almost immediately by both sides.

Following his return to the United States, Marshall reported that the unification of China was being obstructed by extremists in both camps: a party of reactionaries in the Nationalist regime, and zealous Marxist ideologues in the Communist camp. He recommended that the United States attempt to bring about a reconciliation between the progressive elements within the Nationalist regime and the liberal democrats in the Communist fold who had joined Mao because of their disgust with the prevailing corruption and incompetence within Chiang's forces. Marshall also lamented the predominant influence of the military in Chinese politics, which he claimed "accentuates the weakness of civil Government in China." Although Marshall suggested that this coalition government should be headed by Chiang, his recommendation outraged the members of the pro-Chiang CHINA LOBBY in the United States, who opposed any accommodation with the Communists in China. As a means of persuading the two sides to reconcile their differences, Marshall withdrew virtually all American troops from China in January 1947.

In that same month, President Truman appointed Marshall to replace James F. Byrnes as secretary of state. Some political commentators assumed that Marshall might wish to run for president in 1948, but Marshall—who, like many American career military officers, had never voted in an election—stated that he did not wish to be considered for any public office. Certainly he had enough problems in the realm of foreign affairs to occupy his attention during his tenure at State. In February and March 1947, he helped formulate the Truman administration's response to the threat of a Communist takeover in Greece and Turkey; in an address on March 12 which came to be known as the Truman Doctrine, the President vowed to provide $400 million in aid to the two beleaguered nations to keep them from succumbing to Communist pressure.

At Harvard University's commencement exercises on June 3, 1947, Marshall delivered a speech that evolved into the policy known as the Marshall Plan, a program of massive American economic aid—ultimately totaling more than $25 billion—for European recovery. The social and political chaos resulting from World War II had left the nations of Europe vulnerable to totalitarian subversion, and Marshall vowed to use American resources to rebuild the shattered European economies. "Our policy is directed not against any country or doctrine, but against hunger, povery, desperation, and chaos," Marshall declared. "Its purpose should be the revival of a working economy in the world so as to permit the emergence of political and social conditions in which free institutions can exist."

At his own request, Marshall resigned as secretary of state in January 1949 at the end of Truman's first administration. For several months, he served as chairman of the Red Cross, but in the summer of 1949 Marshall agreed to return to government service as secretary of defense, on his condition that he would only stay for six months to a year. During his confirmation hearings, a number of conservative Republicans assailed Marshall for his role in the downfall of Chiang Kai-shek's Nationalist regime in China. (Chiang had resigned the presidency of China in January 1949 and had gone into seclusion.) Senator Robert TAFT, the Republican minority leader, stated that he felt a vote in favor of Marshall's nomination would be tantamount to an approval of a pro-Communist policy in the Far East. It was Senator William JENNER, however, who delivered the most violent anti-Marshall diatribe on the floor of the Senate. Charging that the Truman administration was engaged in an attempt to cover up "its bloody tracks of treason," Jenner stated that the appointment of Marshall was the Democratic Party's effort "to swallow up the treachery of the past in the new treachery they are planning for the future." "General Marshall is not only willing, he is eager to play the role of a front man for traitors," claimed Jenner. "The truth is this is no new role for him, for General George C. Marshall is a living lie. . . . Unless he himself were desperate, he could not possibly agree to continue as an errand boy, a front man, a stooge, or a conspirator for this Administration's crazy assortment of collectivist cutthroat crackpots and communist fellow-travelling appeasers."

Even Taft dissociated himself from Jenner's vituperative rhetoric. Still, fifteen Republican senators voted against Marshall's nomination, which cleared the Senate in September 1949. Six months later, Senator Joseph MCCARTHY of Wisconsin denounced Marshall publicly as "completely incompetent" and "completely unfit." Marshall, McCarthy claimed, had acquired his opinions about China by reading the works of Far East expert Owen LATTIMORE, whom McCarthy had identified in March 1950 as the top Russian spy in the United States.

Following President Truman's dismissal of General Douglas MACARTHUR in April 1951 as commander of the United Nations forces in the KOREAN WAR, McCarthy delivered a full-scale assault upon Marshall. Reading from a speech written primarily by a Washington journalist named Forrest Davis, McCarthy stood on the Senate floor for nearly three hours and inveighed against Marshall, whom he claimed was part of "a conspiracy on a scale so immense as to dwarf any previous such venture in the history of man. A conspiracy of infamy so black that, when it is finally exposed, its principals shall be forever deserving of the maledictions of all honest men." Although most observers agreed with conservative columnist Stewart Alsop, who wrote that McCarthy's charge "is so ridiculous that it may seem silly to discuss it seriously," the speech infuriated Eisenhower, then the leading candidate for the 1952 Republican presidential nomination. McCarthy's vicious attack upon Marshall also galvanized Connecticut Senator William BENTON into introducing a resolution requesting an investigation by the Senate into McCarthy's political and financial activities.

Eisenhower had an opportunity to defend Marshall during the presidential campaign the following year, but decided at the last moment—after meeting with McCarthy privately—to omit the forceful language recommended by his speechwriters. Eisenhower's retreat disillusioned many of his supporters (the candidate's aides referred to it as "the terrible day") and helped convince television news journalist Edward R. MURROW to begin to compile a film dossier on McCarthy for a later expose on the senator. Editorial cartoonist Herbert BLOCK responded to Eisenhower's failure to defend Marshall with a famous cartoon showing a neanderthallike McCarthy standing in a pool of vile filth, holding a sign that read "Anything to Win." Next to him stood a spotless Eisenhower, who explained to a voter that "our differences have nothing to do with the end result we are seeking."

The deteriorating climate of public life in the United States may have strengthened Marshall's determination to retire from office. At the request of President Truman, he had already stayed at Defense far longer than he originally had intended. Marshall resigned in September 1951 and returned to his home in Leesburg, Virginia. He died at Walter Reed Army Hospital eight years later, following a prolonged illness.

**Martin, Joseph W.** (1884–1968)   Speaker of the House of Representatives from 1947 to 1949 and 1951 to 1955, Joseph Martin first entered Congress in 1924. Although he maintained a staunchly conservative stance throughout his congressional career, Martin was known more as a Republican partisan than as a conservative ideologue. He earned a reputation for party loyalty through his support of the Republican administrations of Calvin Coolidge and Herbert Hoover and through his steadfast opposition to the New Deal initiatives of President Franklin Delano Roosevelt. During the congressional elections of 1946, Martin contributed to a Republican landslide by claiming that the Truman administration was infested with Communist sympathizers; the election of a Republican Congress, Martin claimed, was the only way to put an end to the "boring from within by subversionists high up in government."

When the new Republican-dominated Congress convened in January 1947, Martin became speaker of the House. In that role, he supported legislation to slash government spending, cut taxes, increase defense spending, restrict the power of labor unions through the TAFT-HARTLEY ACT, and strengthen the Truman administration's federal employee loyalty program. When Republican presidential candidate Thomas Dewey suffered a surprising defeat in the election of 1948, Martin realized that the moderate wing of the Republican Party had suffered a severe setback. To preserve his authority within Party councils, he accommodated himself to the ensuing pronounced drift to the right

Never a leader in the anti-Communist crusade, Martin did not hesitate to employ the passions aroused by such groups as the CHINA LOBBY to promote the interests of the Republican Party and his own personal political agenda. Frustrated by the Truman administration's un-

willingness to launch an aggressive offensive against the People's Republic of China during the KOREAN WAR, Martin wrote a private letter in February 1951 to General Douglas MACARTHUR, then serving as commander of the United Nations forces in Korea, asking MacArthur for his views on the issue. In his reply, MacArthur agreed that the battle against Communism in Korea was vital to American security interests. "If we lose the war to Communism in Asia," wrote MacArthur, "the fall of Europe is inevitable, win it and Europe most probably would avoid war and yet preserve freedom. . . . There is no substitute for victory." When Martin released MacArthur's letter to the press, Truman decided to remove MacArthur for insubordination. Stung by this insult to the general, Martin, along with a host of other Republican leaders in Congress, responded with a barrage of vitrolic rhetoric against the Truman administration. Following a meeting of the Republican leadership, Martin told reporters that he planned to launch a full-scale investigation of Truman's handling of the Korean War; moreover, he warned that he was considering the impeachment of numerous White House officials. "We might," Martin noted ominously, "want the impeachments of 1 or 50." Specifically, he attacked Secretary of Defense George Catlett MARSHALL, whom he denounced as an "appeaser." Martin subsequently invited MacArthur to address Congress and declared that the general's speech to the assembled legislators was one of the most emotional days of his life in public service.

Following the election of Dwight David EISENHOWER to the presidency in 1952, Martin loyally supported most of the Eisenhower administration's initiatives. He did, however, criticize Eisenhower for consenting to an armistice agreement in Korea that left the nation divided along much the same lines that it had been before the North Korean invasion of June 1950. For the most part, Martin chose not to get intimately involved in the struggle between the White House and Senator Joseph MCCARTHY in 1953–54; instead, he remained on the sidelines, waiting to heal the party's wounds following the Senate's censure of McCarthy in December 1954. Martin remained in Congress until 1960, when he decided not to run for reelection.

**McCarran, Patrick A.** (1876–1954) A native of Reno, Nevada, Patrick McCarran became one of Senator Joseph MCCARTHY's staunchest allies in Congress during the late 1940s and early 1950s. McCarran entered politics in 1903, when he was first elected to the Nevada state legislature. Two years later, he won election as Nye County district attorney and was appointed in 1912 to the Nevada state supreme court. McCarran contested longtime Senator Key Pittman's seat for the U.S. Senate in 1916 but lost overwhelmingly to the popular veteran legislator. Though he lost another Senate primary race in 1926, his perseverance finally paid off when he emerged victorious in his third attempt six years later.

McCarran was known throughout his career as a loner who operated outside the traditional system of party loyalties, without the support of a well-organized Democratic political machine. Shortly after he took his seat in the Senate and obtained a place on the poweful Judiciary and Appropriations committees, McCarran earned national headlines as one of the few Democrats to oppose virtually all of President Franklin D. Roosevelt's New Deal legislative initiatives. When Roosevelt, frustrated by the U.S. Supreme Court's rulings against the New Deal, attempted to circumvent the "nine old men," as he called them, by adding several more justices to the Court, McCarran helped lead the fight to defeat the President's court-packing plan. In foreign affairs, McCarran displayed a pronounced isolationist bias, opposing American involvement in the European war that began with Germany's invasion of Poland in September 1939.

Few people who encountered McCarran came away with neutral feelings about him. Strong-willed and caustic, he ran the powerful Senate Judiciary Committee with an iron hand. McCarran never hesitated to delay federal judiciary appointments to achieve his personal political objectives. He was able to defy the national leaders of the Democratic Party because he employed his patronage power adroitly and always managed to convince his constituents—the state's population was only about 160,000 in 1940—that he put their interests first, above the interests of the nation. McCarran's independence also stemmed from the support he received from Nevada's copper industry and organized gambling interests. By 1946, only five senators had more seniority than McCarran, and perhaps none enjoyed more power.

McCarran was also one of the most ultraconservative members of the Senate. He frequently praised Nationalist Chinese leader CHIANG Kai-shek and dictator Francisco Franco of Spain and lobbied so peristently for American aid to Franco that columnist Drew PEARSON labeled McCarran "the Senator from Madrid." McCarran's attacks upon organized labor and support for corporate business interests also earned him the nickname of "the Senator from Kennecott Copper." Certainly he was not generally well-respected outside Nevada. In 1950, *Time* magazine named him one of the Senate's "most expendable members," characterizing him as "pompous, vindictive and power grabbing," and former Secretary of the Interior Harold Ickes once called him "one of the most socially retarded members of the Senate" and claimed that "it is doubtful whether history, at least during this generation, could offer a rival to McCarran as the most undesirable member of the Senate."

Before 1950, McCarran's primary legislative contribution to the anti-Communist crusade was the McCarran-Walter Immigration Act, which established quotas that favored immigration from Northern and Western Europe, while severely restricting immigration from Southern and Eastern Europe. The measure also prohibited Communists from entering the United States.

When Senator McCarthy launched his attack against Communists in the federal government in February 1950, McCarran willingly joined forces with him. (Poet Archibald MacLeish immortalized their alliance in verse: "Says McCarran to McCarthy / What's platform or party / We sport the same feather / Let's fight this together. . . .") The two shared a committment to rid the United States of Communist influence, but their methods were entirely different. McCarthy employed a scattershot approach, firing off charges wildly with little or no evidence to support him, creating excitement among his admirers and confusion among his enemies, and then moving on to another case before the truth could catch up to him. McCarran, on the other hand, preferred to work within the traditional power structure of the Senate, largely because his chairmanship of the Judiciary Committee provided him with a firm grasp on the levers of authority.

McCarran had long favored some form of internal security legislation to strengthen the government's hand in its fight against Communist subversives. In 1948, he approved the Mundt-Nixon bill that required the registration of Communists—the premise of the bill was that the resulting publicity would sabotage any opportunities for subversion—but that measure died without the Senate taking any definitive action on it. The outbreak of the KOREAN WAR in June 1950 significantly altered the political environment, however, and created a consensus for action on internal security legislation within the Senate. On August 10, McCarran introduced a bill known as S.4037, later referred to as the INTERNAL SECURITY ACT OF 1950 (and popularly known as the MCCARRAN ACT), which combined a revised version of the Mundt-Nixon bill with several provisions proposed by McCarran.

McCarran argued that the bill was essential to "fortify the home front even as we are today fortifying our boys on the battlefield of Korea." Based upon the premise that the Communist movement in the United States consisted of "thousands of adherents, rigidly and ruthlessly disciplined" who were awaiting an opportunity to overthrow the government by force and vio-

lence, the Internal Security Act required the COMMUNIST PARTY and Communist-front organizations to register with a newly established five-person Subversive Activities Control Board. The measure did not, however, outlaw the Communist Party, a tactic which FBI Director J. Edgar HOOVER had long opposed because he feared it would drive the Party underground and render surveillance of its activities more difficult.

A group of liberal Senate Democrats who were weary of Republican charges that they were "soft" on Communism attempted to outflank McCarran by proposing their own internal security measure, which included a provision for placing suspected subversives in detention camps in times of national emergency. Placed in the unusual position of defending American civil liberties, McCarran opposed the Democratic alternative, claiming that it violated the Fifth, Sixth, and possibly the Thirteenth Amendments and that it was clearly "not workable under any of the accepted standards of Americanism." In the end, the Senate combined the detention camp provisions of the Democratic bill with the McCarran legislation and passed the entire measure unanimously. President Truman vetoed the bill, but Congress easily overrode the veto.

When the Senate authorized the Judiciary Committee in December 1950 to organize another subcommittee to investigate subversion, the committee established the Internal Security Subcommittee, with McCarran as its chairman. One of McCarran's top priorities was to continue the investigation of Communist influence in the State Department that his ally McCarthy had begun. On Feburary 10, 1951, McCarran's subcommittee announced that it had obtained thousands of documents belonging to the INSTITUTE FOR PACIFIC RELATIONS from file cabinets located in a barn outside the town of Lee, Massachusetts, where the institute had placed them for storage. Although there was nothing in the material to justify McCarthy's gleeful accusations that the barn had served as a center for Soviet espionage activities in the United

States, McCarran—a dedicated member of the pro-Nationalist CHINA LOBBY—used the documents to launch new attacks upon the Truman administration's Far East policies.

From July 1951 through June 1952, the Internal Security Subcommittee held hearings on the Institute for Pacific Relations, searching for evidence that the institute had turned American policy to the Communists' advantage. The highlight of its investigation was the appearance of Owen LATTIMORE, author and Johns Hopkins University professor, whom McCarthy had earlier identified as the "top Russian espionage agent in the United States." McCarran kept Lattimore on the witness stand for twelve days, questioning him closely on discrepancies between his testimony and the documentary record. The two men clearly disliked each other, and their exchanges were marked by frequent insults; at the end, McCarran described Lattimore's behavior on the stand as "flagrantly defiant . . . consistently evasive, contentious, and belligerent . . . insolent, overbearing, arrogant, and disdainful." Under McCarran's relentless questioning, Lattimore made numerous errors in recollection, thereby lending credence to McCarthy's charges. In its final report on the institute, the subcommittee found that Owen Lattimore (who had edited the institute's journal, *Pacific Affairs*) had been "a conscious articulate instrument of the Soviet conspiracy." McCarran continued his personal vendetta against Lattimore by pressuring the Justice Department to pursue a perjury indictment against him. (McCarran held up the nomination of James McGranary as Attorney General until the administration complied.) Eventually the perjury case collapsed in the courts for lack of evidence.

Beyond its hearings on Lattimore and the institute, McCarran's subcommittee also investigated Communist infiltration of youth organizations in the United States, subversive influence in the entertainment industry, unauthorized travel of suspected Communists in Eastern Europe on U.S. passports, Communist control of the United Public Workers of America, subversive aliens in the United States, Communist infiltration of the telegraph industry, and espionage in embassies and consultates of Communist-dominated nations in the United States. McCarran also called veteran foreign-service officer John Paton DAVIES to testify about his role in formulating U.S. Far East policy and subsequently suggested that Davies, too, had perjured himself in his testimony. Not surprisingly, McCarran was one of the few Democrats to vote with McCarthy in opposition to the Eisenhower administration's appointment of Charles BOHLEN as ambassador to the Soviet Union in March 1954.

When Senator Ralph FLANDERS of Vermont introduced a motion of censure against McCarthy in June 1954, McCarran remained one of McCarthy's most vocal supporters. Before the motion came to a vote in the Senate, however, McCarran died of a heart attack on September 28 during a campaign tour through Nevada.

**McCarran Act**   See INTERNAL SECURITY ACT.

**McCarthy, Joseph R.** (1908–1957)   One of the most controversial figures in American twentieth-century political history, Joseph R. McCarthy was a relatively unknown U.S. senator from Wisconsin who became the leading spokesman of the postwar anti-Communist crusade in 1950–54. Historians have been divided in their assessment of McCarthy's sincerity in adopting a zealous anti-Communist stance, but no one doubts that he had more impact upon American political affairs than any other public figure during the early 1950s.

A native of Wisconsin, McCarthy was born on a farm to Irish-American, Roman Catholic parents who eked out a living in the northeastern corner of the state. Those who knew him during his childhood years agree that McCarthy was a shy and withdrawn boy who clung to his mother. He attended a one-room schoolhouse but did not receive his high school diploma until

Joseph R. McCarthy.

he was well into his twenties. In the summer of 1929, McCarthy left home to manage a grocery store in the town of Manawa, Wisconsin, which seems to have transformed him completely into an outgoing, boisterous, almost excessively aggressive young man. Upon his return to school several months later, he worked so diligently that he completed his high school requirements in a single year. Entering Marquette University in the fall of 1930 and graduating five years later with a degree in law, McCarthy then spent the next three years in private practice in the Appleton, Wisconsin, area.

In 1938, McCarthy decided to run for the position of judge on the tenth circuit court. This was not his first foray into politics; in 1936, he had come in second—running as a Democrat—in a race for district attorney. This time, he threw himself into the campaign as if he had an unlimited store of energy: he crossed the state repeatedly, meeting voters informally and making speeches wherever possible, spreading his slogan of "Justice Is Truth in Action," and achieving a remarkable level of visibility for a candidate for a judicial post. The hard work paid off; McCarthy won the election by more than 4,000 votes.

McCarthy's service on the bench was less than exemplary. Displaying the lack of regard for tradition and established procedure that would characterize his entire political life, he raced through a backlog of cases and continued to set a hectic pace throughout his term. At one point, the Wisconsin Supreme Court cited him for "highly improper" behavior for destroying the transcript of a trial to prevent the higher court from reviewing his conduct of the case.

Shortly after the United States entered World War II in December 1941, McCarthy enlisted in the U.S. Marines. He was dispatched to the Pacific but saw little action in combat. His idleness did not prevent him from attracting publicity to himself by such press-pleasing stunts as firing off 4,700 rounds of ammunition from the back seat of a grounded bomber. McCarthy proudly informed the Appleton, Wisconsin, newspaper that he had been wounded in action, although the story was entirely fictitious. Bored by life in the service and eager to return to the political fray, McCarthy ignored a number of military regulations and Wisconsin statutes prohibiting members of the armed services and judges from running for political office and began a drive to obtain the state's Republican senatorial nomination in 1944. (It was not clear when McCarthy became a Republican, but certainly the change in party affiliation gave him an advantage in a state with a significant Republican majority of voters.) Again he threw himself into the campaign with a frenzy. This time, however, McCarthy was up against veteran Republican Senator Alexander H. Wiley, who had considerable appeal to both Republicans and Democrats. McCarthy fell far short in the primary balloting, though he did manage to garner more than 75,000 votes and a substantial measure of publicity.

Two years later, McCarthy again launched a campaign for the U.S. Senate. This time, his opponent was Robert M. La Follette, Jr., who had served in the Senate since 1925. La Follette, however, had become aloof and unresponsive to the state's electorate, spending most of his time in Washington and seldom listening to the local concerns of his constituents. In the ensuing primary campaign, McCarthy campaigned against the Roosevelt-Truman record, which La Follette had supported, criticizing the New Deal for excessive government regulation of American life and appealing to voters who wanted to return to the simpler, less troubled, more secure world they had known before the Great Depression. When La Follette failed to obtain sufficient crossover support from Democratic labor unions, McCarthy emerged victorious by a narrow margin. In the general election in November 1946, McCarthy raised for the first time the issue of Communism in government by painting his Democratic opponent as "communistically inclined," and a "megaphone being used by the Communist-controlled" political-action committee. The strategy of labeling Democrats as Communists was hardly original or unique to McCarthy, however; similar tactics were used during the 1946 campaigns by Republican candidates across the United States. In the same manner, his victory in the general election was part of a nationwide reaction against fourteen years of Democratic rule in the White House and Congress.

As a freshman senator of the "Class of 1946," McCarthy did nothing to endear himself to his older colleagues in the Senate. He followed a conservative line on domestic affairs, opposing price and rent controls and supporting the anti–labor-union TAFT-HARTLEY ACT. In foreign affairs, McCarthy generally adopted an internationalist approach, favoring the Marshall Plan to rebuild the shattered economies of Western Europe, and supporting the establishment of the North Atlantic Treaty Organization (NATO).

What irritated the Republican Party establishment was his disregard for the unwritten rules and customs of the Senate. McCarthy continually reduced disagreements over policy to personal attacks upon his opponents, often imputing unsavory motives to their actions. He regularly employed harsh, vituperative rhetoric and displayed a stunning disregard for truth whenever the facts stood in the way of his objective.

Consequently, McCarthy found himself shorn of all major committee assignments when the eightieth Congress convened in January 1949. He obtained publicity only by his attack upon the U.S. Army's handling of the so-called "Malmedy Massacre" incident. Late in 1944, during the Battle of the Bulge, German SS guards had murdered hundreds of American prisoners and Belgian civilians behind the lines near the small town of Malmedy. A war crimes court convicted seventy-three SS troopers and sentenced more than forty of them to death; the German defendants appealed to the Supreme Court, claiming that their confessions had been obtained under duress. In the ensuing controversy, McCarthy took up the cause of the convicted German troopers and attacked the U.S. Army's handling of the case. McCarthy's interest in the incident earned him a spot on the Senate subcommittee formed to investigate the Malmedy affair. His conduct on the subcommittee was so obnoxious, however, that the chairman of the subcommittee, Senator Raymond Baldwin of Connecticut, decided to resign from political life altogether.

Meanwhile, McCarthy was experiencing personal financial difficulties and was locked in a battle with the Wisconsin State Department of Taxation over his income tax returns. He had also nearly been disbarred by the Wisconsin State Board of Bar Commissioners for violating in 1944 and 1946 the prohibition against running for political office while retaining his judgeship. His deteriorating relationship with the Senate leadership and his dwindling base of support among his constituents in Wisconsin made McCarthy desperate for a new issue to attract favorable publicity.

On the evening of January 7, 1950, McCarthy found that issue. During the course of a dinner at the Colony Restaurant in downtown Washington, Edmund A. Walsh, dean of the Georgetown School of Foreign Service, suggested that McCarthy take up the growing controversy over Communist influence in the United States. "The government is full of Communists," McCarthy reportedly replied. "The thing to do is hammer at them."

McCarthy launched his crusade against Communists in the federal government on Feburary 9, 1950, during the course of a Lincoln Day speech to the Republican Women's Club in Wheeling, West Virginia. His initial target was the Department of State, which had already been the subject of attacks by conservative Republicans in Congress during the late 1940s. Although no tape recording or verbatim transcript of the Lincoln Day speech exists, reporters who were present at the event claim that McCarthy said, "I have here in my hand a list of 205— a list of names that were made known to the Secretary of State as being members of the Communist Party and who nevertheless are still working and shaping policy in the State Department." Clearly, McCarthy had no list. Nor was the speech in any sense original. McCarthy had simply cut out excerpts from a speech by Representative Richard NIXON, testimony before the Senate Judiciary Committee, and several news articles, and pasted them together.

Press reaction to McCarthy's original charge was muted, and yet there was a larger pool of reporters waiting for McCarthy at his next stop, in Salt Lake City, Utah. There, McCarthy informed reporters that he could not show them the list of Communists in the State Department because he had left it in his baggage on the plane. Nevertheless, he assured his listeners in Salt Lake City that there were 57 "card-carrying Communists" in the State Department, as well as 205 "bad risks." Critics and defenders of McCarthy would argue—and still argue—over the precise numbers and language he used on these occasions and the precise nature of his allegations.

Whatever figures McCarthy had employed, his speeches gave him the attention he had so desperately sought. The Senate established a subcommittee, under the leadership of Maryland Democrat Millard TYDINGS, to investigate McCarthy's charges. Since McCarthy had virtually no evidence to support his initial allegations, he turned to right-wing sources to provide him with names and details. FBI Director J. Edgar HOOVER, who had been furious with McCarthy for making reckless accusations that could discredit the entire anti-Communist crusade, ordered his subordinates to provide McCarthy with any material from FBI files that might prove helpful to the senator. Hoover also dispatched a former bureau investigator, Donald A. Surine, to McCarthy to help him gather incriminating data on possible subversives in the State Department. Meanwhile, millionaire industrialist Alfred KOHLBERG, the head of the CHINA LOBBY—an informal coalition of politicians and businessmen who were ardent supporters of Nationalist Chinese leader CHIANG Kai-shek—met with McCarthy and pledged his support. Kohlberg had long been convinced that Communist sympathizers in the Department of State had subverted the Nationalist cause on the mainland of China, and he viewed McCarthy as a means of finally striking at his adversaries.

The Tydings subcommittee began its hearings on March 8. McCarthy was the first witness. He began by reading through a list of alleged subversives, providing the Senate with details that consisted primarily of rumor and innuendo. At first, Tydings interrupted McCarthy's monologue frequently with questions and requests for elucidation; fearful that the public might perceive his questioning as badgering, however, Tydings soon decided to permit McCarthy to present his case unhindered. On March 13, McCarthy suddenly introduced the name of Owen LATTIMORE into the proceedings when he informed the Tydings subcommittee that Lattimore—whom he claimed was "one of the principal architects of our Far Eastern policy"— was "pro-Communist" and "an extremely bad security risk." Eight days later, McCarthy elaborated on his charges and informed the subcommittee in executive session that Lattimore was "the top Russian espionage agent in the country." "If you crack this case," McCarthy assured his colleagues, "it will be the biggest espionage case in the history of this country." Although McCarthy's accusations against Lattimore were subsequently supported in large measure by ex-Communist Louis BUDENZ, Lattimore appeared before the committee and refuted the charges convincingly.

Others whom McCarthy accused of Communist sympathies included New York attorney Dorothy KENYON and veteran diplomat Philip JESSUP, both of whom were able to convince the subcommittee that they had no affiliation with the COMMUNIST PARTY or any Communist front organization. By that time, however, McCarthy had moved on to present other dozens of cases to the subcommittee and the press. This technique became McCarthy's trademark: repeatedly he made accusations of subversion or disloyalty against individuals and then went on to different cases before those who had been accused could respond or defend themselves.

In its report, released on July 17, 1950, a majority of the Tydings subcommittee stated that McCarthy's allegations were nothing more than "a fraud and a hoax perpetrated on the Senate of the United States and the American people. They represent perhaps the most nefarious campaign of half-truths and untruth in the history of this Republic." For his part, President Harry S. TRUMAN told reporters that McCarthy was nothing more than "a ballyhoo artist who has to cover up his shortcomings by wild charges." "I think," Truman added, "the greatest asset that the Kremlin has is Senator McCarthy." Nevertheless, the Tydings subcommittee hearings had provided McCarthy with an immense amount of publicity, and the Wisconsin senator's office was flooded each day with telegrams and letters from admirers, frequently accompanied by monetary contributions to aid the fight against Communism. His attacks upon the State Department and the "bright young men who are born with silver spoons in their mouths" earned him the support of millions of Americans who had become disillusioned with the domestic and international results of nearly two decades of Democratic rule in Washington.

The outbreak of the KOREAN WAR in June 1950 heightened tensions between American liberals and the growing legions of anti-Communist zealots who blamed the conflict on the Truman administration's alleged unwillingness to take a firm stand against the spread of Communism in the Far East. McCarthy selected as his primary targets Secretary of State Dean ACHESON and Secretary of Defense George C. MARSHALL, who had also served as chief of staff of the U.S. Army during World War II, and as secretary of state in the first Truman administration. Following Truman's dismissal of General Douglas MACARTHUR in April 1951 as commander of the United Nations forces in Korea, McCarthy delivered a full-scale attack upon Marshall that represented one of the most vicious assaults upon any figure in American public life in modern times. During a three-hour speech, he claimed that Marshall—whom he had previously characterized as "completely incompetent" and "completely unfit"—was part of "a conspiracy on a scale so immense as to dwarf any previous such venture in the history of man. A conspiracy of infamy so black that, when it is finally exposed, its principals shall be forever deserving of the maledictions of all honest men."

It was this sort of character assassination (delivered under cover of senatorial immunity against the laws of libel), combined with evidence of financial impropriety, that prompted Senator William BENTON, a Democrat from Connecticut, to submit a resolution in August 1951 calling upon the Senate Rules Committee to launch an investigation into McCarthy's activities, to determine whether he should be expelled from the Senate. "In my opinion," declared Benton, "Senator McCarthy has weakened the respect of decent people for representative government by his attacks upon the character of respectable citizens from the sanctuary of the Senate floor." McCarthy responded in typical fashion, claiming that "Senator Benton has established himself as the hero of every Communist and crook in and out of government." The Senate referred Benton's resolution to a subcommittee headed by Senator Guy Gillette of Iowa. During the ensuing inquiry, McCarthy repeatedly assailed the integrity and motives of the members of the subcommittee. By the end of 1952, the investigation had struggled to an inconclusive end. The subcommittee's final report, issued on January 2, 1953, contained considerable evidence suggesting that McCarthy had engaged in highly questionable financial and political practices and condemned him for deliberately attempting "to thwart any investigation of him by obscuring the real issue and responsibility of the subcommittee by charges of lack of jurisdiction, smear, and Communist-inspired persecution." Yet, the subcommittee failed to recommend any specific action against McCarthy.

When the Republicans regained control of the Senate in the elections of 1952, McCarthy was awarded the chairmanship of the GOVERNMENT OPERATIONS COMMITTEE, as well as the chairmanship of the committee's PERMANENT SUBCOMMITTEE ON INVESTIGATIONS. From those posts he could continue to press forward his inquiries with a relatively free hand, without the responsibility of overseeing one of the larger, legislation-oriented committees. Anyone who expected him to subordinate his crusade to the dictates of party loyalty now that a Republican— Dwight David EISENHOWER—had taken up residence in the White House sorely misjudged the Wisconsin senator. When reporters asked him what had been his main difficulty with the Truman administration in uncovering evidence of disloyalty, McCarthy replied that "the principal hurdle has been the complete, wholehearted opposition from the President on down, the entire Administration, their attempt to protect, to cover up, and their complete refusal to recognize the evidence of subversives when you give it to him." Reporters then asked McCarthy if he intended to continue the search for subver-

sives in government with a Republican administration in power. "Very definitely," McCarthy replied.

Certainly, Eisenhower had little respect for McCarthy or his methods; yet, Eisenhower refused to confront McCarthy directly. "I just will not—I refuse—to get into the gutter with that guy," he told his advisers. As a result, McCarthy became increasingly contemptuous of the Republican leadership in 1953–54. Shortly after Eisenhower took office, McCarthy confronted the President directly over the nomination of Charles BOHLEN—one of Roosevelt's advisers at the YALTA Conference—as U.S. ambassador to the Soviet Union. Bohlen was eventually confirmed, but by campaigning vigorously against the nomination, McCarthy had served notice on the White House that he would not allow the claims of party loyalty to dissuade him from his anti-Communist crusade.

McCarthy subsequently threatened the administration with an investigation of the CENTRAL INTELLIGENCE AGENCY (CIA), which he claimed had been infiltrated by Soviet espionage agents. Vice President Richard Nixon eventually persuaded McCarthy to abandon his inquiry of the CIA, but only at the price of a purge of the agency's personnel. McCarthy then embarked upon an investigation of the INTERNATIONAL INFORMATION AGENCY (IIA), a branch of the State Department that operated the VOICE OF AMERICA as well as dozens of libraries overseas. Claiming that the IIA libraries contained books written by Communists or Communist sympathizers, McCarthy dispatched two of his assistants, Roy COHN and G. David SCHINE, on a tour of Europe to view firsthand the contents of the library shelves. Cohn and Schine disgraced themselves by their raucous behavior on the tour, and the sight of American officials actually burning or destroying books caused such an uproar that Eisenhower found it necessary to issue a statement in defense of intellectual freedom at the commencement exercises at DARTMOUTH COLLEGE in June 1953. At a press conference several days later, however, Eisenhower pointedly refused to name McCarthy as the source of the book-burning controversy.

The climatic confrontation between McCarthy and the Eisenhower administration occurred in the spring of 1954 when McCarthy launched his inquiry into Communist influence in the U.S. Army. For the last several months of 1953, McCarthy had pressed Army officials for access to the Army's confidential files on security and loyalty. Specifically, McCarthy wanted to investigate allegations of espionage among civilian scientists at the Army Signal Corps Engineering Laboratories at FORT MONMOUTH, New Jersey, but few observers believed McCarthy would limit his inquiry to any one locale. Meanwhile, McCarthy's assistant, G. David Schine, had been drafted by the Army, and McCarthy and Cohn had also been pressuring Secretary of the Army Robert T. STEVENS to obtain preferential treatment for Schine. Then, in Feburary 1954, McCarthy learned that an Army dentist, Irving PERESS, had been promoted to the rank of major—following the provisions of the Doctor Draft Law—despite Peress' refusal to answer questions regarding his political beliefs. Peress' invocation of the Fifth Amendment led McCarthy to assume that he was, or had been a Communist, and the senator proclaimed his intention to discover "who promoted Peress." (By that time, Peress had received an early discharge from the Army, but his departure from the service did not dampen McCarthy's ardor to discover who had been responsible for promoting him in the first place.)

McCarthy questioned Brigadier General Ralph ZWICKER on February 18 and insisted that Zwicker provide him with the names of all officers involved in the Peress affair. When Zwicker refused to divulge the names, on the grounds of executive privilege, the senator flew into a rage, shouting that Zwicker was "not fit to wear that uniform" and did not have "the brains of a five-year-old." Secretary of the Army Stevens subsequently ordered Zwicker to stay away from McCarthy's subcommittee. "Just go ahead ahead and try it," McCarthy warned Ste-

vens. "I am going to kick the brains out of anyone who protects Communists! . . . You just go ahead. I will guarantee you that you will live to regret it."

The tangled controversies between the Army and McCarthy were finally resolved during the ARMY-MCCARTHY HEARINGS, which opened on April 22, 1954. The hearings were conducted by the Permanent Subcommittee on Investigations, which normally would have been chaired by McCarthy. Because McCarthy was both the accuser and the defendant in the controversy, however, Senator Karl MUNDT of South Dakota was appointed chairman for the duration of the hearings. Television networks carried the hearings live, which provided millions of Americans with their first opportunity to witness McCarthy's bullying tactics firsthand.

McCarthy's primary antagonist during the hearings was Joseph WELCH, a 63-year-old attorney from Boston who had been named chief counsel for the Army. Welch displayed a dry wit and an avuncular disposition that contrasted sharply with McCarthy's aggressive, blustering image. Part of Welch's strategy was to anger McCarthy, to make the senator lose his temper and commit a tactical blunder that Welch could use to discredit him; by the middle of May, Welch had clearly succeeded in irritating him. The most dramatic confrontation between the two men occurred on June 9, when McCarthy—in an attempt to obtain revenge for the needling of Welch—announced on national television that an associate in Welch's law firm of Hale & Dorr had belonged to the NATIONAL LAWYERS GUILD, which, according to McCarthy, had been identified as "the legal bulwark of the Communist Party." Welch sat disconsolately through McCarthy's diatribe against the young attorney; when he finally composed himself sufficiently to reply, Welch spoke with a measure of sadness and weariness in his voice. "Until this moment, Senator," he said, "I think I never really gauged your cruelty or your recklessness." McCarthy tried to interrupt, but Welch cut him off. "Let us not assassinate this lad further, Senator. You have done enough. Have you no sense of decency, sir, at long last? Have you no sense of decency?"

The incident marked a turning point in McCarthy's fortunes. Although members of the Republican Party had begun to desert McCarthy in the previous weeks, the televised spectacle of the hearings had provided the public with an intimate and ultimately disturbing glimpse into McCarthy's method of operations. At the conclusion of the hearings, President Eisenhower invited Welch to the White House to congratulate him personally.

McCarthy had gone too far, had violated too many rules, and alienated too many of his colleagues in the Senate. On July 20, Senator Ralph FLANDERS, a Republican from Vermont, introduced a resolution calling upon the Senate to censure McCarthy for his actions. On August 2, the Senate voted to refer the question of disciplining him to a six-member select subcommittee that would make recommendations to the entire Senate. The subcommittee was chaired by Senator Arthur WATKINS of Utah, a Republican with an impeccable reputation for honesty and integrity. Specifically, the subcommittee decided to investigate five separate categories of charges against the junior senator from Wisconsin: McCarthy's treatment of the Gillette committee in 1952–53; his invitation to government employees to circumvent the bureaucratic chain of command and provide him personally with classified information that might provide evidence of disloyalty or subversion; his possession of a document during the Army-McCarthy hearings that purported to be a classified letter from J. Edgar Hoover; his verbal "abuses" against several of his colleague in the Senate; and his vituperative attack upon General Zwicker. McCarthy attempted to disrupt the subcommittee's hearings and lead it toward investigations of his critics, but Watkins refused to allow any disruption of the proceedings. On September 27, 1954, the Watkins committee issued its report, recommending that McCarthy be censured for his abusive treatment of other senators and General Zwicker.

After its receipt of the subcommittee's report, the full Senate began to debate the censure resolution on November 8. By this time, McCarthy had lost much of his support among the American public, even among conservative voters. Senate Majority Leader William KNOWLAND of California, under intense pressure from the White House, gradually assembled a sizable bloc of Republican senators in favor of censure. For his part, Minority Leader Lyndon JOHNSON adroitly kept the Democratic bloc in the Senate together by refusing to pressure any senator to vote either for or against censure. On December 2, 1954, the Senate voted 67–22 to condemn McCarthy for contempt and abuse. When reporters asked for his reaction to the Senate's action, McCarthy replied, "Well, it wasn't exactly a vote of confidence."

Although he appeared undaunted by the Senate's condemnation, McCarthy never recovered from the setback. His spirit was broken; always known as a heavy drinker, McCarthy turned to alcohol for solace with increasing frequency. The White House pointedly ignored him, refusing to invite him for conferences with the rest of the Republican leadership. The press, too, began to ignore McCarthy, and the lack of publicity hastened his emotional and physical decline. In the summer of 1956, McCarthy had to be hospitalized several times for detoxification. On April 28, 1957, McCarthy was admitted to Bethesda Naval Hospital with a severe liver ailment caused primarily by excessive consumption of alcohol. Four days later he died, at the age of 49.

**"McCarthyism"** "McCarthyism" was a term first used by Herbert BLOCK in an editorial cartoon in March 1950. Block, the editorial cartoonist for the *Washington Post,* pictured right-wing Republican leaders dragging a reluctant elephant (the cartoonist's symbol for the Republican Party) toward a wavering stack of buckets filled with a dark, tarry substance. Atop the column sat a barrel labeled "McCarthyism." "You mean I'm supposed to stand on that?" asked the incredulous elephant in the caption.

The first appearance of the term in a dictionary occurred in August 1954, when the *American College Dictionary* defined *McCarthyism* as "(1) public accusation of disloyalty . . . unsupported by truth, (2) unfairness in investigative technique."

**McLeod, Scott** (1914–1961)  The top official in the U.S. Department of State's Bureau of Security and Consular Affairs from 1953 to 1957, Scott McLeod inaugurated stricter security and loyalty requirements for State Department employees during the first four years of the Eisenhower administration. Frequently the subject of considerable controversy, McLeod was also accused of forwarding confidential personnel information to Senator Joseph MCCARTHY of Wisconsin to aid the senator in his hunt for Communist sympathizers in the federal government.

A native of Iowa, McLeod pursued a career in reporting before joining the FEDERAL BUREAU OF INVESTIGATION as an agent in 1942. Seven years later, McLeod accepted a position as administrative assistant to Senator Styles BRIDGES, a conservative Republican from New Hampshire. In 1953, McLeod was named chief State Department security officer by Secretary of State John Foster DULLES, who hoped that McLeod could keep the Eisenhower administration clear of the sort of personnel scandals (such as the case of former State Department official Alger HISS) that had damaged President Harry S. TRUMAN.

An avowed conservative, McLeod plunged into his assignment with more vigor than Dulles had expected. One of his first reports questioned the loyalty of Charles BOHLEN, whom Eisenhower had nominated as U.S. ambassador to the Soviet Union. When Dulles decided to maintain his support of Bohlen's nomination,

Scott McLeod, the State Department security chief whose aggressive style alienated moderates and liberals in Washington.

McLeod continued to work behind the scenes to sabotage the nomination. Dulles briefly considered dismissing McLeod but decided that the presence of such a zealous security officer could help deflect criticism of the State Department by McCarthy and his allies. Besides, as President Dwight David EISENHOWER pointed out, the dismissal of McLeod in the emotionally charged atmosphere of mid-1953 would have caused "a great big stink."

For the following four years, McLeod and his subordinates instilled an atmosphere of suspicion and distrust within the State Department. He urged the dismissal on security grounds of scores of employees, most of whom resigned voluntarily rather than endure a formal hearing. McLeod's aggressive tactics engendered considerable resentment, and critics accused him of leaking confidential personnel information to McCarthy to fuel the senator's highly-publicized crusade against Communist infiltration of the federal government. (McLeod reportedly kept a photograph of McCarthy on his desk, with McCarthy's signature above the inscription, "To a Great American.") Finally even Dulles recognized that McLeod was damaging the reputation of the foreign service, and in October 1954 he moved to restrict McLeod's authority.

In 1957, Eisenhower named McLeod ambassador to Ireland, a nomination which drew unusually heavy opposition among senators who still resented McLeod's activities as head of State Department security. Nevertheless, the full Senate approved the nomination, and McLeod served effectively in that post for four years. He resigned following the inauguration of President John F. KENNEDY in 1961 and died of a heart attack in November of that year.

## Meiklejohn, Alexander (1872–1964)

The son of a Scottish laborer, educator Alexander Meiklejohn became one of the strongest advocates of academic freedom in the United States during the McCarthy era.

Born in England and an emigré to the United States with his family when he was eight years old, Meiklejohn completed his undergraduate studies at Brown University and received a Ph.D. in philosophy from Cornell University in 1897. While teaching philosophy and metaphysics at Brown, Meiklejohn acquired a reputation as an educator who insisted that his students critically reexamine a society's traditional verities. From 1891 to 1912, he served as dean at Brown University; he subsequently accepted an appointment to the presidency of Amherst College, where he remained until 1924. After leaving Amherst, Meiklejohn helped found the Experimental College of the University of Wisconsin, where he attempted to create an intellectual community on the model of ancient Athens: he and his colleagues replaced lectures with discussions, eliminated examinations and grades, shared living quarters with students, and min-

Alexander Meikeljohn, defender of academic freedoms.

gled with them at social affairs. In 1938, he retired from Wisconsin as professor emeritus.

Throughout the 1940s and 1950s, Meiklejohn consistently opposed efforts by anti-Communist zealots to stifle academic independence and free speech in the United States. When conservative members of the AMERICAN CIVIL LIBERTIES UNION sought to dismiss Elizabeth Gurley Flynn from its executive board in 1940 because she belonged to the COMMUNIST PARTY, Meiklejohn opposed the action and fought to keep the organization open to Americans of all political persuasions unless they had been convicted of "concrete or verifiable" disloyalty. An idealist in foreign policy, he urged the Western democracies during World War II to stop trying to hold back the new world that "has long seemed powerless to be born." "Can we organize a world society on the principle of human brotherhood?" he asked. "I am sure that we can at least try."

As the hunt for Communists in the United States gathered momentum in 1947, Meiklejohn rejected the notion that there existed a "clear and present danger" that justified infringements on the First Amendment. Indeed, Meiklejohn argued that any danger of subversion that did exist made frank and open criticism of American society more imperative than ever. "The danger of political suppression is greater than the danger of political freedom," he insisted. "Repression is always foolish, freedom is always wise."

In the field of education, Meiklejohn feared that purges of instructors who uttered unpopular opinions in public schools would destroy academic freedom and intellectual honesty in the United States. In a widely publicized debate with Dr. Sidney Hook of New York University, Meiklejohn upheld the right of Communists to teach in American schools. The key to combating Communism, Meiklejohn believed, was the free discussion of political ideals. "Whenever, in the field of ideas, the advocates of freedom and the advocate of suppression meet in fair and unabridged discussion," Meiklejohn predicted, "freedom will win. If that were not true, if the intellectual program of democracy could not hold its own in fair debate, then that program itself would require of us its own abandonment. That chance we believers in self-government have determined to take. We have put our faith in democracy." Meiklejohn also scoffed at the popular view of Communist Party members as ideological slaves of Moscow. If party members were wholly incapable of independent thought, he asked, one would be unable to explain widespread resignations from the party when Moscow changed its policy.

When the actors and directors who became known as the HOLLYWOOD TEN were charged with contempt of Congress in the autumn of 1947, Meiklejohn openly supported their legal battle to stay out of prison. On their behalf, he wrote an amicus curiae (friend of the court) brief that was submitted to both the district court and the court of appeals. Nevertheless, the

Ten were convicted and sentenced to six to twelve months in jail. Meiklejohn subsequently joined with other advocates of academic and artistic freedom to form the National Committee to Abolish the House Un-Activities Affairs Committee. "The only way to fight Communism," he insisted, "is to let it speak itself out. That's true not simply of Communism, it's the only way to fight anything."

In December 1963, after the furor over Communism in America had subsided, Meiklejohn's lifelong dedication to the principles of American democracy were recognized when President Lyndon B. JOHNSON awarded him the prestigious Medal of Freedom. He died of pneumonia one year later.

## Menjou, Adolphe (1890–1963)

A leading member of the anti-Communist community in Hollywood during the late 1940s, Adolphe Menjou was one of the first "friendly" witnesses from the motion picture industry to testify before the HOUSE COMMITTEE ON UN-AMERICAN ACTIVITIES (HUAC) in October 1947.

The son of an Irish mother (a distant cousin of celebrated novelist James Joyce) and a French father who owned restaurants in Pittsburgh, Pennsylvania, and Cleveland, Ohio, Menjou attended Culver Military Academy in Indiana before enrolling at Cornell University in 1912. Rejecting the course of study in engineering that his father had mapped out for him, Menjou flirted with theatrical productions during his college years. Unable to find employment on the stage following graduation, Menjou worked at a series of odd jobs—as a men's clothing salesman, a farm laborer, and a waiter—before finally landing several bit parts in silent films at various New York studios. During World War I, Menjou served in the U.S. Army Ambulance Corps, seeing action in the Meuse-Argonne sector and rising to the rank of captain before returning to the United States in 1919.

Menjou's breakthrough in films came after he moved to the West Coast and obtained a part as King Louis XIII in the Mary Pickford-Douglas

Fairbanks costume epic, *The Three Musketeers*. Roles in *The Sheik* and *A Woman of Paris* solidified Menjou's status as a screen actor; with the advent of talking pictures in 1927, Menjou discovered that his command of several languages (including French, English, and Russian) made him a valuable commodity. Among the hit films of the 1930s and 1940s in which Menjou starred were *The Front Page, A Farewell to Arms, Little Miss Marker, A Star is Born,* and *The Hucksters*. Meanwhile, Menjou had become one of Hollywood's most outspoken conservatives. Menjou later stated that he had become interested in learning more about socialism during World War I; toward that end he had read a condensed version of Karl Marx's critique of capitalism *Das Kapital* because he found perusing the original "a very difficult job." Stories of the Stalinist political purges in the Soviet Union during the 1930s appalled Menjou and confirmed him in his opposition to Communism.

In 1944, Menjou campaigned actively for Republican presidential candidate Thomas E. Dewey and joined with fellow Hollywood conservatives Sam Wood, Walt DISNEY, Gary COOPER, and John WAYNE to found the MOTION PICTURE ALLIANCE FOR THE PRESERVATION OF AMERICAN IDEALS (MPAPAI). When the HUAC—led by chairman J. Parnell THOMAS of New Jersey—announced that it planned to investigate Communist influence in the motion picture industry, Menjou voluntarily met with committee staffers in May 1947 in California and offered to travel to Washington to testify in public session when the committee began its formal hearings in October.

Accordingly, Menjou was the committee's lead witness when it launched its inquiry on October 21, 1947. To establish his credentials, Menjou informed HUAC that he had made a study of "Marxism, Fabian Socialism, Communism, Stalinism, and its probable effects on the American people if they ever gain power here." Although he acknowledged that he had seen no overt Communist propaganda in motion pictures—"such as waving the hammer and

sickle"—he had observed "things that I thought were against what I considered good Americanism, in my feeling." Among the pictures which Menjou believed suspect because they presented a misleading or incomplete picture of life in the Soviet Union were the wartime films *Mission to Moscow* (which failed to include scenes of the Moscow trials) and *North Star,* which, according to Menjou, apparently slandered the Nazis by distorting the effects of the German invasion of the Soviet Union in 1941. Menjou added that Communist sympathizers could easily interject "un-Americanism or subversion" into a motion picture "by a look, by an inflection, by a change in the voice. I have never seen it done," he admitted, "but I think it could be done." Among those in the Hollywood community whom Menjou named as possible Communists were actors Edward G. ROBINSON, Alexander Knox, Paul Henreid, Hume Cronyn, and writer Herbert K. SORRELL, who had recently led a successful strike against Walt Disney's studio.

Menjou assured the members of HUAC that the vigilance of the MPAPAI already had prevented "an enormous amount of sly, subtle un-American class-struggle propaganda from going into pictures." He added that, in his opinon, HUAC itself had "alerted many apathetic people, many people who are not aware of the incredibly serious menace that faces America." Menjou recommended, nevertheless, that Congress outlaw the COMMUNIST PARTY in the United States. The party, he claimed, "is not a political party. It is a conspiracy to take over our Government by force, which would enslave the American people, as the Soviet government—fourteen members of the Politburo—hold the Russian people in abject slavery."

Following his testimony, Menjou continued to act as a self-appointed watchdog of American liberties in Hollywood. In 1948, he clashed with liberal actress Katharine HEPBURN on the set of the film *State of the Union,* accusing her in the presence of reporters of being a Communist sympathizer. Menjou continued to work steadily in films until his death in 1963.

**Miller, Arthur** (1915– )   One of the most successful American playwrights of the twentieth century, Arthur Miller was a left-wing activist in the 1930s and 1940s who subsequently was convicted of contempt of Congress for his failure to provide the HOUSE COMMITTEE ON UN-AMERICAN ACTIVITIES (HUAC) with the names of his former political associates.

Miller grew up in New York City, attended Abraham Lincoln High School, and worked his way through the University of Michigan. While an undergraduate, Miller wrote several plays that received national recognition, including the Theatre Guild's National Award in 1938. Following his graduation from Michigan, Miller joined the Federal Theater Project, though the project's activities were curtailed before it could produce any of his plays.

During the late 1930s, Miller also became involved in several POPULAR FRONT political organizations, including the JOINT ANTI-FASCIST REFUGEE COMMITTEE. As Miller later explained, the line between Communism and liberalism was blurred during that period; all those to the Left of center worked together in the fight against fascism. In 1939 or 1940, Miller attended a Marxist study course in a vacant store in his neighborhood in Brooklyn. "I there signed some form or another," he recalled years later, though he could not remember whether it was an application for membership in the COMMUNIST PARTY. "I understood then that this was to be a study course," Miller stated. "I was there for about three or four times, perhaps. It was of no interest to me and I didn't return."

Exempt from military service because of a football injury he sustained in high school, Miller visited Army camps during World War II to gather background material for a film version of journalist Ernie Pyle's *Story of G.I. Joe.* Meanwhile, he continued to write for the theater. In November 1944, Miller's play, *The Man Who Had All the Luck,* opened on Broadway, and—despite complimentary notices—closed soon thereafter. His second Broadway play, *All My Sons,* directed by Elia KAZAN, made its debut in

Arthur Miller, author of *The Crucible* and *After the Fall.*

February 1947 and won the New York Drama Critics' Circle Award and the Tony Award for Best Play of the year. Two years later, his play *Death of a Salesman* won a Pulizer Prize for Drama; it, too, was staged on Broadway by Kazan.

By that time, Miller was becoming alarmed at the rising tide of anti-Communism and intolerance in the United States. He opposed the far-ranging investigations of HUAC, supported the right of the Communist Party to function as a legal political party in America, spoke out against the anti-labor TAFT-HARTLEY ACT, and denounced infringements upon an author's right to express himself freely in his literature. "It seemed to me," Miller later stated, "that the then prevalent, rather ceaseless, investigating of artists was creating a pall of apprehension and fear among all kinds of people." There was, however, nothing resembling a blacklist in the theater, largely because there was no single group of powerful producers who could be terrorized by HUAC or other anti-Communist zealots into refusing to employ controversial writers, actors or directors. Further, HUAC had rarely ventured into the theater because investigations of stage actors provided far less publicity than hearings into the Hollywood film community.

In 1947, Miller also attended "five or six" meetings of Communist Party writers. "I attended these meetings," Miller later explained, "in order to locate my ideas in relation to Marxism, because I had been assailed for years by all kinds of interpretations of what Communism was, what Marxism was, and I went there to discover where I stood finally and completely. And I listened and said very little, I think, the four or five times." Miller discovered that his concept of great art—"to see the present remorselessly and truthfully"—conflicted with the duty of a Marxist writer to follow the line of the Communist Party. "I could never do that," Miller noted. "I have not done it." It was largely for that reason that Miller was able to tell HUAC investigators truthfully that he "was never under the discipline of the Communist Party or the Communist cause."

Nevertheless, in March 1954, the State Department refused Miller's application for a passport to address a meeting of the American-Belgian Society in London. The following year, the New York City commissioners—acting on a recommendation from a HUAC staff member—withdrew their offer to cooperate on a film Miller was making about juvenile delinquency. "I'm not calling him a Communist," said one city commissioner. "My objection is he refuses to repent." In the spring of 1956, Miller was subpoenaed to testify before HUAC. By that time, Miller had developed an ambivalent attitude toward the committee's anti-Communist investigations. "Certainly I felt distate for those who groveled before this tawdry tribune of moralistic vote-snatchers," he later wrote, "but I had as much pity as anger toward them. It bothered me much more that with each passing week it became harder to simply and clearly say why the whole procedure was vile." Initially, Miller had applauded those former radicals who, in his words, imagined themselves the heirs of Georgia Dimitrov, the Marxist hero who had defied Nazi persecution during the early 1930s. "The problem," Miller continued, "was that in New York the Committee members had all been elected democratically and were not plotting to take over the republic by violent terror."

> At least some of them, moreover, were genuinely alarmed by the recent Red victory in China, the Russian demonstration of the atomic bomb, and the expansion of Soviet territory into Eastern Europe. The mixture, in other words, of authentic naivete, soundly observed dangers, and unprincipled rabble-rousing was impossible to disentangle, especially when the public exposure of a bunch of actors who had not been politically connected for years would never push one Red Chinaman out of the Forbidden City or a single Russian out of Warsaw or Budapest.

At his hearing, Miller was struck particularly by the image and demeanor of chairman Francis WALTER of Pennsylvania, including Walter's "brown-and-white shoes with perforated wing tips, and his blue blazer, a costume for a wedding in Scranton, Pennsylvania, and his pleasant nod to me as he made his entrance amid the stern faces of his Committee." Miller cooperated fully with the committee when it asked about his own political background. He readily acknowledged signing protests against HUAC and in favor of Popular-Front causes, though the process of answering questions about his past activities also made Miller realize "how fatuous it had all been. I remember thinking that my influence on my own history had been nil. The simple truth," Miller concluded, "was that I myself could barely recall a great many of the organizations or causes to which I had given my support."

Miller assured the committee that he would "not support now a cause or movement which was dominated by Communists," and he acknowledged that his own views toward Communism had changed greatly since the late 1930s and early 1940s. "I was not a Saul of Tarsus walking down a road and struck by a bright light," Miller stated. "It was a slow process that occurred over years really, through my own work and through my own efforts to understand myself and what I was trying to do in the world." He further agreed with the committee that it would be "a disaster and a calamity" if the Communist Party ever assumed control of the United States. Marxism, he noted, was a fundamentally passive doctrine, in which "power is forbidden to the individual and rightfully belongs only to the collective. Thus the individual requires no rights, in the sense of protection from the state, any more than a pious person needs rights against the power of his god."

Yet, Miller steadfastly refused to provide the committee with the names of any of his former associates, and specifically the names of the other writers who attended the 1947 meetings to which Miller had earlier referred. He did not invoke the Fifth Amendment or even the First Amendment. Instead, Miller made his refusal an act of conscience. "I want you to understand," Miller said, "that I am not protecting the communists or the Communist Party. I am trying to, and I will, protect my sense of myself. I could not use the name of another person and bring trouble on him. These were writers, poets, as far as I could see, and the life of a writer, despite what it sometimes seems, is pretty tough. I wouldn't make it any tougher for anybody. . . . I will be perfectly frank with you in anything relating to my activities. I take the responsibility for everything I have done, but I cannot take responsibility for another human being."

For his recalcitrance, Miller received a six-month suspended sentence and a fine of $500. The judgment was reversed several months later on appeal.

Miller's artistic reply to HUAC and the prevailing anti-Communist hysteria may be found in two of his plays: THE CRUCIBLE (1953), and AFTER THE FALL (1964). The former play recounts the story of the Salem witch trials, with obvious parallels to the McCarthy era, and contrasts the goodness of those who chose to keep silence with the perfidy of informants. In *After the Fall*, Miller wrote directly of his experience with HUAC and his decision not to inform on his former associates. "If everyone broke faith there would be no civilization!" shouts one character during the play. "That is why the Committee is the face of the Philistine! And it astounds me that you can speak of truth and justice in relation to that gang of cheap publicity hounds!"

Miller's relationship with Kazan deteriorated after Kazan testified before HUAC in 1952 and provided the committee with names of individuals whom he believed were or had been involved in Communist activities. Kazan and Miller had previously intended to collaborate on a script about corrupt labor unions and the waterfront, but when several studio executives suggested that Miller make the corrupt labor officials Communists instead of organized crime bosses, Miller pulled out of the project. Miller and Kazan reconciled their differences in 1963, when they were invited to serve as resident playwright and director for the first season of Lincoln Center. The play on which they collaborated, was, ironically, *After the Fall*.

## Mostel, Zero (1915–1977)

A popular Broadway comic actor who was BLACKLISTED during the height of Senator Joseph MCCARTHY's influence in the early 1950s, Zero Mostel was born in New York City. Originally named Sam Mostel, "Zero" ("after my financial standing in the community") tried for several years after graduating from college to earn a living as an artist. "I called myself an artist," Mostel later explained. "Maybe I am the only one who did." In 1942, Mostel obtained his first job as an entertainer at a New York nightclub called the

Cafe Society Downtown. After a year's booking there, he began to work in films and the theater. His first Hollywood film, *Du Barry Was a Lady,* proved so successful at the box office that Mostel followed with another movie eight years later.

In July 1955, the HOUSE COMMITTEE ON UN-AMERICAN ACTIVITIES (HUAC) subpoenaed Mostel—who had been named by other witnesses as a Communist—to testify in New York about his political activities. Mostel protested that he could not leave California at that time because he was starring in a theatrical production; accordingly, the committee consented to postpone his appearance for several months.

Mostel finally appeared before the committee in Hollywood on October 14. HUAC investigators confronted him with documents that purported to show his membership or participation in numerous Communist-front organizations from the mid-1930s to the early 1950s, including the Young Communist League, AMERICAN YOUTH FOR DEMOCRACY, the JOINT ANTI-FASCIST REFUGEE COMMITTEE, the Voice of Freedom Committee, and the American Committee for Spanish Freedom. To each question about his past associations, Mostel pleaded the Fifth Amendment. Because he already had been blacklisted ("I am a man of a thousand faces," he once said, "all of them blacklisted"), his refusal to answer would have no bearing upon his prospects for employment.

Mostel did, however, assure the committee that he was not presently a member of the COMMUNIST PARTY, although he declined to tell them when he had left the party. (Such an admission obviously would have been an admission that he had once belonged to the party.) At one point in the hearing, Representative Clyde Doyle suggested to Mostel that "from now on, why don't you get far removed from groups known to be Communist dominated or Communist controlled, that sort of thing?" Mostel replied that he believed "in the idea that a human being should go on the stage and entertain to the best of his ability and say whatever he wants to say, because we live, I hope, in an atmosphere of freedom in this country."

Following his appearance, Mostel remained blacklisted until 1968, when he made a triumphal return to Broadway as the star of the hit musical, *A Funny Thing Happened on the Way to the Forum.* In 1976, he appeared in Woody Allen's film, THE FRONT, a fictional treatment of the blacklisting era in Hollywood. Mostel played a character based in part upon comedian Philip LOEB, who had committeed suicide in 1951 after being blacklisted.

## Motion Picture Alliance for the Preservation of American Ideals   

Organized in February 1944 by a coalition of conservative actors, directors, and producers in Hollywood, the Motion Picture Alliance for the Preservation of American Ideals (MPAPAI) took the lead in opposing what it perceived as a rising tide of Communist influence in the motion picture industry. The MPAPAI's founders included director Sam Wood, who also served as the organization's first president, studio executive Walt DISNEY, actors Gary COOPER, John WAYNE, Adolphe MENJOU, Ward Bond, and columnist Hedda Hopper. In announcing the establishment of the alliance, its members stated that "in our special field of motion pictures, we resent the growing impression that this industry is made up of, and dominated by, Communists, radicals and crack-pots. . . . We believe in, and like, the American way of life . . . the freedom to speak, to think, to live, to worship, to work and to govern ourselves, as individuals, as free men; the right to succeed or fail as free men, according to the measure of our ability and our strength. Believing in these things, we find ourselves in sharp revolt against a rising tide of Communism, Fascism and kindred beliefs, that seek by subversive means to undermine and change this way of life."

The alliance believed that Communists and Communist sympathizers were attempting to inject pro-Soviet propaganda into motion pictures. Specifically, Wood and his colleagues—many of whom also were dedicated foes of President Franklin D. Roosevelt and the New Deal—

objected to such films as *Mission to Moscow* and *North Star,* both of which portrayed the Soviet Union in a favorable light. The fact that Roosevelt had urged Hollywood to produce such films during World War II when the Soviet Union was allied with the United States, deterred the founders of the alliance not at all. Instead, they swore "to fight, with every means at our organized command, any effort of any group or individual, to divert the loyalty of the screen from the free America that gave it birth."

Shortly after the MPAPAI was founded, several of its officers (including vice president Walt Disney) sent a letter to Congress alerting Washington to the "flagrant manner in which the motion picture industrialists of Hollywood have been coddling Communists" and so-called totalitarian-minded groups "working in the industry for 'the dissemination of un-American ideas and beliefs.'" The letter virtually invited a congressional investigation of Communist infiltration of the motion picture industry. At the same time, the alliance opened lines of communication with such staunchly anti-Communist national organizations as the AMERICAN LEGION and the Knights of Columbus.

When the HOUSE COMMITTEE ON UN-AMERICAN ACTIVITIES (HUAC) announced in early 1947 that it intended to pursue an investigation of Communist influence in Hollywood, the MPAPAI reportedly provided the committee with the names of alleged Communists or Communist sympathizers in the industry. Prominent members of the alliance—including Wood, Menjou, Bond, and actor Robert TAYLOR—also volunteered to appear before HUAC as "friendly" witnesses, and did indeed testify when the hearings opened in Washington in October 1947. HUAC subsequently prosecuted ten "unfriendly" witnesses, who came to be known as the HOLLYWOOD TEN, for their refusal to answer the committee's questions about their past political activities and associations.

The outbreak of the KOREAN WAR in June 1950 encouraged the alliance to redouble its efforts to drive left-wing influences out of Hollywood. In September 1950, MPAPAI president

John Wayne cited "the heightening realization in motion picture circles of the need for tightening our ranks to defend liberty." "There are now and were then [in 1944] a tight group of Communist conspirators in our midst, treasonably obeying the dictates of a foreign tyranny. Time and history have furnished the proof. . . . We didn't make 'Hollywood' and 'Red' synonymous—the Communists, their fellow travelers and their dupes did that damaging job. We foresaw this result and tried to persuade our fellow workers of the need for cleaning our own house. We intend to continue doing so, since, even yet, too few people recognize that need."

Throughout the McCarthy era, the alliance also played a significant role in the BLACKLISTING and "rehabilitation" of actors, writers, and directors accused of Communist sympathies. When an artist accused of subversion—not infrequently, accused by the alliance itself—wished to establish his or her credentials as a loyal American, the alliance offered to review the subject's record and, if satisfied, issue a clearance to the studios. This procedure placed the MPAPAI in the unique position of serving as arbiter of political correctness in the Hollywood community. As political passions cooled in the late 1950s, MPAPAI gradually lost its influence, though the organization remained in existence long after the demise of Senator Joseph MCCARTHY.

**Mundt, Karl E.** (1900–1974)  A leading member of the conservative Republican bloc in Congress during the McCarthy era, Karl Mundt was born and raised in a prosperous agricultural region of South Dakota. He received a B.A. degree from Carleton College in Minnesota in 1923 and an M.A. from Columbia University in New York. Mundt originally embarked upon a career in education, serving as a high school teacher and school superintendent in South Dakota. From 1927 to 1936, Mundt taught speech and social science at Beadle State Teachers College in Madison, South Dakota, while also helping to run his family's insurance and home-loan businesses.

Senator Karl Mundt, one of the Congress' fore-most anti-Communist crusaders.

Mundt entered public service in 1931, as a member of South Dakota's Fish and Game Commission. Seven years later, he was elected to the U.S. House of Representatives for the first time. Although he joined the isolationist opposition to President Franklin D. Roosevelt's lend-lease legislation in early 1941, Mundt supported the U.S. war effort wholeheartedly following the Japanese air attack upon Pearl Harbor in December 1941. In the closing years of the war, Mundt adopted an internationalist stand, favoring American membership in the United Nations Refugee and Relief Association, and sponsoring legislation that committed Congress to the participation of the United States in the United Nations Economic and Social Council (UNESCO).

Mundt became a member of the HOUSE COMMITTEE ON UN-AMERICAN ACTIVITIES (HUAC) in 1943. After completing an official tour of Moscow, Warsaw, and Belgrade in the fall of 1945—during which he grew "highly critical of Soviet activities in Czechoslovakia and Poland and of ineffective American effort(s) to counteract them"—Mundt submitted a report that called upon the United States to immediately abandon "any semblance of appeasement" toward the Soviet Union. Instead, he recommended a "frank, across-the-table exchange of sentiment between President Harry S. TRUMAN

and Soviet dictator Joseph STALIN. While he opposed American involvement in European political or economic affairs, Mundt supported the less costly alternative of expanded U.S. propaganda warfare; specifically, he urged the expansion of the broadcasts and educational activities of the State Department's INTERNATIONAL INFORMATION AGENCY.

By the beginning of 1948, Mundt had become convinced that the threat posed to the United States by the Soviet Union was at least as grave as the danger Nazi Germany had presented. "It is pretty hard," he once declared, "to find any basic distinction between Fascism and Communism as Communism is practiced by the Stalinists in Moscow and as they direct the activities of the American Communist Party." In the early spring of 1948, Mundt co-sponsored with Representative Richard M. NIXON of California a bill that made it a crime "to attempt in any manner to establish in the United States a totalitarian dictatorship, the direction and control of which is to be vested in or exercised by, or under the domination or control of any foreign government, foreign organization, or foreign individual." The Mundt-Nixon bill stated that since the COMMUNIST PARTY OF THE UNITED STATES OF AMERICA was under the domination of a foreign government, members of the party would be required to register with the Department of Justice. Mundt's proposal also barred members of the Communist Party and Communist-front organizations from holding passports or obtaining employment with the federal government. The Mundt-Nixon bill did not, however, declare the Communist Party illegal; Mundt contended that such action would make the party's activities more difficult to monitor. "I have been one of those who have not looked with favor upon proposals to outlaw the communist party," noted Mundt. "What I want to do is to drive the Communist functionaries out in the open."

Although the House of Representatives approved the Mundt-Nixon bill by an overwhelming majority on May 19, 1948, the measure died for lack of support in the Senate. Two years later, however, the measure was revived following the invasion of South Korea by the Communist government of North Korea. After minor modifications, an amended measure entitled the INTERNAL SECURITY ACT OF 1950 (popularly known as the MCCARRAN ACT, for Senator PATRICK MCCARRAN of Nevada), passed both houses.

During the summer of 1948, Mundt chaired hearings of the HUAC in the absence of Representative J. Parnell THOMAS, who had been hospitalized for a brief time. Mundt led the committee's initial questioning of ex-Communist Whittaker CHAMBERS, who accused former State Department official Alger HISS of membership in the Communist Party. During the hearings, Mundt declared that "there is reason to believe that [Hiss] organized with that Department one of the Communist cells which endeavored to influence our Chinese policy and bring about the condemnation of [Chinese Nationalist leader] CHIANG Kai-shek. . . . Certainly there is no hope for world peace under the leadership of men like Alger Hiss." Following the conclusion of the hearings, Mundt appointed Nixon to head a subcommittee that questioned Chambers again, this time in executive session. Mundt also forwarded to a New York grand jury information on Hiss' testimony before HUAC, and it was largely on the basis of that material that the grand jury eventually indicted Hiss for perjury—specifically on Hiss' claim that he had never belonged to the Communist Party.

In 1948, Mundt won election to the U.S. Senate, where he soon earned a reputation as one of the staunchest supporters of Senator Joseph MCCARTHY of Wisconsin. During the presidential campaign of 1952, Mundt developed the "scientific" formula known as K(1)C(2)—Korea, Communism, and corruption—to summarize the Republican Party's complaints against the record of the Truman administration. Mundt's dedication to the anti-Communist crusade overrode his sense of party loyalty, however. When the Republican administration

of President Dwight David EISENHOWER nominated Charles E. BOHLEN as U.S. ambassador to the Soviet Union in 1953, Mundt joined McCarthy in opposing the nomination. "Rubber-stamp government in America died when President Eisenhower took office," Mundt declared following his vote against Bohlen.

In 1953, Mundt obtained a seat on the Senate's Permanent Committee on Investigations, chaired by McCarthy. One year later, when the committee launched its inquiry into the controversy between McCarthy and officials of the U.S. Army, Mundt—as the ranking Republican on the committee behind McCarthy—chaired the hearings. (Mundt accepted the position reluctantly, after pleading with his Senate colleagues to allow another committee to conduct the investigation.) Although McCarthy had counted upon Mundt to support him in the inquiry, which came to be known as the ARMY-MCCARTHY HEARINGS, Mundt attempted to run the hearings with an impartial hand, occasionally voting with the Democratic minority to suppress McCarthy's attempts to disrupt the hearings and browbeat witnesses.

When McCarthy's performance during the hearings led Senator Ralph FLANDERS of Vermont to introduce a motion of censure against the Wisconsin senator, Mundt sought unsuccessfully to substitute a weaker compromise measure. In the end, Mundt voted against the measure of censure. Following McCarthy's censure, Mundt continued to serve as a leader of the conservative Republican bloc in the Senate, though he did not pursue the anti-Communist crusade with the same vigor as before.

**Murray, Philip** (1886–1953) Leader of the drive to oust Communists from the CONGRESS OF INDUSTRIAL ORGANIZATIONS (CIO) in 1949, Philip Murray was born in Blantyre, Scotland, the son of a Scottish coal miner and labor-union official. Murray himself went to work in the mines at the age of ten. In 1902, Murray's family emigrated to the United States

CIO chief Philip Murray (right), who helped expel Communist-led unions from the CIO.

and settled in western Pennsylvania, where Murray went to work in the coal mines in Westmoreland County. His vocal opposition to unfair management practices earned him the presidency of his local union; to make himself a better leader, Murray—who had only a few years of formal schooling—began to educate himself by taking correspondence courses. In 1912, Murray was elected to the executive board of the UNITED MINE WORKERS (UMW). He rose rapidly through the union's hierarchy, and in 1919 was voted vice-president of the International UMW, which at that time was headed by John L. LEWIS.

A calm, quiet man who acquired a reputation as a peacemaker, Murray provided an excellent counterpoint to the flamboyant, temperamental Lewis. In 1935, President Franklin D. Roosevelt appointed Murray to the Labor and Industry Advisory Board of the National Recovery Administration. Later that year, Murray joined with Lewis and other left-wing labor leaders to found the Congress of Industrial Organizations, a coalition of unions that had grown impatient with the conservative political stance of the American Federation of Labor. Elected to the post of vice president of the CIO, Murray was assigned the task of organizing the nation's steel workers. In 1937, Murray became president of the United Steel Workers of America; under his leadership, the union grew spectacularly, numbering over 930,000 members by 1950.

As Europe drifted toward war in 1939, Murray broke with Lewis on the question of American foreign policy toward Europe. Lewis favored an isolationist stance, and following the announcement of the NAZI-SOVIET PACT in August 1939, Lewis was joined by Communist elements in the CIO. Murray, on the other hand, maintained that the interests of labor would be better served by continued opposition to the fascist powers of Europe, and at the 1939 CIO convention he helped push through a resolution that unequivocally condemned Communism. That same year, Murray helped lead a drive to oust Communists from the leadership of the UNITED AUTO WORKERS, one of the largest unions in the CIO coalition. In 1940, Murray was elected president of the CIO, displacing Lewis. For the following twelve years, Murray was reelected to the presidency of both the CIO and the United Steel Workers.

Yet there still existed a powerful faction of Communists within the CIO. Although Congressman Martin DIES, chairman of the HOUSE COMMITTEE ON UN-AMERICAN ACTIVITIES, was certainly not an unbiased observer, there was truth to Dies' statement in 1941 that "communists have obtained such a stranglehold on many of the unions in the C.I.O. that it is now beyond the power of Mr. Philip Murray or anyone else in the organization's leadership to do anything about the matter."

During World War II, Murray agreed not to strike for the duration of the war. "When your country is involved in war," he declared, "your country must come first." Following the war, Murray fervently opposed the TAFT-HARTLEY ACT, an attempt by conservatives to roll back the gains made by organized labor during the New Deal and the war years. Shortly after the Taft-Hartley Act was passed by Congress in 1947 over the veto of President Harry S. TRUMAN, Murray was indicted for violating its prohibition on political expenditures by labor unions; the indictment was subsequently dismissed by the courts, which ruled the prohibition unconstitutional. Despite his opposition to the presence of Communists in the American labor movement, Murray also denounced the provision in the Taft-Hartley Act that required labor-union leaders to sign affadavits swearing that they were not members of the COMMUNIST PARTY.

Meanwhile, Murray—who recognized that radical rhetoric would doom the labor movement to impotence in the conservative atmosphere of the immediate postwar era—continued his battle to oust Communists from the leadership of the CIO and its member unions, though he sought to avoid any open break that would destroy the liberal-radical alliance that had proved so beneficial to labor in the years before the war. At the 1946 annual CIO convention, Murray had pushed through a resolution denouncing Communist interference in the organization's affairs. Murray also supported the election of anti-Communist Walter REUTHER to the presidency of the United Auto Workers.

In 1948, Murray helped swing the CIO behind the reelection effort of President Truman, claiming that the Progressive Party candidacy of former vice president Henry A. WALLACE could "only divide labor." At the 1948 CIO convention, Murray also accused the Communists of creating dissension within the ranks of organized labor and seeking the ultimate destruction of the union movement. The Communists had, Murray charged, betrayed "every decent movement into which they have infiltrated themselves." "Under no circumstances," vowed Murray, "am I going to permit Communistic infiltration into the national C.I.O. movement." Finally, in 1949 Murray engineered the ouster of eleven Communist-led unions from the CIO, including the Farm Equipment Workers and the UNITED ELECTRICAL WORKERS. The expulsion, combined with government prosecution of Communist labor officials, served to break the power of radical union leaders and effectively destroyed Communist influence within the American labor-union movement.

Murray further validated his credentials as an anti-Communist union leader in June 1950 when he joined Reuther in publicly praising Truman's decision to employ American military forces to repel the invasion of South Korea. The following year, he led the United Steel Workers in a massive strike that turned into the longest and most costly confrontation in the history of the American steel industry.

## Murrow, Edward R. (1908–1965)

The most famous and highly respected American journalist of his generation, Edward R. Murrow was one of the few members of the press willing to confront Senator Joseph MCCARTHY publicly at the height of McCarthy's political influence.

Born in Greensboro, North Carolina, and raised in the state of Washington, Murrow attended Washington State University because it offered the nation's only collegiate course in radio broadcasting. He graduated in 1929, just before the stock-market crash that ushered in the Great Depression. Murrow spent the next five years working for various student and educational organizations, including the Institute of International Education, which provided Murrow a chance to make his first journey to Europe to arrange summer student seminars. There he obtained a crash course in the realities of European politics in the early 1930s, including the xenophobic attitude of Stalinist Russia and the rising tide of racism and militarism in Nazi Germany.

In 1935, Murrow joined the Columbia Broadcasting System at its headquarters in New York; two years later, he was appointed head of the CBS European Bureau. In that role, Murrow personally witnessed many of the crucial events in Eastern Europe as the world drifted toward war. He was in Vienna when Nazi troops entered the Austrian capital; with journalist William Shirer, Murrow covered the fateful conference between Hitler and British Prime Minister Neville Chamberlain at Munich, and the ensuing German invasion of Czechoslovakia. Murrow firmly established his reputation as a first-rate radio reporter, however, during the blitz of London in 1940–41. As the Nazi Luftwaffe pounded the city nightly, Murrow stood on the roof of the British Broadcasting Com-

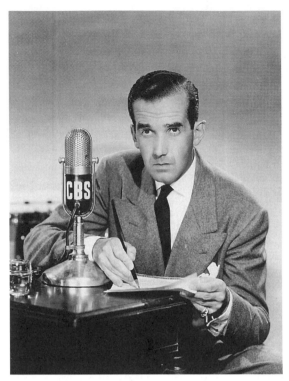

Edward R. Murrow, CBS newscaster, publicly attacked McCarthy for his irresponsible tactics in a famous episode of the *See It Now* television series.

pany's office building, describing the sights and sounds of the assault for his American listeners: "Earlier this evening we heard a number of bombs go sliding and slithering across, to fall several blocks away. Just overhead now the burst of the antiaircraft fire. Still the nearby guns are not working. The searchlights now are feeling almost directly overhead. Now you'll hear two bursts a little nearer in a moment. There they are! That hard stony sound."

At the end of the war, CBS appointed Murrow to the position of vice president, but—uncomfortable in the executive suite—he returned to a reportorial role two years later. Murrow made the switch to television in 1951 with the debut of his program *See It Now*, which featured Murrow's interviews and reports from locations around the world. In December 1952,

Murrow did a show from a foxhole in Korea to show American viewers what life was like for the troops on the front line. His interview subjects in the early 1950s included President Harry S. TRUMAN, scientist J. Robert OPPENHEIMER, General Douglas MACARTHUR, and Soviet leader Nikita KHRUSHCHEV. Murrow also investigated allegations made by Senator Joseph MCCARTHY about Communist influence in the federal government; specifically, Murrow examined the cases of Harry Dexter WHITE, Irving PERESS, and Lieutenant Milo Radulovich. A dedicated defender of civil liberties, Murrow opposed efforts by conservative Congressmen to outlaw the Communist Party, warning his listeners that "we can't legislate loyalty."

Murrow's first attack upon McCarthy's methods of combating Communism occurred in December 1951 when Murrow devoted five minutes of a *See It Now* program to film clips that began by showing McCarthy's complaints of unfair treatment by the press ("We've been kicked around and bullwhipped," claimed McCarthy) during a speech in Milwaukee, followed by examples of McCarthy himself bullying witnesses and making reckless accusations of treason or criminal conduct against Owen LATTIMORE, Secretary of State Dean ACHESON, and former Secretary of State General George Catlett MARSHALL. McCarthy's treatment of Marshall particularly upset Murrow, who had revered Marshall since he first came to know the general during World War II. During the presidential campaign of 1952, when Republican candidate Dwight David EISENHOWER refused to issue a strong defense of Marshall in response to McCarthy's allegations, Murrow began to assemble a comprehensive film dossier on McCarthy.

In October 1953, Murrow dedicated a *See It Now* program to the case of Lieutenant Milo Radulovich, an Air Force Reserve meterologist who had been identified as a security risk because his sister and father had previously been associated with Communist-front organizations. The program marked one of the few times since the start of McCarthy's anti-Communist crusade that the victim of a questionable security decision had enjoyed an opportunity to present his side of the issue to the American public. Murrow illustrated clearly in stark human terms the cost of the Air Force's ruling against Radulovitch: "Are [my children] going to be judged on what their father was labeled?" asked Radulovitch on camera. "Are they going to have to explain to their friends . . . why their father's a security risk? . . . I see a chain reaction that has no end." In his commentary at the close of the program, Murrow observed that "whatever happens in this whole area of the relationship between the individual and the state, we will do it ourselves—it cannot be blamed upon [Soviet Premier] Malenkov, or MAO Tse-tung (Zedong), or even our allies."

The success of the Radulovitch program encouraged Murrow to proceed with a full show devoted to Senator McCarthy himself. While he and his staff compiled the footage for the show, Murrow occasionally suffered pangs of conscience over the ethics of a journalist using the power of the media to attack an individual. Nevertheless, planning for the show proceeded, and when McCarthy launched his investigation of Communist infiltration of the U.S. Army in the late winter of 1954, Murrow decided the time had come to air the program. CBS executives—who wanted to distance themselves from the program—provided Murrow with sole control over the content of the program; the network refused to provide advertisements for it and refused even to preview the show prior to air time. The CBS information office did, however, notify FBI Director J. Edgar HOOVER of the date and time of the program.

At 10:30 on the evening of March 9, 1954, Murrow opened his weekly edition of *See It Now* with a statement that the entire thirty minutes would be dedicated to a report on Senator McCarthy, "told mainly in his [that is, McCarthy's] own words and pictures." Murrow was careful to point out that the network would provide McCarthy an opportunity "to answer himself" if he so desired. The program consisted primarily of taped footage of McCarthy badgering witnesses, defying the military hierarchy and the White House, brandishing "secret" evidence (a committee-hearing transcript, explained Murrow, available to the general public for two dollars a copy), employing half-truths and innuendo, and complaining that the nation's media was treating him unfairly. At numerous points during the program, Murrow interrupted to provide viewers with the facts behind McCarthy's accusations; for instance, after showing a tape of McCarthy asking a witness whether he knew "the CIVIL LIBERTIES UNION has been listed as a front for . . . the COMMUNIST PARTY" Murrow followed with the statement that "the Attorney General's List does not and never has listed the A.C.L.U. as subversive. Nor does the F.B.I. or any other federal government agency." After numerous illustrations of McCarthy's recklessness, Murrow reminded his audience that it did no good to wonder what caused the nation to "huddle, herd-like," before the phenomenon known as MCCARTHYISM. Quoting Shakespeare, Murrow concluded that " 'the fault, Dear Brutus, is not in our stars, but in ourselves.' "

At the end of the program, Murrow delivered his personal commentary on Senator McCarthy:

> We will not walk in fear, one of another. We will not be driven by fear into an age of unreason, if we dig deep in our history and our doctrine; and remember that we are not descended from fearful men. Not from men who feared to write, to speak, to associate, and to defend causes that were for the moment unpopular.
>
> This is not time for men who oppose Senator McCarthy's methods to keep silent—or for those who approve. We can deny our heritage and our history but we cannot escape responsibility for the result. There is no way for a citizen of a republic to abdicate his reponsibility. . . .

Although the immediate reaction among network executives was not encouraging (Murrow later characterized their attitude as "Good show. Sorry you did it.") the public response to the program was overwhelmingly favorable. CBS reported that it received 12,924 calls in favor of the telecast within 48 hours, and only 1,367 opposing it. Telegrams supported Murrow by a margin of more than 10–1. Murrow received congratulatory messages from a broad range of admirers, including scientist Albert EINSTEIN, U.S. Supreme Court Chief Justice Earl WARREN, Congressman Adam Clayton Powell, Jr., former Truman administration adviser Clark Clifford, and author John Gunther. For his part, McCarthy claimed that he had not even bothered to watch the program. "I never listen to the extreme left-wing, bleeding heart elements of radio and TV," he declared. McCarthy initially refused to accept the network's offer of rebuttal time, and so Vice President Richard M. NIXON delivered a response in his place, spending most of his time imploring McCarthy to cease his attacks on the Eisenhower administration.

Eventually McCarthy did reply to Murrow, first on the radio show of ultraconservative commentator Fulton Lewis, Jr., and then during a twenty-two-minute monologue on CBS on April 6. Describing Murrow as "a symbol, the leader and the cleverest of the jackal pack which is always found at the throat of anyone who dares to expose individual Communists and traitors," McCarthy reviewed Murrow's background, pointing out that the newsman had belonged in his youth to the Institute of International Education (which McCarthy identified as "a representative of a Soviet agency [chosen] to do a job which would normally be done by the Russian secret police") and the Industrial Workers of the World, a radical labor organization that had flourished briefly in the Pacific Northwest in the first two decades of the twentieth century. At the end, McCarthy urged Americans not to be deluded or dissuaded from the anti-Communist crusade by "the Murrows, the Lattimores . . . the *DAILY WORKER*, or the Communist Party itself."

Following McCarthy's televised attack, the anti-Communist publication *COUNTERATTACK* observed that Murrow—though not a Communist himself—apparently was "confused on communist issues and defends those involved in communist causes." Further, the FBI increased its surveillance of Murrow and began to compile a thick dossier of his activities and past political associations.

Yet, Murrow weathered the storm. At a White House press conference the day after McCarthy's televised appearance, Eisenhower's press secretary told reporters that the President still considered Murrow a friend, a significant indication of support that made headlines throughout the country. Murrow's sponsor, the Aluminum Company of America (ALCOA), maintained its support of *See It Now*. Freedom House awarded Murrow its annual award, with a citation that read, "Free men were heartened by his courage in exposing those who would divide us by exploiting our fears."

Murrow's program undoubtedly encouraged other critics of McCarthy to speak out, though over the following three months the senator from Wisconsin contributed significantly to his own political demise through his actions in the nationally televised ARMY-MCCARTHY HEARINGS. Meanwhile, *See It Now* continued to feature inquiries into the effects of the anti-Communist hysteria in the United States.

In response to decisions at the network executive level, the focus of Murrow's programs gradually shifted during the late 1950s away from hard news and toward entertainment. In 1960, Murrow accepted an invitation by President John F. KENNEDY to serve as director of the UNITED STATES INFORMATION AGENCY. He was no happier in that role, however, than he had been as a CBS executive in the years immediately after World War II, and so Murrow subsequently returned to television with a program called *CBS Reports,* which was eventually replaced by a situation comedy about a talking horse called *Mister Ed.* An inveterate cigarette smoker, Murrow died of lung cancer on April 27, 1965.

**My Son John**   Another simplistic screen treatment of the Communist espionage threat, *My Son John* was released by Paramount Studios in the spring of 1952. It starred Robert Walker—who died shortly before the film was completed—as John Jefferson, a federal government worker who was also either a COMMUNIST PARTY member or a Communist sympathizer. (The film never quite made the distinction clear.) Jefferson was involved romantically with a suspected female Soviet agent, and when his mother (played by Helen Hayes, in her first movie role in 17 years) inadvertently discovered a key to the girl's apartment in her son's pocket, she dutifully alerted the FEDERAL BUREAU OF INVESTIGATION (FBI).

The message of the film, like that of *I MARRIED A COMMUNIST,* was that nobody was ever allowed to leave the Communist Party alive. At a critical moment in the film, Jefferson decided to renounce his Communist associations, but during a wild automobile chase through the streets of Washington, D.C., he was shot by his former party comrades. He managed to make it as far as the steps of the Lincoln Memorial, but there he died. In a taped confession played at the commencement ceremony of his alma mater, Jefferson acknowledged that he had been "an enemy of my country—and the servant of a foreign power," and he urged the graduating college seniors to "hold fast to honor."

The film endowed Jefferson with stereotypical traits of suspected Communists; for instance, he did not play football in college (unlike his two brothers), he scoffed at religion, he associated with highbrow college professors, and he used "two-dollar" words in conversations with his honest, patriotic parents. All these characteristics particularly irritated Jefferson's American Legionnaire father, played by Dean Jagger, who at one point displayed his displeasure by hitting his son over the head with a Bible. Most reviews singled out actor Van Heflin for praise, for his subdued portrayal of a no-nonsense FBI agent.

# N

**National Association for the Advancement of Colored People**   Founded in 1909 by a coalition of African Americans and white liberals, the National Association for the Advancement of Colored People (NAACP) condemned the HOUSE COMMITTEE ON UN-AMERICAN ACTIVITIES (HUAC) in 1947 for its purported violation of civil liberties in its hunt for Communist subversives. In the same year, the national convention of the NAACP also passed a resolution condemning Communism. Nevertheless, Representative John RANKIN of Alabama, a dedicated racist and member of HUAC, attempted to persuade the rest of the committee to condemn the NAACP as a Communist-front organization. Rankin's effort was stoutly blocked, however, by HUAC chairman J. Parnell THOMAS, who pointed out that "there are a lot of other people [who] condemn this committee, but that doesn't mean they are Communists."

The issue of ties between the NAACP and the Communist movement was raised once again in 1956, when FBI Director J. Edgar HOOVER charged that Communist agents were attempting to infiltrate southern chapters of the NAACP. The Communists, Hoover charged, wanted to lead the NAACP to put pressure on the federal government to act more expeditiously in enforcing the recent Supreme Court decision of *Brown vs. Board of Education of Topeka, Kansas,* which ruled that separate-but-equal public-school systems were unconstitutional. While Hoover readily acknowledged that the NAACP's national organization was staunchly anti-Communist, he persisted in making a connection between Communist subversives and the civil-rights movement. If the Eisenhower administration made no move to launch a full-scale investigation of the NAACP as a result of Hoover's charges, still the hint of any tie between Communists and the civil rights movement appeared to some administration of-ficials to justify Eisenhower's "gradualist" approach to the granting of full civil rights to African Americans.

**National Lawyers Guild**   Founded in 1936 by a group of New Deal lawyers who resented the American Bar Association's (ABA) opposition to many of President Franklin Delano Roosevelt's programs, the guild originally devoted itself to the support of a variety of liberal social and political causes. Although there were a substantial number of Communist sympathizers in the guild from the start, the organization's membership also included many attorneys who opposed Communism and the repressive Stalinist regime in the Soviet Union. Further, many African-American lawyers joined the guild in its early years, because the ABA refused to admit them. In 1939, the guild publicly condemned the invasion of Finland by the Soviet Union; shortly thereafter, however, a struggle for power within the guild left pro-Communist elements in control, and a number of the guild's prominent non-Communist members subsequently left the organization.

Cited as a Communist front in 1944 and 1950 by the HOUSE COMMITTEE ON UN-AMERICAN ACTIVITIES (HUAC), the guild was described by Attorney General Herbert BROWNELL, Jr., in August 1953 as "the legal mouthpiece of the Communist party." In a speech before the ABA, Brownell announced his intention to place the guild on the attorney general's list of subversive organizations, but the guild promptly filed suit in federal court to block the government from holding hearings to determine its loyalty. During the ARMY-MCCARTHY HEARINGS of April—June 1954, the guild made headlines once again when Senator Joseph R. MCCARTHY attacked a young lawyer named Frederick J. Fisher, Jr.—a member of the same law firm as Army special counsel Joseph N.

WELCH—for his membership in the guild during the 1930s.

Guild attorneys often represented clients accused of disloyalty in hearings before HUAC throughout the 1950s. Occasionally, the attorneys would take the Fifth Amendment themselves at the outset of the hearings and then advise their clients to do the same. In 1955, seventeen guild attorneys who formerly had worked for the National Labor Relations Board were called to testify before HUAC; all availed themselves of their Fifth Amendment rights and refused to answer any questions about their political beliefs.

**Nazi-Soviet Pact**  On August 23, 1939, Soviet dictator Joseph STALIN and German Foreign Minister Joachim von Ribbentrop signed a Non-Aggression Pact—popularly known as the Nazi-Soviet Pact—pledging their nations to respect the other's territorial integrity. At the same time, the two nations privately agreed to a series of "supplementary protocols" that effectively divided up Poland and the Baltic states of Estonia, Latvia, and Lithuania between Germany and the USSR.

Hitler's primary objective in signing the pact was to free the German general staff from the burden of fighting a two-front war. With the Soviet Union effectively immobilized, Germany launched an assault on Poland on September 1, 1939. Then, in the spring of 1940, the Wehrmacht's blitzkrieg tore through Western Europe: Norway and Denmark fell in April, the Netherlands and Belgium in May, and, in June, France.

For his part, Stalin had long been obsessed by a fear that the Western democracies would encourage Nazi Germany to fulfill its expansionist ambitions at the expense of the Soviet Union so that they could then stand back and watch the two renegade totalitarian nations of Europe decimate each other. Throughout the early months of 1939, Stalin had pursued negotiations for a defensive alliance with Britain in a desultory manner, but by summer he had become convinced that the British government of Neville Chamberlain had no intention of agreeing to any effective military arrangement with the Soviet Union. In this, Stalin was correct. "I must confess to the most profound distrust of Russia," wrote Chamberlain in March 1939. "I have no belief whatever in her ability to maintain an effective offensive, even if she wanted to. And I distrust her motives, which seem to me to have little connection with our ideas of liberty, and to be concerned only with getting everyone else by the ears." Standing alone against Germany would have entailed severe risks for the USSR, and thus Stalin consented to the Non-Aggression Pact with Germany as the best protection for Soviet interests. Still, Stalin made it clear that the pact was born of expediency and not affection. He refused to consent to the insertion in the preamble to the pact of a paragraph describing relations between the two nations as amicable. "The Soviet Government," Stalin declared, "could not suddenly present to the public assurances of friendship after they had been covered with pails of manure by the Nazi government for six years."

But it was precisely this interpretation of the pact as an abrupt about-face in German-Soviet relations that created severe strains throughout the international Communist movement. Beginning in 1933, when the Nazi Party first rose to ascendancy in Germany, the Soviet Union had been one of Hitler's most implacable enemies. Throughout Western Europe and the United States, Communists joined with liberals and socialists to form a POPULAR FRONT against the fascist powers of Germany and Italy. The coalition suffered a setback in the Spanish Civil War when the Nationalist armies of General Francisco Franco, aided by Nazi Germany, defeated the Republican forces. Nevertheless, the broad support among American liberals for the Republican cause in Spain testified to the success of the Communists' collaborationist policy.

All this changed with the announcement of the Nazi-Soviet Pact. Suddenly, Moscow instructed loyal members of the COMMUNIST

PARTY IN THE UNITED STATES to cease all anti-fascist activities. Instead, they were directed to work against the Roosevelt administration's rearmament program, to become isolationists, and to lead the fight for American neutrality in the emerging conflict in Europe. Earl BROWDER, then the head of the Communist Party in the United States, described the pact as a "very big concession by Hitler" that served America's strategic interests. Opposition to the pact, Browder claimed, "would be a demonstration of a most serious lack of understanding of politics, and a serious disregard of the national interests of America which have been helped by the pact."

The change was too abrupt and too severe. American liberals interpreted the Nazi-Soviet Pact as a cynical betrayal of the anti-fascist cause. For them, the Communist Party no longer was an instrument of social justice; it had become nothing more than a tool to serve the selfish interests of the Soviet Union. As one left-wing author explained, the pact "gave visible substance to the reality that lay behind the fictitious account of Soviet affairs that we took to be a true account in that age of faith." Disillusioned, liberals resigned en masse from Popular Front organizations, and the Communist Party was effectively destroyed as a viable political force in the United States. "If they had only admitted their ignorance," wrote former Communist academician Granville HICKS, "the Communist Party would be intact today. But instead they insisted that the Soviet-German nonaggression pact was the greatest possible contribution to peace and democracy and offered anything that came into their heads as proof. They rushed into print with apologies completely devoid of clarity and logic. . . . The leaders of the Communist Party have tried to appear omniscient, and they have succeeded in being ridiculous. They have clutched at straws, juggled sophistries, shut their eyes to facts. . . ."

Not only did liberals scorn further cooperation with Communists; many assuaged their feelings of betrayal by becoming even more vigilant than the conservative Right in searching out and destroying Communist influence in the United States. Moreover, suspicions of the Soviet Union's intentions lingered through World War II, even after Hitler violated the pact by attacking the Soviet Union in June 1941. Wartime American aid to the USSR was limited in part by the fear that Stalin—having already signed one pact with Germany—might eventually do so again.

**Nicholson, Donald** (1888–1968)  A former FBI agent, Donald Nicholson became chief of security in the U.S. Department of State in 1948. In that post, Nicholson's responsibilities included supervision of investigations into the background and present political activities of State Department employees who were accused of disloyalty or subversion. During Nicholson's tenure as chief of security, accusations were made against such prominent diplomats as Alger HISS, John Carter VINCENT, and John Stewart SERVICE. Despite the charges of anti-Communist members of Congress such as Senator Joseph MCCARTHY of Wisconsin and Repre-

Donald Nicholson, the State Department official who defended the department's loyalty and security review programs.

sentative Richard M. NIXON of California, Nicholson steadfastly denied that the State Department was sheltering Communists or Communist sympathizers.

Following McCarthy's February 10, 1950, speech in which he claimed that there were card-carrying Communists in the State Department, the Senate formed a special committee headed by Senator Millard TYDINGS of Maryland to investigate McCarthy's allegations. On April 5, 1950, Nicholson appeared before the Tydings committee and outlined for the senators the State Department's rigorous security program. "As far as we know," Nicholson stated, "there is no card-carrying Communist in the State Department. If there were, they would be terminated by noon."

Nicholson's assurances did not persuade McCarthy and his colleagues to call off their own investigation, however, and in the final two-and-a-half years of the Truman administration, the State Department's loyalty program came under increasingly heavy attack. Indeed, the unwillingness of Nicholson's superior, Secretary of State Dean ACHESON, to sacrifice individual rights in the search for disloyal employees cost the Democrats dearly in the elections of 1952.

Richard M. Nixon, former member of HUAC, rode to national political fame on the issue of Communism in government.

## Nixon, Richard M. (1913–1994)

Second in prominence only to Senator Joseph MCCARTHY among leaders of the American anti-Communist crusade in the early years of the COLD WAR, Richard M. Nixon used the issue of Communism to help win the Republican vice presidential nomination in 1952. Although he subsequently lost the presidential election of 1960 to Senator John F. KENNEDY of Massachusetts, Nixon launched a political comeback in the late 1960s to become the nation's thirty-seventh President (1969–1974).

The son of devout Quakers, he was born in Yorba Linda, California. In 1922, the Nixon family moved to Whittier, California, where his father opened a grocery store. Nixon himself worked at a variety of odd jobs as a teenager, and later helped put himself through Whittier College by working as bookkeeper at his father's store. Following his graduation from Whittier in 1934, he won a scholarship to Duke University School of Law, where he was elected president of the student law association. He received his law degree in 1937, but because legal jobs were scarce during the Great Depression, Nixon found it necessary to return to Whittier, where he joined a private law firm.

During World War II, Nixon served in a naval transport unit in the Pacific. When he returned to civilian life after the surrender of Japan in August 1945, Nixon was able to persuade the Republican Party leaders of his home congressional district to nominate him to run against the Democratic incumbent, Jerry Voorhis. Although political professionals gave him little chance to defeat Voorhis, Nixon ran an extremely aggressive campaign in which he implied that Voorhis was a Communist sympathizer.

The use of the Communist issue certainly did not originate with Nixon in 1946; in fact, it was a common theme of Republican candidates in many congressional campaigns that year. For Nixon, it proved the key to victory, as he was swept into office as part of the Republican landslide that resulted from widespread public discontent with the policies of the Truman administration.

When he took his seat in Congress in January 1947, Nixon was assigned to the HOUSE COMMITTEE ON UN-AMERICAN ACTIVITIES (HUAC). At that time, HUAC was not regarded as a choice committee assignment, and most of its members were known more for their love of the spotlight than for any solid political accomplishments. At the outset, however, Nixon brought to the committee a sober dedication to hard work and a determination to discover the truth that elevated HUAC's investigations to a higher and more productive level. Early in 1948, Nixon chaired a subcommittee that investigated the possibility of legislation to outlaw the COMMUNIST PARTY. The product of these hearings was the Mundt-Nixon bill, which was passed by the House of Representatives in 1948 but allowed to die in the Senate. Two years later, however, it was resurrected, and served as the basis for the INTERNAL SECURITY ACT OF 1950, also known as the MCCARRAN ACT.

Nixon first gained national prominence in the summer of 1948, during the committee's inquiry into the affairs of a former State Department official named Alger HISS, who had been identified as a Communist by an ex-Communist journalist named Whittaker CHAMBERS. In August 1948, Hiss appeared before HUAC to deny Chambers' allegations. His denials convinced everyone on the committee except Nixon, who had developed an intense personal dislike for the urbane Hiss. With the assistance of HUAC counsel Robert STRIPLING, Nixon persuaded his colleagues to permit him to question Chambers once again. In a secret meeting in New York on August 7, Chambers proved to Nixon's satisfaction that he had, in fact, been closely acquainted with Hiss.

When Hiss appeared for a second time before HUAC in September 1948, he appeared to retreat from his original denials. From that point on, Nixon acted as Hiss's unofficial prosecutor, pressing the case forward, until Hiss was finally convicted of perjury in January 1950. Hiss later claimed that Nixon's motives had been almost entirely political. "Seeking to build his career on getting a conviction in my case," Hiss charged, Nixon had "from the days of the congressional committee hearings constantly issued public statements and leaks to the press against me."

Nixon's attacks upon Hiss—and the Truman administration's defense of the former State Department official—led Nixon to become increasingly partisan in his search for Communists in government. Nixon assailed the administration for its defense of Hiss and its conduct of the case against him; "the entire Truman Administration," Nixon charged, "was extremely anxious that nothing bad happen" to Hiss. When the government arrested Department of Justice employee Judith COPLON on espionage charges in 1949, Nixon publicly demanded an investigation of the department, stating that "in my opinion this case shows why the Department may be unfit and unqualified to carry out the responsibility of protecting the national security against Communist infiltration."

When Senator McCarthy made his famous speech at Wheeling, West Virginia, on February 9, 1950, charging that the Truman administration was harboring more than 200 Communists or Communist sympathizers in the State Department, his speech was actually nothing more than a pasted-up copy of several other speeches and publications, including an address delivered by Nixon in Congress on January 26, 1950. Once McCarthy came under attack for an alleged lack of evidence to support his assertions, Nixon allowed McCarthy to use his files of suspected subversives to defend himself in the ensuing Senate investigation.

In the autumn of 1950, Nixon decided to run for the U.S. Senate. His opponent was Helen Gahagan DOUGLAS, who had assembled a liberal voting record in her three terms in the House. Nixon organized his campaign around the theme of Douglas as a Communist sympathizer. Calling her "the Pink Lady"—"pink down to her underwear"—Nixon accused Douglas of following the Communist line "in voting time after time against measures that are for the security of this country." To emphasize the point, Nixon's campaign workers distributed more than a half-million copies of Douglas' voting record printed on sheets of pink paper. Nixon further charged that if Douglas had been responsible for investigating disloyalty, "the Communist conspiracy in the United States would never have been exposed."

Nixon's fame as a staunch anti-Communist helped earn him the Republican vice-presidential nomination in 1952. Because Republican presidential candidate Dwight David EISENHOWER preferred to present the appearance of remaining above the partisan fray, Nixon served as the aggressive member of the national ticket. Early in the campaign, he pledged to make Communist subversion "the theme of every speech from now until the election." The Democratic administrations of Truman and Franklin Delano Roosevelt, he said, were responsible for "the unimpeded growth of the Communist conspiracy within the United States."

Following the Republican victory, strains within the party arose between Eisenhower and his moderate advisers, on one side, and McCarthy and his conservative supporters in the Senate on the other. Caught in the middle of this controversy, Nixon urged that the Eisenhower administration refrain from attacking McCarthy directly. Any attempt to curb or condemn McCarthy, Nixon argued, would only divide the Republican Party and provide McCarthy with more publicity. Partly as a result of Nixon's advice, Eisenhower refused to publicly criticize McCarthy, even when the senator openly at-

tacked administration policy. During the following 18 months, Nixon strove to keep open the lines of communication and often served as the principal intermediary between the White House and McCarthy. In the spring of 1953, for instance, Nixon helped persuade McCarthy to tone down his attacks upon Eisenhower's nomination of Charles BOHLEN as U.S. ambassador to the Soviet Union. Nixon also convinced McCarthy to abandon his threats to launch an investigation of the CENTRAL INTELLIGENCE AGENCY (CIA), although McCarthy did insist upon a thorough purge of the agency's personnel roster; when McCarthy moved toward an investigation of the U.S. Army in February 1954, it was Nixon who urged—unsuccessfully—conservative Republicans in the Senate to persuade McCarthy to forgo a direct confrontation.

Nixon attempted to employ the theme of anti-Communism once again in the congressional election campaigns of 1954, but this time, charges that the Democrats were "bending to the Red wind" had become shopworn. As public concern faded over the issue of Communist infiltration of the federal government, Nixon began to move toward the political center, although he remained considerably to the right of Eisenhower. In 1960, Nixon managed to capture the Republican presidential nomination, despite only lukewarm support from Eisenhower. After losing to John F. Kennedy in one of the closest presidential contests in American history, Nixon returned to California. In 1962, he ran for governor of his home state, but when he lost that race, too, Nixon bitterly announced his resignation from politics.

He never retreated entirely from the political arena, however, and in 1968 Nixon again won the Republican presidential nomination. Once more Nixon attempted to capitalize on public disenchantment with the liberal domestic policies and disastrous foreign policies of a Democratic administration. This time the effort proved successful, as Nixon narrowly defeated Democratic nominee Hubert HUMPHREY in a three-way race that also included independent candidate George Wallace. Four years later, Nixon won reelection in a landslide victory over Senator George McGovern of South Dakota. In August 1974, however, Nixon resigned from office in the wake of revelations about his role in the Watergate scandal. After a brief period away from intense public scrutiny, Nixon emerged as a respected elder statesman in the Republican Party. He continued to write and speak on political affairs until his death in 1994.

**Nizer, Louis** (1902–1994)   An attorney, author, and analyst of public affairs, Louis Nizer achieved considerable fame through his representation of clients in the motion picture industry. One of Nizer's clients was blacklisted radio personality John Henry FAULK, who sued AWARE, INC. in 1956 for organizing the industrywide boycott that kept Faulk off the air because of his anti-BLACKLIST activities. When the case finally came to trial in 1962, Nizer helped Faulk win a substantial financial settlement from the blacklisters.

Despite his willingness to attack blacklisting in the entertainment industry, Nizer also supported legislation to outlaw the COMMUNIST PARTY IN THE UNITED STATES, or at least to require its members to register as foreign agents. In fact, in May 1950 Nizer publicly called for a "drastic revision" in the American judicial system to permit the courts to deal "firmly" with accused Communists. He thereby took his place among other left-wing anti-Communists in the McCarthy era who attempted to combine a stout defense of non-Communist liberals with an enthusiastic assault upon Communism itself, and particularly the Soviet Union.

# O

**Odets, Clifford** (1906–1963) One of America's leading playwrights during the 1930s and 1940s, Clifford Odets helped found the radical Group Theatre in 1931. It was a time, Odets later recalled, of desperate poverty, when he lived on an income of ten cents a day. It was also a time when the catastrophic effects of the Great Depression led many Americans, including Odets and his fellow actors in the Group Theatre (notably Elia KAZAN), to discuss possible radical changes in the nation's political and economic system.

In 1934 Odets embarked upon his career as a playwright. His first effort, *Awake and Sing*—the story of a poor Jewish family in New York during the Depression—was not produced until he had acquired a reputation. It was his second

Playwright Clifford Odets abjured his Communist past during testimony before HUAC.

play, *Waiting for Lefty*, that won Odets national recognition in 1935. A one-act drama centering around a taxi-drivers' strike in Chicago, *Waiting for Lefty* quickly became a staple in the reportory of socially progressive theatre groups. Odets' later plays included *Golden Boy* (1937) and *The Country Girl* (1950).

In 1935, Odets agreed to go to Hollywood to try his hand at writing screenplays. He later acknowledged that he had been drawn to movies primarily for the money. Odets completed only three scripts before he returned to New York, and only one of these screenplays *(The General Died at Dawn)* ever made it to the theaters. He divided his time over the next decade between the East and West coasts, working in Hollywood as a script doctor to improve other writers' screenplays.

Partly as a response to the social unrest that swirled around New York during the Depression, Odets had joined the COMMUNIST PARTY sometime around 1935, while he was a member of the Group Theatre. At approximately the same time, he joined the Marxist League of American Writers, which also included Earl BROWDER, Theodore Dreiser, and John Howard LAWSON, among others. Odets' stay in the Communist Party was a brief one. According to his own account, Odets left the party six or eight months after he joined because its critics published mercilessly uncomplimentary reviews of his plays in the *DAILY WORKER* and *New Masses*. He was especially upset when the *Daily Worker* called him "a hack writer" who wasted his time on trivial matters instead of focusing solely on proletarian themes. "I don't know how you categorize this sort of criticism," Odets complained, "but I call it very severe and very shocking."

In April 1948, the HOUSE COMMITTEE ON UN-AMERICAN ACTIVITIES (HUAC) subpoenaed Odets to testify in closed session after motion picture executive Jack Warner identified him as one of a dozen Communists he had fired from his studio. The committee subsequently called upon Odets to repeat his testimony in public the following month. In his testimony, Odets insisted that he had not consciously adopted a Marxist stance in his plays; "When I wrote, sir," he told one committee member, "it was out of central, personal things. I did not learn my hatred of poverty, sir, out of Communism." Odets also informed the committee that the bureaucracy of the Hollywood studio system, whereby directors, producers, and other executives all tampered with a screenplay before or during filming, made it virtually impossible for Communist writers to inject Marxist doctrine into a movie.

Odets provided HUAC with six names of individuals whom he identified as Communists (including Kazan). His cooperation earned him the scorn of many in the motion picture community who considered him an informer. Odets, on the other hand, preferred to emphasize the way he aggressively defended his radical past to the committee, and he resented the fact that many of his associates overlooked everything except those six names. "For the most part," Odets wrote, "the judgments (so judgmental everyone is!) of what I did and said in Washington have been disgustingly mechanical, based on a few lines printed in newspapers, right or left, when actually there were three hundred pages of typed transcripts. Personally I find this a disturbingly immoral time and this immorality exists as much on the left as on the right."

Following his appearance before HUAC, Odets returned to Hollywood, where he worked as a moderately successful screenwriter for the rest of his life, unhindered by his former radical political activities.

**One Hundred Things You Should Know about Communism** A series of pamphlets issued by the HOUSE COMMITTEE ON UN-AMERI-CAN ACTIVITIES (HUAC) in 1948 and 1949, *One Hundred Things You Should Know about*

*Communism* was divided into six separate topics, entitled *One Hundred Things You Should Know about Communism in the U.S.A., One Hundred Things You Should Know about Communism and Religion, One Hundred Things You Should Know about Communism and Labor, One Hundred Things You Should Know about Communism and Government, One Hundred Things You Should Know about Communism and Education,* and *Spotlight on Spies.* (Hence there were, in fact, 600 things that the American public needed to know about Communism.)

The pamphlets were not actually written by HUAC staffers; the committee's Chief of Staff Robert STRIPLING acknowledged that the pamphlets had been prepared with "the considerable aid" of Frank Waldrop, editor of the Washington *Times-Herald,* a steadfast journalistic supporter of HUAC. For the committee, the series represented an attempt to summarize and disseminate its findings to the American public. The pamphlets appeared at a time when the Committee's public image had been buffeted by the conviction of former chairman J. Parnell THOMAS on charges of accepting bribes from relatives whom he had placed on his office staff. The committee had failed to uncover concrete evidence of Soviet espionage in America, and President Harry S. TRUMAN appeared ready to recommend that the House of Representatives cut off funding to HUAC when the eighty-first Congress convened in 1949.

Hence the overwhelming public enthusiasm for the *One Hundred Things . . .* pamphlets must have been gratifying to the committee and its staff. In little more than twelve months, the committee distributed approximately 850,000 copies of the pamphlets free of charge; they proved so popular that another 320,000 copies were sold by the Government Printing Office at a cost of ten cents apiece.

The breezy style and question-and-answer format of the pamphlets led the authors to oversimplify both the threat posed by Communism in the United States in the late 1940s and proposed solutions. The introduction to the first pamphlet, *One Hundred Things You Should Know About Communism in the U.S.A.*, for instance, claimed that "these questions and answers are intended to help you know a Communist when you hear him speak and when you see him work. If you ever find youself in open debate with a Communist, the facts here given can be used to destroy his arguments completely and expose him as he is for all to see." The question "What is Communism?" received a one-sentence answer: "A system by which one small group seeks to rule the world."

In a similar vein, the pamphlets posed and answered the following questions:

3.  Are Communists spies?

    Anytime they are ordered to be by their Party.

6.  Are there any Communists in our Government now?

    We hate to say it, but nobody knows whether there are 3 or 3,000, even though $17,000,000 have been spent by the President in the last two years to find out. Read on for details.

10. What do the Communists want?

    To dominate your life from the cradle to the grave, in every detail.

24. Is everybody a Communist who defends Russia?

    Oh, no. Some of the loudest Russia lovers are only fellow travelers and members of Communist fronts.

27. Was Marx crazy?

    Perhaps. But Marx was not the first evil and crazy man to start a terrible world upheaval, nor was he the last. Hitler was ·like that, too, but look at what he did.

97. How can we combat them?

    Reread this pamphlet. Show it to others. Become as interested in protecting your religion as the Communists are in destroying it.

100. Can the Communists win in all this?

    It's up to you.

## Oppenheimer, J. Robert (1904–1967)

The most famous American scientist in the post-World War II era, J. Robert Oppenheimer was best known for directing the scientific research team which worked on the Manhattan Project, the top-secret wartime (1943–45) American effort to develop an atomic bomb. During the early 1950s, questions were raised about Oppenheimer's loyalty to the United States, despite his record of dedicated wartime service.

A brilliant physicist, Oppenheimer had graduated from Harvard University in three years and went on to obtain his graduate degree at Cambridge University in Great Britain. In 1929, Oppenheimer returned to the United States to take a position as an instructor at the University of California at Berkeley. Until 1936, he had not shown much interest in political affairs, but during that year Oppenheimer became outraged over the plight of the Jews in Nazi Germany. He also displayed increasing sympathy for the Loyalist cause in the Spanish Civil War and contributed freely to committees dedicated to helping the Loyalists.

Oppenheimer's brother, Frank, joined the COMMUNIST PARTY in 1936. Although Robert Oppenheimer himself was never a party member, he did become involved with the American Committee for Democracy and Intellectual Freedom, an organization with strong ties to the Communist movement in the United States. During his tenure at Berkeley, Oppenheimer also helped launch a Left-leaning teacher's union at the university, and subscribed to a radical journal, *People's World*. In short, Oppenheimer chose to associate himself with a number of left-wing groups, some of which were linked with the Communist Party, and he maintained those ties until 1941. One must remember, however, that the lines between liberalism and Communism were often blurred during the 1930s when POPULAR FRONT activities brought together individuals who were united only by their determination to defeat fascism.

In 1942, Oppenheimer began to work full-time on the Manhattan Project, the secret American initiative to develop an atomic bomb. Near the end of the year, Brigadier General Leslie R. Groves, the head of the project, selected Oppenheimer to lead the team of research scientists he had assembled to work on the bomb at a laboratory at Los Alamos, New Mexico. At that point, Groves personally read the documentation on Oppenheimer's background in the Army's files and decided that the scientist's value to the Manhattan Project far outweighed any questions about his past political associations. Nevertheless, doubts about Oppenheimer's loyalties—based upon his left-wing activities in the 1930s—precluded a security clearance through normal channels, and Groves had to order personally a clearance for Oppenheimer in December 1942.

Two months later, a colleague at Berkeley with ties to a Soviet espionage network suggested to Oppenheimer that he could pass on scientific data from the Manhattan Project to the Soviet government. Oppenheimer immediately refused, though he failed to report the contact to military security officials, a slip that would later come back to haunt him.

After the successful detonation of two atomic bombs over the Japanese cities of Hiroshima and Nagasaki, Oppenheimer left Los Alamos in October 1945, unsure whether the development of nuclear weapons had been worth the human cost. He served for a brief time as a science adviser to the United Nations Atomic Energy Commission, in hopes of obtaining some viable means of international control of atomic energy. In 1947, Oppenheimer accepted a position as director of the Institute for Advanced Study at Princeton University. During that same year, he agreed to serve as chairman of the General Advisory Committee of the newly established ATOMIC ENERGY COMMISSION (AEC), the federal-government agency responsible for supervising both the peaceful uses of atomic power and the continued research and development of nuclear weapons. Once again there was a formal investigation of Oppenheimer's political background, and once again he was cleared, despite the fact that FBI director J. Edgar HOOVER had

personally sent a report about Oppenheimer's past radical associations to AEC chairman David Lilienthal.

The HOUSE COMMITTEE ON UN-AMERICAN ACTIVITIES (HUAC) undertook an investigation of Oppenheimer's background in 1949 and called both Oppenheimer and his brother (who had quit the Communist Party in 1941, prior to joining the Manhattan Project) as witnesses. Robert Oppenheimer testified before the committee in June 1949 and apparently allayed any suspicions its members may have had; Congressman Richard M. NIXON, for one, announced that he was "tremendously impressed" with Oppenheimer's achievements and was "mighty happy" to have the scientist working for the AEC.

There matters rested until 1953, when Oppenheimer—who by that time was only a consultant to the AEC—voiced his opposition to the Eisenhower administration's "New Look" defense strategy, which included a reliance on massive retaliation and strategic bombing with nuclear weapons. Oppenheimer further alienated certain elements within the national security hierarchy by his refusal to support Eisenhower's decision to speed up research on a hydrogen (fusion) bomb.

Disagreements over national security policy soon turned into doubts about Oppenheimer's loyalty. In reviewing both Oppenheimer's criticism of the H-bomb program and the material in Oppenheimer's file on his associations with Communists in the 1930s, William Borden, the former executive director of the Joint Congressional Committee on Atomic Energy, decided that "more probably than not J. Robert Oppenheimer is an agent of the Soviet Union." From 1939 on, Borden concluded, Oppenheimer had "acted under a Soviet directive in influencing United States military, atomic energy, intelligence and diplomatic policy."

The FBI forwarded Borden's report to President Dwight D. EISENHOWER, who promptly revoked Oppenheimer's security clearance pending an investigation by the AEC. In Eisenhower's words, he wanted Oppenheimer separated from AEC secrets by a "blank wall." Oppenheimer was given a chance to resign without further investigation, but he refused. So while most of the nation watched the ARMY-MCCARTHY HEARINGS on television in April and May 1954, a special Personnel Security Board carried out yet another probe into Oppenheimer's background.

On June 1, 1954, the Board ruled 2–1 against Oppenheimer. Although they acknowledged that Oppenheimer clearly was "a loyal citizen," the two board members who voted against Oppenheimer were troubled by his past radical associations and his continuing adverse criticism of the H-bomb program. "We find that Dr. Oppenheimer's continuing conduct and associations have reflected a serious disregard for the requirements of the security system," they declared. Further, "we find his conduct in the hydrogen-bomb program sufficiently disturbing as to raise a doubt as to whether his future participation . . . would be clearly consistent with the best interests of security."

The AEC commissioners followed suit and, on June 29, voted 4–1 to revoke Oppenheimer's security clearance. Admiral Lewis Strauss, one of the four commissioners to cast a negative vote, explained that he had been persuaded by Oppenheimer's "fundamental defects of character and imprudent dangerous associations," though the commissioners made it clear that they did not question Oppenheimer's present loyalty to the United States.

While President Eisenhower refused to comment on the AEC's decision, many scientists—including Albert EINSTEIN—announced their support for Oppenheimer. Critics of the AEC charged that the Eisenhower administration had made Oppenheimer a scapegoat for the lack of substantive progress on the H-bomb project; others suggested that the administration had sacrificed Oppenheimer to McCarthy in an attempt to persuade the senator not to interfere with the H-bomb research effort.

Oppenheimer never held another position with the federal government. In recognition of his contributions to the nation's security, however, President Lyndon Johnson presented Oppenheimer in December 1963 with the Fermi Award, the highest honor awarded annually by the AEC. Ill with cancer, Oppenheimer spent the remainder of his life at Princeton University teaching part-time and supervising research projects.

**Ordeal by Slander** Published by Little, Brown & Company in 1950, *Ordeal by Slander* represented a 236-page, detailed defense by Owen LATTIMORE against the charges leveled against him by Senator Joseph MCCARTHY. *Ordeal* was written quickly, in the space of four weeks, while Lattimore's name was still front-page news.

Despite Lattimore's protestations of objectivity, *Ordeal* was a one-sided account of his experiences in the spring of 1950 after McCarthy identified him as "the top Russian espionage agent in the country." Lattimore portrays himself as an innocent victim of McCarthy's reckless and blustering charges. "Like a dream that begins with something ridiculous, and then branches and sprawls and crawls into horror and terror," wrote Lattimore, "the nightmare began to grow." The book was not necessarily enhanced by the insights which Lattimore provides into his emotional state during the ordeal: "At first my anger had been boiling hot," he claimed with self-righteous indignation. "By now it had grown cold and sharp-edged."

*Ordeal* opened in Afghanistan—where Lattimore was serving with a United Nations Technical Assistance Commission—with Lattimore's receipt of a telegram advising him of McCarthy's charges. It followed Lattimore as he returned to the United States, confronted McCarthy (with the aid of his wife, Eleanor, and attorney Abe FORTAS), and convincingly disposed of the accusations against him. It concluded with the hearings held by the TYDINGS subcommittee, which had been established by the Senate to investigate McCarthy's charges of Communists in the State Department. Much of the latter part of the book consisted of verbatim copies of Lattimore's statements to the Tydings subcommittee.

Along the way, Lattimore provided his own assessment of Joseph McCarthy. "The newspaper picture of McCarthy," Lattimore wrote, "is misleading. It does not begin to reveal how dangerous he really is. He is usually described as a reckless political gambler and a wild-swinging bruiser who charges into a brawl without sizing up the situation. The truth is that every move he makes is coldly calculated, and that he is the master of a formidable technique." McCarthy's "technique of vilification," as Lattimore described it, included "the repeated lie, renewing a charge after it has been disproved"; "the alternative lie, switching from one unsupported charge to another"; and the use of innuendo and misrepresentation in such volume that "it was impossible to deal in full detail with the whole mass."

*Ordeal* concluded with a plea to the American public to resist attempts by men "hungry for dictatorial power to impose upon us a regimented conformity of belief and opinion. . . . It is more than our democratic right to oppose these men. It is the most sacred of our duties." When *Ordeal by Slander* was originally published, many reviewers praised Lattimore's willingness to engage McCarthy in debate. Despite brisk sales in the first year following publication, the book had no appreciable negative effect on McCarthy's anti-Communist crusade.

## Ornitz, Samuel (1891–1957)

A left-wing writer and long-time radical, Samuel Ornitz was the oldest member of the group of motion picture screenwriters and directors known as the HOLLYWOOD TEN. The son of a successful merchant, Ornitz rejected a career in business (both of his brothers became top executives of steel companies) to dedicate his life to social work and the promotion of political causes through his writing.

His first major literary success was a humorous novel of Jewish immigrant life entitled *Haunch, Paunch and Jowl,* published in 1923. Its success earned Ornitz an invitation to Hollywood to write screenplays, but he never distinguished himself by his work for films. He spent most of his movie career writing "B" movies—compiling twenty-five screenplay credits between 1929 and 1949—and by the end of World War II he had slipped out of favor among the studios.

Ornitz was, however, one of the leading Communists in Hollywood, having joined the COMMUNIST PARTY in New York in the 1920s. He campaigned for left-wing candidate William Z. FOSTER in the presidential campaign of 1932, participated in numerous POPULAR FRONT (that is, antifascist) organizations in the 1930s, and served—along with John Howard LAWSON and Lester COLE—as one of the founders of the SCREEN WRITERS' GUILD in 1934. When the HOUSE COMMITTEE ON UN-AMERICAN ACTIVITIES (HUAC) first threatened to investigate Communism in Hollywood in 1940, Ornitz was one of the witnesses scheduled to testify. The inquiry never made much progress, and the committee was soon distracted by the outbreak of war in December 1941.

When HUAC returned to probe the motion picture industry more closely in 1947, Ornitz was one of the nineteen "unfriendly" witnesses the committee considered calling to testify. When he appeared to testify on October 29, 1947, Ornitz asked to read a statement in which he accused HUAC of anti-Semitism and racism, comparing the threat of contempt to a concentration camp. Chairman J. Parnell THOMAS refused to allow Ornitz to enter the statement into the record and flew into such a rage while Ornitz was testifying that he ordered Ornitz to leave the stand even before a committee investigator could ask the critical question, "Are you now, or have you ever been a member of the Communist Party?" When Thomas recovered his composure and allowed the question to be asked, Ornitz refused to answer. He was subsequently cited for contempt of Congress, convicted, and sentenced to one year in prison and a fine of $1,000.

Already ill with cancer, Ornitz served his entire sentence in the hospital of the federal prison in Springfield, Massachusetts. He spent part of the time reviewing the proofs for his final novel, *Bride of the Sabbath,* published in 1951. Ornitz died six years later.

## Oxnam, Garfield Bromley (1891–1963)

A Methodist bishop, G. Bromley Oxnam was the most prominent ecclesiastical critic of Senator Joseph MCCARTHY and his fellow zealots in the anti-Communist crusade in the United States during the late 1940s and early 1950s. At that time, Bromley was one of the nation's leading clergymen and a longtime supporter of liberal political causes. He was resident bishop of New York from 1944 to 1952 and bishop of Washington between 1952 and 1960. From 1948 to 1954, Bromley was president of the World Council of Churches for North and South America.

Shortly after Representative Harold VELDE assumed the chairmanship of the HOUSE COMMITTEE ON UN-AMERICAN ACTIVITIES (HUAC) in 1953, the committee ventured for the first time to investigate the ties between Communism and organized religion in the United States. Their primary target was Oxnam, who had frequently criticized the irresponsible methods employed by the committee in its investigations, as well as the prevailing atmosphere of stifling political and social conformism. Oxnam particularly deplored the intrusion of political affairs into the realm of the church. "There are some," Oxnam charged, "who insist that the hallelujahs of religion shall always support the hurrahs of the state." In reply, Congressman Donald L. Jackson of California, a member of HUAC, announced on the floor of the House of Representatives that "Bishop Bromley Oxnam has been to the Communist front what Man o' War was to thoroughbred horseracing, and no one except the good Bishop pays much attention to his fulminations these days. Having served God on Sunday and the Communist front for the balance of the week over such a long period of time, it is no wonder that the Bishop sees an investigating committee in every vestry."

Oxnam responded with a challenge to the committee to "name one clergyman who holds a position of large responsibility in any Protestant church who is a member of the COMMUNIST PARTY." He also insisted upon a full and public hearing before the committee of all the allegations that had been made against him by previous witnesses or unnamed informants. (Over the previous seven years, the committee had released to the press information about Oxnam from its files from time to time, despite the fact that much of the material was nothing more than unsubstantiated hearsay or gossip.)

The committee granted Oxnam's request, and the hearing took place on July 21, 1953. Oxnam was permitted only fifteen minutes to make an opening statement; the ensuing questioning took nearly ten hours and the testimony filled more than 200 pages. Velde commenced the hearing by disclaiming any intention of launching an investigation of religion in America. "It is incidental to this hearing," he stated, "that the witness is a man of the cloth." In his prepared statement, Oxnam bitterly denounced the committee for releasing material that had been "prepared in a way capable of creating the impression that I have been and am sympathetic to Communism, and therefore subversive." Bromley thereupon proceeded to make it perfectly clear that his religious faith precluded any belief in Communism whatsoever. "As a result of long study and of prayer," he noted, "I am by conviction pledged to the free way of life and opposed to all forms of totalitarianism, left or right, and to all tendencies toward such practices at home or abroad. Consequently, I have been actively opposed to Communism all my life. I have never been a member of the Communist Party. My opposition to Communism is a matter of public record in books, numerous articles, addresses, and sermons, and in resolutions I have drafted or sponsored in which powerful religious agencies have been put on record as opposed to Communism."

Bromley then launched into an attack upon the committee's method of conducting its inquiries. HUAC, he charged, frequently released on official letterhead—with a signature by an official clerk—unverified and unevaluated material to citizens, organizations, and other members of Congress. Although the committee assumed no responsibility for the accuracy of the information it released, Bromley argued that it was not surprising that many recipients assumed it represented the Committee's conclusions. "The preparation and publication of these files puts into the hands of irresponsible individuals and agencies a wicked tool," continued Bromley. "It gives rise to a new and vicious expression of Ku-Kluxism, in which an innocent person may be beaten by unknown assailants, who are cloaked in anonymity and at times immunity, and whose whips are cleverly constructed lists of so-called subversive organizations and whose floggings appear all too often to be sadistic in spirit rather than patriotic in purpose."

The committee then proceeded to demonstrate the validity of Oxnam's charges. In confronting Bromley with the material they had assembled in its file on him, committee investigators failed to prove that Oxnam had ever knowingly supported a Communist-front organization. Instead, their charges demonstrated that they did not understand the very organizations that they claimed were Communist fronts. For instance, HUAC attorney Robert L. Kunzig noted that Oxnam had been an active member of the AMERICAN CIVIL LIBERTIES UNION (ACLU) since 1946, although the ACLU had thrown out all its Communist members in 1940. Oxnam acknowledged that he had served as "editorial adviser" of the *Protestant Digest* in

1940, but had resigned in 1942—five years before the attorney general identified the *Digest* as a subversive publication—when an associate told him the journal was run by Communists. Representative Francis WALTER even taxed Oxnam for not turning in a former professor from the Boston School of Theology to the FBI when he learned that his teacher had Communist sympathies.

By the time the hearing finally limped to a conclusion, it had become obvious that much of the material in the committee's files on Oxnam had been clipped from various sources, including the *DAILY WORKER* and that no one from HUAC had taken the time to investigate the validity of the information. Public reaction appeared to be decidedly in Oxnam's favor, and the incident certainly dampened Velde's enthusiasm for launching a full-fledged inquiry into the American organized religion establishment. Yet Congressman Walter, for one, refused to acknowledge that Oxnam had been cleared of suspicion of pro-Communist beliefs. "I don't know why anyone would say he was cleared because no one ever charged him with anything," huffed Walter. "I think the hearing demonstrated very clearly that the Communists are using well known and highly placed persons as dupes and the bigger name the better for their cause. I place Bishop Oxnam as being in this category."

Following his appearance before the HUAC, Oxnam returned to his work as bishop of the Washington, D.C., metropolitan area. He retired from that position in 1960, and died three years later.

# P

**Papp, Joseph** (1921–1991)   A leading producer of Shakespearean theatre in the United States, Joseph Papp was a victim of the anti-Communist crusade as it lingered into the late 1950s and early 1960s.

Born Joseph Papirofsky, the son of a trunk-maker, Papp grew up in Brooklyn's slums. To help support his family, he worked nights in a laundry while attending high school during the day. He became interested in theatre and was deeply impressed by such organizations as the Group Theatre, which attempted to stage socially relevant dramas at prices that the working class could afford.

From 1938 to 1946, Papp served in the U.S. Navy, and was discharged as chief petty officer at the end of World War II, and used the G.I. Bill of Rights benefits, to study acting and directing at the Actors' Laboratory Theatre in Hollywood, California, from 1946 to 1948. While teaching acting to workers at the California Labor School, he worked for the Actors' Laboratory for two more years.

In 1950, he joined the prestigious National Company and toured the country as assistant stage manager for its production of *Death of a Salesman*. Papp finally returned to New York in 1951 to direct several one-act plays by Sean O'Casey in off-Broadway theaters; during that same year, he stage managed for CBS-TV, where his responsibilities included the network's dramatic anthology program *Studio One* and the *I've Got a Secret* quiz show

Papp used his CBS job to support his family while working in his free time to establish the New York Shakespeare Festival. He envisioned a free Shakespeare theatre for New Yorkers—a classical version of the Group Theatre he had known as a boy in the 1930s. Papp served as producer and director of the festival in its early years, staging its productions at the Emmanuel Presbyterian Church in downtown Manhattan. Bereft of financial support, he employed an in-novative approach to traditional Shakespearean drama to compensate for the absence of expensive sets and costumes. Besides its productions for the general public, the festival also presented Shakespeare to high school students in the New York area free of charge.

On April 16, 1958, Papp received a subpoena from the HOUSE COMMITTEE ON UN-AMERICAN ACTIVITIES (HUAC) and appeared before the committee on June 19 of that year to inform the committee that he was not at that time a member of the COMMUNIST PARTY; he refused, however, to answer any questions about his political activities prior to February 1955, pleading the Fifth Amendment. When a committee investigator charged that the California Labor School where Papp had taught for several years was "controlled by the Communist conspiracy," he replied that he had not been aware of that fact. Papp stated that he had not attempted to recruit any other entertainers into the Communist Party and scoffed at the suggestion that he had used his "glamour and prestige" to promote noncooperation with HUAC: "I have no glamour and prestige," Papp insisted. "I think it is a misnomer to use that."

Papp acknowledged that he had joined with fellow members of the Actors Laboratory to denounce HUAC's 1951 investigation into Communist influence in the entertainment industry, describing the committee's actions as "star chamber proceedings," and he admitted that he had criticized actor Larry PARKS for his controversial decision to name numerous former political associates as Communists or Communist sympathizers in his testimony before HUAC in 1951. "The feeling I would have about Mr. Parks," said Papp, "would be the same feeling I would have about anybody who would gratuitously injure the people who work with him in the way he did." Not surprisingly, Papp refused to provide the committee with the names of any of his own former political associates. "You know there is a blacklisting device in the industry," noted Papp, "and the naming of people this way does deny these people the right to work, which I think is terribly unfair and un-American."

The committee's inquiry into Papp's activities reached its nadir when HUAC Chairman Morgan Moulder of West Virginia asked whether Papp tried to "intentionally control the operation of the entertainment which you produce or supervise"—that is, Shakespearean drama—"for the purpose of influencing sympathy toward Communism?" Papp replied that the answer to Moulder's question was obviously no, though he did acknowledge that some of Shakespeare's plays "might be considered propagandistic."

HUAC's unenlightening confrontation with Papp revealed the depths to which the committee had sunk in its attempts to uncover new evidence of Communist infiltration of the entertainment industry in the late 1950s. Yet Papp's appearance also testified to the continuing power of the BLACKLIST, for shortly after invoking the Fifth Amendment in his HUAC testimony, he was fired by CBS from his stage manager's job. The network later reinstated him after an arbitrator ruled that its decision to dismiss him had been capricious and unjust.

Papp subsequently earned a national reputation as an innovative producer of Shakespearean drama and avant-garde plays. Among his most famous productions between 1966 and 1990 were *Hair, Sticks and Bones,* and *A Chorus Line.* Papp never lost his commitment to social justice and artistic freedom; in 1990, he rejected a grant from the National Endowment of the Arts because of an antiobscenity restriction on the award. Papp died of prostate cancer in 1991.

**Parks, Larry** (1914–1975)  The first Hollywood celebrity to admit publicly that he had been a Communist, Larry Parks saw his once-promising acting career disintegrate following his appearance before the HOUSE COMMITTEE ON UN-AMERICAN ACTIVITIES.

A native of Kansas, Parks had studied chemistry and physics at the University of Illinois, from which he received his B.A. in 1936. He opted for a career in the theater, however, and became a member of the left-wing Group Theatre in the late 1930s. In 1941, Parks moved to Hollywood, where he became a contract player with Columbia Pictures. He appeared in several dozen low-budget films while working with the Actors' Laboratory Theater, a combined drama school/repertory theater that occasionally performed plays with liberal political themes.

By his own admission, Parks joined the COMMUNIST PARTY in 1941 and remained a member until late 1944 or early 1945. As he later explained, "being a member of the Communist Party fulfilled certain needs of a young man that was liberal in thought, idealistic, who was for the underprivileged, the underdog. I felt that it fulfilled these particular needs." Parks claimed that after he joined the party, he attended very few meetings and gradually drifted out altogether.

Following the end of World War II, Parks received his big break when Columbia chose him for the title role in *The Jolson Story,* a film biography of singer-actor Al Jolson. The enormous popular success of *The Jolson Story* gave him the opportunity to play in other major films, including *Down to Earth* and *Jolson Sings Again.* His career came to a screeching halt in 1951, however, when he was called to testify before the HUAC as part of its renewed investigation of Communist influence in the motion picture industry.

Parks appeared before the committee on March 21, 1951. In response to questions from committee members and staff, he readily acknowledged that he had been a Communist a decade earlier but stoutly maintained that he felt he had done nothing wrong. He also expressed his willingness to answer any questions about his own past political activities and associations but repeatedly begged the committee not to ask him questions about other individuals whom it suspected of being Communists, especially because HUAC investigators already had obtained information that tended to incriminate them. "I would prefer not to mention names, if it is at all possible," Parks told the committee. "I don't think it is fair to people to do this. I have come to you at your request. I will tell you everything that I know about myself, because I feel I have done nothing wrong, and I will answer any question that you would like to put to me about myself. I would prefer, if you will allow me, not to mention other people's names."

As the committee continued to press him to reveal the names of his former associates in the Communist Party, Parks grew increasingly frantic. At last he was reduced to a tearful plea that is still painful to read. "I have two boys," Parks told the committee, "one thirteen months, one two weeks."

> Is this the kind of heritage that I must hand down to them? Is this the kind of heritage that you would like to hand down to your children? And for what purpose? children as innocent as I am or you are, people you already know . . .
>
> I think my career has been ruined because of this, and I would appreciate not having to— Don't present me with the choice of either being in contempt of this Committee and going to jail or forcing me to really crawl through the mud to be an informer. For what purpose? I don't think this is a choice at all. I don't think this is really sportsmanlike. I don't think this is American. I don't think this is American justice. . . .
>
> I chose to come and tell the truth. If you do this to me, I think it will impair the usefulness of this Committee to a great extent, because it will make it almost impossible for a person to come to you, as I have done, and open himself to you and tell you the truth. So I beg of you not to force me to do this.

The committee insisted, and finally—during a meeting in executive session—Parks provided HUAC with the names of seven individuals whom he identified as members of the Communist Party cell to which he had belonged in the

early 1940s, including Gale SONDERGAARD, Ann Revere, and Lee J. COBB.

As Parks predicted, his career was ruined by his testimony before HUAC: the Hollywood studios and the public shunned him for his Communist past, and liberal members of the motion picture industry scorned him for providing the committee with the names of former associates. For the remainder of his life, Parks appeared in only a handful of motion pictures, many of which were made outside the United States. His last performance was in John Huston's film *Freud,* which appeared in 1963. Parks died of a heart attack at his home in California on April 13, 1975, at the age of 60.

**Pauling, Linus C.** (1901–1994)   The only individual to win two Nobel Prizes on his own (Marie Curie won one and shared another), Linus Pauling combined a career in scientific research with a commitment to world peace and the cessation of nuclear testing.

Born in Portland, Oregon, and graduated from Oregon State College in 1922 with majors in chemistry and physics, Pauling pursued graduate study at the California Institute of Technology, from which he received a Ph.D. in 1925. The following year, a Guggenheim Fellowship enabled him to study in Europe with Arnold Summerfield, Erwin Schrödinger, and Niels Bohr.

Early in his career, while he was teaching at the California Institute of Technology, Pauling explored the nature of the chemical bond in inorganic and complex organic molecules. He employed the new method of wave mechanics to develop a resonance theory to explain the structure of certain complicated substances. Pauling's findings in this field—published in numerous papers and his first book, *The Nature of the Chemical Bond and the Structure of Molecules and Crystals* (1939)—led eventually to the development of numerous new drugs, plastics, and synthetic fibers.

During World War II, Pauling worked in the explosives division of the National Defense

Research Commission, and on a medical research committee of the Office of Scientific Research and Development. In 1942, he and two colleagues produced the first synthetic antibodies, and in 1945 he chaired a project that developed a substitute for blood plasma from gelatin. For his wartime work, Pauling was awarded the Presidential Medal for Merit.

Continuing his research into the nature of molecular structures after the war, Pauling and Robert B. Corey announced in 1951 that they had discovered the structure of several different types of protein molecules. For this and his subsequent discoveries in the field, Pauling was awarded the Nobel Prize for Chemistry in 1954.

By that time, Pauling's views on contemporary political affairs had made him an object of considerable suspicion among the leaders of the anti-Communist crusade in the United States. Following the use by the United States of two nuclear weapons against Japan in 1945, Pauling became an active opponent of nuclear testing and a proponent of multilateral disarmament, warning that continued nuclear testing would endanger the health of millions of children of the present and future generations through the long-term effects of radiation. Together with Albert EINSTEIN and J. Robert OPPENHEIMER, Pauling helped found the BULLETIN OF ATOMIC SCIENTISTS, which attempted to convey the political and social concerns of scientists to the lay public. In 1947, Pauling joined actor Charlie CHAPLIN in protesting the vigorous investigation of composer Hanns EISLER by the HOUSE COMMITTEE ON UN-AMERICAN ACTIVITIES (HUAC). In 1949, Pauling and Einstein established the antiwar Committee for Peaceful Alternatives, and the following year Pauling spoke out strongly against the passage of the INTERNAL SECURITY ACT OF 1950. When the California state legislature imposed a LOYALTY OATH on all employees of the University of California, Pauling ventured to Sacramento to oppose the measure in person. The oath—which was also opposed by then-Governor Earl WARREN—eventually was declared unconstitutional.

By 1952, Pauling's political activities had become so objectionable to the anti-Communist crusaders in the United States that the State Department refused to issue him a passport to travel to Britain to address the Royal Society. In response to charges by Senator Joseph MCCARTHY and ex-Communist Louis BUDENZ, Pauling swore that he had never been a member of the COMMUNIST PARTY. (In fact, he swore it on six different occasions.) He denied that he was a Communist or an agent of the Soviet Union. "I am not even a theoretical Marxist," he stated, adding that "nobody tells me what to think except Mrs. Pauling." Pauling assured State Department officials that some of his theories were considered heresy in the Soviet Union and even telephoned and wrote personal letters to President Harry S. TRUMAN and Secretary of State Dean ACHESON—to no avail; the State Department adamantly refused to grant him permission to travel abroad, informing him that it suspected him of being a "secret Communist." When Pauling won the Nobel Prize in 1954, however, the State Department reversed itself at the last moment and allowed him to go to Oslo to accept the prize from King Olaf of Norway.

In 1958, Pauling joined philosopher Bertrand Russell and former Socialist Party presidential candidate Norman Thomas in filing suit against the Defense Department and the ATOMIC ENERGY COMMISSION to cease nuclear testing. Pauling also gathered the signatures of 35 Nobel laureates and more than 9,000 other scientists on a petition to stop nuclear tests and presented the document to the United Nations. Nuclear fallout, he warned, did not respect territorial boundaries or political ideologies, and thus the issue of safety "must not be confused by minor problems such as Communism vs. Capitalism." But because the Soviet Union had long supported the notion of a test-ban treaty, Pauling's advocacy of a test ban made him suspect as a tool of the international Communist movement. Two years later, the Senate Internal Security Subcommittee—which had listed Pauling as a "typical sponsor of Communist fronts" in one of his publications—pressed Pauling to provide it with the names of the individuals who had helped him circulate his petitions for nuclear disarmament. He flatly refused.

In 1961, Pauling sent a message to the Soviet government via Radio Free Europe, urging it, too, to cease nuclear testing. On October 10, 1963, the day that a partial test ban treaty between the United States and the USSR went into effect, the Nobel Prize committee announced that Pauling had won the 1962 Nobel Peace Prize, which had not been awarded the previous year. When reporters asked him which of his two Novel Prizes he deemed more significant, Pauling replied, "Today's, I think, perhaps because I feel so strongly about the need for peace and an end to human suffering from wars." Several weeks later, Pauling received 2,400 write-in votes in the California gubernatorial election.

Pauling took a leave of absence from the California Insitute of Technology in 1963 to join the Center for the Study of Democratic Institutions, though he continued to supervise research projects at Caltech. He subsequently became an outspoken opponent of American involvement in the Vietnam War.

## Pearson, Drew (1897–1969)   In the early 1950s, Drew Pearson was the most widely read newspaper columnist in the United States. A graduate of Phillips Exeter Academy and Swarthmore College, Pearson had originally planned a career as a diplomat. Following World War I, he served as director of relief in the Balkans for the British Red Cross. For the next ten years, Pearson worked at a variety of jobs: teaching at the University of Pennsylvania and Columbia University, sailing on the crew of merchant ships in the Far East and Australia, and writing newspaper articles as a freelance journalist.

Pearson joined the staff of the Baltimore *Sun* in 1929 and subsequently became head of its Washington bureau. Together with Robert S.

Columnist Drew Pearson frequently attacked Senator Joseph McCarthy; McCarthy physically assaulted Pearson in 1950.

Allen of the *Christian Science Monitor,* Pearson published anonymously several books—*Washington Merry-Go-Round* (1931) and *More Merry-Go-Round* (1932)—that used the sort of gossip newspapers would not print. When their authorship of the books became known, Pearson and Allen were fired by their newspapers. They decided to continue publishing inside information as part of a regular column; distributed by United Features syndicate, it had become by 1941 the most widely read political column in the nation. Following Allen's departure from the partnership in 1942, Pearson added a weekly radio show which also featured his "predictions of things to come."

By 1950, Pearson had earned a reputation as a fearless investigator with excellent sources of information and an admirable record for uncovering corruption in the federal government. "My chief motive," he told another reporter, "is to try to make the Government a little cleaner, a little more efficient, and I would say also, in foreign affairs, to try to work for peace."

Yet, Pearson was perhaps also the most hated man in Washington. Prominent figures from both major political parties openly despised the columnist. President Franklin D. Roosevelt once referred to him as "a chronic liar;" President Harry S. TRUMAN called Pearson an "S.O.B." and refused to invite him to the White House after Pearson wrote a column critical of Truman's wife, Bess. Pearson was sued by General Douglas MACARTHUR for $1.75 million for claiming that MacArthur had lobbied for his own promotion, and Senator Kenneth McKellar of Tennessee was so outraged by one Pearson column that he denounced the journalist as "an ignorant liar, a pusillanimous liar, a peewee liar . . . a revolting, constitutional, unmitigated, infamous liar." Pearson appeared totally undaunted by the assaults on his character. "I suppose I've got more enemies per square inch on Capitol Hill," he noted with pride, "than any place else in the world."

Given his prominence in Washington journalistic circles, it was not surprising that Pearson was involved in the initial furor over Senator Joseph MCCARTHY's charges of Communists in the State Department. On February 18, 1950, Pearson became the first nationally syndicated columnist to bring McCarthy's charges to the attention of a national audience, and it was Pearson who broke the news on March 26 that Owen LATTIMORE was the man whom McCarthy had named as "the top Russian espionage agent in America." For the most part, Pearson presented evidence that contradicted McCarthy's charges, revealing that the lists of alleged subversives upon which McCarthy relied had been discredited by other, more discriminating investigators. "Every man on the McCarthy list has already been scrutinized by the House Un-American Activities Committee or by a House appropriations subcommittee," Pearson charged. "This writer, who has covered the State Department for about 20 years, has been considered the career boys' severest critic. However,

knowing something about State Department personnel, it is my opinion that Sen. McCarthy is way off-base."

Pearson maintained his attacks upon McCarthy's veracity throughout the rest of that year. On December 12, the two men met face-to-face at a dinner party at the upstairs ballroom of the Sulgrave Club in downtown Washington. According to Pearson, McCarthy greeted him "with a sort of mock effusiveness. . . . He pretended to be very cordial. He said, 'I'm really going to tear you apart on the Senate floor tomorrow. . . . I'm really going to tear you to pieces.'" McCarthy continued to threaten Pearson throughout the evening; at one point he invited Pearson, who was considerably older and smaller than McCarthy, to step outside and settle their differences with their fists.

Following dinner, while most of the guests were on the dance floor, McCarthy and Pearson were left at a table with Representatives Richard M. NIXON (who had just been elected to the Senate) and Charles Bennett. McCarthy repeated his threat to criticize Pearson in the Senate, "to say some things the country should know." Pearson replied that he planned to say plenty of things about McCarthy in his forthcoming columns; "I've never gone after a man yet that I haven't gotten in the end," he warned. McCarthy invited Pearson to write whatever he pleased—"I've been called everything in the world," the senator declared—and Pearson responded by taunting McCarthy about his personal financial difficulties. "Joe, how is your income tax case coming along?" Pearson asked. "When are they going to put you in jail?"

At that point, McCarthy grabbed the fifty-four-year-old Pearson by the back of the neck. Bennett broke up the confrontation, but McCarthy and Pearson met again in the cloakroom at the end of the evening. As Pearson reached into his pocket for his coat check, McCarthy apparently thought that he was reaching for some sort of weapon. Shouting, "Don't you reach into your pocket like that," he pinned Pearson's arms behind him and kneed him twice in the groin. Gasping for breath, Pearson asked when someone was finally going to put McCarthy "in the booby hatch." McCarthy then slapped Pearson twice hard across the face, knocking the columnist to the ground. Nixon—who claimed that he had never seen anyone slapped as hard as McCarthy struck Pearson—stepped between the two men, but McCarthy refused to leave the cloakroom until Pearson was gone. "I won't turn my back on that son of a bitch," McCarthy said. "He's got to go first."

Over the next two weeks, McCarthy bragged to numerous admirers about his assault upon Pearson, for which he reportedly received congratulations from two dozen senators. On December 15, McCarthy delivered his promised denunciation of the columnist, describing Pearson as the "voice of international communism" and a "Moscow-directed character assassin." "It appears that Pearson never actually signed up as a member of the COMMUNIST PARTY and never paid dues," McCarthy admitted, but he claimed that Pearson and his associates had been disseminating Soviet propaganda. If newspaper publishers and radio-station owners refused to buy Pearson's column, McCarthy promised, "this disguised, sugar-coated voice of Russia . . . would disappear." McCarthy concluded by threatening a boycott against the Adam Hat company, the sponsor of Pearson's radio broadcasts: "Anyone who buys an Adams [sic] hat, any store that stocks an Adams hat, anyone who buys from a store that stocks an Adams hat, is unknowingly and innocently contributing to the cause of international Communism by keeping this Communist spokesman on the air."

Pearson asked Senator Lyndon Baines JOHNSON to clear his name with a speech from the Senate floor, but Johnson refused. Pearson then attempted to repudiate McCarthy's accusations by arguing that his record of fighting communism was considerably more impressive than the Wisconsin senator's, but on December 30, a spokesman for the Adam Hat company announced that it was withdrawing as the sponsor

of the columnist's broadcasts. McCarthy continued to pursue Pearson, urging newspapers to refuse to carry the columns of "an exposed, known, deliberate liar." Pearson retaliated in March 1951 by filing suit against McCarthy and several of his right-wing associates in the media. Requesting $5.1 million in damages, Pearson accused McCarthy of assault (at the Sulgrave Club), libel, and conspiracy. Since McCarthy was immune from libel charges for any statements he made in the Senate, Pearson had virtually no chance to prove his case, and he dropped the lawsuit in 1954.

In the final years of McCarthy's life, the senator attempted to settle his differences with Pearson. Pearson later claimed that the "silent treatment" afforded McCarthy by journalists following his censure by the Senate in December 1954 had hastened McCarthy's death. "The exhilarating stimulus of the crowds, of the headlines, of the klieg lights ruined Joe's effectiveness in his earlier days," Pearson wrote. "The exhilarating stimulus of alcohol ruined his effectiveness in recent days. . . . I'm afraid Joe wanted to die. He would not have stuck to his diet of whiskey had he wanted to live."

Pearson survived McCarthy's allegations; such attacks, he acknowledged, were "part of the business." Pearson's weekly radio broadcast soon acquired another sponsor, and by 1969 his daily column was appearing in nearly 600 newspapers. In later years, Pearson supplemented his income from journalism by selling manure from a herd of 200 cattle on his farm in Maryland and from the Chicago stockyards. Marketed under the name of "Drew Pearson's Best Manure," the fertilizer was touted as even "better than in the column."

Pearson died of a heart attack on September 1, 1969.

**Pegler, Westbrook** (1894–1963)   An Englishman who emigrated to the United States and became a noted journalist for the *New York Daily Mirror,* Westbrook Pegler was one of the most widely read newspaper columnists in

America in the 1940s and 1950s. He entered the journalism business via the United Press syndicate at the age of 16. After returning to high school to complete his education, he worked for newspapers in Iowa, Missouri, and Texas before joining the United Press staff in London as a foreign correspondent. During World War I, the congenitally contentious Pegler—who was acquiring a reputation as "the man who made dissension a philosophy"—managed to antagonize General John "Black Jack" Pershing; Pershing subsequently ordered Pegler's employers to ship him back to the United States.

Following the conclusion of the war, Pegler became a sportswriter because, he explained, "the big salaries on newspapers usually were paid to the sports men." In 1925, the Chicago *Tribune* hired Pegler to write a daily syndicated sports column. On days when he ran out of sports topics, Pegler began to write about national political events. His column proved so popular that the New York *World Telegram* hired him to write a syndicated column in 1933; by 1940, his column was carried in 114 newspapers across the United States with a total circulation of 6.5 million readers.

A man who consistently expressed his opinions in abusive and vitriolic prose, Pegler managed to outrage virtually all his readers at one time or another in his career. During the 1930s he despised European fascism and once described Adolf Hitler and Benito Mussolini as racketeers; he also denounced the New Deal, characterizing President Franklin Delano Roosevelt as a "mamma's boy." Other Pegler targets included flamboyant Governor Huey Long of Louisiana, muckraking novelist Upton Sinclair, former Secretary of the Interior Harold Ickes, publisher William Randolph Hearst (whom he termed a "never to be adequately damned demagogue and historic scoundrel"), and virtually every leader of organized labor in the United States. Pegler regularly attacked the CONGRESS OF INDUSTRIAL ORGANIZATIONS, claiming that

its member unions were led either by Communists or organized crime bosses.

By 1950, Pegler had become one of America's most prominent right-wing columnists. Writing for the Hearst Corporation's chain of newspapers, Pegler posed as an opponent of popular democracy. He referred to American voters as "faceless boobs," suggested that the state of Arizona would be far better off if it jettisoned the outmoded practice of popular elections and allowed businessmen to run its affairs, and supported the revival of the terrorist racist organization known as the Ku Klux Klan. "I am not interested in democracy," he told a congressional committee in 1949, "except to oppose it." On February 8, 1950, one day before Senator Joseph MCCARTHY spoke in Wheeling, West Virginia, alleging Communist influence in the State Department, Pegler recommended in his column that the Republican Party should coalesce around the slogan, "Democracy is no good, so to hell with it."

Pegler served as one of McCarthy's earliest and most consistent supporters. "Joe McCarthy is so right it hurts," he told his readers in May 1952. If they wished to know the truth about McCarthy and his activities, Pegler told his readers to read an article by McCarthy in *Cosmopolitan* magazine that answered "the whole pack of lies about [McCarthy's] anti-Communist crusade that have been circulated by the Communists in our government and our journalism and by their allies, the anti-anti-Communists." Pegler also joined with Pennsylvania Governor James Duff in urging that known Communists be hanged; CBS television newsman Edward MURROW became one of his prime targets after Murrow broadcast a program critical of McCarthy and his investigative methods.

American liberals generally viewed Pegler as a member of the fascist lunatic fringe. Hollywood screenwriter Dalton TRUMBO, for instance, claimed in 1948 that "Westbrook Pegler is one of the most dangerous, malicious, and outspoken anti-Semites in the country."

Pegler's ultraconservative tirades eventually fell out of favor during the placid middle years of the Eisenhower administrations, however, and his influence as a political columnist declined accordingly. He died in 1963 at the age of 69.

*Pennsylvania v. Nelson*   In April 1956, the U.S. Supreme Court reversed the conviction of Steven Nelson, a COMMUNIST PARTY official who had been convicted under the state of Pennsylvania's sedition law. As expressed in Chief Justice Earl WARREN's majority opinion, the Court held that Congress had preempted the states from the field of internal-security legislation; because sedition was a federal crime and not a state or local offense, only federal courts could try sedition cases.

The Court's ruling effectively undercut the support that the federal government had received from state and local courts in the area of employee-loyalty programs. Further, conservative Southern senators saw the decision as an invasion of states' rights, and, therefore, it solidified the alliance between Senator Joseph MCCARTHY and Senator Joseph McClellan of Arkansas, the leader of the Southern bloc in the Senate.

**Peress, Irving** (1918– )   An army dentist who refused to answer questions about his left-wing political beliefs, Major Irving Peress briefly became the focus of Senator Joseph MCCARTHY's search for Communists in the U.S. Army in the winter of 1954. After entering the Army in January 1953 and completing basic training, Peress was awarded the rank of captain and assigned to Camp Kilmer, New Jersey. But when he was asked to complete a routine form stating whether he belonged to any organizations that the Army classified as subversive, Peress demurred and simply wrote "federal constitutional privilege" across the form.

Despite the fact that both the Federal Bureau of Investigation and the Army were investigating him as a possible security risk (he was, in fact, a member of the radical American Labor Party), Peress received a promotion to the rank of major in September 1953. The promotion stunned the commanding general of Camp Kilmer, Brigadier General Ralph W. ZWICKER. After recommending that Peress be relieved of duty, Zwicker alerted Senator McCarthy of the alleged irregularities in the dentist's case.

McCarthy, who already had launched his own investigation of Communist infiltration of the U.S. Army, did not react until after the Army announced in January 1954 that it was granting Peress an honorable discharge. Then McCarthy decided to use Peress's case to force the Army to bring members of its Loyalty and Security Appeals Board before his Senate GOVERNMENT OPERATIONS COMMITTEE so that he could interrogate them about their allegedly lax standards in weeding out security risks. "We intend," declared McCarthy, "to have those twenty persons, who cleared the Communists and sent them back to handle secret material, appear before the committee, so as to ascertain who hired them, who promoted them to those jobs, and why they cleared Communists." For a while, the cry of "Who promoted Peress?" echoed through the nation's newspapers, demonstrating both the fervor of the anti-Communist zealots and the ultimate absurdity of McCarthy's campaign.

McCarthy also insisted that the Army court-martial Peress. Punishment of the dentist, McCarthy argued, "is the only way to notify every Army officer that twenty years of treason are past and that this really is a new day." Peress, meanwhile, received his honorable discharge and returned to civilian life. Nevertheless, McCarthy subpoenaed him to testify before the Government Operations Committee. When Peress appeared on February 18, 1954, McCarthy denounced him as a Communist agent and viciously berated Peress for refusing to answer questions about his own political beliefs or to provide the committee with the names of family members whom it might also prosecute. For his part, Peress quoted to McCarthy an excerpt from the Book of Psalms: "His mischief shall return upon his own head and his violence shall come down upon his own pate."

In the end, the Army concluded that it could not court-martial Peress because it possessed insufficient evidence linking him with any subversive activity. But the affair had been marked by such bureaucratic bungling that it gave the impression of impropriety and provided McCarthy with a convenient weapon to use against the Army. The senator subsequently called General Zwicker to testify about the Peress case and then proceeded to lose his temper completely during the hearings. McCarthy's abusive treatment of Zwicker eventually redounded against him, however, and formed one of the charges in the Senate's motion of censure that effectively ended McCarthy's political career in December 1954.

## Permanent Subcommittee on Investigations

A subcommittee of the Senate COMMITTEE ON GOVERNMENT OPERATIONS, the Permanent Subcommittee on Investigations was established in 1946 as part of the Legislative Reorganization Act. In 1948, the subcommittee was used by Senator Homer Ferguson of Indiana to conduct an inquiry into the loyalty of federal employees. As part of his investigation, Ferguson called ex-Communist Elizabeth BENTLEY to testify. Then, using Bentley's allegations of Communist espionage to substantiate his request, Ferguson asked the Truman administration to turn over its files on alleged Communist William REMINGTON, who at that time was employed by the Department of Commerce. Ferguson's request touched off a full-scale confrontation between the subcommittee and the White House, which refused to turn over its files and characterized the subcommittee's hearings as a "red herring" that was "doing irreparable harm." Nevertheless, the Truman administration was able to fend off the subcommittee only by assigning the FEDERAL BUREAU OF INVESTIGATION additional investigatory authority against potential subversive activities in the United States.

In 1949–50, Senator Clyde HOEY of North Carolina assumed the chairmanship of the permanent subcommittee and used it to initiate an investigation of homosexuals in the federal government. Hoey justified his inquiry by claiming that homosexuals were potential security risks because they were liable to blackmail by Communists who threatened to expose their unconventional lifestyle.

It was Senator Joseph MCCARTHY of Wisconsin, however, who brought the permanent subcommittee to the height of its powers in 1953–54. Using the subcommittee's investigative staff and its considerable discretionary authority to his full advantage, McCarthy used the permanent subcommittee to continue his assault upon the Department of State, while also launching probes into the CENTRAL INTELLIGENCE AGENCY, the INTERNATIONAL INFORMATION AGENCY, and the U.S. Army. In effect, the Permanent Subcommittee on Investigations represented the legislative foundation of McCarthy's power in the Senate; without the personnel and authority of the subcommittee, McCarthy likely would have been unable to conduct the sort of wide-ranging investigations which characterized his anti-Communist crusade.

## Philbrick, Herbert A. (1915– )

Author of the best-selling book I LED THREE LIVES, Herbert Philbrick spent nine years in various Communist-front organizations as an undercover agent for the FEDERAL BUREAU OF INVESTIGATION (FBI). A native of New England, Philbrick worked his way through college in a variety of odd jobs, including a plumber's assistant, soap salesman, construction worker, chauffeur, and interior decorator's helper. After graduating from the Lincoln Technical Institute of Northeastern University with a degree in civil engineering, Philbrick was unable to find employment in his chosen field. Instead, he embarked upon a career in sales and advertising,

Herbert Philbrick (right), whose undercover work for the FBI led to the hit television series, *I Led Three Lives*, with Elizabeth Bentley (left).

obtaining a job with the Holmes Direct Mail Service in Cambridge, Massachusetts.

During the course of a sales call at the offices of the Massachusetts Youth Council in 1940, Philbrick expressed an interest in the Council's extensive program of antiwar propaganda. (Following the announcement of the NAZI-SOVIET PACT in 1939, the COMMUNIST PARTY OF THE UNITED STATES had adopted a policy opposing American intervention in the European war.) Officials of the Youth Council subsequently helped him establish a chapter of the organization in Cambridge, though it soon became clear to Philbrick that the policies and literature of the council bore a close resemblance to certain

Communist Party material that the leaders of the council had also distributed to him. Gradually, Philbrick came to realize that the council was, in fact, a Communist-front organization. He informed the FBI of his suspicions and was instructed by bureau agents to remain within the council to provide the government with inside information about the organization's activities.

Following the entry of the United States into World War II, the pacifist policies of the Youth Council were no longer tenable, and the organization collapsed. The council's former leaders directed Philbrick to join instead a chapter of the Young Communist League (YCL) in Wakefield,

Massachusetts. When the YCL, too, was dissolved in 1943, Philbrick became a member of the successor organization known as AMERICAN YOUTH FOR DEMOCRACY. By this time, Philbrick had become a veteran member of Communist fronts in the Boston area, and so he accepted an invitation to join the Communist Party itself in 1944. To enhance his usefulness as a future teacher within the party, Philbrick was selected to attend study groups in the process of indoctrination in Marxist ideology. Gradually, Philbrick grew closer to the inner circle of the Communist Party in New England, serving as a member of a "professional" cell that directed labor organizing drives and industrial espionage activities. In 1948, Philbrick was detailed to the Progressive Party presidential campaign of former Vice President Henry A. WALLACE as a publicist and speechwriter.

When Attorney General Tom CLARK—in an attempt to prove that the Democratic administration of President Harry S. TRUMAN was not "soft" on Communism—inaugurated the prosecution of eleven leaders of the Communist Party in the summer of 1948, the FBI asked Philbrick to provide it with material against the defendants. On April 6, 1949, Philbrick appeared as a surprise witness in the trial of the eleven party officials in New York. Drawing upon his experience over the previous nine years, Philbrick testified that the program of the Communist Party of the United States had been reformulated in 1945 upon instructions from Moscow to abandon the wartime policy of collaboration and return to the previous policy of political revolution. Philbrick also outlined the measures taken by the Party in 1947–48 to enhance its internal security and weed out potential informers. According to Philbrick, one of the Boston-area Communist organizations to which he belonged had split itself into cells of five for security reasons; members employed only their first names and were prohibited from contacting members of other cells; and practice mobilizations were staged to determine whether the party could mobilize its resources quickly and reliably in times of crisis.

Based in part upon Philbrick's testimony, which allegedly helped demonstrate that the Communist Party was constructing an underground organization specifically designed to promote violent revolution, prosecutors were able to obtain convictions of the defendants under the terms of the SMITH ACT. In the months that followed, Philbrick also provided federal authorities with the names of more than fifty other individuals whom he identified as members of the Communist Party, including academics, labor union organizers (particularly from the UNITED ELECTRICAL WORKERS), and clergymen, though he later acknowledged that he lacked firm evidence in the case of certain church leaders. It was Philbrick's testimony that revealed the left-wing background of Mrs. Mary Knowles, the former Boston-area librarian who found herself in the middle of a controversy in 1955 between right-wing zealots and the FUND FOR THE REPUBLIC after Knowles was hired by the Quaker Meeting in Plymouth, Pennsylvania.

In 1951, Philbrick accepted an offer from the publisher of the New York *Herald Tribune* to write an account of his undercover adventures. The material was serialized in the newspaper and formed the basis for the book-length version, entitled *I Led Three Lives*. The book, in turn, was subsequently turned into a television series starring Richard Carlson that was broadcast each Sunday evening on the NBC network from September 1953 to May 1956. Following the publication of his book, Philbrick continued to write for the *Herald Tribune* as author of a column entitled "The Red Underground"; at one point, his column ran in more than 500 newspapers.

As the anti-Communist fervor in the United States declined in the late 1950s, Philbrick continued to tour the country as a lecturer. His Washington-based newsletter was published on a regular basis through 1981.

**Popular Front**   During the period 1935–39, American Communists joined with liberals and socialists to form the Popular Front, an informal coalition of left-wing elements opposed to the spread of fascism and reaction at home and abroad. The formation of the Popular Front followed a drastic change in the strategy of the international Communist movement. Facing the threat of aggression from the fascist regimes of Adolf Hitler in Germany and Benito Mussolini in Italy, the Seventh World Congress of the Communist International in Moscow decided in July–August 1935 to abandon temporarily its policy of extremism and violent revolution. Instead, it sought to form a united front with progressive working-class elements everywhere, with the goal of "mass action locally, to be carried out by the local organizations through local agreements."

In the United States, the Communist Party during this period—under the leadership of Earl BROWDER—moved toward the Right and attempted to portray itself as the heir of traditional American liberal values. Revolutionary rhetoric virtually disappeared, as Browder claimed that the party no longer took its marching orders from the Soviet Union. The line between the American Communist and Socialist parties became blurred, much to the confusion and eventual detriment of the Socialist movement. The COMMUNIST PARTY OF THE UNITED STATES abandoned its harsh criticism of the New Deal programs of President Franklin Delano Roosevelt, and proclaimed its support for legislation in favor of public-works projects, unemployment compensation, civil rights, and labor's right to organize and bargain collectively.

The party's shift in strategy coincided with a lurch toward the Left in American domestic politics, largely as a result of the desperate economic conditions produced by the Great Depression of 1929–40. Numerous American liberals and labor leaders readily joined hands with the Communists to achieve their objectives. The rise of Nazism in Germany had alarmed American liberals and intellectuals almost as much as it terrified the leaders of the Soviet Union, and the Communist Party—with its tempered rhetoric—seemed a viable ally against the anti-Semitic, militaristic regime in Berlin. Con-

sequently, American liberals cooperated with Communists and, in some cases, knowingly joined the party or Communist-front organizations. The Spanish Civil War of 1936–37, which pitted the leftist Loyalist regime (supported by the Soviet Union) against the fascist forces of General Francisco Franco (who received aid from Nazi Germany), provided perhaps the decade's most obvious opportunity for Communists and liberals to join together to oppose the trend of reaction abroad. Besides those who enlisted in the Loyalist Republican army in Spain, thousands of American liberals joined such organizations as the JOINT ANTI-FASCIST REFUGEE COMMITTEE, which purportedly had been formed to assist refugees from the Spanish conflict as Franco's forces gradually emerged victorious.

The Popular Front was shattered by the announcement of the NAZI-SOVIET PACT of August 1939, a nonaggression agreement between the Soviet Union and Nazi Germany. The treaty clearly served the short-term interests of the Soviets by deflecting German aggression and buying the Soviet Union time to rebuild its military forces following the Stalinist purges of the 1930's, but American radicals were shattered by what they considered to be a betrayal of the antifascist cause. Thousands who had joined the party or its front organizations denounced the pact and deserted their erstwhile Communist allies. Yet, the legacy of the Popular Front period would create havoc a decade later when ultraconservative zealots in the United States would look back to the 1930s and uncover evidence of liberal-Communist cooperation. To the leaders of the anti-Communist crusade who operated in the vastly different atmosphere of U.S.–Soviet hostility during the early years of the COLD WAR, the willingness of liberals to cooperate with Communists during the Popular Front period appeared to be evidence of disloyalty or subversion and led to numerous prosecutions of individuals who had been guilty of nothing more than poor judgment or excessive dedication to the antifascist cause.

**Pressman, Lee** (1906– )   Former general counsel of the CONGRESS OF INDUSTRIAL ORGANIZATIONS, (CIO), Lee Pressman was one of the most prominent Communist sympathizers in the American labor movement in the 1930s and 1940s.

The son of Russian immigrants, Pressman was born in New York City, where he graduated from Stuyvesant High School in 1922, received his B.A. from Cornell University four years later; in 1929, graduated from Harvard Law School and entered private practice with the firm of Stanchfield and Levy. There he joined with other Harvard Law School graduates, who called themselves the International Juridical Association, to publish a journal dealing with the legal problems of farmers, workers, and liberal reformers.

Shortly after the inauguration of President Franklin D. Roosevelt in March 1933, Pressman accepted an offer to serve as assistant general counsel for the Department of Agriculture, then headed by Henry A. WALLACE. Over the next few years, Pressman became part of a group of enthusiastic young political and social reformers in Washington, a group that also included Alger HISS. From 1935–36, he served as general counsel for both the Works Progress Administration, a New Deal agency led by the iconoclastic Harry Hopkins, and the Resettlement Administration, which later became known as the Farm Security Administration.

Sometime during 1934, Pressman apparently joined a Communist study group, partly because of his concern for the dispossessed in the United States but even more because he considered the Soviet Union and the international Communist movement the most dedicated foes of Adolf Hitler and European fascism. Pressman reportedly left his Communist group the following year, though he continued to avail himself of the assistance of Communists in pursuit of his liberal goals.

In 1936, Pressman was named general counsel of the CIO, which had been established a year earlier when labor union chieftain John L.

LEWIS resigned from the American Federation of Labor out of disgust with its conservative policies. Pressman's responsibilities were primarily to represent the CIO in federal litigation and to testify on the organization's behalf before Congress and executive agencies. At the same time, he agreed to serve as general counsel for the United Steelworkers of America, headed by Philip MURRAY. Pressman soon gained a reputation for ruthlessness; as the United States edged closer toward war, Pressman warned in November 1940 (after the signing of the NAZI-SOVIET PACT had forced American Communists to favor isolationism rather than intervention) that steelworkers and other CIO unions would not voluntarily refrain from striking in a national defense emergency. By mid-1943, however, the United States and the Soviet Union were bound in an alliance against the Axis Powers, and Pressman had undergone a change in heart. At that time, he urged union members to accept Roosevelt's call for wage freezes as "one of the greatest contributions which could be made to the war effort." These shifts in Pressman's attitude toward the war effort looked suspiciously as if they had been dictated by Moscow. Certainly, other union officials did not receive Roosevelt's plea with the same urgent enthusiasm as Pressman.

Following the war, Pressman continued to press for radical reform by joining such prominent Communist sympathizers as singer Paul ROBESON and Congressman Vito Marcantonio to establish the Civil Rights Congress through a merger of the International Labor Defense and the National Federation for Constitutional Liberties. In 1947, after the Republican Party had gained control of both houses of Congress, he attempted to block the passage of the antilabor union TAFT-HARTLEY ACT, which he claimed would "chop the heart of the Wagner Act and the Norris-La Guardia Act." When the measure passed Congress easily over the veto of President Harry S. TRUMAN, Pressman supervised the publication of a lengthy analysis of the Taft-Hartley Act, complete with instructions on how labor unions could circumvent the measure. For Pressman, one of the most troubling sections of the Taft-Hartley legislation was its insistence that labor-union officials sign affadavits swearing they were not Communists. Under his direction, the CIO protested the decertification of two member unions whose leaders had refused to take the non-Communist oath.

Pressman left the CIO in 1948 when he became intimately involved in the Progressive Party presidential candidacy of Henry Wallace, his former boss at the Department of Agriculture. Under the leadership of Philip Murray, the CIO remained firmly committed to the Democratic Party; besides, Murray was engaged in a determined effort to remove Communist influences from the CIO's national board and member unions, and Pressman was one of his primary targets. Not surprisingly, the HOUSE COMMITTEE ON UN-AMERICAN ACTIVITIES (HUAC) subpoenaed Pressman to testify in 1948 after it had heard Whittaker CHAMBERS identify him as one of the young Communist sympathizers he had met in Washington in the early years of the New Deal. During his first appearance, Pressman refused to answer questions about his past political associations, though he did denounce the committee's inquiries as a political assault upon Wallace and a thinly veiled attempt to divert the public's attention from the failures of the Republican-controlled Congress.

Two years later, in August 1950, the committee—which by this time had helped maneuver Pressman's college friend Alger Hiss into a citation for perjury—recalled Pressman. By this time, he had broken irrevocably with his colleagues in the Progressive Party over their opposition to American involvement in the KOREAN WAR. (Marcantonio caustically claimed that Pressman had left the Progressive alliance because he had been "disappointed in the amount of fees he expected to get from the Progressive movement when he left the CIO.") During this second round of testimony, Pressman admitted that he had belonged to a Communist group in Washington in 1934–35, though he stated that he had "no knowledge regarding the political beliefs or affiliations of Alger Hiss." Pressman refused to volunteer the names of other members of the group, though he made it clear to the committee that he would do so if they insisted. Pressed by Representative Richard M. NIXON of California, Pressman duly named three other individuals who had belonged to his Communist organization. Although all three already had refused to testify to HUAC, all were subsequently subpoenaed by the Committee, and all three invoked the Fifth Amendment once more. Although Nixon believed that Pressman still had not told everything he knew about the extent of Communist activities in Washington in the mid-1930s, Pressman's decision to turn informant earned him the enmity of his former left-wing colleagues. In fact, Pressman was the only member of the group to acknowledge that he had been a Communist, and he remained the only one who repented. Scorned by both Left and Right, Pressman ended his public career in 1950 and returned to private practice.

**Pumpkin Papers**   See CHAMBERS, Whittaker.

# R

**Radulovich, Milo**   See MURROW, Edward R.

**Rand, Ayn** (1905–1982)   Born in St. Petersburg, Russia, Ayn Rand left her native land in 1926 to visit the United States. She never returned. Rand's hatred of Communism shone through in her novels, from her first work, *We, The Living* (1936) through the best-selling *The Fountainhead* (1943) to *Atlas Shrugged* (1957). For Rand, the supreme human virtues were self-interest and the fulfillment of one's individual potential; her philosophy, which came to be known as Objectivism, extolled the merits of the capitalist system as the most favorable economic environment for self-fulfillment.

Rand began her career as a screenwriter in Hollywood in 1926, leaving eight years later to devote herself full-time to her novels. She returned to the motion picture industry in 1944. Among her screen credits were the scripts for *Love Letters, You Came Along,* and the film version of *The Fountainhead.*

When the HOUSE COMMITTEE ON UN-AMERICAN ACTIVITIES (HUAC) inaugurated its investigation of Communist influence in the motion picture industry in 1947, Rand was one of the "friendly" witnesses the committee called to testify. She appeared on October 20, 1947, and spent much of her time on the stand criticizing a wartime film, *SONG OF RUSSIA,* for its unrealistic portrayal of conditions in the Soviet Union. To Rand, the film was nothing more than Communist propaganda, which she defined as "anything which gives a good impression of Communism as a way of life." Specifically, Rand objected to the film's depiction of Moscow ("big, prosperous-looking, clean buildings"), Russian children ("happy little children in white blouses running around"), Russian peasant women ("manicured starlets driving tractors and the happy women who come from work singing"), and a Soviet border-guard station with "a very lovely mod-

ernistic sign saying U.S.S.R." "I would just like to remind you," Rand told the committee, "that that is the border where probably thousands of people have died trying to escape out of this lovely paradise."

Compared to the cheerful peasants portrayed in the film, Rand's description of life in the Soviet Union was so dismal and grim that one committee member finally asked her whether anyone in Russia ever smiled. "Not quite that way, no," replied Rand. "If they do, it is privately and accidentally. Certainly, it is not social. They don't smile in approval of their system."

Beyond her testimony to HUAC, Rand offered her expertise to the Hollywood studios in a pamphlet, *Screen Guide for Americans,* which contained such advice as "Don't Smear the Free Enterprise System," "Don't Glorify the Collective," "Don't Smear Industrialists," "Don't Deify the 'Common Man,' " and "Don't Smear Success."

**Rankin, John** (1882–1960)   An avowed racist and anti-Semite, Congressman John Rankin of Mississipppi was one of the most widely recognized members of the HOUSE COMMITTEE ON UN-AMERICAN ACTIVITIES (HUAC) during the late 1940s.

Born and raised in Mississippi, Rankin graduated from the University of Mississippi and embarked first upon a career in journalism. When the newspaper for which he was working folded for financial reasons, Rankin returned to his studies and earned a degree from the University of Mississippi Law School in 1910. He served as a prosecuting attorney from 1911 to 1914 and then established a private practice in the town of Tupelo, Mississippi. During World War I, Rankin served in the U.S. Army for the final twenty-one days of the conflict, most of which he spent at an officers' training camp.

In 1920, Rankin was elected to the U.S. House of Representatives from a district in northeastern Mississippi. During the following thirty-two years, Rankin established a reputation as a formidable parliamentarian, one of the leading white supremacists in Congress (he once proposed a bill that would have outlawed interracial marriages in the District of Columbia), a dedicated supporter of veterans' legislation, and a fervent anti-Communist. During the early years of the New Deal, Rankin sponsored the House bill that established the Tennessee Valley Authority, which brought inexpensive electric power to the rural areas of northern Mississippi.

Rankin was assigned a seat on the HUAC in 1945. Prior to that time, the committee had been designated as a special committee, with no permanent standing. Rankin, however, caught the House leadership by surprise on the opening day of the seventy-ninth Congress on January 3, 1945, by offering a motion to make HUAC a standing committee of the House, with considerable discretion on the subjects it would investigate and the methods it would employ. Because Rankin insisted upon a roll-call vote on his motion, few Congressmen were willing to have a negative vote recorded, and so Rankin's motion passed easily.

For the next two years, Rankin dominated the committee's activities, often serving as acting chairman, although HUAC was officially chaired in 1945–46 first by New Jersey Democrat Edward Hart and subsequently by the quiet, unassuming Representative John WOOD of Georgia. Using his position on the committee, Rankin assailed the Office of Price Administration (OPA), which was one of the Truman administration's primary weapons in attempting to curb postwar inflation. To Rankin, however, the OPA was an agent of creeping socialism. "It is about time we got rid of the OPA," Rankin declared. "I am tired of those commissars attempting to tell the American people how naked they shall go." Rankin also claimed to discern subversive propaganda in the films emerging from Hollywood in those years. In announcing HUAC's plans to investigate the motion picture industry, Rankin charged that he intended to uncover

"one of the most dangerous plots ever instigated for the overthrow of the government . . . the greatest hotbed of subversive activities in the United States." "We're on the trail of the tarantula," Rankin told his colleagues in the Senate, "and we're going to follow through."

More than anything else, Rankin was disturbed by the number of Jewish artists involved in the production of motion pictures. A vocal religious bigot, Rankin repeatedly and openly expressed his contempt for Jews. "I have no quarrel with any man about his religion," he once said. "Any man who believes in the fundamental principles of Christianity and lives up to them, whether he is Catholic or Protestant, certainly deserves the respect and confidence of mankind." To Rankin, columnist Walter Winchell was "a little slime-mongering kike," and Anna Marie ROSENBERG a "little Yiddish woman." Rankin even categorized Communists according to their religious backgrounds; for instance, he held Leon Trotsky, a Jew, responsible for the excesses of the Russian Revolution, while Soviet dictator Joseph STALIN became in his view a reformer who helped restore religion to the Russian masses.

In his unique fashion, Rankin managed to combine a hatred of Jews and Communists through a perverse interpretation of the early years of Christianity. "Communism," he declared, "hounded and persecuted the Savior during his earthly ministry, inspired his crucifixion, derided him in his dying agony, and then gambled for his garments at the foot of the cross." Continuing his xenophobic theme into the present, Rankin charged that "these alien-minded communistic enemies of Christianity, and their stooges, are trying to get control of the press of the country. Many of our great daily newspapers have now changed hands and gone over to them. . . . They are trying to take over the radio. Listen to their lying broadcasts in broken English and you can almost smell them." On other occasions, Rankin linked Communism with the ascendancy of nonwhite races. Communism, he claimed, was "nothing but a system of abject slavery, dominated by a racial minority that has seized control [in the Soviet Union], as members of the Politburo."

During Rankin's tenure on HUAC, the Committee launched investigations into the radio broadcasting industry, the Jewish Anti-Fascist Refugee Committee, the pro-civil rights SOUTHERN CONFERENCE FOR HUMAN WELFARE, and, under the leadership of J. Parnell THOMAS, the Hollywood film industry. Rankin's contributions to these hearings were seldom constructive. Often, he appeared to be dozing through the testimony, only to awake with a start and interrupt with an irrelevant interjection, occasionally on topics that had already been covered in depth.

Following the 1950 census, the state of Mississippi lost a seat in the House of Representatives. Rankin's district was combined with six counties of another district, and Rankin was defeated in the first primary election under the redistricted system in August 1952. He died eight years later, following a lengthy illness.

## Reagan, Ronald (1911– )

A leading anti-Communist member of the Hollywood motion picture community, Ronald Reagan gradually moved further toward political conservatism during the late 1940s and 1950s, in large measure due to his involvement in the anti-Communist crusade.

Born in Illinois, Ronald Reagan graduated from Eureka College and worked for five years as a sportscaster before embarking upon a career as an actor in motion pictures. Reagan arrived in Hollywood in 1937 and obtained steady work in films; fan magazines chose him as one of Hollywood's "stars of tomorrow," and in 1941 Warner Brothers studios rewarded him with a new contract at $3,000 per week.

Reagan did not become active in political affairs in Hollywood until December 1945, when he joined the Hollywood Independent Citizens Committee of Arts, Sciences and Professions (HICCASP), an organization that initially included a wide range of moderate to

Ronald Reagan, president of the Screen Actor's Guild during the 1950s, whose involvement with conservative politics began during the McCarthy era.

liberal performers and writers. At that point in his career, Reagan considered himself a liberal Democrat who believed that the United States still possessed an obligation to serve as a beacon of democracy to the rest of the world. A dedicated antifascist during World War II, Reagan later claimed that he was naive about the threat Communism posed to the United States in the immediate postwar years.

By early 1947, Reagan had become concerned about the extent of left-wing activity in Hollywood, and he withdrew from the HICCASP because he feared it was dominated by Communists. In March 1947, Reagan was elected president of the Screen Actors Guild (SAG); one month later, FBI agents visited him and asked if he would be willing to provide them with names of SAG members whom he suspected of contributing to the Communist infiltration of the motion picture industry. Reagan agreed to do so, and told them that he was already aware of "two cliques within the Guild that on all questions of policy follow the COMMUNIST PARTY line." Yet, Reagan still opposed efforts to outlaw the Communist Party ("If we ban the communists from the polls we set a precedent. Tomorrow it may be the Democratic or the Republican Party that gets the ax"), and he urged the public not to smear all liberal organizations with accusations of Communist sympathies.

In September 1947, the HOUSE COMMITTEE ON UN-AMERICAN ACTIVITIES (HUAC) subpoenaed Reagan to testify as a "friendly" witness as part of its investigation of Communist influence in the motion picture industry. Reagan appeared before the committee in Washington on October 25 and told them that while he suspected that a small group of Screen Actors Guild members were associated with the Communist Party, he had no direct knowledge of any party members in the organization. In response to questions about the extent of Communist infiltration of the industry, Reagan replied that "99 percent of us are pretty well aware of what is going on, and . . . on that basis we have exposed their lies when we came across them, we have opposed their propaganda, and I can certainly testify that in the case of the Screen Actors Guild we have been eminently successful in preventing them from, with their usual tactics, trying to run a majority of an organization with a well-organized minority." In short, concluded Reagan, "I do not believe the Communists have ever at any time been able to use the motion-picture screen as a sounding board for their philosophy or ideology."

Yet, Reagan grew increasingly militant on this issue. Two weeks after his testimony before HUAC, the executive board of the SAG—under Reagan's leadership—adopted a resolution requiring every officer and board member of SAG to sign an affadavit that he or she was not a member of the Communist Party or affiliated with the party. Shortly thereafter, the SAG also decided to require each member of the organization to sign a LOYALTY OATH. Performers who refused to cooperate with congressional investigations were banned from membership. Convinced that American liberals were being duped by the Communists, Reagan continued his drift toward the right in 1948, when he abandoned his longtime political support of U.S. Senator Helen Gahagan DOUGLAS in favor of her Republican challenger, Congressman Richard M. NIXON.

On January 22, 1951, Reagan set forth his political views at length in *Fortnight* magazine, in an article entitled "How Do You Fight Communism?" After noting that Communists had "sought to infiltrate and control certain key industries" and had persuaded "confused 'liberals' to front for them at all times," Reagan suggested that the nation dispense with quibbling over the rights of Communists and focus instead on the real threat, which he defined as "Russian agression aimed at world conquest." "The so-called 'Communist party,' " concluded Reagan "is nothing more or less than a 'Russian-American Bund' owing allegiance to Russia and supporting Russia in its plan to conquer the world."

In September 1954, Reagan's nearly moribund acting career received a significant boost when he was offered a job as host of a new television series, *General Electric Theater*. From time to time, Reagan—who also starred in occasional episodes—employed his new position to dispense anti-Communist messages to his audience. In one script, he insisted that a writer insert a scene where a Communist mother slapped her child because she found him praying. In another, Reagan starred as a member of the U.S. Information Service battling Communists who burned down an American library in "a strife-torn Asian village."

During the early 1960s, Reagan devoted an increasing percentage of his time to political affairs. He continued to press the issue of Communist infiltration of the motion picture industry after HUAC had concluded its investigations, and he toured the nation as a spokesman for General Electric, warning that Communists were "crawling out from under the rocks, and memories being as short as they are, there are plenty of well-meaning but misguided people willing to give them a hand." Reagan subsequently joined the Republican Party in 1962, served two terms as governor of California (1966–74), and defeated incumbent Democrat Jimmy Carter in the presidential election of 1980. In 1984, Reagan won a second term in the White House.

***Red Channels***   First issued on June 22, 1950, *Red Channels* was a 215-page handbook from American Business Consultants, the same firm that published the weekly newsletter COUNTER-ATTACK. The original edition of *Red Channels* listed 151 entertainers and authors who allegedly belonged to one or more organizations that the editors had identified as Communist fronts. These individuals, the editors argued, should be barred from television, radio, movies, and the theater until they "proved anti-Communist by word or deed." Among the prominent show business personalities on the original list were Orson Welles, Edward G. ROBINSON, Garson Kanin, Jose FERRER, Abe BURROWS, Henry Morgan, and Gypsy Rose LEE.

Upon closer examination, however, the procedures employed by the editors of *Red Channels* contained serious flaws. Its definition of Communist-front organizations was far broader than that employed by the attorney general in compiling the federal government's official list of subversive organizations. In fact, *Red Channels* obtained its list of front organizations from reports of congressional committees, the California State Un-American Acitivities Committee, and old copies of the COMMUNIST PARTY PUBLICATION, the *DAILY WORKER*. Once it identified an organization as a Communist front, any individual listed on that organization's letterhead or cited by a source as a member was automatically deemed a member of the group, whether or not that person had given approval for the use of his or her name.

Nor did the editors of *Red Channels* make any attempt to determine whether an individual had actually belonged to a Communist-front organization. If an informant or a congressional report identified someone as a member, that was sufficient. The editors did not believe that their job included assessing the accuracy of the reports that came into their office. An attorney for *Red Channels* compared his client's product to the financial-ratings service that Dun & Bradstreet provided to the corporate community; the only difference, he claimed, was that *Red Channels* and *Counterattack* provided a sort of "political credit-rating service."

Among the organizations cited by *Red Channels* as Communist fronts were Consumers Union (the publisher of *Consumer Reports*), Freedom from Fear, the Civil Rights Congress, the LEAGUE OF WOMEN SHOPPERS, the JOINT ANTI-FASCIST REFUGEE COMMITTEE, and the National Council of the Arts, Sciences, and Professions. Public support for the 1948 presidential candidacy of Progressive Party candidate (and former Vice President) Henry WALLACE automatically made one suspect in the eyes of the editors, as did any vocal opposition to the efforts of anti-Communist crusaders. One writer was cited for being the author of a Book Find Club selection; another performer was listed as the sponsor of a national committee to combat anti-Semitism.

Network executives and corporate sponsors soon discovered that the path of least resistance (and greater profits) was to accede quietly to the loyalty judgments delivered by *Red Channels*. The relevant slogan among advertising agencies on Madison Avenue was, "Why buy yourself a headache?" By 1951, virtually no one whose name was listed in the handbook could find employment in radio or television. "Nobody has to tell me not to use anybody listed in *Red Channels*," explained one advertising agency executive. "I just know not to."

One of the first victories for *Red Channels* was the dismissal in 1950 of actress Jean Muir from the television series, *The Aldrich Family.* Muir was listed in the handbook as a member of four Communist-front organizations, despite the fact that she had once denounced the Communist Party as "vicious." She was not given a chance to clear herself; instead, the show's sponsor, General Foods, told the producer to find a new Mrs. Aldrich because it did not want to present "controversial personalities."

In the same fashion, actress Mady CHRISTIANS, the star of the stage version of *I Remember Mama,* was listed in *Red Channels* for her humanitarian work on behalf of political refugees in the United States. Bewildered by the charges against her, Christians suffered a nervous breakdown and died of a cerebral hemorrhage less than a year later. When *Red Channels* cited actor Philip LOEB, who played Papa on the hugely popular television show *The Goldbergs,* the sponsor ordered Gertrude Berg, the owner and star of the show, to fire him. When Berg refused, CBS dropped the show, and no other sponsor stepped forward to pick it up. Loeb subsequently committed suicide.

Writers and performers who were victims of this BLACKLIST usually were not told the real reason why they suddenly became unemployable. As one contemporary industry critic explained, "The sponsor or advertising agency simply does not hire a person listed in *Red Channels* or does not renew a contract upon its expiration. The individual is not even told in so many words that the *Red Channels* listing is reponsible. Any number of perfectly normal excuses—a change of cast, etc.—suffice. The individual is just out of a job. To be sure, there are some exceptions among employers who still have regard for fair play, but they are distressingly few and far between."

### Red Plot against America, The

Written by Robert STRIPLING, secretary and chief of staff of the HOUSE COMMITTEE ON UN-AMERICAN ACTIVITIES (HUAC) between 1939 and 1955, and edited by veteran journalist Bob Considine, *The Red Plot against America* (1949) purported to be an expose of "the Communist conspiracy against the Government and people of the United States." "That such a conspiracy exists is more than obvious," claimed Striping, "though the conspirators, who are anything but fools, have been able to spread devious doubt about [the] nature of their continuing activities."

In *The Red Plot,* which appeared in serial form in newspapers prior to its publication, Striping recounted the activities of HUAC from its inception in 1938 through the indictment of Alger HISS for perjury in 1948. Stripling focused his narrative on the committee's highest visibility hearings, including its investigations of Joseph LASH, former head of the American Student Union; Comintern representative Gerhart EISLER and his brother, Hanns EISLER, one of the twentieth century's most accomplished composers; the screenwriters and directors known as the HOLLYWOOD TEN; and the Hiss–Whittaker CHAMBERS controversy.

Before concluding his account, Stripling—who left the committee in 1955 for a career in the oil industry—complained that HUAC "has never known a period when it was not under attack." Describing his position with HUAC to "working in what amounts to a necessary sewer project," Stripling complained that it seemed "unfashionable, if that is the word, to be primarily interested in America and the preservation of its liberties. Apparently it is in bad taste to expose the fact that Government documents of great importance are being stolen; . . . that a number of Government officials, by their admission or refusal to answer, have been mixed up with a gang of cold-blooded subversives; that choice military secrets, including A-bomb data, have been passed on to the leaders of a country which since V-E day has overrun Poland, Hungary, Bulgaria, Romania, Czechoslovakia, Finland, Albania and most of China."

At the end of the book, Stripling reprinted five pamphlets from the committee's *ONE HUN-*

*DRED THINGS YOU SHOULD KNOW ABOUT COMMUNISM* series, originally printed and distributed in 1948. *The Red Plot* itself was subsequently reprinted by the Arno Press in 1977 as part of its "Anti-Movements in America" series.

## Remington, William Walter (1918–1954)

Between 1948 and 1951, the case of William W. Remington was one of the most conspicuous successes of the HOUSE COMMITTEE ON UN-AMERICAN AFFAIRS (HUAC) in its drive to seek out Communist subversion in the federal government.

The story began in 1936–37, when Remington worked as a messenger for the Tennessee Valley Authority during his summer vacations from his studies at Dartmouth College. At that time, he shared a post-office box with four other men, three of whom were known to federal investigators as members of the COMMUNIST PARTY.

Following his graduation from Dartmouth, Remington obtained employment with the federal government. During World War II, he worked for the War Production Board and headed an important interdepartmental committee with jurisdiction over the licensing of American exports. Meanwhile, he married Anne Moos, whose mother, Elizabeth Moos, was a longtime worker for Communist causes. After the war, Remington obtained a prominent position in the Office of International Trade in the Department of Commerce.

Remington's name surfaced in several investigations of Communist influence in the postwar years. In April 1947, a New York grand jury looking into allegations of Communist subversion in the federal government summoned him to testify, but he was not indicted. During the summer of 1948, however, a former Soviet courier named Elizabeth BENTLEY informed a Senate subcommittee that Remington had supplied her with classified information from government agency files during World War II. She added that she had later dropped him from her list of

contacts because his information was virtually worthless. Bentley then repeated her charges to the HUAC. As a result, Remington's case was reviewed by the Department of Commerce, and he was suspended from his job in August 1948. Six months later, the LOYALTY REVIEW BOARD ordered him reinstated, in part because Bentley did not appear before the board to confirm her charges.

Bentley had, however, repeated her accusations on the NBC radio program *Meet the Press,* an action that led Remington to file a suit for libel. Although he admitted knowing her during the war, Remington said that he was under the impression that she was a journalist and insisted that he had never passed her any classified material. Besides, he said, he had never been a member of the Communist Party. In February 1950, NBC and General Foods, the main sponsor of *Meet the Press,* settled the libel suit out of court and awarded Remington $9,000.

The case did not end there, however. HUAC staffers found the three men with whom Remington had shared the post-office box in Tennessee, and while one refused to answer any questions and another stated that he did not know whether Remington was a Communist, the third man—an assistant professor at Tufts College named Howard A. Bridgman—testified that he and Remington had both been members of a Communist Party group in Knoxville. HUAC then subpoenaed Remington, and in public hearings on May 4 and 5, 1950, he again stated under oath that he had never been a member of the Communist Party. It was possible, he acknowledged, that he might have been friends with people who were or had been Communists; he maintained, however, that "it is impossible for me ever to have been a Communist."

Remington repeated that assertion to a federal grand jury in New York, but apparently he was not convincing in his denials for he was indicted on June 8, 1950, for perjury—he had lied, the grand jury charged, about his past membership in the Communist Party. The government's case was aided by the testimony of Remington's estranged wife, Ann Moos Remington. In an extraordinary display of zeal, prosecutors subjected Mrs. Remington to a lengthy cross-examination behind closed doors without benefit of counsel, informing her that she had no right to refuse to answer the questions of the grand jury. And as Judge Learned Hand later pointed out in his critique of the case, the prosecution clearly violated the confidentiality of communications between husband and wife by insisting that she testify to what Remington had told her while they were still married.

Early in 1951, Remington was convicted of perjury. An appeals court overturned the verdict on a legal technicality. The grand jury then indicted him again, and in January 1953 Remington was once more convicted of two counts of perjury. During his stay in prison, Remington was murdered by another inmate.

**"Report on Blacklisting"**    See FUND FOR THE REPUBLIC.

**Reuther, Walter** (1907–1970)   A visionary and militantly anti-Communist labor leader, Walter Reuther helped build the UNITED AUTO WORKERS (UAW) into one of the most successful and innovative labor unions in the United States.

The son of a union organizer who once ran for Congress on the Socialist Party ticket, Reuther grew up in an environment where controversial social and political problems were the subjects of family discussions at dinnertime. At the age of 16, Reuther quit school to take a job as an apprentice in a steel plant in Wheeling, West Virginia. He was fired after staging a protest against the company's policy of requiring employees to work on Sundays and holidays. Three years later, Reuther and his brother, Victor, arrived in Detroit, where Walter eventually became a foreman at a Ford Motor Company plant. After taking night courses to finish high school, Reuther enrolled at Wayne University; there he led antimilitary demonstrations against

Walter Reuther, leading anti-Communist labor union official and head of the United Auto Workers.

the school's Reserve Officer Training Corps program. Fired from his job at Ford for his labor-organizing activities and his vocal support of the presidential candidacy of Socialist Norman Thomas in 1932, Reuther spent the next three years in Europe with Victor. Together, they worked for nearly two years at a Ford plant in the city of Gorki in the Soviet Union, where Walter developed an admiration for the "genuine proletarian democracy" he found there. His experiences in Russia led Reuther to praise the fortitude of the Soviet people and their ability to adapt to technical innovations, but he completely rejected the ideology of Communism.

Following his return to the United States, Reuther was elected president of the local unit of the United Auto Workers in Ternstedt, Michigan. He successfully engineered a sit-down strike that won his union members a minimum wage of 75 cents an hour, and his local's membership suddenly leaped from 78 to 2,400. In December 1936, the UAW launched a sit-down strike against General Motors that turned into one of the most bitter labor confrontations in American history. After two months of intense negotiations, Reuther won recognition for the UAW as the bargaining agent for General Motors' workers. A similar challenge to Ford resulted in a physical assault upon Reuther by company-hired assailants in May 1937 and subsequent threats upon Reuther's life, but the company finally recognized the UAW in 1941.

During the POPULAR FRONT period of the mid-1930s, when the COMMUNIST PARTY in the United States pursued an accommodationist strategy with American liberals, Communist influence had been growing within the leadership of the UAW. Communist labor organizers possessed valuable experience in vital union activities such as conducting strikes, publishing and distributing newspapers and leaflets, responding to government injunctions, mobilizing outside aid, and fighting back-to-work movements. Although the number of actual party members within the UAW was relatively small (probably never more than 1,100 at any one time), many other workers respected the dedication and tenacity of the Communists within their locals.

Reuther had risen through the ranks of the UAW with Communist support, but the announcement of the NAZI-SOVIET PACT in August 1939 ended any cooperation between Reuther's faction within the union and the Communists. At the national convention of the CONGRESS OF INDUSTRIAL ORGANIZATIONS (CIO) in St. Louis in 1940, Reuther denounced Communists as "colonial agents for a foreign government" and sponsored a resolution condemning Germany, Italy, and the Soviet Union for their "brutal dictatorships and wars of aggression." The following year, he and his brother pushed through another resolution at the UAW convention that barred from union office anyone who was "a member or subservient to any political organization, such as the Communist, Fascist or Nazi organization." At the same convention, Reuth-

er's allies captured a majority of seats on the UAW executive board.

During the wartime period of Soviet-American alliance between 1941 and 1945, the Communist membership of the UAW supported efforts to increase productivity by adopting a no-strike pledge and accepting the automobile industry's offer of incentive pay. Reuther and his allies opposed both policies, claiming that they represented a sell-out of American workers' interests by labor officials who were subservient to Moscow. Reuther was able to manipulate the no-strike and incentive pay issues to isolate the Communists within the UAW. Once peace returned, he launched an effort to purge the union of all Communist influence. Aided by favorable publicity in *Fortune, Time,* and *Life* magazines—all of which were published by the even more zealously anti-Communist Henry LUCE—Reuther narrowly won election to the presidency of the UAW in March 1946.

At the union's 1947 convention, Reuther routed his Communist opponents. As one contemporary observer noted, "the left-wingers sat glum and silent, while Reuther's anti-Communist steamroller clanked over them." In his opening address, Reuther observed that the answer to labor's problems in the postwar period "will not be found in any of the so-called magic totalitarian formulas where you trade freedom for bread. The answer will be found in making democracy work." He urged the union to reaffirm its rejection of Communist interference and successfully promoted a resolution endorsing union compliance with the TAFT-HARTLEY ACT, which required union officials to sign anti-Communist affadavits. For the first time, Reuther's faction won control of the executive board of the UAW. He immediately began to dismiss all Communist sympathizers from the international board of the union, and subsequently attempted to purge UAW locals of Communist influence.

For all his energetic attacks upon Communists in his union, Reuther remained one of the nation's leading liberal activists. He enthusiastically supported the Truman administration's foreign-policy initiatives, including the Marshall Plan's massive infusion of foreign aid to the war-torn nations of Europe. In 1947, he helped establish the AMERICANS FOR DEMOCRATIC ACTION, the organization that sought to distance mainstream American liberalism from Communism in the early postwar years. The following year, Reuther authored an article in *Collier's* magazine entitled "How to Beat the Communists." For Reuther, the key was to make democracy work more effectively, to defeat Communism in "the market place of ideas" through "exposure" rather than "repression." In an attack upon the tactics of the HOUSE COMMITTEE ON UN-AMERICAN ACTIVITIES (HUAC), Reuther denounced "the stupid and indiscriminate DIES-RANKIN-THOMAS brand of Red-baiting," which he claimed actually performed a valuable service to the Communists by smearing "decent unionists and honest liberals." In 1953, Reuther reported that during a six-week tour across the United States, he had met "not one person who wasn't willing to admit privately that Joe MCCARTHY has done more to strengthen the Communist movement than any other one person in history."

In his negotiations with the auto manufacturers, Reuther revealed a unique vision of political and economic democracy that verged close to socialism. He urged management to give organized labor a greater voice in planning through the establishment of industrial councils and insisted that the auto companies "open up their books" so he could determine precisely how much profit they were making. In 1955, Reuther won a guaranteed annual wage for his members to supplement their conventional unemployment insurance. "If fighting for a more equal and equitable distribution of the wealth of this country is socialistic," Reuther once said, "I stand guilty of being a Socialist."

Reuther's opponents once again responded with violence. In April 1948, Reuther was gunned down in the kitchen of his home by an assassin who fired both barrels of a shotgun at the labor leader at close range, striking Reuther in the chest and right arm. Reuther survived but never recovered the full use of his arm. (Victor Reuther was the victim of a similar shotgun attack, which broke his collarbone and destroyed his right eye.)

In 1955, Reuther served as one of the architects of the merger between the CIO and the American Federation of Labor, though he withdrew the UAW from the AFL–CIO eleven years later, charging that the national labor movement had grown stagnant under the leadership of George Meany. On May 9, 1970, Reuther and his wife were killed in a plane crash near Pellston, Michigan.

**Richardson, Seth** (1880–1953)   A veteran Republican attorney and government official, Seth Richardson was selected by President Harry S. TRUMAN in 1947 to head the LOYALTY REVIEW BOARD, which served as an appeals board for federal employees accused of disloyalty by individual government departments or agencies. Prior to his service with the Truman administration, Richardson had served as assistant attorney general under President Herbert Hoover, as counsel for the American Medical Association, and, in 1946, as chief counsel for the congressional committee that investigated the bombing of Pearl Harbor.

Seth Richardson, head of the Subversive Activities Control Board.

Truman appointed Richardson to head the Loyalty Review Board in hopes of allaying Republican criticism of his federal employee-security policies. Richardson, however, antagonized the ultraconservatives in Congress by attempting to operate the board in an impartial fashion, with due regard for the rights of individuals accused of disloyalty. Specifically, the board's reversal of a Treasury Department decision against accused Communist agent William REMINGTON infuriated anti-Communist zealots.

To help identify Communist agents and sympathizers in the United States, the INTERNAL SECURITY ACT OF 1950 called for the establishment of a Subversive Activities Control Board (SACB). The primary purpose of the SACB was to identify organizations that should be listed with the attorney general as Communist-action or Communist-front groups. Impressed with Richardson's handling of his responsibilities on the Loyalty Review Board, Truman nominated Richardson as the first chairman of the SACB. Richardson accepted the assignment, albeit reluctantly. "If I wasn't 70 and curious to see whether the President or Congress is right about the workability of the law," he told reporters, "I wouldn't have touched this job with a ten-foot pole." Richardson had so antagonized Senate Republican conservatives, however, that they delayed his nomination and finally blocked it altogether in 1951.

By that time, Richardson's health was failing. Early in 1953, however, he criticized the Eisenhower administration's decision to abolish the Loyalty Review Board because it would take authority away from the Executive Branch and lodge it in the courts instead. Several weeks later, on March 17, 1953, Richardson died at his home after a lengthy hospital stay.

**Robbins, Jerome** (1918–  )   A leading American choreographer and dancer, Jerome Robbins was a member of the COMMUNIST PARTY from approximately 1943 to 1947.

After attending New York University for one year, Robbins worked as a dancer from 1937 to 1944. He first achieved fame as a choreographer with his ballet *Fancy Free*, which was an immediate success after its debut on Broadway in April 1944. Robbins subsequently served as choreographer for a number of ballets and Broadway musicals, including *The King and I, Two's Company, West Side Story,* and *Fiddler on the Roof.*

In his testimony before the HOUSE COMMITTEE ON UN-AMERICAN ACTIVITIES (HUAC) on May 5, 1953, Robbins acknowledged that he had joined the party—which he referred to as the Communist Political Association—largely because of its stance in favor of minorities and in opposition to fascism and anti-Semitism. He was uncomfortable with the ideological restrictions which the Communists attempted to place upon creative artists, however, and left the party after it abandoned its wartime strategy of cooperation and returned to a hard-line policy of secrecy and confrontation.

During his testimony before HUAC, Robbins provided the committee with the names of more than a half-dozen individuals with whom he had been associated in the Communist movement. He explained his willingness to name names by stating that "I think I made a great mistake before in entering the Communist Party, and I feel that I am doing the right thing as an American." The committee duly congratulated Robbins on his decision, and suggested that he continue to promote "Americanism" through his art and music.

**Robeson, Paul** (1898–1976)   The most famous African American of his generation, singer-actor Paul Robeson earned the enmity of the anti-Communist crusaders of the McCarthy era through his militant support of both Marxist causes and the civil-rights movement. Robeson attended Rutgers University (he was the only African-American student there at the time), earning a Phi Beta Kappa key and recognition as an All-American football player. He subsequently obtained a law degree from Columbia University, supporting himself by playing professional football on the weekends.

Robeson abandoned the law for the stage and in 1924 earned tremendous critical praise for his role as the title character in Eugene O'Neill's *The Emperor Jones.* Robeson's majestic bass voice brought him fame in the stage version of *Show Boat,* in which he made the song "Ol' Man River" the dramatic highlight of the show. In 1929, Robeson left the United States, complaining of racial prejudice, and took up residence in London, where he starred in a production of *Othello.*

Convinced that Communists were the natural allies of African Americans in their struggle for full equality, Robeson became intimately involved in a number of left-wing causes during the 1930s. In 1934 he made the first of several visits to the Soviet Union. "For the first time here," he wrote to a friend from Moscow, "I, the son of a slave, walk this earth in complete dignity." From Russia, Robeson traveled to Spain, where he entertained Republican troops during the Spanish Civil War.

Robeson returned to the United States in 1939. He was frequently featured on the CBS radio network and spent much time giving concerts and singing at rallies for liberal causes. Robeson made eleven films for the major studios in Hollywood but gave up his movie career in 1942 because he was weary of the film industry's tendency to stereotype blacks as "plantation Hallelujah shouters."

By the end of World War II, Robeson had alienated much of white America by his bitter condemnation of racism in the United States and his unabashed enthusiasm for the Soviet Union, which continued unabated in the postwar years. Few campaign slanders were more effective than to accuse one's opponent of being a friend of Paul Robeson. Actor Adolphe MENJOU once went so far as to define a Communist as one who enjoyed listening to Robeson's music.

When the California state legislature's Committee on Un-American Activities called Robeson as a witness in 1946, he stated flatly that he was not a member of the COMMUNIST PARTY.

After that appearance, however, Robeson steadfastly refused to answer any questions about his political affiliation. Not surprisingly, he was BLACKLISTED in the United States. Again Robeson went abroad, to England, France, Sweden, Czechoslovakia, and the Soviet Union, where he wrote that "now, after many years, I am here again in Moscow, in the country I love more than any other."

Robeson returned to the United States in 1949 and resumed his support for radical causes. The following year, the State Department revoked Robeson's passport. When he applied for a new passport, government officials informed Robeson that he could only obtain one if he would sign an affadavit swearing that he was not a Communist. That Robeson flatly refused to do. "There is no mystery involved in this refusal," Robeson noted. "As the witchhunt developed, it became clear that an important issue of Constitutional rights was involved in the making of such inquiries, and the film writers and directors who became known as the HOLLYWOOD TEN challenged the right of any inquisitors to violate the First Amendment's provisions of free speech and conscience. . . . I have made it a matter of principle," Robeson concluded, "to refuse to comply with any demand of legislative committees or departmental officials that infringes upon the Constitutional rights of all Americans."

Robeson was subpoenaed by the HOUSE COMMITTEE ON UN-AMERICAN ACTIVITIES (HUAC) in the spring of 1956 and gave his testimony on June 12. Throughout the proceedings, Robeson was openly hostile to the committee members, who reciprocated by badgering Robeson until the hearing degenerated into an unseemly exchange of insults. Each time the committee asked Robeson whether he had belonged to a Communist-front organization or was acquainted with an individual who did, Robeson invoked the Fifth Amendment. "I have no desire to consider anything," he told the committee's staff director at one point. "I invoke the Fifth Amendment, and it is none of your business what I would like to do, and I invoke the Fifth Amendment. And forget it."

During the hearing, Robeson accused the State Department of revoking his passport because he had spoken out in favor of "independence of the colonial peoples of Africa" and because "when I am abroad I speak out against the injustices against the Negro people of this land." When a committee member asked why he had not remained in the Soviet Union if he found life there so congenial, Robeson replied, "Because my father was a slave, and my people died to build this country, and I am going to stay here, and have a part of it just like you. And no Fascist-minded people will drive me from it. Is that clear?"

Robeson's defiance won him no consideration from HUAC or the State Department. In 1958, however, the U.S. Supreme Court ruled that the State Department could not deny a passport to an applicant because of his or her "beliefs and associations." Robeson promptly received a new passport in June 1958 and spent most of the next few years in London, East Germany, and the Soviet Union.

Robeson returned to the United States in December 1963. He suffered from poor health for much of the rest of his life. As memories of the McCarthy era faded, Americans began to honor Robeson as the rest of the world had long done. In 1973, fifteen years after its original publication, Robeson's autobiography, *Here I Stand,* was reviewed for the first time by *The New York Times.*

## Robinson, Edward G. (1893–1973)

An active member of several POPULAR FRONT organizations in Hollywood during the 1930s, Edward G. Robinson was born Emmanuel Goldberg in Bucharest, Rumania, and arrived in the United States with his family in 1903. After a brief period of studying law, Robinson turned to the theater. Although Robinson, a liberal Democrat, was never a member of the COMMUNIST PARTY, some of the organizations to which he belonged—such as the Hollywood Indepen-

dent Citizens Committee of the Arts, Sciences, and Professions—did include Communists. Further, California state Senator Jack Tenney, head of the state legislature's Committee on un-American Activities, accused Robinson publicly in 1947 of aiding the Communist cause. Robinson's past association with suspect organizations led the editors of the entertainment industry's BLACKLIST bible, *RED CHANNELS,* to list him in 1950 as a Communist sympathizer. Because a listing in *Red Channels* made it virtually impossible for an actor to obtain work, Robinson asked the HOUSE COMMITTEE ON UN-AMERICAN ACTIVITIES (HUAC) for permission to appear in person and rebut the false accusations about his loyalty.

Before Robinson testified, he met with a member of the Community Relations Council (CRC) a Los Angeles-based organization that helped non-Communist Jewish artists clear their names of disloyalty charges. The CRC representative went through Robinson's check stubs and assured him that his donations to organizations declared subversive after the fact did not prove that he was a Communist, especially because numerous other undoubtedly loyal Americans had contributed to the same causes.

Robinson first appeared before HUAC in December 1950 and assured the committee that he was not and had never been a member of the Communist Party, nor did he support Communist causes. The committee accepted his assurances; in fact, Representative Francis WALTER of Pennsylvania was so gratified by Robinson's appearance that he decided that HUAC should return to Hollywood, which it had initially investigated in 1947, and inaugurate a second round of hearings into Communist infiltration of the motion picture industry. "The time has arrived," stated Walter, "when we should find out what influences have been at work in Hollywood, who was reponsible for the charges of Communism, and who is and who is not a Red."

Consequently, HUAC launched another investigation of Hollywood in 1951. In the ensuing hearings, several witnesses mentioned

Robinson's name, and the actor again found it necessary to request another appearance before HUAC to clear himself. When Robinson testified in executive session on April 30, 1952, he made a point of telling the committee that he had just finished appearing for the 250th time in the play, *Darkness at Noon,* based on the novel by ex-Communist author Arthur KOESTLER. According to Robinson, the play (which provided a frightening glimpse of the Stalinist purge trials of the 1930s) represented perhaps "the strongest indictment of Communism ever presented. I am sure it had a profound and lasting effect on all who saw it."

Robinson denied once more that he was or had ever been a Communist "or knowingly a fellow traveler." He acknowledged that he had been duped by Communists into supporting causes that he had deemed worthy at that time, but Robinson insisted that he had never been disloyal or dishonest. "The revelations that persons whom I thought were sincere liberals were, in fact, Communists, has shocked me more than I can tell you," he stated. "I bitterly resent their false assertions of liberalism and honesty through which they imposed upon me and exploited my sincere desire to help my fellow men." As proof of his loyalty, Robinson cited his support for the William Allen White Committee to Aid the Allies in 1940–41 at a time when the official Communist Party line favored a policy of American isolation.

"It is a serious matter to have one's loyalty questioned," Robinson concluded. "Life is less dear to me than my loyalty to democracy and the United States. I ask favors of no one. All I ask is that the record be kept straight and that I be permitted to live free of false charges." Following this appearance and further negotiations with HUAC, Robinson was permitted to resume his film career.

## Roosevelt, Eleanor (1884–1962) The

wife of President Franklin Delano Roosevelt, Eleanor Roosevelt remained a spokesperson for liberal causes after the death of her husband in

Eleanor Roosevelt, whose work on behalf of liberal causes antagonized conservatives in Congress.

1945 and served as a delegate to the United Nations (UN) General Assembly from 1945 to 1951. Accordingly, she became one of the prime targets of the anti-Communist crusaders in Congress during the late 1940s. Members of the HOUSE COMMITTEE ON UN-AMERICAN ACTIVITIES (HUAC) criticized her bitterly for writing a letter in 1939 suggesting that U.S. State Department officials permit composer Hanns EISLER (a suspected Communist and the brother of Communist espionage agent Gerhart EISLER) to enter the United States. During the committee's subsequent investigation of Hanns Eisler in 1947, Congressman John RANKIN of Alabama described an article written by Eleanor Roosevelt for the *Ladies' Home Journal* as "the most insulting, Communistic piece of propaganda that was ever thrown in the faces of the women in America," apparently because Roosevelt had recommended that southern voters replace their conservative representatives with liberals. Presumably Rankin would have been equally appalled by Eleanor Roosevelt's decision in 1947 to become one of the founding members of the AMERICANS FOR DEMOCRATIC ACTION (ADA), the leading anti-Communist liberal organization in the postwar United States.

Not surprisingly, Roosevelt placed herself in the forefront of opposition to the anti-Communist crusade of Senator Joseph MCCARTHY in 1950–54. When McCarthy launched his campaign by accusing the State Department of harboring Communists and Communist sympathizers, one of the first names he mentioned was Dorothy KENYON, a New York attorney who allegedly had belonged to several wartime organizations dedicated to encouraging good relations between the United States and its ally, the Soviet Union. Roosevelt responded to the allegations with scorn. "If all of the honorable senator's 'subversives' are as subversive as Miss Kenyon," Roosevelt wrote in her syndicated newspaper column, "I think the State Department is extremely safe and the nation will continue on an even keel." Indeed, subsequent investigations revealed that there was absolutely no evidence linking Kenyon to any type of subversive activities.

As McCarthy gained in power and prominence, Roosevelt occasionally served as the target of the senator's wrath, as when he accused her of supporting the circulation of writings by suspected Communist author Howard FAST. For her part, Roosevelt responded by comparing McCarthy's tactics with the strategy employed by German Nazi leader Adolf HITLER.

In 1961, President John F. KENNEDY reappointed Roosevelt to the U.S. delegation to the UN General Assembly. He later appointed her head of the federal government's special Commission on the Status of Women. Her published writings include *This Is My Story* (1937), *This I Remember* (1950), *On My Own* (1958), and *Tomorrow Is Now,* which was published posthumously in 1963.

## Rosenberg, Anna Marie (1902–1983)

The highest-ranking woman to serve in the American military establishment through the 1950s, Anna Marie Rosenberg was a prominent

Department of Defense official Anna Rosenberg, attacked by anti-Communist zealots on grossly insufficient evidence.

target of anti-Communist zealots during the McCarthy era.

Born in Budapest, then a part of the Austro-Hungarian Empire, Rosenberg emigrated to the United States with her family in 1912. After serving as a student nurse during World War I, she embarked upon a career in personnel management. During Franklin D. Roosevelt's two terms as governor of New York (1929–33), he frequently consulted Rosenberg on personnel matters. In 1934, the New York regional director of the National Recovery Administration, Nathan Straus, Jr., selected Rosenberg as his assistant, and in 1936 she succeeded Straus as director. In 1937, Rosenberg also became a regional director of the Social Security Board.

During World War II, Rosenberg served with the Office of Defense Health and Welfare Services and the War Manpower Commission. In 1944, President Roosevelt sent Rosenberg to Europe to determine the special needs American soldiers would have when they returned to the United States at the conclusion of the war. Rosenberg informed Roosevelt that the top priority of the GIs appeared to be education, and her report later helped persuade Roosevelt to support the GI Bill of Rights. Upon her return to private life in 1945, Rosenberg founded Anna M. Rosenberg Associates, a marketing consulting and public relations firm in New York City.

In November 1950, Secretary of Defense George Catlett MARSHALL persuaded Rosenberg to take a leave of absence from her business and return to government service as assistant secretary of defense to assist him in solving a host of manpower problems that had arisen during the early months of the KOREAN WAR. Within days, conservative radio commentator Fulton Lewis, Jr., had announced on his program that Rosenberg had formerly belonged to a Communist-dominated John Reed Club, and anti-Communist zealots in Washington had distributed pamphlets to every member in Congress accusing Rosenberg of membership in several different Communist-front organizations. When Rosenberg testified in her own defense before the Senate Armed Services Committee, she pointed out that there were forty-six people in the New York metropolitan area named "Anna Rosenberg" and that one of the other Anna Rosenbergs—and not she—had been associated with the Communist organizations.

The Armed Services Committee approved Rosenberg's nomination unanimously. Undaunted, a virulently anti-Semitic zealot named Benjamin Freedman, who had helped distribute the original charges against Rosenberg, met in Washington with Gerald L. K. Smith, a notorious American fascist demagogue, and Congressman John E. RANKIN of Alabama, a member of the HOUSE COMMITTEE ON UN-AMERICAN ACTIVITIES (HUAC) and a noted anti-Semite in his own right. (Rankin once described Mrs. Rosenberg as a "little Yiddish woman.") Together they drafted a letter protesting Rosen-

berg's appointment. The fact that Rosenberg had been proposed by Marshall, a favorite target of the CHINA LOBBY, brought Wisconsin Senator Joseph MCCARTHY into the affair; McCarthy detailed one of his chief investigators, Don Surine, to assist Freedman, Smith, and Rankin.

Surine subsequently was introduced to Ralph de Sola, an ex-Communist and former circulation manager for *Freedman* magazine, an anti-Communist journal sponsored by wealthy businessman Alfred KOHLBERG, the unofficial head of the China Lobby. De Sola swore that he had once sat next to Anna Rosenberg at a meeting of a John Reed Club in the late 1930s and that he was told at that time that she was a member of the COMMUNIST PARTY. Someone leaked de Sola's testimony to Fulton Lewis, Jr., who broadcast the charges on his radio program.

To clear the air, the Senate Armed Services Committee reopened its hearing on the Rosenberg nomination. During the ensuing testimony, De Sola revealed himself to be quite irresponsible, if not hysterical. He warned the senators that if Rosenberg were confirmed, she would "pack the Pentagon with her Moscow-indoctrinated mob," and would "reduce America to the shambling status of England . . . with its sneak attack against individualism and free American enterprise, [and] bring us to socialism, which is the main corridor to communism and chaos." When the FBI traced the thirty-five witnesses whom de Sola said would collaborate his story, all of them repudiated him, and several described de Sola as unstable. None of the other witnesses whom the committee heard produced viable evidence against Rosenberg. On the other hand, a host of distinguished citizens—including General Dwight David EISENHOWER, Secretary of State James Byrnes, and Senators Stuart SYMINGTON and William BENTON sent letters and telegrams supporting Rosenberg.

A thorough investigation by the FBI revealed that the Anna Rosenberg who had attended the John Reed Club meetings was indeed an entirely different individual than the nominee. The record seemed so clear that even Senator McCarthy eventually professed himself satisfied of Rosenberg's loyalty. Yet, the incident revealed that in the atmosphere of hysteria that gripped the United States during the McCarthy era, a few misguided or malicious individuals had the power to ruin reputations; many of those accused of disloyalty had fewer resources to defend themselves than Rosenberg.

Following the Rosenberg fiasco, Senator Harry CAIN of Washington, hitherto one of the Senate's most zealous anti-Communists, voiced his concern over the path the investigation had taken. "Among the chief witnesses," Cain told his colleagues, "were some who sought to inflict deep injury on Mrs. Rosenberg and further divided the nation by giving false testimony under oath. . . . These witnesses call themselves men, but they were cowardly, dishonest and traitorous in their conduct and testimony before the committee. I have urged the committee to seek to prefer perjury charges against these individuals."

Rosenberg served as assistant secretary of defense from 1950 to 1953 and received the Medal for Merit from President Truman for her dedicated service. When the Eisenhower administration took office, Rosenberg returned to her own public-relations agency, though Eisenhower recognized her contributions by awarding her the prestigious Medal of Freedom. Rosenberg remained active in New York City municipal affairs, serving on the Board of Hospitals, the Business Advisory Council, and the Board of Education, and as a member of various other government and philanthropic organizations in the late 1950s and early 1960s. In 1962, she married Paul G. Hoffman, a prominent Eisenhower Republican who had served as first administrator of the Marshall Plan following World War II. Rosenberg died of pneumonia in 1983 at the age of 81.

## Rosenberg, Ethel Greenglass (1915–1953)

The wife of Julius ROSENBERG and sister of David GREENGLASS, Ethel Greenglass Rosenberg was convicted and executed on

Ethel Rosenberg (left), executed for her alleged role in the Fuchs-Rosenberg atomic espionage ring.

charges of espionage during wartime. She and her husband were the only Americans ever put to death for espionage in the history of the United States civil-court system.

Born in New York City, Ethel Greenglass grew up in an atmosphere of political activism and became a radical herself during the late 1930s. There is, however, no conclusive evidence that she ever joined the COMMUNIST PARTY, though her brother David did join the Young Communist League. An excellent singer who once had hopes of a career in opera, Ethel Greenglass was working as a secretary when she met Julius Rosenberg, who was then an engineering student at City College of New York. They were married on June 18, 1939, and moved into an apartment in Brooklyn. Ethel continued to work as a secretary, while Julius studied for a civil-service position; shortly thereafter, he received an appointment as a junior engineer in the Army Signal Corps.

During World War II, Ethel Rosenberg served as a civil-defense worker and a volunteer at a local settlement house on Henry Street. In 1944, according to the testimony of David Greenglass (who had meanwhile joined the U.S. Army), both Julius and Ethel persuaded him to join a conspiracy to commit espionage by transmitting atomic secrets to the Soviet Union, and by Greenglass's account, he did deliver such secrets to the Rosenbergs the following year.

On February 3, 1950, the British government arrested Klaus FUCHS, a German-born British nuclear physicist. Fuchs confessed to transmitting atomic information to the Soviet Union, and authorities subsequently used Fuchs' confession to trace and arrest several other members of his espionage ring, including Harry GOLD and David Greenglass. Primarily on the strength of Greenglass' statements, FBI agents arrested Julius Rosenberg on July 11, 1950. When Rosenberg refused to cooperate with the investigation, the FBI also arrested Ethel. It seems clear that Ethel, whose part in the plot appeared relatively insignificant by all accounts (Greenglass accused her of typing the material he had stolen on the design of the atomic bomb), was charged with espionage primarily to persuade her husband to confess and provide further information about the alleged spy ring.

The plot did not succeed, and on March 6, 1951, Julius and Ethel Rosenberg were brought to trial before U.S. District Judge Irving R. Kaufman in the Federal Court House in Foley Square, New York. Like her husband, Ethel denied the allegations against her but refused to answer questions about her political beliefs. On March 29, after deliberating for slightly more than eight hours, the jury delivered a verdict of guilty for both defendants, and Kaufman

sentenced Ethel and Julius Rosenberg to death. The U.S. Circuit Court of Appeals upheld the verdict on February 23, 1952, and on October 13 of the same year the U.S. Supreme Court declined to review the case.

For nearly a year, legal and political maneuvering delayed the execution of the sentence. Appeals for clemency or a reduced sentence were signed by prominent scientists such as Albert EINSTEIN and Harold Urey, as well as by thousands of religious leaders in both the Jewish and Christian communities in the United States and abroad. Twice President Dwight David EISENHOWER refused to grant clemency to the Rosenbergs. On June 19, 1953, as 10,000 people gathered in Union Square, New York, to protest the execution, Ethel and Julius Rosenberg were electrocuted at Sing Sing Prison. Ethel followed her husband to the electric chair, but while he was killed immediately, the first jolt of electricity failed to kill Ethel. Authorities had to increase the voltage before she died at 8:08 P.M. She left behind two children, ages ten and six.

**Rosenberg, Julius** (1918–1953)   An engineer by profession, Julius Rosenberg was convicted in April 1951 of espionage as part of a Soviet spy ring that also allegedly included Harry GOLD, David GREENGLASS, and Klaus FUCHS. During World War II, Rosenberg reportedly was recruited by Anatoli A. Yakovlev, an official with the Soviet consulate in New York, to help provide the Soviet Union with information about the American atomic-bomb research effort (the "Manhattan Project") in Los Alamos, New Mexico. According to the sworn testimony of government witnesses, Rosenberg subsequently enlisted the aid of Greenglass, his brother-in-law, a machinist and technical sergeant at Los Alamos who enjoyed access to highly classified research data. Greenglass acknowledged that Rosenberg gave him detailed instructions on the sort of information the Russian government wished him to provide. Further, Greenglass claimed that Rosenberg gave him half of a raspberry Jell-O box that he had

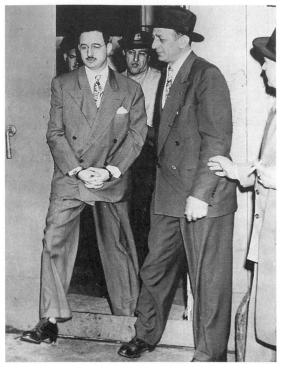

**Julius Rosenberg (left) was executed in 1953 for his atomic espionage activities.**

torn in two; the other half allegedly was handed to a Soviet courier—Gold—so that Gold could identify himself to Greenglass.

Rosenberg himself collected additional information from Greenglass on the trigger mechanism that had been employed in the atomic bomb dropped upon Nagasaki in August 1945, as well as data about a highly classified American satellite research project. According to Greenglass, Rosenberg also stole the design of a secret proximity fuse employed in artillery shells and passed it along to the Soviet Union.

Following the arrest of Gold on May 23, 1950, Rosenberg visited Greenglass and told him to flee the United States. He ordered Greenglass to go first to Mexico and then to Prague, and he provided his brother-in-law with $1,000 in cash to make the journey. Greenglass hesitated, however, and was arrested and charged with conspiracy to commit espionage.

Greenglass's confession on June 15, 1950, implicated Rosenberg, who was arrested less than a month later on conspiracy charges. FBI agents later recalled that when they took Rosenberg into custody, he told them that he had done "the work he felt he was slated for" to "directly help Russia."

In an attempt to force a confession from Julius Rosenberg, the FBI arrested his wife, Ethel, a month later and charged her, too, with conspiracy to commit espionage. The evidence against Ethel Rosenberg was far weaker than that against her husband, and even FBI Director J. Edgar HOOVER acknowledged that she had been brought into the case because "proceeding against his wife might serve as a lever" against Julius. Both Rosenbergs refused to admit any wrongdoing, however, and they were both brought to trial in March 1951. In the ensuing trial—conducted in the emotional atmosphere created by the KOREAN WAR; the detonation by the Soviet Union of its first nuclear device; the Communist victory in the Chinese civil war; and revelations of Communist infiltration of American labor unions, educational institutions, the motion picture industry, and the federal government itself—it became extremely difficult to separate fact from hysteria.

The rhetoric employed by both sides during the trial of the Rosenbergs reflected the tensions emanating from the COLD WAR and the outbreak of open hostilities in Korea in June 1950. The level of emotion generated by the courtroom drama may be glimpsed in the April 5, 1951, speech of the trial judge, Judge Irving Kaufman, when he sentenced both Julius and Ethel Rosenberg to death. Kaufman pointed out that the defendants had "made a choice of devoting themselves to the Russian ideology of denial of God, denial of the sanctity of the individual, and aggression against free men everywhere instead of serving the cause of liberty and freedom." For Kaufman, the United States was "engaged in a life and death struggle with a completely different system. . . . I believe that never at any time in our history were we ever confronted to the same degree with such a challenge to our very existence."

Because Soviet possession of the atomic bomb might potentially lead to the deaths of millions of Americans, Kaufman considered the Rosenbergs' crime "worse than murder." "In your case," he informed the defendants, "I believe your conduct in putting into the hands of the Russians the A-bomb years before our best scientists predicted Russia would perfect the bomb has already caused, in my opinion, the Communist aggression in Korea, with the resultant casualties exceeding 50,000 and who knows but that millions more of innocent people may pay the price of your treason."

Kaufman sentenced the Rosenbergs to death. The couple was incarcerated in Sing Sing Prison in Ossining, New York, while their attorneys appealed their case. On February 23, 1952, the U.S. Circuit Court of Appeals upheld their conviction. The Supreme Court refused to hear the case. After further delays and pleas for clemency—the most fervent protests against the sentence came from abroad—the defendants were electrocuted on June 19, 1953.

Both Julius and Ethel Rosenberg maintained their innocence until the end, claiming that they were "the victims of growing neo-fascism." In a letter to his wife nineteen days before their execution, Julius wrote that "the wishes of certain madmen are being followed in order to use this case as a coercive bludgeon against all dissenters."

It is likely that the FBI never intended to kill the Rosenbergs; rather, the prosecution employed the threat of the death penalty to attempt to extract a confession from one or both of the defendants. Certainly FBI Director J. Edgar Hoover had serious misgivings about executing Ethel Rosenberg, whose role in the affair was minimal at best. Yet the real significance of the Rosenberg affair lay less in the question of guilt—for the evidence indicated that Julius Rosenberg, at least, had been involved in the Fuchs espionage ring—than in the government's nearly hysterical response to a breach of atomic security. Eisenhower, for instance, claimed that the Rosenbergs were guilty of "immeasurably increasing the chances of atomic war" and that their activities "could very well result in the deaths of many, many thousands of innocent citizens." Although there were demonstrations in many U.S. cities against the execution of the Rosenbergs on June 20, 1953, the anti-Communist crusade and the steady stream of revelations of disloyalty and subversion over the previous seven years had left American public opinion in no mood to sympathize with convicted spies.

# S

**Schary, Dore** (1905–1980)   A screenwriter and producer who strove to introduce social themes in his films, Isidore Schary was one of Hollywood's leading liberal spokesmen during the McCarthy era.

The son of Eastern European immigrants, Schary grew up in Newark, New Jersey. His family operated a hotel and a kosher catering business, and Schary frequently performed in the amateur theatrical productions his parents staged for their guests. He quit school at 14 to work at odd jobs; after he returned and completed the equivalent of four years of high school in ten months, Schary joined the *Newark Call* as a reporter. Shortly thereafter, he joined a theater group, shortened his first name to "Dore" (pronounced with two syllables) and began to write plays. In 1932, Columbia Pictures producer Walter Wanger attended one of Schary's dramas and was so impressed that he offered the author (whom he referred to as "Miss Schary") a screenwriting job in Hollywood at a salary of $100 per week.

During his first year in Hollywood, the energetic Schary wrote eleven movie scripts, an achievement that earned him a reputation as a rapid and reliable craftsman. In 1938, he joined Metro-Goldwyn-Mayer Studios, where he became head of a unit responsible for turning out low-budget films. Schary proved so adept at selecting quality scripts, combining them with compatible actors and directors, and producing first-rate films on tight budgets that he was most eagerly sought-after by the motion picture industry. Among his top films at MGM were *Boys Town,* for which he won an Academy Award for best screenplay, *Bataan,* and *Lassie Come Home.* Schary subsequently joined RKO studios, where he doubled the studio's profits while supervising the production of several excellent serious social dramas, including *Crossfire* (a powerful condemnation of anti-Semitism directed by Edward DMYTRYK and produced by Robert

Adrian SCOTT) and *The Boy With Green Hair,* a plea for tolerance of diversity that was diluted considerably by Howard HUGHES after the eccentric and fervently anti-Communist Hughes purchased RKO in 1948.

During the 1930s and 1940s, Schary was a leading liberal activist: he was a member of the Hollywood Anti-Nazi League (a POPULAR FRONT organization whose membership ranged from politically moderate studio executives to Communist writers), the Hollywood Independent Citizens Committee of the Arts, Sciences and Professions, and the AMERICAN YOUTH FOR DEMOCRACY. When the HOUSE COMMITTEE ON UN-AMERICAN ACTIVITIES (HUAC) launched its investigation of Communist influence in the motion picture industry in 1947, Schary was subpoenaed and testified that the committee had no right to infringe upon an individual's right of free speech, no matter how unpopular his opinions. Schary's stand in favor of civil liberties, however, was lost in the controversy created when the committee clashed with a group of hostile witnesses, actors and directors (including Scott and Dmytryk) who had joined the COMMUNIST PARTY but refused to testify about their political beliefs or activities, citing their First Amendment right of free speech. All ten witnesses—who became known collectively as the HOLLYWOOD TEN—were convicted of contempt of Congress, fined, and sentenced to prison. Schary later claimed that he attempted to rescue Scott's career by asking him to sign a statement that he was not a Communist, which Schary could then show to the RKO Board of Directors. "He said he would sign an affidavit that he did not sympathize with any party which sought to overthrow the government by violence," recalled Schary, "but he would not say that he had never been a Communist."

Fearing an adverse public reaction against motion pictures caused by the Ten and eager to prove to Congress that the industry could police itself, major studio executives drafted the WALD-ORF STATEMENT, proclaiming that they would not hire any of the Ten until he was acquitted or purged himself of contempt and declared under oath that he was not a Communist. They further declared that they would not "knowingly employ a communist or a member of any party of group which advocates the overthrow of the Government of the United States by force or by illegal or unconstitutional methods." Schary later stated that he tried to persuade the studio heads to word the declaration in a way that would not induce panic or "create an atmosphere of fear," but the repressive significance of the statement seemed clear.

Although he had voted against the motion to fire the Hollywood Ten, Schary was given the task of reporting the Waldorf decision to the SCREEN WRITERS' GUILD. At RKO, Schary refused to fire Scott or Dmytryk—"despite the fact that they had lied to me about their having been members of the Communist Party"—but the studio dismissed them anyway. Despite his disagreement with his studio's actions, Schary decided not to resign his position in protest. "I was faced with the alternative of supporting the stand taken by my company or of quitting my job," Schary explained. "I like making pictures. I want to stay in the industry. I like it." Furthermore, Schary opposed the uncompromising strategy employed by the Ten, who seemed to believe that the film industry would rise up en masse in defense of their recalcitrant attitude toward HUAC; their attitude turned a potential tragedy into something very farcical. "I felt that Committee acted with absolute banality," observed Schary, "the producers acted cowardly, but the Ten acted stupidly—they were trying by their hysterical acting to get the Committee to admit error. They should have quietly but firmly refused to cooperate with the Committee and then held a dignified press conference where they said eight of us are Communists, but all of us are Americans and patriots, and the public and the press would have backed them one hundred percent."

In March 1949, Schary and several studio executives and artists (including Ronald REAGAN) organized the Motion Picture Industry Council in an attempt to combat the growing industry practice of BLACKLISTING. By that time, Schary had left RKO following a dispute with Hughes, who had little use for films with socially relevant messages. Schary returned to MGM, where he produced nearly 250 films during the following ten years, including *Blackboard Jungle* and *Bad Day at Black Rock*. His increasing commitment to political activism led to his dismissal from the studio in the late 1950s, and he returned to writing plays for the Broadway stage. In 1960, his drama, *Sunrise at Campobello*, the story of Franklin D. Roosevelt's battle with polio, was named Best Play and won five Tony Awards.

**Schine, Gerard David** (1927– )   A top aide to Senator Joseph MCCARTHY in the spring and summer of 1953, Gerard David Schine later became, quite unwittingly, one of the instruments of McCarthy's political downfall.

The son of a millionaire businessman who owned a chain of radio stations, movie theaters, and hotels, Schine's extremely handsome appearance and affluence made him conspicuous even at Harvard University, where he kept a valet and a black convertible with a two-way radio.

While an undergraduate at Harvard, Schine became interested in contemporary affairs, although he always remained a political dilettante. At one point, he managed to confuse Marx with Lenin and Trotsky with Stalin, while assigning the wrong dates to the Russian Revolution and the founding of the Communist Party in his six-page pamphlet entitled *Definition of Communism*. Upon graduation, Schine was made president of his own company, Schine Hotels Inc.; he promptly arranged for a copy of *Definition of Communism* to be placed in each room of the hotel chain.

Late in 1952, Schine met Roy COHN, an aspiring young attorney in the Justice Department who already had made a reputation prosecuting Communists. Shortly afterward, McCarthy hired Cohn as chief counsel of the GOVERNMENT OPERATIONS COMMITTEE. Cohn, in turn, convinced McCarthy to retain Schine as the committee's "chief consultant" on psychological warfare. McCarthy consented to place him on the committee staff to placate Cohn, especially because Schine agreed to serve without pay.

Operating out of Schine's office at the Waldorf Towers in New York, Cohn and Schine embarked upon an investigation of Communist influence in the VOICE OF AMERICA (VOA), a branch of the U.S. Department of State's INTERNATIONAL INFORMATION AGENCY (IIA). After staging a series of televised hearings on the VOA, Schine and Cohn departed for Europe, where they spent several weeks on a highly publicized tour allegedly to search for Communist literature on IIA bookshelves. Their childish pranks—at one point, Cohn chased Schine through the lobby of a plush hotel, hitting him with a rolled-up newsmagazine—and their blatant intimidation of respected IIA employees made the two men the object of scorn in the European press and held them up to ridicule in the United States. Years later, Cohn acknowledged that the junket had been a mistake.

Much to Cohn's dismay, Schine was drafted by the U.S. Army in July 1953. After attempting unsuccessfully to wangle a commission for Schine, Cohn embarked upon a concerted campaign to earn special privileges for his friend. Army officials, intimidated by indications that McCarthy intended to investigate Communist infiltration of the armed services, readily acceded to most of Cohn's requests: Schine received a pass every weekend, for instance, and was routinely excused from drill to allow him to make long-distance telephone calls. By December, word of the Army's preferential treatment of Schine had reached columnist Drew PEARSON, who broke the story in his nationally syndicated column.

The Schine affair threatened to embarrass McCarthy, who, ironically, was really not particu-

larly fond of Schine. In fact, McCarthy informed Secretary of the Army Robert STEVENS in December 1953 that Schine was "a good boy but there is nothing indispensable about him" and that McCarthy would be quite content if Schine were not reassigned to his Senate committee. Nevertheless, Cohn continued to browbeat Army officials on Schine's behalf.

Meanwhile, McCarthy had decided to launch a full-scale investigation into Communist infiltration of the Army, particularly after receiving information that officials at the Army Signal Corps base at FORT MONMOUTH, New Jersey, had routinely promoted a dentist, Irving PERESS, who refused to answer questions about his political beliefs. For several weeks in the spring of 1954, the Army attempted to accommodate McCarthy, but the senator's insistence on reviewing confidential Army personnel files, coupled with his vicious verbal attacks on Brigadier General Ralph W. ZWICKER, the commander of Fort Monmouth, finally convinced Eisenhower and Secretary Stevens that they needed to take a stand against McCarthy's demands.

The campaign by McCarthy and Cohn to obtain special considerations for Schine provided Army officials with a weapon, and they used it to make McCarthy's investigation seem like an attempt by McCarthy to punish the Army for drafting his former aide. During the ensuing ARMY-MCCARTHY HEARINGS, Schine's name repeatedly entered into the testimony of numerous witnesses. At one point, McCarthy attempted to introduce a photograph that purported to show Secretary Stevens with his arm around Schine in a gesture of friendly familiarity. Army special counsel Joseph WELCH, however, proved that the photograph was a forgery and that the original had been cropped to put Schine in the place of someone else.

By the end of the hearings, Welch had used the awkward Cohn-Schine relationship to lead McCarthy into a series of embarrassing emotional outbursts. The nationally televised spectacle had provided the American public with its first close look at McCarthy's arrogant tactics and marked the beginning of the Senator's downfall. For his part, Cohn was forced to resign as chief counsel of the Government Operations Committee once the press learned of his efforts to influence the Army on Schine's behalf.

Schine remained in the Army for the rest of his two-year commitment and then returned to his private business ventures. He returned to public view briefly in 1971, when he served as a producer for the hit movie, *The French Connection.*

### Schlesinger, Arthur Jr. (1917– )

An historian and educator, Arthur Schlesinger Jr. was a founding member of the liberal anti-Communist organization AMERICANS FOR DEMOCRATIC ACTION (ADA). Like numerous other prominent members of ADA, Schlesinger condemned both Communism and the zealous anti-Communist tactics of Senator Joseph MCCARTHY and his colleagues.

In 1946, Schlesinger wrote an article for *Life* magazine in which he claimed that the best way to defeat Communists in the United States was "not to pass repressive legislation or return [Texas Congressman] Martin DIES to public service, but to prevent [another] depression and to correct the faults and injustices in our present system which make even freedom loving Americans look wistfully at Russia. If conservatives spent more time doing this and less time smearing other people who are trying to do it as Communists, they would get much further in the job of returning the [COMMUNIST PARTY OF THE UNITED STATES OF AMERICA] CPUSA to its proper place beside the Buchmanites and Holy Rollers."

When Schlesinger voiced his support for Democratic presidential candidate Adlai STEVENSON in 1952, McCarthy attacked Schlesinger as a Communist sympathizer. The following year, McCarthy included Schlesinger's name on a list of "Communist" authors whose books, the senator charged, should be removed from the libraries of the INTERNATIONAL INFORMATION AGENCY.

Following the election of John F. KENNEDY to the presidency in 1960, Schlesinger was named

Arthur Schlesinger Jr., one of the founders of the Americans for Democratic Action.

special assistant to the President, a position that he held until 1964. Two years later, Schlesinger was appointed to the faculty of City University of New York. In 1946 and 1966, Schlesinger won Pulitzer Prizes for history and biography, respectively; in 1966 and 1979, he also won National Book Awards for history and biography.

### Schulberg, Budd (1914– )

A prominent novelist and ex-Communist screenwriter, Budd Schulberg grew up in Hollywood as the son of B.P. Schulberg, who served as head of Paramount Studios during the 1920s. After graduating from Los Angeles High School, Budd Schulberg attended Dartmouth College. He spent the summer of 1934 visiting the Soviet Union, where he attended a writer's congress. In 1936, Schulberg received a B.A. degree from Dartmouth and later that summer returned to

Hollywood to work as a "reader" in a motion picture studio: for $25 a week, Schulberg read an average of one novel per day and wrote a 25-page synopsis of the plot, characters, and structure. "Promoted" to junior writer, which Schulberg later defined as "a kind of excess baggage—you are supposed to sit around and mature, and nobody much fancies the idea of letting you work with them"—and dissatisfied with the slow progress of his writing career, Schulberg began to write short stories, several of which were subsequently published in popular magazines such as *Collier's, Liberty,* and *The Saturday Evening Post.* Their success persuaded Schulberg to turn one of his stories, "What Makes Sammy Run"—a newspaper office boy rises to become the powerful head of a Hollywood motion picture studio—into a full-length novel. In 1939 he broke his contract with the studio and dedicated himself to writing the novel on a full-time basis.

By this time, Schulberg had become a member of a Marxist study group in Hollywood which, according to Schulberg's later testimony, gradually evolved into a sort of youth group unit of the COMMUNIST PARTY. Disturbed by the continuing unemployment problem in the United States and the rising tide of fascist aggression in Europe, Schulberg eagerly responded to an invitation by Stanley Lawrence, a Communist Party recruiter in Hollywood. "I joined," Schulberg explained, "because at the time I felt that the political issues that they seemed to be in favor of—mostly I recall the opposition to the Nazis and to Mussolini and a feeling that something should be done about it—those things attracted me, and there were some others, too." Other members of the group, according to Schulberg, included screenwriters Ring LARDNER Jr., Paul Jarrico, and Richard Collins.

Schulberg chafed under the artistic discipline exacted by the Communist Party, however. He resented receiving directions from older members of the party about the content and style of his short stories. "By early 1939," Schulberg claimed, "I was definitely backsliding. I was trying to avoid as many meetings as I could and as many responsibilities as I could. I wasn't seeing the right people. Most of the people I was seeing were writers. Some of these writers might have been strongly opposed to the Party. Some perhaps had not even heard of the Party." Members of his youth group expressed opposition to his proposed novel, arguing that it did not show "the progressive forces in Hollywood," and they recommended that Schulberg discuss the matter with party authorities before proceeding further. Schulberg refused and left Hollywood in 1939 for Norwich, Vermont, where he finished the novel early the following year. The announcement of the NAZI-SOVIET PACT in August 1939 completed his disillusionment with the Communist movement.

When Schulberg returned to Hollywood in the late winter of 1940, Collins confronted him, informing him that he should not have left California without the approval of the youth group and suggesting that he visit veteran screenwriter John Howard LAWSON, generally regarded as the elder statesmen of Communist writers in Hollywood, to learn how to write "proletarian novels" with pro-Communist themes. Schulberg eventually consented to a meeting with Lawson, who told him that he was "not functioning as a Communist writer." When the novel *What Makes Sammy Run* was published in 1941, a reviewer for the Communist newspaper the DAILY WORKER initially praised it but later retracted his compliments and published a second, more negative review under party orders.

Schulberg had meanwhile accepted a job as a screenwriter for Metro-Goldwyn-Mayer. During World War II, he served in the U.S. Navy and the Office of Strategic Services. Following the war, he joined the staff of Associate Supreme Court Justice Robert Jackson's staff at Nuremberg, Germany, where he examined secret German films for evidence of war crimes. His second novel, *The Harder They Fall,* an expose of the prizefighting business, was published in 1947.

Despite his break with the Communist Party, Schulberg continued to support left-wing causes. In 1948, he favored the presidential candidacy of Progressive Party nominee Henry WALLACE. Following the conviction of a group of radical screenwriters and directors known as the HOLLYWOOD TEN on charges of contempt of Congress, for their refusal to testify before the HOUSE COMMITTEE ON UN-AMERICAN ACTIVITIES (HUAC), Schulberg endorsed an attempt by the Council of Arts, Sciences, and Professions to abolish HUAC. He later signed an amicus curiae (friend of the court) brief filed in the U.S. Supreme Court in support of the appeal of the Hollywood Ten.

On April 12, 1951, Richard Collins testified before HUAC and identified Schulberg as a former member of the Communist Party. Schulberg subsequently sent a telegram to Representative John WOOD, then chairman of the committee, stating his "opposition to Communists and Soviet dictatorship" and volunteering to cooperate with HUAC "in any way I can." Schulberg appeared before HUAC on May 23, 1951, and reviewed his past association with Communists in Hollywood, naming more than a dozen individuals—including Herbert BIBERMAN, Ring LARDNER, Jr., and Lester COLE—whom he had known in the party. He advised others with similar pasts to come forward and "make a clean breast of it." Schulberg acknowledged that he could understand the reluctance of the American public to forgive actors and directors with Communist backgrounds, a statement which some observers interpreted as an indirect endorsement of the practice of BLACKLISTING. He retreated from his previous endorsement of the move to abolish HUAC, noting that perhaps "people should be called in and their political views should be inquired into." Schulberg added, however, that he did believe it was possible that there were "innocents" in the Communist Party who might not know "the whole story of what Communism and the Communist Party is," and who "might become loyal Americans." Schulberg also

pointed out to the committee that he was a co-founder with Arthur KOESTLER of Funds for Intellectual Freedom, an organization devoted to the support of authors in totalitarian countries struggling with official censorship.

Schulberg's eagerness to provide HUAC with names earned him considerable criticism within left-wing circles in the motion picture industry. "I testified because I felt guilty for having contributed unwittingly to intellectual and artistic as well as racial oppression," Schulberg explained several decades later. "The Communist Party is a totalitarian society. . . . I also had doubts about the idea of a clandestine organization in our democracy, and Communist Party members were not telling the truth when they spoke out as 'liberals' on the KOREAN WAR." Schulberg bitterly criticized writers Lillian HELLMAN and Dalton TRUMBO for their failure to speak out against the Stalinist death camps and for their silence about the disappearance of numerous anti-Stalinist writers during the 1930s and 1940s. "I thought what was happening in Russia was more repressive than anything we were doing in this country," Schulberg stated, "and I didn't trust people who didn't want to fight it. All of that affected what I did before the Committee. . . . They question our talking. I question their silence. There were premature anti-fascists [liberals who opposed fascism before the Communist Party officially altered its stand against the Axis Powers in 1941], but there were also premature anti-Stalinists."

## Scott, Robert Adrian (1913–1973)  One of the members of the leftist group of motion picture writers and directors known as the HOLLYWOOD TEN, Robert Adrian Scott was one of the rising stars in Hollywood in 1947 when the HOUSE COMMITTEE ON UN-AMERICAN ACTIVITIES (HUAC) launched its investigation of Communist influence in the motion picture industry. He had written numerous screenplays, including the popular *Mr. Lucky,* and had produced a half-dozen films for RKO studios. His most notable successes were the anti-fascist film

*Cornered, Murder My Sweet,* and the critically acclaimed and commercially successful *Crossfire* (directed by Edward DMYTRYK), Hollywood's first attempt to confront openly the evils of anti-Semitism.

Because of his involvement in radical activities in Hollywood, Scott was one of the nineteen "unfriendly" witnesses whom HUAC subpoenaed to testify in October 1947. Although Scott was not as dedicated nor as active a COMMUNIST PARTY member as several of the other witnesses, he still refused to answer the committee's standard question, "Are you now, or have you ever been a member of the Communist Party?" His failure to answer the committee's queries earned him a citation for contempt of Congress; along with the other nine "unfriendly" witnesses who refused to answer the same question, he became known as one of the Hollywood Ten. His actions also resulted in a divorce. Scott's wife, actress Anne Shirley, pleaded with him to cooperate with the committee, and when he did not, she left him.

For several weeks following his appearance before HUAC, Scott returned to work at RKO. To help Scott save his job, one of the studio's top executives, Dore SCHARY, asked Scott to sign a statement swearing that he was not a Communist. Scott consented to state that he did not sympathize with any group that attempted to overthrow the U.S. government by force, but he refused to say that he had never been a Communist. After the studios adopted the WALDORF STATEMENT, RKO fired Scott on the grounds that he had brought himself into disrepute by his defiance of HUAC and "the institutions of the United States Government."

Scott was subsequently convicted on the contempt charge and sentenced to a year in prison and a fine of $1,000. While he awaited the completion of the appeals process, Scott went to Paris and began to arrange a motion picture deal. His passport expired after five months, however, and the State Department refused to renew it. He might have remained in Europe indefinitely, but he decided to return to the United States to show his solidarity with the rest of the Ten.

After the U.S. Supreme Court refused to hear his appeal, Scott served his term in the federal penitentiary in Ashland, Kentucky, living in the same dormitory as two other members of the Ten, John Howard LAWSON and Dalton TRUMBO. From 1954 to 1961, Scott supported himself by writing scripts for television. Because he could not obtain work openly under his own name, all his scripts were submitted under the name of his partner, writer Joan LaCour, who received the screen credit and 50 percent of the income. Eventually their "partnership" evolved into a true collaborative effort.

When Trumbo formed his own production company, Robert Rich Productions, Inc., he named Scott as its first president in 1959. Two years later, Scott moved to London to become executive assistant to the chief of M-G-M's British operations. He returned to the United States in 1968 and finally began to produce films for major Hollywood studios again in 1970. Scott died of cancer in 1973.

***Scoundrel Time*** Published in 1969, *Scoundrel Time* represents playwright Lillian HELLMAN's personal account of the era of anti-Communist hysteria in the United States. In her book, Hellman contended that while many anti-Communists in the United States were sincere, the political leaders of the movement—including Richard NIXON, Senator Joseph MCCARTHY, Senator Patrick MCCARRAN, and Representatives Francis WALTER and John S. WOOD—were motivated primarily by opportunism. "I do not think they believed much, if anything, of what they said," Hellman wrote. "The time was ripe for a new wave in America, and they seized their political chance to lead it along each day's opportunity, spit-balling whatever and with whoever came into view."

In a brief account of her involvement in left-wing political affairs in the late 1930s and early 1940s, Hellman claimed that she never joined the COMMUNIST PARTY, even though she was approached by former Communist Party secretary general Earl BROWDER himself. Hellman acknowledged, however, that "whether I signed a Party card or didn't was of little importance to me." In any event, she was subpoenaed by the HOUSE COMMITTEE ON UN-AMERICAN ACTIVITIES (HUAC) in early 1952 to testify about her past political associations. In *Scoundrel Time*, Hellman provides a lengthy account of her decision to send the chairman of HUAC, Congressman Wood, a letter stating that she would agree to testify about herself but would refuse to testify about any other individuals. "Most of the Communists I had met," she wrote, "seemed to me people who wanted to make a better world; many of them were silly people and a few of them were genuine nuts, but that doesn't make for denunciation or furnish enough reason for turning them over for punishment to men who wanted nothing more than newspaper headlines that could help their own careers."

According to Hellman, the idea for such a stance originally came from attorney Abe FORTAS, who was representing Far East expert Owen LATTIMORE at that time. Although Hellman's lover Dashiel HAMMETT opposed the strategy, Hellman decided to adopt the gambit. When the committee refused to accept her letter, Hellman found it necessary to invoke the Fifth Amendment to avoid implicating any of her former associates, but the principle enunciated in her letter was later praised by many observers in the press. Nevertheless, Hellman's use of the Fifth Amendment led her to be BLACKLISTED from employment in the motion picture industry for nearly six years. Her income dwindled from $140,000 a year to $10,000, most of which was taken by the Internal Revenue Department as settlement of a dispute over back taxes, and Hellman found it necessary to sell her farm in Westchester, New York. She supported herself by moving temporarily to Europe, where she wrote screenplays under another name. In 1958, Hellman was finally offered employment under her own name, and the success of her play *Toys*

*in the Attic* in 1960 finally restored her to financial security.

For Hellman, the "scoundrel time" ended because Americans grew bored with the anti-Communist witch hunters, including McCarthy and his allies. "We were not shocked at the damage McCarthy had done, or the ruin he brought on many people," Hellman wrote. "It was simply and plainly that most of America was sick of him. . . ." Hellman concluded her account of the McCarthy era with a parting shot at the intellectuals and writers who failed to stand up and defend those—including Hammett—who were accused by the witch hunters. "In every civilized country," noted Hellman, "people have always come forward to defend those in political trouble. . . . And there were a few here who did just that, but not many, and when one reads them now the words seem slightly timid, or at best too reasonable."

**Screen Writers' Guild**   Founded in April 1933, the Screen Writers' Guild (SWG) became the most active and influential trade union in Hollywood, originally established to obtain practical goals such as higher wages, standardized contracts, shorter hours, and impartial arbitration. Its first president was John Henry LAWSON, who had not yet adopted the radical left-wing ideology that came to dominate his professional life as a screenwriter. As Lawson later explained, he was elected primarily because "I was almost the only person who was totally trusted by all the groups within the Guild. They all felt that . . . I would serve only the interests of the writer and that I would be perfectly honest with everybody."

The guild's willingness to confront the autocratic hierarchy of the movie studios produced a rapid increase in its membership. By the end of October 1934, the guild had 750 members. From the beginning, however, the membership was divided between an older, well-established group of conservative writers and a more politically active band of younger, liberal writers. In 1936, the Right wing of the guild broke away and formed a separate union, known as Screen Playwrights, Inc.

The departure of the conservatives, along with the guild's struggles with the major film studios—including a lengthy, bitter battle in 1937—and the guild's growing sense of solidarity with other American labor unions led the SWG leadership into involvement in national and international political affairs. By 1938, several officers of the guild had joined the COMMUNIST PARTY, while others enthusiastically joined a variety of POPULAR FRONT organizations designed to combat the spread of fascism.

Following the end of World War II and the demise of the wartime alliance between the Soviet Union and the United States, a substantial bloc of the officers and members of the guild began to grow increasingly wary of the radical leftist element within the SWG. The threat by the HOUSE COMMITTEE ON UN-AMERICAN ACTIVITIES (HUAC) to investigate Communist infiltration of the motion picture industry galvanized the moderate and the non-Communist Left of the SWG into action. Despite the fact that the liberals on the SWG executive board detested HUAC and its methods, they refused to endorse the recalcitrant attitude adopted by the screenwriters and directors known as the HOLLYWOOD TEN, led by Lawson.

In effect, the Guild refused to involve itself officially in the controversy between HUAC and the Ten. "In the matter of individual activities of Guild members," noted SWG President Emmet LAVERY, a leader of the anti-Communist liberals, "either within or outside the industry, the individual defense or individual presentation is a matter for each individual witness. As the chief executive officer of the Guild, it is not my purpose at Washington to act either as 'prosecutor' or as 'defending counsel' for individual witnesses before the Committee."

Daunted, perhaps, by the increasing anti-Ten backlash among the public and the studios—as illustrated by the outcome of the WALDORF CONFERENCE—the Screen Writers' Guild elected a moderate slate of candidates to its executive board in November 1947. During the following twelve months, the SWG removed most of the Communists and radicals from its committees and administrative offices.

**Seeger, Pete** (1919– ) A popular folksinger with a record of support for liberal political causes, Pete Seeger was a prominent target of the HOUSE COMMITTEE ON UN-AMERICAN ACTIVITIES (HUAC) in 1955. Called to testify on August 18, 1955, Seeger informed the committee that he would willingly testify about his political and prolabor songs (and even sing them) but that he would not discuss his "associations and opinions." "I feel these questions are improper," Seeger argued, "and I feel they are immoral to ask any American this kind of question."

Pressed by HUAC investigators to state whether he had performed on specific occasions for Communist-front organizations or fundraisers, Seeger replied that "I have sung for Americans of every political persuasion, and I am proud that I never refuse to sing to an audience, no matter what religion or color of their skin, or situation in life. I have sung in hobo jungles, and I have sung for the Rockefellers, and I am proud that I have never refused to sing for anybody. That is the only answer I can give along that line." When asked at the end of his testimony whether he was a member of the COMMUNIST PARTY, Seeger refused to reply on the grounds that "my associations, whatever they are, are my own private affairs."

The committee recommended that Seeger be cited for contempt, and he was subsequently sentenced to a year in jail. Seeger appealed his conviction, and after a seven-year battle the decision was reversed. In the meantime, Seeger was banned from network television as part of the entertainment industry's BLACKLIST. He did not appear on television until 1967, when he was a guest star on *The Smothers Brothers Comedy Hour;* not surprisingly, Seeger took that opportunity to sing a song of protest about U.S. involvement in the Vietnam War.

**Service, John Stewart** (1910– )  A veteran American diplomat who tried to alert the U.S. Department of State to the failings of CHIANG Kai-shek's regime in China, John Stewart Service was one of the earliest targets of Senator Joseph MCCARTHY of Wisconsin. Service, whose parents were missionaries in China, was a member of the group of U.S. foreign-service officers known as "China hands"—diplomats with extensive firsthand experience in China who recognized that Chiang's corrupt and inefficient Nationalist regime would not long survive the onslaught of MAO Zedong's Communist rebels. Service, along with John Carter VINCENT and John Patton DAVIES, urged the Roosevelt administration in 1944–45 to reduce its commitment to Chiang or risk being trapped in the inevitable decline and fall of the Nationalist government.

In April 1945, General Patrick J. Hurley, then serving as American ambassador to China, demanded that Service be recalled to Washington. Shortly after his return to the United States, Service provided personal copies of his political reports on Chinese affairs to a journalist named Philip Jaffe. Clearly, Service intended to use Jaffe to publicize information detrimental to the Nationalist cause. Unknown to Service, Jaffe—the publisher of a left-wing journal known as *AMERASIA*—was under investigation by the FEDERAL BUREAU OF INVESTIGATION (FBI) as a possible Soviet espionage agent. The FBI subsequently arrested Service on June 6, 1945, for conspiring to commit espionage; in part because of behind-the-scenes maneuvering by the Truman administration, however, the federal grand jury decided not to indict Service.

The following year, Service was investigated by a State Department loyalty review board but, in the absence of reliable evidence against him, was permitted to continue his diplomatic career. Nevertheless, the pro-Chiang CHINA LOBBY remained convinced that Service was a security risk and maintained a constant campaign against him in conservative journals. By 1950, he had undergone investigations by two more loyalty review boards, both of which cleared him. In February 1950, however, when Service was en route to New Delhi to assume the position of U.S. consul-general in India, McCarthy publicly accused Service—whom he called "one of the dozen top policymakers in the entire Department of State on Far Eastern policy"—of being "a known associate and collaborator with Communists and pro-Communists."

Recalled to Washington to testify before the Senate committee (chaired by Senator Millard TYDINGS of Maryland) which was established to investigate McCarthy's charges, Lattimore explained that his association with Jaffe was "innocent and incidental." The State Department, he claimed, encouraged returning diplomats to provide journalists with background material to keep the American public informed of contemporary events abroad. Service said he had no idea that Jaffe had any connections with Communists; he assumed that the journalist was a reputable publisher with an academic interest in Chinese affairs. Service concluded his statement by asserting that he was neither a Communist nor a Communist sympathizer, though he acknowledged that he had been guilty of "indiscretion." The Tydings Committee subsequently cleared Service of any wrongdoing, though it did criticize him for being "extremely indiscreet."

Undaunted, McCarthy persisted in his attack upon Service. During a speech to his Wisconsin constituents, McCarthy asked whether the American people wanted on the State Department payroll "a man who admits turning government secrets over to a Communist and who was caught by the FBI giving secret military information to a convicted Communist thief of government top secrets." As part of its continuing campaign against Service, the China Lobby provided additional material to the State Department loyalty review board. Twice more in 1950 Service was subjected to departmental investigations; both times he was cleared.

Finally, the Civil Service Commission's LOYALTY REVIEW BOARD, chaired by Hiram BING-

HAM, examined the case of John Stewart Service in late 1951. This time, the board added a charge of "intentional, unauthorized disclosure" of confidential documents "under circumstances which may indicate disloyalty"—a clear reference to the *Amerasia* incident. The Loyalty Review Board's findings persuaded Secretary of State Dean ACHESON, under heavy pressure from conservatives in Congress, to fire Service in December 1951 as a security risk.

Service subsequently sued the Department of State for improperly dismissing him, and in 1957, after the passions and paranoia of the McCarthy era had subsided, the U.S. Supreme Court ruled in Service's favor.

**Sinatra, Frank** (1917– )    A prominent liberal in the entertainment community during the McCarthy era, Frank Sinatra briefly became a target of anti-Communist crusaders for his political activities and his outspoken support of the HOLLYWOOD TEN, a group of writers and directors who were convicted of contempt of Congress in 1947. The son of Italian immigrants, Sinatra grew up in Hoboken, New Jersey, and briefly attended Drake Institute before embarking upon a career as a singer. (He appears to have decided to become a singer on a whim, after hearing a concert by Bing Crosby.) As a result of his 1937 appearance as a member of the Hoboken Four on the radio talent show, *Major Bowes' Original Amateur Hour,* Sinatra signed as a vocalist with trumpet player Harry James' band in 1939; several months later, he left James and joined Tommy Dorsey's band and then in 1942 struck out on a solo career. The combination of a unique singing style and adroit publicity soon earned him the adulation of thousands of teenage girls across the United States.

In 1943, Sinatra launched his film career with an appearance in *Higher and Higher.* Subsequent roles in such movies as *Anchors Aweigh, On the Town,* and *Till the Clouds Roll By* established him as a major Hollywood star. During World War II, Sinatra also became involved in political affairs, campaigning actively for President Franklin D. Roosevelt in the election of 1944. Following the war, Sinatra continued to work for liberal causes, particularly the battle against racial and religious bigotry. In 1945, he donated his services to RKO Studios for the film *The House I Live In,* an eloquent cinematic plea for tolerance of diversity in American society. Two years later, Sinatra joined the COMMITTEE FOR THE FIRST AMENDMENT (CFA), the short-lived Hollywood organization that sought to organize public support for a group of radical screenwriters and directors before their testimony to the HOUSE COMMITTEE ON UN-AMERICAN ACTIVITIES (HUAC). Along with other members of the CFA, he flew to Washington in late October 1947 to lend his influence to the anti-HUAC movement. Following the witnesses' conviction on contempt charges and the film studios' intransigent stand against employing anyone suspected of Communist leanings, however, the CFA quickly collapsed.

Sinatra's dedication to left-wing causes earned him the enmity of numerous anti-Communist zealots, including California state legislator Jack Tenney, launcher of an abortive probe of Communism in Hollywood in the late 1930s, and the bigoted fascist Gerald L. K. Smith. The denunciation at a HUAC hearing of Sinatra as a Communist sympathizer coincided with a downturn in the singer's career, the result in part of serious medical problems. Film offers disappeared for nearly four years. Not until he accepted a role in the movie *From Here to Eternity* (1953) for a minimal salary did Sinatra begin his comeback. His performance in that film earned Sinatra considerable critical praise, an Academy Award as Best Supporting Actor, and additional roles in such hits as *The Man with the Golden Arm, Suddenly,* and *High Society.*

In 1960, Sinatra sought to strike a blow against the insidious Hollywood practice of BLACKLISTING suspected Communists by announcing in *Variety* magazine that he had hired Albert MALTZ, a member of the Hollywood Ten, as the screenwriter for his proposed film version of a World War II drama entitled *The Execution of Private Slovik.* The resulting outcry of protest from veterans' groups—and possibly a request from Democratic presidential candidate John F. KENNEDY, who was for a time a close friend of Sinatra—led Sinatra to change his mind and jettison Maltz. Several years later, Sinatra starred in director John Frankenheimer's production of *The Manchurian Candidate,* a movie about the presidential ambitions of a senator modeled closely on Senator Joseph MCCARTHY of Wisconsin.

## Smedley, Agnes (1892–1950)

An American journalist who combined a career in reporting with radical political activism, Agnes Smedley avidly supported such causes as birth control, anticolonialism, women's rights, and Indian independence. She grew up in poverty and maintained a steadfast opposition to capitalism throughout her life.

In 1929, Smedley traveled to Shanghai, China, as a correspondent for a German newspaper. There, she established contact with the underground Communist revolutionary movement. She also began a personal relationship with a Soviet spy named Richard Sorge, who later became famous as the head of a Soviet spy ring in Japan from 1937–41.

Smedley spent most of the years between 1936 and 1940 traveling through the interior of China, gathering material for articles on Chinese political affairs and speaking at rallies to garner international support for China's armed struggle against the Japanese invasion. In 1941, Smedley returned to the United States and embarked on a speaking tour to awaken the American public to the plight of China. By this time, Smedley had come to believe that "the Chinese Communist Party represents the most democratic force in China." Yet, because Smedley refused to condemn the Guomindang forces of CHIANG Kaishek, who were also fighting the Japanese imperialists, Chinese Communist officials rejected her application for party membership.

In the closing months of World War II, Smedley's connections with the Communist movement in China led the FBI to launch an investigation of her activities in the United States. In May 1945, Whittaker CHAMBERS told FBI agents that he was certain that Smedley was a Communist; even though he had no actual evidence to support the accusation, Chambers insisted that "there is absolutely no question about it." As the conflict between the Guomindang and the armies of MAO Zedong deteriorated into open civil war, Smedley's support for the Chinese Communists led the FBI to intensify its probe of her activities. The bureau seemed especially determined to prove that Smedley was a Soviet espionage agent.

On February 10, 1949, the U.S. Army—prompted by the headquarters of General Douglas MACARTHUR in Tokyo—released a report that described Smedley as "a spy and agent of the Soviet government" and "one of the early perpetrators, if not the originator, of the hoax that the Chinese Communists were not Communists at all, but only local agrarian revolutionaries innocent of any Soviet connections." Smedley adamantly denied the charges. Two weeks later, the Army retracted its accusations and issued a public apology. Meanwhile, members of the pro-Chiang CHINA LOBBY, including industrialist Alfred KOHLBERG, continued to press the government to build a case against Smedley because of her pro-Communist sympathies. Increasingly isolated from her former associates who reportedly found themselves harassed by the federal government because of their relationship with her, Smedley left the United States for Europe in November 1949. She died in England six months later of complications from a stomach ulcer.

Following Smedley's death, Representative Harold VELDE of the HOUSE COMMITTEE ON UN-AMERICAN ACTIVITIES declared that Communist agents had murdered her because she was preparing to return to the United States and provide the government with information about a major international espionage ring. In

June 1952, the FBI finally laid to rest its case against Smedley with an admission that there was no evidence that she had ever belonged to the COMMUNIST PARTY. "No facts have been developed," noted the FBI report, "which would indicate that subject was engaged in espionage activity on behalf of a foreign government, nor have any further facts been developed as to her alleged espionage activity in the Far East."

## Smith Act (Alien Registration Act of 1940)

Eleven top CPUSA officials were convicted under the terms of the Smith Act.

Passed by the seventy-eighth Congress in 1940, the Smith Act (formally known as the Alien Registration Act) was the first peacetime sedition legislation in the United States since the Sedition Act of 1798. The heart of the act was Section 2, which made it unlawful for any person (1) "to knowingly or willfully advocate, abet, advise, or teach the duty, necessity, desirability, or propriety of overthrowing or destroying any government in the United States by force of violence, or by the assassination of any officer of such government"; (2) "to print, publish, edit, issue, circulate, sell, distribute, or publicly display any written or printed matter advocating, advising, or teaching the duty, necessity, desirability, or propriety of overthrowing or destroying any government in the United States by force of violence"; or (3) "to organize or help to organize any society, group, or assembly of persons who teach, advocate, or encourage the overthrow or destruction of any government in the United States by force or violence, or to be or become a member of, or affiliate with, any such society, group or assembly of persons, knowing the purposes thereof." Section 3 of the act made it a crime for anyone to attempt or conspire to commit any of the proscribed acts.

Because the Smith Act focused on the threat of violent revolution, it reflected a psychology dominated by memories of the Bolshevik insurgencies in Europe following World War I and the fascist putsches of the early 1930s. Had there been a time when the United States was vulnerable to a forceful overthrow of the government, it would have been the mid-1930s when the despair evoked by the misery of the Great Depression caused a significant minority of Americans to doubt the virtues of the capitalist system.

The Smith Act was therefore already outdated by the time it was passed. The only occasion upon which it was employed prior to 1948 was the indictment of several leaders of the radical-fringe Trotskyist Socialist Workers Party (which considered the Communist Party a tool of capitalist stooges) in 1940. Any threat to the security of the United States in the 1940s and 1950s would necessarily have been more subtle and sophisticated, and it was not at all clear how useful the Smith Act would be to combat Communist subversion in the postwar era.

It remained, however, one of the few weapons available to the Justice Department when the Truman administration decided to launch a campaign against the Communist Party in the United States during the early years of the COLD WAR. Although the federal government wished to destroy the power of the Communist Party in the United States, it resisted attempts to declare the party illegal, fearing that such legislation—even if it were constitutional—would create a dangerous precedent and would attract strenuous objections from liberals and civil libertarians. Besides, the FBI feared that if the party were driven underground, it would make it far more difficult to infiltrate.

FBI Director J. Edgar HOOVER preferred to fight the Communist Party through the courts, using well-publicized trials to alert the American people to the threat of internal subversion. Therefore, Hoover successfully persuaded Attorney General Tom CLARK in 1948 to use the Smith Act to prosecute selected Communist Party leaders. On July 20, 1948, the government issued warrants for the arrest of twelve Communist Party officials—including General Secretary of the COMMUNIST PARTY OF THE UNITED STATES OF AMERICA Eugene Dennis—charging them with conspiracy to teach and advocate the violent overthrow of the U.S. government.

During the ensuing trial, which became exceptionally rancorous at times, the language of the Smith Act determined the prosecution's strategy. Because the act required a finding of intent to overthrow the government by force, prosecutors were forced to rely on excerpts from the literary evidence—primarily militant Marxist-Leninist writings—that advocated violent revolution. The trial judge, Harold Medina, ruled that the government had proven its case, and the defendants were sentenced to five years in prison and a fine of $10,000 apiece. In 1951, the case was appealed to the Supreme Court, which decided by a 6–2 majority (DENNIS V. UNITED STATES), to sustain the lower court.

The outcome of the *Dennis* case encouraged the Justice Department to rely upon the Smith Act in future litigation against Communist Party officials. By 1956, 150 cases under the act had been filed by prosecutors. State government officials adopted a similar strategy, enacting their own sedition statutes and using them against Communist Party leaders in their regions. President Harry S. TRUMAN, meanwhile, argued that the successful prosecutions under the Smith Act rendered unnecessary further legislative sanctions against the Communist Party. Nevertheless, Congress passed first the INTERNAL SECURITY ACT OF 1950 (also known as the

MCCARRAN ACT) and then the COMMUNIST CONTROL ACT OF 1954.

This additional legislation, combined with the Supreme Court's modification of its *Dennis* decision in YATES V. UNITED STATES (1957) and the subsidence of anti-Communist hysteria after 1954, effectively ended the useful life of the Smith Act in the fight against Communism in the United States. The prosecutions had achieved precisely what the FBI had sought to avoid in the first place: the Communist Party was driven underground. Because informants had provided most of the evidence in the Smith Act trials, party leaders became obsessed with secrecy, purging membership rolls of unreliables, halting recruiting efforts, and restructuring the party. The end result, nevertheless, was the demise of the Communist Party as an effective force in American political life.

## Smith, Margaret Chase (1897–1995)

One of the first Republicans in Congress to openly criticize Senator Joseph MCCARTHY of Wisconsin, Senator Margaret Chase Smith was a business executive who entered politics in 1930 as a member of the Maine State Republican Committee. From 1937 to 1940, she served as secretary to her husband, Clyde H. Smith, a Republican member of the House of Representatives from Maine. Upon his death, Smith was elected to fill his unexpired term, and served in the House until 1948, when she won a seat in the U.S. Senate.

At the opening of the eighty-first Congress in January 1949, Smith was assigned to the Executive Expenditures Committee, which later became known as the GOVERNMENT OPERATIONS COMMITTEE. The ranking Republican on the committee was Joseph McCarthy, and he and Smith established a reasonably cordial working relationship. In his Lincoln Day speech of February 10, 1950, McCarthy claimed to have proof that the State Department was sheltering Communists and Communist sympathizers. Smith supported McCarthy against subsequent

Senator Margaret Chase Smith of Maine, whose "Declaration of Conscience" attacked the irresponsible tactics of Senator Joseph McCarthy.

Democratic attacks, but as she pressed McCarthy for evidence to support her charges, she grew skeptical. "The more I listened to Joe and the more I read the papers he held in his hands," Smith later admitted, "the less I could understand what he was up to. . . . It was then that I began to wonder about the validity, accuracy, credibility, and fairness of Joseph McCarthy's charges."

Reluctant to speak out against McCarthy's irresponsible allegations, Smith discovered to her dismay at the fact that virtually the entire Democratic contingent in Congress was too frightened to challenge McCarthy publicly. She subsequently prepared a brief statement deploring his tactics and invited six other moderate and liberal Republican senators to sign the statement. All six—Aiken (Vermont), Tobey (New Hampshire), Morse (Oregon), Ives (New York), Thye (Minnesota), and Hendrickson (New Jersey)—agreed to sign the document. On June 1,

1950, Smith rose in the Senate to deliver her DECLARATION OF CONSCIENCE, which criticized both major parties for their role in the sharply intensifying controversy over Communism in government. "As an American," Smith said, "I condemn a Republican 'Fascist' just as much as I condemn a Democrat 'Communist.' I condemn a Democrat 'Fascist' just as much as I condemn a Republican 'Communist.' They are equally dangerous to you and me and to our country. As an American, I want to see our nation recapture the strength and unity it once had when we fought the enemy instead of ourselves." By fighting the issue of Communism in America along partisan lines, Smith added, "Democrats and Republicans alike have unwittingly, but undeniably, played directly into the Communist design of 'confuse, divide, and conquer.' "

Public reaction to Smith's speech was overwhelmingly favorable. Nevertheless, McCarthy soon struck back by removing her from the PERMANENT SUBCOMMITTEE ON INVESTIGATIONS of the Government Operations Committee. Relations between Smith and McCarthy deteriorated further when McCarthy launched a blistering attack on June 14, 1951, against General George Catlett MARSHALL, who had served the Truman administration as both secretary of state and secretary of defense. In response, Smith reaffirmed the principles of her Declaration of Conscience and defended Marshall against McCarthy's vicious charges.

Early in 1952, one of McCarthy's leading allies, a journalist named Lee Mortimer, attacked Smith in a book entitled U.S.A. Confidential. Mortimer claimed that Smith was a Communist sympathizer, a fellow traveler and associate of a suspected Communist agent, and a "left-wing apologist" who was "under the influence of a coterie of left-wing writers." Smith promptly filed suit for libel; when the case finally reached the courts four years later, Mortimer issued a retraction, publicly apologized for his statements, and paid damages to Smith.

Frustrated by his inability to strike back against Smith, McCarthy finally attempted to remove his antagonist from the Senate by throwing his support behind a challenge to Smith in the Maine Republican primary elections of 1954. In previous campaigns, McCarthy's influence had helped defeat senators such as Millard TYDINGS of Maryland and William BENTON of Connecticut. This time, however, McCarthy's strategy misfired. Smith easily won the Republican primary by a margin of 5–1. In the process, she established a new record total of votes in a Maine state primary.

The results of the Maine election helped bolster the political courage of other Senate Republicans during the debate in the autumn of 1954 over a motion to censure McCarthy for his irresponsible behavior. When the motion came to a vote on December 2, 1954, half of the Republicans in the Senate voted in favor of censure; Smith, who had meanwhile handily won reelection in the general election campaign, was one of those who voted for the measure. She was subsequently reelected to the Senate for two additional terms in 1960 and 1966.

## Sobell, Morton (1927– )

One of the alleged members of the Soviet espionage ring that also included Harry GOLD, Klaus FUCHS, David GREENGLASS, and Julius and Ethel ROSENBERG, Morton Sobell was an electrical engineer who had worked for the U.S. Navy's Bureau of Ordnance during World War II. Before the war, Sobell had attended City College of New York where he met and became close friends with classmate Julius Rosenberg. Sobell's wartime work for the Navy included the design of radar apparatus and research on advanced electronic devices, and he continued that research after the war at a General Electric plant in Schenectady, New York. In 1947, Sobell accepted a position at the Reeves Instrument Corporation in Manhattan where he and his colleagues began to construct a computer to evaluate the efficacy of airplane and guided-missiles designs.

On June 16, 1950, FBI agents arrested Greenglass—who had been implicated by Gold—and charged him with passing atomic secrets to the Soviet Union. That was the last

Morton Sobell (center), convicted of atomic espionage as part of the Fuchs-Rosenberg spy ring.

day Sobell reported to work at Reeves Instrument. Leaving a brand-new 1950 Buick sedan in the locked garage of his home, in Flushing, New York, Sobell took his wife and two children and boarded an airplane for Mexico City. Meanwhile, FBI agents reportedly obtained his name as a member of the espionage ring from another suspect, Max Elitcher, who had been a close friend of Sobell but had later perjured himself in a loyalty hearing, thus opening himself to threats of prosecution.

Reports of the FBI's arrest of Julius Rosenberg frightened Sobell into an attempt to acquire passports under a false name so that his family could flee to Europe. Before he could leave, however, FBI agents in Mexico tracked him to his Mexico City apartment. The agents reportedly beat Sobell into unconsciousness and took him (along with his wife and children) back across the border to Laredo, Texas, where he was held on $100,000 bail and charged with five counts of conspiring with Rosenberg to send defense secrets to the Soviet Union. At that time, Sobell was the eighth American to be arrested as part of the Fuchs-Rosenberg ring.

Sobell was tried with the Rosenbergs in March 1951. Although the evidence against him consisted almost entirely of the uncorroborated testimony of Elitcher, Sobell declined to testify on his own behalf. He was found guilty and sentenced to thirty years in the federal prison at

Alcatraz, in California. He appealed the verdict several times, but each appeal was denied, and in 1956 the U.S. Supreme Court refused to hear his case. FBI agents visited Sobell in prison and told him that he might obtain a reduced sentence if he provided names of other Soviet spies, but Sobell refused. "A person must live with himself," he wrote to his wife from his cell at Alcatraz. "There is no slightly soiled dirt, all dirt is dirty."

Sobell served five years in Alcatraz, and then was transferred to a federal prison in Atlanta. He was released after serving eighteen and a half years of his sentence. In 1974, Sobell published a memoir of his life in prison, entitled *On Doing Time*. He always maintained he was innocent of the charges against him.

## Sokolsky, George (1893–1962)

A leading conservative newspaper columnist during the 1940s and 1950s, George Sokolsky maintained close ties with FBI Director J. Edgar HOOVER, Senator Joseph MCCARTHY, McCarthy aide Roy COHN, and other leaders of the anti-Communist crusade in the United States.

A native of Utica, New York, Sokolsky left Columbia University to travel to Russia in 1917 to view the Russian Revolution firsthand. He spent several months in Petrograd, editing an English-language daily newspaper, but was forced to flee to China following the victory of the Bolshevik forces led by Vladimir Ilyich Lenin in 1919.

Sokolsky remained in China for eleven years, serving as a political correspondent for several American newspapers and as editor of *The Far Eastern Review*. During his stay in China, Sokolsky developed an admiration for CHIANG Kaishek, whom he considered the leading apostle of democracy in the Far East. In 1930, Sokolsky returned to the United States and began to write a column of political commentary for the New York *Herald Tribune*. Beginning in 1944, his daily column was distributed across the nation by William Randolph Hearst's King Features Syndicate; at the height of his influence,

Sokolsky's column appeared in nearly 300 newspapers.

Always a devout conservative, Sokolsky—a leading member of the CHINA LOBBY—used his column to promote the fortunes of Chiang's Nationalist regime in China. Sokolsky also maintained close ties with J. Edgar Hoover, who supplied Sokolsky with material for his column; in return, Sokolsky passed on tips to Hoover. When the HOUSE COMMITTEE ON UN-AMERICAN ACTIVITIES launched its investigation of Communist influence in Hollywood in 1947, Sokolsky jumped eagerly into the fray, publishing allegations of disloyalty or subversion against motion picture actors, writers, and directors. Soon, Sokolsky had established himself as a self-appointed blacklister and confessor of performers suspected of Communist sympathies. As one observer pointed out, Sokolsky "indicted, convicted, pardoned, paroled, and granted clemency according to his own rules of evidence."

When Humphrey BOGART sent Sokolsky a copy of a letter in late 1947 admitting that he had been duped by Communists in the past, Sokolsky reprinted Bogart's letter and praised the actor for acknowledging his error, but he added a warning that "next time, however, I hope you will look before you leap. Things are not always what they seem. . . . For instance, you people out in Hollywood had an idea . . . that this country had an ally during the war. . . . That was never true. Soviet Russia was never an ally. Germany's war on Russia coincided, more or less, with our war on Germany and the Russians were ready and willing to take advantage of that situation."

As a leader in the China Lobby, Sokolsky took every opportunity to criticize the Truman administration's Far East policy. For Sokolsky, the fall of Chiang's Nationalist regime in 1949 could only be explained by subversion within the U.S. Department of State, and he drew a direct line between the disloyalty of State Department officials such as John Carter VINCENT and Alger HISS and the outbreak of the KOREAN WAR in June 1950. "If our far eastern policy was not betrayed," wondered Sokolsky, "why are we fighting in Korea?"

Once Senator McCarthy publicly charged the State Department with harboring Communist sympathizers, Sokolsky readily passed along copies of his own files on suspected subversives to provide McCarthy with additional ammunition. It was Sokolsky who introduced McCarthy to Roy COHN, the brilliant and ambitious young attorney who became McCarthy's chief aide. During the early years of the Eisenhower administration, Sokolsky served as a conduit between the White House and McCarthy, passing along to the Wisconsin senator peace feelers or offers of compromise to avoid intraparty confrontations.

The Senate's censure of McCarthy in December 1954 did little to dampen Sokolsky's enthusiasm for the crusade against Communism. Indeed, by the time of his death from a heart attack in 1962, many of his admirers still considered Sokolsky the "high priest of anti-Communism."

**Sondergaard, Gale** (1899–1985)  Noted for her portrayals of mysterious, wicked villainesses, Gale Sondergaard was one of Hollywood's leading character actresses in the 1930s and 1940s, winning an Academy Award as Best Supporting Actress in 1936 for her role in the turgid melodrama *Anthony Adverse;* among her other well-known films were *Anna and the King of Siam, The Spider Woman,* and *The Letter.*

Like her husband, director Herbert BIBER-MAN, Sondergaard was an active member of numerous left-wing Hollywood organizations between 1937 and 1951. An avid supporter of the Loyalist cause in the Spanish Civil War, she was one of the founders of the Hollywood chapter of the JOINT ANTI-FASCIST REFUGEE COMMITTEE and the Motion Picture Artists Committee to aid Republican Spain. When Martin DIES, first chairman of the HOUSE COMMIT-TEE ON UN-AMERICAN ACTIVITIES (HUAC) launched his one-man probe of Communist influence in the motion picture community in

1939, Sondergaard was one of the initial witnesses. After a cursory examination of her background, Dies issued her a clearance.

When HUAC returned to Hollywood in 1947 under the leadership of chairman J. Parnell THOMAS, the committee subpoenaed Sondergaard's husband as an "unfriendly" witness. Like the other members of the HOLLY-WOOD TEN, Biberman refused to answer the committee's questions and was subsequently fined and sentenced to prison for contempt of Congress. To raise defense funds for the appeals of the Ten—and to arouse public support for their stand against the committee—Sondergaard narrated a twenty-minute documentary film entitled *The Hollywood Ten.* The industry promptly BLACKLISTED the film as well as the performers, forcing Sondergaard and the spouses of the other members of the Ten to travel around the country, showing the film in auditoriums and meeting halls.

When HUAC launched its second full-scale investigation of the motion picture industry in 1951, it summoned Sondergaard to testify. On March 13, eight days before she was scheduled to appear before the committee, Sondergaard addressed an open letter to the officers and board members of the Screen Actors Guild (SAG) (including Ronald REAGAN, then serving as SAG president). In her note, which she published as a paid advertisement in the trade paper *Variety,* Sondergaard admitted that her career as an actress could end with her testimony; if the committee asked about her past political associations and activities, she intended to invoke the Fifth Amendment, and she recognized that she would probably be blacklisted as a result. "I must appeal to the Board, to my fellow actors, to consider whether it will not be proper and necessary for it to make a public declaration that it will not tolerate any industry blacklist," Sondergaard concluded. "I can find no reason in my conduct as an actress or union member why I should have to contemplate a severing of the main artery of my life—my career as a performer—because I hold to views for which during the last war I was an esteemed member of the Victory Committee and the recipient of the thanks of my government, industry, and union."

The board of the SAG replied with a ringing defense of the anti-Communist crusade. "This is not the time for dialectic fencing," it stated. "Like the overwhelming majority of the American people, we believe that a 'clear and present danger' to our nation exists. The Guild Board believes that all participants in the international Communist Party conspiracy against our nation should be exposed for what they are—enemies of our country and of our form of government."

Bereft of support from the guild, Sondergaard appeared before the committee, pleaded the Fifth Amendment, and was dismissed from the stand. All of her performance contracts were canceled, and she did not work again as an actress for nearly fifteen years.

**Song of Russia**   Released in 1943, *Song of Russia* was one of three wartime pro-Soviet motion pictures that the HOUSE COMMITTEE ON UN-AMERICAN ACTIVITIES chose to review during its October 1947 investigation of Communist influence in the film industry. (The other films were *Mission to Moscow* and *North Star.*) Specifically, the committee sought to determine whether Communists or their sympathizers had deliberately inserted material favorable to the Soviet Union or Communism in these films.

*Song of Russia*—which opened with a rendition of *The Star-Spangled Banner* played by a Soviet orchestra—starred Robert Taylor as an orchestra conductor who toured the Soviet Union in the spring of 1941 and fell in love with a Russian pianist. They visited her native village, where they were welcomed by a brass band and cheerful, well-fed peasants equipped with their own radios and tractors. Shortly after Taylor and the heroine were married, the Nazi armies attacked; Taylor urged his wife to leave, but she refused to abandon her homeland in its hour of need. Taylor's manager, nicely underplayed by humorist and sometime actor Robert

Benchley, informed the young lady that "You are a fool, but a lot of fools like you died on the village green at Lexington." In the end, one of the Russians convinced Taylor and the girl to return to the United States, so they could tell the American people "what you have seen, and you will see the truth both in speech and in music."

Clearly the film painted an unrealistic portrait of life in the Soviet Union in 1941, but it really was no more exaggerated than most fluffy Hollywood treatments of middle-class life in the United States. When it was released, one reviewer noted that "many U.S. soldiers find this naive propaganda one long howl of laughter. Many civilians may find bits of it acceptable." The best part of the movie was the musical score, which was described as "a boundary-melting pleasure to hear."

Because *Song of Russia* had been made by Metro-Goldwyn-Mayer, the committee questioned first Louis B. Mayer, head of the studio. In the preliminary statement he submitted to the committee, Mayer admitted that the film was "friendly to Russia." "Of course it was," Mayer said. "It was made to be friendly. . . . It seemed a good medium of entertainment and at the same time offered an opportunity for a pat on the back for our then ally, Russia. It also offered an opportunity to use the music of Tschaikowsky. We mentioned this to the Government coordinators and they agreed with us that it would be a good idea to make the picture." The final script, noted Mayer, "was little more than a pleasant musical romance—the story of a boy and girl that, except for the music of Tschaikowsky, might just as well have taken place in Switzerland or England or any other country on the earth." When asked if he believed the film accurately represented conditions in the Soviet Union in 1947, Mayer replied that "I didn't make it as it is today, I made it when they were our ally in 1943."

Mayer was followed to the stand by author Ayn RAND, who proceeded to deliver a detailed, 4,000-word denunciation of the film, claiming that it gave a wholly unrealistic view of life in the Soviet Union and was nothing more than Communist propaganda. This proved too much even for several members of the committee, who reminded Rand that the USSR had been an American ally in World War II and that it might have been in the interest of the United States to keep Russia in the war. "I don't think," Rand answered, "it was necessary to deceive the American people about the nature of Russia." Rand's protestations not withstanding, the committee thereupon abandoned its analysis of the film and moved on to more substantive matters.

**Sorrell, Herbert K.** See DISNEY, Walter E.

**Southern Conference on Human Welfare**
Perhaps the leading liberal political organization in the southern United States during the 1940s, the Southern Conference on Human Welfare (SCHW) was founded in 1938 for the purpose of promoting civil rights and ameliorating the social and economic problems of the South. Nearly 2,000 delegates attended the first meeting in Birmingham, Alabama, where local police made certain that white and black delegates sat on opposite sides of the hall. The conference's first chairman was Dr. Frank Graham, president of the University of North Carolina.

As an indication of the wide range of issues in which the SCHW was interested, its 1938 conference adopted resolutions on such varied subjects as farm tenancy, the HOUSE COMMITTEE ON UN-AMERICAN ACTIVITIES (the SCHW condemned the committee, also known as HUAC), freight-rate differential, public health, social security, penal reform, agricultural credit, and the controversial case of the Scottsboro boys, a group of nine young black men accused of rape. Between 1938 and 1947, the SCHW held a convention every other year (except in 1944) and published on a regular basis a journal entitled *The Southern Patriot*.

While there were a handful of Communists among the organization's membership, they were not sufficiently influential to persuade the

SCHW to adopt the Moscow line on vital issues. For instance, at its 1940 conference—following the NAZI-SOVIET PACT, which allowed Germany and the Soviet Union to carve up Poland—the SCHW approved the following resolution: "We deplore the rise of dictators anywhere, the suppression of civil liberties, the persecution of minorities, aggression against small and weak nations, the violation of the neutral rights and the democratic liberties of the peoples by all fascist, nazi, communist and imperialist powers alike which resort to force and aggression instead of to the processes of law, freedom, democracy and international cooperation."

In 1947, the HUAC conducted an investigation of the SCHW. The committee's report, issued in June 1947 (not coincidentally, on the eve of a major SCHW rally in support of former Vice President Henry WALLACE), sought to prove that the conference followed the COMMUNIST PARTY line and was linked in various ways to a mysterious, ill-defined parent international Communist organization based in Moscow. The committee did not hold public hearings on the SCHW before issuing its report.

HUAC's report on the SCHW began with the accusation that "the Southern Conference for Human Welfare is an organization which seeks to attract southern liberals on the basis of its seeming interest in the problems of the South. . . . Careful examination of its official publication and its activities will disclose that the conference actually is being used in devious ways to further basic Soviet and Communist policy. Decisive and key posts are in most instances controlled by persons whose record is faithful to the line of the Communist Party and the Soviet Union." Specifically, the report charged that the conference "shows unswerving loyalty to the basic principle of Soviet foreign policy"; "has consistently refused to take sharp issue with the activities and policies of either the Communist Party, USA, or the Soviet Union"; "has maintained in decisive posts persons who have the confidence of the Communist press"; and "has displayed consistent anti-American bias and pro-Soviet bias, despite professions, in generalities, of love for America."

As evidence, the committee noted that the SCHW adopted the Communist Party line when it supported the Scottsboro boys and denounced HUAC's record under Martin DIES. Further, the conference allegedly had displayed a "strict and unvarying conformance to the line of the Communist Party" in the field of foreign policy when it joined the war effort enthusiastically during World War II, demanding that all "join in a great offensive now, to work, to produce, to sacrifice, to win." This, claimed the committee, was precisely the line adopted by Communists everywhere; the committee neglected to point out that it was also the line followed by all patriotic Americans as well. The HUAC report added that "a significant number of the leading lights of the Southern Conference" had ties to Communist organizations and causes. Among the sixty-two individuals cited in this list were Dr. Graham, former Vice President Wallace, and former Secretary of the Interior Harold Ickes.

Perhaps recognizing that its case against the SCHW was rather insubstantial, the report closed with the allegation that "the SCHW is perhaps the most deviously camouflaged Communist-front organization." Shortly after the HUAC report appeared, Professor Lawrence Gellhorn of the Columbia University Law School conducted an in-depth analysis of its contents and methodology. "The report demonstrates," Gellhorn concluded, "not that the Southern Conference is a corrupt organization, but that the Committee has been either intolerably incompetent or designedly intent upon publicizing misinformation."

Nevertheless, the report led to the demise of the SCHW. By the end of 1947, the conference had ceased to exist as a viable organization. Its work was subsequently taken up by the Southern Conference Educational Fund.

**Stalin, Joseph** (1879–1953)   Dictator of the Soviet Union from 1929 until his death in 1953, Joseph Stalin forced the USSR into the twentieth century through his relentless campaigns of industrialization and modernization of the nation's military forces.

Born in the southwestern province of Georgia, Stalin's real name was Josif Vissarionovich Djugashvili. Stalin joined the Communist Party in 1904 as a hired thug and proceeded to make himself indispensable by robbing czarist bank messengers to finance subversive Bolshevik activities. Although party intellectuals dismissed him as an uncouth, uneducated young tough, Stalin possessed the sort of native cunning and joy in deceit that carried him unscathed through the vicious internecine power struggles that continued to plague the Soviet Communist movement after the overthrow of the czar's government in 1917. He gradually consolidated his hold on the party machinery by installing his own loyal subordinates—men who owed their careers solely to Stalin's favor—in critical posts. When he finally grasped the reins of power firmly in his own hands, he began to eliminate his most prominent rivals.

First, he turned against the threat from the Left and, in particular, Leon Trotsky. In January 1929, Stalin deported his chief enemy to Constantinople and launched a widespread drive to root out all vestiges of deviationist Trotskyite sentiment in the Soviet bureaucracy. Then Stalin turned against his rivals on the Right, notably the trio of Nikolai Bukharin, Alexis Rykov, and Michael Tomsky. In February 1929, Bukharin, Tomsky, and Rykov—all of whom had criticized Stalin's obsessive drive toward the forced collectivization of Soviet agriculture—were unceremoniously stripped of power for "persisting in their mistakes"; they were replaced on the Politburo by pro-Stalinist loyalists. With all political opposition effectively crushed, Stalin at last could hurl the full force of his tenacious and megalomaniacal personality into the ambitious and murderous crusade to drag the Soviet Union into the twentieth century.

The Soviet Union had already embarked, in the previous year, on its first Five-Year Plan to increase industrial production. In August 1929, the party's Central Committee approved Stalin's plan for "mass and rapid [agricultural] collectivization of whole regions." The campaign would be carried out with brutal vigor; no misplaced concern for the welfare of individuals would be permitted to endanger the success of the grand experiment.

Until 1935, Stalin favored an aggressive international policy to spread the Communist revolution abroad. The rise to power of the fascist powers of Germany and Italy, however, persuaded Stalin to modify the rhetoric of revolution in favor of a policy of accommodation with liberals in the Western democracies. For the following four years, the Comintern (Communist International) supported the establishment of a POPULAR FRONT of left-wing elements in Europe and the United States. As a result, American liberals often found themselves allied with Communist elements in the pursuit of reform. The period of the Popular Front ended abruptly when Stalin signed the NAZI-SOVIET PACT in September 1939. The pact clearly was designed to serve the national strategic interests of the Soviet Union, but the vision of Stalin embracing the leaders of Nazi Germany struck substantial numbers of Communists and liberals in the West as a betrayal of the leftist cause. The process of disillusionment was accelerated as news of the bloody Stalinist purges of the Soviet political and military hierarchy—which began in 1935 and continued into 1939—reached the West.

Following the German attack upon the Soviet Union in June 1941 and the Japanese strike at Pearl Harbor six months later, the United States and the Soviet Union found themselves allied against the Axis powers. During World War II, Stalin met on several occasions with President Franklin D. Roosevelt and British Prime Minister Winston Churchill to discuss wartime strategy and, beginning in 1943, to begin to plan for the postwar world. Once peace returned in August 1945, however, Stalin abandoned his policy of accommodation, seeking instead security through the military control of satellite governments in Eastern Europe. The Soviet takeover of the Eastern European nations, along with the revival of Soviet revolutionary rhetoric, provided ammunition for the anti-Communist crusade in the United States and helped focus public attention on the hunt for Soviet agents and Communist sympathizers in the federal government. For the next eight years, Stalin continued to exert pressure on the West through propaganda, threats, and support of military aggression (as in the North Korean invasion of South Korea in June 1950).

On March 5, 1953, Stalin died of a massive brain hemorrhage suffered four days earlier.

## Stevens, Robert Ten Broeck (1899–1983)

Former chairman and president of J. P. Stevens and Company, one of the largest textile manufacturing firms in the United States, Robert T. Stevens was named secretary of the Army by President Dwight D. EISENHOWER in 1953. Secretary Stevens became embroiled almost immediately in a controversy with Senator Joseph MCCARTHY of Wisconsin who charged that the Army was shielding Communist sympathizers in its ranks.

Initially, Stevens attempted to placate McCarthy by promising to cooperate with a Senate investigation of Communist influence in the Army. For instance, after McCarthy claimed to have uncovered evidence of Communist subversion at the Army Signal Corps base at FORT MONMOUTH, New Jersey, Stevens took McCarthy and his investigative staff on a personal tour of the facility. Stevens also provided extra privileges to McCarthy's aide, G. David SCHINE after Schine was drafted into the Army in 1953. Yet, Stevens refused to accede to McCarthy's demand for access to the confidential personnel files of allegedly disloyal Army employees.

The confrontation between Stevens and McCarthy escalated in the winter of 1953–54, when McCarthy learned that the Army had routinely promoted a dentist, Major Irving PERESS, who refused to answer questions about his political beliefs. To McCarthy, the Peress affair symbolized the Army's cover-up of Communist sympathizers. To help defuse the situation, Stevens—who had virtually no experience in practical political negotiations—met with McCarthy and other conservative Republican senators on February 24; in return for his promise to provide McCarthy with the names of the officials who had been responsible for Peress' promotion, Stevens allegedly received the senators' assurance that Army officials who testified in congressional investigations would receive "fair and courteous treatment." The press release that the senators issued following the meeting, however, mentioned only Stevens' concession, which gave the public the impression that the Eisenhower administration had caved in completely to McCarthy's demands.

Stevens offered to resign to avoid further embarrassment to the White House, but Vice President Richard M. NIXON convinced him to stay at his post. Yet, Stevens' political inexperience continued to hamper the administration's handling of the Army-McCarthy controversy, particularly during the ARMY-MCCARTHY HEARINGS, which began in April 1954. One of the first witnesses to testify, Stevens appeared uneasy and unwilling to answer McCarthy's questions directly. Perhaps Stevens' most significant contribution to the hearings was his decision to retain attorney Joseph WELCH as special counsel for the Army. It was Welch—a superb actor—who ultimately unmasked McCarthy as an unprincipled bully for his savage attack on an associate in Welch's law firm.

For his part, Stevens refused to agree to any compromise with McCarthy that did not completely clear his reputation or the reputation of the Army. Although the hearings ended inconclusively, they did not bear out McCarthy's charges of widespread Communist infiltration of the U.S. armed services. Further, McCarthy's tirades during the inquiry gave a nationwide television audience its first look at the senator's brusque and reckless tactics.

Stevens' reputation also had been shaken, and after a decent interval he resigned in 1955 to return to J. P. Stevens and Company. He returned briefly to government service as a civilian aide to the Army. In 1961, Stevens became a member of the Board of Visitors of the U.S. Military Academy at West Point, a position that he held for two years. He retired from active participation in business ventures in 1974 after being named director emeritus of J. P. Stevens and Company.

**Stevenson, Adlai E.** (1900–1963)  As the Democratic presidential nominee in 1952 and 1956, Adlai Stevenson became one of the favorite targets of conservative Republican partisans during the McCarthy era.

Stevenson grew up in Illinois, the son of a journalist and the grandson of former Vice President Adlai Stevenson, who served in the second administration of President Grover Cleveland (1888–1892). After completing his studies at Choate Academy in Connecticut—where his education was interrupted briefly by service in a naval training unit during World War I—Stevenson entered Princeton University in 1919. At Princeton, Stevenson majored in history and became managing editor of the college newspaper, the *Daily Princetonian*. He obtained a B.A. in 1922, but after two years at Harvard Law School, Stevenson found it necessary to return to Illinois to help manage a family newspaper following the death of his uncle. Stevenson completed his law studies at Northwestern University, receiving a J.D. degree in 1926.

In the summer of 1926, while still undecided whether to pursue a career in journalism or law, Stevenson journeyed to the USSR to see firsthand the results of the Soviet experiment. His experiences in Moscow left Stevenson with a life-long detestation of Communism. "The atmosphere of fear was palpable," he told a friend several decades later, "as palpable as the abject poverty of the masses. I never knew whether or not I was being followed, but I did know that people were afraid to be seen talking to me. . . . I have always been very thankful

Democratic presidential candidate Adlai E. Stevenson.

for that trip. After what I saw there, I could never believe, as so many did in the early 1930s, that Soviet Russia's way was a good way for any state to go. Some men, from the highest humanitarian motives, became Communists or fellow travellers during the Depression, but I felt that I had seen at first hand what Communism really meant, in terms of terror and brutality."

From 1927 to 1931, Stevenson was an associate with the Chicago law firm of Cutting, Moore & Sidley. In 1933, he was appointed special counsel in the recently formed Agricultural Adjustment Administration, though he remained in Washington for only one year before returning to his private law practice. Stevenson's interest in international affairs had led him to become involved in the work of the Chicago Council on International Relations, and as the United States drifted closer to war in 1939–41, Stevenson helped counteract isolationist sentiment in the Midwest by assuming the chairman-

ship of the Chicago chapter of the Committee to Defend America by Aiding the Allies. In the summer of 1941, Stevenson returned to Washington to serve as special assistant and counsel to Secretary of the Navy Frank Knox.

Stevenson remained in that position for most of the war, but as the defeat of Germany grew certain, he became closely involved with planning for a postwar international organization. As an assistant to Secretary of State Edward Stettinius, Jr., Stevenson helped organize the United Nations Conference in San Francisco in the summer of 1945. At the conference itself, Stevenson served as press spokesman for the United States delegation. When the United Nations General Assembly held its first meeting in London in January 1946, Stevenson attended as senior U.S. adviser and later served as a U.S. delegate at subsequent General Assembly sessions in New York in 1946–47.

By that time, Stevenson had become a highly visible public figure, and so the Illinois Democratic leadership prevailed upon him to enter the state gubernatorial race in 1948. Stevenson rolled up a record margin in winning that election and immediately embarked upon an ambitious program of reform over the following four years. He largely rid the state of corruption in its police force, thereby bringing an end to the power of organized gambling interests in Illinois (and particularly in Cook County, which had been the stronghold of Al Capone a decade earlier). Stevenson doubled state expenditures to education, slashed more than a thousand unnecessary jobs from the state-government payroll, fashioned an exemplary system of state mental hospitals, and initiated an impressive program of state-highway construction.

In January 1952, President Harry S. TRUMAN invited Stevenson to the White House to discuss a possible run for the presidency, but Stevenson remained reluctant to enter national politics. More than anything else, he wished to serve a second term as governor of Illinois; "I just [want] to keep my commitments to my friends and followers in Illinois and finish the work we have started," Stevenson declared. "Illinois means a great deal to me. . . . I'll be content if I can leave the state government a lot better than I found it and I think I can." When Democratic Party leaders pointed out that the party faced a dearth of viable candidates at the national level in 1952, Stevenson replied that "great political parties, like great nations, have no indispensable man." Clearly Stevenson's reluctance was quite real and not merely a ploy to encourage a groundswell of support without committing himself.

Yet, the Democratic National Convention proceeded to draft Stevenson as its presidential candidate on the third ballot. Nor surprisingly, in light of the Republican Party's previous assaults upon the record of the Truman administration, Senator Joseph MCCARTHY and Republican vice presidential candidate Richard M. NIXON attempted to portray the Democratic nominee as "soft" on Communism, the same charge they had leveled at President Truman and his advisers. Stevenson detested McCarthy, whom he considered a "sick man"; yet, he reportedly loathed Nixon even more because he felt that Nixon had cynically exploited the issue of Communism in government for personal and partisan political gain. Throughout the campaign, Nixon cited the formula "C(2)K(1)"— "Communism, corruption, and Korea"—which he had borrowed from Senator Karl MUNDT of South Dakota. The election of Adlai Stevenson, Nixon argued, would lead to "more Alger Hisses, more atomic spies, more crises." For his part, McCarthy pretended to confuse the Democratic presidential candidate with former State Department employee Alger HISS, who had recently been convicted of perjury for denying that he had ever been a member of the COMMUNIST PARTY. In speaking at Republican gatherings, McCarthy repeatedly referred with a smirk to "Alger—I mean, Adlai—Stevenson." McCarthy also claimed at one point that if he were put on board the Democratic presidential nominee's campaign train with a club, he might

be able to make a good American out of Stevenson.

Certainly, Stevenson did not hesitate to attack McCarthy and Nixon directly during the election campaign. On October 8, Stevenson told an audience at the University of Wisconsin— McCarthy's home state—that "history shows that almost all tyrants have been demagogues who gained favor with the people by their accusations of the nobles." "Disturbing things have taken place in our own land," he added. "The pillorying of the innocent has caused the wise to stammer and the timid to retreat"—a pointed reference to Eisenhower's failure to defend former Secretary of Defense George Catlett MARSHALL against McCarthy's charges that Marshall headed a Soviet conspiracy within the federal government.

Near the end of the campaign, Stevenson again chided Eisenhower for his unwillingness to disown the reckless, slanderous tactics of McCarthy. "I believe with all my heart that those who would beguile the voters by lies or half-truths, or corrupt them by fear and falsehood, are committing spiritual treason against our institutions," declared Stevenson. "They are doing the work of our enemies. . . . Even worse, they undermine our basic spiritual values. For in the final accounting, 'What shall it profit a man if he shall gain the whole world, and lose his own soul?' "

On Election Day, however, Eisenhower defeated Stevenson in a landslide of near-record proportions, capturing more than 55 percent of the popular vote and winning 442 electoral votes to Stevenson's 89. Despite his overwhelming defeat at the polls, Stevenson continued to denounce McCarthy and the zealots among the anti-Communist crusaders across the nation. In response to Republican charges that the administrations of Franklin D. Roosevelt and Harry Truman had amounted to "twenty years of treason," Stevenson delivered on March 7, 1954, a stinging assessment of the appalling impact of MCCARTHYISM upon American institutions.

"Our State Department has been abused and demoralized," he informed a Miami audience. "The American voice abroad has been enfeebled. Our educational system has been attacked; our press threatened; our servants of God impugned; a former President maligned; the executive departments invaded; our foreign policy confused; the President himself patronized; and the integrity, loyalty and morale of the United States Army assailed."

> And why, you ask, do demagogues triumph so often? The answer is inescapable: because a group of political plungers has persuaded the President that McCarthyism is the best Republican formula for political success. Had the Eisenhower administration chosen to act in defense of itself and of the nation which it must govern, it would have had the grateful and dedicated support of all but a tiny and deluded minority of our people.
>
> Yet, clear as the issue is, and unmistakable as the support, the administration appears to be helpless. Why? . . . A political party divided against itself, half McCarthy and half Eisenhower, cannot produce national unity—cannot govern with confidence and purpose. And it demonstrates that, so long as it attempts to share power with its enemies, it will inexorably lose power to its enemies.

In the spring and summer of 1954, Stevenson was one of the few Democratic Party leaders on the national level who were willing to denounce McCarthy openly. As the Wisconsin Senator's power waned following the ARMY-MCCARTHY HEARINGS, collapsing finally after the Senate voted a motion of censure on December 2, 1954, Stevenson's status within the party rose accordingly. Stevenson was easily nominated as the Democratic presidential standard bearer once again at the party's national convention in August 1956, but probably no Democrat could have defeated the popular Eisenhower in the President's bid for reelection. Once more, Stevenson was swept aside in a flood of Republican

votes; this time, Eisenhower's electoral margin was 457–73.

Stevenson, meanwhile, had accepted in 1955 a position as partner in the Chicago law firm of Stevenson, Rifkind & Wirtz. He spent the following four years traveling abroad extensively—including a 1958 journey to the Soviet Union—and writing articles and commentaries on foreign affairs. In December 1960, President-elect John F. KENNEDY named Stevenson as U.S. ambassador to the United Nations. As part of his administration's Alliance for Progress program, Kennedy also dispatched Stevenson on a fact-finding tour of ten South American nations in the summer of 1961. Stevenson returned convinced that the region required a massive infusion of American economic aid to combat the rising tide of poverty and political instability that offered a fertile ground for Communist agitation.

On July 14, 1965, Adlai Stevenson died of a heart attack while walking along the streets of New York. Shortly before his death, he had planned to resign his position at the United Nations in protest over the growing American military involvement in Vietnam.

**Stone, I.F.** (1908–1989)   One of the leading independent journalists in the United States in the post-World War II era, I.F. Stone carried on a relentless crusade against Senator Joseph MCCARTHY and his ultraconservative allies in the anti-Communist crusade during the early 1950s.

Stone, who grew up in New Jersey, became interested in the newspaper business and, at fourteen, was publishing his own paper. While still in school, he worked for a local weekly newspaper and served as a correspondent for a city daily; although Stone majored in philosophy in college, he devoted many of his afternoons and evenings to rewriting articles and editing copy for the *Philadelphia Inquirer*.

Repelled by the notion of a college teaching career—he apparently found the atmosphere of academia far too stifling for his taste—Stone decided to pursue a full-time career in journalism. From 1932 to 1939, he served as an editorial writer on the *Philadelphia Record* and the *New York Post,* both of which were staunch editorial supporters of President Franklin D. Roosevelt's New Deal legislation. In 1940 he journeyed to Washington to become the Washington editor of the liberal weekly publication, *The Nation.* Subsequently, Stone worked as a columnist and reporter for the short-lived afternoon daily, *PM,* the *New York Star,* and the *New York Compass.*

Meanwhile, Stone had also adopted a pronounced left-wing political philosophy; according to his own account, he had been converted to radicalism by reading novelist Jack London, political economist Herbert Spencer, Russian anarchist Peter Kropotkin, and Karl Marx. While still in college, Stone joined the Socialist Party and was elected to the party's New Jersey State Committee. He also campaigned for Socialist presidential candidate Norman THOMAS in the election of 1928 but abandoned organized political life because of what he called "the sectarianism of the left." "Moreover," Stone later wrote, "I felt that party affiliation was incompatible with independent journalism, and I wanted to be free to help the unjustly treated, to defend everyone's civil liberty and to work for social reform without concern for leftist infighting."

Certainly, Stone's decision to cut his ties to the Socialist Party resulted in no diminution of his commitment to liberal causes: He supported former Vice President Henry A. WALLACE's bid for the presidency in 1948, supported a policy of peace and coexistence with the Soviet Union, defended the civil liberties of Communists, opposed the Truman administration's loyalty review board program, denounced the actions of the HOUSE COMMITTEE ON UN-AMERICAN ACTIVITIES (HUAC), and despised FBI Director J. Edgar HOOVER and the two foremost anti-Communist zealots in the U.S. Senate, Republican Joseph MCCARTHY of Wisconsin, and Dem-

ocrat Patrick MCCARRAN of Nevada. Stone also claimed the honor of having written the first newspaper editorial against the SMITH ACT in 1940. "There was nothing to the left of me," claimed Stone, "but the DAILY WORKER."

When the *New York Compass* folded in 1952, Stone decided to embark upon his own publishing venture, a four-page weekly journal that he entitled *I.F. Stone's Weekly.* Aided by the mailing lists of several liberal newspapers, Stone obtained sufficient subscriptions to get the paper off the ground. Much to his relief, he encountered no difficulties in obtaining a second-class-mail permit for his venture, despite the obvious leftist leanings of the *Weekly.* Beginning with the first issue in January 1953, Stone wrote all the articles himself and published the journal privately. Stone's independence was bolstered by his decision not to accept advertising of any sort, thereby removing any potential source of financial pressure to alter his editorial stance. Within ten years, the readership of his *Weekly* had grown from 5,000 to 20,000.

When Stone began publication, McCarthy stood at the zenith of his power. And the senator thus became Stone's first target. On January 17, 1953, Stone lamented the decision by the Senate—which had recently passed into the control of the Republican Party in the wake of the Eisenhower landslide of November 1952—to name McCarthy chairman of the GOVERNMENT OPERATIONS COMMITTEE. "The Senator who is now chairman of the Senate's key watchdog committee," wrote Stone, "is the Senator who most needs watching. The report made on McCarthy by the Senate subcommittee on privileges and elections [dealing with alleged abuses by McCarthy during the Maryland senatorial campaign of 1950] is a monument to the ineptitude of gentlemen in dealing with a brawler who pays no attention to the rules, Queensberry or otherwise."

Stone's descriptions of McCarthy's personal appearance painted a vivid picture to readers who had not yet had the opportunity to witness the Wisconsin senator on television. Observing

McCarthy enter a Senate hearing room, Stone noted that "he had his left hand in his pocket and walked with what was meant to be a modest slouch, a self-conscious grin on his face. The gray jailbird complexion, the covert look of a smart fox, were unchanged. In that gravelly voice, bored, impersonal and inexorable, like the detective hero in a soap opera, McCarthy called the meeting to order." For Stone, one of the most dangerous aspects of McCarthy's activities was his attempt to create "a kind of dictatorship for himself within the framework of established government, to make himself the recipient of complaints from assorted crackpots and malcontents, to build up a secret ring of informants within the government, to use their reports in unscrupulous smear campaigns, and to make officials more fearful of him than of their own superiors."

Stone watched, bemused, as the Republican establishment attempted to control McCarthy following Eisenhower's election to the presidency. Yet, Stone saw nothing amusing in the alliance between McCarthy and FBI Director J. Edgar HOOVER, whom Stone believed to be perhaps the guiding force behind the anti-Communist crusade in the United States. "There are indications," he wrote, "that the FBI and the congressional witch hunt committees were synchronized in the thought control drive, that FBI men moved in to staff the committees, and that the FBI's informers and undercover operatives were released to the committees as witnesses when their usefulness as agents had been ended by exposure. . . ."

Not surprisingly, Stone rejoiced when the Republican leadership in the Senate finally concluded that it had to "smash" McCarthy to prove that the party was not "soft" on Communism. Yet, Stone remained horrified by the legacy of MCCARTHYISM, particularly the federal-employee security program, which conducted its investigations without due regard for the rights of suspected individuals and which encouraged secret allegations by undisclosed informants.

Following the Senate's censure of McCarthy, Stone continued to attack what he perceived as government assaults upon the civil liberties and civil rights of American citizens. During the Vietnam War, *I.F. Stone's Weekly* became one of the leading journalistic opponents of American military involvement in Southeast Asia.

**Strauss, Lewis** (1896–1974)   One of the five original commissioners of the ATOMIC ENERGY COMMISSION (AEC), millionaire financier Lewis Strauss was a zealous advocate of the development of thermonuclear weapons and a dedicated foe of J. Robert OPPENHEIMER, the physicist who had led the wartime Manhattan Project.

The son of a successful businessman, Strauss entered the world of finance in 1917 as an economic analyst for Herbert Hoover, who was then serving as head of the U.S. Food Administration. Two years later, Strauss was offered a position in the Wall Street banking firm of Kuhn, Loeb, and Company. His activities for this company earned him a personal fortune and also brought him into contact with several prominent physical scientists in Europe and the United States. It was partly through his acquain-

Lewis Straus, chairman of the Atomic Energy Commission in the Eisenhower administration.

tance with Danish scientist Niels Bohr that Strauss, who later claimed that he had really wanted to be a physicist, became deeply interested in studies of radioactivity.

During World War II, Strauss served in the U.S. Navy as staff assistant to the chief of ordnance and as assistant chief of the office of procurement and material. In August 1944, he was named special assistant to Secretary of the Navy James Forrestal, and in recognition of Strauss' wartime services, President Harry S. TRUMAN elevated him to the rank of rear admiral in November 1945.

Before he returned to civilian life in December 1945, Strauss represented the Navy on the Interdepartmental Committee on Atomic Energy. Following the passage of the McMahon Atomic Energy Act of 1946, which established the AEC to oversee all production and research into atomic energy in the United States, Truman nominated Strauss to serve as one of the AEC's five commissioners. Truman may have regretted his action when Strauss became one of the most vocal advocates for the development of thermonuclear weapons, particularly after the Soviet Union announced in September 1949 that it had successfully exploded its first nuclear device. Over the objections of scientist J. Robert Oppenheimer and AEC chairman David Lilienthal, the Truman administration subsequently approved a research program to produce a hydrogen bomb, albeit not with the same degree of enthusiasm for the project as Strauss displayed. Strauss never forgot—or forgave—Oppenheimer for his opposition to the H-bomb program.

In July 1953, President Dwight David EISENHOWER appointed Strauss chairman of the AEC. In that position, Strauss campaigned vigorously against all efforts at disarmament, despite Eisenhower's public statements favoring the exploration of alternatives designed to reduce the growing stockpiles of nuclear weapons in the United States and the Soviet Union. Strauss also seized the opportunity to remove Oppenheimer from the U.S. nuclear-research effort by providing Eisenhower with information that seemed to prove that Oppenheimer had attempted to delay the hydrogen-bomb program. While Eisenhower respected Oppenheimer's abilities as a physicist, he felt he could not countenance any opposition to a policy once it had been approved by the White House. After further investigation, a special committee established by Eisenhower concluded that while Oppenheimer was not disloyal, he did possess certain "defects of character" that might prove detrimental to the U.S. atomic-research program. Therefore, the committee recommended the revocation of Oppenheimer's security clearance, and in the spring of 1954, the AEC commissioners—led by Strauss—voted 4–1 to uphold the committee's decision. Oppenheimer's defenders later suggested that Strauss's eagerness to remove Oppenheimer was largely a ploy to placate Senator Joseph MCCARTHY and to deflect McCarthy from further investigations into the AEC's security program.

In 1958, Eisenhower nominated Strauss as secretary of commerce, but the Senate refused to confirm the nomination.

**Stripling, Robert**  See HOUSE COMMITTEE ON UN-AMERICAN ACTIVITIES.

**Symington, (William) Stuart** (1901–1988)  A leading opponent of Senator Joseph MCCARTHY, particularly during the ARMY-MC-CARTHY HEARINGS of April–June 1954, Democratic Senator Stuart Symington of Missouri had acquired a reputation as an excellent and resourceful administrator in both business and government before his election to the U.S. Senate in 1952.

A native of Amherst, Massachusetts, Symington grew up in Baltimore, Maryland, where his father practiced law. At the age of 17, Symington joined the U.S. Army and served briefly before the armistice brought World War I to a close in November 1918. Following his return to civilian life, Symington attended Yale College, graduating with a B.A. degree in 1923. He then embarked upon a business career, serving as an

Democratic senator Stuart Symington of Missouri, a vocal opponent of Joseph McCarthy.

executive with numerous companies, including the Gould Car Lighting Company, the Colonial Radio Company, the Symington Company, the Rustless Iron and Steel Company, and the Emerson Electrical Manufacturing Company. As president and chairman of the board of Emerson Electrical, Symington established excellent working relations with a previously hostile, radical-dominated union by offering workers a profit-sharing plan which brought labor 30 percent of the company's annual profits.

During World War II, President Harry S. TRUMAN employed Symington as an airplane-armament expert. In July 1945, Symington was named chairman of the Surplus Property Board, the organization which had the difficult job of disposing of billions of dollars' worth of surplus war property. When Congress established the U.S. Air Force in July 1946 under the terms of the National Security Act, Truman appointed Symington the nation's first secretary of the Air Force. In that post, Symington pressed consistently for increased funding for U.S. air power, arguing that the Soviet Union already possessed superior land and sea resources. Frustrated by the Truman administration's refusal to meet his funding requests, Symington resigned in March 1950 in protest of what he termed "drastic armaments reductions for the sake of budget balancing." Truman subsequently named Symington chairman of the National Security Resources Board in April 1950; it was Symington, therefore, who bore the responsibility for mobilizing American military resources to meet the North Korean invasion of South Korea two months later.

In the autumn of 1952, Symington ran as the Democratic candidate for the United States Senate from Missouri. Despite the nationwide landslide for Republican presidential candidate Dwight D. EISENHOWER (who also carried Missouri by a narrow margin), Symington emerged victorious. When the Eighty-Second Congress convened in January 1953, Symington's primary assignment was the Senate Armed Services Committee. He was also assigned, however, to the GOVERNMENT OPERATIONS COMMITTEE (chaired by Senator McCarthy) in part because Senate Minority Leader Lyndon JOHNSON felt that Symington—having just won an election—would be relatively impervious to threats of political pressure by McCarthy and his zealous anti-Communist supporters.

Although Symington resigned from the Government Operations Committee in July 1953 in protest against what he considered to be Senator McCarthy's "one-man rule" of the committee, Symington agreed to return to the Government Operations Committee in 1954. In April of that year, the committee began its investigation of the controversy between McCarthy and U.S. Army officials. During the ensuing hearings, the openly partisan Symington acted as one of McCarthy's chief critics, repeatedly goading the Wisconsin senator into emotional outbursts of frustration. Privately, Symington advised Secretary of the Army Robert T. STEVENS that Mc-

Carthy "might be sick, you know. . . . If you are going to play with McCarthy, you have got to forget about any of these Marquis of Queensberry rules." Publicly, a nationwide television audience was treated to vicious verbal exchanges between Symington and McCarthy. McCarthy termed Symington "an alleged man" and "sanctimonious Stu," and charged that he was "unfit" to serve on the Government Operations Committee. For his part, Symington complained about McCarthy's blustering, delaying tactics—"End run of diversion Number 1,620," he once scoffed—and once suggested to McCarthy that "you better go to a psychiatrist."

Symington clearly got the better of the repartee. His reputation as a foe of defense-spending cuts made it difficult for McCarthy to attack Symington's patriotism, and Symington's calm demeanor contrasted favorably with McCarthy's temperamental blustering. Further, Symington's barbs upset McCarthy so much that he became an easy target for the rapier wit of Army Special Counsel Joseph WELCH.

Along with every other Democrat in the Senate, Symington voted in favor of the motion to censure McCarthy in December 1954. To prevent similar abuses of the congressional investigative process in the future, Symington recommended a complete "housecleaning" of the Government Operations Committee and its subcommittees.

Much to the discomfiture of President Eisenhower, Symington continued to attack the administration's efforts to reduce defense spending. In February 1956, he warned the American public that the Soviets led the United States in the field of ballistics missiles. "They have fired long-range missiles hundreds of miles further than we have," Symington claimed. One month later, Symington became chairman of a subcommittee charged with investigating the so-called missile gap between the United States and the Soviet Union. "We want to find out whether the relative air strength of the United States, present and planned, is adequate—as against Russia's estimated strength—to be able to take a sudden, devastating nuclear attack and then come back to destroy the possible enemy," Symington explained. Not surprisingly, the ensuing hearings led advocates of air power to call for increased funds for the development of long-range missiles. The issue of the relative air strength of the United States and the USSR remained a controversial topic throughout the last years of the Eisenhower administration and served as one of the most significant issues in the 1960 presidential campaign between Vice President Richard NIXON and the Democratic nominee, Senator John F. KENNEDY.

Symington continued to serve in the Senate until 1976 when he retired to return to private life. He died December 14, 1988.

# T

**Taft, Robert A.** (1889–1953) One of the leading conservative Republican statesmen of the twentieth century, Robert A. Taft served as minority leader in the U.S. Senate from 1947 to 1953 and as majority leader from January 1953 until his death on July 31 of that year.

The son of President William Howard Taft (1909–1913), Robert Taft was born in Cincinnati, Ohio, and spent four years of his childhood in the Philippine Islands while his father was governor-general of the Philippines. Following his return to the United States, Taft attended Yale University and Harvard Law School, from which he received an LL.B. in 1913. For four years, Taft practiced law as a member of the Cincinnati firm of Maxwell and Ramsey. From 1917 to 1919, Taft served as assistant counsel to the U.S. Food Administration, the agency that had been established to regulate prices and production during World War I. After the armistice, Taft journeyed to Europe, where he became counsel for the American Relief Administration under the direction of Herbert Hoover.

Taft returned to the private practice of law in 1922. The firm he founded with his brother—Taft, Stettinius, and Hollister—became the largest and most affluent firm in the city of Cincinnati. Although he had never been a gregarious man at ease with the give and take of politics, Taft decided in the early 1920s to embark upon a political career. From 1922 to 1926, he served in the Ohio state legislature, rising to the position of speaker before moving on to a two-year career in the state Senate. In 1938, Taft won election to the U.S. Senate for the first time and quickly established a reputation as an isolationist through his opposition to the Selective Service Act and Lend-Lease measures. Taft also opposed most of the Roosevelt administration's New Deal reform measures and consistently pressed for the reduction of federal spending.

The public reaction against the Truman administration in the congressional elections of 1946 provided Taft with much-needed conservative support in the Senate and confirmed him in his determination to roll back the tide of New Deal reforms. The following year, Taft successfully negotiated the passage of an anti-union labor measure, the TAFT-HARTLEY ACT, which also required labor-union officials to sign affidavits swearing that they were not members of the COMMUNIST PARTY. In fact, the apparent rightward shift of the nation in the postwar years encouraged Taft to make a strenuous effort to obtain the Republican presidential nomination in 1948, though he eventually lost to the moderate favorite, Governor Thomas E. Dewey of New York.

Senator Robert A. Taft told Joseph McCarthy that "if one case doesn't work, try again."

359

In international affairs, Taft continued to lead the Republican isolationist bloc in the Senate in the postwar era. Although he supported the United Nations, Taft strongly suggested that the United States abandon world leadership except to "set an example of living so well at home that all other nations would wonder, envy, and decide to emulate us." In the face of the Soviet occupation of Eastern Europe, Taft argued that the United States should "resist communism but not interfere in the private concerns of other nations."

When Senator Joseph MCCARTHY of Wisconsin claimed in February 1950 that the Department of State was sheltering card-carrying Communists among its employees, Taft openly supported McCarthy and privately suggested that McCarthy employ a scattershot approach to the issue of Communists in government. "Keep talking," Taft said, "and if one case doesn't work out . . . proceed with another." In response to Democratic criticisms of McCarthy, Taft described his Wisconsin colleague as "a fighting Marine who risked his life to preserve the liberties of the United States." In contrast, Taft argued that "the greatest Kremlin asset in our history has been the pro-Communist group in the State Department."

Although Taft initially supported the Truman administration's decision to commit American military forces to resist the North Korean invasion of South Korea in June 1950, he blamed the debacle on the Democrats' "weak" Far East policy, which he claimed had invited Communist aggression. Taft continued to sound the same theme in his reelection campaign in the autumn of 1950. "Because of the Administration's strong Communist sympathies, which apparently existed before and about the time of the YALTA Conference" he stated, "we have placed Russia in a commanding presence in Europe . . . and in China."

By 1952, however, Taft had begun to distance himself from the excesses of McCarthy and the anti-Communist crusade. Specifically, he deplored the attacks by McCarthy and Senator William JENNER of Indiana upon General George C. MARSHALL, who had served as secretary of state and secretary of defense in the Truman administration. Taft's reticence to give McCarthy his full support was due in no small measure to his desire to obtain the Republican presidential nomination of 1952. Already the overwhelming choice of the ideological conservative wing of the party, Taft realized that he would need to appeal to the moderate and liberal elements to emerge victorious at the convention in Chicago. It was Taft's misfortune, however, to face the emotional, human appeal of General Dwight David EISENHOWER, who—in an extremely bitter convention fight—won the presidential nomination on the first ballot.

Disappointed, Taft nevertheless loyally supported the Eisenhower administration in the few months of life that remained to him. To ease any tensions between McCarthy and the White House, Taft maneuvered McCarthy out of the chairmanship of the Senate Internal Security Subcommittee, substituting instead the presumably more manageable Jenner. Nevertheless, a potentially disastrous confrontation between McCarthy and Eisenhower arose when the President appointed Charles BOHLEN—a former adviser to Roosevelt at the Yalta Conference—as ambassador to the Soviet Union. Taft dutifully worked to obtain Senate confirmation of the controversial nomination, although the violence of the ensuing battle with McCarthy and eleven other members of the right-wing Republican bloc led Taft to send a warning to the White House: "No more Bohlens."

As Majority Leader, Taft had represented Eisenhower's best hope to control McCarthy and the Republican right wing. Taft's death in July 1953 threatened to lead to an irrevocable split within the party ranks. In an acknowledgment of Taft's tremendous prestige and influence within the Senate, Eisenhower declared that the United States had lost "a truly great citizen and I have lost a wise counsellor and a valued friend." When he called upon Taft's widow, Eisenhower murmured, "I don't know what I'll do without him." Less than a year later, the administration and McCarthy were locked in a grim struggle for control of the party that ended in the dramatic ARMY-MCCARTHY HEARINGS of April–June 1954 and, ultimately, in the censure of McCarthy by the Senate in December 1954.

**Taft-Hartley Act** The Taft-Hartley Act, formally known as the Labor-Management Relations Act of 1947, was a measure designed to reduce the power of labor unions in the United States. Co-sponsored by Senator Robert A. TAFT (Ohio) and Representative Fred A. Hartley (New Jersey), the bill revised the National Labor Relations Act of 1935, popularly known as the Wagner Act. The Wagner Act had antagonized many business leaders and conservative members of congress by providing federal guarantees to labor's right to organize, bargain collectively, and strike. Public resentment against the rash of work stoppages that plagued American industry in the readustment period of 1945–46, along with high prices and reports of Communist infiltration of labor unions, added to the growing pressure for restrictions on the activities of organized labor. When the Republican Party gained control of Congress in the elections of 1946, it was not surprising that labor reform became one of the first objectives of the new Republican majority.

The bill that first emerged from the House Committee on Labor and Education, chaired by Hartley, was too severe even for the conservative Taft. The Senate subsequently approved a slightly less draconian measure, and the differences were resolved in a conference committee. The final bill that Congress sent to President Harry S. TRUMAN on June 9, 1947, outlawed the closed shop (a labor tactic that made membership in a union a prerequisite for obtaining employment at a particular plant), prohibited union and corporation contributions to federal elections, required unions to submit financial reports, banned secondary boycotts and jurisdictional strikes, made unions liable in federal courts for violation of contract, and enabled the National Labor Relations Board (NLRB) to protect businesses against unfair labor practices. The measure further granted the President of the United States authority to declare a national emergency whenever a potential or actual strike threatened to "imperil the national health or safety." In that event, the President would prohibit the strike for eighty days, while the Federal Mediation and Conciliation Service attempted to resolve the dispute.

The Taft-Hartley Act also reflected the rising concern with Communist influence in the United States by requiring all union officials to sign annually an affidavit that they were not Communists. If the officials refused to sign, their unions would forfeit the right to bargain collectively under the protection of the National Labor Relations Board, and to participate in NLRB representation elections.

According to Representative Hartley, the provision requiring anti-Communist affidavits grew out of his committee's investigation of a strike by Local 248 of the UNITED AUTO WORKERS (UAW) against the Allis-Chalmers company. Hartley claimed that Local 248, which was one of the most militant and left-wing locals in the UAW, had led "Moscow-ordered" strikes in 1941 and 1946 that "seriously hampered our nation's reconversion effort, and conversely aided Russian foreign policy." Freshman Wisconsin Senator Joseph MCCARTHY of Wisconsin volunteered an amendment to the bill that would have given employers the right to fire workers who had *previously* been expelled from unions because of Communist sympathies or membership in the COMMUNIST PARTY. Taft rejected the amendment as "unnecessary and irrelevant."

Virtually all leaders—both Communist and non-Communist—of the American Federation of Labor and the CONGRESS OF INDUSTRIAL ORGANIZATIONS (CIO) strenuously opposed the Taft-Hartley Act, as did a narrow majority of Democratic national committee members. Most of Truman's cabinet urged him to approve the bill, but the President, who had antagonized organized labor the previous year by calling out federal troops to break a strike in the steel industry, finally decided to veto the Taft-Hartley Act on the grounds that it would weaken the trade-union movement in the United States. The House of Representatives overrode the veto within twenty-four hours, with more Democrats voting against the President than with him. The Senate followed suit several days later.

Some non-Communist labor leaders such as Walter REUTHER used the affidavit provision of Taft-Hartley to drive their Communist opponents from union office. Others, like CIO President Philip MURRAY, opposed the concept of the affidavit as unconstitutional. Because the wording was vague and prohibited "belief in" and "association with" Communism, the act provoked legal questions that could only by decided by the federal judiciary. By 1949, it was clear that the Supreme Court would not overturn the Taft-Hartley Act, but the measure never completely accomplished its anti-Communist objectives. Numerous Communist labor officials signed the Taft-Hartley affidavits anyway, swearing that they were not members of the Communist Party. The NLRB refused to accept their affidavits as sincere and attempted to decertify their unions; the NLRB also persuaded the Justice Department to issue indictments for perjury.

In the end, only a few Communist labor leaders were convicted of perjury, and no unions were decertified. Congress, meanwhile, opted to pursue its anti-Communist drive through the INTERNAL SECURITY ACT OF 1950 and the COMMUNIST CONTROL ACT OF 1954. In 1959, Congress modified the Taft-Hartley Act by passing the Landum-Griffin Act, which further restricted trade-union activities and strengthened federal regulation of trade unions to eliminate corruption and crime and protect the rights of rank-and-file union members.

**Taylor, Robert** (1911–1969)  One of the first "friendly" witnesses to appear before the HOUSE COMMITTEE ON UN-AMERICAN ACTIVI-

Motion picture star Robert Taylor, a "friendly" witness before HUAC.

TIES (HUAC) during its investigation of Communist influences in the motion picture industry, actor Robert Taylor testified in Washington on October 22, 1947. Taylor informed the committee that during his movie career, he had noticed elements of Communist propaganda in various movie scripts; "I have seen things from time to time," Taylor claimed, "which appeared to me to be slightly on the pink side, shall we say." Moreover, Taylor maintained that the signs of Communist activity had been increasing over the past four or five years. He had, for instance, noticed bits of Communist propaganda in one of his wartime films, SONG OF RUSSIA, although he admitted that many things to which he objected had been eliminated by the studio.

Taylor said that he had never performed—and would never perform—in any picture with any individuals whom he considered disloyal to the United States. "If I were even suspicious of a person being a Communist with whom I was scheduled to work," Taylor noted, "I am afraid it would have to be him or me, because life is a little too short to be around people who annoy me as much as these fellow travelers and Communists do." He did, however, voice concern that there were members of the Screen Actors Guild who had been acting in a rather suspicious manner. "If they are not Communists," Taylor offered darkly, "they are working awfully hard to be Communists. I don't know. Their tactics and their philosophies seem to me to be pretty much Party-line stuff." When asked to name individuals of whose loyalty he was doubtful, Taylor provided the committee with the names of actor Howard DA SILVA and actress Karen Morley.

When asked by Representative Richard M. NIXON whether he was aware that his testimony against Communists might subject him to ridicule and criticism from left-wing quarters in Hollywood, Taylor said he would take such criticism "as a compliment, because I really enjoy their displeasure." Nor did he fear that his testimony might detract from his popularity at the box office. "I happen to believe strongly enough in the American people and in what the American people believe in," Taylor added, "to think that they will go along with anybody who prefers America and the American form of government over any other subversive ideologies which might be presented and by whom [sic] I might be criticized." In response to a final question from HUAC Chairman J. Parnell THOMAS, Taylor declared himself in favor of legislation outlawing the COMMUNIST PARTY, if such a measure "would solve the Communist threat in this country."

**Thomas, J. Parnell** (1895–1970) As chairman of the HOUSE COMMITTEE ON UN-AMERICAN ACTIVITIES (HUAC) from 1947–49, John Parnell Thomas—born John Parnell Feeney, Jr.—led the committee's investigations of Communist influence in American labor unions and the motion picture industry.

A native of New Jersey, Feeney attended the University of Pennsylvania's Wharton School of Finance and Commerce and New York University Law School before enlisting in the U.S. Army shortly after the nation's entry into World War I in February 1917. Discharged with the rank of captain, Feeney became a bond salesman for the Wall Street investment house of Paine, Webber and Company in 1919. Sometime around 1920, he obtained a court order changing his name from Feeney to Thomas, which had been his mother's maiden name.

After serving as mayor of his hometown of Allendale, New Jersey, and as a legislator in the New Jersey Assembly, Thomas won election to the U.S. Congress in 1936 as representative of the Seventh District of New Jersey. He quickly established himself as one of the most vociferous congressional opponents of President Franklin D. Roosevelt's New Deal. Convinced that the United States needed "more business in Government, and less Government in business," Thomas stated that "New Dealism to me is . . . not far different from the socialism of Hitler, that of Mussolini, and the communism of Stalin." One of Thomas's primary targets in the Roosevelt administration was Secretary of Labor Frances Perkins, whose impeachment he advocated in 1939. Apart from his assaults upon the New Deal, Thomas devoted much of his time in Congress to sponsoring legislation favoring veterans' interests. Thomas did, however, support the administration's defense-preparedness initiatives, including the Selective Service Act of 1940 and Lend-Lease (1941).

When the House of Representatives created a Special Committee to Investigate Un-American Activities under the chairmanship of Texas Democrat Martin DIES, Thomas was named as one of the original seven members. Although the committee was assigned the task of investigating both fascist and Communist propaganda, Thomas always considered Communism the more significant, insidious threat. In a 1940 radio broadcast, he claimed that "many Communists and Communist 'fellow travelers' have been appointed to key positions in our Government. . . . Only Communists or those approved by Communists could procure employment on certain Federal projects." When Attorney General Robert H. Jackson argued that the highly publicized investigations of Dies and Thomas made it more difficult for the government to pursue its counterespionage activities, Thomas responded with a public attack upon Jackson's loyalty.

As the senior member of the HUAC, Thomas became its chairman in 1947. Although he initially claimed that HUAC had been "too melodramatic" in the past, he proceeded to conduct hearings in an even more flamboyant fashion, interjecting his own prejudices into the proceedings and stating even before an investigation began that he was certain that un-American activity would be uncovered. At the outset of the committee's inquiry into Communist infiltration of labor unions in 1947, Thomas predicted that "we are not going to fail, we are going to succeed as no committee of Congress has ever succeeded before in this respect. That is, to expose the un-American activities, not only in unionism but in other fields, education, the films, government. We are going to expose them like they have never been exposed before."

Confronted with hostile witnesses, Thomas—a stout man, about five feet seven inches tall, with a florid complexion—reacted petulantly, pounding his gavel and matching their truculence with vituperative responses of his own. His encounters with the leftist writers and directors known as the HOLLYWOOD TEN during HUAC's headline-making inquiry into the motion picture industry in the autumn of 1947 quickly degenerated into farce. At one point, Thomas dismissed a witness from the stand even before committee investigators could ask whether he had ever been a member of the COMMUNIST PARTY. Initial public reaction to the Hollywood fiasco was so negative that Thomas suspended the hearings in November and never resumed them.

Thomas refused to acknowledge that any witness had a constitutional right to refuse to cooperate with his committee; such a defense, he advised the House, was nothing more than "a concerted effort on the part of the Communists, their fellow-travelers, their dupes, and paid apologists to create a lot of fog about constitutional rights, the First Amendment, and so forth." He enjoyed ridiculing his opponents, and once claimed that Frank SINATRA was "sort of a Mrs. Roosevelt in pants."

Yet, Thomas did generally attempt to keep the committee's inquiries focused on the search for Communist influence in the United States, intervening when a line of questioning appeared to be veering too far afield from the primary issue. He rejected attempts by the notoriously racist Alabama Congressman John RANKIN to paint the NATIONAL ASSOCIATION FOR THE ADVANCEMENT OF COLORED PEOPLE as a Communist-front organization and prevented committee investigators from recklessly impugning the loyalty of certain labor-union officials.

In August 1948, columnist Drew PEARSON accused Thomas of accepting kickbacks from members of his congressional office staff. At a grand jury hearing on November 4, Thomas refused to testify about the charges against him, pleading the Fifth Amendment. He was convicted of bribery, resigned from Congress, and was sentenced to the federal penitentiary in Danbury, Connecticut. There he encountered Ring LARDNER, Jr., and Lester COLE, two members of the Hollywood Ten who had been convicted of contempt of Congress for their refusal to testify before Parnell's committee. As Cole passed Thomas, who was cleaning the prison's chicken coop, he made a political remark. "I see that you are still spouting radical nonsense," muttered Thomas. "And I see," replied Cole, "that you are still shoveling chicken shit."

**Thomas, Norman** (1884–1969)  The elder statesman of American socialism, Norman Thomas abandoned the Socialist Party's uneasy alliance with the Communists in the 1930s and turned strongly against the Soviet Union, favoring repressive measures against American Communists during the McCarthy era.

Originally a social worker who also was an ordained Presbyterian minister, Thomas joined the Socialist Party in 1918 out of disgust with the social injustice and exploitation he witnessed in the slums of New York City. In 1924, Thomas ran unsuccessfully for governor of New York on the Socialist Party ticket. He subsequently served as the Socialist Party candidate for President in the elections of 1928, 1932, 1936, 1940, 1944, and 1948.

Although Thomas had endorsed the notion of a POPULAR FRONT against fascism, a trip to Moscow in 1937—at the height of the Stalinist purge trials—weakened his faith in the Soviet system, and the announcement of the NAZI-SOVIET PACT in August 1939 completed his disillusionment. Like many mainstream American liberals, Thomas (who was always more of a Christian liberal than a devout Marxist) sought to distance himself and the Socialist Party from Communists in the postwar period. He bitterly criticized former Vice President Henry WALLACE, the Progressive Party candidate for the presidency in 1948, for Wallace's refusal to recognize that the Progressive Party was dominated by Communists.

Norman Thomas, leader of the Socialist Party of the United States.

Thomas rejected the witch-hunting tactics of anti-Communist zealots such as Senator Joseph MCCARTHY of Wisconsin and the HOUSE COMMITTEE ON UN-AMERICAN ACTIVITIES; yet, he also defended the government's right to investigate subversive activities and to bar Communists from sensitive positions of national security. Thomas also agreed with conservatives in Congress that Communists should not be permitted to teach at American colleges and universities. "The right of the Communist to teach should be denied," insisted Thomas, "because he has given away his freedom in the quest for truth."

Throughout the 1960s, Thomas continued to press for social reform in the United States, for increased American humanitarian aid abroad, and for multilateral disarmament and an end to the COLD WAR.

**Truman, Harry S.** (1884–1972) Succeeding to the presidency on April 12, 1945, following President Franklin Delano Roosevelt's death, Harry S. Truman's initial months in the White House were marked by indecisiveness and clumsy errors—attributable largely to the fact that he had been shut out of the decision-making process during the Roosevelt administration. However, he quickly came to understand the complexities of the domestic and international problems that faced the United States in the postwar era.

Born in Lamar, Missouri, Truman grew up on a farm outside the town of Grandview and moved with his family to Independence, Missouri, at the age of six. He aspired to a military career, but his poor eyesight kept him from entering the U.S. Military Academy at West Point. Instead, Truman briefly attended business school and then spent five years moving from one job to another: construction on the Atchison, Topeka, and Santa Fe Railroad, bookkeeping for several Kansas City banks, and the mailroom of the Kansas City *Star*. In 1906, Truman returned to Grandview to help his father operate the family farm. His few minor investments in oil and mining properties turned out quite badly—a foretaste of Truman's consistent lack of business success.

When the United States entered World War I in 1917, Truman enlisted and rose to the rank of lieutenant. His field-artillery regiment was assigned to France, where he commanded an artillery battery in the Meuse-Argonnes, Vosges, and Sommedieu campaigns. The lethargic pace of the Paris peace negotiations kept Truman in France until early 1919, much to his dismay: At this point in his life, he had no political aspirations and certainly no overriding interest in world affairs. In early 1919, he expressed his frustration in a letter to his fiancee, Bess Wallace: "I don't give a whoop (to put it mildly) whether there's a League of Nations or whether Russia has a Red government or a Purple one, and if the President of the Czecho-Slovaks wants to pry the throne out from under the King of Bohemia, let him pry but send us home. . . ."

Back in the United States, Truman joined with businessman Eddie Jacobson to purchase a men's clothing store in Kansas City in May 1919. The store failed in the recession of 1921, however, and Truman at last forsook a business career and entered politics. He obtained Kansas City Democratic Party boss Thomas Pendergast's support in an election campaign for Jackson County judge. After ten years as presiding county judge, Truman was elected to the U.S. Senate in 1934; during his second Senate term, he became chairman of the Committee to Investigate the National Defense Program, especially formed by the Senate to seek out corruption and inefficiency that had resulted from the vast increase in federal defense spending in World War II. Truman's reputation for honesty and toughness, along with his record of loyalty to the administration and his midwestern background, persuaded Roosevelt to select him as the Democratic vice-presidential nominee in 1944 in place of Vice President Henry A. WALLACE.

Almost from the start, Truman evinced a disposition to confront the Soviet Union over its desire to obtain as much territory as possible during the closing months of the war. Indeed, it is likely that one of the reasons he decided to employ two atomic bombs against Japan in 1945 was the effect such a display of American military might would have upon the USSR and Soviet dictator Josef STALIN.

In the postwar period, Truman chose to adopt a policy of containment in an attempt to prevent the Soviets from gaining further territory in Southern and Eastern Europe; to bolster the defensive capability of the democracies of Western Europe, Truman endorsed the organization of the North Atlantic Treaty Organization (NATO), sponsored the Marshall Plan to rebuild shattered European economies, and promulgated the Truman Doctrine, which specifically pledged the United States to resist the subversion of legitimate democratic governments in Greece and Turkey.

Yet, Truman was unwilling to risk another world war to challenge Soviet control of Eastern Europe, nor was he willing to commit the United States to a land war in the Far East in an attempt to save the corrupt and inefficient Nationalist Chinese government of CHIANG Kai-shek in a civil war against the Communist forces of MAO Zedong. Truman's realistic approach to American goals and resources infuriated conservative Republicans in Congress, who commenced to assault the administration verbally for its alleged failure to "get tough" with the Soviets and the Chinese Communists. The confrontation was heightened by Republican opposition to Truman's domestic policies of liberal social and political reform, known collectively as "the Fair Deal." When the Republican Party captured control of both houses of Congress in the elections of 1946, hostility between the executive and legislative branches reached new heights.

By the late autumn of 1946, revelations of Soviet espionage in Canada had combined with conservative hostility to the Truman administration's foreign and domestic policies to encourage Republican politicians to raise the issue of Communist subversion in American society.

Specifically, the HOUSE COMMITTEE ON UN-AMERICAN ACTIVITIES (HUAC) under the chairmanship of Congressman J. Parnell THOMAS of New Jersey charged the Truman administration with sheltering pro-Soviet advisers in the White House and the State Department. On March 22, 1947, in an attempt to defuse the issue of Communism in government, Truman issued EXECUTIVE ORDER 9835, which established the nation's first comprehensive federal-employee loyalty program. The measure set up separate loyalty boards within each executive department and created a Civil Service Commission LOYALTY REVIEW BOARD—headed by conservative Republican Seth RICHARDSON—with appellate jurisdiction over the individual department boards. Whenever the Civil Service Commission became aware of information indicating present disloyalty (questionable past political associations were deemed insufficient evidence) on the part of a federal employee, the commission requested the FEDERAL BUREAU OF INVESTIGATION to carry out a full field investigation that was intended to determine whether the individual in question belonged to any subversive organizations. The attorney general was granted sole authority to determine which organizations would be listed as subversive or Communist fronts. Once its field investigation was completed, the FBI forwarded its findings to the relevant department review board; employees who were dismissed could appeal the decision to the head of the department and finally to the Civil Service Loyalty Review Board.

In introducing this program to the public, Truman took pains to point out that it was not intended to set off a witch hunt. "Rumor, gossip or suspicion will not be sufficient to lead to the dismissal of any employee for disloyalty," Truman announced. "The Government, as the largest employer in the United States, must be the model of a fair employer. It must guarantee that the civil rights of all employees of the Government shall be protected properly and adequately." Yet, when Executive Order 9835 failed to uncover extensive evidence of subver-

sion within the federal government, Truman eventually bowed to pressure from Senator Joseph MCCARTHY and other anti-Communist zealots to promulgate EXECUTIVE ORDER 10241, which tightened the standards of the loyalty-review program. Under the revised program, federal employees could be dismissed if the government decided that there existed "reasonable doubt" of their loyalty at any time in the past.

Meanwhile, the case of Alger HISS provoked increased Republican criticism of the Truman administration for being "soft" on Communism. On August 4, 1948, *Time* magazine editor Whittaker CHAMBERS told HUAC that Hiss, a former federal government official who had served for fourteen years in the State Department, had been a member of a Soviet espionage network. Although Chambers' accusations caused a storm of controversy in Washington—Speaker of the House Sam Rayburn of Texas noted that there was "political dynamite in this Communist investigation"—Truman appeared to shrug off the charges. In a press conference the following day, Truman announced that HUAC's hearings were only "a 'red herring' to keep [Congress] from doing what they ought to do. . . . They are slandering a lot of people that don't deserve it." When Hiss was subsequently convicted of perjury (for denying that he had ever belonged to the COMMUNIST PARTY) in January 1950, the anti-Communist crusaders in Congress received further ammunition to use against Truman.

By that time, the victory of the Communist armies in the Chinese civil war—despite massive infusions of American military and economic assistance—had provoked further suspicion of the Truman administration's commitment to the campaign against the spread of Communism abroad. In August 1949, Truman and his secretary of state, Dean ACHESON, released the CHINA WHITE PAPER, a voluminous study of American-Chinese relations since World War II, designed to prove that the fall of Chiang's Nationalist government was due to "the military ineptitude of the Nationalist leaders, their defections and surrenders, and the absence among their forces of the will to fight." Their explanations did not, however, satisfy the members of the pro-Chiang CHINA LOBBY in the United States. This loose coalition of conservative businessmen and politicians charged that Chiang had been betrayed by willful pro-Communist decisions within the Truman administration and specifically within the State Department. The announcement in September 1949 that the Soviet Union had successfully exploded its first nuclear device—followed by revelations of an atomic espionage ring that purportedly had operated within the United States between 1945 and 1948—cast further doubt about the competence (if not the loyalty) of Truman and his advisers in the minds of the anti-Communist crusaders.

It was not surprising, therefore, that Senator Joseph McCarthy struck a responsive chord when he accused President Truman in February 1950 of harboring a number of "card-carrying Communists" within the State Department. Without attacking the President directly, McCarthy charged that Truman was the "prisoner of a bunch of twisted intellectuals" who failed to tell him the truth about the Communist threat. In response, Truman—whose approval rating among American voters had slipped to 37 percent by this time—told reporters that McCarthy was nothing more than "a ballyhoo artist who has to cover up his shortcomings by wild charges." "I think," Truman added, "the greatest asset that the Kremlin has is Senator McCarthy." To the sister of Owen LATTIMORE, the Far East expert whom McCarthy had identified as the top Soviet espionage agent in the United States, Truman predicted that "our friend McCarthy will eventually get all that is coming to him. He has no sense of decency or honor."

Yet, McCarthy and his allies would wreak great political damage upon Truman and his administration over the following two years. The outbreak of the KOREAN WAR in June 1950 added further fuel to McCarthy's charges, despite Truman's decision on June 30 to authorize the commitment of U.S. ground troops to combat in Korea. If Truman had been more steadfast in his support of Chiang in China, the Republican argument ran, the forces of international Communism would not have dared to attack in Korea. The war also lent added urgency to the drive by anti-Communist crusaders in Congress to strengthen federal laws against domestic subversion. In August 1950, Senator Patrick MCCARRAN of Nevada, chairman of the Senate Judiciary Committee, introduced a bill that required members of the Communist Party and Communist-front organizations to register with the federal government. The measure, which came to be known as the INTERNAL SECURITY ACT OF 1950, further barred Communists from employment in the federal government and the defense industry. The bill was necessary, claimed McCarran, to "fortify the home front even as we are today fortifying our boys on the battlefield of Korea."

Although Congress supported the measure overwhelmingly, Truman vetoed the Internal Security Act on September 22, 1950, arguing that it would help, rather than hurt the Communist cause by forcing the Communist Party underground. "It would actually weaken our existing internal security measures," Truman stated, "and would seriously hamper the Federal Bureau of Investigation and our other security agencies. It would help the Communists in their efforts to create dissension and confusion within our borders. It would help the communist propagandists throughout the world who are trying to undermine freedom by discrediting as hypocrisy the efforts of the United States on behalf of freedom." The concept of requiring Communist organizations to divulge information about themselves, added Truman, was "about as practical as requiring thieves to register with the sheriff." In an attempt to rally Senate Democratic support behind his veto and deal a blow to the fanatical anti-Communist movement, Truman declared that "this is a time when we must marshall all our resouces and all the moral strength of our free system in self-defense against the threat of Communist aggression. We will fail in this, and we will destroy all that we seek to preserve, if we sacrifice the liberties of our citizens in a misguided attempt to achieve national security."

Truman's eloquence notwithstanding, Congressional Democrats who were weary of being caught on the unpopular side of the Communist issue deserted the administration in droves. Both houses easily passed the Internal Security Act over Truman's veto, though the President was later vindicated when the U.S. Supreme Court ruled in 1964 that the measure was unconstitutional.

Truman's decision in March 1951 to remove General Douglas MACARTHUR as U.S. commander in Korea unleashed yet another round of denunciations from Republican conservatives in Congress. Although MacArthur clearly had behaved in an insubordinate manner by sabotaging a U.S. peace initiative, his supporters in Congress were outraged at Truman's treatment of the general. Senator William JENNER of Indiana declared that "this country today is in the hands of a secret coterie which is directed by agents of the Soviet Union. . . . Our only choice is to impeach President Truman and find out who is the secret invisible government which has so cleverly led our country down the road to destruction." House Republican Minority Leader Joseph MARTIN told reporters that the House GOP Caucus had discussed the question of Truman's impeachment. For his part, McCarthy announced that Truman was "a son of a bitch" for his treatment of MacArthur.

The attacks of the anti-Communist zealots seriously wounded Truman's ability to conduct the affairs of the nation in his final year in the White House, and the administration limped to a close identified in the minds of many Americans with the Republican formula—first introduced by Senator Karl MUNDT of South Dakota—of K (1) C (2): Korea, Communism, and corruption. Truman's choice as Democratic standard bearer in the presidential election of 1952 was Governor Adlai STEVENSON of Illinois, and although he was initially reluctant to run, Stevenson eventually accepted the draft of the Democratic presidential nominating convention. In a vote that revealed both the personal popularity of the Republican candidate, General Dwight David EISENHOWER and the public's disenchantment with the legacy of the Truman administration, Stevenson was buried in a landslide of near-record proportions.

Following his departure from the White House on January 20, 1953, Truman retired to his home in Independence, Missouri. He subsequently published two volumes of memoirs—*Year of Decisions* (1955) and *Years of Trial and Hope* (1956)—and remained active in Democratic Party affairs. The passage of time and the cooling of the passions of the McCarthy Era led to the public rehabilitation of Truman's image, as historians began to publish favorable assessments of his forthright leadership style and the accomplishments of his administration. On December 26, 1972, Truman died of complications from severe lung congestion.

**Trumbo, Dalton** (1905–1976)   A member of the left-wing group of motion picture writers and directors known as the HOLLYWOOD TEN, Dalton Trumbo was one of the most successful screenwriters in Hollywood when the HOUSE COMMITTEE ON UN-AMERICAN ACTIVITIES (HUAC) launched its investigation in 1947 of Communist influence in the movie industry.

Born and raised in Colorado, Trumbo attended the University of Colorado for one year before family financial problems forced him to leave school. He took a job at the Davis Perfection Bakery in Los Angeles but managed to attend classes at the University of Southern California while working. Trumbo also found time to supplement his income by trafficking in bootleg whiskey during the waning days of Prohibition. His brief bootlegging career formed the basis for his first short story, published in *Vanity Fair* magazine in 1932.

Although he desired to carve out a career as an author of serious fiction, Trumbo accepted a position as a junior screenwriter with Warner Brothers studio in 1935 to earn a living while he pursued his literary endeavors. He was dismissed the following year when he refused to leave the SCREEN WRITERS' GUILD and join a studio-sponsored union instead. During the next three years, Trumbo wrote for Columbia studios, MGM, and RKO, writing grade-B movies while completing the draft of a powerful antiwar novel entitled *Johnny Got His Gun*.

The success of this novel, along with his screenplays for such highly regarded films as *Kitty Foyle* (for which he was nominated for an Academy Award in 1941) and *Thirty Seconds Over Tokyo*, made Trumbo one of the highest-paid screenwriters in Hollywood at the end of World War II. His unique contract gave him the right to hold story conferences in his house, where he slept during the day and worked at night while sitting in his bathtub, balancing his typewriter upon a specially designed crossboard.

Trumbo's work on behalf of the Screen Writers' Guild and the pacifist movement in the prewar period had brought him into contact with most of Hollywood's prominent left-wing activists, and it was his friendship with and admiration for these individuals that convinced him to join the COMMUNIST PARTY in 1943. "To me it was not a matter of great consequence," he stated several decades later. "It represented no significant change in my thought or in my life. . . . To me, it was an essential part of being alive and part of the time at a very significant period in history, probably the most significant period of this century, certainly the most catastrophic."

When HUAC commenced its investigation into Communist influence in the motion picture industry, Trumbo was subpoenaed and called to Washington as an "unfriendly" witness. Together with Ring LARDNER, Jr., he helped fashion the strategy that the ten unfriendly witnesses (the HOLLYWOOD TEN) adopted: they would all refuse to answer questions about their past or present political affiliations and activities, basing their silence on the rights afforded them under the First Amendment. On October 29, 1947, Trumbo appeared before the committee, bearing copies of twenty of his film scripts, challenging the committee members to find evidence of Communist propaganda therein. When the chairman of the Committee, J. Parnell THOMAS, refused to allow Trumbo to read a prepared statement, in which Trumbo compared Washington to the German capital of Berlin on the eve of the Reichstag fire, Trumbo castigated the hearings as "the beginning . . . of an American concentration camp."

After being forcibly evicted from the committee hearing room, Trumbo was charged with contempt of Congress, convicted, and sentenced to one year in prison and a fine of $1,000. He served his sentence in the federal penitentiary in Ashland, Kentucky, living in the same dormitory with two other members of the Hollywood Ten, John Howard LAWSON and Adrian SCOTT. Between his conviction and the time he entered prison in 1950, Trumbo left the Communist Party. "I just drifted away," he explained years later. "I changed no beliefs. I just quit going to meetings and never went back—with no more feeling of separation than I had before I started with the Communist Party."

After serving his sentence (with two months off for good behavior), Trumbo went into self-imposed exile in Mexico City, staying with Lardner and two other expatriate American writers. By 1953, however, he was back in the United States. Because he was still on the motion picture studios' BLACKLIST, Trumbo had to find other writers to FRONT for him; that is, to agree to put their names on the scripts that Trumbo wrote. In his first eighteen months back in the United States, Trumbo finished a dozen scripts in this fashion, including the popular film, *Roman Holiday*. He then began to use pseudonyms for his scripts. In 1957, Trumbo—writing under the name of Robert Rich—won an Academy Award for his script for *The Brave One*. This state of affairs struck many observers as incongruous, if not slightly ridiculous, and it marked the beginning of the end of the blacklist. After the Academy of Motion Picture Arts and Sciences refused to give Trumbo his Oscar, he launched a one-man crusade against the blacklist, going so far as to found his own production company, Robert Rich Productions, Inc., to make independent films.

Finally, in January 1960, producer Otto Preminger announced publicly that he had hired Trumbo to write the screenplay for his new project, a film version of the best-selling Leon Uris novel, *Exodus*. Although other members of the Ten still found it difficult to find work under their own names, Trumbo no longer needed to hide behind a front or a pseudonym. His later screenwriting projects included *The Sandpiper*, *Hawaii*, *The Fixer*, and *Papillon*.

In an act of symbolic recognition that Trumbo had been ill-treated during the McCarthy era, in 1975 the Academy of Motion Picture Arts and Sciences awarded Trumbo a replica of the Oscar he had won for *The Brave One* nearly twenty years earlier—this time with his real name inscribed on the award. Trumbo died the following year.

## Tydings, Millard E. (1891–1961)   A four-term United States Senator from Maryland, Democrat Millard E. Tydings was one of the first and most prominent political victims of the anti-Communist hysteria created by Senator Joseph MCCARTHY of Wisconsin during the early 1950s.

A native of Maryland and a graduate of Loyola College, Tydings was admitted to the Maryland bar in 1913. He embarked upon a political career almost at once, winning election to the Maryland House of Delegates in 1916. The following year, he enlisted in the U.S. Army, serving in the Mexican border campaign with General John "Black Jack" Pershing before going overseas to join the American Expeditionary Force in World War I. By the end of the war, Tydings had risen to the rank of lieutenant

Senator Millard Tydings of Maryland (center), an early foe and victim of Joseph McCarthy.

colonel, with a Distinguished Service Medal, a Distinguished Service Cross, and three citations.

Tydings resumed his political career in 1924, when he won election to the U.S. House of Representatives. Two years later, he was elected to the Senate, where he soon established himself as one of the leading intellectuals in the chamber. Although he generally supported the Roosevelt administration on foreign affairs, adopting an internationalist stance, Tydings was a dedicated conservative in domestic affairs and became a harsh critic of the New Deal. Roosevelt became so enraged at Tydings' opposition to his plan to enlarge the U.S. Supreme Court that he vowed to campaign against the Maryland senator in the primary election of 1938. Despite—or perhaps because of—Roosevelt's interference in Maryland's internal political affairs, Tydings won a landslide victory in the primary and an equally overwhelming win in the general election.

By 1950, Tydings had become chairman of the powerful Senate Armed Services Committee; he also served on the Foreign Affairs Committee and the Joint Committee on Atomic Energy. His reputation as a national statesman led *Time* magazine to name him as one of the Senate's ten "most valuable" members, and his name had been mentioned as a potential presidential or vice-presidential Democratic candidate in 1952. Tydings' career was about to suffer a devastating reverse, however.

In a speech in Wheeling, West Virginia, on February 9, 1950, Senator McCarthy accused the State Department of harboring a number of "card-carrying Communists" among its employees. In an attempt to pursue these accusations in an orderly fashion, the Senate adopted on Feburary 21 a resolution directing the Foreign Relations Committee to "conduct a full and complete study and investigation as to whether persons who are disloyal to the United States are employed by the Department of State as charged by the Senator from Wisconsin (Mr. McCarthy)." Twice, Senate Majority Leader Scott Lucas of Illinois asked Tydings to head the subcommittee that would carry out the investigation; Tydings refused but finally consented when Lucas asked him a third time. Tydings had previously bested McCarthy in a debate over the loyalty of Admiral Louis E. Denfeld, and the Democratic leadership—including Foreign Relations Committee chairman Tom CONNALLY—felt that Tydings' conservative reputation and national stature made him an excellent choice to head the inquiry. Tydings later claimed that the Democratic leadership had erred in forming a subcommittee to investigate McCarthy's charges "without asking McCarthy to make out a prima facie case to support his statements." The Senate, Tydings noted, should at least have called McCarthy before the full Foreign Relations Committee to ascertain "if he had the facts to justify investigation of his charges."

Nevertheless, Tydings opened his subcommittee's hearings on McCarthy's accusations on March 8, 1950. Initially, he and the other Democrats on the subcommittee attempted to confront McCarthy directly, interrogating him on his broad charges of subversion and arguing with the Wisconsin senator on specific cases. Their hostile conduct was criticized by numerous observers who believed that McCarthy deserved a chance to make his case without

interruption. Tydings consequently muted his criticism of McCarthy for the duration of the hearings. When McCarthy appeared to score points with his accusations of disloyalty and espionage against Far East expert Owen LATTIMORE, Tydings implored President Harry S. TRUMAN to provide the subcommittee with Lattimore's FBI files, as well as the files on all eighty-one individuals whom McCarthy had identified as security risks. When Truman hesitated to turn over the files, Senate Republicans termed the Tydings subcommittee's investigation a "whitewash" of McCarthy's charges.

By early May, Tydings had grown distressed over the course the investigation had taken. McCarthy had manipulated the hearings to obtain more publicity for his allegations, moving from one case to another before the subcommittee could reach any final conclusions. Tydings therefore recommended that the Truman administration establish a special loyalty-review commission to investigate all of McCarthy's charges, but Truman again deferred action.

In early July, Tydings decided that his subcommittee had completed its assigned task. The majority report, issued on July 17, was a strongly partisan attack upon McCarthy, accusing the Wisconsin senator of perpetrating "a fraud and a hoax" and "perhaps the most nefarious campaign of half-truths and untruth in the history of this Republic." McCarthy's charges, most of which already had been raised during the previous session of Congress, were deemed baseless. All the individuals whom McCarthy had named were exonerated, although several were cited for minor transgressions or poor judgment. When he defended his subcommittee's report to the Senate, Tydings again accused McCarthy of employing deception and falsehoods in his accusations.

In the end, the subcommittee's report probably had little effect on American public opinion. Tydings' obvious disdain for McCarthy was interpreted by some as partisanship, an attempt to cover up the shortcomings of the Truman administration. Tydings himself later acknowledged that he should have pursued a more disciplined course in handling McCarthy: "My mistake was in allowing him to wander all over the map, out of Senatorial courtesy, instead of holding his feet to the fire."

Tydings soon discovered the political cost of confronting Joseph McCarthy. During the subcommittee's hearings, McCarthy's admirers in Maryland—many of whom were conservatives who had supported Tydings in previous elections—began to circulate charges that Tydings was conducting a coverup. Confident that he would win reelection with only minimal effort, Tydings refused to heed warnings that his chairmanship of the subcommittee was eroding his political base at home. He easily defeated his primary opponents in 1950 and captured the Democratic nomination for the Senate, but his Republican opponent, John Marshall Butler, already had met with McCarthy in July to map their campaign strategy. Accordingly, Butler assailed Tydings for "the thoroughly disgraceful manner in which he whitewashed the State Department employee loyalty investigation," and termed the subcommittee report a "blotch on the integrity of Maryland."

During the general election campaign, McCarthy visited Maryland on several occasions, accusing Tydings of protecting Communists, and denouncing Tydings and his Democratic allies in the Senate as "men of little minds" and "Commiecrats." Contributions from McCarthy supporters such as CHINA LOBBY head Alfred KOHLBERG and Texas oil millionaire Clint Murchison poured into Butler's campaign coffers. The campaign reached a low point on the weekend before election day, when McCarthy's staff helped produce and distribute a tabloid entitled "From the Record," which linked Tydings with Lattimore and others whom McCarthy had accused of disloyalty. The pamphlet also featured a composite photograph of Tydings with Earl BROWDER, secretary general of the COMMUNIST PARTY OF THE UNITED STATES OF AMERICA. Two photographs had been carefully cropped and combined to make it appear as if Tydings and Browder were engaged in close conversation; actually, the Tydings half of the photo was nothing more than a shot of the senator listening to 1938 election returns.

Tydings assailed the tabloid as a "new all-time low" in the Republicans' "false, malicious and vicious smear campaign" against him. He defended his record of fighting Communism and reminded voters that he had consistently followed a conservative line in domestic policy. But Butler's tactics, combined with an increase in Republican voter registration in Maryland and widespread desertions of Tydings by the state's black voters (who were weary of his persistent refusal to support civil-rights legislation), led to a Republican victory at the polls. On November 7, Butler defeated Tydings by a margin of 53–47 percent. Tydings subsequently filed a complaint with the Senate's subcommittee on privileges and elections, charging Butler with "willfully and deliberately" printing and disseminating "false and deceiving statements." Although the ensuing inquiry found numerous examples of questionable campaign practices and specifically condemned "From the Record" as an example of the sort of campaign literature that "eats away like acid at the very fabric of American life," the subcommittee declined to overturn the results of the election. The subcommittee's report did, however, inspire Senator William BENTON to introduce a resolution calling for an investigation into McCarthy's behavior.

Tydings briefly considered another run for the Senate in 1958, but ill health forced him to withdraw. He died of pneumonia in 1961.

# U

**United Auto Workers** See REUTHER, Walter.

**United Electrical, Radio and Machine Workers** As early as 1939, the HOUSE COMMITTEE ON UN-AMERICAN ACTIVITIES (HUAC) identified the United Electrical, Radio and Machine Workers (UE) as one of a dozen labor unions in the United States that were "more than tinged with Communism." Like numerous other unions within the CONGRESS OF INDUSTRIAL ORGANIZATIONS (CIO), the UE had employed Communists as organizers in the 1930s, at a time when the Communist movement in the United States advocated collaboration with non-Marxist liberals.

By the end of the decade, Communists were solidly entrenched at the highest levels of the UE's national leadership. UE president James Carey (who was *not* a Communist) explained that he had only been able to spot the Communists "because of their flip-flop on the war" following the announcement of the NAZI-SOVIET PACT in August 1939. "As months passed," Carey added, "I discovered that they were in complete control of the national office; they dominated the executive committee, ran the union paper and were strongly entrenched in the locals and districts. All the organizers were Party-liners."

In 1946, an anti-Communist group led by Carey lost a critical union election to the Communist-led slate. The following year, HUAC initiated another probe into Communist infiltration of labor unions. Its attention was drawn to the UE in July 1947 when two officers of Bridgeport, Connecticut, local testified that they had led a successful campaign to oust Communists from the local and its executive board. In retaliation, the national union had attempted to revoke the charter of the Bridgeport local.

Under vigorous questioning by Congressman Richard M. NIXON, the techniques employed by

Communists to gain control of the UE became clear. According to union members' testimony, the Communists had placed their men in key leadership positions in the union, exerted "iron discipline" over their members, worked indefatigably toward their goals, and manipulated the seemingly routine election of delegates to the union's national conventions.

A strike by the UE against the Bucyrus-Erie Company in Evansville, Indiana, in 1948 resulted in a thorough defeat for the union. Because the UE's leaders refused to sign the anti-Communist affidavit required by the TAFT-HARTLEY ACT, the company was legally entitled to refuse to negotiate with the union. The National Labor Relations Board subsequently called for a new election (in which the UE could not participate), and a House subcommittee published accusations of Communist influence in the union. Company supervisors and foremen (supported by local veterans' organizations and the Catholic church) encouraged anti-Communist sentiment among the union's rank-and-file membership. Finally, the strike collapsed, and the UE lost its authorization to negotiate with Bucyrus-Erie.

Following further hearings by HUAC into Communist infiltration of the Pittsburgh local of the UE, the CIO expelled the UE at its national convention in November 1949. It was replaced by the recently established International Electrical Workers Union under Carey's leadership. Shaken by defections to Carey's union, the UE suffered another blow when FBI informant Herbert PHILBRICK identified a number of UE executives as Communists in his testimony to HUAC in the fall of 1952. Later that year, HUAC staff members traveled to Chicago to hear testimony from union members who had left the COMMUNIST PARTY. UE leaders responded by accusing HUAC of timing its investigation to subvert the union's massive strike against International Harvester, and a band of anti-HUAC pickets stormed into the Federal Building in Chicago and disrupted the committee's deliberations by pounding on the hearing-room door. Undaunted, HUAC subpoenaed three leading UE negotiators, who duly appeared but invoked the Fifth Amendment.

No more cooperative was John T. Goljack, vice president of the UE, when he was summoned to testify before HUAC in 1955. Goljack denounced HUAC's hearings as a "union busting venture," characterized the witnesses against him as liars, lunatics, and stool pigeons, and described Carey's International Electrical Workers Union as "the only McCarthyite union in America." Goljack refused to answer when a HUAC investigator asked if he had been a Communist in 1949 when the CIO expelled the UE; he was cited for contempt, but the Supreme Court overturned his conviction in 1962. Goljack was then reindicted for refusing to tell the committee if he was a member of the Communist Party; again, the Supreme Court threw out the conviction, this time by a unanimous vote in 1966.

## United States Information Agency. See INTERNATIONAL INFORMATION AGENCY.

## Utley, Freda (1898–1978)   A British journalist and ex-Communist, Freda Utley served as one of the leading witnesses against Far East expert Owen LATTIMORE during the hearings conducted by the Tydings subcommittee in the spring of 1950. A native of London, Utley completed her undergraduate work in history at King's College, London University in 1923 and later earned an M.A. from the London School of Economics. (Her thesis dealt with trade guilds in the later Roman Empire.) She also joined the British Communist Party during this time. In 1928, Utley accepted an assignment as special correspondent in Japan for the *Manchester Guardian*. Her experiences there provided the material for her first book, *Japan's Feet of Clay*, published in 1937 and banned in Japan.

In 1930, Utley took up residence in the Soviet Union, following her marriage to a Russian named Arcadi Berdichevsky. For five years she worked at various Soviet government posts in the Comintern (International Communist Party), the Commissariat of Foreign Trade, and the Institute of World Economy and Politics, where she served as senior scientific researcher after receiving her Ph.D. from the Academy of Sciences in Moscow. In 1936, during the Stalinist purge trials, Berdichevsky was arrested and imprisoned. Four years later, Utley realized that he almost certainly had been murdered, and, leaving Moscow, she eventually settled in London where she published an account of her disillusionment with Communism, *The Dream We Lost: Soviet Russia Then and Now* (1940). In *The Dream We Lost,* which philosopher Bertrand Russell described as a "detailed, documented and intimate indictment of Stalin's government," Utley explained the appeal of Communism for young idealists like herself who had lost their faith in Christianity. "I failed in my youth to perceive that Communism is a substitute for religion," she wrote. "The instinctive desire for a religion was the compelling force leading me step by step into the Communist trap." Utley's motives for joining the COMMUNIST PARTY were therefore quite similar to those of the six intellectuals who recounted their own disillusioning experiences with Communism in THE GOD THAT FAILED, published in 1948.

After she left Moscow following the arrest of her husband, Utley traveled to China to cover the Sino-Japanese war as special correspondent for the London *News Chronicle*. There she gathered material for two additional books, *China At War* (1939) and *Japan's Gamble in China* (1939). In 1940, she moved to the United States to become economic adviser to a New York-based corporation and a member of the advisory council of the department of politics at Princeton University. Four years later, Utley accepted an offer to serve as a consultant for the Chinese Supply Commission, an agency of CHIANG Kai-shek's Nationalist Chinese government. In 1945 she resumed her journalistic career as a correspondent for *Reader's Digest* in China and Germany.

Utley's personal experiences with the terrorist policies of the Stalinist regime, along with her contacts with the Nationalist government and the CHINA LOBBY, the pro-Chiang coalition of American politicians and businessmen headed by industrialist Alfred KOHLBERG, made her one of the favorite witnesses of congressional committees investigating Communist influence in the federal government in the late 1940s and early 1950s. Although she bitterly assailed State Department officers who had characterized the Communist Chinese forces led by MAO Zedong as democratic, agrarian reformers, Utley herself had written in 1939–40 that the Chinese Communist Party's goal "has genuinely become social and political reform along capitalist and democratic lines," and that Communism in China, "having become almost entirely an agrarian movement, had by 1935 been transmuted by the logic of history into a movement of peasant emancipation." Since that time, however, Utley had become a zealous member of the China Lobby, for whom she wrote numerous pamphlets supporting the Nationalist cause.

Following Senator Joseph MCCARTHY's charges in March 1950 that Owen LATTIMORE was "the top Russian espionage agent in America," Utley was summoned to testify before the Senate subcommittee—chaired by Maryland Senator Millard TYDINGS—that had been established to assess the validity of McCarthy's accusations. Utley had previously sworn in an affidavit that she had met Lattimore in Moscow when he "was receiving instructions from the Soviet government," but when she testified before the subcommittee on May 1, Utley claimed that McCarthy was mistaken in his allegation that Lattimore was the Soviet government's foremost espionage agent in the United States. Utley also stated that McCarthy might have been wrong in accusing Lattimore of being "the 'architect' of the disastrous China policy pur-

sued by the administration." In fact, Utley was not even certain whether Lattimore was a member of the Communist Party at all, although she added that "his attitudes and actions seemed to me . . . practically indistinguishable from those of a Communist." Yet Utley swore unequivocally that American policy in the Far East—a policy that, according to the China Lobby, had betrayed Chiang and favored the Communist cause—had been "inspired by Mr. Lattimore and his disciples, proteges, and friends." She described Lattimore as a "Judas cow," an "out-and-out defender of the Soviet government," and a man who "can be said to have done more than anyone else to poison the wells of opinion with regard to China." "His function," she argued, "has been to lead us unknowingly to destruction."

In fact, Utley suggested that Lattimore's service to the Communist cause as a left-wing policy analyst far transcended any minor role he could have played in an espionage ring. "To suggest that Mr. Lattimore's great talents have been utilized in espionage," she stated, "seems to me as absurd as to suggest that Mr. Gromyko or Mr. Molotov employ their leisure hours at Lake Success, or at international conferences, in snitching documents." Utley testified against Lattimore a second time when the Johns Hopkins University professor was investigated by the Senate Internal Security subcommittee chaired by Senator Patrick MCCARRAN of Nevada. Her book, *The China Story,* published in 1951, was widely regarded as a rebuttal to Lattimore's account of his ORDEAL BY SLANDER (1950). In her work, Utley contended that the United States "lost China by default and opened the way to the Communist conquest of the Far East."

In 1952, Utley toured the overseas libraries of the United States Department of State, searching for pro-Communist publications. On April 1, 1953, she testified before McCarthy's GOVERNMENT OPERATIONS COMMITTEE on what she had discovered: the selection of books on the shelves did not provide an accurate picture of American life and society. She had found only a few overtly anti-Communist books in the libraries, and even those were difficult to identify from the catalogues. Worse, Utley claimed that she had seen numerous publications by Communists or Communist sympathizers. The libraries, she concluded, were "loaded up with what you might call anti-anti-communist material, not fellow-traveller or Communist-sympathizer material but people who are extremely anti those who are doing anything against the Communists."

Following the downfall of Senator McCarthy and the gradual subsidence of anti-Communist hysteria in the United States, Utley resumed her journalistic career, and spent seveal years studying the Arab-Israeli conflict in the Middle East. In 1957, she published her insights into the region in a book entitled *Will the Middle East Go West?*

# V

**Velde, Harold H.** (1910–1985) A former FEDERAL BUREAU OF INVESTIGATION (FBI) agent who became chairman of the HOUSE COMMITTEE ON UN-AMERICAN ACTIVITIES (HUAC), Harold Velde graduated from Northwestern University in 1931. He spent the next four years teaching high school in Hillsdale, Illinois, while attending the University of Illinois Law School in the evenings. After receiving his law degree in 1937, Velde practiced law for five years, until he enlisted as a private in the U.S. Army Signal Corps. Discharged from the Army in 1943, Velde became a special agent in the FBI's division of sabotage and counterespionage. He served for a year in the bureau's San Francisco office as a wiretap specialist, during which time he helped gather evidence against "Scientist X," a former University of California physicist named Joseph Weinberg who was accused of passing atomic secrets to the Soviet Union. Velde left the FBI in 1946 when he was appointed county judge of Tazewell County, Illinois, and two years later, he won election as a Republican candidate to the House of Representatives with the slogan, "Get the Reds out of Washington and Washington out of the Red," thereby combining anti-Communism with a determination to slash federal spending.

Velde's experience in hunting subversives won him a seat on the HUAC. He quickly acquired a reputation as a fervent anti-Communist who specialized in espionage matters. In May 1949, he testified before a special federal grand jury investigating subversive activities that he favored legislation to extend the time limit for prosecution of espionage cases. When the Soviet Union announced in September of that year that it had successfully detonated a nuclear weapon, Velde declared that the Soviets had "undoubtedly gained three to five years in producing the atomic bomb" because of a "soft" attitude toward Communism during the past fifteen years of Democratic administrations, "from the White House down." Warning that "Soviet espionage agents are still highly active in the continental United States," Velde called upon American voters to "throw out of office those incompetents who regard their political lives as more important than our national security." Along with Congressman Richard M. NIXON of California, Velde criticized Judge Samuel F. Kaufman's handling of the perjury trial of Alger HISS, though he conceded that Kaufman must have been under "terrific pressure" from Hiss' sympathizers in the administration.

When HUAC launched its second investigation into Communist infiltration of the entertainment industry in 1951 (the first investigation having foundered in 1947 for lack of evidence of actual Communist propaganda in motion pictures), Velde announced that he was still convinced that "Communist propaganda had been put into films—perhaps not in an open manner, but in the way the writers think if they are Communists." Dissatisfied with the Truman administration's loyalty-review program for federal employees, Velde also urged Congress to investigate the "entire security set-up" of the federal government. Indeed, Velde apparently assumed that his primary function as a congressman was to investigate subversion. Virtually, the only two pieces of legislation he proposed during his early years in Congress were a bill to require LOYALTY OATHS for voters in national elections, and another measure requiring the Librarian of Congress to list all books that could be defined as "subversive."

When the Republican Party swept to victory in the 1952 elections, capturing the White House and both houses of Congress, Velde warned that the Communists might attempt to infiltrate the party's inner councils now that it had regained national power. The Republican landslide made Velde chairman of HUAC, and during his tenure as chairman Velde established a record for the number and duration of the committee's investigations, taking a total of 178 days of testimony from more than 650 witnesses. By establishing subcommittes and dispatching them throughout the nation, Velde succeeded in investigating simultaneously the UNITED ELECTRICAL WORKERS, the automobile industry, union officials in Chicago, New York State employees, and an assorted band of alleged subversives in San Diego, California. Velde himself continued HUAC's inquiry into the entertainment industry, calling such prominent artists as musician Artie Shaw (who claimed that he had been duped by Communists), actor Lionel Stander, choreographer Jerome ROBBINS, and director Robert Rossen. Velde's standard of conduct for investigations was not calculated to win any support from civil libertarians. "It's a lot better to wrongly accuse one person of being a Communist," he announced, "than to allow so many to get away with such Communist acts as those that have brought us to the brink of World War Three."

As chairman, Velde focused his attention on investigating Communist influence in the fields of education and religion. In January 1953, he told *The New York Times* that "I feel that we should look into the field of education. That has been largely left untouched up till now. I realize, of course, that we're going to have a lot of opposition from various educators, particularly from the 'left-wing' educators, but I believe that is a very fertile field for investigation and that it should be done." Velde denied that he sought to limit academic freedom in any manner, though his critics—cognizant of his legislative record on this matter—greeted his protestations with skepticism. "In my opinion," Velde declared, "any person can think anything he wants to, as long as he doesn't do or perform any overt act which would be considered disloyal, and therefore, as far as freedom of thought is concerned, I think we'll make no inroads on that freedom whatever by our investigations."

Velde promptly launched an inquiry into Communist activities at Harvard University in the late 1930s. Among the witnesses from academia who admitted their past membership in the COMMUNIST PARTY were writer Granville HICKS, historian Daniel BOORSTIN, and English professor Robert Gorham DAVIS. The example set by Velde's committee inspired numerous communities to establish their own investigations into Communist infiltration of universities and local public school systems, leading to the dismissal or resignation of hundreds of teachers.

On March 9, 1953, Velde ventured into the sensitive field of organized religion when he informed a national radio audience that he might pursue an investigation into Communist influence in the nation's churches. Several years earlier, HUAC had noted "with dismay the inordinately large proportion of clerics among the persons who are aiding or supporting the Communist 'peace' campaign in this country." But President Dwight D. EISENHOWER made it clear that he saw no point in questioning the loyalty of the nation's churches, and the other members of HUAC appeared almost equally unenthusiastic about Velde's proposal. Following an unsatisfactory confrontation with G. Bromley OXNAM, the Methodist Bishop of Washington and a president of the World Council of Churches, Velde abandoned his inquiry. Later in 1953 he attempted to gain further publicity for HUAC by reopening the case of the late Harry Dexter WHITE, but the Eisenhower administration quashed his efforts to subpoena witnesses.

Chastened, Velde maintained a low profile during his second year as chairman of HUAC. When the Democrats regained control of the House of Representatives in the 1954 congressional elections, Velde was forced to relinquish his chairmanship of the committee to Congressman Francis WALTER of Pennsylvania. He served one more term in the House of Representatives, and then retired from Congress in 1957.

## Vincent, John Carter (1900–1972)   One of the State Department's leading experts on Chinese affairs in the 1940s, and hence a prominent target of Senator Joseph MCCARTHY and

the CHINA LOBBY, John Carter Vincent was born in Kansas and educated at Mercer University in Macon, Georgia. After vacillating between a career in the U.S. Consular Service and a life as a Baptist missionary, Vincent—a dedicated disciple of President Woodrow Wilson, who inspired him with a sense of idealism—joined the foreign service in 1925. For the following ten years, he served as a diplomatic officer in China; his stations included the cities of Ch'ang-sha, Hankow, Peking, Mukden, and Dairen. In 1936, Vincent was transferred to the State Department, where he served on the China desk of the Far East Division. He grew increasingly concerned over the threat of Japanese imperialism in Asia, and repeatedly—and unsuccessfully—pressed his superiors to implement policies to thwart that nation's expansionist campaign in China.

In the summer of 1940, Vincent was transferred to Shanghai, China, as American consul. After a brief stay in that city, he moved on to the capital of Chungking as first secretary of the U.S. embassy. There Vincent became closely acquainted with Nationalist Chinese leader CHIANG Kai-shek and to recognize the deep and abiding enmity that existed between the Nationalist regime and the Chinese Communist forces of MAO Zedong, then sheltered in northern China. During the next several years, Vincent became increasingly frustrated with the unwillingness of corrupt and inefficient Nationalist officials to adopt any "effective meaures for agrarian reform, equitable taxation, and . . . promotion of home industries"—in short, to implement the sort of policies that would "cut the ground from under the Communists" and enable Chiang to unify China in the face of continuing Japanese aggression. Vincent also urged the State Department in Washington to use its military- and economic-assistance programs to create a democratic and progressive regime in China that would enable that nation to become a source of stability in the Far East, rather than a disruptive influence.

When Vice President Henry WALLACE arrived in China on a fact-finding mission in 1944, Vincent accompanied the vice president for most of his tour. Vincent's analysis of Chinese politics clearly influenced Wallace's conclusions at the end of his mission, recommending U.S. support for a coalition of "western trained men whose outlook is not limited to the perpetuation of the old, landlord-dominated rural society of China, and the considerable group of Generals and other officers who are neither subservient to the landlords nor afraid of the peasantry." Wallace's report, did not, however, produce any significant change in the internal situation in China, where civil war between the Nationalist and Communist forces resumed following the surrender of Japan in August 1945.

While Vincent warned policymakers in Washington to limit American involvement in the Chinese civil war, he attempted to persuade Chiang Kai-shek to resolve his differences with the Communists in an attempt to form a united, non-Marxist coalition government. "A National Government moving ahead with American support in the job of rehabilitation and reconstruction," Vincent wrote on September 9, 1946, "would have a better chance to cut the ground out from under the communists, even though they were in the Government, than it would have of doing so by keeping them out of the government and endeavoring to eliminate them by force." Vincent's recommendations fell on deaf ears in Chungking, however, and the Nationalists persisted in their efforts to annihilate the Communists. Faced with this sort of obduracy, Vincent argued that extensive U.S. aid to Chiang Kai-shek would be wasted because an unreformed Nationalist government was doomed to failure.

In January 1947, the Truman administration nominated Vincent to the rank of career minister, but the nomination ran afoul of opposition by the China Lobby, a loosely organized coalition of pro-Chiang politicians and businessmen headed by millionaire industrialist Alfred KOHL-

BERG. New Hampshire Republican Senator Styles BRIDGES, a member of the Senate Foreign Relations Committee, charged that Vincent had "notoriously and harmfully distorted the American position" in China through his pro-leftist sentiments. Several months later, the China Lobby publication *Plain Talk* claimed that Vincent had "sabotaged the traditional American policy in China and has been fronting for the Soviet viewpoint." Instead of confronting the opposition directly, the administration decided to appoint Vincent to a less-controversial diplomatic post in Switzerland, where he remained for the next three years.

On February 20, 1950, Vincent's loyalty was again questioned by anti-Communist zealots when Senator McCarthy identified him in a Senate speech as one of the leading Soviet agents in the U.S. State Department. (Vincent was, in fact, "number two" on McCarthy's list of eighty-one alleged Communists in the State Department.) Without mentioning Vincent by name, McCarthy noted that "the file shows that this particular individual, who has held one of the most important positions at one of the listening posts in Europe, was shadowed, that he was found to have contacted a Soviet agent, and that the Soviet agent was then followed to the Soviet Embassy, where the agent turned the material over to the Soviet Embassy." Actually, McCarthy was reading from a dossier assembled by a team of investigators several years earlier; yet, the senator's accusations persuaded FBI Director J. Edgar HOOVER to launch a full-scale investigation of Vincent's background.

Vincent, meanwhile, stoutly maintained his innocence of all charges of disloyalty or espionage. "I have never acted directly or indirectly to provide espionage agents of Russia or any other country with information in the State Department or from any other governmental source," Vincent told the State Department's chief of security. "The Senator's story is simply not true. . . . I have never joined any political organization, 'front,' or political party. I am a

Jeffersonian democrat, a Lincolnian republican, and an admirer since youth of Woodrow Wilson. . . . I have never knowingly associated with American Communists or Communist sympathizers." After hearing testimony on the matter, the special Senate subcommittee formed to investigate McCarthy's accusations cleared Vincent, describing the charges against him as "absurd."

Nevertheless, the Truman administration again bowed to pressure in March 1951 when it decided not to name Vincent ambassador to Costa Rica, as it had intended but to send him instead to Morocco because that position did not require Senate confirmation. Yet, even there Vincent could not escape controversy. In testimony before the Senate Subcommittee on Internal Security in August 1951, ex-Communist Louis BUDENZ identified Vincent as a former fellow member of the COMMUNIST PARTY. Budenz said that in 1944, he had "heard in official Communist Party circles that John Carter Vincent and Owen LATTIMORE were members of the Communist Party traveling with Henry Wallace" as part of the vice-president's mission to China. Vincent immediately wrote to subcommittee chairman Patrick MCCARRAN of Nevada, asking for an opportunity to clear his name. During the interim, the State Department's Loyalty Security Board formally notified Vincent that he was under investigation on charges that he had been "pro-Communist in [his] views and sympathies in the period 1940–1947," that he had belonged to the Communist Party, and that he had had "contact or association with individuals concerning whom the Board has certain derogatory information."

In late January 1952, Vincent was finally permitted to testify before the Senate Internal Security Subcommittee. His testimony lasted for six days, during which time the State Department completed its own investigation and cleared Vincent of the charges against him. The Internal Security Subcommittee's report was less favorable, concluding that Vincent had

**Voice of America, the radio broadcast arm of the International Information Agency.**

joined with Lattimore to bring about "a change in United States policy in 1945 favorable to the Chinese Communists." Partly as a result of the subcommittee's findings, the Civil Service Commission's LOYALTY REVIEW BOARD, headed by former Senator Hiram BINGHAM, decided to launch its own investigation of Vincent's activities. On December 15, 1952, the board notified Vincent that although it had not found him guilty of disloyalty, it had decided by a 3–2 margin that "his conduct in office, as clearly indicated by the record, forces us reluctantly to conclude that there is reasonable doubt as to his loyalty to the Government of the U.S." Consequently, Vincent was suspended immediately by the State Department pending yet another investigation.

Before he left the White House in January 1953, President Harry S. TRUMAN appointed a special commission headed by Judge Learned Hand to examine Vincent's record. But before

the commission could complete its task, Secretary of State John Foster DULLES suspended the inquiry and determined on his own initiative that Vincent had been guilty of poor judgment and "a failure to meet the standard which is demanded of a Foreign Service officer." Dulles allowed Vincent the opportunity to resign and keep his pension; if Vincent refused, he would be dismissed. Vincent agreed to resign and quit the foreign service at the end of February 1953. Dulles' action outraged former Secretary of State Dean ACHESON, who commented that "Mr. Dulles's six predecessors, under all of whom Mr. Vincent had served in the China field, did not find his judgment or services defective or substandard. On the contrary, they relied on him and promoted him."

For the following several years, Vincent earned a living as a speaker and columnist on foreign affairs. Throughout the 1960s, he steadfastly opposed the escalating American involvement in Vietnam, advocating instead a policy designed to keep Southeast Asia neutral. In December 1972, Vincent died of lung failure following a brief illness.

**Voice of America**   The radio broadcast arm of the INTERNATIONAL INFORMATION AGENCY (IIA), the Voice of America (VOA) came under attack by Senator Joseph MCCARTHY in early 1953 for allegedly employing "Communists, left-wingers, New Dealers, radicals and pinkos" among the 10,000 members of its staff. When McCarthy launched a full-scale Senate investigation of both VOA and the IIA in February 1953, Eisenhower refused to issue a statement of support for the personnel of either agency; as a result, the head of VOA resigned under pressure shortly after McCarthy's PERMANENT SUBCOMMITTEE ON INVESTIGATIONS began a series of secret hearings. Pressed by reporters to comment on McCarthy's charges against VOA, Eisenhower dodged the question, replying that "I think it would be completely inappropriate for me to comment specifically on individuals in Congress and their methods, because presumably the Congress approves these, or they wouldn't go on."

McCarthy subsequently dispatched two of his assistants, Roy COHN and G. David SCHINE, to Europe to investigate VOA offices and IIA libraries abroad. When they claimed to discover evidence of pro-Communist sympathies among the agencies' personnel, Secretary of State John Foster DULLES dismissed more than 800 VOA employees. As a result of the climate of fear fostered by McCarthy and his subordinates, VOA officials in Europe actually began to burn books that had been identified by right-wing zealots as pro-Communist or subversive.

At a speech on June 14, 1953, at DARTMOUTH COLLEGE, President Eisenhower appeared to chastise McCarthy and his followers for their attack on VOA and IIA. "Don't join the book burners," Eisenhower urged his listeners. "Don't think you are going to conceal faults by concealing evidence that they ever existed. Don't be afraid to go in your library and read every book." Several days later, however, Eisenhower retreated from any implied criticism of McCarthy, and Dulles followed suit by charging that VOA employees were burning books in a vindictive attempt to embarrass him for cooperating with McCarthy. (See also DARTMOUTH COLLEGE SPEECH.)

# W

**Waldorf Statement** A proclamation that banned members of the left-wing screenwriters and directors known as the HOLLYWOOD TEN from further employment in the motion picture industry, the Waldorf Statement represented an attempt by the major film studios to avoid further congressional interference in their affairs.

Following the initial phase of the investigation by the HOUSE COMMITTEE ON UN-AMERICAN AFFAIRS into the motion picture industry in October 1947, Hollywood's leading film producers and studio executives met at the Waldorf-Astoria Hotel in New York City on November 24–25, 1947, to frame a joint policy toward the committee's efforts. The leading force behind the meeting was Eric Johnston, president of the Motion Picture Producers Association of America. At the opening session, Johnston informed the assembled executives that they needed to take a formal stand in favor of the hearings. The public, according to Johnston, already had begun to turn against films involving artists accused of Communist sympathies. As evidence, Johnston cited newspaper editorials attacking the Hollywood Ten, threats of boycotts by the AMERICAN LEGION against such films, and violent audience reaction in one North Carolina community against a film featuring Katharine HEPBURN, a member of the COMMITTEE FOR THE FIRST AMENDMENT.

Johnston recommended that the studios make a public gesture in favor of anti-Communism by either dismissing or refusing to employ all members of the Hollywood Ten. In fact, RKO and Twentieth Century-Fox had already decided to fire three members of the Ten: Edward DMYTRYK, Robert Adrian SCOTT, and Ring LARDNER Jr. Although Samuel GOLDWYN protested that there was not yet sufficient evidence to justify such action, the other studio heads voted to adopt Johnston's suggestion. To further reduce the heat from HUAC, the assembled executives announced that they would launch an extensive self-regulation policy to keep Communists out of the motion picture industry.

On December 3, 1947, a formal three-paragraph announcement—the Waldorf Statement (named for the hotel in which it was written)—was released to the public. The studios deplored the actions of the Hollywood Ten in refusing to answer the questions of a duly constituted committee of Congress and declared that their actions had "impaired their usefulness to the industry." They pledged to dismiss or suspend any of the Ten currently in their employ (as it turned out, only five of the Ten were currently on a studio payroll) and promised not to rehire any members of the Ten until they had been acquitted, purged themselves of contempt, or swore under oath that they were not Communists.

The studios further promised not to knowingly employ Communists or members of any group that advocated the overthrow of the U.S. government by force or illegal means. They concluded by urging the Hollywood writers' and directors' guilds to work voluntarily with the Motion Picture Producers Association to root out subversives and protect free speech.

In the increasingly tense atmosphere of the late 1940s, the anti-subversive portions of the Waldorf Statement took on greater weight than its cursory acknowledgment of First Amendment rights. Following the issuance of the statement, film studios began to question employees more rigorously about their political affiliations and denied work to applicants who gave unsatisfactory answers. Not surprisingly, the major studios also began to produce fewer films with liberal social themes. Only with the passage of time and the subsidence of political paranoia did the studios relax their vigilance against left-wing employees, and no member of the Hollywood Ten was openly employed until Otto Preminger hired Dalton TRUMBO in 1960.

**Wallace, Henry A.** (1888–1965) Vice-president in Franklin D. Roosevelt's third administration (1941–45) and Progressive Party candidate for president in the 1948 election, Henry Wallace was the best-known liberal American politician in the 1940s. Wallace's father had served Presidents Harding and Coolidge as secretary of agriculture in the 1920s, and he himself began his own professional career as an agriculturalist. Before entering politics, Wallace edited the popular and prestigious farm journal *Wallace's Farmer* and achieved significant breakthroughs as a plant geneticist, particularly with hybrid strains of corn.

Roosevelt appointed Wallace as his secretary of agriculture in his first two administrations (1933–41) and then selected him as his running mate for the 1940 presidential campaign. Wallace had long been known as an idealistic liberal in domestic politics, enthusiastically supporting the more radical New Deal initiatives; he wished to apply religious ethics to political problems and to help transform capitalism into a more humane economic system. In foreign affairs, Wallace was an internationalist, backing the League of Nations in its efforts to stimulate international cooperation. During World War II, Roosevelt assigned Wallace the task of running the Board of Economic Warfare, which coordinated American imports and exports and selected economically vital enemy targets for strategic bombing.

On May 8, 1942, Wallace delivered his most famous wartime speech, which later became known as "The Century of the Common Man." It proved so popular that hundreds of thousands of copies were distributed within weeks. In this address, Wallace linked the American revolution with similar struggles for political and economic independence throughout the world, culminating in the Russian Revolution of 1917. He then presented his vision of the postwar world: "Everywhere the common man must learn to build his own industries with his own hands in a practical fashion. Everywhere the common man must learn to increase his productivity so

that he and his children can eventually pay to the world community all that they have received. No nation will have the God-given right to exploit other nations. . . . The methods of the nineteenth century will not work in the people's century which is now about to begin."

Such visionary rhetoric was not calculated to endear Wallace to conservative American politicians who felt the United States should pursue its own strategic interests in the postwar world. No more pleasing to militant anti-Communists was Wallace's call for the continuation of Soviet-American cooperation after the war. In 1944, Roosevelt elected to replace Wallace with less controversial (and more conservative) Missouri Senator Harry S. TRUMAN as his running mate. Wallace remained with the administration as secretary of commerce, fulfilling the same cabinet role in the early months of the Truman presidency.

When Wallace criticized Truman in 1946 for moving toward a tougher policy toward Soviet expansion, however, Truman fired him. That same year, Wallace also earned the distinction of becoming one of the first targets of little-known Wisconsin Representative Joseph MCCARTHY, who was then seeking his first term in the U.S. Senate. Upon learning that Wallace was planning to deliver a speech in Wisconsin on foreign affairs, McCarthy warned Wallace "that the people of Wisconsin completely understand only one language—the American language, and Mr. Wallace does not speak that language."

Wallace ran for the presidency himself in 1948 as the candidate of the newly organized Progressive Party. The campaign—which also featured Truman as the Democratic nominee, Thomas E. Dewey as the Republican candidate, and South Carolina Senator Strom Thurmond as the standardbearer of the newly organized "Dixiecrat" party—was notable for its extraordinarily vitriolic tone. Seeking to establish their own anti-Communist credentials, Democratic candidates accused Wallace of surrounding himself with Communist sympathizers; Wallace himself, they charged, was nothing more than a puppet for the COMMUNIST PARTY. (The Communist Party did, in fact, support Wallace in 1948.)

Wallace responded that the issue of Communists in government was a "red herring," an attempt to divert the American people from the real issues of inflation and consumer shortages, and he reminded the electorate that he was the only presidential candidate who had been a successful businessman. Still, Wallace's public statements provided the opposition with plenty of ammunition. At the start of the campaign, Wallace described the HOLLYWOOD TEN, who had recently been convicted of contempt of Congress, as "most adept at carrying truth to the American people." He also described the late Harry Dexter WHITE, a former State Department official who had been accused of Soviet espionage activities, as "my good friend and close associate on many New Deal committees," and he attributed White's death from a coronary attack to the inquisitorial excesses of the HOUSE COMMITTEE ON UN-AMERICAN ACTIVITIES.

In the election in November, Wallace gathered only slightly more than a million votes. He continued to speak out against Truman's foreign policies, and criticized the formation of NATO in 1949, but as time passed, Wallace grew increasingly bitter toward his erstwhile Communist allies whom he felt had cost him the 1948 election. He broke with the Progressive Party in 1950 and publicly voiced his support for Truman's commitment of American combat troops to Korea. Wallace then retired from political affairs and devoted the remainder of his life to the cause of agricultural research.

## Walter, Francis (1894–1963)

A Democratic congressman from eastern Pennsylvania, Francis Walter served as chairman of the HOUSE COMMITTEE ON UN-AMERICAN ACTIVITIES (HUAC) for eight years, longer than any other individual.

Walter grew up in the industrial city of Easton, Pennsylvania, and attended nearby Lehigh University for several years before transferring to

George Washington University in Washington, D.C. In 1919, Walter completed his studies at Georgetown University School of Law and returned to Pennsylvania to enter private practice.

Walter first won election to Congress in 1932 during the nadir of the Great Depression. He devoted his early years in Congress to serving the specific needs of his home district. Thereafter, Walter established a record as a Democratic moderate, respected by members on both sides of the ideological battles that raged over President Franklin D. Roosevelt's New Deal reforms. Walter's first significant foray into the field of national legislation came in 1939 when he cosponsored a bill providing for judicial review of regulations issued by New Deal agencies. During World War II, Walter introduced legislation authorizing federal courts to postpone labor

Representative Francis Walter of Pennsylvania, longtime chairman of the House Committee on Un-American activities.

strikes that threatened the national defense. Walter's primary interest, however, was in the field of immigration. Following World War II, he sponsored legislation increasing the number of war refugees from Western Europe allowed admission into the United States. In 1952, however, Walter joined with Senator Patrick MCCARRAN in sponsoring legislation that established immigration quotas based on national origin; the measure was clearly designed to severely restrict immigration from Southern and Eastern Europe and from all parts of Asia.

In part, Walter was motivated to introduce this legislation by his fear that aliens from those proscribed areas would be subversives devoted to the propagation of their Communist beliefs. Since 1949, Walter had served as second-ranking Democrat the HUAC, a post he reportedly did not desire and one which he accepted only under pressure from the Truman administration. Walter's position on the committee appeared to intensify greatly his existing aversion to Communism. In March 1949, he introduced a measure to deprive COMMUNIST PARTY members of U.S. citizenship, even if they were born in the United States. The following year, he served as acting chairman when HUAC held hearings in Hawaii to ascertain the extent of Communist influence in the islands. In August 1950, Walter sponsored legislation requiring the Communist Party to register its members and report on their activities, on the premise that Communism was an international conspiracy dedicated to the violent overthrow of democratic government. When HUAC turned its attention once again to Hollywood in the spring of 1951, it was Walter who chaired most of the committee's hearings into Communist influence in the motion picture industry.

Walter reportedly was deeply offended by the opposition of liberals—and both the Republican and Democratic 1952 presidential candidates, General Dwight David EISENHOWER and Governor Adlai STEVENSON—to the McCarran-Walter Act of 1952, and he began to view criticism of his legislation as evidence of subversion. Never-

theless, when Walter assumed the chairmanship of HUAC in 1955, the committee abandoned certain excesses that had marred its previous anti-Communist investigations. After taking the almost unheard-of step of reducing his committee's funding and staffing, Walter convened a meeting of HUAC members and staffers to discuss fair treatment of witnesses. He further declared that the committee would not pursue inquiries of subversion in any particular profession, but would instead "go after Communists as Communists," wherever it might find them. Committee hearings lost the acrimonious tone they had assumed under previous chairmen Harold VELDE and J. Parnell THOMAS, becoming instead almost models of courtesy. Most of the credit for this transformation belonged to Walter. When playwright Arthur MILLER appeared before HUAC in 1956, he noted Walter's pleasant demeanor and his unassuming and conventionally middle-class outfit: a blue blazer which he had worn to a wedding in Scranton, Pennsylvania, and brown-and-white shoes with perforated wing tips. To ease tensions further, Walter repeatedly reminded zealous supporters of HUAC's investigations that he hoped they would be "traditionally American and withhold judgment" about the guilt of witnesses "until they know what all the facts are."

Nevertheless, Walter continued to press the anti-Communist crusade forward, despite the fact that the Senate's censure of Senator Joseph MCCARTHY in December 1954 had dampened the public's enthusiasm for the issue. In 1955–56, Walter initiated an investigation into the entertainment industry on Broadway, held hearings on Communist infiltration of the National Labor Relations Board, and looked into the case of a $5,000 payment by the FUND FOR THE REPUBLIC to the Quaker Plymouth Meeting for its willingness to hire a librarian who previously had invoked the Fifth Amendment during a loyalty hearing. In the spring of 1956, Walter introduced a bill authorizing the secretary of state to refuse passports to any U.S. citizen against whom there was "adverse security information." During the ensuing hearings, Walter engaged in particularly acrimonious exchanges with singer-actor Paul ROBESON, who repeatedly provoked the chairman with charges of racism.

Gradually, Walter's gracious attitude deteriorated into hostility. Continuing demands for liberalization of his immigration bill led him to brand reformers as Communist sympathizers. Moreover, the thaw in American-Soviet relations that accompanied the rise of Nikita Khrushchev to power in the post-Stalinist era of the late 1950s troubled Walter deeply. "The menace of Communism remains unabated," reported HUAC in 1956. "Anti-Stalinism," Walter suggested, "is but a political artifice, fraudulent and more dangerous than any other produced by the Kremlin thus far." When the Eisenhower administration opened talks with the Soviet Union on a nuclear test ban, Walter bemoaned "the sorry spectacle of otherwise intelligent American leaders willing to negotiate with Communism's masters at international conference tables as if there were a real foundation of sincerity and good faith."

Between 1957 and 1960, HUAC uncovered few fertile fields for further investigation. Walter pursued inquiries into the American National Exhibition of art in Moscow, allegations of Communist influence in the recently published revised standard version of the Bible, purported Communist sympathizers in New York City's arts and music circles (including Shakespeare producer Joseph PAPP, who lost his job as a stage manager at CBS-TV after invoking the Fifth Amendment in his testimony before HUAC in 1958), and a defunct Marxist educational institution known as the Jefferson School of Social Science, also located in New York.

With the inauguration of President John F. KENNEDY in 1961, Walter forsook his obsession with the Communist threat and assumed a key role as liaison between the administration and Congress. In the twilight of Walter's congressional career, Speaker of the House Sam Rayburn paid tribute to his service on HUAC by praising Walter for having "dug out more dens

of disloyalty than any man who has ever lived in the United States." HUAC held far fewer hearings over the following two years, the last full session of Congress which Walter attended.

On May 31, 1963, Walter died of leukemia. His record more-than-thirty years of congressional service was extraordinarily complex. While the staff of HUAC noted that "his many contributions in the field of national security will be an everlasting monument to his memory and will serve as a living inspiration to all those who serve after him," an analysis of his voting record revealed that he had voted consistently with the liberal bloc in the House on both foreign and domestic measures.

**Warren, Earl** (1891–1974)  Chief Justice of the U.S. Supreme Court Earl Warren infuriated conservative anti-Communists such as Senators Joseph MCCARTHY and William JENNER of Indiana through his support of civil liberties for individuals accused of political radicalism.

A native of California, Earl Warren received a law degree from the University of California Law School in 1914 and worked his way up through state government service to become attorney general of California in 1939. Three years later, he won the Republican gubernatorial nomination and, despite the heavy predominance of Democratic voters in California, emerged victorious in a stunning upset. By courting the political center, Warren managed to garner both the Republican and the Democratic nominations for governor in 1946.

During his second term as governor, Warren confronted the issue of LOYALTY OATHS for state employees when several members of the Board of Regents of the University of California—prompted by the California legislature's Committee on Un-American Affairs—introduced a resolution requiring all members of the university's faculty to take a test oath asserting their loyalty, disavowing Communism, and disclosing their membership in all academic and scientific organizations. Warren strongly opposed the concept of a loyalty oath, arguing that it was

**U.S. Supreme Court Chief Justice Earl Warren, whose rulings in favor of civil liberties for suspected Communists infuriated conservatives.**

unnecessary (faculty already were required to take an oath "to support and defend the Constitution and laws of the United States and of the State of California") and unenforceable; because the oath would not be required by state law, the university could not even impose a perjury penalty for taking a false oath.

Despite Warren's opposition, the Board of Regents adopted the resolution. When sixty-eight faculty members refused to take the oath, they were summarily dismissed from their teaching positions. As Warren predicted, the professors appealed for reinstatement through the court system and eventually won their case when the California State Supreme Court invalidated the loyalty oath.

Seeking an ideologically compatible and geographically complimentary vice-presidential running mate, Republican presidential nominee Thomas E. Dewey selected Warren as his running mate in the 1948 election campaign. Warren joined in the Republican attack upon the Truman administration's handling of the issue of Communist sympathizers in government, accusing the White House of "coddling Communists." After Truman staged his dramatic upset victory, Warren returned to California and won a third term as governor in 1950. He entered the national political arena again in 1952, seeking the presidential nomination for himself, but was swept aside by the entrance of General Dwight David EISENHOWER into the race.

Upon the death of U.S. Supreme Court Chief Justice Fred Vinson in 1954, Eisenhower selected Warren to lead the nation's highest court, despite the vehement objections of the President's conservative advisers. In his first few months on the Court, Warren surprised his right-wing detractors by voting to uphold the government's attempts to prosecute alleged subversives; in *Galyan v. Press,* for instance, Warren agreed that an alien could be deported on the grounds that he had once been a member of the COMMUNIST PARTY, even if he had subsequently renounced his Party membership.

With the Court's ruling in *Peters v. Hobby* in June 1955, however, Warren began to carve out a record as a defender of the rights of accused individuals, particularly in cases that involved the government's increasingly rigorous internal security programs. In PENNSYLVANIA V. NELSON (1956), Warren joined the Court's majority in ruling that Communists could not be tried for sedition in state or local courts because sedition was solely a federal offense. Later that year, the chief justice took government prosecutors to task in *Mesarosh v. United States* for their reliance on the testimony of paid informants—whose veracity was highly suspect—to infiltrate the Communist Party and then provide evidence against alleged subversives. "The dignity of the United States Government will not permit the conviction of any person on tainted testimony," Warren wrote. "[We must] see that the waters of justice are not polluted."

By the summer of 1957, the anti-Communist hysteria that had grabbed the nation during the McCarthy era had subsided, but the legal cases that had begun in the early years of the decade were still wending their way through the courts. On June 17, 1957, the Supreme Court handed down three rulings that so diminished the government's ability to prosecute suspected Communists that conservative critics dubbed the day "Red Monday." In WATKINS V. UNITED STATES, Warren served notice that the Court would tolerate no further abuses of the investigative process by congressional committees such as the HOUSE COMMITTEE ON UN-AMERICAN ACTIVITIES.

Similarly, in *Sweeney v. New Hampshire*, the Court overturned the conviction for contempt of a teacher at the University of New Hampshire who had refused to answer questions about his past political associations. Charging that the professor's privacy and academic freedom had been violated, Warren claimed that "mere unorthodoxy or dissent from the prevailing mores is not to be condemned: The absence of such voices would be a symptom of grave illness." And in YATES V. UNITED STATES, the Court overturned by a 6–1 majority the convictions of fourteen Communists under the SMITH ACT. In its decision, the Court declared that an "abstract advocacy" of the violent overthrow of the government was not sufficient evidence of a "clear and present danger." By doing so, the Court reversed the stand it had taken in 1951 in a similar case, DENNIS V. UNITED STATES.

In one of its final rulings against government excesses in the anti-Communist crusade, the Warren Court ruled in 1958 that the State Department could not legally deny a passport to an individual merely because that person refused to sign an affidavit swearing that he was not a member of the Communist Party. This ruling, in *Kent v. Dulles,* freed actor-singer Paul ROBESON to leave the United States for Europe after an eight-year struggle.

Given these decisions by the Warren Court, it was not surprising that Senator McCarthy once remarked on the floor of the Senate that "I will not say that Earl Warren is a Communist, but I will say he is the best friend of Communism in the United States." President Eisenhower also believed that Warren and his colleagues had gone too far toward protecting the rights of Communists and reportedly complained that his appointment of Warren as chief justice was "the biggest damn fool thing I ever did."

**Watkins, Arthur V.** (1886–1973)  As a second-term Republican senator from the state of Utah, Arthur Watkins served as chairman of the special subcommittee established by the U.S. Senate in 1954 to hold hearings into charges of misconduct by Senator Joseph MCCARTHY of Wisconsin.

The grandson of Mormon immigrants from England and Switzerland, Watkins had been born in Midway, Utah, when that state was still very much a part of the western frontier; he later recalled that his "first associations were with the rugged pioneer life of the time, Indians, saw mills, logging, hunting and fishing; with the toil of homesteading." As a youth, Watkins worked on his family's farm at Vernal, in the sparsely settled northeastern section of the state. An outstanding basketball player in high school and college, he attended Brigham Young University for three years before moving to New York to fulfill his obligations as a missionary for the Church of Latter Day Saints. "I ran into a good deal of prejudice and misunderstanding," Watkins noted, calling the experience "eye-opening for a country boy." He remained in New York to complete his studies and received an LL. B. degree from Columbia University in 1912.

Upon his return to Utah, Watkins entered private law practice and in 1914 became assistant county attorney of Salt Lake County. After suffering a duodenal ulcer and a massive hemorrhage, he resigned from the stressful practice of law and took over the management of a 600-

Senator Arthur V. Watkins (right), chairman of the Senate committee that approved the resolution of censure against Joseph McCarthy.

acre commercial orchard in northern Utah. As he recovered his health, Watkins once again became active in legal and political affairs. From 1929 to 1933, he served as judge for the Fourth Judicial District of Utah.

Watkins was defeated in his first venture into national politics when he lost a bid for a seat in the U.S. House of Representatives in 1936; ten years later, however, he took advantage of the nationwide voter reaction against the Truman administration when he won election to the U.S. Senate as part of the Republican "Class of 1946." He had campaigned with virtually no outside financial assistance and only a skeletal organization. Therefore, when he arrived in Washington, the fiercely independent Utah Re-

publican found himself indebted to no special interest groups.

Watkins quickly established a reputation in the Senate as a moderate on domestic affairs and a conservative in foreign policy. When the Truman administration introduced legislation establishing the North Atlantic Treaty Organization (NATO), Watkins urged the addition of reservations to ensure that the United States would retain its freedom of action in time of war. Specifically, Watkins joined with fellow Republicans Robert TAFT of Ohio and Kenneth Wherry of Nebraska in insisting that Congress approve any use of military force to support other members of the alliance. When the Senate rejected his amendments, Watkins joined twelve other Republicans in voting against the NATO initiative.

A man of impeccable personal integrity, Watkins was frequently critical of the Truman administration's foreign policy but refused to participate in the sort of publicity-seeking witch hunts for subversives in the federal government that were being orchestrated by congressional anti-Communist zealots in the early 1950s. Following the inauguration of President Dwight D. EISENHOWER in January 1953, Watkins became a loyal supporter of Republican foreign policy. He sponsored, for instance, the Refugee Act of 1953 for Eisenhower, which allowed over 200,000 homeless war refugees to settle in the United States.

When the Senate established the Internal Security Subcommittee in December 1950, Watkins was selected as one of the three original Republican members of the panel, during his service on the subcommittee, becoming close friends with chairman Patrick MCCARRAN of Nevada. Watkins was especially active in the subcommittee's inquiries into Communist infiltration of labor unions; of particular interest to the Utah Republican were the subcommittee's investigations of Communist influence in the copper mining industry of his home state. Unlike several other members of the subcommittee, Watkins attempted to conduct his inquiries "with a minimum of pain and embarrassment to innocent victims and bystanders," although he acknowledged later that "there was, admittedly, some anguish among those whose careless actions and muddy thinking were so resolutely probed." In speaking of Far East expert Owen LATTIMORE, one of the principal targets of the Internal Security Subcommittee's investigations and the man whom McCarthy had termed the foremost Soviet espionage agent in the United States, Watkins concluded that while Lattimore had advocated conciliation with the Chinese Communists, there was no proof that Lattimore had participated in any type of espionage activity.

Until the summer of 1954, Watkins—preoccupied with the work of the Internal Security Subcommittee and the need to bring affordable electric power to his constitutents—had not become intimately involved in the mounting controversy over the actions of Senator McCarthy. He had noticed that McCarthy employed slipshod investigatory methods and supplied his gullible audiences—who accepted his charges of Communist subversion in the federal government—with evidence of dubious legal value. Watkins had also noted with growing dismay McCarthy's discourteous treatment of his fellow senators, including Millard TYDINGS of Maryland, William BENTON of Connecticut, and J. William FULBRIGHT of Arkansas: "While I was not particularly concerned with Joe's 'MCCARTHYISM,' " Watkins later observed, "there were a number of Senators who had been offended aesthetically, professionally, and personally by the Wisconsin Senator's roughshod methods and sometimes abrasive personality. The Republicans among this group were also concerned with the effect that McCarthy was having on party image and effectiveness."

Following Senator Ralph FLANDERS' introduction on July 16, 1954, of a resolution recommending the censure of McCarthy, the Senate established on August 2 a select committee to investigate the specific charges supplied by Flanders, Fulbright, and Oregon Republican Wayne Morse. The subcommittee consisted of six senators, three Democrats and three Republicans. Much to Watkins' dismay, Senate Majority Leader William KNOWLAND of California informed Watkins that he had been selected as a member of the committee; moreover, as a senior Republican and an experienced attorney and judge, he had been named its chairman. Unwilling to shirk what he considered to be a responsibility "I would have preferred to dodge," Watkins dutifully accepted the appointment, though he later referred to it as "the most unpleasant task I have ever had to perform in all my public life."

No objective critic could have questioned Watkins' patriotism, honesty, or credentials as a dedicated opponent of Communism. Although columnist Stewart Alsop described him as an "elderly mouse," Watkins possessed an intense devotion to the integrity of the Senate and the U.S. Constitution that, under the circumstances, portended considerable trouble for McCarthy: "Paramount to my personal view and reactions to the entire McCarthy episode—and very possibly of relevance to my appointment to the censure Committee," stated Watkins, "is my strong belief that the Constitution of the United States. . . . Those institutions which derive from the Constitution (and this includes specifically the Senate of the United States, in the present context) are entitled to the respect and honor of every citizen. It was and is my stand that a Senator, above all, should in his speech and actions demonstrate this same conviction to contribute to and uphold the dignity of the Senate." Noting that senators are required to answer only to their colleagues for their performance on the floor of the Senate, Watkins concluded that "unless the Senate itself protects this unique privilege, any individual Senator with less regard for his obligations and his honor can greatly misuse his prerogatives."

When Watkins commenced hearings on the Flanders motion on August 31, McCarthy and his attorney Edward Bennett WILLIAMS immediately attempted to derail the proceedings by challenging the impartiality of one of the committee's Democratic members, Senator Edwin O. Johnson of Colorado. In gaveling McCarthy into silence—for one of the first times in the Wisconsin senator's career—Watkins ruled that because McCarthy had retained Williams as counsel, he was not entitled to interject his own objections or opinions into matters already discussed by Williams. Thus McCarthy was precluded from staging the sort of disruptive performance that had diverted previous investigations into his behavior. Moreover, Watkins insisted that the committee maintain its focus solely on the narrow grounds of the resolution of censure; because that document dealt specifically with McCarthy's behavior in the Senate—a matter of public record—Watkins' ruling essentially guaranteed that the committee would reach a verdict unfavorable to McCarthy.

Realizing that he had little chance to divert the committee from its appointed task, McCarthy inaugurated a campaign to take his case to the American people. When the committee paused to take a break from its hearings, McCarthy rushed into the hallway where television cameras were waiting—to avoid a circus atmosphere, Watkins had banned television and movie cameras from the hearing room—and denounced the select committee as a "kangaroo court" and a "packed jury." Thousands of letters and postcards subsequently poured into Watkins' Senate office; although Watkins refused to read them at the time because he did not wish to be influenced by public opinon, his staff later estimated that reaction was running about 35–1 in favor of McCarthy. Right-wing columnists in newspapers across the nation complained that the work of the Watkins Committee would hamper the fight against Communist subversion in the United States.

On November 11—Veterans' Day—McCarthy addressed a crowd of 3,000 supporters at Constitution Hall in Washington, D.C.: "You are the victims of a massive appeasement that has been going on for years," shouted McCarthy. "It knows no political bounds. . . . Regardless of what the Senate may do, this fight to expose those who would destroy this Nation will go on and on and on." Later that month, another pro-McCarthy rally in New York city attracted 13,000 supporters. A national group that called itself Ten Million Americans Mobilizing for Justice obtained more than a million signatures on petitions to the Senate on behalf of McCarthy and, with great fanfare, delivered the boxes containing the petitions into the office of Vice President Richard M. NIXON, who accepted them on behalf of the Senate and promptly sent them back to New York.

Undaunted, the select committee issued its report on November 8, 1954, recommending the censure of McCarthy on two counts. The first was his adamant and contemptuous refusal to respond to the inquiry chaired by Senator Guy Gillette investigating Senator Benton's charges of improper conduct. During the inquiry, McCarthy had also personally insulted several of his colleagues; one senator, he claimed, was "a living miracle without brains or guts." "It is our opinon," argued the Watkins Committee, "that the failure of Senator McCarthy to explain to the Senate these matters: (1) Whether funds collected to fight communism were diverted to other purposes inuring to his personal advantage; (2) whether certain of his official activities were motivated by self-interest; and (3) whether certain of his activities in senatorial campaigns involved violations of the law; was conduct contumacious toward the Senate and injurious to its effectiveness, dignity, responsibilities, processes and prestige."

The second count involved McCarthy's conduct in the ARMY-MCCARTHY HEARINGS and particularly his public denunciations of General Ralph ZWICKER, one of the Army's chief witnesses. "The conduct of Senator McCarthy toward General Zwicker was not proper," concluded the committee. "We do not think that this conduct would have been proper in the case of any witness, whether a general or a private citizen, testifying in a similar situation. . . . The conduct of Senator McCarthy toward General Zwicker in reprimanding and ridiculing him, in holding him up to public scorn and contumely, and in disclosing the proceedings of the executive session in violation of the rules of his own committee, was inexcusable."

Following the select committee's presentation of its report to the Senate, McCarthy began to refer to Watkins as a "coward." Watkins' performance during the hearings, McCarthy charged, was the "most unusual, most cowardly thing I've heard of so far." (Another version claimed that McCarthy actually said that Watkins' ruling against him on the first day of hearings was "the most unheard of thing I've ever heard of.") Later, McCarthy wrote—but never delivered—a speech that claimed that "when the Watkins committee announced its recommendation of censure, the Communists made no attempt to conceal their joy."

During the debate on the censure motion, Watkins responded to McCarthy with, he said, "more sorrow than anger." After detailing the charges against McCarthy that led to his committee's recommendations, Watkins pointed out that "in our own presence, here in the Senate, we have seen another example of the Senator's hit-and-run attack. Senators have seen what I have called to their attention, an attack on their representative, their agent. They have seen an attack made on that agent's courage and intelligence. They have heard the junior Senator from Wisconsin say that I am both stupid and a coward. I am asking all my colleagues in the Senate . . . What are you going to do about it?"

Following Watkins' speech, the Senate was completely silent for a moment; then both Watkins' colleagues and the spectators in the galleries broke into applause. When the Senate voted on the motion of censure on December 1, 1954, Wakins joined sixty-six other senators in voting in favor; twenty-two voted against the motion.

On the day after the censure vote, Watkins was summoned to the White House where President Eisenhower expressed his appreciation to Watkins for conducting a fair and orderly hearing into McCarthy's activities. Watkins thanked Eisenhower but added that the select committee still wanted the Army to forward to the relevant Senate committee the names of the individuals responsible for promoting Dr. Irving PERESS, an Army dentist who allegedly was a Communist sympathizer. Eisenhower was surprised—and angered—by Watkins' unexpected request, but the administration later sent the material to Congress.

Even though Watkins did not run for reelection until 1958, four years after the Senate's censure of McCarthy, die-hard McCarthy supporters coalesced behind the independent candidacy of former Governor Bracken Lee to defeat Watkins by a narrow margin. Eisenhower subsequently appointed Watkins chief commissioner of the Indian Claims Committee. Years later, in his published account of his role in the McCarthy era—entitled *Enough Rope* (1969)—Watkins claimed that his defeat by Lee led him to adopt a "quieter, more healthful" lifestyle, and undoubtedly added years to his life.

## Watkins v. United States (1957)

John Watkins was a UNITED AUTO WORKERS (UAW) executive who had been cited for contempt of Congress for refusing to answer questions before the HOUSE COMMITTEE ON UN-AMERICAN ACTIVITIES (HUAC). Watkins told the committee that he was not a Communist, although he acknowledged that he had collaborated with Communists in the past to achieve the UAW's objectives. When the committee asked him to name those Communists, Watkins refused to discuss anyone who was not, as far as he knew, currently a Communist. The committee subsequently cited him for contempt.

Chief Justice Earl WARREN wrote the majority opinion for the U.S. Supreme Court in overturning Watkins' conviction in 1957. The Court's decision was actually based upon relatively narrow grounds; the committee, it charged, had failed to make clear to Watkins the "pertinacy" of its questions. As Justice Felix Frankfurther later explained, "The witness should have been given a chance to see the relevance. The burden is on the committee to show it." All members of the Court, save Justice Tom CLARK, concurred in this part of Warren's opinion.

Warren, however, went beyond this argument in announcing the Court's decision. The chief justice also put forth his belief that Congress, and by extension its committees, did not possess unlimited investigative powers. "There is no congressional power to expose for the sake of exposure," Warren wrote. Without a valid legislative function, a congressional committee lacked sanction for its actions.

Clearly the ruling struck at the wide-ranging investigations conducted by HUAC and Senator Joseph MCCARTHY's PERMANENT SUBCOMMITTEE ON INVESTIGATIONS of the Senate GOVERNMENT OPERATIONS COMMITTEE. On reading Warren's opinion, one outraged conservative member of Congress exclaimed that the Watkins decision represented a greater Soviet victory than any they had achieved "on any battlefield since World War II."

## Wayne, John (1907–1979)

As a three-time president of the Motion Picture Alliance for the Preservation of American Ideals (MPAPAI), an organization established in 1944 to combat Communist influence in the motion picture industry, John Wayne (born Marion Morrison) was one of Hollywood's most indefatigable anti-Communist crusaders. Even before the HOUSE COMMITTEE ON UN-AMERICAN ACTIVITIES began its investigation into subversives in the motion picture industry, Wayne and his fellow Hollywood conservatives—including actors Adolphe MENJOU and Ward Bond—had urged the major studios to clean house and rid themselves of Communists and Marxist sympathizers.

In September 1950, Wayne publicly pledged the MPAPAI's assistance in the fight to help "rouse Southern California and the film colony to the grim and present danger of our times." "There are now," Wayne warned, "a tight group of Communist conspirators in our midst, treasonably obeying the dictates of a foreign tyranny." At the eighth annual meeting of the Alliance in March 1951, Wayne told an enthusiastic audience of 1,000 film actors, writers, and technicians that the recent procession of former left-wing actors and writers who were renouncing Communism without providing the House committee with the names of their former associates should be regarded with a healthy skepticism. "Let no one say that a Communist can be tolerated in American society and particularly in our industry," noted Wayne. "We do not want to associate with traitors. We want patriotism and justice. We hate no one. We hope those who have changed their view will cooperate to the fullest extent. By that I mean names and places, so that they can come back to the fellowship of loyal Americans."

Wayne also played starring roles in several movies with anti-Communist themes, including *Big Jim McClain,* based on HUAC investigator William Wheeler's experiences in battling Communism in Hawaii, and *Jet Pilot,* in which Wayne played an American intelligence officer who flew to the USSR with Soviet defector Janet Leigh, obtained secret information, and fled back to the United States with Soviet MIGs in hot pursuit.

### *The Way We Were* (1973)

A hit movie that deals in part with the era of the BLACKLIST in Hollywood, *The Way We Were* starred Robert Redford as a nonpolitical college student who fell in love with a Communist student activist played by Barbra Streisand (with frizzy hair). When the movie opens in the late 1930s, Streisand is attempting (with the help of James Woods) to organize a peace strike on campus, undoubtedly as a result of the new Moscow line that emerged in the aftermath of the NAZI-SOVIET PACT. Redford at first scoffs at the intensity of Streisand's political commitment but eventually falls in love with her, despite the fact that she never seems to know when to stop spouting proletarian propaganda. Once the United States is dragged into the war as an ally of the Soviet Union, the two find that their politics have become sufficiently compatible to enable them to get married.

When the movie resumes in the late 1940s, Redford has become a successful screenwriter in Hollywood; Streisand has a less-glamorous job reading screenplays and writing plot synopses for the studios. Soon the threat of hearings by the HOUSE COMMITTEE ON UN-AMERICAN ACTIVITIES (HUAC) into Communist influence in Hollywood infringes upon the happiness of the couple and their friends, and the movie spends several scenes depicting the movie community's debate over whether it would be more noble to defy the committee or to testify and name the names of past radical political associates. Much like the COMMITTEE FOR THE FIRST AMENDMENT in 1947, Streisand and her radical friends travel to Washington to organize a protest of the HOLLYWOOD TEN hearings. Upon her return to Los Angeles, Redford goes to the train station to pick up Streisand and becomes involved in a fistfight with an angry anti-Communist zealot.

Redford, meanwhile, becomes outraged when a studio alters his script to remove any possible hint of left-wing propaganda. He soon becomes disillusioned with both the HUAC reactionary crusaders and the ex-Communists who want to use the hearings to make a political point about political repression in the United States. "People," he shouts at Streisand, "are more important than any goddamn witch-hunt." Redford ends by leaving Streisand shortly after their first child is born. In the last scene of the movie, they encounter each other years later and reminisce about the happy times they had and "the way they were" before the McCarthy era.

### Welch, Joseph Nye (1890–1960)

An attorney who confronted Senator Joseph MCCARTHY directly on national television at the height of McCarthy's power, Joseph Nye Welch was largely unkown to the American people prior to his involvement in the ARMY-MCCARTHY HEARINGS in the spring of 1954.

Born in Primghar, Iowa, on October 22, 1890, Welch worked his way through Grinnell College, graduating in 1914 with a bachelor's degree and a scholarship to Harvard Law School. By the time he completed his studies at Harvard in 1917, the United States had entered World War I. Welch enlisted in the Army and was assigned to Officer Training School, but the war ended before he received his commission as a second lieutenant.

Upon his return to civilian life, Welch was admitted to the Massachusetts bar and the following year (1919) joined the prestigious Boston law firm of Hale & Dorr, becoming a partner in 1923. In the next three decades, Welch established a reputation within the legal profession as one of the top civil-trial attorneys in the nation. Known especially for his thorough and meticulous preparation of cases, he was often called upon for consultation by other law firms.

On April 2, 1954, the Army announced that it had appointed Welch special counsel to handle its case in hearings before the Senate PERMA-

NENT SUBCOMMITTEE ON INVESTIGATIONS. During the preceding six months, Senator McCarthy had accused the Army of harboring Communist infiltrators. The Army countered with charges that McCarthy and his chief aide, Roy COHN, had pressured military officials to obtain preferential treatment for Private G. David SCHINE, a close associate of Cohn's who had been drafted in the summer of 1953. In accepting the appointment as special counsel, Welch claimed that he had never been active in partisan political affairs and that he had formed no opinion either for or against Senator McCarthy. "I am a registered Republican and a trial lawyer," he told reporters. "I'm just for facts." Initially, Welch intended to bring two associates from Hale & Dorr—Frederick J. Fisher, Jr., and James D. St. Clair—to Washington as his assistants. Upon learning, however, that Fisher had belonged to the NATIONAL LAWYERS GUILD in the 1930s, Welch decided not to expose him to the publicity that would attend the hearings. Instead, Fisher remained in Boston, while Welch and St. Clair proceeded to Washington.

When the Army-McCarthy Hearings opened amid intense public excitement on April 22, a national television audience received its first glimpse of Joseph Welch. Tall, stoop-shouldered, and slightly portly, the sixty-three-year-old Welch displayed a dry wit and avuncular disposition that contrasted sharply with McCarthy's aggressive, blustering image. *The New York Times* described Welch as "a happy leprechaun," while other observers compared him to a character out of a Charles Dickens novel. Sitting through hours of testimony with his chin resting on his hand, invariably clad in a three-piece suit and bow tie (he later acknowledged that he owned more than 150 bow ties), Welch initially appeared somewhat bemused by the proceedings, as if he could not quite believe the drama of human frailty that was unfolding before his eyes. But as time went on, viewers learned to expect the sharp rejoinders and pointed questions that lurked just beneath Welch's folksy charm and gentlemanly demeanor.

Welch delighted especially in needling McCarthy. Part of his strategy during the hearings was to anger McCarthy to make the senator lose his temper and commit a tactical blunder that Welch could use to discredit McCarthy. He scored his first major victory on the fourth day of testimony, when he revealed that a piece of evidence submitted by McCarthy and Cohn, a photograph of Secretary of the Army Robert T. STEVENS smiling at Private Schine, had been altered to remove a third individual standing between Stevens and Schine. No one would admit to tampering with the picture. In questioning one of McCarthy's investigators about the origin of the doctored photo, Welch asked if he thought the picture had been delivered by "a pixie." McCarthy immediately jumped into the fray, asking Welch to define for him what a pixie was. Without missing a beat, Welch replied, "Yes. I should say, Mr. Senator, that a pixie is a close relative of a fairy." Since rumors about the precise nature of the relationship between Cohn and Schine had been swirling around Washington for months, Welch's remark stung McCarthy and left the senator waiting for an opportunity to even the score.

To counter McCarthy's charges that Secretary Stevens had impeded investigations into alleged Communist sympathizers at FORT MONMOUTH, New Jersey, Welch produced documents on May 4 demonstrating Stevens' cooperative attitude. In response, McCarthy immediately pulled out a two-and-a-half-page letter that he claimed was a note from FBI Director J. Edgar HOOVER to an Army general, alerting him to security problems at a number of military laboratories as early as 1951. McCarthy insisted that Stevens had done nothing about the situation since that time. Welch asked that Hoover verify the contents of the letter, and the following day, an FBI official testified that McCarthy's document was actually a retyped, abridged copy of Hoover's original 15-page note. Again, Welch had demonstrated that someone on McCarthy's staff had altered evidence to suit the senator's purpose. Furthermore, the act of retyping any part of an FBI document that bore the notation "Personal and Confidential" was a palpable violation of security regulations.

When McCarthy took the witness stand to defend his use of the controversial document, he adamantly refused to tell Welch from whom he had obtained the letter. Welch reminded the senator that he had taken an oath to tell "the truth, the whole truth, and nothing but the truth." Still, McCarthy refused to divulge his source. Welch asked if McCarthy had adopted "some mental reservation, some Fifth- or Sixth-Amendment notion that you could measure what you would tell?" Angrily, McCarthy swore that he never took the Fifth Amendment (which he had frequently characterized as the last refuge of accused traitors) and that he had no reservation about telling the whole truth. "Thank you, sir," Welch said politely. "Then tell us who delivered the document to you." Again McCarthy refused.

By the middle of May, Welch had so angered McCarthy that the senator delivered a lengthy diatribe accusing the special counsel, whom he termed a "clever little lawyer" (actually, Welch stood 6'3" tall), of trying to turn the hearings into a farce, to prevent a full-scale investigation of Communist influence in the Army. The climactic confrontation between the two men occurred on June 9, the thirtieth day of the hearings, during Welch's persistent cross-examination of Roy Cohn. Again and again, Welch pressed Cohn to explain precisely how he and Schine had conducted their inquiries into reports of disloyalty in Army bases in the United States and abroad. Although Cohn held up reasonably well against Welch's questions, McCarthy was growing visibly upset. Finally, McCarthy interrupted Welch's questions with a speech of his own. Without looking directly at Welch, McCarthy announced on national television that he had obtained evidence that revealed that an associate in Welch's law firm of Hale & Dorr—namely, Frederick J. Fisher, Jr.—had belonged to the National Lawyers Guild, which, according

to McCarthy, had been identified as "the legal bulwark of the COMMUNIST PARTY."

McCarthy's outburst violated a private agreement that Cohn and Welch had negotiated two days earlier: Welch had promised not to ask Cohn about his military record (Cohn had failed the physical entrance exam at West Point) in return for a pledge to keep Fisher's name out of the hearings. McCarthy had accepted that agreement, but now the senator had broken the bargain by naming Fisher as a former member of the guild in an apparent attempt to settle a personal score with Welch.

While McCarthy continued to press his point, Welch sat disconsolately nearby, holding his head in his hands. When he finally composed himself sufficiently to reply, Welch spoke with a measure of sadness and weariness in his voice. "Until this moment, Senator," he said, "I think I never really gauged your cruelty or your recklessness." Welch acknowledged that he had known that Fisher had belonged to the National Lawyers Guild and that this former association was the reason he had decided to leave Fisher in Boston in the first place. He then proceeded to inform McCarthy that Fisher currently served as secretary of his local chapter of the Young Republicans League and appeared to have a brilliant future as an attorney at Hale & Dorr. "It is, I regret to say, equally true that I fear he shall always bear a scar needlessly inflicted by you," continued Welch. "If it were in my power to forgive you for your reckless cruelty, I would do so. I like to think I am a gentle man, but your forgiveness will have to come from someone other than me." When McCarthy attempted to resume his attack, Welch cut him off. "Let us not assassinate this lad further, Senator. You have done enough. Have you no sense of decency, sir, at long last? Have you left no sense of decency?"

A long moment of silence followed. Then the spectators in the hearing room rose to their feet and burst into applause, and reporters rushed out the door to telephone the story to their editors In the hallway outside, photographers snapped pictures of a clearly distraught Welch wiping tears from his eyes. Inside, McCarthy turned to an onlooker and raised his hands, asking, "What did I do?" The incident marked a turning point in the senator's fortunes. Although members of the Republican Party had begun to desert McCarthy in the previous weeks, the televised spectacle of the hearings had provided the public with an intimate and ultimately disturbing glimpse into McCarthy's method of operations. At the conclusion of the hearings, President EISENHOWER invited Welch to the White House to congratulate him personally.

The Army-McCarthy Hearings made Welch a national celebrity. He was invited to appear on numerous television shows, and film director Otto Preminger cast him as a trial judge in the 1959 movie *Anatomy of a Murder*. Welch said he accepted Preminger's offer because "all my life I've wanted to be a judge. When I was a younger man, I never attracted enough attention to be appointed. Now I'm 68, and this is about as close as I'll come." Critics generally admired his dramatic performance in the role. On October 6, 1960, Joseph Welch died of a heart attack in Cape Cod Hospital at Hyannis, Massachusetts.

**White, Harry Dexter** (1892–1948) A brilliant economist and high-ranking Treasury Department official during the Roosevelt and Truman administrations, Harry Dexter White was accused by Congressional investigators of aiding the careers of Communist espionage agents in the federal civil service.

Born in Boston, White entered the business world immediately upon graduating from high school. Not until he returned from service in the U.S. Army in World War I did he complete his undergraduate education, receiving a B.A. degree from Stanford University in 1924 and an M.A. the following year. White then served as an instructor in economics at Harvard University and Lawrence College (Wisconsin) before resuming his graduate studies at Harvard, where he received a Ph.D. in 1935.

In 1934, White entered government service as director of monetary research, a newly created position in the Treasury Department. He subsequently became one of the nation's leading experts in international financial affairs, and advanced to the position of assistant secretary of the Treasury. During World War II, White fashioned proposals for global currency stabilization that were later incorporated in the World Bank and the Bretton Woods Monetary Plan of 1944; looking toward the place of Germany in postwar Europe, he also contributed significantly to the development of the Morgenthau Plan, which recommended, inter alia, that the cause of European stability would best be served if Germany were dismembered after the war and substantial portions of the region devoted to agriculture rather than industry.

In 1946, President Harry S. TRUMAN named White executive director of the International Monetary Fund. By that time, the FEDERAL BUREAU OF INVESTIGATION (FBI) was pursuing leads that seemed to indicate that White was closely associated with several federal government officials whom the bureau claimed were part of a Soviet espionage ring. The issue became public at the end of July 1948 when self-proclaimed former Communist spy Elizabeth BENTLEY told the HOUSE COMMITTEE ON UN-AMERICAN ACTIVITIES (HUAC) that White—whom Bentley admitted she had never met—was part of an "elite" Communist cell in Washington. According to Bentley, White had used his influence as assistant secretary to promote COMMUNIST PARTY members and sympathizers to influential positions within the government bureaucracy. Bentley's charges thus made White the highest-ranking federal employee ever implicated in a Communist espionage plot.

White immediately denied Bentley's accusations and branded her statement before the committee "the most fantastic thing I ever heard of." He appeared before HUAC himself to refute the allegations and to defend the reputations of others implicated by Bentley. Suffering from a serious heart condition, White asked the committee for frequent rests during his testimony; Chairman J. Parnell THOMAS granted White's request, albeit with ill grace and a snide comment that "for a person who had a severe heart condition, you certainly play a lot of sports." White answered all the committee's questions, refusing—unlike others named by Bentley—to take refuge in the Fifth Amendment. He swore that he was not and never had been a Communist and that he never had committed any disloyal act.

Less than two weeks later, on August 16, 1948, White died of a heart attack at his farm in New Hampshire. It was not clear how much his appearance before HUAC had precipitated the fatal attack, although former Vice President Henry WALLACE commented bitterly that White, a close personal friend, died "a victim of the Un-American Activities committee."

After White's death, ex-Communist Whittaker CHAMBERS also identified him as a member of a wartime Soviet spy ring. It seemed clear that White had, in fact, advanced the careers of certain individuals who later came under suspicion for espionage, although no evidence other than the testimony of Bentley and Chambers was ever produced to directly implicate White in any breach of security.

The case of Harry Dexter White outlived White himself. Conservative Republicans in Congress denounced President Truman for failing to remove White—indeed, for promoting him—after the FBI had uncovered evidence that appeared to cast doubts upon his loyalty. In 1953, Herbert BROWNELL, attorney general in the administration of President Dwight David EISENHOWER, briefly revived the White case by threatening to launch an inquiry into the affair. For Brownell, the case was a means of establishing the Eisenhower administration's anti-Communist credentials and preempting a challenge from Senator Joseph MCCARTHY of Wisconsin.

Brownell considered issuing a subpoena to former President Truman to testify before Congress, but Truman replied scornfully that he would ignore any subpoena, and Brownell subsequently abandoned the proposed investigation.

## Williams, Edward Bennett (1920–1989)

When Senator Joseph MCCARTHY selected Edward Bennett Williams to defend him against a lawsuit filed by columnist Drew PEARSON, Williams was a young Washington attorney just starting his own practice. Pearson filed suit against McCarthy in December 1950 for assault—the senator had punched Pearson at a Washington night club—and defamation of character. As Williams negotiated a settlement with Pearson's attorneys, he agreed to represent McCarthy in another libel action in 1952; this time, McCarthy himself was suing another member of the U.S. Senate, William BENTON of Connecticut, for uncomplimentary remarks Benton had made about McCarthy. McCarthy withdrew the action two years later.

Meanwhile, Williams also represented several witnesses in their appearances before the HOUSE COMMITTEE ON UN-AMERICAN ACTIVITIES (HUAC). All of Williams' clients whom he accompanied to HUAC hearings provided the committee with the names of former associates in left-wing political activities; none of them pleaded the Fifth Amendment. Because Williams was representing witnesses in HUAC's inquiry at the same time he was defending Senator McCarthy, then the most prominent anti-Communist crusader in the nation, some contemporary observers criticized him for playing both sides of the issue.

McCarthy asked Williams to serve as his counsel at the ARMY-MCCARTHY HEARINGS as well, but Williams refused. It was clear, Williams later recalled, that McCarthy "just wanted me to carry his briefcase and that he wanted to run the hearings himself." Williams did, however, meet with McCarthy privately at night during the hearings to provide the senator with advice.

McCarthy's behavior in the Army-McCarthy Hearings and in hearings and debates in the Senate led his critics within Congress to introduce a resolution censuring him for his conduct. On August 2, 1954, the Senate voted to refer the question of disciplining McCarthy to a six-member committee that would make recommendations to the entire Senate. Again McCarthy asked Williams to defend him, and Williams agreed on the condition that McCarthy give him complete control of the case. In fact, Williams instructed McCarthy to remain silent during the committee's hearings, except when he was testifying. Because the evidence appeared to be solidly against McCarthy, Williams focused his defense on procedural matters. He argued that the committee lacked legal authority to investigate McCarthy's behavior; that a member of Congress could not be censured for actions in a previous session of Congress; and that McCarthy, in calling for government employees to provide him with evidence of subversion, was only doing what other congressional internal security committees had already done. Senator Arthur WATKINS, who was chairing the hearings, rejected all of Williams' arguments.

Near the end of the hearings, when it became apparent that the committee would vote to recommend censure, Williams tried to arrange a compromise. Instead of censuring McCarthy, Williams suggested, the Senate would only note that it did not "condone" McCarthy's behavior. Refusing to concede anything to his critics, McCarthy sabotaged the compromise. Accordingly, the Senate voted in December 1954 to censure McCarthy.

Williams remained friends with McCarthy for the remaining few years of the senator's life. He represented McCarthy in an Internal Revenue Service audit and finally concluded a settlement of the Pearson case in 1956.

## Winant, John G. (1889–1947)   A moderate Republican statesman, John Winant was one of the first casualties of the anti-Communist crusade in the United States in the late 1940s.

A graduate of St. Paul's School in Concord, New Hampshire, Winant majored in American history and politics at Princeton University, where he studied under future president Woodrow Wilson, then a history professor at Princeton. Winant obtained an M.A. from Princeton in 1915 and an LL.D. from the University of New Hampshire in 1916. He was elected to the New Hampshire House of Representatives in 1917, but enlisted in the American Expeditionary Force later that year following the entry of the United State into World War I. At the end of the conflict, he was discharged as a captain in command of an air observation squadron.

Winant returned to politics, winning election to the New Hampshire State Senate in 1921 and the state House of Representatives in 1923. Two years later, he served his first term as Governor of New Hampshire. During the Great Depression, Winant served two additional two-year terms as governor, from 1931 to 1935. Unlike many of his Republican colleagues across the nation, Winant supported much of President Franklin D. Roosevelt's New Deal legislation designed to expand the authority of the federal government in the nation's economy, including the controversial National Recovery Administration. Winant also proposed his own social- and labor-reform measures on the state level, notably a minimum-wage law, the creation of a state planning board, a state relief bill, and assistance to dependent children.

In 1941, Roosevelt appointed Winant as U.S. ambassador to Great Britain, replacing Joseph P. Kennedy. Winant remained in that post throughout World War II; during the latter years of the war he also served as the U.S. representative on the European Supervisory Council. In March 1946, President Harry S. TRUMAN named Winant permanent U.S. representative to the United Nations Economic and Social Council (UNESCO).

Early in 1947, Winant came under attack from conservative Republicans in Congress for allegedly conspiring to allow Soviet troops into

Berlin in the closing days of the war before American or British troops could arrive in the German capital. Questions based solely on suspicion and conjecture were raised as to Winant's loyalty. On November 3, 1947—two weeks after he delivered a speech promoting political and social freedom at a conference sponsored by the New York *Herald Tribune*—John Winant committed suicide at his home in Concord, New Hampshire.

**Wood, John Stephen** (1885–1968)   Chairman of the HOUSE COMMITTEE ON UN-AMERICAN ACTIVITIES (HUAC) from 1945 to 1947 and 1949 to 1951, John Wood was born in Cherokee County, Georgia. As one of fourteen children in a family living in one of the poorest agricultural regions of the state, Wood was forced to work his way through college as a factory hand and teacher. Shortly after he received his LL.B. from Mercer University, the United States entered World War I; Wood put aside his private law practice to serve as a lieutenant in the U.S. Army Air Force. Following the war, Wood won election to the Georgia House of Representatives and was subsequently appointed judge of the Blue Ridge Judicial Circuit Court of Appeals.

In 1931, Wood was elected to the U.S. House of Representatives for the first time, defeating the dean of the state's congressional delegation. He supported most of President Franklin Delano Roosevelt's New Deal initiatives, although he balked at federal civil-rights legislation. Wood resigned from Congress in 1935 to resume his private law practice but ran again and won election in 1945. Not surprisingly, considering the fact that Wood's district was one of the most isolated congressional districts in the nation, he exhibited a xenophobic attitude toward many of the Truman administration's diplomatic initiatives in the postwar period; he opposed, for example, legislation allowing the State Department to establish a foreign student exchange program. In the 1945–47 session of Congress,

Wood also introduced legislation to regulate subversive propaganda in the United States.

When Representative Edward J. Hart of New Jersey resigned as chairman of HUAC in July 1945, Wood assumed the leadership of the committee. Unlike previous committee chairman Martin DIES, Wood displayed no love for the publicity spotlight. A gentle, decent man who seemed more comfortable in the well-ordered environment of a courtroom than in the hurly-burly of national politics, Wood refrained from taking a leading role in the questioning of witnesses. Upon his accession to the chairmanship of HUAC, he promised to make "no attempt at either 'whitewashing' or witch-hunting," and declared that "in my book all Americans are good ones until they are proved otherwise." Wood's passivity, however, allowed Congressman John RANKIN, the second highest-ranking Democrat on the committee, to usurp the leadership of the anti-Communist crusade in the House temporarily.

During Wood's first term as chairman of HUAC, the committee initiated investigations into the activities of the JOINT ANTI-FASCIST REFUGEE COMMITTEE and the radio news-broadcast industry; the latter inquiry prompted Wood to introduce a bill designed to control news commentators and radio stations. (The bill was opposed by the Truman administration and the Federal Communications Commission and failed to pass the House.) After the Republican Party captured control of the House of Representatives in the 1946 elections, Wood retained his membership on HUAC, though he rarely attended the committee's investigative sessions. He became chairman once again in 1949 when the Democrats regained control of Congress. Much to the relief of observers who had grown disgusted with the flamboyant theatrics of Republican Representative J. Parnell THOMAS, who had served as chairman during the interim, Wood declared that he would abolish the more sensational aspects of HUAC's hearings. He also promised to provide Dr. Edward U. CONDON, director of the National Bureau of Standards, with a hearing into the charges of disloyalty that had been made against him.

During 1949, Wood introduced legislation which made it a criminal offense for any government employee or any individual "employed in connection with any national defense contract" to belong to the COMMUNIST PARTY or contribute to the party or any other subversive group. On June 8, 1949, Wood announced that as a result of charges made by a group of anti-Communist zealots known as the National Sons of the American Revolution, HUAC had dispatched letters to more than seventy colleges, high schools, and state boards of education, requesting them to supply lists of textbooks used. The purpose of the inquiry, according to Wood, was to determine whether any textbooks were written from a Communist perspective.

Although Wood—who apparently took this action on his own initiative, without clearing it with his fellow Committee members—claimed that he had no idea that anyone would object to such an inquiry, his letters provoked a storm of criticism from educators and members of his own committee. Wood was subsequently forced to issue a disclaimer explaining that "no investigation" of academic institutions was intended and that it was "of no concern to the committee if the Communist Manifesto or any other book or document containing the tenets of communism is being studied for comparative purposes in our educational institutions."

A private man who released few details about his personal life, Wood announced his resignation from Congress in 1952 and spent the last sixteen years of his life in retirement.

# Y

**Yalta Conference** In February 1945, President Franklin Delano Roosevelt, British Prime Minister Winston Churchill, and Soviet dictator Joseph STALIN met at Yalta in the Crimean peninsula of the USSR to discuss the future of Eastern Europe. Yalta was the last of the Allied summit conferences of World War II; by this time, German resistance was crumbling along both the Western and Eastern fronts, and it was clear that the final collapse of the Nazi regime was only a matter of time.

Given the huge losses suffered by the Red Army along the Eastern front during the war, it was not surprising that Stalin already had decided to turn Eastern Europe into a Soviet sphere of influence in an attempt to prevent another German invasion of the USSR in the future. Roosevelt realized that the U.S.' ability to influence the postwar settlement in Eastern Europe was therefore quite limited. Nevertheless, the President sought to bind Stalin by persuading him to sign a statement of principles known as the Declaration on Liberated Europe. Under this agreement, often referred to as the Yalta Charter, the United States, Britain, and the USSR pledged themselves to assist the former Nazi satellite regimes in Europe "to solve by democratic means their pressing political and economic problems" and to acknowledge "the right of all people to choose the form of government under which they will live."

At least one of Roosevelt's advisers, Harry Hopkins, was convinced that Stalin fully intended to carry out this pledge. "We really believed," wrote Hopkins later, "that this was the dawn of a new day. . . . We were *absolutely certain* that we had won the first great victory of the peace. . . . The Russians had proved that they could be reasonable and farseeing and *there wasn't any doubt* in the minds of the President or any of us that we could live with them and get along with them peacefully for as far into the future as any of us could imagine."

Armed with the Yalta Charter and anxious to obtain Soviet assistance in the war against Japan, Roosevelt refused to press Stalin further over the future of Poland and the rest of Eastern Europe. Within a year, it had become clear that the Soviet Union had no intention of honoring the Yalta Charter. The subsequent establishment of Soviet satellite regimes in Eastern Europe infuriated American conservatives as well as Americans of Eastern European heritage and made *Yalta* a code word for the betrayal of freedom during the McCarthy era. Nearly a decade later, several of Roosevelt's advisers at Yalta (notably Charles BOHLEN and Alger HISS) found themselves under attack by Senator Joseph MCCARTHY and his right-wing allies for their role at the conference.

**_Yates v. United States_** In *Yates v. United States* (1957), the U.S. Supreme Court ruled that an individual could not be punished solely for the abstract advocacy of the overthrow of the government by force in the absence of actual incitement or recruitment toward that end. It therefore modified an earlier ruling of the Court in a similar case, in *DENNIS V. UNITED STATES*.

The Yates case originated in the U.S. District Court for the Southern District of California in 1951, with the conviction of fourteen members of the COMMUNIST PARTY OF THE UNITED STATES OF AMERICA (CPUSA) for violations of the SMITH ACT. Each defendant was sentenced to five years' imprisonment and fined $10,000. The motive behind the prosecution clearly appeared to be the elimination of the Communist Party as an active and effective force in American society.

Specifically, the government charged the defendants with a single count of conspiring to advocate and teach the duty of overthrowing the government by force as speedily as circumstances would permit and with organizing a society of persons (the CPUSA) who so advo-

The Big Three (from left, Winston Churchill, Franklin D. Roosevelt, and Joseph Stalin) at the Yalta Conference in February, 1945.

cated and taught. The indictment further claimed that in carrying out their conspiracy, the defendants had (1) become members of the Communist Party and assumed leadership in carrying out its policies; (2) caused units of the party to be organized in California and elsewhere; (3) written and published in party organs such as the *DAILY WORKER* articles on the proscribed teachings; (4) conducted schools in the indoctrination of party members in the proscribed teachings; and (5) recruited new party members, particularly among employees of key industries of the United States.

Although the U.S. Court of Appeals upheld the verdict, the Supreme Court overturned the ruling and ordered the lower court to throw out the convictions of five of the defendants and provide new trials for the other nine. In the majority opinion, delivered on June 17, 1957— a date that became known among conservative critics of the Court as "Red Monday" because three separate anti-Communist cases were reversed—Justice John Harlan explained that the defendants had not "organized" the CPUSA in 1951; the party had been organized in 1945, and by 1951 the three-year statute of limitations against such organization had expired. More significant for future cases was Harlan's unequivocal statement that the advocacy of doctrines alone was not sufficient for conviction:

The legislative history of the Smith Act and related bills shows beyond all question that Congress was aware of the distinction between the advocacy or teaching of abstract doctrine and the advocacy or teaching of action, and that it did not intend to disregard it. The statute was aimed at the advocacy and teaching of concrete action for the forcible overthrow of the Government, and not of principles divorced from action.

In a strongly worded concurring opinion, Justice Hugo Black, joined by Justice William Douglas, noted that the defendants had, in essence, been tried and convicted on a charge "that they believe in and want to foist upon this country a different and to us a despicable form of authoritarian government in which voices criticizing the existing order are summarily silenced. I fear that the present type of prosecutions are more in line with the philosophy of authoritarian government than with that expressed by our First Amendment."

It was the Court's decision in *Yates v. United States* that led President Dwight David EISENHOWER, who believed the Supreme Court had gone too far in protecting the rights of Communists, to complain that his appointment of Earl Warren to be chief justice was "the biggest damn fool thing I ever did."

Following the Yates decision, prosecutors found it virtually impossible to obtain convictions under the Smith Act. Eighty-one outstanding indictments of Communists were dismissed. After 1957, only one Communist went to prison in the United States for his or her political activities.

# Z

**Zwicker, Ralph W.** See ARMY-MCCARTHY HEARINGS.

# Chronology

## 1919
**August:** Formation of Communist Party of the United States of America
**September:** American Legion founded by World War I veterans
**November:** Attorney General Palmer names J. Edgar Hoover to head antiradical General Intelligence Division of Department of Justice

## 1928
**July–September:** Sixth World Congress of Communist International in Moscow urges hard line against capitalist democracies.

## 1933
**March:** Franklin Delano Roosevelt inaugurated as President of United States; start of New Deal
**July:** John Howard Lawson elected first president of Screen Writers' Guild

## 1935
**July–August:** Seventh World Congress of Communist International in Moscow urges co-operation with Western democracies as part of a Popular Front against fascism
**October:** Formation of Congress of Industrial Organizations (CIO)

## 1938
**June 7:** Congress establishes House Committee on Un-American Activities (HUAC)

## 1939
**August 23:** Representatives of Germany and Soviet Union sign Nazi-Soviet Pact, destroying Popular Front
**September:** Whittaker Chambers informs Assistant Secretary of State Adolf Berle of the presence of Communist sympathizers in the federal government

## 1940
**June 28:** Smith Act (Alien Registration Act) signed into law.

## 1941
**June 22:** Germany invades Soviet Union
**December 7:** Japan attacks U.S. Navy at Pearl Harbor

## 1944
**February:** Hollywood conservatives found the Motion Picture Alliance for the Preservation of American Ideals
**June 6:** Allies begin invasion of Europe with landings at Normandy

## 1945
**February:** Yalta Conference to determine postwar settlement for Eastern Europe
**April 12:** Death of Franklin Roosevelt; Harry S. Truman assumes presidency
**May 8:** V-E Day; surrender of Germany
**June 6:** Arrest of six suspects in *Amerasia* case
**July:** Communist Party of the United States readopts hard line versus capitalism and expels Earl Browder
**August 13:** V-J Day; surrender of Japan

**August:** Elizabeth Bentley testifies to FBI about Soviet espionage

**September:** Igor Gouzenko defects from Soviet consultate in Canada, and makes allegations of Soviet espionage in the United States

## 1946

**November:** Congressional elections return substantial Republican majority to both U.S. Senate and House of Representatives; newly elected members include Joseph McCarthy and Richard Nixon

**November:** Louis Budenz testifies before HUAC

## 1947

**January:** Formation of Americans for Democratic Action

**January:** J. Parnell Thomas assumes chairmanship of HUAC

**March:** Ronald Reagan elected president of Screen Actors Guild

**March 22:** Truman issues Executive Order 9835, creating first loyalty program for federal employees

**June 18:** Congress passes Taft-Hartley Act over Truman's veto, requiring labor union officials to sign affidavits swearing they are not Communists

**September:** Formation of the Committee for the First Amendment

**October 27–30:** HUAC holds hearings in Washington on Communist influence in motion picture industry; Hollywood Ten refuse to testify

**November:** Attorney General releases list of purportedly subversive groups

**December 3:** Waldorf Statement issued by motion picture studio executives

## 1948

**April–May:** Hollywood Ten convicted of contempt of Congress

**July:** Elizabeth Bentley testifies before HUAC

**July 20:** Twelve leaders of Communist Party of the United States arrested

**August:** Whittaker Chambers and Alger Hiss testify before HUAC

**November:** President Truman wins reelection

**December 2:** Whittaker Chambers leads HUAC investigators to stolen government documents hidden in pumpkin field

**December 15:** Alger Hiss indicted for perjury

## 1949

**January:** Trial of twelve Communist Party leaders begins in District Court

**March 4:** Justice Department employee Judith Coplon arrested on charges of espionage

**July:** Alger Hiss trial ends in hung jury

**August:** Communist forces under Mao Zedong assume control of mainland China

**August:** U.S. Department of State issues China White Paper

**August:** Soviet Union explodes its first nuclear device

**November:** National convention of CIO under leadership of Walter Reuther and Philip Murray expels Communist-led unions, including United Electrical Workers

**December:** Nationalist Chinese leader Chiang Kai-shek flees to Formosa

## 1950

**January 21:** Alger Hiss convicted of perjury

**February 2:** Klaus Fuchs arrested in Great Britain on charges of espionage

**February 9:** Joseph McCarthy delivers speech in Wheeling, West Virginia, charging that the Truman administration includes Communists and Communist sympathizers in influential positions

**March 1:** Klaus Fuchs sentenced to fourteen years in prison

**March 8:** Senate committee under chairmanship of Millard Tydings begins inquiry into McCarthy's charges of Communists in the federal government

**April 10:** U.S. Supreme Court refuses to review the cases of the Hollywood Ten

**May 23:** Harry Gold arrested on charges of espionage

**June 1:**  Senator Margaret Chase Smith issues Declaration of Conscience

**June 8:**  William Remington indicted for perjury

**June 15:**  David Greenglass, brother-in-law of Julius Rosenberg, confesses to charges of espionage and identifies Rosenberg as accomplice

**June 22:**  First issue of *Red Channels* published

**June 25:**  North Korea launches massive military attack against South Korea

**July 14:**  Tydings Committee issues majority report condemning McCarthy's charges as "a fraud."

**July 17:**  FBI agents arrest Julius Rosenberg on charges of espionage

**September:**  Director Edward Dmytryk issues statement from prison declaring he was not a member of the Communist Party

**September 22:**  Congress passes Internal Security Act over veto of President Truman, requiring registration of Communist organizations

**November:**  Richard Nixon elected to U.S. Senate

**1951**

**March 6:**  Trial of Julius and Ethel Rosenberg begins

**April  5:** Julius and Ethel Rosenberg sentenced to death

**April  28:**  Truman issues Executive Order 10241

**June 4:**  U. S. Supreme Court upholds convictions of Communist Party officials in *Dennis v. U.S.*

**July:**  Senate Internal Security Subcommittee commences hearings on Institute for Pacific Relations

**December 13:**  John Stewart Service dismissed from U.S. State Department

**1952**

**May 21:**  Lillian Hellman testifies before HUAC

**November 1:**  United States detonates first thermonuclear device

**November:**  Dwight David Eisenhower defeats Adlai Stevenson in presidential election; Joseph McCarthy reelected to U.S. Senate

**November 13:**  Death of Abraham Feller

**December:**  Owen Lattimore indicted for perjury

**1953:**

**January:**  Joseph McCarthy assumes chairmanship of Senate Committee on Government Operations

**January:**  Secretary of State John Foster Dulles demands resignation of John Carter Vincent

**February:**  Eisenhower nominates Charles Bohlen as ambassador to Soviet Union

**March:**  Death of Joseph Stalin

**April 27:**  Eisenhower administration issues Executive Order 10450

**June 14:**  President Eisenhower delivers commencement speech at Dartmouth College, condemning censorship and "book burners"

**June 19:**  Execution of Julius and Ethel Rosenberg

**July 27:**  Armistice ends Korean War

**September:**  *I Led Three Lives* debuts on network television

**1954**

**March 9:**  Edward R. Murrow attacks McCarthy on television program, *See It Now*

**April:**  Army-McCarthy hearings begin

**May 7:**  Dien Bien Phu falls to Vietnamese rebels

**June 9:**  Confrontation between McCarthy and Joseph Welch over political associations of Frederick J. Fisher

**June 29:**  Atomic Energy Commission revokes security clearance of J. Robert Oppenheimer

**July 16:**  Senator Ralph Flanders introduces resolution of censure against Senator McCarthy

**August 2:**  Senate establishes select committee, chaired by Arthur Watkins, to investigate charges against McCarthy

**August 19:**  Communist Control Act establishes Subversive Activities Control Board

**December 2:**  U.S. Senate approves resolution of censure against McCarthy

## 1956
**April:**   U.S. Supreme Court reverses conviction of Communist Party official Steven Nelson (*Nelson v. U.S.*)

## 1957
**May 2:**   Death of Senator Joseph McCarthy
**June 17:**   U.S. Supreme Court reverses conviction of fourteen Communist Party officials under Smith Act (*Yates v. U.S.*) and warns it will tolerate no abuses of congressional investigative powers (*Watkins v. U.S.*)

## 1960
**January:**   Otto Preminger announces he has hired formerly blacklisted screenwriter Dalton Trumbo to write script for *Exodus*
**November:**   John F. Kennedy defeats Richard Nixon in U.S. presidential election

# Bibliography

Readers who desire to conduct further research in the McCarthy era may wish to consult the following volumes.

Acheson, Dean. *Present at the Creation.* New York: W. W. Norton & Co., 1969.

Adams, John G. *Without Precedent: The Story of the Decline of McCarthyism.* New York: W. W. Norton & Company, 1983.

Ambrose, Stephen. *Eisenhower: The President.* New York: Simon and Schuster, 1984.

Anderson, Jack, and Ronald W. May. *McCarthy: The Man, the Senator, the "Ism"* Boston: Beacon Press, 1952.

Bayley, Edwin R. *Joe McCarthy and the Press.* Madison: University of Wisconsin Press, 1981.

Bentley, Eric, ed. *Thirty Years of Treason: Excerpts from Hearings before the House Committee on Un-American Activities, 1938–1968.* New York: Viking Press, 1971.

Branyan, Robert L., and L. H. Larsen, eds. *The Eisenhower Administration 1953–1961: A Documentary History.* New York: Random House, 1971.

Broadwater, Jeff. *Eisenhower and the Anti-Communist Crusade.* Chapel Hill: University of North Carolina Press, 1992.

Buckley, William F., et al. *The Committee and Its Critics.* New York: G. P. Putnam's Sons, 1962.

Caridi, Ronald J. *The Korean War and American Politics.* Philadelphia: University of Pennsylvania Press, 1968.

Carr, Robert K. *The House Committee on Un-American Activities, 1945–1950.* Ithaca, N.Y.: Cornell University Press, 1952.

Caute, David. *The Great Fear.* New York: Simon and Schuster, 1978.

Ceplair, Larry, and Steven Englund. *The Inquisition in Hollywood.* Garden City, NY: Doubleday, 1980.

Cohn, Roy. *McCarthy.* New York: New American Library, 1968.

Cook, Fred J. *The Nightmare Decade.* New York: Random House, 1971.

Crosby, Donald F., S.J. *God, Church, and Flag: Senator Joseph R. McCarthy and the Catholic Church, 1950–1957.* Chapel Hill: University of North Carolina Press, 1978.

Donner, Frank. *The Age of Surveillance.* New York: Knopf, 1981.

Draper, Theodore. *The Roots of American Communism.* New York: Viking, 1957.

Eisele, Albert. *Almost to the Presidency.* Blue Earth, Minn.: The Piper Company, 1972.

Flynn, John T. *The Lattimore Story.* New York: Devin-Adair, 1953.

Freeland, Richard. *The Truman Doctrine and the Origins of McCarthyism.* New York: Knopf, 1971.

Fried, Richard. *Men Against McCarthy.* New York: Columbia University Press, 1976.

———. *Nightmare in Red: The McCarthy Era in Perspective.* New York: Oxford University Press, 1990.

Gelhorn, Walter. *Security, Loyalty, and Science.* Ithaca, N.Y.: Cornell University Press, 1950.

Gellermann, William. *Martin Dies.* New York: John Day Co., 1944.

Goldstein, Alvin H. *The Unquiet Death of Julius and Ethel Rosenberg.* New York: Lawrence Hill and Co., 1975.

Goodman, Walter. *The Committee.* New York: Farrar, Straus and Giroux, 1968.

Griffith, Robert. *The Politics of Fear.* Amherst: University of Massachusetts Press, 1970.

Guttmann, Allen, and Benjamin M. Ziegler, eds. *Communism, the Courts and the Constitution.* Lexington, Ky.: D.C. Heath & Co., 1964.

Hiss, Alger. *Recollections of a Life.* New York: Henry Holt, 1988.

Hoopes, Townsend. *The Devil and John Foster Dulles.* Boston: Little Brown and Company, 1973.

Kahn, E.J. *The China Hands.* New York: Viking, 1975.

Kahn, Gordon. *Hollywood on Trial*. New York: Boni & Garr, 1948.

Keeran, Roger. *The Communist Party and the Auto Workers Unions*. Bloomington: University of Indiana Press, 1980.

Klehr, Harvey, and John E. Haynes. *The American Communist Movement*. Boston: Twayne, 1992.

Landis, Mark. *Joseph McCarthy*. Cranbury, NJ: Associated University Presses, 1987.

Latham, Earl. *The Communist Controversy in Washington*. Cambridge, MA: Harvard University Press, 1966.

Lattimore, Owen. *Ordeal by Slander*. Boston: Little, Brown and Co., 1950.

Levenstein, Harvey. *Communism, Anticommunism, and the CIO*. Westport, Conn.: Greenwood Press, 1981.

Matusow, Allen J., ed. *Joseph R. McCarthy*. Englewood Cliffs, NJ: Prentice-Hall, Inc., 1970.

May, Gary. *China Scapegoat: The Diplomatic Ordeal of John Carter Vincent*. Washington, D.C.: New Republic Books, 1979.

McCullough, David. *Truman*. New York: Simon and Schuster, 1992.

Navasky, Victor S. *Naming Names*. New York: Viking Press, 1980.

O'Reilly, Kenneth. *Hoover and the Un-Americans: The FBI, HUAC, and the Red Menace*. Philadelphia: Temple University Press, 1983.

Oshinsky, David. *A Conspiracy So Immense*. New York: Free Press, 1983.

Powers, Richard Gid. *Secrecy and Power: The Life of J. Edgar Hoover*. New York: Free Press, 1987.

Radosh, Ronald, and Joyce Milton. *The Rosenberg File*. New York: Holt, Rinehart and Winston, 1983.

Reeves, Thomas C. *The Life and Times of Joe McCarthy*. New York: Stein and Day, 1982.

Rogin, Michael P. *The Intellectuals and McCarthy*. Cambridge, Mass.: MIT Press, 1967.

Schrecker, Ellen. *The Age of McCarthyism*. New York: St. Martin's Press, 1994.

Smith, John Chabot. *Alger Hiss: The True Story*. New York: Holt, Rinehart and Winston, 1976.

Smith, Margaret Chase, with William C. Lewis, Jr. *Declaration of Conscience*. Garden City, N.Y.: Doubleday, 1972.

Steinberg, Peter L. *The Great 'Red Menace.'* Westport, Conn.: Greenwood Press, 1984.

Stern, Philip M. *The Oppenheimer Case: Security on Trial*. New York: Harper & Row, 1969.

Stripling, Robert. *The Red Plot Against America*. New York: Arno Press, 1977.

Theoharis, Athan G. *Seeds of Repression: Harry S. Truman and the Origins of McCarthyism*. Chicago: Quadrangle, 1971.

Thomas, Lately. *When Even Angels Wept*. New York: William Morrow & Company, 1973.

Von Hoffman, Nicholas. *Citizen Cohn*. New York: Doubleday, 1988.

Watkins, Arthur V. *Enough Rope*. Englewood Cliffs: Prentice-Hall, Inc., 1969.

Weinstein, Allan. *Perjury: The Hiss-Chambers Case*. New York: Knopf, 1978.

Wexley, John. *The Judgment of Julius and Ethel Rosenberg*. New York: Cameron & Kahn, 1955.

Weyl, Nathaniel. *The Battle Against Disloyalty*. New York: Thomas Y. Crowell Company, 1951.

# Appendix I: Executive Order 9835
# March 21, 1947

**PART I—INVESTIGATION OF APPLICANTS**

1. There shall be a loyalty investigation of every person entering the civilian employment of any department or agency of the executive branch of the Federal Government
   a. Investigations of persons entering the competitive service shall be conducted by the Civil Service Commission, except in such cases as are covered by a special agreement between the Commission and any given department or agency.
   b. Investigations of persons other than those entering the competitive service shall be conducted by the employing department or agency. Departments and agencies without investigative organizations shall utilize the investigative facilities of the Civil Service Commission.
2. The investigations of persons entering the employ of the executive branch may be conducted after any such person enters upon actual employment therein, but in any such case the appointment of such person shall be conditioned upon a favorable determination with respect to his loyalty. . . .
3. An investigation shall be made of all applicants at all available pertinent sources of information and shall include reference to:
   a. Federal Bureau of Investigation files.
   b. Civil Service Commission files.
   c. Military and naval intelligence files.
   d. The files of any other appropriate government investigative or intelligence agency.
   e. House Committee on Un-American Activities files.
   f. Local law-enforcement files at the place of residence and employment of the applicant, including municipal, county, and State law-enforcement files.
   g. Schools and colleges attended by applicant.
   h. Former employers of applicant.
   i. References given by applicant.
   j. Any other appropriate source.
4. Whenever derogatory information with respect to loyalty of an applicant is revealed a full field investigation shall be conducted. A full field investigation shall also be conducted of those applicants, or of applicants for particular positions, as may be designated by the head of the employing department or agency, such designations to be based on the determination by any such head of the best interests of national security. . . .

**PART II—INVESTIGATION OF EMPLOYEES**

   a. An officer or employee who is charged with being disloyal shall have a right to an administrative hearing before a loyalty board in the employing department or agency. He may appear before such board personally, accompanied by counsel or representative of his own choosing, and present evidence on his own behalf, through witnesses or by affidavit.
   b. The officer or employee shall be served with a written notice of such hearing in sufficient time, and shall be informed therein of the nature of the charges against him in sufficient detail, so that he will be enabled to prepare his defense. The charges shall be stated as specifically and completely as, in the discretion of the employing department or agency, security considerations permit. . . .
3. A recommendation of removal by a loyalty board shall be subject to appeal by the officer or employee affected, prior to his removal, to the head of the employing department or agency or to such person or persons as may be designated by such head, under such regulations as may be prescribed by him, and the decision of the department or

agency concerned shall be subject to appeal to the Civil Service Commission's Loyalty Review Board, hereinafter provided for, for an advisory recommendation. . . .

## PART III—RESPONSIBILITIES OF CIVIL SERVICE COMMISSION

1. There shall be established in the Civil Service Commission a Loyalty Review Board of not less than three impartial persons, the members of which shall be officers or employees of the Commission. . . .
3. The Loyalty Review Board shall currently be furnished by the Department of Justice the name of each foreign or domestic organization, association, movement, group or combination of persons which the Attorney General, after appropriate investigation and determination, designates as totalitarian, fascist, communist or subversive, or as having adopted a policy of advocating or approving the commission of acts of force or violence to deny others their rights under the Constitution of the United States, or as seeking to alter the form of government of the United States by unconstitutional means.
   a. The Loyalty Review Board shall disseminate such information to all departments and agencies.

## PART IV—SECURITY MEASURES IN INVESTIGATIONS

1. At the request of the head of any department or agency of the executive branch an investigative agency shall make available to such head, personally, all investigative material and information collected by the investigative agency concerning any employee or prospective employee of the requesting department or agency, or shall make such material and information available to any officer or officers designated by such head and approved by the investigative agency.
2. Notwithstanding the foregoing requirement, however, the investigative agency may refuse to disclose the names of confidential informants, provided it furnishes sufficient information about such informants on the basis of which the requesting department or agency can make an adequate evaluation of the information furnished by them and provided it advises the requesting department or agency in writing that it is essential to the protection of the informants or to the investigation of other cases that the identity of the informants not be revealed. Investigative agencies shall not use this discretion to decline to reveal sources of information where such action is not essential.

3. Each department and agency of the executive branch should develop and maintain, for the collection and analysis of information relating to the loyalty of its employees and prospective employees, a staff specially trained in security techniques, and an effective security control system for protecting such information generally and for protecting confidential sources of such information particularly.

## PART V—STANDARDS

1. The standard for the refusal of employment or the removal from employment in an executive department or agency on grounds relating to loyalty shall be that, on all the evidence, reasonable grounds exist for belief that the person involved is disloyal to the Government of the United States.
2. Activities and associations of an applicant or employee which may be considered in connection with the determination of disloyalty may include one or more of the following:
   a. Sabotage, espionage, or attempts or preparations therefor, or knowingly associating with spies or saboteurs;
   b. Treason or sedition or advocacy thereof;
   c. Advocacy of revolution or force or violence to alter the constitutional form of government of the United States;
   d. Intentional, unauthorized disclosure to any person, under circumstances which may indicate disloyalty to the United States, of documents or information of a confidential or nonpublic character obtained by the person making the disclosure as a result of his employment by the Government of the United States;
   e. Performing or attempting to perform his duties, or otherwise acting so as to serve the interests of another government in preference to the interests of the United States;
   f. Membership in, affiliation with or sympathetic association with any foreign or domestic organization, association, movement, group or combination of persons, designated by the Attorney General as totalitanan, fascist, communist, or subversive, or as having adopted a policy of advocating or approving the commission of acts of force or violence to deny other persons their rights under the Constitution of the United States, or as seeking to alter the form of government of the United States by unconstitutional means.

## PART VI—MISCELLANEOUS

1. Each department and agency of the executive branch, to the extent that it has not already done

so, shall submit to the Federal Bureau of Investigation of the Department of Justice, either directly or through the Civil Service Commission, the names (and such other necessary identifying material as the Federal Bureau of Investigation may require) of all of its incumbent employees.

a. The Federal Bureau of Investigation shall check such names against its records of persons concerning whom there is substantial evidence of being within the purview of paragraph 2 of Part V hereof, and shall notify each department and agency of such information.

b. Upon receipt of the above-mentioned information from the Federal Bureau of Investigation, each department and agency shall make, or cause to be made by the Civil Service Commission, such investigation of those employees as the head of the department or agency shall deem advisable. . . .

# Appendix II: Testimony before HUAC

*J. Edgar Hoover*

. . . The aims and responsibilities of the House Committee on Un-American Activities and the Federal Bureau of Investigation are the same—the protection of the internal security of this Nation. The methods whereby this goal may be accomplished differ, however. I have always felt that the greatest contribution this committee could make is the public disclosure of the forces that menace America—Communist and Fascist. . . . This committee renders a distinct service when it publicly reveals the diabolic machinations of sinister figures engaged in un-American activities. . . .

The Communist movement in the United States began to manifest itself in 1919. Since then it has changed its name and its party line whenever expedient and tactical. But always it comes back to fundamentals and bills itself as the party of Marxism-Leninism. As such, it stands for the destruction of our American form of government; it stands for the destruction of American democracy; it stands for the destruction of free enterprise; and it stands for the creation of a "Soviet of the United States" and ultimate world revolution.

The historic mission: The preamble of the latest constitution of the Communist Party of the United States, filled with Marxian "double talk" proclaims that the party "educates the working class, in the course of its day-to-day struggles, for its historic mission, the establishment of socialism."

The phrase "historic mission" has a sinister meaning. To the uninformed person it bespeaks tradition, but to the Communist, using his own words, it is "achieving the dictatorship of the proletariat"; "to throw off the yoke of imperialism and establish the proletarian dictatorship"; "to raise these revolutionary forces to the surface and hurl them like a devastating avalanche upon the united forces of bourgeois reaction, frenzied at the presentment of their rapidly approaching doom."

In recent years, the Communists have been very cautious about using such phrases as "force and violence"; nevertheless, it is the subject of much discussion in their schools and in party caucus where they readily admit that the only way in which they can defeat the present ruling class is by world revolution.

The Communist, once he is fully trained and indoctrinated, realizes that he can create his order in the United States only by "bloody revolution."

Their chief textbook, *The History of the Communist Party of the Soviet Union*, is used as a basis for planning their revolution. Their tactics require that to be successful they must have:

1. The will and sympathy of the people.
2. Military aid and assistance.
3. Plenty of guns and ammunition.
4. A program for extermination of the police as they are the most important enemy and are termed "trained Fascists."
5. Seizure of all communications, buses, railroads, radio stations, and other forms of communications and transportation.

They evade the question of force and violence publicly. They hold that when Marxists speak of force and violence they will not be responsible—that force and violence will be the responsibility of their enemies. They adopt the novel premise that they do not advocate force and violence publicly but that when their class resists to defend themselves then they are thus accused of using force and violence. A lot of double talk. . . .

. . . The American Communist, like the leopard, cannot change his spots.

The party line: The Communist Party line changes from day to day. The one cardinal rule that can always be applied to what the party line is or will be is found in the fundamental principle of Communist teachings that the support of Soviet Russia is the duty of Communists of all countries.

One thing is certain. The American progress which

all good citizens seek, such as old-age security, houses for veterans, child assistance, and a host of others is being adopted as window dressing by the Communists to conceal their true aims and entrap gullible followers. . . .

The numerical strength of the party's enrolled membership is insignificant. But it is well known that there are many actual members who because of their position are not carried on party rolls.

. . . The *Daily Worker* boasts of 74,000 members on the rolls.

What is important is the claim of the Communists themselves that for every party member there are 10 others ready, willing, and able to do the party's work. Herein lies the greatest menace of communism. For these are the people who infiltrate and corrupt various spheres of American life. So rather than the size of the Communist Party, the way to weigh its true importance is by testing its influence, its ability to infiltrate.

The size of the party is relatively unimportant because of the enthusiasm and iron-clad discipline under which they operate. In this connection, it might be of interest to observe that in 1917 when the Communists overthrew the Russian Government there was one Communist for every 2,277 persons in Russia. In the United States today there is one Communist for every 1,814 persons in the country.

One who accepts the aims, principles, and program of the party, who attends meetings, who reads the party press and literature, who pays dues, and who is active on behalf of the party "shall be considered a member." The open, avowed Communist who carries a card and pays dues is no different from a security standpoint than the person who does the party's work but pays no dues, carries no card, and is not on the party rolls. In fact, the latter is a greater menace because of his opportunity to work in stealth.

Identifying undercover Communists, fellow travelers, and sympathizers: The burden of proof is placed upon those who consistently follow the ever-changing, twisting party line. Fellow travelers and sympathizers can deny party membership but they can never escape the undeniable fact that they have played into the Communist hands thus furthering the Communist cause by playing the role of innocent, gullible, or willful allies. . . .

The Communist propaganda technique is designed to promote emotional response with the hope that the victim will be attracted by what he is told the Communist way of life holds in store for him. The objective, of course, is to develop discontent and hasten the day when the Communists can gather sufficient support and following to overthrow the American way of life.

Communist propaganda is always slanted in the hope that the Communist may be alined [*sic*] with liberal progressive causes. The honest liberal and progressive should be alert to this, and I believe the Communists' most effective foes can be the real liberals and progressives who understand their devious machinations.

The deceptiveness of the Communist "double talk" fulfills the useful propaganda technique of confusion. In fact, Lenin referred to their peculiar brand of phraseology as ". . . that cursed Assopian [*sic*] language . . . which . . . compelled all revolutionaries to have recourse, whenever they took up their pens to write a legal work."

Lenin used it for the purpose of avoiding "censorship." Communists today use it to mislead the public.

The use of the term "democracy" by the Communists, we have learned to our sorrow, does not have the meaning to them that it does to us. To them it means communism and totalitarianism and our understanding of the term is regarded by them as imperialistic and Fascist. . . .

Motion pictures: The American Communists launched a furtive attack on Hollywood in 1935 by the issuance of a directive calling for a concentration in Hollywood. The orders called for action on two fronts. (1) An effort to infiltrate the labor unions; (2) infiltrate the so-called intellectual and creative fields. . . .

. . . The entire industry faces serious embarrassment because it could become a springboard for Communist activities. Communist activity in Hollywood is effective and is furthered by Communists and sympathizers using the prestige of prominent persons to serve, often unwittingly, the Communist cause.

The party is content and highly pleased if it is possible to have inserted in a picture a line, a scene, a sequence, conveying the Communist lesson, and more particularly, if they can keep out anti-Communist lessons.

Infiltration: The Communist tactic of infiltrating labor unions stems from the earliest teachings of Marx, which have been reiterated by party spokesmen down through the years. They resort to all means to gain their point and often succeed in penetrating and literally taking over labor unions before the rank and file of members are aware of what has occurred.

With few exceptions the following admonitions of Lenin have been followed:

It is necessary to be able to withstand all this, to agree to any and every sacrifice, and even—if need be—to resort to all sorts of devices, maneuvers, and illegal methods, to evasion and subterfuge, in order to penetrate into the trade-unions, to remain in them, and to carry on Communist work in them at all costs. (p. 38, Left-Wing Communism, an Infantile Disorder. V. I. Lenin, 1934, International Publishers Co., Inc.)

I am convinced that the great masses of union men and women are patriotic American citizens interested chiefly in security for their families and themselves. They have no use for the American Communists but in those instances where Communists have taken control of unions, it has been because too many union men and women have been outwitted, outmaneuvered, and outwaited by Communists.

The Communists have never relied on numerical strength to dominate a labor organization. Through infiltration tactics they have in too many instances captured positions of authority. Communists have boasted that with 5 percent of the membership the Communists with their military, superior organizational ability and discipline could control the union. . . .

If more union members took a more active role and asserted themselves it would become increasingly difficult for Communists to gain control. Patriotic union members can easily spot sympathizers and party members in conventions and union meetings because invariably the latter strive to establish the party line instead of serving the best interests of the union and the country. . . .

Government: The recent Canadian spy trials revealed the necessity of alertness in keeping Communists and sympathizers out of Government services. . . .

Since July 1, 1941, the FBI has investigated 6,193 cases under the Hatch Act, which forbids membership upon the part of any Government employee in any organization advocating the overthrow of the government of the United States. . . .

One hundred and one Federal employees were discharged as a result of our investigation, 21 resigned during the investigation, and in 75 cases administrative action was taken by the departments. A total of 1,906 individuals are no longer employed by the Government while 122 cases are presently pending consideration in various Government agencies.

The FBI does not make recommendations; it merely reports facts, and it is up to the interested Government department to make a decision. Almost invariably, of course, subjects of investigations deny affiliation with subversive groups, often despite strong evidence to the contrary. . . .

Mass and front organizations: . . . The Communist Party in the United States immediately took up the [united front] program and a systematic plan was worked out of infiltrating existing organizations with Communists. . . .

. . . Front organizations . . . solicited and used names of prominent persons. Literally hundreds of groups and organizations have either been infiltrated or organized primarily to accomplish the purposes of promoting the interests of the Soviet Union in the United States, the promotion of Soviet war and peace aims, the exploitation of Negroes in the United States, work among foreign-language groups, and to secure a favorable viewpoint toward the Communists in domestic, political, social, and economic issues.

The first requisite for front organizations is an idealistic sounding title. Hundreds of such organizations have come into being and have gone out of existence when their true purposes have become known or exposed while others with high-sounding names are continually springing up. . . .

The Communist Party of the United States is a fifth column if there ever was one. It is far better organized than were the Nazis in occupied countries prior to their capitulation.

They are seeking to weaken America just as they did in their era of obstruction when they were alined [sic] with the Nazis. Their goal is the overthrow of our Government.

There is no doubt as to where a real Communist's loyalty rests. Their allegiance is to Russia, not the United States. . . .

. . . What can we do? And what should be our course of action? The best antidote to communism is vigorous, intelligent, old-fashioned Americanism with eternal vigilance. I do not favor any course of action which would give the Communists cause to portray and pity themselves as martyrs. I do favor unrelenting prosecution wherever they are found to be violating our country's laws.

As Americans, our most effective defense is a workable democracy that guarantees and preserves our cherished freedoms.

I would have no fears if more Americans possessed the zeal, the fervor, the persistence, and the industry to learn about this menace of Red fascism I do fear for the liberal and progressive who has been hoodwinked and duped into joining hands with the Communists. I confess to a real apprehension so long as Communists are able to secure ministers of the gospel to promote their evil work and espouse a cause that is alien to the religion of Christ and Judaism. I do fear so long as school boards and parents tolerate conditions whereby Communists and fellow travelers, under the guise of academic freedom, can teach our youth a way of life that eventually will destroy the sanctity of the home, that undermine[s] faith in God, that causes them to scorn respect for constituted authority and sabotage our revered Constitution.

I do fear so long as American labor groups are infiltrated, dominated, or saturated with the virus of communism. I do fear the palliation and weasel-worded gestures against communism indulged in by some of our labor leaders who should know better but who have become pawns in the hands of sinister but astute manipulations for the Communist cause.

I fear for ignorance on the part of all our people who may take the poisonous pills of Communist propaganda. . . .

The Communists have been, still are, and always will be a menace to freedom, to democratic ideals, to the worship of God, and to America's way of life.

I feel that once public opinion is thoroughly aroused as it is today, the fight against communism is well on its way. Victory will be assured once Communists are identified and exposed, because the public will take the first step of quarantining them so they can do no harm. Communism, in reality, is not a political party. It is a way of life—an evil and malignant way of life. It reveals a condition akin to disease that spreads like an epidemic and like an epidemic a quarantine is necessary to keep it from infecting the Nation.

OCTOBER 23, 1947:

### Ronald Reagan

The Committee met at 10:30 A.M., the Honorable J. Parnell Thomas (Chairman) presiding.

THE CHAIRMAN: The record will show that Mr. McDowell, Mr. Vail, Mr. Nixon, and Mr. Thomas are present. A Subcommittee is sitting.

Staff members present: Mr. Robert E. Stripling, Chief Investigator; Messrs. Louis J. Russell, H. A. Smith, and Robert B. Gaston, Investigators; and Mr. Benjamin Mandel, Director of Research.

MR. STRIPLING: When and where were you born, Mr. Reagan?

MR. REAGAN: Tampico, Illinois, February 6, 1911.

MR. STRIPLING: What is your present occupation?

MR. REAGAN: Motion-picture actor.

MR. STRIPLING: How long have you been engaged in that profession?

MR. REAGAN: Since June 1937, with a brief interlude of three and a half years—that at the time didn't seem very brief.

MR. STRIPLING: What period was that?

MR. REAGAN: That was during the late war.

MR. STRIPLING: What branch of the service were you in?

MR. REAGAN: Well, sir, I had been for several years in the Reserve as an officer in the United States Cavalry, but I was assigned to the Air Corps.

MR. STRIPLING: That is kind of typical of the Army, isn't it?

MR. REAGAN: Yes, sir. The first thing the Air Corps did was loan me to the Signal Corps.

MR. McDOWELL: You didn't wear spurs?

MR. REAGAN: I did for a short while.

THE CHAIRMAN: I think this has little to do with the facts we are seeking. Proceed.

MR. STRIPLING: Mr. Reagan, are you a member of any guild?

MR. REAGAN: Yes, sir, the Screen Actors Guild.

MR. STRIPLING: How long have you been a member?

MR. REAGAN: Since June 1937.

MR. STRIPLING: Are you the president of the guild at the present time?

MR. REAGAN: Yes, sir.

MR. STRIPLING: When were you elected?

MR. REAGAN: That was several months ago. I was elected to replace Mr. [Robert] Montgomery when he resigned.

MR. STRIPLING: When does your term expire?

MR. REAGAN: The elections come up next month.

MR. STRIPLING: Have you ever held any other position in the Screen Actors Guild?

MR. REAGAN: Yes, sir. Just prior to the war I was a member of the board of directors, and just after the war, prior to my being elected president, I was a member of the board of directors.

MR. STRIPLING: As a member of the board of directors, as president of the Screen Actors Guild, and as an active member, have you at any time observed or noted within the organization a clique of either Communists or Fascists who were attempting to exert influence or pressure on the guild?

MR. REAGAN: Well, sir, my testimony must be very similar to that of Mr. [George] Murphy and Mr. [Robert] Montgomery. There has been a small group within the Screen Actors Guild which has consistently opposed the policy of the guild board and officers of the guild, as evidenced by the vote on various issues. That small clique referred to has been suspected of more or less following the tactics that we associate with the Communist Party.

MR. STRIPLING: Would you refer to them as a disruptive influence within the guild?

MR. REAGAN: I would say that at times they have attempted to be a disruptive influence.

MR. STRIPLING: You have no knowledge yourself as to whether or not any of them are members of the Communist Party?

MR. REAGAN: No, sir, I have no investigative force, or anything, and I do not know.

MR. STRIPLING: Has it ever been reported to you that certain members of the guild were Communists?

MR. REAGAN: Yes, sir, I have heard different discussions and some of them tagged as Communists.

MR. STRIPLING: Would you say that this clique has attempted to dominate the guild?

MR. REAGAN: Well, sir, by attempting to put over their own particular views on various issues, I guess you would have to say that our side was attempting to dominate, too, because we were fighting just as hard to put over our views, and I think we were proven correct by the figures—Mr. Murphy gave the figures—and those figures were always approximately the same, an average of ninety per cent or better of the Screen Actors Guild voted in favor of those matters now guild policy.

MR. STRIPLING: Mr. Reagan, there has been testimony to the effect here that numerous Communist-front organizations have been set up in Hollywood. Have you ever been solicited to join any of those organizations or any organization which you considered to be a Communist-front organization?

MR. REAGAN: Well, sir, I have received literature from an organization called the Committee for a Far-Eastern Democratic Policy. I don't know whether it is Communist or not. I only know that I didn't like their views and as a result I didn't want to have anything to do with them.

MR. STRIPLING: Were you ever solicited to sponsor the Joint Anti-Fascist Refugee Committee?

MR. REAGAN: No, sir, I was never solicited to do that, but I found myself misled into being a sponsor on another occasion for a function that was held under the auspices of the Joint Anti-Fascist Refugee Committee.

MR. STRIPLING: Did you knowingly give your name as a sponsor?

MR. REAGAN: Not knowingly. Could I explain what that occasion was?

MR. STRIPLING: Yes, sir.

MR. REAGAN: I was called several weeks ago. There happened to be a financial drive on to raise money to build a badly needed hospital called the All Nations Hospital. I think the purpose of the building is so obvious by the title that it has the support of most of the people of Los Angeles. Certainly of most of the doctors. Some time ago I was called to the telephone. A woman introduced herself by name. I didn't make any particular note of her name, and I couldn't give it now. She told me that there would be a recital held at which Paul Robeson would sing, and she said that all the money for the tickets would go to the hospital, and asked if she could use my name as one of the sponsors. I hesitated for a mo-

ment, because I don't think that Mr. Robeson's and my political views coincide at all, and then I thought I was being a little stupid because, I thought, Here is an occasion where Mr. Robeson is perhaps appearing as an artist, and certainly the object, raising money, is above any political consideration: it is a hospital supported by everyone. I have contributed money myself. So I felt a little bit as if I had been stuffy for a minute, and I said, "Certainly, you can use my name." I left town for a couple of weeks and, when I returned, I was handed a newspaper story that said that this recital was held at the Shrine Auditorium in Los Angeles under the auspices of the Joint Anti-Fascist Refugee Committee. The principal speaker was Emil Lustig [Ludwig?], Robert Burman took up a collection, and remnants of the Abraham Lincoln Brigade were paraded on the platform. I did not, in the newspaper story, see one word about the hospital. I called the newspaper and said I am not accustomed to writing to editors but would like to explain my position, and he laughed and said, "You needn't bother, you are about the fiftieth person that has called with the same idea, including most of the legitimate doctors who had also been listed as sponsors of that affair."

MR. STRIPLING: Would you say from your observation that that is typical of the tactics or strategy of the Communists, to solicit and use the names of prominent people to either raise money or gain support?

MR. REAGAN: I think it is in keeping with their tactics, yes, sir.

MR. STRIPLING: Do you think there is anything democratic about those tactics?

MR. REAGAN: I do not, sir.

MR. STRIPLING: As president of the Screen Actors Guild, you are familiar with the jurisdictional strike which has been going on in Hollywood for some time?

MR. REAGAN: Yes, sir.

MR. STRIPLING: Have you ever had any conferences with any of the labor officials regarding this strike?

MR. REAGAN: Yes, sir.

MR. STRIPLING: Do you know whether the Communists have participated in any way in this strike?

MR. REAGAN: Sir, the first time that this word "Communist" was ever injected into any of the meetings concerning the strike was at a meeting in Chicago with Mr. William Hutchinson, president of the carpenters' union, who were on strike at the time. He asked the Screen Actors Guild to submit terms to Mr. [Richard] Walsh, and he told us to tell Mr. Walsh that, if he would give in on these terms, he in turn would run this Sorrell and the other Commies out—

I am quoting him—and break it up. I might add that Mr. Walsh and Mr. Sorrell were running the strike for Mr. Hutchinson in Hollywood.

MR. STRIPLING: Mr. Reagan, what is your feeling about what steps should be taken to rid the motion-picture industry of any Communist influences?

MR. REAGAN: Well, sir, ninety-nine per cent of us are pretty well aware of what is going on, and I think, within the bounds of our democratic rights and never once stepping over the rights given us by democracy, we have done a pretty good job in our business of keeping those people's activities curtailed. After all, we must recognize them at present as a political party. On that basis we have exposed their lies when we came across them, we have opposed their propaganda, and I can certainly testify that in the case of the Screen Actors Guild we have been eminently successful in preventing them from, with their usual tactics, trying to run a majority of an organization with a well-organized minority. In opposing those people, the best thing to do is make democracy work. In the Screen Actors Guild we make it work by insuring everyone a vote and by keeping everyone informed. I believe that, as Thomas Jefferson put it, if all the American people know all of the facts they will never make a mistake. Whether the Party should be outlawed, that is a matter for the Government to decide. As a citizen, I would hesitate to see any political party outlawed on the basis of its political ideology. We have spent a hundred and seventy years in this country on the basis that democracy is strong enough to stand up and fight against the inroads of any ideology. However, if it is proven that an organization is an agent of a foreign power, or in any way not a legitimate political party—and I think the Government is capable of proving that—then that is another matter. I happen to be very proud of the industry in which I work; I happen to be very proud of the way in which we conducted the fight. I do not believe the Communists have ever at any time been able to use the motion-picture screen as a sounding board for their philosophy or ideology.

\* \* \*

MR. CHAIRMAN: There is one thing that you said that interested me very much. That was the quotation from Jefferson. That is just why this Committee was created by the House of Representatives: to acquaint the American people with the facts. Once the American people are acquainted with the facts there is no question but what the American people will do the kind of a job that they want done: that is, to make America just as pure as we can possibly make it. We want to thank you very much for coming here today.

MR. REAGAN: Sir, I detest, I abhor their philosophy, but I detest more than that their tactics, which are those of the fifth column, and are dishonest, but at the same time I never as a citizen want to see our country become urged, by either fear or resentment of this group, that we ever compromise with any of our democratic principles through that fear or resentment. I still think that democracy can do it.

OCTOBER 27, 1947:

### John Howard Lawson

The Committee met at 10:30 A.M., the Honorable J. Parnell Thomas (Chairman) presiding.

Staff members present: Mr. Robert E. Stripling, Chief Investigator; Messrs. Louis J. Russell, H. A. Smith, and Robert B. Gaston, Investigators; and Mr. Benjamin Mandel, Director of Research.

THE CHAIRMAN: The record will show that a Subcommittee is present, consisting of Mr. Vail, Mr. McDowell, and Mr. Thomas.

MR. LAWSON: Mr. Chairman, I have a statement here which I wish to make—

THE CHAIRMAN: Well, all right, let me see your statement.

(Statement* handed to the Chairman.)

THE CHAIRMAN: I don't care to read any more of the statement. The statement will not be read. I read the first line.

MR. LAWSON: You have spent one week vilifying me before the American public—

THE CHAIRMAN: Just a minute—

MR. LAWSON: —and you refuse to allow me to make a statement on my rights as an American citizen.

THE CHAIRMAN: I refuse to let you make the statement because of the first sentence. That statement is not pertinent to the inquiry. Now, this is a Congressional Committee set up by law. We must have orderly procedure, and we are going to have orderly procedure. Mr. Stripling, identify the witness.

MR. LAWSON: The rights of American citizens are important in this room here, and I intend to stand up for those rights, Congressman Thomas.

MR. STRIPLING: Mr. Lawson, will you state your full name, please?

MR. LAWSON: I wish to protest against the unwillingness of this Committee to read a statement, when you permitted Mr. Warner, Mr. Mayer, and others to read statements in this room. My name is John Howard Lawson.

MR. STRIPLING: When and where were you born?

*The statement is printed below, right after the testimony.—E. B.

MR. LAWSON: New York City.

MR. STRIPLING: What year?

MR. LAWSON: 1894.

MR. STRIPLING: Give us the exact date.

MR. LAWSON: September 25.

MR. STRIPLING: Mr. Lawson, you are here in response to a subpoena which was served upon you on September 19, 1947; is that true?

MR. LAWSON: That is correct.

MR. STRIPLING: What is your occupation, Mr. Lawson?

MR. LAWSON: I am a writer.

MR. STRIPLING: How long have you been a writer?

MR. LAWSON: All my life—at least thirty-five years—my adult life.

MR. STRIPLING: Are you a member of the Screen Writers Guild?

MR. LAWSON: The raising of any question here in regard to membership, political beliefs, or affiliation—

MR. STRIPLING: Mr. Chairman—

MR. LAWSON: —is absolutely beyond the powers of this Committee.

MR. STRIPLING: Mr. Chairman—

MR. LAWSON: But—

(*The Chairman pounding gavel.*)

MR. LAWSON: It is a matter of public record that I am a member of the Screen Writers Guild.

MR. STRIPLING: I ask—

(*Applause.*)

THE CHAIRMAN: I want to caution the people in the audience: You are the guests of this Committee and you will have to maintain order at all times. I do not care for any applause or any demonstrations of one kind or another.

MR. STRIPLING: Now, Mr. Chairman, I am also going to request that you instruct the witness to be responsive to the questions.

THE CHAIRMAN: I think the witness will be more responsive to the questions.

MR. LAWSON: Mr. Chairman, you permitted—

THE CHAIRMAN (*pounding gavel*): Never mind—

MR. LAWSON: —witnesses in this room to make answers of three or four or five hundred words to questions here.

THE CHAIRMAN: Mr. Lawson, you will please be responsive to these questions and not continue to try to disrupt these hearings.

MR. LAWSON: I am not on trial here, Mr. Chairman. This Committee is on trial here before the American people. Let us get that straight.

THE CHAIRMAN: We don't want you to be on trial.

MR. STRIPLING: Mr. Lawson, how long have you been a member of the Screen Writers Guild?

MR. LAWSON: Since it was founded in its present form, in 1933.

MR. STRIPLING: Have you ever held any office in the guild?

MR. LAWSON: The question of whether I have held office is also a question which is beyond the purview of this Committee.

(*The Chairman pounding gavel.*)

MR. LAWSON: It is an invasion of the right of association under the Bill of Rights of this country.

THE CHAIRMAN: Please be responsive to the question.

MR. LAWSON: It is also a matter—

(*The Chairman pounding gavel.*)

MR. LAWSON: —of public record—

THE CHAIRMAN: You asked to be heard. Through your attorney, you asked to be heard, and we want you to be heard. And if you don't care to be heard, then we will excuse you, and we will put the record in without your answers.

MR. LAWSON: I wish to frame my own answers to your questions, Mr. Chairman, and I intend to do so.

THE CHAIRMAN: And you will be responsive to the questions or you will be excused from the witness stand.

MR. LAWSON: I will frame my own answers, Mr. Chairman.

THE CHAIRMAN: Go ahead, Mr. Stripling.

MR. STRIPLING: I repeat the question, Mr. Lawson: Have you ever held any position in the Screen Writers Guild?

MR. LAWSON: I stated that it is outside the purview of the rights of this Committee to inquire into any form of association—

THE CHAIRMAN: The Chair will determine what is in the purview of this Committee.

MR. LAWSON: My rights as an American citizen are no less than the responsibilities of this Committee of Congress.

THE CHAIRMAN: Now, you are just making a big scene for yourself and getting all "het up." (*Laughter.*) Be responsive to the questioning, just the same as all the witnesses have. You are no different from the rest. Go ahead, Mr. Stripling.

MR. LAWSON: I am being treated differently from the rest.

THE CHAIRMAN: You are not being treated differently.

MR. LAWSON: Other witnesses have made statements, which included quotations from books, references to material which had no connection whatsoever with the interest of this Committee.

THE CHAIRMAN: We will determine whether it has connection. Now, you go ahead—

MR. LAWSON: It is absolutely beyond the power of this Committee to inquire into my association in any organization.

THE CHAIRMAN: Mr. Lawson, you will have to stop or you will leave the witness stand. And you will leave the witness stand because you are in contempt. That is why you will leave the witness stand. And if you are just trying to force me to put you in contempt, you won't have to try much harder. You know what has happened to a lot of people that have been in contempt of this Committee this year, don't you?

MR. LAWSON: I am glad you have made it perfectly clear that you are going to threaten and intimidate the witnesses, Mr. Chairman.

(The Chairman pounding gavel.)

MR. LAWSON: I am an American and I am not at all easy to intimidate, and don't think I am.

(The Chairman pounding gavel.)

MR. STRIPLING: Mr. Lawson, I repeat the question. Have you ever held any position in the Screen Writers Guild?

MR. LAWSON: I have stated that the question is illegal. But it is a matter of public record that I have held many offices in the Screen Writers Guild. I was its first president in 1933, and I have held office on the board of directors of the Screen Writers Guild at other times.

MR. STRIPLING: You have been employed in the motion-picture industry, have you not?

MR. LAWSON: I have.

MR. STRIPLING: Would you state some of the studios where you have been employed?

MR. LAWSON: Practically all of the studios, all the major studios.

MR. STRIPLING: As a screen writer?

MR. LAWSON: That is correct.

MR. STRIPLING: Would you list some of the pictures which you have written the script for?

MR. LAWSON: I must state again that you are now inquiring into the freedom of press and communications, over which you have no control whatsoever. You don't have to bring me here three thousand miles to find out what pictures I have written. The pictures that I have written are very well known. They are such pictures as *Action in the North Atlantic, Sahara,*—

MR. STRIPLING: Mr. Lawson—

MR. LAWSON: —such pictures as *Blockade,* of which I am very proud, and in which I introduced the danger that this democracy faced from the attempt to destroy democracy in Spain in 1937. These matters are all matters of public record.

MR. STRIPLING: Mr. Lawson, would you object if I read a list of the pictures, and then you can either state whether or not you did write the scripts?

MR. LAWSON: I have no objection at all.

MR. STRIPLING: Did you write *Dynamite,* by M-G-M?

MR. LAWSON: I preface my answer, again, by saying that it is outside of the province of this Committee, but it is well known that I did.

MR. STRIPLING: *The Sea Bat,* by M-G-M?

MR. LAWSON: It is well known that I did.

MR. STRIPLING: *Success at Any Price,* RKO?

MR. LAWSON: Yes, that is from a play of mine, *Success Story.*

MR. STRIPLING: *Party Wire,* Columbia?

MR. LAWSON: Yes, I did.

MR. STRIPLING: *Blockade,* United Artists, Wanger?

MR. LAWSON: That is correct.

MR. STRIPLING: *Algiers,* United Artists, Wanger?

MR. LAWSON: Correct.

MR. STRIPLING: *Earth Bound,* Twentieth Century-Fox.

MR. LAWSON: Correct.

MR. STRIPLING: *Counterattack,* Columbia.

MR. LAWSON: Correct.

MR. STRIPLING: You have probably written others, have you not, Mr. Lawson?

MR. LAWSON: Many others. You have missed a lot of them.

MR. STRIPLING: You don't care to furnish them to the Committee, do you?

MR. LAWSON: Not in the least interested.

MR. STRIPLING: Mr. Lawson, are you now or have you ever been a member of the Communist Party of the United States?

MR. LAWSON: In framing my answer to that question I must emphasize the points that I have raised before. The question of Communism is in no way related to this inquiry, which is an attempt to get control of the screen and to invade the basic rights of American citizens in all fields.

MR. MCDOWELL: Now, I must object—

MR. STRIPLING: Mr. Chairman—

(The Chairman pounding gavel.)

MR. LAWSON: The question here relates not only to the question of my membership in any political organization, but this Committee is attempting to establish the right—

(The Chairman pounding gavel.)

MR. LAWSON: —which has been historically denied to any committee of this sort, to invade the rights and privileges and immunity of American citizens, whether they be Protestant, Methodist, Jewish, or Catholic, whether they be Republicans or Democrats or anything else.

THE CHAIRMAN (*pounding gavel*): Mr. Lawson, just quiet down again. Mr. Lawson, the most pertinent question that we can ask is whether or not you have ever been a member of the Communist Party. Now, do you care to answer that question?

MR. LAWSON: You are using the old technique, which was used in Hitler Germany in order to create a scare here—

THE CHAIRMAN (*pounding gavel*): Oh—

MR. LAWSON: —in order to create an entirely false atmosphere in which this hearing is conducted—

(*The Chairman pounding gavel.*)

MR. LAWSON: —in order that you can then smear the motion-picture industry, and you can proceed to the press, to any form of communication in this country.

THE CHAIRMAN: You have learned—

MR. LAWSON: The Bill of Rights was established precisely to prevent the operation of any committee which could invade the basic rights of Americans. Now, if you want to know—

MR. STRIPLING: Mr. Chairman, the witness is not answering the question.

MR. LAWSON: If you want to know—

(*The Chairman pounding gavel.*)

MR. LAWSON: —about the perjury that has been committed here and the perjury that is planned—

THE CHAIRMAN: Mr. Lawson—

MR. LAWSON: —permit me and my attorneys to bring in here the witnesses that testified last week and permit us to cross-examine these witnesses, and we will show up the whole tissue of lies—

THE CHAIRMAN (*pounding gavel*): We are going to get the answer to that question if we have to stay here for a week. Are you a member of the Communist Party, or have you ever been a member of the Communist Party?

MR. LAWSON: It is unfortunate and tragic that I have to teach this Committee the basic principles of American—

THE CHAIRMAN (*pounding gavel*): That is not the question. That is not the question. The question is: Have you ever been a member of the Communist Party?

MR. LAWSON: I am framing my answer in the only way in which any American citizen can frame his answer to a question which absolutely invades his rights.

THE CHAIRMAN: Then you refuse to answer that question; is that correct?

MR. LAWSON: I have told you that I will offer my beliefs, affiliations, and everything else to the American public, and they will know where I stand.

THE CHAIRMAN (*pounding gavel*): Excuse the witness—

MR. LAWSON: As they do from what I have written.

THE CHAIRMAN (*pounding gavel*): Stand away from the stand—

MR. LAWSON: I have written Americanism for many years, and I shall continue to fight for the Bill of Rights, which you are trying to destroy.

THE CHAIRMAN: Officers, take this man away from the stand—

(*Applause and boos.*)*

THE CHAIRMAN (*pounding gavel*): There will be no demonstrations. No demonstrations, for or against. Everyone will please be seated. All right, go ahead, Mr. Stripling. Proceed.

MR. STRIPLING: Mr. Chairman, the Committee has made exhaustive investigation and research into the Communist affiliations of Mr. John Howard Lawson. Numerous witnesses under oath have identified Mr. Lawson as a member of the Communist Party. I have here a nine-page memorandum which details at length his affiliations with the Communist Party and its various front organizations. I now ask that Mr. Louis J. Russell, an Investigator for the Committee, take the stand.

In order to give the Committee the type of affiliations that Mr. Lawson has had with the Communist Party, I should like to refer, Mr. Chairman, to an article which appeared in the *Daily Worker,* the official organ of the Communist Party. This article is dated September 6, 1935, and appears on page 5 of the *Daily Worker.* Under the headline "Artists, writers," it says: "We cannot let the *Daily* go under—" referring to the *Daily Worker.* It says: "Need for *Daily Worker* has grown a thousand times since 1934." By John Howard Lawson. The article bears a picture of Mr. Lawson, and it appears on the front page of the *Daily Worker.* Under the *Daily Worker* heading, the following language appears: "*The Daily* Worker— central organ of the Communist Party of the United States, section of the Communist International." I have here, Mr. Chairman, another article from the *Daily Worker* by John Howard Lawson, dated February 26, 1935, page 5: "The Story of William Z. Foster, a tribute on the occasion of his fifty-fourth birthday, by John Howard Lawson." I have here, Mr. Chairman, over one hundred exhibits showing Mr. Lawson's affiliations with the party.

Your name is Louis J. Russell?

MR. RUSSELL: That is right.

MR. STRIPLING: You are a member of the investigative staff of the Committee on Un-American Activities?

MR. RUSSELL: I am.

MR. STRIPLING: You were formerly with the FBI for ten years?

* As Lawson is taken away by officers.—E. B.

MR. RUSSELL: I was.

MR. STRIPLING: Were you detailed to make an investigation as to the Communist Party affiliations of John Howard Lawson?

MR. RUSSELL: I was.

MR. STRIPLING: What did your investigation disclose?

MR. RUSSELL: We were furnished—or I was—with copies of Communist Party registration cards pertaining to certain individuals for the year 1944.

THE CHAIRMAN: Speak louder, please.

MR. RUSSELL: One of those cards bears the number 47275 and is made out in the name of John Howard Lawson, 4542 Coldwater Canyon; City, Los Angeles; County, Los Angeles; State, California. There is a notation contained on this registration card: "New card issued on December 10, 1944." Other information contained on this card, which referred to the personal description of the John Howard Lawson mentioned, on Communist Party registration No. 47275—the description is as follows: "Male, white. Occupation, writer. Industry, motion pictures. Member of CIO–A. F. of L." "Independent union or no union," "Independent union" is checked. There is a question asked on this registration card: "Is member club subscriber for *Daily Worker?*" The answer, "Yes," is checked.

MR. STRIPLING: That is all, Mr. Russell. Now, Mr. Chairman, what is the Committee's pleasure with regard to the nine-page memorandum? Do you want it read into the record or do you want it made a part of the record?

THE CHAIRMAN: The Committee wants you to read it.

MR. STRIPLING:

INFORMATION FROM THE FILES OF THE COMMITTEE ON UN-AMERICAN ACTIVITIES, UNITED STATES HOUSE OF REPRESENTATIVES,

ON THE COMMUNIST AFFILIATIONS OF JOHN HOWARD LAWSON

John Howard Lawson is a screen writer and one of the most active Communists in the Hollywood movie industry. . . .

The files of the House Committee on Un-American Activities show that—

1. Rena M. Vale, a former member of the Communist Party and a screen writer, testified before the Special Committee on Un-American Activities on July 22, 1940, that Mr. Lawson had been identified to her as a Communist Party member when she met him at a Communist Party fraction meeting. She further testified that Mr. Lawson during the meeting gave advice on inserting the Communist Party line into drama.

The State legislative committee investigating un-American activities in California has cited Mr. Lawson as "one of the most important Marxist strategists in southern California," in its 1945 report, page 118. The California report notes on the same page that Rena M. Vale also testified before the State legislative committee and that the witness identified Lawson as a member of the Communist Party fraction of the Screen Writers Guild who had given advice on the Communist Party program in the writing of the play *Sun Rises in the West.* The State legislative committee states further, in its 1947 report, page 260, that Mr. Lawson directed a Communist bloc of about sixty-five members in local 47, the Hollywood local of the American Federation of Musicians, AFL, between the years 1937 and 1940.

2. The Communist Party has been publicly defended by John Howard Lawson. The *Daily Worker,* in an article on April 16, 1947, page 2, and reprinted in the Sunday edition of April 20, 1947, page 8, announced that Mr. Lawson was one of the signers of a statement opposing any legislative attempts to restrict the activities of the Communist Party. The organization sponsoring the statement was the Civil Rights Congress, which the House Committee on Un-American Activities, in a report published September 2, 1947, declared to be "dedicated not to the broader issues of civil liberties, but specifically to the defense of individual Communists and the Communist Party." The Civil Rights Congress is now defending such persons as Gerhart Eisler, an agent of the Communist International convicted of passport fraud, and Eugene Dennis, Communist Party general secretary, convicted of contempt of Congress. The Civil Rights Congress is the successor to the International Labor Defense, former legal arm of the Communist Party, according to former Attorney General Francis Biddle. John Howard Lawson also came to the support of the Communist Party on another occasion, according to the *Daily Worker* for March 18, 1945, page 2. Mr. Lawson was listed in this issue as one of the signers of a statement hailing a War Department order allowing military commissions for Communists. Sponsor of the statement was the National Federation for Constitutional Liberties, which was cited as a Communist front organization by former Attorney General Biddle. Biddle pointed out the organization's defense of such prominent Communist leaders as Sam Darcy and Robert Wood, party secretaries for Pennsylvania and Oklahoma, respectively. The organization was

also cited as a Communist front by the Special Committee on Un-American Activities on June 25, 1942, and March 29, 1944.

3. John Howard Lawson has given his support to a number of individual Communists. The *People's World,* official west coast Communist organ, reported on October 22, 1942, page 2, that Mr. Lawson was backing Mrs. LaRue McCormick, a candidate for the California State Senate on the Communist Party ticket. Mr. Lawson was one of the signers of a statement in defense of the Comintern agent Gerhart Eisler, according to the *Daily Worker* for February 28, 1947, page 2. The organization sponsoring this statement in behalf of Eisler was the Civil Rights Congress.

The following is the "statement," which Lawson was not allowed to read into the record:

### A Statement by John Howard Lawson

For a week, this Committee has conducted an illegal and indecent trial of American citizens, whom the Committee has selected to be publicly pilloried and smeared. I am not here to defend myself, or to answer the agglomeration of falsehoods that has been heaped upon me, I believe lawyers describe this material, rather mildly, as "hearsay evidence." To the American public, it has a shorter name: dirt. Rational people don't argue with dirt. I feel like a man who has had truckloads of filth heaped upon him; I am now asked to struggle to my feet and talk while more truckloads pour more filth around my head.

No, you don't argue with dirt. But you try to find out where it comes from. And to stop the evil deluge before it buries you—and others. The immediate source is obvious. The so-called "evidence" comes from a parade of stool-pigeons, neurotics, publicity-seeking clowns, Gestapo agents, paid informers, and a few ignorant and frightened Hollywood artists. I am not going to discuss this perjured testimony. Let these people live with their consciences, with the knowledge that they have violated their country's most sacred principles.

These individuals are not important. As an individual, I am not important. The obvious fact that the Committee is trying to destroy me personally and professionally, to deprive me of my livelihood and what is far dearer to me—my honor as an American—gains significance only because it opens the way to similar destruction of any citizen whom the Committee selects for annihilation.

I am not going to touch on the gross violation of the Constitution of the United States, and especially of its First and Fifth Amendments, that is taking place here. The proof is so overwhelming that it needs no elaboration. The Un-American Activities Committee stands convicted in the court of public opinion.

I want to speak here as a writer and a citizen.

It is not surprising that writers and artists are selected for this indecent smear. Writers, artists, scientists, educators, are always the first victims of attack by those who hate democracy. The writer has a special responsibility to serve democracy, to further the free exchange of ideas. I am proud to be singled out for attack by men who are obviously—by their own admission on the record—out to stifle ideas and censor communication.

I want to speak of a writer's integrity—the integrity and professional ethics that have been so irresponsibly impugned at these hearings. In its illegal attempt to establish a political dictatorship over the motion picture industry, the Committee has tried to justify its probing into the thought and conscience of individuals on the ground that these individuals insert allegedly "subversive" lines or scenes in motion pictures. From the viewpoint of the motion picture producer, this charge is a fantasy out of the Arabian Nights. But it is also a sweeping indictment of the writer's integrity and professional conduct. When I am employed to write a motion picture, my whole purpose is to make it a vital, entertaining creative portrayal of the segment of life with which it deals. Many problems arise in writing a picture. Like all honest writers, I never write a line or develop a situation, without fully discussing its implications, its meaning, its tendency, with the men in charge of production. Where a line or a situation might relate to controversial issues, I am particularly insistent on full discussion, because such issues affect studio policy, critical response and popularity of the picture.

My political and social views are well known. My deep faith in the motion picture as a popular art is also well known. I don't "sneak ideas" into pictures. I never make a contract to write a picture unless I am convinced that it serves democracy and the interests of the American people. I will never permit what I write and think to be subject to the orders of self-appointed dictators, ambitious politicians, thought-control gestapos, or any other form of censorship this Un-American Committee may attempt to devise. My freedom to speak and write is not for sale in return for a card signed by J. Parnell Thomas saying "O.K. for employment until further notice."

Pictures written by me have been seen and approved by millions of Americans. A subpoena for me is a subpoena for all those who have enjoyed these pictures and recognized them as an honest portrayal of our American life.

Thus, my integrity as a writer is obviously an integral part of my integrity as a citizen. As a citizen I am not alone here. I am not only one of nineteen men who have been subpoenaed. I am forced to appear here as a representative of one hundred and thirty million Americans because the illegal conduct of this Committee has linked me with every citizen. If I can be destroyed no American is safe. You can subpoena a farmer in a field, a lumberjack in the woods, a worker at a machine, a doctor in his office—you can deprive them of a livelihood, deprive them of their honor as Americans.

Let no one think that this is an idle or thoughtless statement. This is the course that the Un-American Activities Committee has charted. Millions of Americans who may as yet be unconscious of what may be in store for them will find that the warning I speak today is literally fulfilled. No American will be safe if the Committee is not stopped in its illegal enterprise.

I am like most Americans in resenting interference with my conscience and belief. I am like most Americans in insisting on my right to serve my country in the way that seems to me most helpful and effective. I am like most Americans in feeling that loyalty to the United States and pride in its traditions is the guiding principle of my life. I am like most Americans in believing that divided loyalty—which is another word for treason—is the most despicable crime of which any man or woman can be accused.

It is my profound conviction that it is precisely because I hold these beliefs that I have been hailed before this illegal court. These are the beliefs that the so-called Un-American Activities Committee is seeking to root out in order to subvert orderly government and establish an autocratic dictatorship.

I am not suggesting that J. Parnell Thomas aspires to be the man on horseback. He is a petty politician, serving more powerful forces. Those forces are trying to introduce fascism in this country. They know that the only way to trick the American people into abandoning their rights and liberties is to manufacture an imaginary danger, to frighten the people into accepting repressive laws which are supposedly for their protection.

To anyone familiar with history the pattern for the seizure of dictatorial power is well known. Manufactured charges against "reds," "communists," "enemies of law and order" have been made repeatedly over the centuries. In every case, from the Star Chamber in Stuart England to the burning of the Reichstag in Nazi Germany, the charges have included everyone

with democratic sympathies; in every case the charges have been proven false; in every case, the charges have been used to cover an arbitrary seizure of power.

In the terrible wave of repression that swept England at the end of the eighteenth century, Charles James Fox asked a simple question: "We have seen and heard of revolutions in other states. Were they owing to the freedom of popular opinions? Were they owing to the facility of popular meetings? No, sir, they were owing to the reverse of these." The writers and thinkers who were jailed and silenced at that time were all cleared a few years later. The great scientist, Priestley, whose home was burned, was forced to flee to America where he was honored as an apostle of liberty. The persecutions under the Alien and Sedition Acts in our own country in 1798 were all proved to be the irresponsible means by which a reactionary political party sought to maintain itself in power. Congress officially repaid all the fines collected under the Sedition Act. The cry of sedition was again raised through the land in 1919 in order to build up the illusion of a nonexistent national emergency and thus justify wholesale violations of the Bill of Rights, designed solely to crush labor, prevent American participation in the League of Nations, and keep reaction in power.

Today, we face a serious crisis in the determination of national policy. The only way to solve that crisis is by free discussion. Americans must know the facts. The only plot against American safety is the plot to conceal facts. I am plastered with mud because I happen to be an American who expresses opinions that the House Un-American Activities Committee does not like. But my opinions are not an issue in this case. The issue is my right to have opinions. The Committee's logic is obviously: Lawson's opinions are properly subject to censorship; he writes for the motion picture industry, so the industry is properly subject to censorship; the industry makes pictures for the American people, so the minds of the people must be censored and controlled.

Why? What are J. Parnell Thomas and the Un-American interests he serves, afraid of? They're afraid of the American people. They don't want to muzzle me. They want to muzzle public opinion. They want to muzzle the great Voice of democracy. Because they're conspiring against the American way of life. They want to cut living standards, introduce an economy of poverty, wipe out labor's rights, attack Negroes, Jews, and other minorities, drive us into a disastrous and unnecessary war.

The struggle between thought-control and freedom of expression is the struggle between the people and a greedy unpatriotic minority which hates and fears the people. I wish to present as an integral part of this statement, a paper which I read at a Conference on Thought Control in the United States held in Hollywood on July 9th to 13th. The paper presents the historical background of the threatening situation that we face today, and shows that the attack on freedom of communication is, and has always been, an attack on the American people.

The American people will know how to answer that attack. They will rally, as they have always rallied, to protect their birthright.

# Appendix III: The Waldorf Statement December 3, 1947

Members of the Association of Motion Picture Producers deplore the action of the ten Hollywood men who have been cited for contempt. We do not desire to prejudge their legal rights, but their actions have been a disservice to their employers and have impaired their usefulness to the industry.

We will forthwith discharge or suspend without compensation those in (our employ and we will not re-employ any of the ten until such time as he is acquitted or has purged himself of contempt and declares under oath that he is not a Communist.

On the broader issues of alleged subversive and disloyal elements in Hollywood, our members are likewise prepared to take positive action.

We will not knowingly employ a Communist or a member of any party or group which advocates the overthrow of the Government of the United States by force or by illegal or unconstitutional methods. In pursuing this policy, we are not going to be swayed by hysteria or intimidation from any source. We are frank to recognize that such a policy involves dangers and risks. There is the danger of hurting innocent people. There is the risk of creating an atmosphere of fear. Creative work at its best cannot be carried on in an atmosphere of fear. We will guard against this danger, this risk, this fear. To this end we will invite the Hollywood talent guilds to work with us to eliminate any subversives, to protect the innocent, and to safeguard free speech and a free screen wherever threatened.

# Appendix IV: Whittaker Chambers' Statement to the FBI December 3, 1948

I, Jay David Whittaker Chambers, make the following statement to Floyd L. Jones and Daniel F. X. Callahan, whom I know to be Special Agents of the Federal Bureau of Investigation. I understand that any statement that I make can be used against me in a court of law. No threats or promises have been made to me in connection with this statement. I have been advised that I have a right of counsel, but I have waived same after consulting with my counsel in connection with the making of this statement.

I am presently a defendant in a civil action brought against me by ALGER HISS in Federal Court in Baltimore, Maryland. In connection with a pre-trial deposition being taken at the request of counsel for Mr. HISS, on November 17, 1948, I produced in evidence 65 typewritten documents and 4 small pieces of white paper on which appeared handwriting that, according to my recollection, is the handwriting of ALGER HISS. The 65 pages of documents were copies or condensations of State Department documents which were turned over to me by ALGER HISS during the latter part of 1937 and early 1938. These documents have been in the possession of NATHAN LEVINE, my wife's nephew, who now resides on Sterling Place in Brooklyn, New York. He is a lawyer and has an office on 42nd Street near Broadway, believed to be in the Newsweek Building. When I gave him these documents shortly after I broke with the Party in 1938, he was living in his mother's house at 260 Rochester Avenue, Brooklyn, New York. When I gave them to him, I asked him to hide them for me and, if anything happened to me, that he should open them and make them public. He didn't know the contents of these documents or where they came from. They were in a brown manila envelope. I got them from him on Sunday, November 14, 1948, at his mother's house in Brooklyn. They were hidden in a dumb waiter shaft in his mother's house. There were also contained in this envelope three cans of undeveloped film and two strips of developed film which I will mention later. I went to LEVINE'S house to get the small pieces of paper containing HISS' handwriting and had forgotten about the documents and the film until they were turned over to me.

Also included in this brown envelope were four yellow-lined sheets of paper in the handwriting of HARRY DEXTER WHITE. I had mentioned this handwriting in my deposition on November 17, 1948. The reason I did not introduce the three cans of film at the deposition was because it was undeveloped. I did not introduce the two strips of developed negative film was because I wanted to keep all the film together and possibly have the film developed and made readable at a later date.

I did not introduce the handwritten pages turned over to me by HARRY DEXTER WHITE on advice of counsel because they thought it was irrelevant. The handwriting of HARRY DEXTER WHITE described above has been in the possession of my attorneys since November 17, 1948, the date of the pre-trial deposition. The three cans of undeveloped film as well as the two strips of developed negative film were turned over by me to two investigators of the House Committee on Un-American Activities at my home in Westminster, Maryland, on Thursday night, December 2, 1948, in response to a subpoena presented by them to me on that date.

I have no other documents whatever of this nature now.

As far as I can recall, the undeveloped film in the cans described above contained photographs of original documents that came out of the State Department and the Bureau of Standards. The bulk of the documents from the State Department were turned over to me by ALGER HISS. Others were turned over to me possibly by JULIAN WADLEIGH. I assume that these were classified Confidential and Strictly Confidential, the same as some of the documents that I presented on November 17, 1948.

The documents that were presented by me at the deposition were copies or condensations of State Department documents. These copies were turned over to me by ALGER HISS during the latter part of 1937 and the first part of 1938 as indicated by the dates on the documents. These documents were given to me for delivery to a Colonel BYKOV, who had previously been introduced to ALGER HISS, at which time ALGER HISS agreed to furnish documents from the State Department to me for delivery to Colonel BYKOV. ALGER HISS was well aware that Colonel BYKOV was the head of a Soviet underground organization. It is possible that some of the 65 documents I presented at the deposition were photographed and copies of the photographs were turned over to Colonel BYKOV. I didn't destroy the documents because I was preparing to break with the Party in about April, 1938.

Some of the documents supplied by HISS were copied on a typewriter in ALGER HISS' home by him or his wife, and then turned over to me. In other instances, original documents from the State Department were turned over to me by ALGER HISS and taken by me in most instances to photographers to be copied, the original documents then being returned to ALGER HISS the same night to be returned by him to the State Department. . . . ALGER HISS was aware of the fact that the documents were being photographed for delivery to Colonel BYKOV. . . .

. . . Colonel BYKOV wanted to know something about the personnel in the apparatus [the Communist underground] and questioned me very closely about them. He wanted to meet some of them.

The first person that he met in the apparatus was ALGER HISS. In the spring of 1937, I arranged a meeting between ALGER HISS and Colonel BYKOV. HISS went to New York where I met him at a place somewhere near the Brooklyn Bridge. We then proceeded to a movie house quite a distance out in Brooklyn. HISS and I waited on a bench in the mezzanine of the theater, and BYKOV emerged from the audience and I introduced him to ALGER HISS. . . .

At the time of the meeting with HISS, after leaving the theater Colonel BYKOV raised the question of procuring documents from the State Department, and ALGER HISS agreed. Following the meeting, ALGER HISS began to supply a consistent flow of material from the State Department, such as the type of documents that I presented at the pre-trial deposition on November 17, 1948. I want to say that as far as I can remember, I have never discussed the existence of the documents that I presented at the pre-trial deposition with anyone. Neither have I told any Governmental agency or Government body concerning the existence of these documents. I have never discussed with anyone the procuring of any documents from Government agencies for transmittal to Colonel BYKOV.

In testifying to various Government agencies over the last ten years, I have had two purposes in mind. The first was to stop the Communist conspiracy. The second was to try to preserve the human elements involved. In this sense, I was shielding these people. For these reasons, I have not previously mentioned the procuring and passing of any documents.

I have read the above statement . . . and to the best of my knowledge and recollection, I declare it is the truth.

# Appendix V: Speech at Wheeling, West Virginia, Senator Joseph McCarthy February 9, 1950*

Six years ago, at the time of the first conference to map out the peace—Dumbarton Oaks—there was within the Soviet orbit 180,000,000 people. Lined up on the antitotalitarian side there were in the world at that time roughly 1,625,000,000 people. Today, only six years later, there are 800,000,000 people under the absolute domination of Soviet Russia—an increase of over 400 percent. On our side, the figure has shrunk to around 500,000,000. In other words, in less than six years the odds have changed from nine to one in our favor to eight to five against us. This indicates the swiftness of the tempo of Communist victories and American defeats in the cold war. As one of our outstanding historical figures once said, "When a great democracy is destroyed, it will not be because of enemies from without, but rather because of enemies from within."

The truth of this statement is becoming terrifyingly clear as we see this country each day losing on every front.

At war's end we were physically the strongest nation on earth and, at least potentially, the most powerful intellectually and morally. Ours could have been the honor of being a beacon in the desert of destruction, a shining living proof that civilization was not yet ready to destroy itself. Unfortunately, we have failed miserably and tragically to arise to the opportunity.

The reason why we find ourselves in a position of impotency is not because our only powerful potential enemy has sent men to invade our shores, but rather because of the traitorous actions of those who have been treated so well by this Nation. It has not been the less fortunate or members of minority groups who have been selling this Nation out, but rather those who have had all the benefits that the wealthiest nation on earth has had to offer—the finest homes, the finest college education, and the finest jobs in Government we can give.

This is glaringly true in the State Department. There the bright young men who are born with silver spoons in their mouths are the ones who have been worst.

Now I know it is very easy for anyone to condemn a particular bureau or department in general terms. Therefore, I would like to cite one rather unusual case—the case of a man who has done much to shape our foreign policy.

When Chiang Kai-shek was fighting our war, the State Department had in China a young man named John S. Service. His task, obviously, was not to work for the communization of China. Strangely, however, he sent official reports back to the State Department urging that we torpedo our ally Chiang Kai-shek and stating, in effect, that communism was the best hope of China.

Later, this man—John Service—was picked up by the Federal Bureau of Investigation for turning over to the Communists secret State Department information. Strangely, however, he was never prosecuted. However, Joseph Grew, the Under Secretary of State, who insisted on his prosecution, was forced to resign. Two days after Grew's successor, Dean Acheson, took over as Under Secretary of State, this man—John Service—who had been picked up by the FBI and who had previously urged that communism was the best hope of China, was not only reinstated in the State Department but promoted. And finally, under Acheson, placed in charge of all placements and promotions.

Today, ladies and gentlemen, this man Service is on his way to represent the State Department and

*The following is one version of McCarthy's speech, as entered into the *Congressional Record*. There is still controversy over the precise text of the speech as delivered.

Acheson in Calcutta—by far and away the most important listening post in the Far East. . . .

Another interesting case was that of Julian H. Wadleigh, economist in the Trade Agreements Section of the State Department for 11 years [who] was sent to Turkey and Italy and other countries as United States representative. After the statute of limitations had run so he could not be prosecuted for treason, he openly and brazenly not only admitted but proclaimed that he had been a member of the Communist Party, . . . that while working for the State Department he stole a vast number of secret documents . . . and furnished these documents to the Russian spy ring of which he was a part.

This, ladies and gentlemen, gives you somewhat of a picture of the type of individuals who have been helping to shape our foreign policy. In my opinion the State Department, which is one of the most important government departments, is thoroughly infested with Communists.

I have in my hand fifty-seven cases of individuals who would appear to be either card carrying members or certainly loyal to the Communist Party, but who nevertheless are still helping to shape our foreign policy.

One thing to remember in discussing the Communists in our Government is that we are not dealing with spies who get thirty pieces of silver to steal the blueprints of a new weapon. We are dealing with a far more sinister type of activity because it permits the enemy to guide and shape our policy. . . .

This brings us down to the case of one Alger Hiss who is important not as an individual any more, but rather because he is so representative of a group in the State Department. It is unnecessary to go over the sordid events showing how he sold out the Nation which had given him so much. Those are rather fresh in all of our minds.

However, it should be remembered that the facts in regard to his connection with this international Communist spy ring were made known to the then Under Secretary of State Berle three days after Hitler and Stalin signed the Russo-German alliance pact. . . .

Under Secretary Berle promptly contacted Dean Acheson and received word in return that Acheson (and I quote) "could vouch for Hiss absolutely"—at which time the matter was dropped. . . .

Again in 1943, the FBI had occasion to investigate the facts surrounding Hiss' contacts with the Russian spy ring. But even after that FBI report was submitted, nothing was done.

Then late in 1948—on August 5—when the Un American Activities Committee called Alger Hiss to give an accounting, President Truman at once issued a Presidential directive ordering all Government agencies to refuse to turn over any information whatsoever in regard to the Communist activities of any Government employee to a congressional committee. . . .

If time permitted, it might be well to go into detail about the fact that Hiss was Roosevelt's chief adviser at Yalta when Roosevelt was admittedly in ill health and tired physically and mentally . . . and when, according to the Secretary of State, Hiss and Gromyko drafted the report on the conference. . . .

Of the results of this conference, Arthur Bliss Lane of the State Department had this to say: "As I glanced over the document, I could not believe my eyes. To me, almost every one spoke of a surrender to Stalin."

As you hear this story of high treason, I know that you are saying to yourself, "Well, why doesn't the Congress do something about it?" Actually, ladies and gentlemen, one of the important reasons for the graft, the corruption, the dishonesty, the disloyalty, the treason in high Government positions—one of the most important reasons why this continues is a lack of moral uprising on the part of the 140,000,000 American people. . . .

As you know, very recently the Secretary of State proclaimed his loyalty to a man guilty of what has always been considered as the most abominable of all crimes—of being a traitor to the people who gave him a position of great trust. The Secretary of State in attempting to justify his continued devotion to the man who sold out the Christian world to the atheistic world, referred to Christ's Sermon on the Mount as a justification and reason therefor, and the reaction of the American people to this would have made the heart of Abraham Lincoln happy.

When this pompous diplomat in striped pants, with a phony British accent, proclaimed to the American people that Christ on the Mount endorsed communism, high treason, and betrayal of a sacred trust, the blasphemy was so great that it awakened the dormant indignation of the American people.

He has lighted the spark which is resulting in a moral uprising and will end only when the whole sorry mess of twisted, warped thinkers are swept from the national scene so that we may have a new birth of national honesty and decency in Government.

# Appendix VI: Declaration of Conscience Speech, Margaret Chase Smith June 1, 1950

I would like to speak briefly and simply about a serious national condition. It is a national feeling of fear and frustration that could result in national suicide and the end of everything that we Americans hold dear. It is a condition that comes from the lack of effective leadership in either the Legislative Branch or the Executive Branch of our Government.

That leadership is so lacking that serious and responsible proposals are being made that national advisory commissions be appointed to provide such critically needed leadership.

I speak as briefly as possible because too much harm has already been done with irresponsible words of bitterness and selfish political opportunism. I speak as simply as possible because the issue is too great to be obscured by eloquence. I speak simply and briefly in the hope that my words will be taken to heart.

I speak as a Republican. I speak as a woman. I speak as a United States Senator. I speak as an American.

The United States Senate has long enjoyed worldwide respect as the greatest deliberative body in the world. But recently that deliberative character has too often been debased to the level of a forum of hate and character assassination sheltered by the shield of congressional immunity.

It is ironical that we Senators can in debate in the Senate directly or indirectly, by any form of words, impute to any American who is not a Senator any conduct or motive unworthy or unbecoming an American—and without that non-Senator American having any legal redress against us—yet if we say the same thing in the Senate about our colleagues we can be stopped on the grounds of being out of order.

It is strange that we can verbally attack anyone else without restraint and with full protection and yet we hold ourselves above the same type of criticism here on the Senate Floor. Surely the United States Senate is big enough to take self-criticism and self-appraisal. Surely we should be able to take the same kind of character attacks that we "dish out" to outsiders.

I think that it is high time for the United States Senate and its members to do some soul-searching—for us to weigh our consciences—on the manner in which we are performing our duty to the people of America—on the manner in which we are using or abusing our individual powers and privileges.

I think that it is high time that we remembered that we have sworn to uphold and defend the Constitution. I think that it is high time that we remembered that the Constitution, as amended, speaks not only of the freedom of speech but also of trial by jury instead of trial by accusation.

Whether it be a criminal prosecution in court or a character prosecution in the Senate, there is little practical distinction when the life of a person has been ruined.

Those of us who shout the loudest about Americanism in making character assassinations are all too frequently those who, by our own words and acts, ignore some of the basic principles of Americanism:

The right to criticize;

The right to hold unpopular beliefs;

The right to protest;

The right of independent thought.

The exercise of these rights should not cost one single American citizen his reputation or his right to a livelihood nor should he be in danger of losing his reputation or livelihood merely because he happens to know someone who holds unpopular beliefs. Who of us doesn't? Otherwise none of us could call our souls our own. Otherwise thought control would have set in.

The American people are sick and tired of being afraid to speak their minds lest they be politically smeared as "Communists" or "Fascists" by their opponents. Freedom of speech is not what it used to be in America It has been so abused by some that it is not exercised by others.

The American people are sick and tired of seeing innocent people smeared and guilty people whitewashed. But there have been enough proved cases, such as the Amerasia case, the Hiss case, the Coplon case, the Gold case, to cause nationwide distrust and strong suspicion that there may be something to the unproved, sensational accusations.

As a Republican, I say to my colleagues on this side of the aisle that the Republican Party faces a challenge today that is not unlike the challenge that it faced back in Lincoln's day. The Republican Party so successfully met that challenge that it emerged from the Civil War as the champion of a united nation—in addition to being a Party that unrelentingly fought loose spending and loose programs.

Today our country is being psychologically divided by the confusion and the suspicions that are bred in the United States Senate to spread like cancerous tentacles of "know nothing, suspect everything" attitudes. Today we have a Democratic Administration that has developed a mania for loose spending and loose programs. History is repeating itself—and the Republican Party again has the opportunity to emerge as the champion of unity and prudence.

The record of the present Democratic Administration has provided us with sufficient campaign issues without the necessity of resorting to political smears. America is rapidly losing its position as leader of the world simply because the Democratic Administration has pitifully failed to provide effective leadership.

The Democratic Administration has completely confused the American people by its daily contradictory grave warnings and optimistic assurances—that show the people that our Democratic Administration has no idea of where it is going.

The Democratic Administration has greatly lost the confidence of the American people by its complacency to the threat of communism here at home and the leak of vital secrets to Russia through key officials of the Democratic Administration. There are enough proved cases to make this point without diluting our criticism with unproved charges.

Surely these are sufficient reasons to make it clear to the American people that it is time for a change and that a Republican victory is necessary to the security of this country. Surely it is clear that this nation will continue to suffer as long as it is governed by the present ineffective Democratic Administration.

Yet to displace it with a Republican regime embracing a philosophy that lacks political integrity or intellectual honesty would prove equally disastrous to this nation. The nation sorely needs a Republican victory. But I don't want to see the Republican Party ride to political victory on the Four Horsemen of Calumny—Fear, Ignorance, Bigotry, and Smear.

I doubt if the Republican Party could—simply because I don't believe the American people will uphold any political party that puts political exploitation above national interest. Surely we Republicans aren't that desperate for victory.

I don't want to see the Republican Party win that way. While it might be a fleeting victory for the Republican Party, it would be a more lasting defeat for the American people. Surely it would ultimately be suicide for the Republican Party and the two-party system that has protected our American liberties from the dictatorship of a one party system.

As members of the Minority Party, we do not have the primary authority to formulate the policy of our Government. But we do have the responsibility of rendering constructive criticism, of clarifying issues, of allaying fears by acting as responsible citizens.

As a woman, I wonder how the mothers, wives, sisters, and daughters feel about the way in which members of their families have been politically mangled in Senate debate—and I use the word "debate" advisedly.

As a United States Senator, I am not proud of the way in which the Senate has been made a publicity platform for irresponsible sensationalism. I am not proud of the reckless abandon in which unproved charges have been hurled from this side of the aisle. I am not proud of the obviously staged, undignified countercharges that have been attempted in retaliation from the other side of the aisle.

I don't like the way the Senate has been made a rendezvous for vilification, for selfish political gain at the sacrifice of individual reputations and national unity. I am not proud of the way we smear outsiders from the Floor of the Senate and hide behind the cloak of congressional immunity and still place ourselves beyond criticism on the Floor of the Senate.

As an American, I am shocked at the way Republicans and Democrats alike are playing directly into the Communist design of "confuse, divide, and conquer." As an American, I don't want a Democratic Administration "whitewash" or "cover-up" any more than I want a Republican smear or witch hunt.

As an American, I condemn a Republican "Fascist" just as much as I condemn a Democrat "Communist." I condemn a Democrat "Fascist" just as much as I condemn a Republican "Communist." They are equally dangerous to you and me and to our country. As an American, I want to see our nation recapture the strength and unity it once had when we fought the enemy instead of ourselves.

It is with these thoughts that I have drafted what I call a "Declaration of Conscience." I am gratified that Senator Tobey, Senator Aiken, Senator Morse, Senator Ives, Senator Thye, and Senator Hendrickson have concurred in that declaration and have authorized me to announce their concurrence.

# Appendix VII: The McCarran Act [Internal Security Act of 1950] (excerpts)

To protect the United States against certain un-American and subversive activities by requiring registration of Communist organizations, and for other purposes. . . .

SEC. 1. (b) Nothing in this Act shall be construed to authorize, require or establish military or civilian censorship or in any way to limit or infringe upon freedom of the press or of speech as guaranteed by the Constitution of the United States and no regulation shall be promulgated hereunder having that effect.

### NECESSITY FOR LEGISLATION

SEC. 2. As a result of evidence adduced before various committees of the Senate and House of Representatives, the Congress hereby finds that—

(1) There exists a world Communist movement which, in its origins, its development, and its present practice, is a world-wide revolutionary movement whose purpose it is, by treachery, deceit, infiltration into other groups (governmental and otherwise), espionage, sabotage, terrorism, and any other means deemed necessary, to establish a Communist totalitarian dictatorship in the countries throughout the world through the medium of a world-wide Communist organization. . . .

(4) The direction and control of the world Communist movement is vested in and exercised by the Communist dictatorship of a foreign country.

(5) The Communist dictatorship of such foreign country, in exercising such direction and control and in furthering the purposes of the world Communist movement, establishes or causes the establishment of, and utilizes, in various countries, action organizations which are not free and independent organizations, but are sections of a world-wide Communist organization and are controlled, directed, and subject to the discipline of the Communist dictatorship of such foreign country. . . .

(11) The agents of communism have devised clever and ruthless espionage and sabotage tactics which are carried out in many instances in form or manner successfully evasive of existing law. . . .

(15) The Communist movement in the United States is an organization numbering thousands of adherents, rigidly and ruthlessly disciplined. Awaiting and seeking to advance a moment when the United States may be so far extended by foreign engagements, so far divided in counsel, or so far in industrial or financial straits, that overthrow of the Government of the United States by force and violence may seem possible of achievement, it seeks converts far and wide by an extensive system of schooling and indoctrination. Such preparations by Communist organizations in other countries have aided in supplanting existing governments. The Communist organization in the United States, pursuing its stated objectives, the recent successes of Communist methods in other countries, and the nature and control of the world Communist movement itself, present a clear and present danger to the security of the United States and to the existence of free American institutions, and make it necessary that Congress, in order to provide for the common defense, to preserve the sovereignty of the United States as an independent nation, and to guarantee to each State a republican form of government, enact appropriate legislation recognizing the existence of such world-wide conspiracy and designed to prevent it from accomplishing its purpose in the United States.

### REGISTRATION . . . OF COMMUNIST ORGANIZATIONS

SEC. 7. (a) Each Communist-action organization (including any organization required, by a final order of the Board, to register as a Communist-action organization) shall, within the time specified in subsection (c) of this section, register with the Attorney General, on a form prescribed by him by regulations, as a Communist-action organization.

(b) Each Communist-front organization (including any organization required, by a final order of the Board, to register as a Communist-front organization) shall, within the time specified in subsection (c) of this section, register with the Attorney General, on a form prescribed by him by regulations, as a Communist-front organization. . . .

### REGISTRATION OF MEMBERS OF COMMUNIST-ACTION ORGANIZATIONS

SEC. 8. (a) Any individual who is or becomes a member of any organization concerning which (1) there is in effect a final order of the Board requiring such organization to register under section 7 (a) of this title as a communist-action organization, (2) more than thirty days have elapsed since such order has become final, and (3) such organization is not registered under section 7 of this title as a Communist-action organization, shall within sixty days after said order has become final, or within thirty days after becoming a member of such organization, whichever is later, register with the Attorney General as a member of such organization. . . .

# Appendix VIII: Veto of the Internal Security Act of 1950, President Harry S. Truman September 22, 1950

*To the House of Representatives:*

I return herewith, without my approval, H.R. 9490, the proposed "Internal Security Act of 1950." . . .

H.R. 9490 would not hurt the Communists. Instead, it would help them. . . .

It would actually weaken our existing internal security measures and would seriously hamper the Federal Bureau of Investigation and our other security agencies.

It would help the Communists in their efforts to create dissension and confusion within our borders.

It would help the Communist propagandists throughout the world who are trying to undermine freedom by discrediting as hypocrisy the efforts of the United States on behalf of freedom. . . .

. . . Fortunately, we already have on the books strong laws which give us most of the protection we need from the real dangers of treason, espionage, sabotage, and actions looking to the overthrow of our Government by force and violence. Most of the provisions of this bill have no relation to these real dangers. . . .

The idea of requiring Communist organizations to divulge information about themselves is a simple and attractive one. But it is about as practical as requiring thieves to register with the sheriff. Obviously, no such organization as the Communist Party is likely to register voluntarily.

Under the provisions of the bill, if an organization which the Attorney General believes should register does not do so, he must request a five-man Subversive Activities Control Board to order the organization to register. The Attorney General would have to produce proof that the organization in question was in fact a Communist-action or a Communist-front organization. To do this he would have to offer evidence relating to every aspect of the organization's activities. The organization could present opposing evidence. Prolonged hearings would be required to allow both sides to present proof and to cross-examine opposing witnesses.

To estimate the duration of such a proceeding involving the Communist Party, we need only recall that on much narrower issues the trial of the eleven Communist leaders under the Smith Act consumed nine months. In a hearing under this bill, the difficulties of proof would be much greater and would take a much longer time. . . .

. . . Under this bill, the Attorney General would have to attempt the difficult task of producing concrete legal evidence that men have particular ideas or opinions. This would inevitably require the disclosure of many of the FBI's confidential sources of information and thus would damage our national security.

If, eventually, the Attorney General should overcome these difficulties and get a favorable decision from the Board, the Board's decision could be appealed to the courts. . . .

All these proceedings would require great effort and much time. It is almost certain that from two to four years would elapse between the Attorney General's decision to go before the Board with a case, and the final disposition of the matter by the courts.

And when all this time and effort had been spent, it is still most likely that no organization would actually register.

The simple fact is that when the courts at long last found that a particular organization was required to register, all the leaders of the organization would have to do to frustrate the law would be to dissolve the organization and establish a new one with a different name and a new roster of nominal officers. . . .

441

Unfortunately, these provisions are not merely ineffective and unworkable. They represent a clear and present danger to our institutions.

Insofar as the bill would require registration by the Communist Party itself, it does not endanger our traditional liberties. However, the application of the registration requirements to so-called Communist-front organizations can be the greatest danger to freedom of speech, press, and assembly, since the Alien and Sedition Laws of 1798. This danger arises out of the criteria or standards to be applied in determining whether an organization is a Communist-front organization.

There would be no serious problem if the bill required proof that an organization was controlled and financed by the Communist Party. . . . However, recognizing the difficulty of proving those matters, the bill would permit such a determination to be based solely upon the extent to which the positions taken or advanced by it from time to time on matters of policy do not deviate from those of the Communist movement.

This provision could easily be used to classify as a Communist-front organization any organization which is advocating a single policy or objective which is also being urged by the Communist Party. . . . Thus, an organization which advocates low-cost housing for sincere humanitarian reasons might be classified as a Communist-front organization because the Communists regularly exploit slum conditions as one of their fifth-column techniques.

It is not enough to say that this probably would not be done. The mere fact that it could be done shows clearly how the bill would open a Pandora's box of opportunities for official condemnation of organizations and individuals for perfectly honest opinions which happen to be stated also by Communists.

The basic error of these sections is that they move in the direction of suppressing opinion and belief. This would be a very dangerous course to take, not because we have any sympathy for Communist opinions, but because any governmental stifling of the free expression of opinion is a long step toward totalitarianism. . . .

We can and we will prevent espionage, sabotage, or other actions endangering our national security. But we would betray our finest traditions if we attempted, as this bill would attempt, to curb the simple expression of opinion. This we should never do, no matter how distasteful the opinion may be to the vast majority of our people. The course proposed by this bill would delight the Communists, for it would make a mockery of the Bill of Rights and of our claims to stand for freedom in the world.

And what kind of effect would these provisions have on the normal expression of political views? Obviously, if this law were on the statute books, the part of prudence would be to avoid saying anything that might be construed by someone as not deviating sufficiently from the current Communist propaganda line. And since no one could be sure in advance what views were safe to express, the inevitable tendency would be to express no views on controversial subjects.

The result could only be to reduce the vigor and strength of our political life—an outcome that the Communists would happily welcome, but that free men should abhor. . . .

This is a time when we must marshall all our resources and all the moral strength of our free system in self-defense against the threat of Communist aggression. We will fail in this, and we will destroy all that we seek to preserve, if we sacrifice the liberties of our citizens in a misguided attempt to achieve national security.

# Appendix IX: U.S. Attorney General's List of Subversive Organizations, 1950 (excerpt)

## Communist

Abraham Lincoln Brigade

Abraham Lincoln School, Chicago, Illinois

Action Committee to Free Spain Now

American Association for Reconstruction in Yugoslavia, Inc.

American Branch of the Federation of Greek Maritime Unions

American Committee for European Workers' Relief

American Committee for Protection of Foreign Born

American Committee for Spanish Freedom

American Committee for Yugoslav Relief, Inc.

American Council for a Democratic Greece, formerly known as the Greek American Council; Greek American Committee for National Unity

American Council on Soviet Relations

American Croatian Congress

American Jewish Labor Council

American League against War and Fascism

American League for Peace and Democracy

American Peace Mobilization

American Polish Labor Council

American Rescue Ship Mission (a project of the United American Spanish Aid Committee)

American Russian Institute, New York

American Russian Institute, Philadelphia

American Russian Institute (of San Francisco)

American Russian Institute of Southern California, Los Angeles

American Slav Congress

American Youth Congress

American Youth for Democracy

Armenian Progressive League of America

Boston School for Marxist Studies, Boston, Massachusetts

California Labor School, Inc., 216 Market Street, San Francisco, California

Central Council of American Women of Croatian Descent, aka Central Council of American Croatian Women, National Council of Croatian Women

Citizens Committee to Free Earl Browder

Citizens Committee for Harry Bridges

Civil Rights Congress and its affiliated organizations, including:
  —Civil Rights Congress for Texas
  —Veterans against Discrimination of Civil Rights Congress of New York

Comite Coordinador Pro Republica Española

Committee for a Democratic Far Eastern Policy

Commonwealth College, Mena, Arkansas

Communist Party, U.S.A., its subdivisions, subsidiaries and affiliates, including:
  —Citizens Committee of the Upper West Side (New York City)
  —Committee to Aid the Fighting South
  —Daily Workers Press Club
  —Dennis Defense Committee
  —Labor Research Association, Inc.
  —Southern Negro Youth Congress
  —United May Day Committee
  —United Negro and Allied Veterans of America

—Yiddisher Kultur Farband

Communist Political Association, its subdivisions, subsidiaries, and affiliates, including:

—Florida Press and Educational League

—Peoples Educational and Press Association of Texas

—Virginia League for Peoples Education

Connecticut State Youth Conference

Congress of American Revolutionary Writers

Congress of American Women

Council on African Affairs

Council for Pan-American Democracy

Dennis Defense Committee

Detroit Youth Assembly

Emergency Conference to Save Spanish Refugees (founding body of the North American Spanish Aid Committee)

Friends of the Soviet Union

George Washington Carver School, New York City

Hawaii Civil Liberties Committee

Hollywood Writers Mobilization for Defense

Hungarian-American Council for Democracy

Independent Socialist League

International Labor Defense

International Workers Order, its subdivisions, subsidiaries and affiliates, including

—American-Russian Fraternal Society

—Carpatho-Russian Peoples Society

—Cervantes Fraternal Society

—Croatian Benevolent Fraternity

—Finnish-American Mutual Aid Society

—Garibaldi American Fraternal Society

—Hellenic-American Brotherhood

—Hungarian Brotherhood

—Jewish Peoples Fraternal Order

—People's Radio Foundation, Inc.

—Polonia Society of the IWO

—Romanian-American Fraternal Society

—Serbian-American Fraternal Society

—Slovak Workers Society

—Ukranian-American Fraternal Union

Jefferson School of Social Science, New York City

Jewish Peoples Committee

Joint Anti-Fascist Refugee Committee

Joseph Weydemeyer School of Social Science, St. Louis, Missouri

Labor Research Association, Inc.

Labor Youth League

League of American Writers

Macedonian-American People's League

Michigan Civil Rights Federation

Michigan School of Social Science

National Committee for the Defense of Political Prisoners

National Committee to Win the Peace

National Conference on American Policy in China and the Far East (a Conference called by the Committee for a Democratic Far Eastern Policy)

National Council of Americans of Croatian Descent

National Council of American-Soviet Friendship

National Federation for Constitutional Liberties

National Negro Congress

Nature Friends of America (since 1935)

Negro Labor Victory Committee

New Committee for Publications

North American Committee to Aid Spanish Democracy

North American Spanish Aid Committee

Ohio School of Social Sciences

Oklahoma Committee to Defend Political Prisoners

Pacific Northwest Labor School, Seattle, Washington

Partido del Pueblo of Panama (operating in the Canal Zone)

Peoples Educational Association (Incorporated under name Los Angeles Educational Association, Inc.) aka Peoples Educational Center, Peoples University, People's School

People's Institute of Applied Religion

Philadelphia School of Social Science and Art

Photo League (New York City)

Progressive German-Americans, aka Progressive German-Americans of Chicago

Proletarian Party of America

Revolutionary Workers League

Samuel Adams School, Boston, Massachusetts

Schappes Defense Committee

Schneiderman-Darcy Defense Committee
School of Jewish Studies, New York City
Seattle Labor School, Seattle, Washington
Serbian Vidovdan Council
Slovenian-American National Council
Socialist Workers Party, including American Committee for European Workers' Relief
Socialist Youth League
Tom Paine School of Social Science, Philadelphia, Pennsylvania
Tom Paine School of Westchester, New York
Union of American Croatians
United American Spanish Aid Committee
United Committee of South Slavic Americans
United Harlem Tenants and Consumers Organization
Veterans of the Abraham Lincoln Brigade
Walt Whitman School of Social Science, Newark, New Jersey
Washington Bookshop Association
Washington Committee for Democratic Action
Washington Commonwealth Federation
Wisconsin Conference on Social Legislation
Workers Alliance
Workers Party, including Socialist Youth League
Young Communist League

## Subversive

Communist Party, U.S.A., its subdivisions, subsidiaries, and affiliates
Communist Political Association, its subdivisions, subsidiaries, and affiliates, including:
—Florida Press and Educational League
—Peoples Educational and Press Association of Texas
—Virginia League for Peoples Education
German-American Bund
Independent Socialist League
Partido del Pueblo of Panama (operating in the Canal Zone)

Socialist Workers Party
Workers Party
Young Communist League

**Organizations that have "adopted a policy of advocating or approving the commission of acts of force and violence to deny others their rights under the Constitution of the United States"**

American Christian Nationalist Party
Associated Klans of America
Association of Georgia Klans
Columbians
Knights of the White Camellia
Ku Klux Klan
Original Southern Klans, Incorporated
Protestant War Veterans of the U.S., Inc.
Silver Shirt Legion of America

**Organizations that "seek to alter the form of government of the United States by unconstitutional means"**

Communist Party, U.S.A., its subdivisions, subsidiaries, and affiliates Communist Political Association, its subdivisions, subsidiaries, and affiliates, including:
—Florida Press and Educational League
—Peoples Educational and Press Association of Texas
—Virginia League for Peoples Education
Independent Socialist League
Industrial Workers of the World
Nationalist Party of Puerto Rico
Partido del Pueblo of Panama (operating in the Canal Zone)
Socialist Workers Party
Workers Party
Young Communist League

# Appendix X: FBI Files and Memos, Harry Gold and David Greenglass, 1950–51

*December 28, 1950*

MEMO  RE  HARRY GOLD
       ESPIONAGE R
       (65—15324)

GOLD was interviewed in the Tombs (NYCity Prison) on 12/28/50 in the presence of DAVID GREENGLASS. The purpose of this interview was specifically to determine what transpired at their first meeting in Albuquerque.

GREENGLASS stated that GOLD introduced himself to him and his wife as DAVID; GREENGLASS is quite certain about this item and he added that both he and his wife have since recalled that this was the name used by GOLD. Gold asserted that he could not recall definitely what name he used and to this point believed that he had used the name of Kessler. However, in the course of this joint interview with GREENGLASS, GOLD recalls that the name he did use at the time of his first meeting with GREENGLASS was commented upon as being similar or the same as GREENGLASS's name or some relative's name; therefore, GOLD now believes that GREENGLASS's recollection is correct and that he did use the name of "DAVE."

Concerning the reported salutation "Greetings from BEN." GREENGLASS says that he has no recollection of such a statement made by GOLD, pointing out further that the name BEN would mean nothing to him. GREENGLASS proposed that possibly GOLD had said "greetings from Julius" which would of course make sense to GREENGLASS. GOLD's spontaneous comment to this was that possibly GREENGLASS was right that he had mentioned the name of JULIUS rather than BEN. GOLD, however is not at all clear on this point. He asserted that on every occasion of his meeting with a new contact he always "brought greetings" from someone in accordance with prior

instructions; therefore, it is his contention that [he] did bring greetings to GREENGLASS on this occasion.

          J. C. Walsh
          [Special Agent]

*March 5, 1951*

SYNOPSIS OF FACTS:

GOLD now recalls that he brought "greetings from JULIUS" on the occasion of his first meeting with DAVID GREENGLASS and that such was done on instructions of YAKOVLEV. . . .

DETAILS:  RE  JULIUS ROSENBERG

In anticipation of the ROSENBERG trial on March 6, 1951, GOLD was interviewed on a number of occasions by Assistant U.S. Attorneys MILES J. LANE and JAMES B. KILSHEIMER in the presence of [Special Agents] John A. Harrington, William F. Norton, and the writer. . . .

In the course of prior interviews with GOLD in the Tombs (New York City Prison) he was examined closely relative to the specific details of his original contact with DAVID GREENGLASS. GOLD has always maintained that on this occasion he brought "Greetings from BEN," and so testified before the Federal Grand Jury relative to the indictment proceedings in the ROSENBERG matter. GOLD, however, has always admitted that he has not been too clear as to this specific detail, that is, as to the actual name used.

GOLD and GREENGLASS were interviewed simultaneously by the writer for their concerted effort in recalling the incident. GREENGLASS asserted that he could not recall GOLD saying anything about greet-

446

ings and furthermore, if GOLD had brought such greetings, according to GREENGLASS, they were not from BEN. GREENGLASS pointed out that such was an obvious deduction in so far as the name BEN meant nothing to him. He pointed out, however, that it is his belief that if GOLD did bring greetings the only name from whom such greetings would come would be JULIUS, meaning JULIUS ROSENBERG.

Subsequent to these interviews with GREENGLASS and GOLD, the latter averred that after considerable reflection he is quite certain that on the occasion of the first meeting he had with GREENGLASS he brought greetings from JULIUS, and that such was done under the direction of YAKOVLEV.

Joseph C. Walsh

*Handwritten statement by David Greenglass reporting his interrogation by FBI; dated June (17), 1950.*

Saturday
June 1950

These are my approximate statements to the F.B.I.

1. I stated that I met Gold in N. M. at 209 N. High St. my place. They told me that I had told him to come back later because I didn't have it ready. I didn't remember this but I allowed it in the statement. When he came back again I told them that I gave him the envelope with the stuff not expecting payment and then he gave me an envelope. Later I found that it contained $500.

2. I told them that on a visit to me in Nov. 1944 my wife asked me if I would give information. I made sure to tell the F.B.I. that she was transmitting this info from my Brother in Law Julius and was not her own idea. She was doing this because she felt I would be angry if she didn't ask me.

I then mentioned a meeting with a man who I didn't know arranged by Julius. I established the approximate meeting place but no exact date. The place was a car an Olds owned by my father-in-law, at somewhere above 42nd St. on 1st Ave. in Man. I talked to the man but I could recall very little about which we spoke. I thought it might be that he wanted me to think about finding out about H. E. lens's used in experimental tests to determine data on the a bomb.

I made a general statement on my age etc. you know the usual thing.

I mentioned no other meeting with anyone.

One more thing, I identified Gold by a torn or cut piece of card, but I didn't tell them where or how I got it. Also I definitely placed my wife out of the room at the time of Gold's visit.

Also I didn't know who sent Gold to me.

I also made a pencil sketch of an H.E. mold set up for an experiment. But this I'll tell you I can honestly say the information I gave Gold maybe not at all what I said in the statement.

# Appendix XI: Sentencing of Julius and Ethel Rosenberg, Judge Irving Kaufman April 5, 1951

Because of the seriousness of this case and the lack of precedence, I have refrained from asking the Government for a recommendation. The responsibility is so great that I believe that the Court alone should assume this responsibility. . . .

The issue of punishment in this case is presented in a unique framework of history. It is so difficult to make people realize that this country is engaged in a life and death struggle with a completely different system. This struggle is not only manifested externally between these two forces but this case indicates quite clearly that it also involves the employment by the enemy of secret as well as overt outspoken forces among our own people. All of our democratic institutions are, therefore, directly involved in this great conflict. I believe that never at any time in our history were we ever confronted to the same degree that we are today with such a challenge to our very existence. The atom bomb was unknown when the espionage statute was drafted. I emphasize this because we must realize that we are dealing with a missile of destruction which can wipe out millions of Americans.

The competitive advantage held by the United States in super-weapons has put a premium on the services of a new school of spies—the homegrown variety that places allegiance to a foreign power before loyalty to the United States. The punishment to be meted out in this case must therefore serve the maximum interest for the preservation of our society against these traitors in our midst.

It is ironic that the very country which these defendants betrayed and sought to destroy placed every safeguard around them for obtaining a fair and impartial trial, a trial which consumed three weeks in this court. I recall the defendant Julius Rosenberg testifying that our American system of jurisprudence met with his approval and was preferred over Russian justice. Even the defendants realize—by this admission—that this type of trial would not have been afforded to them in Russia. Certainly, to a Russian national accused of a conspiracy to destroy Russia not one day would have been consumed in a trial. It is to America's credit that it took the pains and exerted the effort which it did in the trial of these defendants. Yet, they made a choice of devoting themselves to the Russian ideology of denial of God, denial of the sanctity of the individual, and aggression against free men everywhere instead of serving the cause of liberty and freedom.

I consider your crime worse than murder. Plain deliberate contemplated murder is dwarfed in magnitude by comparison with the crime you have committed. In committing the act of murder, the criminal kills only his victim. The immediate family is brought to grief and when justice is meted out the chapter is closed. But in your case, I believe your conduct in putting into the hands of the Russians the A-bomb years before our best scientists predicted Russia would perfect the bomb has already caused, in my opinion, the Communist aggression in Korea, with the resultant casualties exceeding 50,000 and who knows but that millions more of innocent people may pay the price of your treason. Indeed, by your betrayal you undoubtedly have altered the course of history to the disadvantage of our country. No one can say that we do not live in a constant state of tension. We have evidence of your treachery all around us every day—for the civilian defense activities throughout the nation are aimed at preparing us for an atom bomb attack.

Nor can it be said in mitigation of the offense that the power which set the conspiracy in motion and profited from it was not openly hostile to the United States at the time of the conspiracy. If this was your excuse the error of your ways in setting yourselves above our properly constituted authorities and the decision of those authorities not to share the information with Russia must now be obvious.

The evidence indicated quite clearly that Julius Rosenberg was the prime mover in this conspiracy. However, let no mistake be made about the role which his wife, Ethel Rosenberg, played in this conspiracy. Instead of deterring him from pursuing his ignoble cause, she encouraged and assisted the cause. She was a mature woman—almost three years older than her husband and almost seven years older than her younger brother. She was a full-fledged partner in this crime.

Indeed the defendants Julius and Ethel Rosenberg placed their devotion to their cause above their own personal safety and were conscious that they were sacrificing their own children, should their misdeeds be detected—all of which did not deter them from pursuing their course. Love for their cause dominated their lives—it was even greater than their love for their children.

What I am about to say is not easy for me. I have deliberated for hours, days and nights. I have carefully weighed the evidence. Every nerve, every fiber of my body has been taxed. I am just as human as are the people who have given me the power to impose sentence. I am convinced beyond any doubt of your guilt. I have searched the records—I have searched my conscience—to find some reason for mercy—for it is only human to be merciful and it is natural to try to spare lives. I am convinced, however, that I would violate the solemn and sacred trust that the people of this land have placed in my hands were I to show leniency to the defendants Rosenberg.

It is not in my power, Julius and Ethel Rosenberg, to forgive you. Only the Lord can find mercy for what you have done.

The sentence of the Court upon Julius and Ethel Rosenberg is, for the crime for which you have been convicted, you are hereby sentenced to the punishment of death, and it is ordered upon some day within the week beginning with Monday, May 21st, you shall be executed according to law.

# Appendix XII: Lillian Hellman—Letter to HUAC May 19, 1952

Dear Mr. Wood:

As you know, I am under subpoena to appear before your committee on May 21, 1952.

I am most willing to answer all questions about myself. I have nothing to hide from your committee and there is nothing in my life of which I am ashamed. I have been advised by counsel that under the fifth amendment I have a constitutional privilege to decline to answer any questions about my political opinions, activities, and associations, on the grounds of self-incrimination. I do not wish to claim this privilege. I am ready and willing to testify before the representatives of our Government as to my own opinions and my own actions, regardless of any risks or consequences to myself.

But I am advised by counsel that if I answer the committee's questions about myself, I must also answer questions about other people and that if I refuse to do so, I can be cited for contempt. My counsel tells me that if I answer questions about myself, I will have waived my rights under the fifth amendment and could be forced legally to answer questions about others. This is very difficult for a layman to understand. But there is one principle that I do understand: I am not willing, now or in the future, to bring bad trouble to people who, in my past association with them, were completely innocent of any tallc or any action that was disloyal or subversive. I do not like subversion or disloyalty in any form and if I had ever seen any I would have considered it my duty to have reported it to the proper authorities. But to hurt innocent people whom I knew many years ago in order to save myself is, to me, inhuman and indecent and dishonorable. I cannot and will not cut my conscience to fit this year's fashions, even though I long ago came to the conclusion that I was not a political person and could have no comfortable place in any political group.

I was raised in an old-fashioned American tradition and there were certain homely things that were taught to me: To try to tell the truth, not to bear false witness, not to harm my neighbor, to be loyal to my country, and so on. In general, I respected these ideals of Christian honor and did as well with them as I knew how. It is my belief that you will agree with these simple rules of human decency and will not expect me to violate the good American tradition from which they spring. I would, therefore, like to come before you and speak of myself.

I am prepared to waive the privilege against self-incrimination and to tell you everything you wish to know about my views or actions if your committee will agree to refrain from asking me to name other people. If the committee is unwilling to give me this assurance, I will be forced to plead the privilege of the fifth amendment at the hearing.

A reply to this letter would be appreciated.

Sincerely yours,

Lillian Hellman

## The following is a listing of Lillian Hellman's alleged political affiliations as reported in *Red Channels* (1950).

**LILLIAN HELLMAN**
Playwright, Author
REPORTED AS:

| | |
|---|---|
| Independent Citizens Committee of the Arts, Sciences, and Professions | Speaker, Theatre Panel, Conference of the Arts, Sciences, and Professions, 6/22, 23/45. *Daily Worker*, 6/10/45, p. 14. |

Progressive Citizens of America, National Arts, Sciences, and Professions Council

Participant, Cultural Freedom Conference, 10/25, 26/47. *Daily Worker*, 10/27/47, p. 2.

National Council of American-Soviet Friendship

Signer. Women's Committee. Greetings to women of Soviet Union in celebration of International Women's Day. *Daily Worker*, 3/9/48, p. 5.

National Wallace for President Committee

Member. *Daily Worker*, 3/26/48, p. 7.

Harlem Women for Wallace

Speaker, 6/9/48; gave forceful tribute to Wallace. *Daily Worker*, 6/10/48, p. 6.

"New Party" (Wallace)

Member, Platform Committee, 7/23/48. *Daily Worker*, 7/19/48, p. 5.

Writers for Wallace

Member, Initiating Committee. *Daily Worker*, 9/21/48, p. 7.

Moscow Art Theatre

Sent greetings to directors and members. Celebration of Moscow Art Theatre's 50th Anniversary. *Daily Worker*, 11/1/48, p. 13.

Progressive Party

Attended three-day conference. *Daily Worker*, 11/16/48, p. 5.

National Council of the Arts, Sciences, and Professions

Signer. Statement calling for abolition of House Committee on Un-American Activities. *Daily Worker*, 12/29/48, p. 2.

Scientific and Cultural Conference for World Peace

Signer. Invitation to conference. *Daily Worker*, 1/10/49, p. 11.
Member, Program Committee. *Daily Worker*, 2/28/49, p. 9.

Amicus Curiae Brief

Signer. Petition to Supreme Court to review the conviction of [ John Howard] Lawson and [Dalton] Trumbo.

Moscow Theaters

Plays, *The Watch on the Rhine*, *The Little Foxes*, performed in Moscow theaters. *Soviet Russia Today*, 10/45, p. 32.

American Committee for Democracy and Intellectual Freedom

Signer. Petition to discontinue Dies Committee. *House Un-Am. Act. Com., Appendix 9*, p. 331.

American Committee to Save Refugees; Exiled Writers Committee of the League of American Writers; United American Spanish Aid Committee

Chairman, "Europe Today" dinner forum, 10/9/41. *House Un-Am. Act. Com., Appendix 9*, p. 357.

American League for Peace and Democracy

Sponsor, Refugee Scholarship and Peace Campaign, 8/3/39. *House Un-Am. Act. Com., Appendix 9*, p. 410.

Russian War Relief, Inc.

Signer. Advertisement asking for help on behalf of the Russian people, 10/10/41. *House Un-Am. Act. Com., Appendix 9*, p. 475.

Artists' Front to Win the War

Participant. Meeting, 10/16/42. *House Un-Am. Act. Com., Appendix 9*, p. 575.

Citizens Committee for Harry Bridges

Member and sponsor, 1941. *House Un-Am. Act. Com., Appendix 9*, p. 599.

*Equality*

Member, Editorial Council, 12/39. *House Un-Am. Act. Com., Appendix 9*, p. 698.

Friends of the Abraham Lincoln Brigade

Sponsor, 6/11/38. *House Un-Am. Act. Com., Appendix 9*, pp. 753-56.
Sponsor. Disabled Veterans Fund, 3/22/39. *House Un-Am. Act. Com., Appendix 9*, p. 753.

Joint Anti-Fascist Refugee Committee

Sponsor. Dinner, 10/27/43. *House Un-Am. Act. Com., Appendix 9*, p. 941.

The League of Women Shoppers, Inc.

Vice-president. *House Un-Am. Act. Com., Appendix 9*, pp. 1007–10.

National Emergency Conference for Democratic Rights

Signer. "Open Letter to the United States Senate." *House Un-Am. Act. Com., Appendix 9*, p. 1212.

Progressive Committee to Rebuild the American Labor Party

Member, Executive Committee. *House Un-Am. Act. Com., Appendix 9*, p. 1500.

Statement by American Progressives on the Moscow Trials — Signer, 5/3/38. *House Un-Am. Act. Com., Appendix 9,* p. 1617.

Theatre Arts Committee — Member, Executive Board. *House Un-Am. Act. Com., Appendix 9,* p. 1626.

Frontier Films — Member, Advisory Board, 4/6/37. *Un-Am. Act. in California, 1948,* p. 96.

# Appendix XIII: Memo to President Truman from Dean Acheson re: John Carter Vincent

*Memorandum from Secretary Acheson to President Truman regarding the case of John Carter Vincent, contained in the White House press release of January 3, 1953:*

I have recently been advised by Chairman Bingham of the Loyalty Review Board that a panel of the Loyalty Review Board has considered the case of Mr. John Carter Vincent, a Foreign Service Officer with class of Career Minister. Chairman Bingham also advises me that while the panel did not find Mr. Vincent guilty of disloyalty, it has reluctantly concluded that there is reasonable doubt as to his loyalty to the Government of the United States. Chairman Bingham further advises me that it is therefore the recommendation of the Board that the services of Mr. Vincent be terminated.

Such a recommendation by so distinguished a Board is indeed serious and impressive and must be given great weight. The final responsibility, however, for making a decision as to whether Mr. Vincent should be dismissed is that of the Secretary of State. I am advised that any doubt which might have previously existed on this point has been removed by the recent decision of the United States Circuit Court of Appeals for the District of Columbia in *James Kutcher, Appellant, v. Carl Gray, Jr., Veterans Administration, Appellee.* That case establishes that the action of the Board is a recommendation "just that— nothing more" and that in the last analysis upon the Head of the Department is imposed "the duty to impartially determine on all the evidence" the proper disposition of the case.

A most important item on which I must rely in exercising this responsibility, is the communication from Chairman Bingham in which he advised me of the conclusion reached by his panel. This communication contains elements which raise serious problems.

In the first place, I note a statement that the panel has not accepted or rejected the testimony of Mr. Budenz that he recalls being informed by others that Mr. Vincent was a Communist and under Communist discipline. The panel also states that it does not accept or reject the findings of the Committee on the Judiciary of the Senate with respect to Mr. Vincent and the Institute of Pacific Relations or the findings of the Committee with respect to the participation of Mr. Vincent in the development of United States policy towards China in 1945. The panel, however, proceeds to state that, although it has not accepted or rejected these factors, it has taken them into account. I am unable to interpret what this means. If the panel did take these factors into account, this means that it must have relied upon them in making its final determination. Yet I am unable to understand how these factors could have played a part in the final determination of the panel if these factors were neither accepted nor rejected by the Board.

This is not merely a point of language. It is a point of real substance. It is difficult for me to exercise the responsibility which is mine under the law with the confusion which has been cast as to the weight which the panel gave to the charges of Mr. Budenz or the findings of the Senate Committee.

The communication from the panel raises another issue which goes to the heart of operation of the Department of State and the Foreign Service. It is the issue of accurate reporting. The communication contains the following statement: "The panel notes Mr. Vincent's studied praise of Chinese Communists and equally studied criticism of the Chiang Kai-shek Government throughout a period when it was the declared and established policy of the Government of the United States to support Chiang Kai-shek's Government."

Mr. Vincent's duty was to report the facts as he saw them. It was not merely to report successes of existing policy but also to report on the aspects in which it was failing and the reasons therefor. If this involved reporting that situations existed in the administration of the Chinese Nationalists which had

453

to be corrected if the Nationalist Government was to survive, it was his duty to report this. If this involved a warning not to underestimate the combat potential of the Chinese Communists, or their contribution to the war against Japan, it was his duty to report this. In the hearings which followed the relief of General MacArthur, General Wedemeyer has testified that he has made reports equally as critical of the administration of the Chinese Nationalists.

The great majority of reports which Mr. Vincent drafted were reviewed and signed by Ambassador Gauss, an outstanding expert in the Far East. Ambassador Gauss has made it crystal clear that in his mind the reports drafted by Mr. Vincent were both accurate and objective.

I do not exclude the possibility that in this or in any other case a board might find that the reports of an officer might or might not disclose a bias which might have a bearing on the issue of his loyalty. But in so delicate a matter, affecting so deeply the integrity of the Foreign Service, I should wish to be advised by persons thoroughly familiar with the problems and procedures of the Department of State and the Foreign Service. This involves an issue far greater in importance than the disposition of a loyalty case involving one man. Important as it is to do full justice to the individual concerned, it is essential that we should not by inadvertence take any step which might lower the high traditions of our own Foreign Service to the level established by governments which will permit their diplomats to report to them only what they want to hear.

The memorandum from Mr. Bingham indicates that the Board also took into account "Mr. Vincent's failure properly to discharge his responsibilities as Chairman of the Far Eastern Subcommittee of State, War and Navy to supervise the accuracy or security of State Department documents emanating from that Subcommittee." The statement which refers to the security of the files seems to me to be inadvertent. Presumably it is a reference to the fact that State Department documents were involved in the *Amerasia* case. However, in the many Congressional investigations which have followed that case it has not been suggested that Mr. Vincent had any responsibility for those documents. I have not discovered any such

evidence in the file in this case. The reference to the accuracy of the State Department documents emanating from that Committee is obscure. In any case, while it might be relative to Mr. Vincent's competence in performing his duties, it does not seem to me to have any bearing on the question of loyalty.

The report finally refers to Mr. Vincent's association with numerous persons "who, he had reason to believe," were either Communists or Communist sympathizers. This is indeed a matter which, if unexplained, is of importance and clearly relevant. It involves inquiry as to whether this association arose in the performance of his duties or otherwise. It further involves an inquiry as to the pattern of Mr. Vincent's close personal friends and whether he knew or should have known that any of these might be Communists or Communist sympathizers.

All these matters raised in my mind the necessity for further inquiry. This further inquiry was made possible by the documents in this proceeding which you provided me upon my request. I find upon examining the documents that the recommendation made by the panel of the Loyalty Review Board was made by a majority of one, two of the members believing that no evidence had been produced which led them to have a doubt as to Mr. Vincent's loyalty. In this situation, I believe that I cannot in good conscience and in the exercise of my own judgment, which is my duty under the law, carry out this recommendation of the Board. I do not believe, however, that in the exercise of my responsibility to the Government, I can or should let the matter rest here. I believe that I must ask for further guidance.

I, therefore, ask your permission to seek the advice of some persons who will combine the highest judicial qualifications of weighing the evidence with the greatest possible familiarity of the works and standards of the Department of State and the Foreign Service, both in reporting from the field and making decisions in the Department. If you approve, I should propose to ask [these] persons to examine the record in this case and to advise me as to what disposition in their judgment should be made in this case. . . . [*Department of State Bulletin*, Vol. XXVIII, January 19, 1953, pp. 122–23.]

# Appendix XIV: Executive Order 10450
## April 27, 1953
## [*Federal Register*, XVIII, No. 82 (April 29, 1953), 2489–92]

Whereas the interests of the national security require that all persons privileged to be employed in the departments and agencies of the Government, shall be reliable, trustworthy, of good conduct and character, and of complete and unswerving loyalty to the United States; and

Whereas the American tradition that all persons should receive fair, impartial, and equitable treatment at the hands of the Government requires that all persons seeking the privilege of employment or privileged to be employed in the departments and agencies of the Government be adjudged by mutually consistent and no less than minimum standards and procedures among the departments and agencies governing the employment and retention in employment of persons in the Federal service:

Now, therefore, by virtue of the authority vested in me by the Constitution and statutes of the United States, including section 1753 of the Revised Statutes of the United States (5 U. S. C. 651); the Civil Service Act of 1883 (22 Stat. 403; 5 U. S. C. 632, *et seq.*); section 9A of the act of August 2, 1939, 53 Stat. 1148 (5 U. S. C. 118 j); and the act of August 26, 1950, 64 Stat. 476 (5 U. S. C. 22–1, *et seq.*), and as President of the United States, and deeming such action necessary in the best interests of the national security, it is hereby ordered as follows:

SECTION 1. In addition to the departments and agencies specified in the said act of August 26, 1950, and Executive Order No. 10237 of April 26, 1951, the provisions of that act shall apply to all other departments and agencies of the Government.

SEC. 2. The head of each department and agency of the Government shall be responsible for establishing and maintaining within his department or agency an effective program to insure that the employment and retention in employment of any civilian officer or employee within the department or agency is clearly consistent with the interests of the national security.

SEC. 3. (a) The appointment of each civilian officer or employee in any department or agency of the Government shall be made subject to investigation. The scope of the investigation shall be determined in the first instance according to the degree of adverse effect the occupant of the position sought to be filled could bring about, by virtue of the nature of the position, on the national security, but in no event shall the investigation include less than a national agency check (including a check of the fingerprint files of the Federal Bureau of Investigation), and written inquiries to appropriate local law-enforcement agencies, former employers and supervisors, references, and schools attended by the person under investigation: *Provided,* that upon request of the head of the department or agency concerned, the Civil Service Commission may, in its discretion, authorize such less investigation as may meet the requirements of the national security with respect to per-diem, intermittent, temporary, or seasonal employees, or aliens employed outside the United States. Should there develop at any stage of investigation information indicating that the employment of any such person may not be clearly consistent with the interests of the national security, there shall be conducted with respect to such person a full field investigation, or such less investigation as shall be sufficient to enable the head of the department or agency concerned to determine whether retention of such person is clearly consistent with the interests of the national security.

(b) The head of any department or agency shall designate, or cause to be designated, any position within his department or agency the occupant of which could bring about, by virtue of the nature of the position, a material adverse effect on the national security as a sensitive position. Any position so designated shall be filled or occupied only by a person with respect to whom a full field investigation has been conducted: *Provided,* that a person occupying a sensitive position at the time it is designated as such may continue to occupy such position pending the completion of a full field investigation, subject to the other provisions of this order: *And provided further,* that in case of emergency a sensitive position may be filled for a limited period by a person with respect to whom a full field preappointment investigation has not been completed if the head of the department or agency concerned finds that such action is necessary in the national interest, which finding shall be made a part of the records of such departmenl or agency.

SEC. 4. The head of each department and agency shall review, or cause to be reviewed, the cases of all civilian officers and employees with respect to whom there has been conducted a full field investigation under Executive Order No. 9835 of March 21, 1947, and, after such further investigation as may be appropriate, shall re-adjudicate, or cause to be re-adjudicated, in accordance with the said act of August 26, 1950, such of those cases as have not been adjudicated under a security standard commensurate with that established under this order.

SEC. 5. Whenever there is developed or received by any department or agency information indicating that the retention in employment of any officer or employee of the Government may not be clearly consistent with the interests of the national security, such information shall be forwarded to the head of the employing department or agency or his representative, who, after such investigation as may be appropriate, shall review, or cause to be reviewed, and, where necessary, re-adjudicate, or cause to be re-adjudicated, in accordance with the said act of August 26, 1950, the case of such officer or employee.

SEC. 6. Should there develop at any stage of investigation information indicating that the employment of any officer or employee of the Government may not be clearly consistent with the interests of the national security, the head of the department or agency concerned or his representative shall immediately suspend the employment of the person involved if he deems such suspension necessary in the interests of the national security and, following such investigation and review as he deems necessary, the head of the department or agency concerned shall terminate the employment of such suspended officer or employee whenever he shall determine such termination necessary or advisable in the interests of the national security, in accordance with the said act of August 26, 1950.

SEC. 7. Any person whose employment is suspended or terminated under the authority granted to heads of departments and agencies by or in accordance with the said act of August 26, 1950, or pursuant to the said Executive Order No. 9835 or any other security or loyalty program relating to officers or employees of the Government, shall not be reinstated or restored to duty or reemployed in the same department or agency and shall not be reemployed in any other department or agency, unless the head of the department or agency concerned finds that such reinstatement, restoration, or reemployment is clearly consistent with the interests of the national security, which finding shall be made a part of the records of such department or agency: *Provided,* that no person whose employment has been terminated under such authority thereafter may be employed by any other department or agency except after a determination by the Civil Service Commission that such person is eligible for such employment.

SEC. 8. (a) The investigations conducted pursuant to this order shall be designed to develop information as to whether the employment or retention in employment in the Federal service of the person being investigated is clearly consistent with the interests of the national security. Such information shall relate, but shall not be limited, to the following:

(1) Depending on the relation of the Government employment to the national security:

(i) Any behavior, activities, or associations which tend to show that the individual is not reliable or trustworthy.

(ii) Any deliberate misrepresentations, falsifications, or omissions of material facts.

(iii) Any criminal, infamous, dishonest, immoral, or notoriously disgraceful conduct, habitual use of intoxicants to excess, drug addiction, or sexual perversion.

(iv) An adjudication of insanity, or treatment for serious mental or neurological disorder without satisfactory evidence of cure.

(v) Any facts which furnish reason to believe that the individual may be subjected to coercion, influence, or pressure which may cause him to act contrary to the best interests of the national security.

(2) Commission of any act of sabotage, espionage, treason, or sedition, or attempts thereat or preparation therefor, or conspiring with, or aiding or abetting, another to commit or attempt to commit any act of sabotage, espionage, treason, or sedition.

(3) Establishing or continuing a sympathetic association with a saboteur, spy, traitor, seditionist, anarchist, or revolutionist, or with an espionage or other secret agent or representative of a foreign nation, or any representative of a foreign nation whose interests may be inimical to the interests of the United States,

or with any person who advocates the use of force or violence to overthrow the government of the United States or the alteration of the form of government of the United States by unconstitutional means.

(4) Advocacy of use of force or violence to overthrow the government of the United States, or of the alteration of the form of government of the United States by unconstitutional means.

(5) Membership in, or affiliation or sympathetic association with, any foreign or domestic organization, association, movement, group, or combination of persons which is totalitarian, Fascist, Communist, or subversive, or which has adopted, or shows, a policy of advocating or approving the commission of acts of force or violence to deny other persons their rights under the Constitution of the United States, or which seeks to alter the form of government of the United States by unconstitutional means.

(6) Intentional, unauthorized disclosure to any person of security information, or of other information disclosure of which is prohibited by law, or willful violation or disregard of security regulations.

(7) Performing or attempting to perform his duties, or otherwise acting, so as to serve the interests of another government in preference to the interests of the United States.

(b) The investigation of persons entering or employed in the competitive service shall primarily be the responsibility of the Civil Service Commission, except in cases in which the head of a department or agency assumes that responsibility pursuant to law or by agreement with the Commission. The Commission shall furnish a full investigative report to the department or agency concerned.

(c) The investigation of persons (including consultants, however employed), entering employment of, or employed by, the Government other than in the competitive service shall primarily be the responsibility of the employing department or agency. Departments and agencies without investigative facilities may use the investigative facilities of the Civil Service Commission, and other departments and agencies may use such facilities under agreement with the Commission.

(d) There shall be referred promptly to the Federal Bureau of Investigation all investigations being conducted by any other agencies which develop information indicating that an individual may have been subjected to coercion, influence, or pressure to act contrary to the interests of the national security, or information relating to any of the matters described in subdivisions (2) through (7) of subsection (a) of this section. In cases so referred to it, the Federal Bureau of Investigation shall make a full field investigation.

SEC. 9. (a) There shall be established and maintained in the Civil Service Commission a security-investigations index covering all persons as to whom security investigations have been conducted by any department or agency of the Government under this order. The central index established and maintained by the Commission under Executive Order No. 9835 of March 21, 1947, shall be made a part of the security-investigations index. The security-investigations index shall contain the name of each person investigated, adequate identifying information concerning each such person, and a reference to each department and agency which had conducted an investigation concerning the person involved or has suspended or terminated the employment of such person under the authority granted to heads of departments and agencies by or in accordance with the said act of August 26, 1950.

(b) The heads of all departments and agencies shall furnish promptly to the Civil Service Commission information appropriate for the establishment and maintenance of the security-investigations index.

(c) The reports and other investigative material and information developed by investigations conducted pursuant to any statute, order, or program described in section 7 of this order shall remain the property of the investigative agencies conducting the investigations, but may, subject to considerations of the national security, be retained by the department or agency concerned. Such reports and other investigative material and information shall be maintained in confidence, and no access shall be given thereto except, with the consent of the investigative agency concerned, to other departments and agencies conducting security programs under the authority granted by or in accordance with the said act of August 26, 1950, as may be required for the efficient conduct of Government business.

SEC. 10. Nothing in this order shall be construed as eliminating or modifying in any way the requirement for any investigation or any determination as to security which may be required by law.

SEC. 11. On and after the effective date of this order the Loyalty Review Board established by Executive Order No. 9835 of March 21, 1947, shall not accept agency findings for review, upon appeal or otherwise. Appeals pending before the Loyalty Review Board on such date shall be heard to final determination in accordance with the provisions of the said Executive Order No. 9835, as amended. Agency determinations favorable to the officer or employee concerned pending before the Loyalty Review Board on such date shall be acted upon by such Board, and whenever the Board is not in agreement with such favorable determination the case shall be remanded to the department or agency concerned for determination in accordance with the standards and procedures established pursuant to this order. Cases pending before the regional loyalty boards of the Civil Service Commission on which hearings have not been initiated on such date shall be referred to the department or agency concerned. Cases being heard by regional loyalty boards on such date shall be heard to conclusion, and the determination of the board shall be forwarded to the head of the department or agency concerned: *Provided,* that if no specific department or agency is involved, the case shall be dismissed without prejudice to the applicant. Investigations pending in the Federal Bureau of Investigation or the Civil Service Commission on such date shall be completed, and the reports thereon shall be made to the appropriate department or agency.

SEC. 12. Executive Order No. 9835 of March 21, 1947, as amended, is hereby revoked. For the purposes described in section 11 hereof the Loyalty Review Board and the regional loyalty boards of the Civil Service Commission shall continue to exist and function for a period of one hundred and twenty days from the effective date of this order, and the Department of Justice shall continue to furnish the information described in paragraph 3 of Part III of the said Executive Order No. 9835, but directly to the head of each department and agency.

SEC. 13. The Attorney General is requested to render to the heads of departments and agencies such advice as may be requisite to enable them to establish and maintain an appropriate employee-security program.

SEC. 14. (a) The Civil Service Commission, with the continuing advice and collaboration of representatives of such departments and agencies as the National Security Council may designate, shall make a continuing study of the manner in which this order is being implemented by the departments and agencies of the Government for the purpose of determining:

(1) Deficiencies in the department and agency security programs established under this order which are inconsistent with the interests of, or directly or indirectly weaken, the national security.

(2) Tendencies in such programs to deny to individual employees fair, impartial, and equitable treatment at the hands of the Government, or rights under the Constitution and laws of the United States or this order.

Information affecting any department or agency developed or received during the course of such continuing study shall be furnished immediately to the head of the department or agency concerned. The Civil Service Commission shall report to the National Security Council, at least semiannually, on the results of such study, and shall recommend means to correct any such deficiencies or tendencies.

(b) All departments and agencies of the Government are directed to cooperate with the Civil Service Commission to facilitate the accomplishment of the responsibilities assigned to it by subsection (a) of this section.

SEC. 15. This order shall become effective thirty days after the date hereof.

# Appendix XV: Albert Einstein Letter 1953

**The following is a letter from Albert Einstein to New York schoolteacher William Frauenglass, who had asked Einstein's advice on how to respond to congressional loyalty investigations. Einstein's letter was published in *The New York Times* on June 12, 1953.**

Thank you for your communication. By "remote field" I referred to the theoretical foundations of physics.

The problem with which the intellectuals of this country are confronted is very serious. Reactionary politicians have managed to instill suspicion of all intellectual efforts into the public by dangling before their eyes a danger from without. Having succeeded so far, they are now proceeding to suppress the freedom of teaching and to deprive of their positions all those who do not prove submissive, i.e., to starve them out.

What ought the minority of intellectuals to do against this evil? Frankly, I can only see the revolutionary way of noncooperation in the sense of Gandhi's. Every intellectual who is called before one of the committees ought to refuse to testify, i.e., he must be prepared for jail and economic ruin, in short, for the sacrifice of his personal welfare in the interest of the cultural welfare of his country.

However, this refusal to testify must not be based on the well-known subterfuge of invoking the Fifth Amendment against possible self-incrimination, but on the assertion that it is shameful for a blameless citizen to submit to such an inquisition and that this kind of inquisition violates the spirit of the Constitution.

If enough people are ready to take this grave step they will be successful. If not, then the intellectuals of this country deserve nothing better than the slavery which is intended for them.

P.S. This letter need not be considered "confidential."

# Appendix XVI: Presidential News Conference 1953 (excerpt)

**The following is an excerpt from President Dwight David Eisenhower's press conference on June 17, 1953. Four days earlier, Eisenhower had delivered a speech at Dartmouth College criticizing "book burners." Under questioning at the subsequent news conference, Eisenhower retreated from any implication that his Dartmouth speech had been aimed directly at McCarthy.**

## Presidential News Conference
### June 17, 1953
*[ Public Papers of the Presidents: 1953* (Washington, 1960), 426–27.]

THE PRESIDENT: My speech, I think, should stand by itself, but I will amplify to this extent: by no means am I talking, when I talk about books or the right of dissemination of knowledge, am I talking about any document or any other kind of thing that attempts to persuade or propagandize America into communism. Indeed, our courts found 11 Communists guilty of practically traitorous action; they pointed out that these men were dedicated to the destruction of the United States form of government by force, and that they took orders from a foreign government. So, manifestly, I am not talking about that kind of thing when I talk about free access to knowledge.

I believe the United States is strong enough to expose to the world its differing viewpoints—from those of what we call, almost, the man who has Socialist leanings to the man who is so far to the extreme right that it takes a telescope to find him. But that is America, and let's don't be afraid to show it to the world. Because we believe that form of government, those facts, that kind of thinking, that kind of combination of things, has produced the greatest system of government that the world has produced. That is what we believe; that is what I am talking about. And let no one try to think that I am attempting to propagate Communist beliefs by using governmental money to do it.

Excluding that kind of thing, I am against "book burning" of course—which is, as you well know, an expression to mean suppression of ideas. I just do not believe in suppressing ideas. I believe in dragging them out in the open and taking a look at them. That is what I meant, and I do not intend to be talking personally and in personalities with respect to anyone.

QUESTION. Merriman Smith, *United Press:* Mr. President, your speech this last Sunday at Dartmouth was interpreted or accepted by a great many people as being critical of a school of thought represented by Senator McCarthy; is that right or wrong?

THE PRESIDENT: Now, Merriman, you have been around me long enough to know I never talk personalities. I think that we will get along faster in most of these conferences if we remember that I do not talk personalities; I refuse to do so. . . .

# Appendix XVII: Communist Control Act of 1954 (excerpts)

SEC. 2. The Congress hereby finds and declares that the Communist Party of the United States, although purportedly a political party, is in fact an instrumentality of a conspiracy to overthrow the Government of the United States. It constitutes an authoritarian dictatorship within a republic, demanding for itself the rights and privileges accorded to political parties, but denying to all others the liberties guaranteed by the Constitution. Unlike political parties, which evolve their policies and programs through public means, by the reconciliation of a wide variety of individual views, and submit those policies and programs to the electorate at large for approval or disapproval, the policies and programs of the Communist Party are secretly prescribed for it by the foreign leaders of the world Communist movement. Its members have no part in determining its goals, and are not permitted to voice dissent to party objectives. Unlike members of political parties, members of the Communist Party are recruited for indoctrination with respect to its objectives and methods, and are organized, instructed, and disciplined to carry into action slavishly the assignments given them by their hierarchical chieftains. Unlike political parties, the Communist Party acknowledges no constitutional or statutory limitations upon its conduct or upon that of its members. The Communist Party is relatively small numerically, and gives scant indication of capacity ever to attain its ends by lawful political means. The peril inherent in its operation arises not from its numbers, but from its failure to acknowledge any limitation as to the nature of its activities, and its dedication to the proposition that the present constitutional Government of the United States ultimately must be brought to ruin by any available means, including resort to force and violence. Holding that doctrine, its role as the agency of a hostile foreign power renders its existence a clear present and continuing danger to the security of the United States. It is the means whereby individuals are seduced into the service of the world Communist movement, trained to do its bidding, and directed and controlled in the conspiratorial performance of their revolutionary services. Therefore, the Communist Party should be outlawed.

SEC. 3. The Communist Party of the United States, or any successors of such party regardless of the assumed name, whose object or purpose is to overthrow the Government of the United States, or the government of any State, Territory, District, or possession thereof, or the government of any political subdivision therein by force and violence, are not entitled to any of the rights, privileges, and immunities attendant upon legal bodies created under the jurisdiction of the laws of the United States or any political subdivision thereof; and whatever rights, privileges, and immunities which have heretofore been granted to said party or any subsidiary organization by reason of the laws of the United States or any political subdivision thereof, are hereby terminated: *Provided, however,* That nothing in this section shall be construed as amending the Internal Security Act of 1950, as amended.

P.L. 637–83rd Congress

# Appendix XVIII: Resolution of Censure, Documents 1954

Senate Speech by Ralph Flanders
on the Resolution of Censure
July 30, 1954
U.S. *Congressional Record,* 84th Cong., 2nd Sess.,
1954, C, Part 10, 12729–31.

MR. RALPH FLANDERS (Rep., Vt.): Mr. President, I call up the resolution of censure which lies on the desk.

THE VICE PRESIDENT: The clerk will read the resolution.

THE CHIEF CLERK: The Senator from Vermont proposes the following resolution (S. Res. 301):

> *Resolved,* That the conduct of the Senator from Wisconsin [Mr. McCarthy] is unbecoming a Member of the United States Senate, is contrary to senatorial traditions, and tends to bring the Senate into disrepute, and such conduct is hereby condemned.

MR. WILLIAM KNOWLAND (Rep., Cal.): Mr. President, will the Senator yield at this point?

MR. FLANDERS: I yield.

MR. KNOWLAND: Mr. President, I merely wish to say that we have a large attendance of Senators tonight, and undoubtedly will continue to have during the course of the evening. The galleries are full. A number of persons are standing around the walls of the Chamber. I hope everyone will recognize that the rules of the Senate do not permit indications of approval or disapproval. It will be difficult enough to carry on the debate this evening, and we shall need the cooperation of everyone present in order that there may be no demonstrations of any kind.

MR. FLANDERS: Mr. President—

THE VICE PRESIDENT: The Senator from Vermont is recognized.

MR. FLANDERS: A resolution of censure of one of its Members by the Senate is a serious but not unprecedented matter. The most recent case occurred in 1929 when a Republican Senate censured a Republican Senator for introducing an unauthorized person into the executive sessions of his committee. This matter is indeed a serious one. It is therefore important that a bill of particulars be offered to support the motion of censure. My own list of particulars I now proceed to offer though other Senators will have many other matters in their minds besides those which I am specifying.

Item 1: In my talk on the Senate floor on June 11 I called the attention of the Senate to the fact that in the closing days of the 82d Congress serious charges were made against the junior Senator from Wisconsin. A subcommittee of the Rules Committee felt that those charges were so serious that they addressed to the junior Senator from Wisconsin—hereinafter designated as the Senator—a list of questions. Neither at that time nor now do I pass any judgment on the charges on which these questions were based. What I do charge is that the Senator was repeatedly asked to reply to the questions and that he repeatedly refused or neglected to do so, classing them as smears and ignoring them. In so doing, the Senator showed personal contempt for the subcommittee. He likewise expressed doubts as to their honesty and as to their jurisdiction in the matters concerned.

The Senate itself, by a vote of 60 to 0, upheld the honesty and the jurisdiction of its committee and subcommittee. The personal contempt of the Senator was thereby spread over the Senate as a whole and there it remains to this day.

It may be objected that all of this relates to old and forgotten matters. They are old but not forgotten. The Senator cannot pass them off lightly on that account, however, because he habitually digs up matters of far greater age and does not hesitate to use them against anyone whom he calls before his committee or its subcommittees.

As a matter of fact, there is no statute of limitations which runs against this kind of contempt because it is personal, not legal. It remains upon us indefinitely unless and until the Senator chooses to cleanse himself by answering the questions.

If he continues to refuse answering, he finds himself, however informally, in the same category as the fifth-amendment Communists. He is quite evidently occupying the same ground and can scarcely avoid being called a fifth-amendment Senator.

This first item of the bill of particulars affects the Senate's honor and is therefore pertinent to the resolution which has just been read and supports its importance and validity.

Item 2: In the spring of 1953 the Senator sent abroad a pair of investigators named Cohn and Schine who were instructed, we suppose, to seek for subversion, Communist literature, and other Communist influences in our embassies and operational staffs abroad. He is responsible for the words and acts of these men. He appointed them. He has never repudiated their words and acts.

This ineffable pair was frivolous and irresponsible beyond words to describe. We took that expedition too lightly. We were amused by it, albeit in a rueful sort of way. But Cohn and Schine caused no amusement in Europe. They caused amazement that led to serious doubts as to the seriousness, responsibility, and intelligence of this Government as represented by emissaries of its upper legislative chamber. No one can know the dismay which was spread among our friends abroad unless he has heard it from those friends at first hand.

This calamity came at a time when the responsibility for world leadership could not be escaped by this Nation if we were not to see the world crumble to ruins around us in a destruction which we will ultimately share. Here again the Senate's honor and, in addition, the Nation's honor, have been compromised by the Senator's irresponsible staff and here is another major item in the bill of particulars.

Item 3: The Senator has an habitual contempt for people—

MR. HERMAN WELKER (Rep., Ida.): Mr. President, will the Senator yield?

MR. FLANDERS: I yield.

MR. WELKER: Let me say to the Senator from Vermont that I will not consent to the first sentence of item No. 3. No matter what the Senator from Vermont may think of the Senator from Wisconsin and his investigation of communism, I happen to know that he does not have a contempt for people. He loves my child and my wife, and he loves the children of almost every other Senator. I will not allow that statement to go unchallenged.

MR. FLANDERS: I proceed.

This contempt is so all-pervasive that it appears whenever we hear his words or see him in action. It was displayed on every hour of the televised hearings if I am to believe people who spent more time before the screen than I did. It appears in the press reports of those hearings and of every hearing. It is habitual in his own press releases.

I will give but two examples among a multitude which might be brought to bear on this particular issue. In the Army hearings General Zwicker was badgered to the point where he became, to use the Senator's words, one of the most "arrogant" witnesses that had ever appeared before him. The Senator thereupon used language to him that no man with any human decency would have ever used—particularly one whose own military care is, according to reports, the reverse of illustrious to one whose military services for his country are on full record and are beyond question.

The language was astonishing, the situation extreme, but the contempt was, and is, habitual.

MR. WELKER: Mr. President, will the Senator yield?

MR. FLANDERS: I yield.

MR. WELKER: Is the Senator familiar with the INS news report from Cambridge, Mass., on June 11, after the occurrence of which he has just spoken? I quote it. [Walker then quoted a news report of Zwicker's comments on the subject of coexistence with Communism.]

Is the Senator from Vermont familiar with that report?

MR. FLANDERS: I am not, but I shall go to the sources and examine them.

MR. WELKER: I hand it to the Senator.

MR. FLANDERS: That is not the source. I shall go to the source.

MR. WELKER: Very well.

MR. FLANDERS: I now proceed.

The second instance is one that has happened within the past few days. In trying to explain to the Rules Committee the sweet reasonableness of the procedures which the Senator always uses in his hearings, he made the charge that he knew one Dorothy Kenyon to be a member of the Communist Party on the testimony of 2 witnesses. She has completely denied this under oath. The next step would be to prosecute her for perjury, but the Senator says he contemplates doing nothing about the matter. This, by the way, is from the news report of the hearing.

The fact that he has made charges of such seriousness and lets them hang over the victim for the rest of her life without attempt on his part to prove them or offering her the chance of disproving them, is a direct insult to the personality and the soul of the victim. The astonishing thing is that the Senator does not know that he is insulting.

This thing happens over and over and over again. Unrebuked it casts a blot on the reputation of the Senate itself. It also makes plain the impossibility of controlling exhibitions of innate character by any change in the rules. The Senator can break rules faster than we can make them.

This list will do for an illustration of my own bill of particulars. Any Member of this body will find an inexhaustible mine of incidents from which each can draw his own bill of particulars.

By the way, I hold in my hand an additional list of particulars numbering 33—not 30, not 40, not 128, not 27, but 33.

We now come to a major question which is raised by this sad affair. That question is, who is going to prosecute Communists if the Senator's operations have the shadow of censure cast over them? The answer is simple. There will be no loss at all to the anti-Communist campaign. The Senator's contributions have been minor and comparatively unimportant.

"I have in my hand," to use one of the Senator's pet phrases, a list of the Department of Justice cases under the Smith Act as reported on July 29, 1954. There have been 13 such cases in which 103 persons have been indicted and 72 convicted in the trials already completed. Twenty-eight of the persons indicted are still on trial or awaiting trial. This is an impressive list, but the Senator made no contribution to this successful round-up of Communists.

There has been another series of cases based on grand jury indictment and FBI reports. Some of these are still going on.

In the *Amerasia* case Jaffee pleaded guilty, Larson entered a plea of nolo, and the Ross case was nol prossed. The credit does not go to the junior Senator.

Hiss was indicted, tried, convicted, and sentenced. The credit for that must go to the man who is now our Vice President. It does not go to the Senator.

Remington, after 2 trials, was convicted on 2 counts, and sentenced to 3 years. The Senator had no hand in that.

Julius and Ethel Rosenberg were convicted, sentenced, and executed. The Senator had no hand in that.

Harry Gold entered a plea of guilty for accepting atomic secrets from Dr. Fuchs. He was sentenced to 30 years. The Senator had no hand in this.

Coplon was tried twice with her co-conspirator Gubitchev and both were sentenced. Gubitchev's sentence was suspended if he would return to Russia, which he did. The Coplon sentence was denied by the court, but the case is still pending. The Senator had no hand in bringing this case to the public attention.

Ben Gold, president of the International Fur and Leather Workers Union, was convicted of making false statements in denying that he was a member of the Communist Party. The Senator had no part in this.

Verber and Ponger were convicted of conspiracy to transmit national defense information to Russia. They entered pleas of guilty and were sentenced to periods running from 5 to 15 years. The co-conspirator in the Soviet Embassy was declared persona non grata and departed for Russia. The Senator had no part in this.

The Lattimore case is the only one of the major cases of Communist Party conspiracy and espionage in which the Senator has had a hand. Perjury proceedings are pending in his case but no conviction has been obtained. This is the one major feather in the war bonnet of the Senator.

Here we have the really serious and effective work of ridding the country of communism done by others without the blowing of trumpets or the beating of drums. It has been done quietly, efficiently and thoroughly by the FBI and the Department of Justice.

The Senator's work has resulted in some desirable dismissals. So far as I am aware, he has never claimed credit for a single successful prosecution.

As to the pink dentist, the wide world knows he was the original fuse which set off the 7 weeks fusee of the McCarthy-Army investigations whose net result to date has been the departure of Mr. Cohn. The investigation might never have been held if the Secretary of the Army had not tried to appease the Senator. I think one may say with some assurance that there are three who cannot be appeased. They are, or have been, Hitler, the Kremlin, and the Senator.

Even in the cases that the Senator has turned up, this has been done by "muscling in" on the authorized work of another committee. The job of fighting communism in the Government is the responsibility of the Subcommittee on Internal Security, of the Judiciary Committee, headed by the Senator from Indiana [Mr. Jenner]. It was a case of "double-muscle" when the Senator started his investigation of communism in the unions in the Boston area, for he not only took over the job of the Senator from Indiana, but also the subcommittee job to which the Senator from Maryland [Mr. Butler] had been assigned. No one who knows the Senator from Indiana and the Senator from Maryland can have the slightest fear that the fight against communism will be neglected by them, or carried out otherwise than with efficiency and determination.

Meanwhile the proper work of the Committee on Government Operations was being left undone except as it was carried out by one man without a staff and without an appropriation. I refer, of course, to the Senator from Delaware [Mr. Williams], who has done a tremendous job in ferreting out corruption and bringing it to justice.

Mention should also be made of the work currently going on in the Banking and Currency Committee in investigating the scandals in housing. There is plenty of work for the junior Senator from Wisconsin to do in his appointed field without raiding the jurisdictions of his fellow Senators.

Mr. President, whether as orator or audience, I prefer short speeches. I therefore conclude for the present at this point.

## REPORT ON RESOLUTION TO CENSURE

NOVEMBER 8, 1954—Ordered to be printed

Mr. WATKINS, from the Select Committee To Study Censure Charges, submitted the following

### REPORT

[To accompany S. Res. 301]

The Select Committee To Study Censure Charges, consisting of—

Arthur V. Watkins (chairman)
Edwin C. Johnson (vice chairman)

| | |
|---|---|
| John C. Stennis | Francis Case |
| Frank Carlson | Sam J. Ervin, Jr. |

to which was referred the resolution (S. Res. 301) and amendments, having considered the same, reports thereon and recommends that the resolution be adopted with certain amendments.

### INTRODUCTION

On August 2 (legislative day, July 2), 1954, Senate Resolution 301, to censure the Senator from Wisconsin, Mr. McCarthy, submitted by Senator Flanders on July 30, and amendments proposed thereto, was referred to a select committee to be composed of 3 Republicans and 3 Democrats and named by the Vice President. By said order the select committee was authorized—

(1) To hold hearings;
(2) To sit and act at such times and places during the sessions, recesses, and adjourned periods of the Senate;
(3) To require by subpena or otherwise the attendance of such witnesses and the production of such correspondence, books, papers, and doc-

uments, and to take such testimony as is deemed advisable.

The select committee was instructed to act and to make a report to the Senate prior to the adjournment sine die of the Senate in the 2d session of the 83d Congress.

The order of the Senate is set forth in the hearing record, page 1 et seq.

The Vice President, on August 5, 1954, acting on the recommendations of the majority leader and the minority leader, made the following appointments of members of the select committee: From the majority, the Senator from Utah (Mr. Watkins), the Senator from Kansas (Mr. Carlson), and the Senator from South Dakota (Mr. Case). From the minority, the Senator from Colorado (Mr. Johnson), the Senator from Mississippi (Mr. Stennis), and the Senator from North Carolina (Mr. Ervin). The select committee chose the Senator from Utah (Mr. Watkins) as chairman, and the Senator from Colorado (Mr. Johnson) as vice chairman.

The select committee, on August 24, 1954, served upon the junior Senator from Wisconsin, and other interested persons, a notice of hearings, setting forth 5 categories containing 13 specifications of charges from certain of the proposed amendments, establishing the general procedural rules for the hearings before the select committee, and formally requesting the appearance of Senator McCarthy. The notice of hearings will be found in the hearing record, page 8.

All testimony and evidence taken and received by the select committee was at public hearings attended by Senator McCarthy and his counsel, except the opinion of the Senate Parliamentarian which was obtained pursuant to Senator McCarthy's request.

The public hearings were held in accordance with said notice of hearings, on August 31, September 1, 2, 7, 8, 9, 10, 11, and 13, 1954. The entire testimony, evidence, and proceedings at said public hearings are in the printed record of the hearings.

I

CATEGORY I. INCIDENTS OF CONTEMPT OF THE SENATE OR A SENATORIAL COMMITTEE

A. GENERAL DISCUSSION AND SUMMARY OF EVIDENCE

The evidence on the question whether Senator McCarthy was guilty of contempt of the Senate or a senatorial committee involves his conduct with relation to the Subcommittee on Privileges and Elections of the Senate Committee on Rules and Administration. An analysis of the three amendments referring to this general matter (being amendment (3) proposed by Senator Fulbright, amendment (a) proposed by Senator Morse, and amendment (17) proposed by Senator Flanders) reveals these specific charges:

(1) That Senator McCarthy refused repeated invitations to testify before the subcommittee.

(2) That he declined to comply with a request by letter dated November 21, 1952, from the chairman of the subcommittee to appear to supply information concerning certain specific matters involving his activities as a Member of the Senate.

(3) That he denounced the subcommittee and contemptuously refused to comply with its request.

(4) That he has continued to show his contempt for the Senate by failing to explain in any manner the six charges contained in the Hennings-Hayden-Hendrickson report, which was filed in January 1953.

We have decided to consider and discuss in our report under this category the incident with reference to Senator Hendrickson, since the conduct complained of is related directly to the fact that Senator Hendrickson was a member of the Subcommittee on Privileges and Elections. This incident is referred to in the amendment proposed by Senator Flanders (30), the specific charge being:

(5) That he ridiculed and defamed Senator Hendrickson in vulgar and base language, calling him: "A living miracle without brains or guts."

The report referred to as the Hennings-Hayden-Hendrickson report is the report of the Subcommittee on Privileges and Elections to the Committee on Rules and Administration, pursuant to Senate Resolution 187, 82d Congress, 1st session, and Senate Resolution 304, 82d Congress, 2d session, filed January 2, 1953, and appears in part II of the hearing record. The select committee admitted in evidence the Hennings-Hayden-Hendrickson report for the limited purposes of showing the nature of the charges before that subcommittee, as bearing upon the question of jurisdiction of that subcommittee, and what was the subject matter of the investigation (pp. 55, 121, and 524 of the hearings).

As stated by the chairman (p. 17 of the hearings), the select committee did not construe this category as involving in any way the truth or falsity of any of the charges against Senator McCarthy considered by that subcommittee. These charges, as shown by its report and as stated briefly by the chairman, Senator Hennings, in a letter to Senator McCarthy under date of November 21, 1952 (Hennings-Hayden-Hendrickson report, p. 98), were: [Here follows a summary of the subjects of the subcommittee's inquiry.]

The evidence taken by the select committee under this category consisted of letters and documents, oral testimony by Senator McCarthy and oral testimony by Senator Hayden, and by the Parliamentarian. As to the statement regarding Senator Hendrickson, there is the testimony of a reporter. There is no material contradiction in any of the testimony relating to this category. The sending and receipt of the correspondence is admitted. There is no contradiction of the verbal testimony of Senator McCarthy with reference to his conversations with Chairman Gillette, or of that of Chairman Hayden with reference to the constitution of the Subcommittee on Privileges and Elections and the filing of its report, or of that of Parliamentarian Watkins, discussed fully hereinafter.

The evidence shows that the Subcommittee on Privileges and Elections was proceeding to investigate and report on Senate Resolution 187; that Senator McCarthy was invited to appear to testify before the subcommittee on five separate occasions extending from September 25, 1951, to November 7, 1952, and formally requested to appear by letter and telegram of November 21, 1952; that Senator McCarthy could not appear at the times specified in the request because of his absence in Wisconsin; that Senator McCarthy did not appear before the subcommittee in answer to the matters under investigation regarding his own conduct, but did appear on one occasion in support of his Senate Resolution 304 directed against Senator Benton; that Senator McCarthy accused the subcommittee of acting without power and beyond its jurisdiction, of wasting vast amounts of public money for improper partisan purposes, of proceeding dishonestly, of aiding the cause of communism, and that these accusations were directed toward an official subcommittee of the Senate. The uncontradicted testimony further shows that Senator McCarthy directed and gave to the press an abusive and insulting statement concerning Senator Hendrickson, calculated to wound a colleague, solely because Senator Hendrickson was a member of the subcommittee and performing service required by the Senate.

VIII

RECOMMENDATIONS OF SELECT COMMITTEE UNDER SENATE ORDER PURSUANT TO SENATE RESOLUTION 301

For the reasons and on the facts found in this report, the select committee recommends:

1. That on the charges in the category of "Incidents of Contempt of the Senate or a Sena-

torial Committee," the Senator from Wisconsin, Mr. McCarthy, should be censured.

2. That the charges in the category of "Incidents of Encouragement of United States Employees To Violate the Law and Their Oaths of Office or Executive Orders," do not, under all the evidence, justify a resolution of censure.

3. That the charges in the category of "Incidents Involving Receipt or Use of Confidential or Classified or Other Confidential Information From Executive Files," do not, under all the evidence, justify a resolution of censure.

4. That the charges in the category of "Incidents Involving Abuse of Colleagues in the Senate," except as to those dealt with in the first category, do not, under all the evidence, justify a resolution of censure.

5. That on the charges in the category of "Incident Relating to Ralph W. Zwicker, a general officer of the Army of the United States," the Senator from Wisconsin, Mr. McCarthy, should be censured.

6. That with reference to the amendment to Senate Resolution 301 offered by the Senator from New Jersey, Mr. Smith, this report and the recommendations herein be regarded as having met the purposes of said amendment.

7. That with reference to the amendment to Senate Resolution 301 offered by the Senator from Connecticut, Mr. Bush, that an amendment to the Senate Rules be adopted in accord with the language proposed in part VII of this report.

The chairman of the select committee is authorized in behalf of the committee to present to the Senate appropriate resolutions to give effect to the foregoing recommendations.

Senate Debate on the McCarthy Censure Motion
December 1, 1954
[U.S. *Congressional Record*, 84th Cong., 2nd Sess., 1954, C, Part 12, 15952–54.]

MR RUSSELL LONG (Dem., La.): Mr. President, so much do I dislike the idea of censuring one's colleagues that I cannot conceive of myself ever bringing before the Senate a censure resolution. Nevertheless this unpleasant task has been brought before us, and I have been compelled to reach an unhappy decision. I have been especially troubled because of the possible dangers of the precedent which would be established by voting censure, which is and should always be a most extraordinary action by the Senate. Censure of a colleague in the Senate is a grave matter, and it should not be invoked without clear and unequivocal justification.

It is not enough, in my opinion, to disapprove generally of the personal conduct of a Senator or the manner in which he carries out his duties as a Senator. Specific misconduct is essential as a basis for censure.

I disagree with the statement in the select committee's report to the effect that a Senator does not have the right to impugn the motives of a fellow Senator or a senatorial committee. I believe that all of us have that right, and I would certainly regret to see it otherwise.

Suppose that a committee might in fact be proceeding from wrongful motives and seeking to destroy a Member of the Senate who was engaged in an undertaking essential to our security. It is unquestionably in the national interest that there be freedom to bring forward such charges—and, of course, to be given a chance to prove them. However, any Senator who chooses to exercise that right must clearly do so at his peril, because either an individual Senator or a committee can bring the case before the Senate in the event of such an attack.

The conduct of the junior Senator from Wisconsin toward and his abusive language concerning the Gillette-Hennings committee certainly constituted a challenge which, in my opinion, should have been taken up by that committee. Had it been brought before the Senate at the time it was occurring, I feel certain that I would have voted to sustain the committee and to condemn the attack by the Senator. I am not prepared to censure him now, solely for an action which went unchallenged at the time.

Unfortunately, this is not the only instance in which the junior Senator from Wisconsin has challenged duly constituted committees of the Senate. In most violent form we have witnessed his attitude and attack on the chairman, and indeed all the members, of a select committee of the Senate appointed with the greatest care. The members of this committee are without exception considered by the entire membership of the Senate, except by the Senator from Wisconsin, to be men whose honor and integrity are without question. All of us know also that not one member of this committee served by his own wish or nomination They served as a matter of duty, and an attack on them cannot be treated in any way except as an attack on the Senate as a whole.

Each of us must now decide whether or not we find that the Senator's abusive conduct toward the select committee, and the other committees and individuals which are involved here, has been justified by the evidence which he has produced before the select committee and on the floor of the Senate. I do not believe that he has produced the evidence to support these charges.

He has said that this committee as a whole was serving the cause of communism, but he has produced no evidence supporting this charge, and I emphatically state that I do not believe that any member of this committee knowingly or unknowingly is serving the cause of communism. He has labeled the chairman of this committee as a coward on grounds which I cannot remotely accept. I believe that Senator WATKINS has discharged a disagreeable and onerous responsibility in a manner which has won for him new esteem among us all, and I cannot by my vote do otherwise than express my confidence in him and appreciation for his conscientious effort to serve the Senate in a most unpleasant post.

Therefore, Mr. President, I shall vote in favor of censure. In view of all the circumstances I do not see how I could do otherwise. I wish to make it a matter of record, however, that in doing so I do not consider that I am establishing a precedent which can be used in the future to enforce uniformity in our conduct as individual Senators and representatives of our respective States.

Except for repeated assaults by the junior Senator from Wisconsin on individual Senators and duly constituted committees, which have not been mitigated by any generous expression on his part and which have not been supported by evidence to prove his charges of wrongful motives and harmful actions, I should never have decided to vote for censure in this case. Instead, I should like to again make it clear that I support him fully in his right to impugn the motives of any and all of us; but the fact cannot be escaped that his imputations, as those of any other Senator, must be subjected to scrutiny if they are challenged and brought before the Senate.

In the present case he is clearly found wanting when called upon to support his allegations. This is the test which should be applied in all such cases; and I believe that by the judicious application of this test we can avoid in future instances the very harmful results which have been pointed out most clearly by the junior Senator from Wisconsin [Mr. McCarthy], the Senator from Idaho [Mr. Welker], and others in the debate which is now being concluded. The right to challenge must be undisputed and, equally so, the burden of proof must rest with the challenger when his challenge is accepted. . . .

MR. WILLIAM KNOWLAND (Rep., Cal.): Mr. President, I yield myself 10 minutes.

I said at the session of the Senate last August that the select committee which was appointed commanded my confidence. I have not changed my viewpoint of the integrity, the ability, the loyalty, or the courage of that committee in the slightest degree since that time.

These men I know well. I have served with some of them for a considerable period of time. I have known others in their capacity as public servants or as private citizens. I stated on the floor of the Senate in August, and I repeated my statement during this session, that I would be willing to be tried for my life before this select committee as a group, or before any of them individually. I did not draw the center line when I said that, because my statement applied to the Senator from Mississippi [Mr. Stennis], the Senator from North Carolina [Mr. Ervin], and to the Senator from Colorado [Mr. Johnson], as well as it applied to the Senator from Utah [Mr. Watkins], the Senator from Kansas [Mr. Carlson], and the Senator from South Dakota [Mr. Case]. Any abuse or unfair statements which have been made in relation to this committee or to any of its members I consider to be abuse and unfair statements against the majority leader, and I might add, perhaps, against the minority leader and the Senate of the United States itself.

The investigation was not an easy task for the committee to undertake. I have said privately to some of my colleagues in the Senate that I did not believe I ever had a more difficult or distasteful job than I had on my side of the aisle in asking three Members of this body to undertake what all of us knew would be a difficult task to perform. I express on my own behalf and on behalf of the Senate my deep sense of appreciation that the members of the select committee have been willing to undertake this very difficult work.

I have known and served with the distinguished junior Senator from New Jersey [Mr. Hendrickson] for a considerable period of time. I have served with him during the entire 6 years he has been a Member of the Senate. I am sorry he will not be back with us at the next session, because I admire his intelligence and his courage as a man, as a soldier of his country, and as a Senator. I would have no hesitation about giving my unqualified approval of him for any position for which he might be suggested, because I know he has the ability, courage, and intelligence to undertake and fulfill with great distinction any position which he might be called upon to fill.

When any of my colleagues are treated unfairly, I feel very badly. I do not think it helps the person who makes references to them in an unfair way.

But having said that, Mr. President, I also must say that I have had to search my conscience very deeply before coming to a final conclusion in regard to the matter pending before the Senate. I have finally, and only last night, after some prayerful consideration, arrived at what, at least to me, is a decision in the matter. I shall not vote for the censure resolution.

Mr. President, we are dealing with a body which has existed since the birth of this Republic. I hope we are dealing with a body which will exist long after all of us have gone. As was stated by the Senator from Connecticut [Mr. Purtell] today, I hope that we shall not hand down to those who succeed us a body which will have any less power than had the body as we found it when we came to the Senate.

Mr. President, it is a very difficult decision that Members on both sides of the aisle must make. Certainly we must, and we shall, in my judgment, continue the power of the Senate to conduct investigations into the executive branch of the Government, or into any field involving legislative responsibility. We have a constitutional obligation to do that, and we must resist with all the power at our command, and it is a substantial power, an effort to curtail in the slightest degree that power of investigation.

But, Mr. President, we must be very certain in this body to make sure that if at any time in the future a Senator speaks up, he will not be cut down. Sometimes it is very difficult to draw the line. I have told the junior Senator from Wisconsin, and I am sorry he stepped from the Chamber momentarily, because I have told him privately, and I would not say publicly what I had not said privately, that I do not approve of the language which the junior Senator from Wisconsin used concerning my good friend, and he is my good friend, the Senator from New Jersey [Mr. Hendrickson], or remarks of the junior Senator from Wisconsin regarding the select committee. I stated that any charges made against the committee to the effect that it was the "unwitting handmaiden" of anything in fact implied that the majority leader was also the unwitting handmaiden, and I personally resented it.

However, under the circumstances, and considering the long history of the Senate, I do not believe the Senate should now, in an ex post facto sort of way, adopt a resolution of censure, which has not been done in the entire history of the Senate under the circumstances presently before the Senate.

Mr. President, are we to have no statute of limitations at all? I believe the Senate has to give some consideration to that question. During the address of the junior Senator from Nevada [Mr. Brown], on yesterday, during the time he yielded for questions, I briefly referred to the fact that we might go back to the 1941 Langer case, to be specific. At that time the question arose with regard to the seating of a Member of this body. The question arose as to whether a Senator might be expelled. Certain charges were made. The Senate, in its judgment, determined that

it would not expel a Senator, and would not deny him his seat. However, the charges might still remain.

The period from 1941 to 1954 is 13 years. Are we to establish a precedent that the Senate might go back and draw up charges, after such a long period of time has elapsed, and consider a censure resolution? In some distant day, such a proposal might be politically inspired.

Those who are familiar with history know that during the period of the French Revolution, a member of the French Assembly could rise on one side of the aisle and denounce a colleague on the other side of the aisle, and if standing at his back was a majority, the man who was denounced went to the guillotine. That is an extreme case, to be sure, but we are dealing with this question now for all history, and not alone for the 83d Congress, or merely for the junior Senator from Wisconsin, or for any individual Senator, important as he may be.

I think there is a very real basis for believing that if a censurable act is committed, the action should be taken by the Congress in which that act took place, because otherwise there would be no statute of limitations. I think it is particularly true that when a Senator has committed an alleged act during the term of office for which he has been elected, and he submits his candidacy to the people of his State, and the people of his own State reelect him, and he comes to the bar of the Senate and presents his credentials, and takes his oath of office, the Senate is derelict in its duty if at that particular time it does not raise a question as to his right to be seated. If he is seated, and the point is not made, then I think the statute of limitations runs. If we do not follow some rule of reason in that regard, a transitory, highly political group which might come to power some day in the distant future, after all of us have passed from the scene, might determine, for political purposes, to use the power of the majority to censure a member of the minority, and that member might be a member of the Democratic minority, the Republican minority, the conservative minority, or the liberal minority, because governments of countries have changed over the years. The only protection we have is to go by the landmarks of the Constitution and the precedents of the Senate, which have kept the Senate the greatest, freest deliberative body the world has ever seen.

Mr. President, after a careful search of my conscience, and considering the responsibility which weighs heavily upon me because of the seat I occupy, I have come to this conclusion. I wish it to be understood that if the Senate should vote against the censure resolution, it would be in no sense an approval of the use of the words used by the junior Senator from Wisconsin, for I would not approve of such words. I would not want it so interpreted, and I have told the junior Senator from Wisconsin that he has not in the least been courteous to some of his colleagues in this Chamber.

However, under the conditions I have cited, in fairness to his body, to myself, and to those by whom I have been asked to serve, I feel that I should not vote for censure. . . .

MR. LYNDON JOHNSON (Dem., Tex.): At the outset of the debate it was my intention not to address the Senate on the subject now before the Senate.

I had thought that the question could best be handled through a calm discussion by the participants—the members of our select committee and the declared opponents of the resolution. The senior Senator from Texas believed it would be best to listen to the arguments advanced by the opposing sides, and then express his position by his vote alone.

After all, Mr. President, on an issue of this kind no person's word can be as eloquent as his vote.

Since the debate began, however, there have been developments which have changed my decision as to the course I should pursue. The most important is the attack made upon the select committee chosen by the majority and minority leaders, and I regard it as an attack upon the Senate itself.

The change in my course does not mean I have changed my mind as to how I should vote. A number of days ago I came to the conclusion that sufficient facts were available to permit a reasonably intelligent man to make a reasonably conscientious decision.

On the basis of the evidence, it is my intention to vote for the censure resolution. That is a personal decision on my part. I am not seeking to influence, and I have not sought to influence, the decision of any other Senator.

Mr. President, it is not my purpose to go into a lengthy explanation of the reasons for the vote I shall cast. The report of the select committee and the addresses made by its distinguished members are ample, in the judgment of the senior Senator from Texas. They need no elaboration insofar as I am concerned.

Mr. President, I am rising to speak for one reason only—to make it unmistakably clear, today and tomorrow, and in the years to come, where I stand with respect to the unwarranted attack upon the members of the select committee.

Mr. President, I had a hand in the selection of the members of that great committee. They were not my selection alone, because I sought advice and counsel. I doubt whether there was any Member on this side of the aisle who, during that period of selection, was not approached by me, seeking advice, counsel, and recommendations.

In a very real sense this was truly a committee which represented the whole Senate. In making the selection, Mr. President, we sought men of prudence, men with judicial temperaments, men of unquestionable patriotism, men who could and would succeed in putting their country ahead of any political or partisan consideration.

Mr. President, it is my belief that we succeeded beyond the fondest expectations of the most optimistic.

Mr. President, I wish to have it noted here that I am not confining my personal tribute to the Democratic members of the select committee alone. I think particular praise is due to the very able and the very courageous senior Senator from Utah [Mr. Watkins], a man who will forever deserve the gratitude of the American people for his courageous and his statesmanlike conduct. Although I do not always agree with the political views of the senior Senator from Utah, he will always have my respect and my admiration as a courageous gallant gentleman, a public servant in the highest sense of the word.

Neither he nor any other member of the select committee sought the post. They accepted it, knowing it to be a very disagreeable task. They accepted it solely because it had to be done—because duty was calling; and these six men are the kind of men who always answer the call of duty. From an examination of the record, it is obvious that they approached this unpleasant duty in a judicial frame of mind. They leaned over backwards to give the junior Senator from Wisconsin the benefit of any doubt. They exercised what I consider great restraint and prudence.

Mr. President, it concerned me to find inserted in the CONGRESSIONAL RECORD a statement describing these agents of the Senate—these men who, pursuant to an order of the Senate, were selected upon recommendation of the majority and the minority leaders, as "unwitting handmaidens of communism." I imagine it even came as something of a shock to the most vigorous opponents of the censure resolution.

The use of the word "unwitting" does not change the situation, for, Mr. President, if these are "unwitting" men, then our country is lost, because I do not think any Member will dispute the statement that these six men represent as good as we have in the United States Senate.

Mr. President, I do not intend to have my comments construed as a "defense" of the select committee. It needs no defense. Its members are eminently qualified, as they have so amply demonstrated, to take care of themselves. I am speaking, Mr. President, because I am proud to associate myself with statesmen of their high caliber. I am speaking out of a deep, personal belief that I, as an individual, must reject these imputations against the honor of great Americans with a long, proven record of service to their country.

The words which were used in attacking these men do not belong in the pages of the CONGRESSIONAL RECORD or of the Senate Journal. Such word would be much more fittingly inscribed on the wall of a men's room. But Mr. President, the issue before us is not just the use of harsh language. Men like "Big" ED JOHNSON, the governor-to-be of Colorado, Judge JOHN STENIS, Judge SAM ERVIN, and the other members of the select committee, can handle any personal abuse which may come in their direction.

The real issue, as I see it, Mr. President, is whether the Senate of the United States, the greatest deliberative body in the history of the world, will permit abuse of a duly appointed committee seeking to carry out the will of the Senate.

The issue before us is just that simple.

If we sanction such abuse—whether of this committee, that committee, or another committee—we might just as well turn over our jobs to a small group of men and go back home to plow the south 40 acres.

For myself, I can conceive of no compromise on this question. Like any reasonable man, I am willing to consider language which will improve the resolution, any language which will express better the sense of this body, But on the basic issue of censure or noncensure of the conduct of the junior Senator from Wisconsin, I, as a man devoted to the traditions of this body, feel that there is no choice.

If there were truly an issue involving communism, my attitude would be different. But I can search the record with a fine-tooth comb and, on that question, I can find nothing even remotely connected with the battle against subversion.

Mr. President, many people are strongly in favor of the junior Senator from Wisconsin. Many are strongly opposed to him. I doubt whether any action we take here today or tomorrow will meet with the approval of either group. But the overwhelming majority of the American people, most of them silent as we speak, are concerned with the practices, the policies, and the conduct of the United States Senate.

Our integrity can best be preserved by a straight-out vote. As for myself—and I am speaking for no other Senator—I have made my decision.

Senate Vote on the McCarthy Censure Resolution
December 2, 1954
[U.S. *Congressional Record,* 84th Cong., 2nd Sess., 1954, C, Part 12, 16392.]

YEAS—67

| | | |
|---|---|---|
| Abel | Anderson | Bennett |
| Aiken | Beall | Burke |
| Bush | Green | Morse |
| Byrd | Hayden | Murray |
| Carlson | Hendrickson | Neely |
| Case | Hennings | O'Mahoney |
| Chavez | Hill | Pastore |
| Clements | Holland | Payne |
| Cooper | Humphrey | Potter |
| Cotton | Ives | Robertson |
| Daniel, S. C. | Jackson | Russell |
| Daniel, Tex. | Johnson, Colo. | Saltonstall |
| Douglas | Johnson, Tex. | Scott |
| Duff | Johnson, S. C. | Smith, Maine |
| Eastland | Kefauver | Smith, N. J. |
| Ellender | Kerr | Sparkman |
| Ervin | Kilgore | Stennis |
| Ferguson | Lehman | Symington |
| Flanders | Long | Thye |
| Frear | Magnuson | Watkins |
| Fulbright | Mansfield | Williams |
| George | McClellan | |
| Gillette | Monroney | |

NAYS—22

| | | |
|---|---|---|
| Barrett | Hickenlooper | Millikin |
| Bridges | Hruska | Mundt |
| Brown | Jenner | Purtell |
| Butler | Knowland | Schoeppel |
| Cordon | Kuchel | Welker |
| Dirksen | Langer | Young |
| Dworshak | Malone | |
| Goldwater | Martin | |

NOT VOTING—6

| | | |
|---|---|---|
| Bricker | Gore | Smathers |
| Capehart | Kennedy | Wiley |

ANSWERED "PRESENT"—1

McCarthy

So the resolution (S. Res. 301), as amended, was agreed to, as follows:

*Resolved,* That the Senator from Wisconsin, Mr. McCARTHY, failed to cooperate with the Subcommittee on Privileges and Elections of the Senate Committee on Rules and Administration in clearing up matters referred to that subcommittee which concerned his conduct as a Senator and affected the honor of the Senate and, instead, repeatedly abused the subcommittee, and its members who were trying to carry out assigned duties, thereby obstructing the constitutional processes of the Senate, and that this conduct of the Senator from Wisconsin, Mr. McCAR-THY, is contrary to senatorial traditions and is hereby condemned.

SEC. 2. The Senator from Wisconsin, Mr. McCAR-THY, in writing to the chairman of the Select Committee To Study Censure Charges (Mr. WATKINS) after the select committee had issued its report and before the report was presented to the Senate charging three members of the select committee with "deliberate deception" and "fraud" for failure to disqualify them. selves; in stating to the press on November 4, 1954, that the special Senate session that was to begin November 8, 1954 was a "lynch party"; in repeatedly describing this special Senate session as a "lynch bee" in a nationwide television and radio show on November 7, 1954; in stating to the public press on November 13, 1954, that the chairman of the select committee (Mr. WATKINS) was guilty of "the most unusual, most cowardly thing I've heard of" and stating further: "I expected he would be afraid to answer the questions, but didn't think he'd be stupid enough to make a public statement"; and in characterizing the said committee as the "unwitting handmaiden," "involuntary agent," and "attorneys in fact" of the Communist Party and in charging that the said committee in writing its report "imitated Communist methods—that it distorted, misrepresented, and omitted in its effort to manufacture a plausible rationalization" in support of its recommendations to the Senate, which characterizations and charges were contained in a statement released to the press and inserted in the CONGRESSIONAL RECORD of November 10, 1954, acted contrary to senatorial ethics and tended to bring the Senate into dishonor and disrepute, to obstruct the constitutional processes of the Senate, and to impair its dignity; and such conduct is hereby condemned.

# Index

This index is designed to be used in conjunction with the many cross-references within the A-to-Z entries. The main A-to-Z entries are indicated by **boldface** page references. The general subjects are subdivided by the A-to-Z entries. Illustrations and captions are indicated by *italicized* page references. The chronology is indicated by "c" following the page locator.

## A

AAUP *see* American Association of University Professors

ABC (American Broadcasting Company) 82

ABC (American Business Consultants) *see* American Business Consultants

Abraham Lincoln Brigade 208, 443

Abraham Lincoln School (Chicago, Illinois) 443

academic freedom

American Association of University Professors 7, 8

Einstein, Albert 128, 129

Hicks, Granville 172

Meiklejohn, Alexander 262, 263

Velde, Harold H. 379

Warren, Earl 390

Wood, John Stephen 403

academics *see* professors and educators

Academy of Motion Picture Arts and Sciences 371

ACCF *see* American Committee for Cultural Freedom

Acheson, Dean (1893–1971) *1*, **1–4**

*Amerasia* 6, 7

Berle Jr., Adolf A. 27

Bridges, Styles 42

China 69

China Lobby 70

China White Paper 71

Clubb, Oliver Edmund 74

Dulles, John Foster 123

Eastland, James Oliver 125

Hiss, Alger 176, 177

International Information Agency 198

Korean War 223

Lattimore, Owen 232

McCarthy, Joseph R. 257

Service, John Stewart 338

Truman, Harry S. 367

Vincent, John Carter 382, 453–454

ACLU *see* American Civil Liberties Union

Action Committee to Free Spain Now 443

actors and actresses

Allen, Woody 32, 150

Ball, Lucille **20–21**, *21*

Bogart, Humphrey *35*, **35–36**, 82, 344

Bond, Ward 106, 268, 269, 395

Carlson, Richard 192, 304

Chaplin, Charles Spencer ("Charlie") 32, 56, **63–65**, 135

Christians, Mady 32, 72, 313

Cobb, Lee J. 32, 58, **74–75**, 295

Coburn, Charles **75–76**, 106

Cooper, Gary **92–93**, 172, 268

Da Silva, Howard *99*, **99–100**, 363

Douglas, Helen Gahagan *113*, **113–114**, 114, 283, 311

Douglas, Melvyn 12, 113, **114–115**

Ferrer, Jose 31, **141–142**, 147, 148, 312

Garfield, John 63, **156**

Hayden, Sterling **166**, *166*

Henreid, Paul 82, 264

Hepburn, Katharine 82, *170*, **170–171**, 264, 384

Holliday, Judy **178**

Kaye, Danny 82, 160

Knox, Alexander 81, 264

Leigh, Janet 188, 396

Loeb, Philip 19, 32, 150, 268, 313

March, Fredric **246**

Menjou, Adolphe *see* Menjou, Adolphe

Monroe, Marilyn 5

Mostel, Zero 14, 32, 150, **267–268**

Muir, Jean 32, 313

Parks, Larry 74, 100, 187, 293, **294–295**

Reagan, Ronald 112, 182, *310*, **310–312**, 410c, 421–423

Robeson, Paul 117, 126, 306, **318–320**, 388

Robinson, Edward G.
31, 32, 220, 264, 312,
**320–321**
Sinatra, Frank 32, 81,
245, **338–339**, 364
Sondergaard, Gale 29,
32, 100, 295, **345–346**
Taylor, Robert 99, 100,
269, 346, *362*,
**362–363**
Wayne, John 141, 188,
268, 269, **395–396**
Welles, Orson 31, 119,
312
Actors Laboratory 293
ADA *see* Americans for
Democratic Action
Adam Hat (company)
299
ADL *see*
Anti-Defamation
League
AEC *see* Atomic Energy
Commission
AFL *see* American
Federation of Labor
African Americans *see
also* National
Association for the
Advancement of
Colored People
(NAACP)
Communist Party of the
United States of
America 84, 85
Du Bois, William
Edward Burghardt
**116–118**
National Lawyers Guild
278
Robeson, Paul 117,
126, 306, **318–320**,
388
*After the Fall* (Arthur
Miller play) **4–5**, 267
AFTRA *see* American
Federation of
Television and Radio
Artists
Aiken, George 105

ALA *see* American
Library Association
Alcatraz (California
prison) 344
ALCOA *see* Aluminum
Company of America
*Aldrich Family, The*
(television series) 313
Alerted Americans 155
Alien Registration Act of
1940 *see* Smith Act
Allen, Robert S. 297
Allen, Woody 32, 150
Allis-Chalmers
(company) 361
Alsop, Joseph 53, 83
Alsop, Stewart 83, 249,
392
Aluminum Company of
America (ALCOA) 277
*Amerasia* (journal) **5–7**,
222, 337, 338, 409c
"America First"
(movement) 238
American Association for
Reconstruction in
Yugoslavia, Inc. 443
American Association of
University Professors
(AAUP) **7–8**
American Association of
University Women 47
American Bar
Association 154
American-Belgian
Society 97, 266
American Branch of the
Federation of Greek
Maritime Unions 443
American Broadcasting
Company *see* ABC
American Business
Consultants (ABC)
31, 209, 210 *see also
Counterattack; Red
Channels*
American China Policy
Association 221
American Christian
Nationalist Party 445

American Civil Liberties
Union (ACLU) **8–9**,
138, 166, 167, 262
*American College
Dictionary* 261
American Committee for
Cultural Freedom
(ACCF) **9–10**
American Committee for
Democracy and
Intellectual Freedom
287
American Committee for
European Workers'
Relief 443
American Committee for
Spanish Freedom 443
American Committee for
the Protection of the
Foreign-Born 72, 443
American Committee for
Yugoslav Relief, Inc.
443
American Committee to
Save Refugees 208
American Council for a
Democratic Greece 443
American Council on
Soviet Relations 443
American Croatian
Congress 443
American Federation of
Labor (AFL) 84, 238,
361
American Federation of
Television and Radio
Artists (AFTRA) 19,
140
American Friends
Service Committee 154
American Jewish Labor
Council 443
American Jewish League
against Communism
222
American Labor Party
301
American League against
War and Fascism 443

American League for
Peace and Democracy
443
American Legion
**10–12**, *11*
baseball 22
blacklist 31, 32
Chaplin, Charles
Spencer 64
Douglas, Melvyn 115
Ferrer, Jose 142
founding of 409c
Fund for the Republic
155
Maltz, Albert 245
*American Legion
Magazine* 10, 11
American Library
Association (ALA) **12**
American National
Exhibition 388
American Peace
Mobilization 443
American Polish Labor
Council 443
American Rescue Ship
Mission 443
American-Russian
Fraternal Society 444
American Russian
Institute (New York
City) 443
American Russian
Institute
(Philadelphia) 443
American Russian
Institute (San
Francisco) 443
American Russian
Institute of Southern
California (Los
Angeles) 443
Americans for
Democratic Action
(ADA) **12–13**, 115,
189, 317, 321, 331,
410c
American Slav Congress
443

American-Soviet Science Society (ASSS) **13–14**

American Youth Congress 443

American Youth for Democracy (AYD) **14**, 186, 304, 443

*Anatomy of a Murder* (film) 399

Anderson, Marian 101

Anti-Defamation League (ADL) **14–15**

Appendix Nine (HUAC collection of documents) **15**

Aragon, Louis 135

Armed Services Committee, Senate *see under* Senate, U.S.

Armenian Progressive League of America 443

Army, U.S. *see also* Army-McCarthy hearings; Greenglass, David; MacArthur, Douglas; Marshall, George Catlett; Peress, Irving

Government Operations Committee 162

Institute for Pacific Relations 193

Permanent Subcommittee on Investigations 302

Stevens, Robert Ten Broeck 16, 77, 259, **349–350**, 357, 397

Stillwell, Joseph W. "Vinegar Joe" 66, 67, 102

Zwicker, Ralph W. 16, 18, 143, 259, 301, 302, 394

Army-McCarthy hearings (1954) **15–18**

Brownell, Herbert 45

Cohn, Roy 77

Eisenhower, Dwight David 132

Hoover, J. Edgar 183

Kennedy, Robert F. 215

McCarthy, Joseph R. 259

Mundt, Karl E. 271

National Lawyers Guild 278

Schine, Gerard David 330

Stevens, Robert Ten Broeck 350

Watkins, Arthur V. 394

Welch, Joseph Nye 396, 397, 398, 399

Williams, Edward Bennett 400

Army Signal Corps Engineering Laboratories *see* Fort Monmouth

Arnaz, Desi 21

Arnold, Thurman 147, 169

Artists' Front to Win the War 142, 209

Arts Council (Office of Civilian Defense) 115

Ashland, Kentucky 236, 334, 370

Associated Klans of America 445

Association of Georgia Klans 445

ASSS *see* American-Soviet Science Society

atomic bomb 87, 126, 151, 326, 327

atomic energy 18

Atomic Energy Commission (AEC) **18**

Condon, Edward U. 88

Lilienthal, David 288, 356

Oppenheimer, J. Robert 288, 289, 411c

Pauling, Linus C. 296

Strauss, Lewis 18, 191, 289, *355*, 355–356

Attlee, Clement 215

Attorney General's List of Subversive Organizations 443–445

attorneys *see* courts and legal profession

authors *see* writers

automobile industry 89

AWARE, Inc. **18–19**, 140, 155, 284

AYD *see* American Youth for Democracy

**B**

Bailey, Dorothy (1907– ) **20**

Baldwin, Joseph C. 14

Baldwin, Raymond 255

Ball, Joseph 48

Ball, Lucille (1911–1989) **20–21**, *21*

balloons 97

Barsky, Edward K. 208–209

*Barsky et al. v. United States* 209

baseball **22**

Benchley, Robert 346

Bennett, Charles 298

Bentley, Elizabeth (1909–1965) **22–24**, *50*, *303*

House Committee on Un-American Activities 186, 410c

Institute for Pacific Relations 194

Koestler, Arthur 221

Permanent Subcommittee on Investigations 302

Remington, William Walter 314

White, Harry Dexter 399, 400

Benton, William Burnett (1900–1973) *24*, **24–26**

Buckley Jr., William F. 48

Marshall, George Catlett 249

McCarthy, Joseph R. 257, 258

Rosenberg, Anna Marie 323

Tydings, Millard E. 373

Watkins, Arthur V. 393

Williams, Edward Bennett 400

Berdichevsky, Arcadi 375

Berg, Gertrude 313

Berkeley, Martin 169

Berle Jr., Adolf A. (1895–1971) **26–28**, *27*, 61, 119, 409c

Berlin, Germany 79

Bernardi, Herschel 150

Bernstein, Walter 150

Bessie, Alvah (1904–1985) **28**, 112, 179

Biberman, Herbert (1900–1971) **28–30**, 179, 180, 333

Biddle, Francis 13, 106, 182

Bielaski, Frank 6

*Big Jim McClain* (film) 395

Bingham, Hiram (1876–1956) **30**, 137, 138, 382

Birmingham, Alabama 226

Black, Hugo 34, 107, 196, 226, 406

blacklist **30–32**

AWARE, Inc. 18, 19

Biberman, Herbert 29

Christians, Mady 72

Da Silva, Howard 100

Faulk, John Henry 140

Foreman, Carl 146

*Front* 150

front 149

Hammett, Samuel Dashiell 165

Hellman, Lillian 170

Hepburn, Katharine 171
Hollywood Ten 180
*Joseph Julian v. American
Business Consultants*
(1954) 209, 210
Lardner Jr., Ring 229
Lawson, John Howard
236
Maltz, Albert 244
Mostel, Zero 267, 268
Motion Picture Alliance
for the Preservation of
American Ideals 269
Papp, Joseph 294
*Red Channels* 313
Robeson, Paul 319
Seeger, Pete 336
Sondergaard, Gale 345
Trumbo, Dalton 370,
371
*Way We Were* 396
Blankfort, Michael
(1907–1982) **32–33**
Blau, Patricia 33–34
*Blau v. United States*
(1950) **33–34**
Block, Herbert L. (1909– )
*34,* **34–35,** 131, 249, 260
Bloom, Sol 47
Bloomgarden, Kermit 5
B'nai B'rith *see*
Anti-Defamation
League
Bogart, Humphrey
(1899–1957) *35,*
**35–36,** 82, 344
Bohlen, Charles E.
(1905– ) **36–38,** *37,*
411c
Bridges, Styles 42
Dulles, John Foster 123
Eisenhower, Dwight
David 131
Knowland, William F.
219
McCarran, Patrick A.
253
McCarthy, Joseph R.
258
McLeod, Scott 261

Mundt, Karl E. 271
Nixon, Richard M. 283
Taft, Robert A. 360
Yalta Conference 404
Bohr, Niels 356
Bond, Ward 106, 268,
269, 395
Boorstin, Daniel J.
(1914– ) **38,** 171, 379
Borden, William 288
Boston School for
Marxist Studies 443
Bowles, Chester 24
*Boy with Green Hair, The*
(film) 188, 328
Bozell, Brent 48, 49
Bradley, Omar 191
Brandeis, Louis 1
*Brave One, The* (film)
371
Brecht, Bertolt
(1898–1956) **38–40,**
179
Brennan, William 196
*Bridge Over the River
Kwai, The* (film) 173
Bridges, Harry
(1901–1990) **40–41,**
108, 184
Bridges, Lloyd 172
Bridges, Styles
(1898–1963) *41,*
**41–43,** 69, 70, 261, 381
Bridgman, Howard A.
314
Brookings Institution 43
Browder, Earl
(1891–1973) **43–44,**
409c
Budenz, Louis F. 51
Communist Party of the
United States of
America 85
House Committee on
Un-American
Activities 185
Kennedy, Robert F. 215
Nazi-Soviet Pact 280
Popular Front 305
*Scoundrel Time* 335

Tydings, Millard E. 373
Brownell, Herbert
(1903– ) 37, **44–46,**
57, 131, 278, 400
*Brown v. Board of
Education of Topeka,
Kansas* (1954) 126,
278
Brunauer, Esther
Caulkihn (1901–1959)
30, **46–48**
Brunauer, Stephen
(1903– ) 30, 46, 47,
**48**
Bryan, Helen R. 209
Buckley Jr., William F.
(1925– ) **48–50,** *49,* 78
Bucyrus Erie Company
374
Budenz, Louis F.
(1891–1967) *50,*
**50–53**
Blankfort, Michael 33
Chambers, Whittaker 63
*Daily Worker* 98
*Dennis v. U.S.* (1951)
106
Eisler, Gerhart 133, 134
House Committee on
Un-American
Activities 186, 410c
Institute for Pacific
Relations 194
Lattimore, Owen 231,
232
McCarthy, Joseph R.
257
Pauling, Linus C. 296
Vincent, John Carter
381
Bukharin, Nikolai 133,
348
*Bulletin*
(American-Soviet
Science Society
publication) 14
*Bulletin of Atomic
Scientists* (journal)
**53–54,** 296
Bundy, William 59, 120

Burnham, James
(1905–1987) **54**
Burrows, Abraham
(1910– ) 31, **54–55,**
312
Busbey, Fred 46
Butler, John Marshall
83, 162, 373
Butterworth, W. Walton
71
Byrnes, James 1, 2, 174,
232, 323

**C**

Cain, Harry P.
(1906–1979) **56–58,**
324
California 239, 243, 389
*see also* Committee on
Un-American Activities
California, University of
8, 239, 296, 388
California Labor School,
Inc. (San Francisco)
443
Capehart, Homer 152,
177
Capper, Arthur 14
Capra, Frank 171
Carey, James 374
Carlson, Richard 192,
304
Carnegie Endowment for
International Peace
174
Carpatho-Russian
Peoples Society 444
Cartoonists' Guild 110,
236
Catholic Church 31,
**58–59,** 94, 95
Catholic War Veterans
32, 58
CBS (Columbia
Broadcasting System)
19, 140, 274, 275, 276,
294, 313

Central Council of
American Women of
Croatian Descent 443
Central Intelligence
Agency (CIA) **59**, 131,
162, 258, 283, 302 *see
also* Dulles, Allen W.
"Century of the
Common Man, The"
(Henry Wallace
speech, 1942) 385
Cervantes Fraternal
Society 444
CFA *see* Committee for
the First Amendment
Chamberlain, Neville
157, 279
Chambers, Whittaker
(1901–1964) *59,*
**59–63**, 432–433
    American Committee
    for Cultural
    Freedom 9
    Berle Jr., Adolf A. 26,
    27, 409c
    Budenz, Louis F. 52
    Clubb, Oliver
    Edmund 74
    Dulles, Allen W. 120
    Hiss, Alger 174, 175,
    176
    House Committee on
    Un-American
    Activities 186, 410c
    Koestler, Arthur 221
    Mundt, Karl E. 271
    Pressman, Lee 307
    *Red Plot against
    America* 313
    Smedley, Agnes 339
    White, Harry Dexter
    400
Chaplin, Charles
Spencer ("Charlie")
(1889–1977) 32, 56,
**63–65**, 135
Chennault, Claire Lee 69
Chiang Kai-shek
(1887–1975) *65,*
**65–67**, *67*, 410c

China 67, 68
China Lobby 69, 70
China White Paper 70
Davies Jr., John Paton
102
Hiss, Alger 174
Korean War 223, 225
Lattimore, Owen 230
Luce, Henry R. 240
MacArthur, Douglas
242
Mao Zedong 245
Marshall, George
Catlett 248, 249
McCarran, Patrick A.
251
Service, John Stewart
337
Smedley, Agnes 339
Sokolsky, George 344
Truman, Harry S. 366
Vincent, John Carter
380
Chicago, Illinois 375
Childs, Marquis 130
China **67–69** *see also*
Chiang Kai-shek;
China Lobby; Mao
Zedong
    Acheson, Dean 3
    *Amerasia* 5, 6
    Clubb, Oliver
    Edmund 74
    Davies Jr., John Paton
    102
    Dulles, John Foster
    124
    Institute for Pacific
    Relations 194
    Korean War 223, 226
    Lattimore, Owen 230
China Lobby **69–70**
    Acheson, Dean 3
    *Amerasia* 6
    Chiang Kai-shek 66
    China 68, 69
    Institute for Pacific
    Relations 193
    Knowland, William F.
    219

Kohlberg, Alfred 221,
222
Korean War 223
Lattimore, Owen 230
Luce, Henry R. 240
Mao Zedong 245
Marshall, George
Catlett 248
McCarran, Patrick A.
253
McCarthy, Joseph R.
256
Service, John Stewart
337
Smedley, Agnes 339
Sokolsky, George 344
Truman, Harry S. 368
Utley, Freda 376
Vincent, John Carter
380, 381
*China Monthly* (journal)
70, 222
China Policy Association
70
*China Story, The* (Freda
Utley) 376
China White Paper
**70–72**, 410c
    Acheson, Dean 3
    China 68
    China Lobby 70
    Kohlberg, Alfred 222
    Mao Zedong 246
    Truman, Harry S. 367
Christians, Mady
(1900–1951) 32, *72,*
313
Churchill, Winston 349,
404, *405*
CIA *see* Central
Intelligence Agency
Cincinnati Reds 22
CIO *see* Congress of
Industrial
Organizations
Citizens Committee for
Harry Bridges 443
Citizens Committee of
the Upper West Side
(New York City) 443

Citizens Committee to
Free Earl Browder 443
civil liberties
    Budenz, Louis F. 53
    Clark, Tom C. 73
    Communist Control
    Act (1954) 82
    Douglas, William O.
    115
    Einstein, Albert 128
    Emergency Civil
    Liberties Committee
    136
    Fund for the Republic
    154, 155
    Warren, Earl 388
Civil Rights Congress
(CRC) 142, 165, 178,
186, 306, 312, 443
civil rights movement
125, 126, 278
Civil Service
Commission *see*
Loyalty Review Board
Clark, Tom C.
(1899–1977) *72,*
**72–74**
    American-Soviet
    Science Society 14
    American Youth for
    Democracy 14
    Coplon, Judith 93
    *Dennis v. U.S.* (1951)
    106, 107
    Duggan, Lawrence
    119
    Hoover, J. Edgar 182
    Philbrick, Herbert A.
    304
    Smith Act (Alien
    Registration Act of
    1940) 341
    *Watkins v. United
    States* (1957) 395
"clear and present
danger" standard 107
Clearing House 145
Clifford, Clark 276
Clubb, Oliver Edmund
(1901–1989) 4, 74

Cobb, Lee J.
(1911–1976) 32, 58,
**74–75**, 295
Coburn, Charles
(1877–1961) **75–76**,
106
Cocteau, Jean 135
Cogley, John 32, 155
Cohen, Elliot 9
Cohn, Harry 147
Cohn, Roy (1927–1986)
**76–78**
Army-McCarthy
hearings 16, 17
Dartmouth College
Speech 99
Flanders, Ralph E. 144
Foreman, Carl 147
International
Information Agency
198, 199
Kennedy, Robert F. 215
McCarthy, Joseph R.
258, 259
Schine, Gerard David
329, 330, 331
Sokolsky, George 345
Voice of America 383
Welch, Joseph Nye 397,
398
Cohn, Sidney 146
*Cold Friday* (Whittaker
Chambers) 62, 63
Cold War **78–79**, 86
*Cold War, The* (Walter
Lippmann) 78
Cole, Lester
(1904–1985) **80–81**,
179, 333, 364
*Cole v. United States*
(1956) **81**
*Collier's* (magazine) 317
Collins, Richard 332,
333
Columbia Broadcasting
System *see* CBS
Columbians
(organization) 445

Comintern (Communist
International) 83, 85,
133, 305, 349, 409c
Comite Coordinador Pro
Republica Española
443
*Committee and Its Critics,
The* (*National Review*
editors) 49–50, 54
Committee for a
Democratic Far
Eastern Policy 443
Committee for
Constitutional
Government 222
Committee for Peaceful
Alternatives 296
Committee for the First
Amendment (CFA)
**81–82**
Blankfort, Michael 33
Bogart, Humphrey 35,
36
founding of 410c
Hepburn, Katharine 171
Hollywood Ten 179
March, Fredric 246
Sinatra, Frank 338
Committee of Industrial
Organizations *see*
Congress of Industrial
Organizations
Committee of One
Thousand 82, 127, 246
Committee on
Government
Operations, Senate *see*
Government
Operations
Committee, Senate
Committee on
Un-American
Activities (California)
236, 319, 388
Committee to Aid the
Fighting South 443
Committee to Investigate
the National Defense
Program 366

*Commonweal*
(publication) 58, 193
Commonwealth College
(Mena, Arkansas) 443
Communist Control Act
(1954) 46, **82–83**, 86,
190, 411c, 461
*Communist Front
Organizations with
Special Reference to the
National Citizens
Political Action
Committee see*
Appendix Nine
Communist International
*see* Comintern
Communist Party of the
United States of
America (CPUSA)
**83–86**, *84, 340,* 409c,
410c
American Association of
University Professors 7
Attorney General's List of
Subversive
Organizations 443, 445
Browder, Earl *see*
Browder, Earl
Cohn, Roy 76
Cole, Lester 80
Communist Control Act
(1954) 82, 83
*Daily Worker see Daily
Worker*
*Dennis v. U.S.* (1951)
106, 107
Foster, William Z. 43,
84, 85, **148–149**, 185
Hays, Arthur Garfield
167
Hoover, J. Edgar 181,
182, 183
House Committee on
Un-American
Activities 185
Internal Security Act of
1950 195
Nazi-Soviet Pact 280
Nelson, Steven 301,
412c

Philbrick, Herbert A.
304
Popular Front 305
Smith Act (Alien
Registration Act of
1940) 340, 341
*Yates v. United States*
(1957) 404, 405
*Communist Party v.
Subversive Activities
Control Board* (1961)
196
Communist Political
Association 444, 445
Community Relations
Council (CRC) 320
Conant, James B. 48
Condon, Edward U.
(1902–1974) 14, 53,
61, **86–89**, 215, 402
Congress for Cultural
Freedom 9
Congress of American
Revolutionary Writers
444
Congress of American
Women 444
Congress of Industrial
Organizations (CIO)
**89–90**, 410c
Bridges, Harry 40
Communist Party of the
United States of
America 85
Dies, Martin 108
Flanders, Ralph E. 143
House Committee on
Un-American Activities
184, 185
Lewis, John L. 238
Murray, Philip 271–273
Pegler, Westbrook 300
Pressman, Lee 306, 307
Reuther, Walter 317
Taft-Hartley Act 361
United Electrical, Radio
and Machine Workers
374

Connally, Tom (1877–1963) 73, **90–92**, *91*, 372
Connecticut State Youth Conference 444
Considine, Bob 313
Constitution Hall (Washington, D.C.) 101, *101*
Consumers Union 312
Cooke, Alistair (1908– ) **92**
Cooper, Gary (1901–1961) **92–93**, 172, 268
Cooper, John Sherman 83
Coplon, Judith (1920– ) 73, 79, **93–94**, 215, 282, 410c
Corcoran, Tommy 6, 173
Corey, Robert B. 296
*Cosmopolitan* (magazine) 300
Council for Pan-American Democracy 444
Council on African Affairs 117, 444
*Counterattack* (newsletter) 31, **94–95**, 155, 222, 276
*Court Martial of Billy Mitchell, The* (film) 234
courts and legal profession *see also* Justice, U.S. Department of; Supreme Court, U.S.
  Cohn, Roy *see* Cohn, Roy
  Fisher Jr., Frederick J. 17, 77, 278, 397, 398, 411c
  Fortas, Abraham 9, 141, *147*, **147–148**, 231, 289, 335
  Hand, Learned 14, 94, 226, 315, 382
  Hays, Arthur Garfield **166–167**, 209
  Kaufman, Irving R. 128, 226, 325, 326, 448–449

Kennedy, Robert F. 77, 78, **214–215**
Kenyon, Dorothy **216–217**, 257, 322
McGranery, James P. 76, 159, 194, 233, 253
Medina, Harold 107, 341
Nizer, Louis 140, **284**
Pressman, Lee 60, 173, 174, **306–307**
Stripling, Robert *see* Stripling, Robert
Welch, Joseph Nye *see* Welch, Joseph Nye
Williams, Edward Bennett 26, 393, **400–401**
CPUSA *see* Communist Party of the United States of America
CRC *see* Community Relations Council
*Crisis, The* (journal) 117
Croatian Benevolent Fraternity 444
Cronin, Father John (1908–1994) **95–96**
Cronyn, Hume 264
*Crossfire* (film) 328, 334
Crossman, Richard 156, 157
*Crucible, The* (1953) (Arthur Miller play) **96–97**
Crum, Bartley 179
Crusade for Freedom 97
Cukor, George 135
Currie, Lauchlin 23
"Custodial Detention List" (FBI) 181
Cvetic, Matt 199
*Cyrano de Bergerac* (film) 141
Czechoslovakia 97

**D**

*Daily Worker* (newspaper) *98*, **98–99**

blacklist 31
Blankfort, Michael 33
Budenz, Louis F. 50, 51
Chambers, Whittaker 60
Odets, Clifford 285
*Red Channels* 312
Schulberg, Budd 332
Daily Workers Press Club 443
Danbury, Connecticut 80, 229, 364
DAR *see* Daughters of the American Revolution
*Darkness at Noon* (Arthur Koestler novel) 220
*Darkness at Noon* (play) 321
Dartmouth College Speech (Dwight Eisenhower, 1953) 77, 99, 131, 199, 258, 383, 411c
Da Silva, Howard (1909–1986) *99*, **99–100**, 363
Daughters of the American Revolution (DAR) **100–102**, *101*
Davies Jr., John Paton (1908– ) 4, 30, 69, **102–104**, 123, 124, 253
Davis, Ben *84*
Davis, Forrest 249
Davis, Nathaniel P. 74
Davis, Robert Gorham (1908– ) **104**, 379
Day, Laraine 192
Declaration of Conscience (1950) (Margaret Chase Smith speech) **104–105**, 342, 411c, 436–438
Declaration of Conscience (1953) (manifesto signed by

28 actors and journalists) **105–106**
Declaration on Liberated Europe (Yalta Charter) 404
Decter, Moshe 10
Democratic Party 58, 69, 195 *see also specific political figures*
Denfeld, Louis E. 372
Dennis, Eugene 106, 341
Dennis Defense Committee 443, 444
*Dennis v. U.S.* (1951) **106–107**, 115–116, 226, 341, 390, 411c
de Sola, Ralph 323
Detroit Youth Assembly 444
Dewey, John 9
Dewey, Thomas E. 44, 70, 389
"Did the Movies Really Clean House?" (*American Legion Magazine* article) 11
Dien Bien Phu, fall of (1954) **107–108**, *108*, 411c
Dies, Martin (1900–1972) **108–110**
  Bogart, Humphrey 35
  Bridges, Harry 40
  Congress of Industrial Organizations 90
  House Committee on Un-American Activities 184, 185
  March, Fredric 246
  Murray, Philip 273
  Sondergaard, Gale 345
  Southern Conference on Human Welfare 348
directors (film)
  Allen, Woody 32, 150
  Biberman, Herbert **28–30**, 179, 180, 333

Chaplin, Charles
Spencer ("Charlie")
32, 56, **63–65**, 135
Dmytryk, Edward
**111–112**, 179, 180,
187, 329, 384, 411c
Kazan, Elia *see* Kazan,
Elia
Kramer, Stanley 112,
146, 172
McCarey, Leo 170, 171
Welles, Orson 31, 119,
312
Wood, Sam 268, 269
Dirksen, Everett 145,
162
Disney, Walter E.
(1901–1966) *110,*
**110–111,** 182, 236,
268, 269
Dmytryk, Edward
(1908– ) **111–112,**
179, 180, 187, 329,
384, 411c
documents 415–472 *see
also* Appendix Nine;
China White Paper
Douglas, Helen Gahagan
(1902–1980) *113,*
**113–114,** 114, 283, 311
Douglas, Kirk 32
Douglas, Melvyn
(1901–1981) 12, 113,
**114–115**
Douglas, Paul 189, 195
Douglas, William O.
(1898–1980) 107,
**115–116,** *116,* 196, 406
Doyle, Clyde 268
*Dream We Lost, The:
Soviet Russia Then and
Now* (Freda Utley) 375
Dreiser, Theodore 63
Du Bois, William
Edward Burghardt
(1868–1963) **116–118**
Duclos, Jacques 78, 85,
98
Duff, James 300

Duggan, Lawrence
(1905–1948) 62,
**118–119**
Dukas, Helen 128
Dulles, Allen W.
(1893–1969) 59,
**119–121,** *120*
Dulles, John Foster
(1888–1959) **121–124**
Bohlen, Charles E. 37
Davies Jr., John Paton
103
Dien Bien Phu 108
Eisenhower, Dwight
David 131
Hiss, Alger 174
International
Information Agency
198
McLeod, Scott 261, 262
Vincent, John Carter
382, 411c
Voice of America 383
Dunne, Philip 81
Dworshak, Henry 162

**E**

Eastland, James Oliver
(1904–1988) *125,*
**125–126**
ECLC *see* Emergency
Civil Liberties
Committee
education *see* academic
freedom; loyalty oaths;
professors and
educators
Einstein, Albert
(1879–1955)
**126–129,** *127,* 459
*Bulletin of Atomic
Scientists* 53
Daughters of the
American Revolution
102
Du Bois, William
Edward Burghardt 118

Emergency Civil
Liberties Committee
136
hydrogen bomb 191
Murrow, Edward R. 276
Oppenheimer, J. Robert
289
Rosenberg, Ethel
Greenglass 325
Eisenhower, Dwight
David (1890–1969)
*129,* **129–133,** 460 *see
also* Dartmouth
College Speech
American Library
Association 12
Army-McCarthy
hearings 17
Atomic Energy
Commission 18
Block, Herbert L. 35
Bohlen, Charles E. 36,
37, 38, 411c
Brownell, Herbert 44,
45, 46
Cain, Harry P. 56, 57
Central Intelligence
Agency 59
Cohn, Roy 77
Cold War 79
*Cole v. United States*
(1956) 81
Communist Control Act
(1954) 83
Daughters of the
American Revolution
102
Davies Jr., John Paton
103
Dien Bien Phu 107, 108
Dulles, Allen W. 120
Dulles, John Foster
121, 122, 123
Executive Order 10450
138, 411c
Flanders, Ralph E. 144
Government Operations
Committee 162
Hammett, Samuel
Dashiell 165

Hoover, J. Edgar 183
International
Information Agency
198, 199
Korean War 226
Loyalty Review Board
240
MacArthur, Douglas 243
Marshall, George Catlett
247, 249
Martin, Joseph W. 250
McCarthy, Joseph R.
258, 259, 260
McLeod, Scott 262
National Association for
the Advancement of
Colored People 278
Nixon, Richard M. 283
Oppenheimer, J. Robert
288
Rosenberg, Anna Marie
323
Rosenberg, Ethel
Greenglass 325
Stevens, Robert Ten
Broeck 349
Strauss, Lewis 356
Taft, Robert A. 360
Velde, Harold H. 379
Voice of America 383
Walter, Francis 387
Warren, Earl 389, 390
Watkins, Arthur V.
392, 394
Welch, Joseph Nye 399
*Yates v. United States*
(1957) 406
Eisenhower, Milton 47
Eisenhower Doctrine
124
Eisler, Gerhart
(1897–1968) *133,*
**133–134**
Brecht, Bertolt 39
Budenz, Louis F. 51
House Committee on
Un-American
Activities 186
*I Was a Communist for
the FBI* 199

Joint Anti-Fascist
Refugee Committee
208
*Red Plot against
America* 313
Eisler, Hanns
(1898–1962) **134–136**
Brecht, Bertolt 39
Chaplin, Charles
Spencer 63, 64
House Committee on
Un-American
Activities 186
Pauling, Linus C. 296
*Red Plot against
America* 313
Roosevelt, Eleanor
321
Elitcher, Max 343
Ellender, Allen 154
Emergency Civil
Liberties Committee
(ECLC) **136**
Emergency Committee
of Atomic Scientists 87
Emergency Conference
to Save Spanish
Refugees 444
Emerson, Thomas 136
Employment Service,
U.S. 20
*Enough Rope* (Arthur
Watkins) 394
entertainment industry
*see* motion picture
industry; radio;
television
espionage
Atomic Energy
Commission 18
Bentley, Elizabeth 22,
23
Chambers, Whittaker
60
Coplon, Judith 93, 94
Eisler, Gerhart *see*
Eisler, Gerhart
Fuchs, Klaus
150–152, 158, 159,
161, 191, 410c

Gold, Harry *see* Gold,
Harry
Golos, Jacob 22, 23
Gouzenko, Igor 160
Greenglass, David *see*
Greenglass, David
Gubitchev, Valentin
93, 94
Lattimore, Owen 230,
232
Perlo, Victor 22, 60
Pumpkin Papers 62,
176, 410
Rosenberg, Ethel
Greenglass *see*
Rosenberg, Ethel
Greenglass
Rosenberg, Julius *see*
Rosenberg, Julius
Smedley, Agnes 339
Sobell, Morton *343*,
343–344
*Execution of Private
Slovik, The* (film) 245,
339
Executive Order 9835
(1946) 73, **136–137**,
239, 367, 410c,
415–417
Executive Order 10241
(1951) 30, **137–138**,
226, 367, 411c
Executive Order 10450
(1953) 9, 81, 132,
133, **138**, 411c,
455–458
*Exodus* (film) 32, 180,
371, 412c

**F**

Fair Deal 366
Farm Equipment
Workers 90, 273
Fast, Howard (1914– )
*139*, **139–140**, 198,
209, 322
Faulk, John Henry
(1913–1990) 19, 32,
140, 284

*Fear on Trial* (John
Henry Faulk) 140
Federal Bureau of
Investigation (FBI)
*Amerasia* 6
American Civil
Liberties Union 9
Executive Order 9835
137
Feller, Abraham 141
*I Led Three Lives* 192
informants
Bentley, Elizabeth
410c
Disney, Walter E.
110
Gouzenko, Igor 161
Reagan, Ronald 310
*My Son John* 277
officials and agents
*see* Hoover, J. Edgar;
Philbrick, Herbert A.
Permanent
Subcommittee on
Investigations 302
Smith Act (Alien
Registration Act of
1940) 340
targets
Chaplin, Charles
Spencer 64
Christians, Mady 72
Coplon, Judith 93,
94
Einstein, Albert 128
Fuchs, Klaus 152
Hammett, Samuel
Dashiell 165
Kent, Morton 215
Lennart, Isobel 237
Murrow, Edward R.
277
Service, John
Stewart 337
Smedley, Agnes
339, 340
Sobell, Morton 343,
344
White, Harry Dexter
399

Truman, Harry S. 367
federal employee loyalty
programs *see*
Executive Order 9835;
Executive Order
10241; Executive
Order 10450; Loyalty
Review Board
Federal Mediation and
Conciliation Service
361
Federal Theater Project
233
Federal Trade
Commission 221
Feller, Abraham
(1905–1952)
**140–141**, 411c
Ferguson, Homer 302
Ferrer, Jose (1912–1992)
31, **141–142**, 147, 148,
312
Field, Frederick
Vanderbilt 194
Fifth Amendment 34,
169, 179, 196, 197
*Fifth Amendment Today,
The* (Erwin Griswold)
154
Film Associates, Inc. 29
film directors *see*
directors
film industry *see* motion
picture industry
film producers *see*
producers
films
*Anatomy of a Murder*
399
*Big Jim McClain* 395
*Boy with Green Hair*
188, 328
*Brave One* 371
*Bridge Over the River
Kwai* 173
*Court Martial of Billy
Mitchell* 234
*Crossfire* 328, 334
*Cyrano de Bergerac*
141

*Execution of Private Slovik* 245, 339
*Exodus* 32, 180, 371, 412c
*Front* 32, 150, **150**, 268
*High Noon* **172–173**
*I Married a Communist* 188, **192–193**
*I Was a Communist for the FBI* **199–200**
*Jet Pilot* 188, **395–396**
*Manchurian Candidate* 339
*Mission to Moscow* 264, 269
*Monsieur Verdoux* 64
*Moulin Rouge* 142
*My Son John* 277
*North Star* 168, 264, 269
*Spartacus* 32
*State of the Union* 171, 264
*On the Waterfront* 58
*Way We Were* 396
Films for Democracy 246
Finnish-American Mutual Aid Society 444
*Firing Line* (American Legion publication) 10
*Firing Line* (television program) 50
First Amendment 107, 179, 196
Fischer, Louis 156
Fisher Jr., Frederick J. 17, 77, 278, 397, 398, 411c
Flanders, Ralph E. (1880–1970) 17, *142*, **142–145**, 153, 154, 260, 411c, 462–465
Florida 243
Florida Press and Educational League 444, 445
fluoridation 102
Flynn, Elizabeth Gurley 8, 262

Flynn, John T. 69
Ford, Henry 155
Ford Foundation *see* Fund for the Republic
Ford Motor Company 89, 155, 316
Foreign Relations Committee, Senate *see under* Senate, U.S.
Foreign Service, U.S. *see* State, U.S. Department of
Foreman, Carl (1914–1984) 32, **146–147**, 172, 173
Formosa *see* Taiwan
Forrestal, James 356
Fortas, Abraham (1910–1982) 9, 141, *147*, **147–148**, 231, 289, 335
Fort Monmouth, New Jersey (Army laboratories)
Army-McCarthy hearings 15, 16
Cohn, Roy 77
Jenkins, Ray Howard 201
McCarthy, Joseph R. 259
Schine, Gerard David 330
Stevens, Robert Ten Broeck 349
Welch, Joseph Nye 397
*Fortnight* (magazine) 311
Foster, William Z. (1881–1961) 43, 84, 85, **148–149**, 185
Foy, Brian 199
France *see* Dien Bien Phu, fall of
Franco, Francisco 58, 251, 305
Frankenheimer, John 339
Frankfurter, Felix 1, 173, 196, 395

Frauenglass, William 459
Freedman, Benjamin 323
"freedom bell" 97
Freedom from Fear 29, 312
Freedom House 277
*Freeman, The* (periodical) 222
Friends for Intellectual Freedom 221
Friends of the Soviet Union 444
"From the Record" (Maryland campaign literature) 373
front (cover for screenwriters) **149–150**
*Front, The* (film) 32, **150**, 268
Fruenglass, William 128
Fuchs, Klaus (1911–1988) **150–152**, 158, 159, 161, 191, 410c
Fulbright, James William (1905–1994) 42, **152–154**, *153*
Fund for the Republic 32, 53, **154–155**, 304, 387
Funds for Intellectual Freedom 333
fusion weapons *see* hydrogen bomb

**G**

Galante, Carmine 78
*Galyan v. Press* 389
Garfield, John (1913–1952) 63, **156**
Garibaldi American Fraternal Society 444
Gellhorn, Lawrence 186, 348
General Foods Corporation 313

General Intelligence Division (of Justice Department) 409c
General Motors Corporation (GM) 316
*Generation on Trial, A: U.S.A. v. Alger Hiss* (Alistair Cooke) 92
George Washington Carver School (New York City) 444
German-American Bund 445
Gershwin, Ira 81
Gide, Andre 156
Gilford, Jack 32
Gillette, Guy 25, 393
Girdler, Tom M. 89
GM *see* General Motors Corporation
*God That Failed, The (1949)* (book edited by Richard Crossman) **156–157**, 220
Gold, Harry (1911– ) 151, 152, **157–159**, *158*, 162, 326, 410c, 446–447
*Goldbergs, The* (television series) 313
Goldwyn, Samuel (1879–1974) **159–160**, 168, 384
Goljack, John T. 375
Golos, Jacob 22, 23
Goodwin, William J. 69
Gough, Lloyd 150
Gouzenko, Igor (1915–1982) 78, **160–161**, *161*, 410c
government officials
Acheson, Dean *see* Acheson, Dean
Bailey, Dorothy **20**
Berle Jr., Adolf A. **26–28**, *27*, 61, 119, 409c
Biddle, Francis 13, 106, 182

Bingham, Hiram **30**, 137, 138, 382

Bohlen, Charles E. *see* Bohlen, Charles E.

Brownell, Herbert 37, **44–46**, 57, 131, 278, 400

Brunauer, Esther Caulkihn 30, **46–48**

Brunauer, Stephen 30, 46, 47, **48**

Bundy, William 59, 120

Byrnes, James 1, 2, 174, 232, 323

Clark, Tom C. *see* Clark, Tom C.

Clubb, Oliver Edmund 4, **74**

Cohn, Roy *see* Cohn, Roy

Coplon, Judith 73, 79, **93–94**, 215, 282, 410c

Davies Jr., John Paton 4, 30, 69, **102–104**, 123, 124, 253

Duggan, Lawrence 62, **118–119**

Dulles, Allen W. 59, **119–121**, *120*

Dulles, John Foster *see* Dulles, John Foster

Grew, Joseph 6, 27

Hiss, Alger *see* Hiss, Alger

Hull, Cordell 119, 232

Ickes, Harold 14, 251, 348

Jackson, Robert H. 364

Jessup, Philip C. 70, 71, 153, **203–205**, *204*, 222, 257

Kent, Morton **215–216**

Lattimore, Owen *see* Lattimore, Owen

Marshall, George Catlett *see* Marshall, George Catlett

McGranery, James P. 76, 159, 194, 233, 253

McLeod, Scott 36, 123, *261*, **261–262**

Nicholson, Donald *280*, **280–281**

Perlo, Victor 22, 60

Remington, William Walter 23, 76, 302, **314–315**, 318, 411c

Richardson, Seth 20, 136, 137, *317*, **317–318**, 367

Rosenberg, Anna Marie 56, 309, 322, **322–324**

Service, John Stewart *see* Service, John Stewart

Strauss, Lewis 18, 191, 289, *355*, **355–356**

Vincent, John Carter *see* Vincent, John Carter

White, Harry Dexter *see* White, Harry Dexter

Government Operations Committee, Senate **161–162**, 411c *see also* Permanent Subcommittee on Investigations

Dulles, Allen W. 121

Hoey, Clyde 178

McCarthy, Joseph R. 258

Peress, Irving 301

Smith, Margaret Chase 341

Symington, (William) Stuart 357

Utley, Freda 376

Government Printing Office 162

Graham, Frank 347, 348

*Great Pretense, The* (anti-Communist report) 63

Greece 78

Greek American Committee for National Unity 443

Greenglass, David (1922– ) 152, 158, 159, **162–163**, 325, 326, 411c, 447

Grew, Joseph 6, 27

Griswold, Erwin 154

Group Theatre 156, 235, 285, 294

Groves, Leslie R. 288

Gubitchev, Valentin 93, 94

Gunther, John 276

**H**

Hall, Gus *84*

Hammett, Samuel Dashiell (1894–1961) *164*, **164–165**, 167, 168, 198, 335

Hand, Learned 14, 94, 226, 315, 382

Harding, John 237

Harlan, John 405

Harriman, W. Averell 102

Harrison, Caroline 100

Harry Bridges Defense Fund 41

Hart, Dorothy 199

Hart, Edward J. 185

Hartley, Fred A. 361

Hartnett, Vincent 18, 19, 140

Harvard University (Cambridge, Massachusetts) 38, 104, 171, 172, 187, 379

Hawaii Civil Liberties Committee 444

Hayden, Sterling (1916–1986) **166**, *166*

Hayes, Helen 277

Hays, Arthur Garfield (1881–1954) **166–167**, 209

Health, Education and Welfare, U.S. Department of 81

Hearst, William Randolph 63

Hearst Corporation 300

Heflin, Van 277

Hellenic-American Brotherhood 444

Hellman, Lillian (1905–1984) **167–170** *see also Scoundrel Time*

Cohn, Roy 77

Fortas, Abraham 148

Goldwyn, Samuel 159

Hammett, Samuel Dashiell 164, 165

House Committee on Un-American Activities 187, 411c, 450–452

Schulberg, Budd 333

Hendrickson, Robert 105

Henreid, Paul 82, 264

Hepburn, Katharine (1907– ) 82, *170*, **170–171**, 264, 384

*Herald Tribune* (New York newspaper) 53, 119, 304

Herblock *see* Block, Herbert L.

*Here I Stand* (Paul Robeson) 320

HICCASP *see* Hollywood Independent Citizens Committee of Arts, Sciences and Professions

Hickenlooper, Bourke 216

Hicks, Granville
(1901–1982) 38,
**171–172**, 280, 379
Highlander Folk School
(Monteagle,
Tennessee) 126
*High Noon* (film)
**172–173**
Hilberman, David 111
Hinton, Ed 192
Hiss, Alger (1904– )
**173–177**
  Acheson, Dean 3
  Berle Jr., Adolf A. 26, 27
  Brunauer, Esther
    Caulkihn 47
  Budenz, Louis F. 52
  Chambers, Whittaker
    60, 61, 62
  China Lobby 70
  Cooke, Alistair 92
  Cronin, Father John 95
  Duggan, Lawrence 118
  Dulles, Allen W. 120
  Gouzenko, Igor 161
  House Committee on
    Un-American
    Activities 186, 410c
  Mao Zedong 245
  Mundt, Karl E. 271
  Nicholson, Donald 280
  Nixon, Richard M. 282
  *Red Plot against America*
    313
  Sokolsky, George 344
  Truman, Harry S. 367
  Velde, Harold H. 378
  Yalta Conference 404
Hiss, Donald 60
Hitler, Adolf 85, 157,
  279, 280, 305
Hoey, Clyde
  (1877–1954) 161,
  162, **177–178**, 302
Hoffman, Paul G. 143,
  145, 154
Holliday, Judy
  (1922–1965) **178**

"Hollywood Fights
Back" (radio
broadcast) 82
Hollywood Independent
Citizens Committee of
Arts, Sciences and
Professions
(HICCASP) 310
Hollywood League of
American Writers
School 112
*Hollywood Life* 100, 165,
178
*Hollywood Reporter* 179
Hollywood Ten
**178–180** *see also
names of individual
members of the group
(e.g., Bessie, Alvah)*
  blacklist 31
  Blankfort, Michael 33
  Einstein, Albert 127
  Goldwyn, Samuel 160
  Hepburn, Katharine 171
  House Committee on
    Un-American
    Activities 186, 410c
  Meiklejohn, Alexander
    263
  *Red Plot against America*
    313
  Screen Writers' Guild
    336
  Thomas, J. Parnell 364
  Waldorf Statement 384
*Hollywood Ten, The*
  (documentary film)
  345
Hollywood Writers
Mobilization for
Defense 444
Holmes, Oliver Wendell
173
homosexuality 144, 178,
302
Hook, Sidney 9, 263
Hoover, J. Edgar
  (1895–1973)
  **180–183**, *181*, 409c

Army-McCarthy
hearings 16, 17
Ball, Lucille 21
Central Intelligence
Agency 59
Chambers, Whittaker 61
Communist Control Act
(1954) 83
Condon, Edward U. 87
Disney, Walter E. 111
Einstein, Albert 127
Fund for the Republic
155
House Committee on
Un-American
Activities 418–421
Internal Security Act of
1950 195
Lattimore, Owen 231
McCarthy, Joseph R.
256
Murrow, Edward R. 275
National Association for
the Advancement of
Colored People 278
Oppenheimer, J. Robert
288
Rosenberg, Julius 326,
327
Smith Act (Alien
Registration Act of
1940) 341
Sokolsky, George 344
Stone, I. F. 355
Vincent, John Carter
381
Welch, Joseph Nye 397
Hopkins, Harry 404
Hopper, Hedda 268
Hornbeck, Stanley K.
173, 174
House Committee on
Un-American
Activities (HUAC)
**183–187**, *184*, 409c,
418–430 *see also
Appendix Nine; One
Hundred Things You
Should Know about
Communism*

*After the Fall* 4
American Association of
University Professors
7, 8
American Legion 10
Americans for
Democratic Action 13
American-Soviet Science
Society 14
American Youth for
Democracy 14
AWARE, Inc. 19
blacklist 31, 32
Bridges, Harry 40
Brookings Institution 43
Brunauer, Esther
  Caulkihn 47
Buckley Jr., William F.
  48–50
Christians, Mady 72
Cold War 79
Condon, Edward U.
  86–88
critics
  Chaplin, Charles
    Spencer 64
  Douglas, Helen
    Gahagan 113
  Douglas, Melvyn
    115
  Goldwyn, Samuel
    159, 160
  Hepburn, Katharine
    170
  March, Fredric 246
  Reuther, Walter 317
Cronin, Father John 95
*Daily Worker* 98
Daughters of the
American Revolution
101
Duggan, Lawrence 118
Emergency Civil
Liberties Committee
136
Executive Order 9835
136
Fortas, Abraham 148
*High Noon* 172

Hollywood Ten 178, 179

Hoover, J. Edgar 182

*I Was a Communist for the FBI* 199

Joint Anti-Fascist Refugee Committee 208, 209

Korean War 226

League of Women Shoppers 236

members

Dies, Martin 108, 109

Mundt, Karl E. 270, 271

Nixon, Richard M. 282

Rankin, John 308, 309, 310

Thomas, J. Parnell 364, 410c

Velde, Harold H. 378, 379

Walter, Francis 387

Wood, John Stephen 402

Motion Picture Alliance for the Preservation of American Ideals 269

National Association for the Advancement of Colored People 278

National Lawyers Guild 278, 279

*Red Plot against America* 313

*Scoundrel Time* 335

Screen Writers' Guild 336

*Song of Russia* 346

Southern Conference on Human Welfare 347, 348

Truman, Harry S. 367

United Electrical, Radio and Machine Workers 374, 375

Waldorf Statement 384

*Watkins v. United States* (1957) 395

*Way We Were* 396

Williams, Edward Bennett 400

witnesses

Ball, Lucille 20, 21

Bentley, Elizabeth 22, 23, 24, 410c

Berle Jr., Adolf A. 26, 27

Bessie, Alvah 28

Biberman, Herbert 29

Blankfort, Michael 33

Bogart, Humphrey 35

Boorstin, Daniel J. 38

Brecht, Bertolt 39

Browder, Earl 44

Budenz, Louis F. 51, 52, 410c

Burnham, James 54

Burrows, Abraham 54, 55

Chambers, Whittaker 61, 410c

Clubb, Oliver Edmund 74

Cobb, Lee J. 75

Cole, Lester 80

Cooper, Gary 92

Da Silva, Howard 99, 100

Davis, Robert Gorham 104

Disney, Walter E. 110, 111

Dmytryk, Edward 112

Eisler, Gerhart 133, 134

Eisler, Hanns 135

Fast, Howard 139

Ferrer, Jose 141

Foreman, Carl 146, 147

Foster, William Z. 149

Garfield, John 156

Hayden, Sterling 166

Hays, Arthur Garfield 167

Hellman, Lillian 168–169, 411c

Hicks, Granville 171, 172

Hiss, Alger 174, 410c

Lardner, Ring Jr. 228

Lavery, Emmet 234

Lawson, John Howard 235, 236

Lennart, Isobel 237

Maltz, Albert 244

Menjou, Adolphe 263, 264

Miller, Arthur 265, 266, 267

Mostel, Zero 268

Odets, Clifford 285, 286

Oppenheimer, J. Robert 288

Ornitz, Samuel 290

Oxnam, Garfield Bromley 291, 292

Papp, Joseph 293, 294

Parks, Larry 294, 295

Pressman, Lee 307

Rand, Ayn 308

Reagan, Ronald 311

Remington, William Walter 314

Robbins, Jerome 318

Robeson, Paul 319, 320

Robinson, Edward G. 320

Schary, Dore 328

Schulberg, Budd 333

Scott, Robert Adrian 333, 334

Seeger, Pete 336

Sondergaard, Gale 345

Taylor, Robert 362

Trumbo, Dalton 370

White, Harry Dexter 400

House of Representatives, U.S.

Committee on Un-American Activities *see* House Committee on Un-American Activities (HUAC)

members *see* representatives, U.S.

"How Do You Fight Communism" (Ronald Reagan article) 311

"How to Beat the Communists" (Walter Reuther article) 317

"How You Can Fight Communism" (James F. O'Neil article) 10

Hughes, Howard (1905–1975) 187–188, 329

Hughes, Langston 118, 198

Hull, Cordell 119, 232

Humphrey Jr., Hubert H. (1912–1978) *188,* **188–190**

Americans for Democratic Action 12

Communist Control Act (1954) 82, 83

Government Operations Committee 162

Internal Security Act of 1950 195, 196

Hungarian-American Council for Democracy 444

Hungarian Brotherhood 444

Hungary 58

Hurley, General Patrick J. 337

Huston, John 81

Hutchins, Robert M. 155

hydrogen bomb 127, **190–191**, *191*, 288, 289

**I**

Ickes, Harold 14, 251, 348

*I. F. Stone's Weekly* 354

IIA *see* International Information Agency

*I Led Three Lives* (television series) 182, **192**, 302, 304, 411c

ILWU *see* International Longshoremen's and Warehousemen's Union

*I Married a Communist* (film) 188, **192–193**

Immigration and Naturalization Service 128

"I'm No Communist" (Humphrey Bogart article) 36

Independent Citizens Committee of the Arts, Sciences and Professions 156

Independent Productions Corporation 29

Independent Socialist League 444, 445

Indiana 226

Industrial Workers of the World 276, 445

Information Agency, U.S. *see* International Information Agency

informers *see* Bentley, Elizabeth; Budenz, Louis F.; Chambers, Whittaker; Philbrick, Herbert A.

*Inquisition in Eden* (Alvah Bessie) 28

Institute for Pacific Relations (IPR) **193–194**, 411c
  Budenz, Louis F. 53
  China Lobby 70
  Knowland, William F. 219
  Kohlberg, Alfred 221
  Lattimore, Owen 230, 232, 233
  McCarran, Patrick A. 252, 253

Institute of International Education 118, 276

Internal Revenue Service (IRS) 14, 78, 155, 165

Internal Security Act of 1950 (McCarran Act) **194–197**, 411c, 439–442
  *Blau v. United States* (1950) 34
  Communist Control Act (1954) 83
  Communist Party of the United States of America 86
  Douglas, Helen Gahagan 113
  Humphrey Jr., Hubert H. 189
  Koestler, Arthur 221
  Korean War 225
  McCarran, Patrick A. 252
  Mundt, Karl E. 271
  Pauling, Linus C. 296
  Truman, Harry S. 368, 369

Internal Security Subcommittee, Senate *see under* Senate, U.S.

Internal Security Subcommittee (Senate)
  members
    Eastland, James Oliver 125, 126
    McCarran, Patrick A. 252, 253
    Watkins, Arthur V. 392
  targets
    Davies Jr., John Paton 103
    Institute for Pacific Relations 194, 411c
    Pauling, Linus C. 296–297
    Vincent, John Carter 381
  witnesses
    Budenz, Louis F. 53
    Holliday, Judy 178
    Lattimore, Owen 232, 233
    Utley, Freda 376

International Harvester 374

International Information Agency (IIA) *197*, **197–199** *see also* Voice of America
  Cohn, Roy 76
  Dulles, John Foster 124
  Eisenhower, Dwight David 131
  Fast, Howard 139
  Government Operations Committee 162
  McCarthy, Joseph R. 258
  Permanent Subcommittee on Investigations 302

International Labor Defense 444

International Longshoremen's and Warehousemen's Union (ILWU) 40, 41

International Workers Order 444

IPR *see* Institute for Pacific Relations

IRS *see* Internal Revenue Service

isolationism 360

*It's a Hell of a Life But Not a Bad Living* (Edward Dmytryk) 112

Ives, Irving 105

*I Was a Communist for the FBI* (film) **199–200**

**J**

Jackson, Donald L. 21, 146, 291

Jackson, Henry R. 16, 56, 57, 77, 162, 215

Jackson, Robert H. 364

Jaffe, Philip 5, 6, 7, 337

JAFRC *see* Joint Anti-Fascist Refugee Committee

Jagger, Dean 277

Jarrico, Paul 188, 332

Jefferson School of Social Science (New York City) 165, 388, 444

Jell-O box 158, 162, 163, 325

Jenkins, Ray Howard (1897–1975) **201–202**

Jenner, William (1908–1985) *202*, **202–203**
  Eisenhower, Dwight David 130, 131
  Korean War 225
  MacArthur, Douglas 241
  Marshall, George Catlett 249
  Truman, Harry S. 369

Jessup, Philip C. (1897–1986) 70, 71, 153, **203–205**, *204*, 222, 257

*Jet Pilot* (film) 188, 395–396

Jewish Anti-Fascist Refugee Committee 310

Jewish Peoples
Committee 444
Jewish Peoples Fraternal
Order 444
Jews and Judaism
14–15, 309
Johnson, Edwin O. 393
Johnson, Laurence 140
Johnson, Lyndon Baines
(1908–1973) *206,*
**206–208**
China 69
Fortas, Abraham 148
Government
Operations
Committee 162
Humphrey Jr., Hubert
H. 190
Knowland, William F.
219
McCarthy, Joseph R.
260, 470–471
Pearson, Drew 299
Symington, (William)
Stuart 357
John Steinbeck
Committee to aid
Agricultural
Organizations 113
Johnston, Eric 11, 12,
160, 384
Joint Anti-Fascist
Refugee Committee
(JAFRC) **208–209**
Attorney General's
List of Subversive
Organizations 444
Eisler, Gerhart 134
Fast, Howard 139
Ferrer, Jose 142
Miller, Arthur 265
Popular Front 305
*Red Channels* 312
Sondergaard, Gale
345
Wood, John Stephen
402
Joint Committee against
Communism 222

*Joseph Julian v. American
Business Consultants*
(1954) **209–210**
Joseph Weydemeyer
School of Social
Science (St. Louis) 444
journalists
Alsop, Joseph 53, 83
Alsop, Stewart 83,
249, 392
Block, Herbert L. *34,*
**34–35,** 131, 249,
260
Buckley Jr., William
F. **48–50,** *49,* 78
Cogley, John 32, 155
Cooke, Alistair **92**
Jaffe, Philip 5, 6, 7,
337
Murrow, Edward R.
209, 249, *274,*
**274–277,** 300, 411c
Pearson, Drew *see*
Pearson, Drew
Pegler, Westbrook
78, **299–301**
Smedley, Agnes 74,
**339–340**
Sokolsky, George
**344–345**
Stone, I. F. 136,
**353–355**
Utley, Freda 69,
**375–377**
Waldrop, Frank 187,
286
Winchell, Walter 21,
109, 309
Judd, Walter 69, 177
judges *see* courts and
legal profession
Judiciary Committee,
Senate *see under*
Senate, U.S.
Julian, Joseph 209
Justice, U.S. Department
of
*Amerasia* 7
Biddle, Francis 13,
106, 182

Brownell, Herbert 37,
**44–46,** 57, 131, 278,
400
Cohn, Roy *see* Cohn,
Roy
Communist Control
Act (1954) 83
Coplon, Judith 73,
79, **93–94,** 215, 282,
410c
Eisler, Hanns 135
Hiss, Alger 176
Jackson, Robert H.
364
McCarran, Patrick A.
253
McGranery, James P.
76, 159, 194, 233,
253
Nixon, Richard M.
282
Smith Act (Alien
Registration Act of
1940) 340, 341

**K**

Kaghan, Theodore 199
Kanin, Garson 31, 312
Kaufman, Irving R. 128,
226, 325, 326, 448–449
Kaufman, Samuel F. 378
Kaye, Danny 82, 160
Kazan, Elia (1909– )
*211,* **211–213**
*After the Fall* 4, 5
American Committee
for Cultural
Freedom 9
Catholic Church 58
*Crucible* 96
House Committee on
Un-American
Activities 187
Miller, Arthur 267
Odets, Clifford 286
Kefauver, Estes 83, 189
Kelly, Gene 82
Kelly, Grace 172
Kempton, Murray 180

Kennedy, John F.
(1917–1963) 69, 162,
**213–214,** *214,* 339,
412c
Kennedy, Joseph P. 213,
215
Kennedy, Robert F.
(1925–1968) 77, 78,
**214–215**
Kenney, Robert 179
Kent, Morton
(1901–1949) **215–216**
*Kent v. Dulles* (1958) 390
Kenyon, Dorothy
(1888–1972)
**216–217,** 257, 322
Khrushchev, Nikita
(1894–1971) 41, **217,**
*217,* 275
*Khrushchev Remembers*
(Nikita Khrushchev)
217
Kilgore, Harley 189, 195
Kinsey, Alfred C.
(1894–1956) **217–218**
Knights of Columbus 58
Knights of the White
Camellia 445
Knowland, William F.
(1908–1965) *218,*
**218–220,** 468–470
China Lobby 69, 70
Flanders, Ralph E.
145
Korean War 227
McCarthy, Joseph R.
260
Watkins, Arthur V.
392
Knowles, Mary 155, 304
Knox, Alexander 81, 264
Koestler, Arthur
(1905–1983) 156,
**220–221**
Kohlberg, Alfred
(1886–1960) **221–223**
blacklist 31
Budenz, Louis F. 52
China Lobby 69, 70
Cohn, Roy 78

*Counterattack* 94
Institute for Pacific
Relations 193
Lattimore, Owen 230
McCarthy, Joseph R.
256
Smedley, Agnes 339
Tydings, Millard E. 373
Vincent, John Carter
380–381
Korean War (1950-53)
**223–227**
American Civil Liberties
Union 9
China 69
Feller, Abraham 140
Internal Security Act of
1950 194
MacArthur, Douglas
241–242, 243
Martin, Joseph W. 250
McCarthy, Joseph R.
257
Kramer, Stanley 112,
146, 172
Kristol, Irving 9
Ku Klux Klan 445
Kung, H. H. 69
Kunzig, Robert L. 292

**L**

labor leaders
Bridges, Harry **40–41**,
108, 184
Lewis, John L. 85, 89,
238, **238–239**, 272,
273
Murray, Philip 89, 90,
238, **271–274**, 272,
362, 410c
Reuther, Walter 90,
273, *315*, **315–317**,
362, 410c
Labor-Management
Relations Act of 1947
*see* Taft-Hartley Act
Labor Research
Association, Inc. 443,
444

labor unions *see*
American Federation
of Labor; Congress of
Industrial
Organizations; United
Electrical, Radio and
Machine Workers
Labor Youth League 444
LaCour, Joan 334
La Follette Jr., Robert M.
255
Lamont, Thomas 143
Landon, Alf 85
Landum-Griffin Act
(1959) 362
Langer, William 196
Lardner Jr., Ring
(1915–1983) 179,
**228–229**, 332, 333, 384
Larsen, Emmanuel 6
Lash, Joseph 313
Lasky, Victor 106
*Las Vegas Story, The*
(film) 188
Lattimore, Eleanor 289
Lattimore, Owen
(1900–1988) *229*,
**229–233**, 411c *see also*
*Ordeal by Slander*
American Civil Liberties
Union 9
Browder, Earl 44
Budenz, Louis F. 52, 53
China 69
China Lobby 70
Clubb, Oliver Edmund
74
Cohn, Roy 76
Connally, Tom 91
Declaration of
Conscience (1953) 106
Fortas, Abraham 147,
148
Institute for Pacific
Relations 193, 194
Knowland, William F.
219
Kohlberg, Alfred 222
Mao Zedong 245

Marshall, George Catlett
249
McCarran, Patrick A. 253
McCarthy, Joseph R.
256, 257
Pearson, Drew 298
Tydings, Millard E. 372
Utley, Freda 375, 376
Watkins, Arthur V. 392
Lavery, Emmet
(1902–1986) **233–234**,
336
Lawrence, Stanley 332
Lawson, John Howard
(1894–1977) **235–236**,
423–430
Blankfort, Michael 33
Chaplin, Charles Spencer
63
Cobb, Lee J. 75
Hollywood Ten 179, 180
Lavery, Emmet 234
Schulberg, Budd 332
Screen Writers' Guild
335, 336, 409c
lawyers *see* courts and
legal profession
League of American
Writers 164, 171, 208,
444
League of Women
Shoppers 111, **236**,
312
League of Women
Voters 111, 236
Lee, Gypsy Rose 31, 312
legislation, federal
Communist Control Act
(1954) 46, **82–83**, 86,
190, 411c, 461
Internal Security Act of
1950 (McCarran Act)
*see* Internal Security
Act of 1950
McCarran-Walter Act of
1952 251, 387
Smith Act (Alien
Registration Act of
1940) *see* Smith Act

Summary Suspension
Act of 1950 81
Taft-Hartley Act (1947)
239, 273, 306–307,
359, **361–362**, 410c
Legislative
Reorganization Act
(1946) 302
Lehman, Herbert 25
Leigh, Janet 188, 396
Lenin Peace Prize 118
Lennart, Isobel
(1915–1971) **237–238**
Lewis Jr., Fulton 78,
276, 323
Lewis, John L.
(1880–1969) 85, 89,
238, **238–239**, 272, 273
Lewisburg Federal
Penitentiary 176
*Liberty* (magazine) 246
Lie, Trygve 140, 141
*Life* (magazine) 240, 331
Lilienthal, David 288,
356
Lippmann, Walter 78
Lloyd, David 13
Loeb, Philip 19, 32, 150,
268, 313
Loeb, William 69, 106,
221
Loew's Incorporated 80
Long, Russell 467–468
Los Alamos, New
Mexico *see* Manhattan
Project
Losey, Joseph 188
Lovejoy, Frank 199
loyalty oaths 79, 226,
**239**, 311, 378, 388, 389
loyalty programs *see*
Executive Order 9835;
Executive Order
10241; Executive
Order 10450
Loyalty Review Board (of
Civil Service
Commission) **239–240**
Bailey, Dorothy 20
Bingham, Hiram 30

Cain, Harry P.  57
*Cole v. United States*
   (1956)  81
Dulles, John Foster  123
Executive Order 9835
   136, 137
Executive Order 10241
   137–138
Richardson, Seth  317,
   318
Service, John Stewart
   337–338
Truman, Harry S.  367
Vincent, John Carter
   382
Loyalty Security Board (of
   State Department)  381
Lucas, Scott  372
Luce, Clare Boothe  221
Luce, Henry R.
   (1898–1967)  61, 69,
   **240**, 316

**M**

MacArthur, Douglas
   (1880–1964)  224,
   **241–243**, 242
   Connally, Tom  92
   Eisenhower, Dwight
      David  129
   Korean War  223, 225
   Martin, Joseph W.  250
   Murrow, Edward R.
      275
   Pearson, Drew  298
   Smedley, Agnes  339
   Truman, Harry S.  369
Macedonian-American
   People's League  444
MacLeish, Archibald  1,
   252
Madison Square Garden
   Rally (1945)  208
Malden, Karl  58
Malin, Patrick  9
"Malmedy Massacre"
   (1944)  255

Maltz, Albert
   (1908–1985)  32, 33,
   179, 234, **243–245**, 338
*Manchester Guardian*
   (British newspaper)  76,
   198
*Manchurian Candidate,
   The* (film)  339
Manhattan Project  151,
   162, 287, 288, 325
Mann, Thomas  118, 127
Mansfield, Mike  70
Mao Zedong (1893–1976)
   *245*, **245–246**
   Chiang Kai-shek  66
   China  67, 68, 410c
   China Lobby  69
   China White Paper  70
   Hiss, Alger  174
   Lattimore, Owen  230
   Marshall, George
      Catlett  248
Marcantonio, Vito  306,
   307
March, Fredric
   (1897–1975)  **246**
Marshall, George Catlett
   (1880–1951)  **246–250**,
   247
   China  68, 69
   China Lobby  70
   Dulles, John Foster  122
   Eisenhower, Dwight
      David  130
   Lattimore, Owen  232
   Martin, Joseph W.  250
   McCarthy, Joseph R.
      257
   Murrow, Edward R.
      275
   Rosenberg, Anna Marie
      323
   Smith, Margaret Chase
      342
   Taft, Robert A.  360
Marshall Plan  248, 366
Martin, Joseph W.
   (1884–1968)  225, 241,
   **250–251**, 369

Marxist League of
   American Writers  285
Maryland  373
"massive retaliation"
   122
Matisse, Henri  135
Matsu (island off China
   coast)  69
Matusow, Harvey  194,
   233
Mayer, Louis B.  346
McCarey, Leo  170, 171
McCarran, Patrick A.
   (1876–1954)
   **251–253**
   Block, Herbert L.  34
   Bohlen, Charles E.  37
   Dartmouth College
      Speech  99
   Davies Jr., John Paton
      103
   Eastland, James
      Oliver  125
   Feller, Abraham  141
   Institute for Pacific
      Relations  194
   Internal Security Act
      of 1950  195
   Korean War  224
   Lattimore, Owen
      232, 233
   *Scoundrel Time*  334
   Vincent, John Carter
      381
   Watkins, Arthur V.
      392
McCarran Act  *see*
   Internal Security Act
   of 1950
McCarran-Walter Act of
   1952  251, 387
McCarthy, Joseph R.
   (1908–1957)
   **253–260**, *254*, 410c,
   411c, 412c
   Army-McCarthy
      hearings  *see*
      Army-McCarthy
      hearings

assistants  *see* Cohn,
   Roy; Kennedy,
   Robert F.; Schine,
   Gerard David
censure by Senate
   462–472
   Bridges, Styles  42
   Cronin, Father John
      96
   Eastland, James
      Oliver  125
   Eisenhower, Dwight
      David  132
   Flanders, Ralph E.
      145
   Fulbright, James W.
      153, 154
   Humphrey Jr.,
      Hubert H.  190
   Knowland, William
      F.  219
   McCarran, Patrick
      A.  253
   McCarthy, Joseph
      R.  260
   Mundt, Karl E.  271
   Smith, Margaret
      Chase  343
   Symington,
      (William) Stuart
      358
   Watkins, Arthur V.
      392, 393, 394
court cases
   *Cole v. United States*
      (1956)  81
   *Pennsylvania v.
      Nelson* (1956)  301
critics and opponents
   American
      Committee for
      Cultural Freedom
      10
   American Library
      Association  12
   Americans for
      Democratic
      Action  13
   Benton, William
      Burnett  24, 25, 26

Block, Herbert L.
34, 35
Cain, Harry P. 56
Connally, Tom 91
Cronin, Father John
95, 96
Douglas, Helen
Gahagan 114
Dulles, Allen W.
120, 121
Flanders, Ralph E.
143
Fulbright, James W.
153, 154
Luce, Henry R. 240
Murrow, Edward R.
275, 276
Nicholson, Donald
280, 281
Pearson, Drew 298,
299
Roosevelt, Eleanor
322
Smith, Margaret
Chase 341, 342,
343
Stevens, Robert Ten
Broeck 349, 350
Stevenson, Adlai E.
352
Stone, I. F. 354
Symington,
(William) Stuart
357, 358
Truman, Harry S.
368
Tydings, Millard E.
373
foreign policy role
China 69
China Lobby 70
Cold War 79
Korean War 225,
226
informants
Budenz, Louis F. 52
Chambers,
Whittaker 62
Sokolsky, George
345

legal defense
Williams, Edward
Bennett 400, 401
neutral parties
Eisenhower, Dwight
David 130, 131,
132
Hoover, J. Edgar
183
supporters and
sympathizers
American Legion 11
Bridges, Styles 42
Buckley Jr., William
F. 48, 49
Dies, Martin 110
Dulles, John Foster
123, 124
Eastland, James
Oliver 125
Kohlberg, Alfred
222
McCarran, Patrick
A. 252
McLeod, Scott 261,
262
Mundt, Karl E. 271
Nixon, Richard M.
282, 283
Pegler, Westbrook
300
Taft, Robert A. 360
targets
Acheson, Dean 3,
4
Amerasia 7
Bohlen, Charles E.
37, 38
Bridges, Harry 41
Brunauer, Esther
Caulkihn 46, 47
Brunauer, Stephen
48
Central Intelligence
Agency 59
Clubb, Oliver
Edmund 74
Davies Jr., John
Paton 103
Einstein, Albert 128

Fund for the
Republic 155
Hammett, Samuel
Dashiell 165
Institute for Pacific
Relations 193,
194
International
Information
Agency 197, 198
Kenyon, Dorothy
216
Lattimore, Owen
230, 231, 232
Marshall, George
Catlett 249
National Lawyers
Guild 278
Pauling, Linus C.
296
Peress, Irving 301
Rosenberg, Anna
Marie 324
Schlesinger, Arthur
Jr. 331
Service, John
Stewart 337
Vincent, John
Carter 381
Voice of America
383
Wallace, Henry A.
385
Warren, Earl 390
McCarthy and His
Enemies (William F.
Buckley Jr. and Brent
Bozell) 48–49
McCarthy and the
Communists (Moshe
Decter and James
Rorty) 10
"McCarthyism" 35,
260–261, 352, 353
McCarthyism (Joseph
McCarthy book) 106
McClellan, John L. 162
McClellan, Joseph 301
McGohey, John 73

McGranery, James P.
76, 159, 194, 233, 253
McGrath, J. Howard 64
McGuire, James 118
McKellar, Kenneth 298
McLeod, Scott
(1914–1961) 36, 123,
261, 261–262
McWilliams, Carey 136
Meany, George 317
Medina, Harold 107, 341
Meet the Press (NBC
radio show) 23, 62,
175, 314
Meet the Press (NBC
television show) 145
Meiklejohn, Alexander
(1872–1964) 262,
262–263
Menjou, Adolphe
(1890–1963) 106,
171, 263–264, 268,
269, 319, 395
Mesarosh v. United States
(1956) 389
MGM
(Metro-Goldwyn-Mayer
) (movie studio) 80,
237, 346
Michigan 226, 243
Michigan Civil Rights
Federation 444
Michigan School of
Social Science 444
Midwest Daily Record 51
MI5 (British
counterespionage
agency) 151
Miller, Arthur (1915– )
4–5, 57, 58, 96–97,
265, 265–267, 387
Mill Point, West Virginia
112, 244
Mindszenty, Cardinal
Joseph 58
missile gap 358
Mission to Moscow (film)
264, 269
Mitchell, Kate L. 6
Monroe, Marilyn 5

Monroney, Mike  59, 121
*Monsieur Verdoux* (film)
    64
Moos, Elizabeth  314
Morgan, Henry  312
Morley, Karen  363
Morse, Wayne  105
Mortimer, Lee  342
Mostel, Zero
    (1915–1977)  14, 32,
    150, **267–268**
Motion Picture Alliance
    for the Preservation of
    American Ideals
    (MPAPAI)  **268–269**,
    409c
    Coburn, Charles
        75–76
    Cooper, Gary  92
    Disney, Walter E.  110
    Ferrer, Jose  141
    Menjou, Adolphe  264
    Wayne, John  395
Motion Picture Artists
    Committee to Aid
    Republican Spain  80,
    156, 345
Motion Picture
    Democratic Committee
    115, 164
Motion Picture Guild,
    Inc.  29, 156, 228
motion picture industry
    actors and actresses
        *see* actors and
        actresses
    American Legion
        11–12
    Committee for the
        First Amendment
        (CFA)  *see*
        Committee for the
        First Amendment
    composers  *see* Eisler,
        Hanns
    Declaration of
        Conscience (1953)
        **105–106**
    directors  *see* directors
        (film)

executives  *see* Disney,
    Walter E.; Goldwyn,
    Samuel; Hughes,
    Howard; Johnston,
    Eric
    Hollywood Ten  *see*
        Hollywood Ten
    House Committee on
        Un-American
        Activities  186, 410c
    loyalty oaths  239
    producers  *see*
        producers (film)
    screenwriters  *see*
        screenwriters
    Screen Writers' Guild
        (SWG)  *see* Screen
        Writers' Guild
    studios
        MGM  80, 237, 346
        Paramount  277
        RKO  112, 188, 192,
            329, 334, 384
        Twentieth
            Century-Fox  229,
            384
        United Artists  64
        Universal  165, 245
        Walt Disney  236
        Warner Brothers
            156, 199
    Waldorf Statement
        (1947)  31, 160,
        179, 329, **384**, 410c,
        431
Motion Picture Industry
    Council  329
Motion Picture
    Producers Association
    384
Motion Pictures Arts
    Committee to Aid
    Republican Spain  164
Moulder, Morgan  294
*Moulin Rouge* (film)  142
MPAPAI  *see* Motion
    Picture Alliance for the
    Preservation of
    American Ideals
Muir, Jean  32, 313

Mundt, Karl E.
    (1900–1974)
    **269–271**, *270*
    Army-McCarthy
        hearings  16
    Duggan, Lawrence
        119
    Government
        Operations
        Committee  162
    Hiss, Alger  175
    Internal Security Act
        of 1950  195
    McCarthy, Joseph R.
        259
Mundt-Ferguson-Johnston
    bill (1950)  194, 195
Mundt-Nixon bill (1948)
    194, 252, 270, 282
Murchison, Clint  373
Murray, Philip
    (1886–1953)  89, 90,
    238, **271–274**, *272*,
    362, 410c
Murrow, Edward R.
    (1908–1965)  209,
    249, 274, **274–277**,
    300, 411c
Mussolini, Benito  305
*My Son John* (film)  277

# N

NAACP  *see* National
    Association for the
    Advancement of
    Colored People
*Naming Names* (Victor
    Navasky)  32
*Nation* (magazine)  62
National Association for
    the Advancement of
    Colored People
    (NAACP)  85, 117,
    **278**, 364
National Broadcasting
    Company  *see* NBC
National Catholic
    Welfare Conference  95

National Committee for
    a Free Europe, Inc.
    (NCFE)  97
National Committee for
    the Defense of Political
    Prisoners  444
National Committee to
    Abolish the House
    Un-Activities Affairs
    Committee  263
National Committee to
    Win the Peace  444
National Conference on
    American Policy in
    China and the Far East
    444
National Council of
    Americans of Croatian
    Descent  444
National Council of
    American-Soviet
    Friendship  14, 444
National Council of the
    Arts, Sciences and
    Professions  312
National Federation for
    Constitutional
    Liberties  444
Nationalist Party of
    Puerto Rico  445
National Labor Relations
    Act of 1935  *see*
    Wagner Act
National Labor Relations
    Board (NLRB)  89,
    239, 361, 374, 387
National Lawyers Guild
    109, 185, **278–279**, 398
National Negro Congress
    444
National Recovery Act
    (NRA)  84, 98
*National Review*
    (journal)  49
National Sons of the
    American Revolution
    403
NATO  *see* North
    Atlantic Treaty
    Organization

Nature Friends of America 444

Navasky, Victor 31, 32

*Navigating the Rapids: 1918–1971* (Adolf A. Berle Jr.) 28

Nazi-Soviet Pact (1939) 85, 98, 157, **279–280**, 305, 349, 409c

NBC (National Broadcasting Company) 165, 192

NCFE *see* National Committee for a Free Europe, Inc.

Negro Labor Victory Committee 444

Neibuhr, Reinhold 12

Nelson, Steven 301, 412c

*Nelson v. U.S.* (1956) 412c

New Committee for Publications 444

New Deal
Catholic Church 58
Communist Party of the United States of America 84, 85
*Daily Worker* 98
Daughters of the American Revolution 101
Dies, Martin 108
House Committee on Un-American Activities 184
Popular Front 305

New Look (Eisenhower defense strategy) 288

*New Masses* (Communist publication) 33, 60, 74, 171, 235, 244, 285

New Playwrights Theater 235

New York City 266

*New York Times* (newspaper) 71, 103, 128, 397, 459

Nicholson, Donald (1888–1968) *280,* **280–281**

Nixon, Richard M. (1913–1994) *49, 281,* **281–284**, 410c, 411c, 412c
Acheson, Dean 3
Bridges, Styles 42
Buckley Jr., William F. 50
Central Intelligence Agency 59
Chambers, Whittaker 61
Chiang Kai-shek 67
China Lobby 70
Condon, Edward U. 88
Coplon, Judith 93
Cronin, Father John 95
Douglas, Helen Gahagan 114
Duggan, Lawrence 119
Dulles, Allen W. 120, 121
Eisenhower, Dwight David 131
Eisler, Gerhart 134
Government Operations Committee 161
Hiss, Alger 175–177
House Committee on Un-American Activities 186
Knowland, William F. 219
Mao Zedong 246
McCarthy, Joseph R. 256, 258
Murrow, Edward R. 276
Nicholson, Donald 281
Oppenheimer, J. Robert 288
Pearson, Drew 298, 299
Pressman, Lee 307
Reagan, Ronald 311
*Scoundrel Time* 334
Stevens, Robert Ten Broeck 350
Stevenson, Adlai E. 352
Taylor, Robert 363

United Electrical, Radio and Machine Workers 374
Watkins, Arthur V. 393

Nizer, Louis (1902–1994) 140, **284**

NLRB *see* National Labor Relations Board

Non-Aggression Pact *see* Nazi-Soviet Pact

North American Committee to Aid Spanish Democracy 444

North American Spanish Aid Committee 444

North Atlantic Treaty Organization (NATO) 130, 366

North Carolina 171, 384

*North Star* (film) 168, 264, 269

novelists *see* writers

Novikov, Nikolai 208

NRA *see* National Recovery Act

nuclear weapons *see also* atomic bomb; Atomic Energy Commission; hydrogen bomb; Manhattan Project
*Bulletin of Atomic Scientists* 53
Dulles, John Foster 122
Gold, Harry 158
MacArthur, Douglas 242
Pauling, Linus C. 296

**O**

Objectivism 308

Odets, Clifford (1906–1963) 33, 63, 135, 187, *285,* **285–286**

Office of Price Administration (OPA) 185, 309

Office of Strategic Services (OSS) 5, 6

Ohio 226

Ohio School of Social Sciences 444

Ohio State University 8

Oklahoma, University of 8

Oklahoma Committee to Defend Political Prisoners 444

*One Hundred Things You Should Know about Communism* (HUAC pamphlet series) 187, **286–287**

O'Neil, James F. 10, 12

*On the Waterfront* (film) 58

OPA *see* Office of Price Administration

Oppenheimer, J. Robert (1904–1967) **287–289**
American Committee for Cultural Freedom 9
Atomic Energy Commission 18, 411c
*Bulletin of Atomic Scientists* 53
Condon, Edward U. 86
Einstein, Albert 129
hydrogen bomb 191
Murrow, Edward R. 275
Strauss, Lewis 356

*Ordeal by Slander* (Owen Lattimore) 106, **289–290**

Original Southern Klans, Incorporated 445

Ornitz, Samuel (1891–1957) 179, **290–291**

OSS *see* Office of Strategic Services

*Out of Bondage* (Elizabeth Bentley) 24

Oxnam, Garfield Bromley (1891–1963) **291–292**, 379

**P**

*Pacific Affairs* (journal)
193, 230
Pacific Northwest Labor
School (Seattle,
Washington) 444
Palmer Raids 181
Papp, Joseph
(1921–1991) 32,
**293–294**, 388
Paramount Studios 277
Parks, Larry
(1914–1975) 74, 100,
187, 293, **294–295**
Partido del Pueblo
(Panama) 444, 445
Pauling, Linus C.
(1901–1994) 53,
**295–297**
Peace Information
Center 117
Pearson, Drew
(1897–1969) *297*,
**297–299**
Crusade for Freedom
97
Dies, Martin 109
Lattimore, Owen 231
McCarran, Patrick A.
251
Schine, Gerard David
330
Thomas, J. Parnell
364
Williams, Edward
Bennett 400
Pegler, Westbrook
(1894–1963) 78,
**299–301**
Pendergast, Thomas 366
*Pennsylvania v. Nelson*
(1956) **301**, 389
Peoples Educational and
Press Association of
Texas 444, 445
Peoples Educational
Association 444
People's Education
Center 112

People's Institute of
Applied Religion 444
People's Radio
Foundation, Inc. 444
Peress, Irving (1918– )
**301–302**
Army-McCarthy
hearings 16
Flanders, Ralph E.
143
McCarthy, Joseph R.
259
Murrow, Edward R.
275
Stevens, Robert Ten
Broeck 349, 350
Watkins, Arthur V.
394
Perkins, Frances 363
Perlo, Victor 22, 60
Permanent
Subcommittee on
Investigations, Senate
**302**
Army-McCarthy
hearings 16
Cohn, Roy 76, 77
Kennedy, Robert F.
214
McCarthy, Joseph R.
258, 259
Mundt, Karl E. 271
Smith, Margaret
Chase 342
Voice of America 383
*Watkins v. United
States* (1957) 395
*Peters v. Hobby* (1955)
389
Peurifoy, John 232
Philadelphia School of
Social Science and Art
444
Philbrick, Herbert A.
(1915– ) 155, 182,
192, **302–304**, *303*, 374
Photo League (New York
City) 444
*Photoplay* (magazine) 36

Picasso, Pablo 56, 64,
135
*Plain Talk* (publication)
222, 381
playwrights *see*
Blankfort, Michael;
Brecht, Bertolt;
Hellman, Lillian;
Miller, Arthur; Odets,
Clifford
Plymouth Monthly
Meeting (Quaker
organization) 155
Poland 58
politicians
Aiken, George 105
Benton, William
Burnett *see* Benton,
William Burnett
Bridges, Styles *41*,
**41–43**, 69, 70, 261,
381
Butler, John Marshall
83, 162, 373
Cain, Harry P. **56–58**,
324
Capehart, Homer
152, 177
Connally, Tom 73,
**90–92**, *91*, 372
Dies, Martin *see* Dies,
Martin
Dirksen, Everett 145,
162
Douglas, Helen
Gahagan *113*,
**113–114**, 114, 283,
311
Douglas, Paul 189,
195
Eastland, James Oliver
*125*, **125–126**
Eisenhower, Dwight
David *see*
Eisenhower, Dwight
David
Flanders, Ralph E.
17, *142*, **142–145**,
153, 154, 260, 411c,
462–465

Fulbright, James
William 42,
**152–154**, *153*
Gillette, Guy 25, 393
Hendrickson, Robert
105
Hoey, Clyde 161,
162, **177–178**, 302
Humphrey Jr., Hubert
H. *see* Humphrey
Jr., Hubert H.
Ives, Irving 105
Jackson, Donald L.
21, 146, 291
Jackson, Henry R. 16,
56, 57, 77, 162, 215
Jenner, William *see*
Jenner, William
Johnson, Lyndon
Baines *see* Johnson,
Lyndon Baines
Judd, Walter 69, 177
Kefauver, Estes 83,
189
Kennedy, John F. *see*
Kennedy, John F.
Knowland, William F.
*see* Knowland,
William F.
Martin, Joseph W.
225, 241, **250–251**,
369
McCarran, Patrick A.
*see* McCarran,
Patrick A.
McCarthy, Joseph R.
*see* McCarthy,
Joseph R.
Monroney, Mike 59,
121
Morse, Wayne 105
Mundt, Karl E. *see*
Mundt, Karl E.
Nixon, Richard M. *see*
Nixon, Richard M.
Rankin, John *see*
Rankin, John
Reagan, Ronald 112,
182, *310*, **310–312**,
410c, 421–423

Reynolds, Robert 110
Roosevelt, Franklin D.
    *see* Roosevelt,
    Franklin D.
Smith, Margaret Chase
    162, **341–343**, *342,*
    411c *see also*
    Declaration of
    Conscience (1950)
Stevenson, Adlai E. *see*
    Stevenson, Adlai E.
Symington, (William)
    Stuart 16, 162, 323,
    **356–358**, *357*
Taft, Robert A. *see* Taft,
    Robert A.
Tenney, Jack 110, 234,
    320, 338
Thomas, J. Parnell *see*
    Thomas, J. Parnell
Thomas, Norman 44,
    296, 354, **364–365,**
    *365*
Thye, Edward 105
Tobey, Charles 105
Truman, Harry S. *see*
    Truman, Harry S.
Tydings, Millard E. 7,
    44, 91, *371,* **371–373**
Velde, Harold H. *see*
    Velde, Harold H.
Wallace, Henry A. *see*
    Wallace, Henry A.
Walter, Francis *see*
    Walter, Francis
Warren, Earl *see*
    Warren, Earl
Watkins, Arthur V. *see*
    Watkins, Arthur V.
Wood, John Stephen
    *see* Wood, John
    Stephen
Polonia Society of the
    IWO 444
Popular Front **304–305**
    Communist Party of the
        United States of
        America 85
    *Daily Worker* 98
    Foster, William Z. 149

*God That Failed* 157
    Nazi-Soviet Pact 279,
        409c
    Stalin, Joseph 349
Porter, Cole 1
Porter, Paul 147
Potter, Charles 162
Powell Jr., Adam
    Clayton 276
Preminger, Otto 32,
    180, 371, 399, 412c
Pressman, Lee (1906– )
    60, 173, 174, **306–307**
producers (film)
    Foreman, Carl 32,
        **146–147**, 172, 173
    Hughes, Howard
        **187–188**, 329
    Johnston, Eric 11, 12,
        160, 384
    Kramer, Stanley 112,
        146, 172
    Preminger, Otto 32,
        180, 371, 399, 412c
    Schary, Dore **328–329,**
        334
professors and educators
    Boorstin, Daniel J. **38,**
        171, 379
    Burnham, James **54**
    Davis, Robert Gorham
        **104,** 379
    Du Bois, William
        Edward Burghardt
        **116–118**
    Graham, Frank 347, 348
    Hicks, Granville 38,
        **171–172,** 280, 379
    Hook, Sidney 9, 263
    Lattimore, Owen *see*
        Lattimore, Owen
    Meiklejohn, Alexander
        *262,* **262–263**
    Schlesinger, Arthur Jr.
        9, 12, **331,** *331*
Progressive
    German-Americans
    444
Progressive Party 385

Proletarian Party of
    America 444
*Protestant Digest* 292
Protestant War Veterans
    of the U.S., Inc. 445
Pumpkin Papers 62,
    176, 410

**Q**

Quemoy (island off
    China coast) 69

**R**

Rabinowitch, Eugene 53
radio broadcasts *see*
    Voice of America
    (VOA)
radio personalities
    Burrows, Abraham 31,
        **54–55,** 312
    Faulk, John Henry 19,
        32, **140,** 284
    Lewis Jr., Fulton 78,
        276, 323
Radulovich, Milo 275
Rand, Ayn (1905–1982)
    **308,** 346, 347
Randolph, John 150
Rankin, John
    (1882–1960) **308–310**
    Chaplin, Charles
        Spencer 64
    Daughters of the
        American Revolution
        101
    Duggan, Lawrence 119
    Einstein, Albert 127
    House Committee on
        Un-American
        Activities 185
    Korean War 226
    National Association for
        the Advancement of
        Colored People 278
    Roosevelt, Eleanor 321
    Rosenberg, Anna Marie
        323
    Thomas, J. Parnell 364
Rauh, Joseph 169

Rayburn, Sam 367, 388
Reagan, Ronald (1911– )
    112, 182, *310,* **310–312,**
    410c, 421–423
*Recollections of a Life*
    (Alger Hiss) 177
Red-baiting 110, 317
*Red Channels*
    (periodical) **312–313,**
    411c
    blacklist 31
    Christians, Mady 72
    Ferrer, Jose 141
    Fund for the Republic
        155
    *Joseph Julian v. American
        Business Consultants*
        (1954) 209
    Kohlberg, Alfred 222
    Robinson, Edward G.
        320
Redford, Robert 396
"Red Monday" (June 17,
    1957) 405
*Red Plot against America,
    The* (Robert Stripling
    and Bob Considine)
    187, **313–314**
"Red Scare" 101
Reece, B. Carroll 218
Reeves Instrument
    Corporation 343
religion *see* Catholic
    Church; Oxnam,
    Garfield Bromley
Remington, Anne Moos
    314, 315
Remington, William
    Walter (1918–1954)
    23, 76, 302, **314–315,**
    318, 411c
*Report on Blacklisting*
    (compiled by John
    Cogley) 32, 155
representatives, U.S.
    Dies, Martin *see* Dies,
        Martin
    Douglas, Helen Gahagan
        *113,* **113–114,** 114,
        283, 311

Jackson, Donald L.
21, 146, 291
Judd, Walter 69, 177
Martin, Joseph W.
225, 241, **250–251**,
369
Mundt, Karl E. *see*
Mundt, Karl E.
Nixon, Richard M. *see*
Nixon, Richard M.
Rankin, John *see*
Rankin, John
Thomas, J. Parnell *see*
Thomas, J. Parnell
Velde, Harold H. *see*
Velde, Harold H.
Walter, Francis *see*
Walter, Francis
Wood, John Stephen
*see* Wood, John
Stephen
Republican Party 70,
105 *see also specific*
*people*
Republic Steel 89
Reuther, Walter
(1907–1970) 90, 273,
*315,* **315–317,** 362,
410c
Revere, Ann 295
Revolutionary Workers
League 444
Reynolds, Robert 110
Ribbentrop, Joachim von
279
Rich, Robert *see*
Trumbo, Dalton
Richardson, Seth
(1880–1953) 20, 136,
137, *317,* **317–318,** 367
Ridgway, Matthew B.
224, 226
Ritt, Martin 150
RKO Studios 112, 188,
192, 329, 334, 384
Robards Jr., Jason 4
Robbins, Jerome (1918–
) **318,** 379
Robert Rich Productions,
Inc. 334, 371

Robeson, Paul
(1898–1976) 117,
126, 306, **318–320,** 388
Robinson, Edward G.
(1893–1973) 31, 32,
220, 264, 312, **320–321**
Rockefeller Foundation
14, 218
Rogers, Lela 234
*Rogers v. U.S* 34
Roman Catholic Church
*see* Catholic Church
Romanian-American
Fraternal Society 444
Roosevelt, Eleanor
(1884–1962) 12, 101,
109, *321,* **321–322**
Roosevelt, Franklin D.
*405,* 409c
Acheson, Dean 1
Berle Jr., Adolf A. 26
Catholic Church 58
Chiang Kai-shek 66
Communist Party of
the United States of
America 84, 85
Congress of Industrial
Organizations 89
*Daily Worker* 98
Dies, Martin 109
Douglas, Melvyn 115
Douglas, William O.
115
Duggan, Lawrence
118
Eisenhower, Dwight
David 130
Hellman, Lillian 168
Hoover, J. Edgar 181
House Committee on
Un-American
Activities 184
Lewis, John L. 238
Marshall, George
Catlett 247
Motion Picture
Alliance for the
Preservation of
American Ideals 269
Murray, Philip 272

Pearson, Drew 298
Popular Front 305
Pressman, Lee 306
Rosenberg, Anna
Marie 322, 323
Stalin, Joseph 349
Tydings, Millard E.
371
Wallace, Henry A.
385
Winant, John G. 401
Yalta Conference 404
Rorty, James 10
Rosenberg, Anna Marie
(1902–1983) 56, 309,
*322,* **322–324**
Rosenberg, Ethel
Greenglass
(1915–1953) *324,*
**324–325,** 411c,
448–449
American Civil
Liberties Union 9
American Committee
for Cultural
Freedom 10
Cohn, Roy 76
Cold War 79
*Crucible* 97
Einstein, Albert 128
Fuchs, Klaus 152
Korean War 226
Rosenberg, Julius 326
Rosenberg, Julius
(1918–1953)
**325–327,** *326,* 411c,
448–449
American Civil
Liberties Union 9
American Committee
for Cultural
Freedom 10
Cohn, Roy 76
Cold War 79
*Crucible* 97
Einstein, Albert 128
Fuchs, Klaus 151, 152
Gold, Harry 158, 159
Greenglass, David
162, 163

Korean War 226
Sobell, Morton 343
Rosenwald, Harold 173
Rossen, Robert 379
Rosten, Norman 5
Rules Committee, Senate
*see under* Senate, U.S.
Rusk, Dean 218
Russell, Bertrand 296,
375
Rutgers University (New
Brunswick, New
Jersey) 8
Ryan, Robert 192
Rykov, Alexis 348

**S**

SACB *see* Subversive
Activities Control
Board
*Safeguards for America*
(Knights of Columbus
radio broadcasts) 58
SAG *see* Screen Actors
Guild
St. Clair, James D. 397
*St. Louis Post-Dispatch*
(newspaper) 109
Salem witchcraft trials
96–97
*Salt of the Earth* (film) 29
Samuel Adams School
(Boston,
Massachusetts) 444
*Saturday Evening Post*
(periodical) 112, 229
Saypol, Irving 209, 210
Sayre, Francis B. 173
Schappes Defense
Committee 444
Schary, Dore
(1905–1980)
**328–329,** 334
Schine, Gerard David
(1927– ) **329–331**
Army-McCarthy
hearings 16, 17
Cohn, Roy 76, 77

Dartmouth College Speech 99

Flanders, Ralph E. 144

International Information Agency 198, 199

McCarthy, Joseph R. 258, 259

Stevens, Robert Ten Broeck 349

Voice of America 383

Welch, Joseph Nye 397, 398

Schneiderman-Darcy Defense Committee 445

School of Jewish Studies (New York City) 445

Schulberg, Budd (1914– ) 187, 221, **331–333**

SCHW *see* Southern Conference on Human Welfare

scientists

Condon, Edward U. 14, 53, 61, **86–89**, 215, 402

Einstein, Albert *see* Einstein, Albert

Fuchs, Klaus **150–152**, 158, 159, 161, 191, 410c

Gold, Harry *see* Gold, Harry

Kinsey, Alfred C. **217–218**

Oppenheimer, J. Robert *see* Oppenheimer, J. Robert

Pauling, Linus C. 53, **295–297**

Scott, Robert Adrian (1913–1973) 179, 329, **333–334**, 384

Scottsboro Boys 84–85, 235, 348

*Scoundrel Time* (Lillian Hellman play) 170, **334–335**

Screen Actors Guild (SAG) 156, 310, 311, 345, 346, 410c

Screen Directors Guild 239

*Screen Guide for Americans* (Ayn Rand) 308

screenwriters

Bessie, Alvah **28**, 112, 179

Biberman, Herbert **28–30**, 179, 180, 333

Blankfort, Michael **32–33**

Cole, Lester **80–81**, 179, 333, 364

Collins, Richard 332, 333

Foreman, Carl 32, **146–147**, 172, 173

front 149

Hammett, Samuel Dashiell *164*, **164–165**, 167, 168, 198, 335

Hellman, Lillian *see* Hellman, Lillian

Jarrico, Paul 188, 332

Lardner Jr., Ring 179, **228–229**, 332, 333, 384

Lavery, Emmet **233–234**, 336

Lawson, John Howard *see* Lawson, John Howard

Lennart, Isobel **237–238**

Maltz, Albert 32, 33, 179, 234, **243–245**, 338

Odets, Clifford *see* Odets, Clifford

Ornitz, Samuel 179, **290–291**

Rand, Ayn **308**, 346, 347

Schary, Dore **328–329**, 334

Schulberg, Budd 187, 221, **331–333**

Scott, Robert Adrian 179, 329, **333–334**, 384

Trumbo, Dalton *see* Trumbo, Dalton

Screen Writers' Guild (SWG) **335–336**

Cole, Lester 80

Hollywood Ten 179

Lavery, Emmet 233, 234

Lawson, John Howard 235, 409c

Ornitz, Samuel 290

Schary, Dore 329

Seattle Labor School 445

"Security Index" (FBI) 182

sedition legislation 301 *see also* Smith Act

Seeger, Pete (1919– ) 32, 95, **336**

*See It Now* (television program) 274, 275, 277, 411c

Senate, U.S.

Bill 4037 (1950) 195

committees

Armed Services 357, 371

Foreign Relations 36, 37, 90, 91, 131, 153, 372

Government Operations *see* Government Operations Committee

Judiciary 251, 252

Rules 25

Watkins *see* Watkins Committee

members *see* senators, U.S.

subcommittees

Internal Security *see* Internal Security

Subcommittee (Senate) Permanent Subcommittee on Investigations *see* Permanent Subcommittee on Investigations

Tydings *see* Tydings Subcommittee

*Senator McCarthy* (pamphlet) 222

senators, U.S.

Aiken, George 105

Benton, William Burnett *see* Benton, William Burnett

Bridges, Styles *41*, **41–43**, 69, 70, 261, 381

Butler, John Marshall 83, 162, 373

Cain, Harry P. **56–58**, 324

Capehart, Homer 152, 177

Connally, Tom 73, **90–92**, *91*, 372

Dirksen, Everett 145, 162

Douglas, Paul 189, 195

Eastland, James Oliver *125*, **125–126**

Flanders, Ralph E. *see* Flanders, Ralph E.

Fulbright, James William 42, **152–154**, *153*

Gillette, Guy 25, 393

Hendrickson, Robert 105

Hoey, Clyde 161, 162, **177–178**, 302

Humphrey Jr., Hubert H. *see* Humphrey Jr., Hubert H.

Ives, Irving 105

Jackson, Henry R. 16, 56, 57, 77, 162, 215

Jenner, William *see*
Jenner, William
Johnson, Lyndon
Baines *see* Johnson,
Lyndon Baines
Kefauver, Estes 83,
189
Kennedy, John F. *see*
Kennedy, John F.
Knowland, William F.
*see* Knowland,
William F.
McCarran, Patrick A.
*see* McCarran,
Patrick A.
McCarthy, Joseph R.
*see* McCarthy,
Joseph R.
Monroney, Mike 59,
121
Morse, Wayne 105
Mundt, Karl E. *see*
Mundt, Karl E.
Nixon, Richard M.
*see* Nixon, Richard
M.
Reynolds, Robert 110
Smith, Margaret
Chase 162,
**341–343**, *342*, 411c
*see also* Declaration
of Conscience
(1950)
Symington, (William)
Stuart 16, 162, 323,
**356–358**, *357*
Taft, Robert A. *see*
Taft, Robert A.
Thye, Edward 105
Tobey, Charles 105
Tydings, Millard E. 7,
44, 91, *371*, **371–373**
Watkins, Arthur V.
*see* Watkins, Arthur
V.
Serbian-American
Fraternal Society 444
Serbian Vidovdan
Council 445

Service, John Stewart
(1910–  ) **337–338**,
411c
Acheson, Dean 4
*Amerasia* 6, 7
Bingham, Hiram 30
China 69
China Lobby 70
Kohlberg, Alfred 222
Mao Zedong 245
Nicholson, Donald
280
Seventh World Congress
of the Communist
International
(Moscow, 1935) 305,
409c
*Sexual Behavior in the
Human Female* (Alfred
Kinsey) 218
*Sexual Behavior in the
Human Male* (Alfred
Kinsey) 217–218
"Shadow of Fear, The"
(1948 ACLU report) 8
Shaw, Artie 379
Sheen, Fulton J. 51, 58
Sheen, Martin 245
Shelley, Joshua 150
Shirer, William 136, 274
Shirley, Anne 334
Siam *see* Thailand
Silone, Ignazio 156
Silvermaster, Nathan
Gregory 22
Silver Shirt Legion of
America 445
Sinatra, Frank (1917–  )
32, 81, 245, **338–339**,
364
singers
Robeson, Paul 117,
126, 306, **318–320**,
388
Seeger, Pete 32, 95,
**336**
Sinatra, Frank 32, 81,
245, **338–339**, 364

Sing Sing Prison
(Ossining, New York)
327
*Situation in Asia, The*
(Owen Lattimore) 230
Sixth World Congress of
Communist
International
(Moscow, 1928) 409c
Skardon, James 151
Sloan, Everett 19
Sloane, Alan 19
Slovak Workers Society
444
Slovenian-American
National Council 445
Smedley, Agnes
(1892–1950) 74,
**339–340**
Smith, Gerald L. K. 323,
338
Smith, H. Alexander 105
Smith, Margaret Chase
(1897–1995) 162,
**341–343**, *342*, 411c
*see also* Declaration of
Conscience (1950)
Smith, Walter Bedell 36,
103
Smith Act (Alien
Registration Act of
1940) **340–341**, 409c
American Civil
Liberties Union 8
Bridges, Harry 40
Communist Party of
the United States of
America 86
*Dennis v. U.S.* (1951)
106, 107
Stone, I. F. 354
*Yates v. United States*
(1957) 404, 406
Sobell, Morton (1927–  )
*343*, **343–344**
Socialist Workers Party
445
Socialist Youth League
445

Sokolsky, George
(1893–1962) **344–345**
*Solution in Asia* (Owen
Lattimore) 230
Sondergaard, Gale
(1899–1985) 29, 32,
100, 295, **345–346**
*Song of Russia* (film)
308, **346–347**, 362
Soong, T. V. 69
Sorge, Richard 339
Sorrell, Herbert K. 111,
264
Southern Conference
Education Fund 126
Southern Conference on
Human Welfare
(SCHW) 186, 310,
**347–348**
Southern Negro Youth
Congress 443
*Southern Patriot, The*
(journal) 347
Soviet-American
Women's Conference
113
Soviet Union
Cold War *see* Cold
War
Comintern *see*
Comintern
espionage *see*
espionage
people
Bukharin, Nikolai
133, 348
Golos, Jacob 22, 23
Gouzenko, Igor 78,
**160–161**, *161*,
410c
Gubitchev, Valentin
93, 94
Khrushchev, Nikita
41, **217**, *217*, 275
Stalin, Joseph *see*
Stalin, Joseph
*Song of Russia* 346,
347
*Spain Again* (Alvah
Bessie) 28

Spanish Civil War
 (1936–39) 58, 157,
 208, 279, 305
Spanish Refugee Appeal
 142
Sparkman, John J. 37,
 125
*Spartacus* (film) 32
Spellman, Francis
 Cardinal 58, 78
Spender, Stephen 156
spies *see* espionage
sports *see* baseball
Springfield,
 Massachusetts 290
Stalin, Joseph
 (1879–1953)
 348–349, *405*, 411c
 Block, Herbert L. 35
 Cold War 78
 Communist Party of the
  United States of
  America 84, 85
 House Committee on
  Un-American
  Activities 184
 Nazi-Soviet Pact 279,
  280
 Rankin, John 309
 Yalta Conference 404
Stalin Peace Prize 140
Stander, Lionel 115, 379
Stanky, Eddie 22
*Star of the Red Sea*
 (airplane) 82
Stassen, Harold 97
State, U.S. Department of
 *see also* International
 Information Agency;
 State Department
 officials
 American Library
  Association 12
 Bingham, Hiram 30
 China 68–69
 China Lobby 70
 China White Paper 71,
  72
 Connally, Tom 91
*Crucible* 97

McCarthy, Joseph R.
 256
Miller, Arthur 266
Pauling, Linus C. 296
Permanent
 Subcommittee on
 Investigations 302
Robeson, Paul 319, 320
State Department officials
 Acheson, Dean *see*
  Acheson, Dean
 Berle Jr., Adolf A.
  **26–28**, *27*, 61, 119,
  409c
 Bohlen, Charles E. *see*
  Bohlen, Charles E.
 Brunauer, Esther
  Caulkihn 30, **46–48**
 Byrnes, James 1, 2, 174,
  232, 323
 Clubb, Oliver Edmund
  4, **74**
 Davies Jr., John Paton
  4, 30, 69, **102–104**,
  123, 124, 253
 Duggan, Lawrence 62,
  **118–119**
 Dulles, John Foster *see*
  Dulles, John Foster
 Grew, Joseph 6, 27
 Hiss, Alger *see* Hiss,
  Alger
 Hull, Cordell 119, 232
 Jessup, Philip C. 70, 71,
  153, **203–205**, *204*,
  222, 257
 Marshall, George Catlett
  *see* Marshall, George
  Catlett
 McLeod, Scott 36, 123,
  *261*, **261–262**
 Nicholson, Donald *280*,
  **280–281**
 Service, John Stewart
  *see* Service, John
  Stewart
 Vincent, John Carter
  *see* Vincent, John
  Carter
state employees 226, 301

*State of the Union* (film)
 171, 264
steel industry 89
Steel Workers
 Organizing Committee
 (SWOC) 89
Stefan, Virginia 192
Steiger, Rod 58
Stein, Sol 9
Stettinius Jr., Edward
 351
Stevens, Robert Ten
 Broeck (1899–1983)
 16, 77, 259, **349–350**,
 357, 397
Stevenson, Adlai E.
 (1900–1963) *11*, 13,
 226, **350–353**, *351*,
 369, 387, 411c
Stewart, Donald Ogden
 63
Stillwell, Joseph W.
 "Vinegar Joe" 66, 67,
 102
Stone, I. F. (1908–1989)
 136, **353–355**
Straus Jr., Nathan 322
Strauss, Lewis
 (1896–1974) 18, 191,
 289, *355*, **355–356**
Streisand, Barbra 396
strikes 89
Stripling, Robert
 Brecht, Bertolt 39
 Chambers, Whittaker 61
 Condon, Edward U. 87
 Eisler, Hanns 135
 Hiss, Alger 175
 House Committee on
  Un-American
  Activities 187
 Lavery, Emmet 234
 Nixon, Richard M. 282
*One Hundred Things You*
 *Should Know about*
 *Communism* 286
*Red Plot against America*
 313
Subversive Activities
 Control Board (SACB)

56, 57, 195, 196, 318,
 411c
subversive organizations,
 Attorney General's list
 of *see* Attorney
 General's List of
 Subversive
 Organizations
"Suggested Standards for
 Determining
 Un-American
 Activities" (Brookings
 Institution pamphlet)
 43
suicides
 Feller, Abraham 141
 Kent, Morton 215, 216
 Loeb, Philip 19, 32
 Winant, John G. 402
Summary Suspension
 Act of 1950 81
Sun Yat-sen 65
Supreme Court, U.S.
 Black, Hugo 34, 107,
  196, 226, 406
 *Blau v. United States*
  (1950) **33–34**
 Bridges, Harry 40
 Clark, Tom C. *see*
  Clark, Tom C.
 *Cole v. United States*
  (1956) **81**
 *Communist Party v.*
  *Subversive Activities*
  *Control Board* (1961)
  196
 *Dennis v. U.S.* (1951)
  **106–107**, 115–116,
  226, 341, 390, 411c
 Douglas, William O.
  107, **115–116**, *116*,
  196, 406
 Eastland, James Oliver
  125–126
 Executive Order 10241
  138
 Fast, Howard 139
 Frankfurter, Felix 1,
  173, 196, 395
 *Galyan v. Press* 389

Hollywood Ten  180, 410c
Korean War  226
*Mesarosh v. United States* (1956) 389
*Nelson v. U.S.* (1956) 412c
*Pennsylvania v. Nelson* (1956) **301**, 389
*Peters v. Hobby* (1955) 389
Robeson, Paul  320
Rosenberg, Ethel Greenglass  325
Rosenberg, Julius  327
*Sweeney v. New Hampshire*  390
United Electrical, Radio and Machine Workers  375
Vinson, Fred  73, 107
Warren, Earl  *see* Warren, Earl
*Watkins v. United States* (1957) 390, **395**, 412c
*Yates v. United States* (1957) 73, 116, 390, **404–406**, 412c
Surine, Donald A.  183, 256, 323
*Sweeney v. New Hampshire*  390
SWG  *see* Screen Writers' Guild
SWOC  *see* Steel Workers Organizing Committee
Symington, (William) Stuart (1901–1988) 16, 162, 323, **356–358**, 357

**T**

Taft, Robert A. (1889–1953) *359*, **359–361**
Bohlen, Charles E. 37, 38

Government Operations Committee  161
International Information Agency  197
Marshall, George Catlett  249
Taft-Hartley Act  361
Taft-Hartley Act (1947) 239, 273, 306–307, 359, **361–362**, 410c
Taiwan (Formosa)  66, 68, 69, 70
"Tawny Pippit" (State Department project) 103
Taylor, Robert (1911–1969) 99, 100, 269, 346, *362*, **362–363**
television
    networks  *see* ABC; CBS; NBC
    personalities  *see* Ball, Lucille; Carlson, Richard
    programs
        *Aldrich Family*  313
        *Firing Line*  50
        *Goldbergs*  313
        *I Led Three Lives* 182, **192**, 302, 304, 411c
        *Meet the Press*  145
        *See It Now*  274, 275, 277, 411c
Teller, Edward  191
Temple University (Philadelphia)  8
Temporary Commission on Employee Loyalty 136
Ten Million Americans Mobilizing for Justice 393
Tennessee Valley Authority  314
Tenney, Jack  110, 234, 320, 338

Tenney Committee (California)  234
test-ban treaty  296
Texarkana, Texas  28, 29
Thailand (Siam)  5
theater
    actors and actresses *see* actors and actresses
    directors and producers  *see* Kazan, Elia; Papp, Joseph
    groups  *see* Group Theatre
    playwrights  *see* Blankfort, Michael; Brecht, Bertolt; Hellman, Lillian; Miller, Arthur; Odets, Clifford
Theatre Union  33, 244
*This Is My Story* (Louis F. Budenz)  52
Thomas, J. Parnell (1895–1970) **363–364**
    Atomic Energy Commission  18
    Brecht, Bertolt  39
    Chaplin, Charles Spencer  64
    Cole, Lester  80–81
    Condon, Edward U. 87, 88
    Eisler, Gerhart  134
    Eisler, Hanns  135
    Executive Order 9835 136
    Goldwyn, Samuel  160
    Hepburn, Katharine 170
    Hollywood Ten  179
    House Committee on Un-American Activities  184, 185–186, 410c
    Lardner Jr., Ring  228
    Lavery, Emmet  233, 234

Lawson, John Howard 235
National Association for the Advancement of Colored People  278
*One Hundred Things You Should Know about Communism* 286
Ornitz, Samuel  290
Taylor, Robert  363
Truman, Harry S.  367
Trumbo, Dalton  370
White, Harry Dexter 400
Thomas, Norman (1884–1969) 44, 296, 354, **364–365**, *365*
Thorpe, Elliott R.  193, 232
Thurmond, Strom  125
Thye, Edward  105
*Time* (magazine) 61, 200, 225, 240, 251, 371
*Times* (London newspaper) 152
Tobey, Charles  105
Tom Paine School (Westchester, New York)  445
Tom Paine School of Social Science (Philadelphia)  445
Tomsky, Michael  348
*Toys in the Attic* (Lillian Hellman play)  335
Tracy, Spencer  171
Trade Union Education League  148
Treasury, U.S. Department of the  223 *see also* White, Harry Dexter
Trilling, Diana  9
*Trojan Horse in America, The—A Report to the Nation* (Martin Dies) 109
Trotsky, Leon  309, 348

500    Index

Trotskyist Socialist
  Workers Party 340
Truman, Harry S.
  (1884–1972)
  365–369, 409c, 410c
Acheson, Dean 1, 2,
  453–454
American Legion 10–11
Americans for
  Democratic Action 13
Atomic Energy
  Commission 18
Bentley, Elizabeth 23
Benton, William Burnett
  24
Bingham, Hiram 30
Bridges, Harry 40
Bridges, Styles 42
Chambers, Whittaker 61
China 68
China White Paper
  70–72
Clark, Tom C. 73
Cold War 79
Condon, Edward U. 86,
  88
Congress of Industrial
  Organizations 90
Declaration of
  Conscience 105
Dennis v. U.S. (1951)
  106
Dulles, Allen W. 120
Dulles, John Foster 122
Einstein, Albert 127
Eisenhower, Dwight
  David 130
Executive Order 9835
  136, 137, 410c
Executive Order 10241
  137, 411c
Fortas, Abraham 147
Goldwyn, Samuel 160
Government Operations
  Committee 161
Hiss, Alger 175
Hoover, J. Edgar 182
House Committee on
  Un-American
  Activities 186

Humphrey Jr., Hubert
  H. 189
hydrogen bomb 191
Internal Security Act of
  1950 194–196
Korean War 223, 225,
  226
Lattimore, Owen 231
Loyalty Review Board
  239
MacArthur, Douglas
  241–243
Marshall, George Catlett
  248
McCarthy, Joseph R.
  257
Murray, Philip 273
Murrow, Edward R. 275
One Hundred Things You
  Should Know about
  Communism 286
Pearson, Drew 298
Permanent
  Subcommittee on
  Investigations 302
Richardson, Seth 317,
  318
Smith Act (Alien
  Registration Act of
  1940) 341
Stevenson, Adlai E. 351
Strauss, Lewis 356
Symington, (William)
  Stuart 357
Taft-Hartley Act 361
Tydings, Millard E. 372
Vincent, John Carter
  380–382
White, Harry Dexter
  399
Winant, John G. 401
Trumbo, Dalton
  (1905–1976)
  369–371, 412c
blacklist 32
Blankfort, Michael 33
front 149, 150
Hollywood Ten 179,
  180
Lavery, Emmet 234

Lawson, John Howard
  236
Pegler, Westbrook 300
Schulberg, Budd 333
Trump, Donald 78
Turkey 78
Twentieth Century-Fox
  229, 384
Tydings, Millard E.
  (1891–1961) 7, 44,
  91, 371, 371–373
Tydings Subcommittee
  (Senate)
  Brunauer, Esther
    Caulkihn 47
  Kenyon, Dorothy 216,
    217
  Lattimore, Owen 230,
    231, 232
  McCarthy, Joseph R.
    256, 257, 410c, 411c
  Nicholson, Donald 281
  Ordeal by Slander 289
  Service, John Stewart
    337

U

UAW see United Auto
  Workers
UE see United Electrical,
  Radio and Machine
  Workers
Ukranian-American
  Fraternal Union 444
Unfinished Woman, An
  (Lillian Hellman) 168
Union of American
  Croatians 445
United American
  Spanish Aid
  Committee 208, 445
United Artists 64
United Auto Workers
  (UAW)
  Congress of Industrial
    Organizations 89
  Lardner Jr., Ring 228
  Murray, Philip 273

Reuther, Walter
  315–317
Taft-Hartley Act 361
Watkins v. United States
  (1957) 395
United Committee of
  South Slavic
  Americans 445
United Electrical, Radio
  and Machine Workers
  (UE) 90, 186, 273,
  374–375, 379, 410c
United Harlem Tenants
  and Consumers
  Organization 445
United May Day
  Committee 443
United Mine Workers
  (UMM) 238, 272
United Nations
  Daughters of the
    American Revolution
    102
  Korean War 225, 227
  officials and
    representatives see
    Feller, Abraham; Lie,
    Trygve; Roosevelt,
    Eleanor; Stevenson,
    Adlai E.; Winant, John
    G.
United Nations
  Commission on the
  Status of Women 216
United Negro and Allied
  Veterans of America
  443
United Public Workers
  of America 20, 253
United States Relations
  with China with Special
  Reference to the Period
  1944–1949 see China
  White Paper
United States Steel 89
United Steelworkers of
  America 272, 274, 306
Universal Studios 165,
  245

universities and colleges
*see* academic freedom;
American Association
of University
Professors; loyalty
oaths; professors and
educators
Urey, Harold  325
*U.S.A. Confidential* (Lee
Mortimer)  342
Utley, Freda
(1898–1978)  69,
375–377

**V**

Vandenburg, Arthur  71
Van Dusen, Henry
Pitney  218
*Variety* (magazine)  100,
110, 345
Velde, Harold H.
(1910–1985)  **378–379**
American Association
of University
Professors  7
Boorstin, Daniel J.  38
Condon, Edward U.
88
Davis, Robert Gorham
104
House Committee on
Un-American
Activities  187
Oxnam, Garfield
Bromley  292
Smedley, Agnes  339
Veterans of Foreign
Wars  22
Veterans of the Abraham
Lincoln Brigade  445
Vietnam *see* Dien Bien
Phu
Vincent, John Carter
(1900–1972)  **379–383**
Acheson, Dean  4,
453–454
Budenz, Louis F.  52,
53
China  69

China Lobby  70
Dulles, John Foster
123, 411c
Kohlberg, Alfred  222
Mao Zedong  245
Nicholson, Donald
280
Sokolsky, George  344
Vinson, Fred  73, 107
Vinson, Owen  55
Virginia League for
Peoples Education
444, 445
VOA *see* Voice of
America
Voice of America (VOA)
197, 198, 199, 330,
382, 383
Voorhis, Jerry  281

**W**

Wagner Act (1935)  98,
361
*Waiting for Lefty*
(Clifford Odets play)
285
Waldorf Statement
(1947)  31, 160, 179,
329, **384**, 410c, 431
Waldrop, Frank  187,
286
Walker, Robert  277
Wallace, Henry A.
(1888–1965)  **385–386**
Americans for
Democratic Action
13
Chiang Kai-shek  66
Congress of Industrial
Organizations  90
*Daily Worker*  98
Dies, Martin  109
Du Bois, William
Edward Burghardt
117
Hepburn, Katharine
170
Lattimore, Owen  230

Philbrick, Herbert A.
304
Pressman, Lee  306,
307
*Red Channels*  312
Southern Conference
on Human Welfare
347, 348
Thomas, Norman  365
Vincent, John Carter
380
White, Harry Dexter
400
Walsh, Edmund A.  58,
256
Walt Disney Studios  236
Walter, Francis
(1894–1963)  *386,*
**386–388**
blacklist  32
Burnham, James  54
Foreman, Carl  147
Fund for the Republic
155
House Committee on
Un-American
Activities  187
Miller, Arthur  266
Oxnam, Garfield
Bromley  292
Robinson, Edward G.
320
*Scoundrel Time*  334
Walt Whitman School of
Social Science
(Newark, New Jersey)
445
Wanger, Walter  328
Ware, Harold  60
Warner, Jack  285
Warner Brothers  156,
199
Warren, Earl
(1891–1974)
**388–390**, *389*
Budenz, Louis F.  53
Eastland, James Oliver
126
Internal Security Act
of 1950  196

Knowland, William F.
219
loyalty oaths  239
Murrow, Edward R.
276
Pauling, Linus C.  296
*Pennsylvania v. Nelson*
(1956)  301
*Watkins v. United
States* (1957)  395
*Yates v. United States*
(1957)  406
Washington Bookshop
Association  445
Washington Committee
for Democratic Action
445
Washington
Commonwealth
Federation  445
*Washington Post*
(newspaper)  34, 109,
119, 260
water fluoridation  102
"waterfront priests"  58
Watkins, Arthur V.
(1886–1973)
**390–395**, *391*
Eisenhower, Dwight
David  132, 133
Flanders, Ralph E.
145
McCarthy, Joseph R.
260, 411c
Williams, Edward
Bennett  401
Watkins, John  395
Watkins Committee
(Senate)  145, 394
*Watkins v. United States*
(1957)  390, **395**, 412c
Wayne, John
(1907–1979)  141,
188, 268, 269, **395–396**
*Way We Were, The* (film)
**396**
Weavers, The (music
group)  95
*Web of Subversion, The*
(James Burnham)  54

Weinberg, Joseph 378
Welch, Joseph Nye
    (1890–1960) **396–399**
    Army-McCarthy
        hearings 17
    Cohn, Roy 77
    McCarthy, Joseph R.
        259, 260, 411c
    National Lawyers Guild
        279
    Schine, Gerard David
        330
    Stevens, Robert Ten
        Broeck 350
Welker, Herman 22
Welles, Orson 31, 119,
    312
Welles, Sumner 119, *184*
Wheeler, William 395
Wheeling, West Virginia
    (McCarthy 1950
    speech site) 13, 256,
    410c, 434–435
*Where We Came Out*
    (Granville Hicks) 172
Wherry, Kenneth 70
White, E. B. 127
White, Harry Dexter
    (1892–1948) **399–400**
    Bentley, Elizabeth 23
    Brownell, Herbert 45
    Chambers, Whittaker 60
    China Lobby 70
    Eisenhower, Dwight
        David 131, 132

Murrow, Edward R. 275
Velde, Harold H. 379
Wallace, Henry A. 386
white supremacists 309
Wiley, Alexander H. 254
William Allen White
    Committee to Aid the
    Allies 321
William Morris Agency
    150
Williams, Edward
    Bennett (1920–1989)
    26, 393, **400–401**
Willis, Edwin 187
Wilson, Charles 16
Wilson, Donald 11, 12
Winant, John G.
    (1889–1947) **401–402**
Winchell, Walter 21,
    109, 309
wiretaps 46, 94
Wisconsin 255
Wisconsin Conference
    on Social Legislation
    445
witchcraft *see Crucible,
    The*
*Witness* (Whittaker
    Chambers) 62
Wood, John Stephen
    (1885–1968) **402–403**
    Condon, Edward U. 88
    Hellman, Lillian 169,
        170

House Committee on
    Un-American
    Activities 185, 187
Schulberg, Budd 333
*Scoundrel Time* 334
Wood, Sam 268, 269
Woods, James 396
Workers Alliance 445
Workers and Farmers
    Party 85
Workers Party 445
World Federation 178
World Peace Council
    Prize 118
World War II 349, 404,
    409c *see also* Yalta
    Conference
Wright, Frank Lloyd 136
Wright, Richard 156,
    157
writers
    Blankfort, Michael
        **32–33**
    Buckley Jr., William F.
        **48–50**, *49*, 78
    Fast, Howard *139*,
        **139–140**, 198, 209,
        322
    Hammett, Samuel
        Dashiell *164*,
        **164–165**, 167, 168,
        198, 335
    Koestler, Arthur 156,
        **220–221**
    Mann, Thomas 118, 127

Philbrick, Herbert A.
    *see* Philbrick, Herbert
    A.
Wright, Richard 156,
    157
Writers' Clinic 228
Wyler, William 81, 160

**Y**

Yakovlev, Anatoli A.
    158, 325
Yalta Conference (1945)
    36, **404**, 409c
*Yates v. United States*
    (1957) 73, 116, 390,
    **404–406**, 412c
YCL *see* Young
    Communist League
Yiddisher Kultur
    Farband 444
Young Communist
    League (YCL) 237,
    303, 304, 445
Youngdahl, Luther 233
Young Workers' League
    46, 47
Youth Council 303

**Z**

Zanuck, Darryl 229
Zaremba, John 192
Zwicker, Ralph W. 16,
    18, 143, 259, 301, 302,
    394